Overview

Contents

III The Oracle Tools

IV Design and Construction of an Oracle Database

VI The Care and Feeding of a Production Oracle System

VII   What to Do When It Doesn't Work

About the Authors

Mohammad Asadi has more than 19 years experience in data processing, mostly in data administration, including Oracle, IMS, the DB2 family, and SQL Server databases. Currently he is working with a major software development company supporting Oracle, DB2, and SQL Server databases.

Joe Greene has worked in a variety of fields, from driving submarines to spacecraft design. Along the way, he began to implement computer systems to meet various business needs. This led to a career as a computer consultant with a number of assignments working with Oracle databases. His experience ranges from very large data warehouses (with more than 100GB of data) to small scientific data collection systems, with a wide variety of databases in between. He is the author of *Oracle DBA Survival Guide* (Sams Publishing, 1995, ISBN: 0-672-30681-6).

Renae Rogge-Hoar has been a software engineer for over 12 years, developing and designing systems in finance, manufacturing, health, and marketing. Seven of those years have been in an Oracle environment. She currently is employed as an Oracle DBA for Concepts Direct, Inc. in Longmont, Colorado. In "real life" she is married to the greatest guy in the world, Marty Hoar, and has two incredible kids: Brianna, 14 months, and Zachary, 10 weeks.

Kelly Leigh, with more than ten years experience in the systems administration world, made the jump into database administration over five years ago. Starting out with Informix and moving to Oracle, he has experience in everything from product installation, to database layout, to implementing custom applications. Currently working for a small company in Longmont, Colorado, he is also co-owner of Colorado Business Solutions, a company created to provide small and mid-range business consulting in a wide range of areas including office automation, network installation, database installation, and software training. Outside of work, Kelly is an avid hiker and camper, spending much of his free time in the foothills of the Rocky Mountains.

Kimbra McDonald has more than 15 years experience in data processing, with more than 11 of those in designing and developing Oracle database systems. She is currently the manager of a database management systems technical support team at JD Edwards World Source Company in Denver, Colorado. When she is not working, she enjoys 4-wheeling in the summer and snow skiing in the winter in the Rocky Mountains—just out her back door.

Ken Rogge has successfully led a myriad of database and development projects over the past 14 years. He is currently serving as a client/server technical architect for Oppenheimer Funds in Denver, Colorado. He thoroughly enjoys his work, and also relishes time spent with family, which includes his wife Tammy, and children Adam, Alisha, Maria, and Brennan.

Lave Singh (BSc, ACGI, MBCS) is founder and head of Titanium Computers Ltd., a training and consulting firm that, for the past nine years, has provided Oracle training and consultancy services to organizations in Central Europe, Eastern Europe, North America, and the Middle East. The company specializes in the Oracle family of products, providing training and consulting services specifically in the areas of database administration, application and instance tuning, database auditing and review, and forms and reports (Developer/2000). Lave got his start 15 years ago in a Computational Science course at Imperial College. Since that time, he has been working in the computing field. He was fortunate to become involved with the Oracle product set in its early days in the UK—more than nine years ago. He is slowly breaking his addiction to machines and discovering what is important. His mother Amar, wife Permjit, and children Benisha, Taejen, and Kashmir make it all worthwhile. He wonders at the magic of growth and learns from them constantly. He can be reached on e-mail at lsingh@compuserve.com or by phone at +44 (181) 692 5204.

Gigi Wadley has been involved with Oracle for approximately seven years. Her experience has been obtained through government and private industries. The majority of the work she has done consists of Pro*C and SQL*Forms. She has been married for 15 years and has a 14-year-old daughter. Most of their lives have been spent in Colorado where they enjoy the lifestyle that the state provides.

Joe Zafian III has been working full-time in Information Systems since graduation from New Jersey Institute of Technology with a B.S. in computer science in 1981. Currently a consultant specializing in Oracle database applications with Computer Management Sciences, Inc. (CMSI), he has been working with all versions of the RDBMS and its associated tools since 1986. As a consultant, he has worked with a number of Fortune 500 clients in several industries across a vast array of hardware platforms. This experience qualified him to speak at the International Oracle Users' Week Conferences in 1994 (Predicting Storage Requirements for Large, Dynamic Databases and Advanced Techniques for Dynamic, User-Driven Applications in SQL*Forms 3.0) and in 1995 (Quality Assurance for Oracle Projects and Advanced Techniques for Oracle Forms 4.5 Applications). Additionally, he wrote the section on Oracle Developer/2000 in *Oracle Unleashed* (Sams Publishing, 1996, ISBN: 0-672-30872-X). When not striving to deliver quality Oracle systems, Joe enjoys sports, fishing, and other outdoor activities with his wife, Ruth. Joe is also active with Toastmasters International as a district officer. He can be contacted for training and development opportunities or general Oracle questions through CMSI at (860)633-3608 or through CompuServe at 73744,2713.

Tell Us What You Think!

As a reader, you are the most important critic and commentator of our books. We value your opinion and want to know what we're doing right, what we could do better, what areas you'd like to see us publish in, and any other words of wisdom you're willing to pass our way. You can help us make strong books that meet your needs and give you the computer guidance you require.

Do you have access to CompuServe or the World Wide Web? Then check out our CompuServe forum by typing GO SAMS at any prompt. If you prefer the World Wide Web, check out our site at http://www.mcp.com.

> **NOTE**
>
> If you have a technical question about this book, call the technical support line at 317-581-3833.

As the publishing manager of the group that created this book, I welcome your comments. You can fax, e-mail, or write me directly to let me know what you did or didn't like about this book—as well as what we can do to make our books stronger. Here's the information:

Fax: 317-581-4669

E-mail: enterprise_mgr@sams.samspublishing.com

Mail: Rosemarie Graham
         Sams Publishing
         201 W. 103rd Street
         Indianapolis, IN 46290

Introduction

Welcome to the *Oracle7.3 Developer's Guide*—a book that's been written *by* developers, *for* developers. Each of the people contributing to the book has real-life experience working in the Oracle world. By using the examples, tips, and techniques they provide, you can quickly profit from their cumulative years of practical experience gained the hard way.

The rate of change in the Oracle world is increasing at such a fast pace that at times it's hard to keep up to date with the product names—never mind what those products do. It's now possible to use a number of different technologies (Developer/2000 tools, Visual Basic, PowerBuilder, SQLWindows, C, COBOL, Java, and so on) to work with an Oracle database. With each technology, a fundamental set of skills and methods applies (irrespective of the front-end technology being used) and can be used to ease and accelerate the development cycle. Those skills and methods are what this book aims to cover.

What's in This Book

The primary topics covered by this book include the following:

- The structure and architecture of the Oracle RDBMS
- The more advanced parts of the SQL and PL/SQL languages
- Advanced ways of working with database structures (tables, indexes, clusters, views, database triggers, constraints, and so on)
- The Oracle utilities (such as SQL*Plus, Export, Import, and SQL*Loader)
- Design and construction of a database
- Project management and quality assurance
- Keeping a production system maintained, monitored, protected, and backed up
- Tuning considerations and ideas
- Additional database options (parallel options, Trusted Oracle, National Language Support, and so on)

Even though a few examples in the book relate to a particular platform, the vast majority of the book is platform-independent. The topics and examples will apply to any platform and any tool used to connect to the Oracle database.

Conventions Used in This Book

The following typographic conventions are used in this book:

- Code lines, commands, statements, variables, program output, and any text you see on-screen appear in a special `computer` typeface.

- Placeholders in syntax descriptions appear in an *`italic computer`* typeface. Replace the placeholder with the actual filename, parameter, or whatever element it represents.

- Regular *italics* are used to highlight technical terms when they first appear in the text and are also used to emphasize important points.

 You may notice this icon in a few places in the book. It tells you that the code being discussed at that point has been included on the CD-ROM accompanying this book. Although some code listings have been included on the CD-ROM, it is primarily filled with handy third-party software.

Within most chapters, you will encounter Notes, Tips, and Warnings that help to highlight the important points and aid you in steering clear of the pitfalls.

➡ Sometimes when a code line is too long to fit within the margins of this book, the line is broken; this icon is used to show that the lines should actually be input as one line.

"But I'm Already a Developer . . ."

This book is aimed at the intermediate to advanced developer and assumes that you are already familiar with some of the basics of working with Oracle.

Even though you may already be experienced in the Oracle world, I'm sure you'll gain much from the tips, techniques, and alternative methods presented in this book. You probably haven't had time before to look at a number of the topics in detail, and you may discover some choices you didn't know existed.

While you are reading the book and looking at the examples, be sure to also spend time playing around on a real database. Look at the examples, try them out, and explore the subject area. That way, you'll gain an understanding that goes deeper and lasts longer.

Relax, get comfortable, and let's start developing.

I

Introduction
to Oracle

1

Introduction to Databases

by Lave Singh

This chapter provides a brief overview of what databases are, what the Oracle database provides, and a brief discussion of client/server systems.

What Is a Database?

In one form or another, databases have been around for a long time. This section provides a look at databases in general before you begin to examine the Oracle database specifically.

Before Computers

Databases are just collections of data. In one form or another, they have always been around. Before the advent of computers, information was often recorded on paper and stored in such a way that the information could be easily accessed and searched based on various criteria. Although such a system might be suitable for small amounts of data, once the volume of information grows, managing and searching becomes time-consuming and laborious.

Many organizations still find paper-based information storage to be the best and most suitable system. For a small nursery school class, for example, keeping the names and addresses of the children and their parents on paper is probably the most convenient and simplest method. For a bank, however, recording balances, debits, and credits from accounts on a paper-based system would prove too complex. A computer-based system provides obvious benefits in terms of managing, using, and analyzing the information gathered.

After Computers

With the arrival of computers, information began to be stored in digital format rather than on paper. This change offered many advantages: programs could be written to retrieve, insert, update, and delete information automatically; backup and recovery of the data became easier; the data could be copied to other computers; and the level of information security could be enhanced.

In the early days, without any kind of database management system, data was held in files, and programs had to be written to make use of those files. One drawback was that the programs took longer to write than they currently do (with the SQL language). In addition, if one program performed some processing on data (perhaps a simple retrieval), another program that wanted the same functionality had to duplicate the code or call another program that provided the functionality. When the files of data were first set up, the structure of the file was defined and the program assumed this structure for the data. For example, if a file was to hold information on customers for the system, you could specify that the first 10 bytes were the customer number, the next 80 bytes the name of the customer, the next 10 bytes the phone number, and so on.

However, if the data requirements changed, as they always did, then besides changing the structure of the file, you had to modify and retest all the programs that used that file. As a result, changes were often resisted, and extra time and effort had to be spent "getting it right the first time" to avoid disastrous consequences.

The next advance was the introduction of software that performed some of the mundane data management tasks for you—the database management system (DBMS). A DBMS helps to separate the physical storage and manipulation of data from the programs that use it. With the advent of the DBMS, developers became freer to concentrate on program functionality.

The Different Types of Databases

This section discusses three of the primary DBMS types: hierarchical, network, and relational. Oracle and a number of other vendors use the relational model.

Hierarchical Databases

A hierarchical database model stores data in a tree-like structure, with parent and child relationships between the records in the database (see Figure 1.1).

FIGURE 1.1.
Diagram of data held in a hierarchical database.

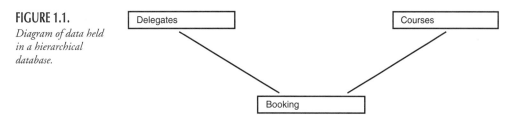

The hierarchical model has a number of drawbacks. Before information can be accessed about a child record, the parent record must be accessed. To overcome this limitation, much repeated and redundant data is normally stored in the database. In addition, a child record can only relate to one parent. Consequently, if you want to model two relationships to a child, you must introduce additional data to show the extra relationships. Another major drawback of the hierarchical model is that relationships between data are hard-coded into the database. When you set up the database, you specify how the parent and child rows relate (using some of the fields as key values).

Network Databases

The network database model can be seen as an extended version of the hierarchical model; it was introduced to overcome some of the limitations of the hierarchical model. The major difference between the two models is that in the network model a record can have predefined relationships to many other records, not just to one parent record. The network model includes two sets of objects: the records themselves and the links between the records. You specify the way in which one set of records relates to another when you first set up the data structures, so it's difficult to change that relationship later. This difficulty stems from the fact that the relationship is hard-coded as part of the database structure and cannot be specified "on-the-fly," unlike a SQL statement written for a relational database. Figure 1.2 illustrates a network database.

FIGURE 1.2.

Diagram of data held in a network database.

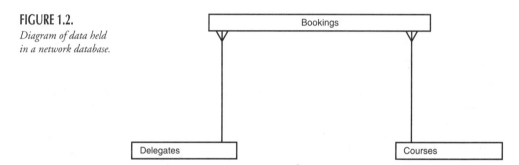

Network databases typically involve more complex coding than relational databases. Programs working on network databases work most often on individual records instead of on sets of records. However, whatever can be implemented in a network database format can be implemented in a relational database format.

Relational Databases

The relational database model resulted from an IBM-sponsored research project by Dr. E.F. Codd. The relational model attempts to overcome some of the failings of the hierarchical and network database models, and provides easy-to-use and flexible data structures. Figure 1.3 shows the representation of the table structures in a relational database.

The relational model includes data structures (tables), operators (the SQL language) that can be used to manage the data in the data structures, and some integrity rules (constraints, and so on) that ensure that the data obeys the business rules defined for the system.

The relational model is based on relational algebra concepts and theory and, in the early days, used some of the same terminology to describe the processing that could be performed on the data structures. For example, relational theory uses the words "relations" to mean tables, "tuples" to mean rows, and "attributes" to mean columns in tables.

FIGURE 1.3.
*Diagram of data held
in a relational
database.*

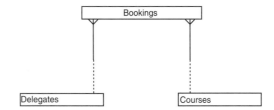

Relational databases are the most common type of database management systems in use today. Created in 1979, Oracle is among the products in this field. Other relational databases include DB2, Ingres, Informix, Sybase, and SQL Server.

The most basic concept in relational databases is the table. A *table* is a two-dimensional object that stores information about one thing of significance (for example, delegates who are to attend a class), as shown in Table 1.1.

Table 1.1. Contents of a sample database table.

Delegate ID	Last Name	First Name	Organization	Sex	
1	Andreas	Connirae	DSS	F	Row shows all information about one delegate
2	Brooks	Michael	US Army	M	
3	Grinder	John	Sequent	M	
4	Connor	Joseph	Bellcore	M	
5	Robbins	Anthony		M	Null value-organization unknown for this row
6	Kaur	Kashmir	Titanium	F	
7	Kaur	Benisha	Titanium	F	Actual column value for a particular row
8	Singh	Taejen	Titanium	M	
9	Samra	Karam	Amari	M	
10	Samra	Kailan	Amari	M	
11	Singh	Harman	DSS	M	
12	Kaur	Amriss	DSS	F	

Column shows one
attribute about delegates

Another important concept in relational databases is that relationships between tables are not hard-coded in the structure of the data; that is, there are no pointers in the data to relate one table to another. This means that you can specify the relationships between two (or more) sets of data at development time rather than when the tables are first created. This greatly improves the flexibility of the database management system.

Relational Database Properties

A relational database management system (RDBMS) has the following properties:

■ Represents data in the form of tables
■ Does not hard-code relationships between tables
■ Doesn't require the user to understand its physical implementation
■ Provides information about its content and structure in system tables
■ Can be manipulated through SQL commands
■ Supports the concept of NULL values

These properties are described in the following sections.

Tables

Data in a relational database is represented in the form of tables, which have the properties described in the following sections.

Rows Must Be Uniquely Identifiable

Any row in any table must be uniquely identifiable; duplicate rows cannot exist in the same table. This theoretical property should be implemented in every table (using primary key and unique constraints) but Oracle does not enforce it.

Column Names Must Be Unique

Each column within a table must have a unique name; you cannot have two columns with the same name in the same table. The same column name can exist in two different tables (and they could represent different meanings if so desired).

Order of Rows Is Insignificant

The order in which rows are stored or retrieved is not significant. If you want to retrieve rows in a specific order, you must specify the order in the statements you use to retrieve the data.

Order of Columns Is Insignificant

The order in which columns are specified for a table is not significant to the workings of application programs. You could re-create a table with columns in a different order and all application programs should still work (if they have been written correctly). The order in which columns are retrieved is specified when writing the statements to retrieve the data.

Values Are Atomic

Each column value is atomic; that is, it cannot be broken down further into smaller components. This is a theoretical requirement; in practice, however, enumerated fields are often specified for a table to make processing easier.

No Hard-Coded Relationships

In a relational database, there are no hard-coded relationships defined between tables—a relationship between two tables can be specified at any time using any column names. (Note that foreign key constraints do specify a relationship between two tables, but the columns used for the foreign key constraint do not have to be used to relate the tables in programs—other columns could be used.)

Physical Implementation Hidden

The physical structure of the database and the access routes to the data are not specified by the user of the database—that's the job of the database management system. The user specifies the *what*; the *how* is determined by the database system software. This makes the database flexible because the data can be moved or physically changed without any recoding of application programs.

System Tables

Users must be able to get information about the structure of the database, including which tables and other structures exist. Relational databases provide this information in a set of system tables that users can access, similar to the way they look up information describing their current system setup.

SQL

Relational database users issue commands in Structured Query Language, an English-like language that is nonprocedural (that is, it works on an entire set of rows at once, rather than by processing one row at a time). SQL is a powerful language capable of handling all access and modification operations. Although Oracle also provides other ways to work with the data in the database, SQL is the most common tool for user interaction with a relational database.

NULL Values

Relational databases must support the concept of NULL values for columns that are unknown or undefined. Null values do not represent spaces or zeros for numeric fields; they are processed differently from normal values for a column.

For example, when you want to enter information about a new customer, you might know his name but not his bank account number. The bank account number column for a new customer record, therefore, would be left at NULL.

Benefits of Oracle

The Oracle database system provides a number of benefits, some of which can also be found in other relational database systems. In addition to the benefits described in the following sections, Oracle and its components run on more than 100 different hardware and operating system platforms (including all the different versions of UNIX from the many different vendors). Oracle Corporation also provides a full suite of development tools, end-user tools, applications, and utilities.

Large Databases

Oracle can support databases ranging in size from a few megabytes to hundreds of gigabytes. The database files can reside either on hard-disk drives or on CD-ROMs, which can be particularly useful for archival or historical data.

Many Users

Without any extra application development effort, an Oracle database can support from one to hundreds of users. All necessary locking and protection of data is done by the database management software. In fact, it is common to see applications being developed on a single-user version of the Oracle database (perhaps Oracle running on Microsoft Windows), and then implemented without any code changes on a bigger machine with many more users.

Large Range of Tools

The Oracle Corporation supplies many tools that provide front-end access to Oracle databases in the form of screens, reports, or even graphs on the data. These tools, though used mostly with Oracle databases, can also be used with non-Oracle data sources. The tool selection expands periodically.

Portable

The Oracle RDBMS software, as already mentioned, runs on more than 100 different hardware and operating system platforms. If you have developed an Oracle application on one machine, it becomes relatively simple to port your system to another machine and operating system. Very little needs to be changed with regards to Oracle application code.

Backup and Recovery

Oracle provides many options when it comes to backing up and recovering data. In fact, if a database and machine have been set up correctly, there is very little that can cause total loss of data. If something does go wrong, depending on the type of failure, the database administrator often needs to do very little to recover the changes saved since the database was last running, ensuring a speedy return to normal work.

Oracle also can perform *hot* backups of database files, which means that a backup can be performed while the files are in use. This feature enables the system to be available 24 hours a day.

Distributed Databases

Oracle enables data physically located in various databases—which may even mean different machines at scattered locations—to be treated as one logical database. The physical structure is hidden from the application programs. The fact that the data does not reside in the database to which they're connected is transparent to the application programs. As far as locking, read-consistency, and rolling back of work is concerned, everything is handled automatically by the database system software. Again, as far as the application developer is concerned, the program behaves as if all the data were physically located in the local database.

Security

Standard Oracle database software provides many security facilities, including controlling access to the database, determining the commands that can be run, limiting the amount of resources that can be used by individual processes, and defining the level of access to data in the database.

If the security privileges of standard Oracle are not enough (it will be for the vast majority of cases), the Trusted Option provides even more privileges.

Database Data Processing

Using the constraints and database triggers facilities of Oracle, much validation and other processing can be defined when tables are first created. This allows you to set up "business rules" as you set up data structures.

The constraints and database triggers remove the need, in theory, for validation and similar processing to be performed in front-end programs. This simplifies the front-end programs, and ensures that the data is always validated regardless of which front-end program makes the changes to it. However, at the time of writing, the way that errors are reported back from these constraints and database triggers is less than ideal. Oracle8, when it comes out, will provide better facilities for reporting these errors in a more user-friendly way.

Client/Server Support

Oracle supports a wide range of client and server machines, offering you a tremendous choice in platforms for the database engine (the server) and front-end programs (either Oracle front-end programs or non-Oracle tools). In addition, Oracle supports a wide number of network protocols and topologies that allow client and server machines to communicate.

Client/Server Systems

The expression *client/server* has different meanings to people (especially depending on which salesman you are talking to!).

Before the advent of client/server computing, one common configuration used dumb terminals connected to a large back-end machine. Every character typed and any other processing required by the dumb terminal had to be processed by the main machine (typically a mainframe-type system). This increased the CPU processing and memory requirements of the main machine.

With the advent of GUI-based operating systems such as MS Windows, users wanted to use their PCs for all processing instead of having to link a dumb terminal to a more powerful mainframe. They also wanted the ease of use, power, and flexibility of GUI platforms.

With a client/server setup, you can run some programs on the client machine (perhaps a PC) and some programs on the server (for example, the Oracle database software on a UNIX machine) with some way of linking the machines together (perhaps a local area network). The programs running on the PC use the CPU processing power and memory of the PC rather than of the main machine. If you want to communicate with the database, you send statements across the network to the server where they are processed, and the results are returned to the client machine.

This is the typical setup with Oracle. The front-end programs that present data to the user (for example, Oracle tools such as Oracle forms, or non-Oracle tools such as Visual Basic) run on the PC with the full GUI capabilities of a PC. The back-end database server machine processes requests from many client machines. The database server machine can be smaller since the processing and memory requirements have been off-loaded. It could even be another PC with a multitasking operating system (Windows NT for example). In between the two machines you need a network with a network protocol (a set of standards for communicating), such as TCP/IP. To set up an interface between Oracle and the network, however, you must use the Oracle SQL*Net product. Figure 1.4 shows a typical client/server setup, with the database server on a UNIX machine and with PCs as client machines.

FIGURE 1.4.

Diagram of a typical client/server setup.

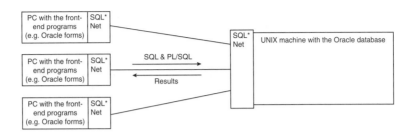

Client/server setups have the following advantages over traditional architectures:

■ *Processing power can be off-loaded from the server machine.*
The machine on which the Oracle database server software and database reside does not need to be as powerful since much of the processing and memory requirements can be off-loaded onto client machines.

■ *A wide choice of client machines is available.*
A number of different client machine and operating system types can be chosen to connect to the database server. For example, with one UNIX machine running the Oracle database we could connect some MS Windows PCs, some Apple Macintosh machines, some X Windows terminals, and even some dumb terminals.

■ *PC-based clients are easier to use.*
More and more users are familiar with PCs and how they operate. Thus when it comes to delivering an application, only training in the application itself and not in the operating system is required. This leads to more productive use of user time in actually getting to know the application.

■ *Better tools are available.*
Typically the range and power of Oracle and non-Oracle tools available on a PC far surpasses the range available on any other platform. The ease of use of these tools, both for the developer and the end-user, allows more effort to be spent satisfying the business requirements for which the application was designed.

■ *Expandability and choice is increased.*
If the server machine becomes overloaded, perhaps due to an increase in business, you can either increase the power of the server machine or change the server machine to a bigger and more powerful model without affecting the client programs at all. In addition, one client machine can connect to many different servers depending on the type of work that is to be performed—again this could be very easy to set up from both the client and the server sides.

Summary

This chapter provided some of the background and history for databases in general and, briefly, for client/server systems. Oracle, as one of the most popular relational databases in use today, provides extra facilities on top of the basic relational model discussed here. Later chapters cover some of the other options provided by the Oracle relational database management system.

Oracle Corporation, even though it's best known for its database product, provides a number of other products, tools, and services, most of which are based on the Oracle database.

The rest of the book covers areas of the Oracle relational database in more detail and with greater analysis.

2

The Oracle Database Architecture

by Lave Singh

This chapter examines the way in which Oracle uses the resources of any machine on which it runs.

Overview of the Oracle Architecture

System architecture determines how a database uses memory, hardware, and networks, and which processes or programs run on any machine. Any computer on which the Oracle database runs will have some memory, a CPU, one or more disk drives, and possibly a network connection. The architecture described in the following pages applies to the smallest PC and to the largest UNIX machine running Oracle. If you understand the Oracle architecture on one machine, you understand it on all machines.

Although it's not absolutely necessary to understand Oracle architecture before developing Oracle systems, a basic understanding will help you resolve cryptic errors, tune the database, and design and develop robust production systems.

Figure 2.1 shows the Oracle architecture as it exists on most machines.

FIGURE 2.1.

Diagram of the Oracle Architecture.

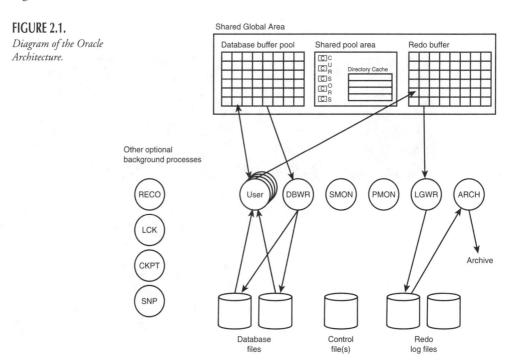

Memory

Oracle uses the machine's memory to hold commonly used information and any Oracle programs that are to be run on the machine. As with any database system, the more memory available to Oracle, the faster it runs. Oracle uses the machine's virtual memory, if available. At the operating system level, Oracle data structures in memory and programs get paged or swapped out to disk. With the Oracle database, you have greater control of how much memory the Oracle database and user processes use than you do with other programs.

Shared Memory

The Oracle shared memory area is known as the Oracle SGA—officially short for *system global area*, although some people think of it as *shared global area*. The SGA holds common information for all users of the database. The bigger you make the SGA (using INIT.ORA parameters), the faster the database runs overall because it can avoid having to read data from disk.

The way that the SGA has been set up and tuned can make significant impacts on performance.

> **TIP**
>
> The larger the amount of memory allocated to the SGA the faster, in general, the database will run. This is because most required information can be accessed directly from memory rather than from disk.

The SGA itself has three main components: the database buffer pool, the shared pool area, and the redo buffer area. In addition, control information for the Oracle system software is held within the shared pool, and in communications areas if the MultiThreaded Server configuration is being used.

Database Buffer Pool

An Oracle database consists of files, usually stored on hard disk. The greater the number of database files, the bigger the database. Oracle formats the files to make it easier to manage their storage. It partitions files into "Oracle blocks." Any database objects that need to use storage measure it in terms of one or more Oracle blocks (more about this later).

For example, the following CREATE TABLE statement creates a table with just one character column of size 1.

```
CREATE TABLE test (mydummy VARCHAR2(1));
```

The table is empty when first created—no rows have yet been inserted. However, the table has already been allocated some Oracle blocks.

```
SELECT  segment_name, blocks
FROM    user_segments
WHERE   segment_name_name = 'TEST';
SEGMENT_NAME        BLOCKS
--------------  ----------
TEST                     5
SQL>
```

Once rows are inserted into the table, the Oracle blocks start to be used.

```
INSERT INTO test VALUES ('a'):
INSERT INTO test VALUES('b');
```

If you want to see the data in the table, you can issue a SELECT statement. However, before the data is shown, the Oracle blocks for the table are read from the database files into memory (if they are not already there).

Assuming that the database was just started in the morning, the database buffer pool will be relatively empty (some Oracle blocks are loaded in when the instance was first started). If you want to access a table (with an INSERT, an UPDATE, or a DELETE statement), the Oracle blocks for that table must be read from disk and into memory. If you access the same table again, it will be faster to get to the data the second time because the Oracle blocks have already been read in from disk (assuming that they remain in memory). Any other user wishing to access the same data will also find that their statements run a little faster because the Oracle blocks are already there in memory.

Oracle database administrators can control how much memory to allocate to the database buffer pool by using a parameter set in the Oracle INIT.ORA file called db_block_buffers. The higher the value of this parameter, the more Oracle blocks in memory, meaning fewer disk reads and, therefore, a faster system. Database administrators can fine-tune this memory area through different utilities.

The database buffer pool is shared by all the processes using the Oracle database. The pool contains the Oracle blocks for tables, indexes, rollback segments, temporary segments, clusters, cache segments—in fact, any Oracle blocks on the database files.

Once an Oracle block is in the database buffer pool, it remains there. If additional Oracle blocks are needed, and there are not enough unused blocks in the database buffer pool, some blocks have to be purged from the pool using a least recently used (LRU) algorithm. Oracle purges only blocks that have not been used recently. Any changes are saved to the database files; then the blocks are discarded and the memory allocated to them is reused.

Shared Pool Area

The shared pool area of the SGA contains two subareas: the cursor area and the data dictionary cache.

Again, as a general rule, the bigger you make the shared pool area the faster your system will run. However, you cannot size the two subareas individually. The database administrator can increase the total size of the shared pool area using the Oracle `INIT.ORA` parameter `shared_pool_size`.

Cursors

Whenever a SQL command is issued, it must be translated. The translation process is called *parsing* and requires a memory area known as a *cursor*. Cursors are stored in the cursor area of the shared pool.

Translation is required when a SQL statement is first run, and it may be required again if memory is low and Oracle needs to reuse cursors in the shared pool for another SQL statement. The bigger the shared pool area, the more cursors it can hold and the fewer translation operations required. Unnecessary retranslations slow down the system.

Before translating a statement, Oracle checks whether the statement has already been translated into a cursor in the shared pool. If it has (either by your user process or by another user issuing the same statement), Oracle reuses the executable version of the statement in the cursor.

The algorithm for figuring out whether a statement already exists in the shared pool requires that the statements being compared will return a success only if the two statements look *exactly* the same—even the case and spacing must be the same. For example, the following two statements are considered to be different. The second statement cannot reuse the translated version of the first in the cursor, so another cursor must be used.

```
SELECT * FROM test;
select * from test;
```

> **TIP**
>
> To make optimal use of the cursor area of the shared pool, you should set up and follow departmental coding standards to make sure that your SQL statements look exactly the same.

By using procedures, functions, and packages to produce reusable code, and by passing the actual value of parameters, you save work. Reusable code also helps ensure that fewer cursors are used.

Here's an example: In a typical production system, more than one user interacts with the database through a screen interface. The very first user to issue commands causes the code to be translated into cursors. Later users issuing the same commands (by using the same screens), reuse the translated versions of the statements, thereby saving overhead by not reparsing. Earlier versions of Oracle (up to version 6) could not offer this savings because their cursors were not shared.

Data Dictionary Cache

The data dictionary cache part of the shared pool area holds information originally retrieved from the Oracle data dictionary (the system tables in the database files). When an instance is first started, the data dictionary cache area is relatively empty (and some entries are loaded at that point).

The system tables hold just about everything one needs to know about the database. They are used when any DDL statement is issued, when further extents are required for database objects, and when statements need to be parsed.

When an SQL statement is issued, the syntax and object names are validated during the parsing stage. Syntax checking is the easy part: The Oracle optimizer checks that the order, sequence, and spelling of the Oracle statement is correct. If the syntax is OK, the object names are checked to ensure that the tables and columns actually exist, and that the user has appropriate privileges for the objects accessed. This applies not just to tables but to other objects being accessed.

To check that the table names, column names, and security privileges are valid, the Oracle system tables are used. When an instance is first brought up, the system tables are read from the database files and loaded into the shared pool area of the SGA. This is performed using SQL in a process known as *recursive SQL*. Once the information from the system tables has been read from the database files, it is kept in the data dictionary section of the shared pool area.

If the same object names are required again, the system tables do not need to be accessed again because the information required is in the dictionary area of the shared pool area. The data dictionary cache grows to use more and more of the shared pool area (up to a certain limit). If there is not enough memory to hold all the information read from the system tables, some of the entries are removed to make room for more. If the removed entries are needed again, further recursive SQL runs automatically to access the system tables.

You can use the v$rowcache dynamic memory table to find out how well the data dictionary cache is doing.

```
SQL> r
  1* select  parameter, count, usage, fixed, gets, getmisses from v$rowcache
```

PARAMETER	COUNT	USAGE	FIXED	GETS	GETMISSES
dc_free_extents	23	10	0	65	29
dc_used_extents	35	19	0	19	19
dc_segments	25	21	0	419	21
dc_tablespaces	7	2	0	55	2
dc_tablespaces	11	2	0	26	2
dc_tablespace_quotas	21	1	0	36	1
dc_files	1	0	0	0	0
dc_users	17	6	0	500	6
dc_rollback_segments	35	19	1	172	18
dc_objects	146	140	43	756	97
dc_constraints	39	23	0	44	23
dc_object_ids	41	31	0	296	31

```
dc_truncates                     1          0          0          0          0
dc_tables                       74         64         22       1426         42
dc_synonyms                     12          8          0         14          8
dc_sequences                    14          4          0          5          4
dc_usernames                    20          3          0        133          3
dc_database_links                1          0          0          0          0
dc_histogram_defs                1          0          0          0          0
dc_profiles                      1          0          0          0          0
dc_users                         1          0          0          0          0
dc_columns                     540        523        197       8183        235
dc_table_grants                124         20          0         48         20
dc_column_grants                 1          0          0          0          0
dc_indexes                      49         48         21        592         20
dc_constraint_defs              70         56          0        677         34
dc_constraint_defs               5          4          0          0          0
dc_sequence_grants               1          0          0          0          0
dc_histogram_data                1          0          0          0          0
dc_user_grants                  49          5          0        327          5

30 rows selected.

SQL>
```

In the preceding example, you can see the use of the 30 dictionary caches from v$rowcache. The dc_columns cache, for example, has a size of 540, which means that it can hold definitions of 540 columns out of which 197 are fixed (these are column definitions for some of the core dictionary tables that must always be left in the cache). In addition, you can see that 523 of the entries in the dc_columns cache have been used. The gets column shows how many times it attempted to access the cache—8183 times. It would attempt to access the cache, for example, when it parses a statement and needs to determine whether the column definition exists. Out of the 8183 times it attempted to access the cache, it failed to find the definition in the cache 235 times (the getmisses column), requiring that the column definition be loaded from the data dictionary tables in the database files.

Redo Buffers

The redo buffers area of the SGA contains entries that are to be written to the redo log files. The redo log entries essentially contain before and after images of any bytes in Oracle blocks that have changed, along with other entries such as when a commit, rollback, or checkpoint is performed.

These entries are produced continually whenever data is changed. Every time an INSERT, UPDATE, or DELETE statement is run, the old and new values for those bytes that have changed in the Oracle block for the table being modified are recorded in the redo logs. In addition, the rollback segments record the old version of the Oracle block, and the rows that are affected are locked. Whenever other statements such as COMMIT or ROLLBACK are issued, they are also recorded in the redo buffer area. Whenever a DDL statement is issued, the system table blocks affected are recorded in the redo buffers area.

The entries in the redo buffer are written to the redo log files, as already mentioned, when changes are committed. The buffer area is also written to the redo log files when the buffer area is filled and further changes need to be recorded in the redo buffer area.

The redo buffers are essentially a staging area for the redo log files.

User Process Memory

Oracle user processes each require an area in memory known as the PGA—officially short for *program global area,* but some people think of it as the *process global area.* The SGA provides memory that can be shared between different processes that use the Oracle instance; the PGA is memory that can only be used by *one* process. The size of the PGA varies from operating system to operating system, and it is allocated on the database server machine—the same machine as the SGA.

Using the MultiThreaded Server can reduce the amount of memory required for the PGA since some of the more shareable elements that would be in the PGA can be moved over to the SGA. This is only possible, however, if the MultiThreaded Server configuration has been set up, as the next section describes.

MultiThreaded Server (MTS)

In the default client/server setup for Oracle (and on most UNIX-type platforms), each front-end process (for example, an Oracle tool running on a PC) has a "partner" process on the database server machine that performs the work for the client program. Each front-end has a corresponding back-end process doing the work for it. This back-end process is known as the *shadow process.* So, for example, if 100 users are connected to the database, there are 100 shadow processes.

Usually, the shadow processes are idle much of the time (depending on how active and busy the front-end processes are), and they consume the database server's resources and memory.

Instead of using the default setup, you can set up the MultiThreaded Server configuration, which requires that SQL*NET version 2 be installed. With the MultiThreaded Server, you have *shared* server processes. These do the work that would otherwise have been performed by shadow processes; however, there are far fewer shared server processes and, if more are required, Oracle automatically allocates them. When new shared server processes are created, Oracle automatically deallocates any shared server processes above a minimum level set by the database administrator.

Using the MultiThreaded Server configuration can significantly reduce the overhead of having many shadow processes managed by the operating system. The MultiThreaded Server configuration is set up by the database administrator who configures SQL*NET and then configures the Oracle instance in this mode.

In the MultiThreaded Server configuration, a user process can still attach to the instance through a dedicated server, which is especially useful for avoiding the overhead of going through the background processes associated with the MultiThreaded Server. This approach is useful for batch runs, large loads, and so on.

Figure 2.2 shows a conceptual view of the MultiThreaded Server.

FIGURE 2.2.

Diagram showing the MultiThreaded Server configuration.

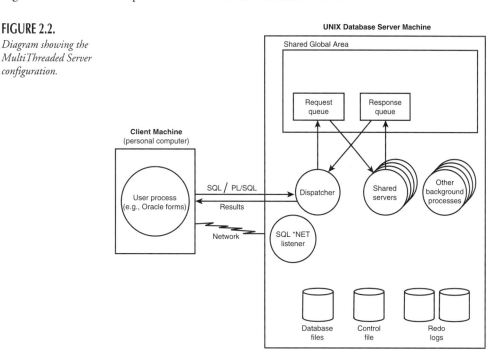

Memory for Running Programs

Every program needs memory to run, whether it's Oracle or not. On the database server, the Oracle kernel software can be loaded just once and shared by all processes that need to call the core software. It is a re-entrant program that allows calls from many other processes.

The memory requirements for the database server are reduced in a client/server configuration because the client programs use the CPU and memory on the client machine.

Paging and Swapping Out Memory

Virtual memory allows more memory to be used than is really available. The operating system, if it supports virtual memory, uses areas on the hard disk as extensions to the real memory. This may not make the system run faster, but it does increase the amount of memory areas that can be addressed by the application programs and allows more programs to be loaded into memory.

If the operating system supports virtual memory, the Oracle memory structures may, if required, get paged and swapped out to disk. Paging and swapping out is something that is performed at the operating system level and involves moving program or other memory areas from real memory to hard disk. If the same memory areas need to be reaccessed, the memory written out to disk must be reloaded from disk to the machine's real memory. More real memory is beneficial to the performance of Oracle and other programs running on the machine.

Processes

In this section, you examine some of the processes that may be running on any machine on which the Oracle database runs. The actual implementation may vary from machine to machine, but the fundamentals are the same.

System Processes

The Oracle system processes are also known as the Oracle background processes. Four need to be up and running all the time, otherwise the database won't be accessible. Others are optional. These processes are initiated when the instance is first started and are stopped when the instance is shut down.

The Four Mandatory System Processes

As you learn in this section, the following four processes must always be up and running for the database to be usable:

- Database writer
- Log writer
- System monitor
- Process monitor

The Database Writer (DBWR)

The database writer writes out Oracle blocks from the database buffer pool back to the database files. Only those Oracle blocks that have changed need to be written back to the database. It can write out the Oracle blocks at various times—for example, when the instance is shut down, when the database buffer pool does not have any free blocks to load new database blocks, when a checkpoint occurs, and periodically when the system is idle.

The Log Writer (LGWR)

The log writer background process writes changes in the redo log buffer pool to the redo log files. The online redo log files are written to in turn—when one online redo log file is filled, the other is written to. The redo log write writes out the redo log buffer when the redo log buffer pool is full and free space is required. It also writes out the entries in the redo log buffer pool when a transaction commits changes or when changes are rolled back.

The System Monitor (SMON)

The system monitor process performs instance recovery automatically when the instance or machine crashes. It automatically rolls back any changes that were pending when the instance crashed, and ensures that changes that had received the commit successful message when the instance was last up remain committed even if the database buffer pool blocks had not yet been written to the database files.

In addition, the system monitor process removes temporary segments that are created when additional sort areas are required. Additional sort areas may be required for many reasons—for example, when an attempt is made to sort a large number of rows.

The system monitor background process also compacts contiguous areas of free storage in the database files, so that the number of entries seen in, for example, the dba_free_space data dictionary view are reduced.

The Process Monitor (PMON)

The process monitor background process cleans up after user processes fail, perhaps because the user process was killed. It rolls back any work that the user process was in the middle of performing, releases any locks, and releases any other system resources that the user process had acquired before the failure. This is performed automatically as the PMON process periodically wakes up.

Optional System Processes

In addition to the four mandatory Oracle background processes, a number of other Oracle background processes can be initialized if certain extra facilities of the Oracle database software are used.

The Archiver (ARCH)

The archiver background process automatically copies the online redo log files to an offline location if the database has been set up by the database administrator to run in archivelog mode. This copying takes place whenever the redo log files fill up and switch from one file to another, or when the database administrator manually switches from one online redo log file to another.

The Recoverer (RECO)

The recoverer background process automatically synchronizes the recovery of failed distributed transactions. These are transactions that make changes on more than one database. If these transactions fail, actions such as committing can be handled automatically by this process on all databases involved.

The Checkpointer (CKPT)

The checkpointer process can, if enabled, update the file headers of the database files with information about the checkpoint that has been reached. Ordinarily this action is performed by the log writer, but CKPT can reduce the load on the log writer process when a large number of database files need to be updated at the checkpoint.

Snapshot (SNP)

Snapshots are copies of tables that are made automatically. They usually are copies of tables on another database. Once created, snapshots are refreshed automatically at an interval specified when the snapshot is created. The snapshot refresh process helps in speeding up the refreshing process.

Lock (LCK)

The parallel server version of the Oracle database allows the creation of multiple Oracle instances on different processors to increase the CPU processing power available to Oracle. If this setup is used, a process using one instance of Oracle could have a row locked and another process using a separate instance of Oracle wishing to lock the same row would still find the row locked. This synchronization between two or more instances in an Oracle parallel server setup is handled by the locking background process.

Dispatchers

If the Oracle MultiThreaded Server configuration is used, the dispatcher processes receive requests from front-end programs for work to be performed on the database (SQL and PL/SQL), and this process dispatches the statements to one of the shared servers.

Shared Servers

Oracle shared servers are part of the MultiThreaded Server configuration; they receive requests from a dispatcher for some work and perform the work. If more shared servers are required because of more load on the database, more shared server processes are allocated automatically. They communicate with the dispatcher processes using memory.

User Processes

User processes are the front-end programs through which the user connects to the database. If a client/server configuration is not in place, the user processes run on the same machine as the database server and they take up CPU power and memory. If a client/server configuration is being used, the user process runs on the client machine and communicates with the database server whenever required. It either communicates with a shadow process or with the shared server processes that are part of the MultiThreaded Server configuration.

Physical Files

The physical architecture of Oracle includes a number of files on disk, of which only three types are required. These files are described in the following sections.

Database Files

The database files are the database; other files support the database system's architecture. There may, as a minimum, be only one file that holds the entire database, including all tables, indexes, and other structures for all users.

Database files are formatted by Oracle into Oracle blocks to manage the storage within the files. The Oracle block size is set when the database is first created and cannot be changed for that database. Oracle blocks are the smallest storage unit used in the database and are the same blocks that are loaded into the database buffer pool of the SGA. The bigger the database files, the more Oracle blocks available for holding tables, indexes, and other data. Oracle files can range in size from a minimum of about 3.5 megabytes (MB) up to a number of terabytes (TB).

Oracle manages the storage within the database files when a table is created or extended. However, storage parameters should be specified whenever any database object that needs to use storage is created (this is not mandatory).

By default, Oracle uses fixed-size files. From release 7.2 onward, however, the database files can be configured to grow automatically when more storage is required. In addition, the database administrator can manually force the database files to shrink in size.

Oracle also can use database files that are on CD-ROM. These files are treated as read-only files because changes cannot be written (in most cases) to a CD-ROM drive. CD-ROMs can be especially useful for holding large amounts of archive data that you know will not change.

Control File

The control file is a small file that holds control information for the database. It includes the name of the database, the names of the database files, the names of the redo log files, and synchronization information.

When an instance is first started, the control file is used to locate the names and locations of the database and redo log files; if the control file is not present, the instance cannot start. It is easy for database administrators to keep multiple copies of the control file so that it can be kept updated by the Oracle instance. Such copies should probably be stored on separate disk drives to guard against loss of the entire database. Even if the only copy of the control file is lost, however, it can be manually re-created by the database administrator.

Redo Logs

There must be a minimum of two redo log files for any database. These files are known as the *online redo log files*. The database administrator can create more than two, if needed. The redo log files hold information that used to be in the redo log buffer area of the SGA. Any changes made to database blocks are recorded in the redo log files, such as the old and new values of any changes, along with other entries recording that a commit, rollback, or checkpoint was performed.

Here's a simple scenario: If an instance should crash after a commit successful message is received but before the database blocks are written to the database files, the entries in the redo log files are used to reapply the changes (or to roll back any changes, if required).

A redo log file has a sequence number that is incremented by one as it fills up one redo log file and moves to the other log file. These sequence numbers are recorded in the very first block of each database file and also in the redo log files. They are used to ensure that all the files that make up the database are in sync when the instance is first started.

The database administrator can easily multiplex the redo log files to ensure that when one copy of the redo log files is written to, a mirror copy is also kept. Disk mirroring does not have to be available at the operating system level. Mirror copies of the redo log files should be kept on separate disk drives to guard against loss of the entire disk device.

Offline Redo Logs

The database can be set up to run in archivelog mode, which means that whenever the online redo log files fill, they are copied to an archive destination. The location and names of the offline redo log files can be specified by the database administrator. The offline redo log files are exact copies of the online redo log files. Since the online redo log files record all changes made to the database files, by archiving these files in the offline destination you can have a complete record available of all changes made to the database.

The offline redo log files would only be required in the event a recovery became necessary, and only if one or more of the other database files had been lost. The database administrator can use the online and offline redo log files to reapply all changes made to the database since the last backup. This means that even if the database files are lost (deleted, corrupted, or the whole disk lost), you can recover to an old copy of the database files. Instead of restoring all the database files from a backup, you can restore only those that had actually been lost. This speeds up the recovery process because changes need to be reapplied to fewer database files.

CPU

With the Oracle parallel server option of the database, Oracle software can make use of multiple CPU machines or machines that have been clustered together. An Oracle instance (which is the combination of the SGA and the background processes) can be set to run on all available CPUs. If the CPU processing power is a bottleneck, this change can significantly increase performance.

Network

Oracle software runs on top of many network protocols—TCP/IP, IPX/SPX, DECNET, SNA, and so on. For example, a Microsoft Windows client machine running an Oracle tool can connect to a UNIX database server machine with TCP/IP as the network protocol allowing the two machines to communicate. The Oracle SQL*NET software for the network protocol chosen must be installed on both sides to allow Oracle to communicate with the networking software.

This means that you need not tie yourself to one networking protocol, but instead can produce systems that run on any combination of client/server machines with a multitude of network protocols and topologies.

System Tables

Oracle system tables are also known as the Oracle data dictionary and are created when the database is first created. These system tables are always owned by the Oracle user SYS, and everyone has privileges on some of the system tables. You should never attempt to manually change these system tables; use DDL commands (such as CREATE, ALTER, and DROP) to make changes to these tables.

These core system tables have names such as OBJ$, TAB$, IND$, and so on. Direct access to these tables is not required since a set of data dictionary views is created to make information retrieval much easier. There are over 250 data dictionary views (depending on the release of the Oracle software), and you can obtain a list of the view names by selecting the DICT table.

```
SELECT * FROM DICT;
```

The view names are divided into five main categories, which are described in the following sections.

USER_ Views

Data dictionary views that begin with USER_ show information on objects that the current Oracle user owns. These are accessible to every user, by default.

For example, the following code fragment gets information about the tables owned by the current Oracle user.

```
SELECT * FROM user_tables;
```

ALL_ Views

Views beginning with ALL_ show information on objects owned by the Oracle user and information on which the user has access to. (For example, a user might give SELECT access on his table to another Oracle user.)

The following code will display all the tables the user owns or can access.

```
SELECT * FROM all_tables;
```

This view is available to all Oracle users, regardless of system privilege level.

DBA_ Views

Views beginning with DBA_ are ordinarily accessible only to Oracle database administrators and show information on all objects in the database.

This view allows a database administrator to ascertain which objects currently exist on the database and who owns them.

```
SELECT * FROM dba_tables;
```

All the USER_, ALL_, and DBA_ views are owned by the Oracle user SYS. Public synonyms are created to allow every Oracle user to access those views that begin with the USER_ and ALL_ prefixes, and public synonyms are not created for these DBA_ views. This means that the SYS table owner prefix must be applied before using these views (even as a database administrator) unless you are logged in to the SYS user. The DBASYN Oracle-supplied script can be run to create private synonyms for these views in every database administrator account that needs access to these.

There are some extra views beginning with DBA_ that do not have an equivalent view beginning with ALL_ or USER_. Most of these show information about the structure of the database that ordinary Oracle users are not allowed to access.

For example, the following code retrieves the names, sizes, and locations of the physical database files that constitute the database.

```
SELECT * FROM dba_data_files;
```

V$ Views

The V$ views are not really data dictionary tables stored on the database. They are in-memory tables that show useful information about the way that the instance has been set up to run or how well the instance is performing.

These views can be useful to the database administrator in determining how much memory has been allocated to the SGA, for example, or for tuning the instance itself. Many of these views change from second to second and show dynamic information about how well the instance is performing.

The following code example displays the amount of memory that is allocated to the different memory structures within the SGA and that will not change until the instance is restarted (and the parameters used to start the instance are modified).

```
SELECT * FROM v$sga;
```

The following view shows instance-wide statistics and can be useful to the database administrator in determining why the instance is not performing as well as it could.

```
SELECT * FROM v$sysstat;
```

Others Views

A number of views are created to provide ANSI-standard view names that show information in the ANSI-standard way. Or they have been created for backward compatibility with previous versions of the Oracle database.

The ANSI-standard view names do not show full information about the Oracle database, since there are major differences in the Oracle architecture that are not reflected in the ANSI-standard views.

For example, the following code is another way of finding out which tables have been created.

```
SELECT * FROM tab;
```

Oracle Users

A single database may have many Oracle users, each of whom have their own copies of tables (common in a development-type environment) or who may access a central copy of the tables. In a production database, it is common to have only one Oracle user who owns the tables for the whole system and many other Oracle users who have access to the central copy of the tables. However, for large and complex systems, there may be many Oracle users who own the tables—perhaps one owns the tables for the sales subsystem, another owns the tables for the marketing subsystem, and so on.

There are always two Oracle users created when the database is first created. The first is SYS, who owns the core data dictionary tables, and the other is SYSTEM, who owns the product-specific tables (such as the tables that allow Oracle Reports programs to be saved to the database). Both of these users are more privileged users (database administrators), and they can do just about anything on the database.

Each Oracle user can be protected with a password, and this password must be provided when you want to connect to the database with that username. The same Oracle username can be used to connect to Oracle from any tool—whether it be an Oracle tool or a non-Oracle tool.

An Oracle user can only use a command if he has been given the system privilege for that command by the database administrator. For example, an Oracle user can only create procedures on the database if she has been given the "create procedure" system privilege. In addition, Oracle users can work with other people's tables if they have access to the table—for example, select and update access.

If you have access to a database administrator account, you can look at the list of Oracle users that currently exist in the database by using the following code:

```
SELECT * FROM dba_users;
```

Logical Structures

This section examines the logical structures that make up a database, including structures that hold your data and other structures that are essentially present to support the Oracle database architecture.

Tables

Tables are the primary database objects; they hold the data for the system. Tables take up space in the database files—maybe just a few Oracle blocks or up to millions of Oracle blocks. When tables are first created, storage parameters should be specified to indicate exactly how much storage space a table is to take. Setting parameters helps avoid the overhead of having to allocate more storage later and keeps all the data for a table together in the database files, which improves performance when accessing the data. Once some Oracle blocks have been allocated to a table, they are not released until either the table is dropped or the truncate command is used against it.

Indexes

Indexes are essentially quick lookup tables that make it easier to find rows in the tables. Indexes are stored in the database blocks in the database files and are internally held in a binary tree structure that is always balanced. This means that even if the key values are skewed, the system still goes through the same number of accesses through the index entries to get any key values. In addition, indexes are internally held by ascending key value, which helps the Oracle software look up key values—doing a binary chop-type sort on the index data.

Once created, table indexes are managed automatically by Oracle every time a row is inserted, updated, or deleted. No manual maintenance is necessary.

There may be one or more columns that make up the index, and there may be many indexes set up on a table. It's unusual to have more than about five indexes on a table, however, because inserts, updates, and deletes are slowed down since each change causes every index to be modified.

Indexes are of two types: unique and non-unique. If a unique index is created on a column or a set of columns, the Oracle RDBMS software ensures that no duplicate key values appear in that column or set of columns. Non-unique indexes are created primarily for performance reasons—to ensure that there is a quicker way of looking up data rather than doing a full-table scan of all the rows in the table.

When a primary key or unique key constraint is added and enabled for a table, a unique index is automatically created on the primary key or unique key columns. In fact, when a primary key or unique key constraint is enabled, the indexes are created, and when the constraint is disabled, the indexes are dropped.

> **TIP**
>
> Use primary key and unique key constraints to create unique indexes rather than using the "create unique index" command.

Indexes are one of the most important tools in helping to speed up access to data.

> **CAUTION**
>
> Unique indexes are dropped when primary key and unique key constraints are disabled.

Sequences

A sequence is a database object that can be used to provide very quick generation of unique numbers. There may be more than one person at a time generating numbers from a sequence, with very little lock waiting occurring. In fact, to improve performance further, the database administrator can decide to cache numbers from sequences on the database.

One drawback of sequences, however, is that a ROLLBACK statement will not roll back a sequence. This means that once a number has been generated from a sequence, the sequence carries on generating higher numbers even if a rollback is done. Numbers generated from a sequence would be lost if not used.

Clusters

A cluster is a way of storing data in a location that can be determined by its key value. This does not affect the SQL statements that run against the table—whether or not the table is clustered does not affect the workings of the application programs. It is another physical way of holding the data for a table.

Two types of clusters are discussed in the following sections.

Index Clusters

Index clusters are database objects that hold data (usually) from two or more tables in the same Oracle blocks. To do this, a cluster must be created, an index created on the cluster, and then, at the end of the CREATE TABLE statements, the tables to be held in the cluster must be specified. The cluster key is usually based on the column or columns used to join two or more tables together. This means that if you want to use data from both tables, accessing one Oracle block usually provides the data from both tables—you don't have to access the blocks for one table and then the other. In fact, before the index cluster blocks are accessed, the index created on the cluster is used to locate the Oracle block(s) with the key value required.

Hash Clusters

A hash cluster is very similar to an index cluster in that the data is stored based on a key value. Using a hashing algorithm (which can be specified by the developer or the database administrator), Oracle knows where to look for a row when an exact key value search is required. This can speed up access to the data since, without using any kind of index structure, Oracle can go quickly to the Oracle block that contains the data.

Views

A view is a SELECT statement stored in the database. Every time the view name is used in a SQL statement, the underlying SELECT statement for the view is used to get to the data. A view does not hold a separate copy of the data, but instead runs the underlying SQL statement every time the view name is used. This means that the version of the data seen through the view is always up to date.

Views can make it easier for users to interrogate data in an ad hoc way through end-user query tools such as Oracle's Data Browser. Without the user having to know how the tables relate, you can write a view that joins the tables. The user just performs a simple select on the tables and the join happens automatically. In addition, a view could be used to show a summary version of the data. Since no separate copy of the data is kept, the summary is always up to date.

The Oracle data dictionary views (USER_TABLES, for example) show information from many different real data dictionary tables.

Synonyms

A synonym is an alias for a database object—that is, another name by which the object may be known. Synonyms can be of two types: private or public. A private synonym can only be used by the Oracle user that created it. A public synonym can only be created by the database administrator, but it can be accessed by anyone (the Oracle user still needs privileges on the underlying object to be able to make use of it).

Synonyms allow you to avoid hard-coding the owners of any objects in code, which means that just by changing the synonym (and without changing the code) you can make programs work on a different table (perhaps in a different Oracle user).

Synonyms can be created on many types of objects, including database procedures.

```
CREATE SYNONYM mysyn FOR mary.hertable;
```

Database Links

A database link is a database object (very much like a synonym) that defines the connection parameters that allow us to use tables and other objects on another database. For example, within a single SELECT statement, you can access tables, views, and synonyms—not just in the database to which you're connected, but in other databases to which you have some kind of network link.

Snapshots

Snapshots are tables created from other tables that exist on databases other than the ones to which you're connected. Once the snapshot is created, the table is automatically kept up to date by Oracle at intervals defined when the snapshot is created. This allows you to avoid network calls to gain access to data on other databases; instead you have your own local, automatically refreshed copy of the table. In fact, updatable snapshots can be created that allow two or more databases to make changes to the table; the changes are propagated to all other snapshots of the table.

Summary

This chapter covered how Oracle operates on just about any platform on which it runs. Understanding how all the pieces fit together and some of the options available from the Oracle database can help to reduce the amount of time and effort required in developing and maintaining an application system. This is especially useful because many Oracle error messages point to underlying parts of the architecture. With a basic understanding, you can start to look in the right areas to resolve any questions or problems.

II

Oracle Fundamentals

3

The Elements of the SQL Language

by Joe Zafian III

The usefulness of any database management system comes from its capability to store information efficiently and its capacity to access and manipulate the data in the database. The Oracle relational database management system (RDBMS) provides the structures and mechanisms to process a vast array of information requirements. Structured Query Language (SQL) is the mechanism that an Oracle database uses to define and access data.

The American National Standards Institute (ANSI) has adopted the SQL standard as the language used to interface with relational databases, and Oracle complies with ANSI's SQL89 standard. This chapter describes the various database objects that organize the data objects in an Oracle database and also introduces the SQL language commands for building and accessing each object.

> **NOTE**
>
> This chapter introduces the concept of Oracle queries (or SELECT statements) with little or no explanation of the statement syntax. The next several chapters explore queries in detail. I am including several queries in this chapter because I believe that using them will help you to understand the database objects and how these objects fit into a database.

The Database Objects

The Oracle RDBMS organizes your data within several well-defined structures that facilitate efficient storage and retrieval of information. Proper definition of these objects will assure a high-quality, usable database.

Tablespaces

The primary structures in an Oracle database are the tablespaces. A tablespace is not specifically a database object, but is rather the repository for your database objects. Tablespaces consist of one or more operating system files (or devices) that are allocated to your tablespace.

Creating Tablespaces

Typically, the database administrator (DBA) defines tablespaces for the database by using the CREATE TABLESPACE command.

> **NOTE**
>
> Although the DBA usually creates tablespaces, I have encountered several instances when the developer may need to perform some of the traditional so-called DBA

functions. Therefore, I am including in this book the DBA information relevant to developers. I believe that if you, as a developer of Oracle applications, understand the background and details of many of the DBA tasks, you can use Oracle's powerful database more efficiently.

```
CREATE TABLESPACE tablespace_name
DATAFILE filespec
 [DEFAULT STORAGE storage]
 [ONLINE ¦ OFFLINE]
```

In the preceding CREATE TABLESPACE command, the tablespace name can be any combination of alphanumeric characters and underscores and can contain up to 30 characters. The file spec to define the name and size of the operating system file is

```
'filename' SIZE integer [K¦M] [REUSE]
 [AUTOEXTEND OFF¦
 AUTOEXTEND ON [NEXT integer [K¦M]
 [MAXSIZE UNLIMITED¦integer [K¦M]]
```

where *filename* is any valid operating system file (include the full path name) and *integer* defines the size of the file with an optional kilobyte or megabyte multiplier. The optional REUSE parameter is required if the file to be used already exists. If the REUSE parameter is used, the file size may not be changed.

> **NOTE**
>
> When you use the REUSE parameter, the existing file will be overwritten. Thus, indiscriminate use of this parameter can severely damage your database if you specify the wrong filename. Oracle does not check whether a file is in use for a different tablespace before overwriting it. It's usually advisable to use the REUSE parameter only when you are rebuilding a database or tablespace.

The AUTOEXTEND clause was added to the filespec definition in Oracle version 7.2. By specifying the AUTOEXTEND clause, the tablespace automatically allocates more storage from the operating system if the tablespace is full. Prior to version 7.2, tablespaces were fixed in size, and the DBA was required to extend the tablespaces when they became full. If the NEXT and MAXSIZE parameters are specified, the file will be extended by increments equal to the NEXT size up to the specified MAXSIZE.

The default storage clause in the CREATE TABLESPACE command defines the amount of space that newly created objects will occupy within the tablespace. The format of the storage clause follows.

```
(INITIAL integer [K¦M] NEXT integer [K¦M] PCTINCREASE integer
 MINEXTENTS integer MAXEXTENTS integer)
```

When they are used, the elements of the storage clause define the initial size and growth parameters that are defined within the tablespace. The initial size of an object is the amount of space the first extent for any object occupies. The next size defines how much more space additional extents for the object occupy. The PCTINCREASE parameter (a value between 0 and 100) determines the growth rate for each additional extent. The MINEXTENTS parameter defines the minimum number of extents that should be initially created for an object, and MAXEXTENTS limits the growth of a table to a maximum number of extents. The maximum value for MAXEXTENTS is operating system-dependent based on the standard block size for the database. Finally, the database may be created ONLINE or OFFLINE (in other words, open to be accessed or closed).

The following example creates a USER_TOOLS online tablespace using a 250MB file. The default table sizes will have an initial size of 256KB and additional extents will be added at 64KB with a growth rate of 50 percent.

```
CREATE TABLESPACE USER TOOLS
 DATAFILE 'o:\dbs\tools.dbf' SIZE 250M AUTOEXTEND ON NEXT 50M MAXSIZE UNLIMITED
 DEFAULT STORAGE (INITIAL 256K NEXT 64K PCTINCREASE 50
 MINEXTENTS 1 MAXEXTENTS 249)
 ONLINE;
```

If a table is added to this tablespace using the default parameters, the extents will be added as shown in Table 3.1.

Table 3.1. Growth of objects in a tablespace.

Extent	Size (in 4K blocks)
1	64
2	16
3	24
4	36
5	54
6	72
7	108
8	162
9	244
10	366

As shown in Table 3.1, the PCTINCREASE parameter can cause database objects to grow out of control. Therefore, this parameter should be 0 unless you have a good reason for using another value. Unfortunately, the SYSTEM tablespace in your database probably uses Oracle's default value of 50 percent. I have seen many instances of database failure due to out-of-control growth of the SYSTEM tablespace objects.

Examining Tablespaces

Generally, tablespaces are created on separate physical devices to ensure maximum performance. With a thorough knowledge of the tablespaces in the database and their purpose, you can construct your database to maximize its performance. In theory, if a query can access multiple physical drives simultaneously, the query will perform better than if only one device is used. To determine the accessible tablespaces and their default storage parameters, issue the following query. (The syntax for SQL queries will be discussed later in this book.)

```
select tablespace_name,
 initial_extent INITIAL,
 next_extent NEXT,
 min_extents MIN,
 max_extents MAX,
 pct_increase PCT,
 status
 from user_tablespaces;
```

This query returns a report similar to Listing 3.1.

Listing 3.1. List of available tablespaces.

TABLESPACE_NAME	INITIAL	NEXT	MIN	MAX	PCT	STATUS
SYSTEM	20480	8192	1	249	50	ONLINE
ROLLSPACE	131072	131072	1	249	0	ONLINE
USER_TOOLS	40960	16384	1	249	0	ONLINE
USER_TABS	20480	8192	1	249	0	ONLINE
USER_NDX	20480	8192	1	125	0	ONLINE
USER_REFERENCE	20480	8192	1	5	0	READ ONLY
USER_OTHER	20480	8192	1	249	0	OFFLINE

As Listing 3.1 shows, the database has seven available tablespaces. Any objects that are added to the database will use the default storage parameters shown in the report. Also, note in the STATUS column, the status of a tablespace may be ONLINE, OFFLINE, or READ ONLY. New objects and data may be written into an ONLINE tablespace only, and a READ ONLY tablespace cannot be written to until its status changes to ONLINE.

To allocate storage space for database objects, contiguous free space must exist in the specified tablespace. To determine the amount of available free space for a tablespace, issue the following query:

```
select tablespace_name,
 file_id,
 block_id,
 bytes,
 blocks
 from user_free_space
 where tablespace_name = 'USER_TABS'
 order by file_id, block_id;
```

As shown in Listing 3.2, this query returns three segments of available space (50, 80, and 175 blocks, respectively) in the USER_TABS tablespace.

Listing 3.2. Available free space.

TABLESPACE_NAME	FILE_ID	BLOCK_ID	BYTES	BLOCKS
USER_TABS	3	178	204800	50
USER_TABS	3	228	327860	80
USER_TABS	3	51026	716800	175

As extents are added to the database, the RDBMS will first attempt to locate the extent within a single existing free space segment. If no single segment is found, the RDBMS will try to find an existing contiguous space among several free segments for the extent. Finally, if no contiguous space exists, the datafile will be extended as specified by the AUTOEXTEND option for the tablespace. If AUTOEXTEND is not allowed, the extension will fail and an error will be issued.

Using the preceding example, suppose that you need to create an object with an initial size of 100 data blocks. A 100-block segment exists, and the object will be placed at BLOCK_ID 51026. If you need a second 100-block object , the 50-block and 80-block segments are merged and the new object is stored at position 178, leaving free space segments at BLOCK_ID 278 (30 blocks) and BLOCK_ID 51126 (75 blocks). If you need a third 100-block extent, the datafile would be extended if possible. As you can see, you must be very careful when you are creating and removing objects from the database.

Modifying Tablespaces

As your database evolves, you may have to modify objects within it to reflect the changes. You can use the ALTER TABLESPACE command to change various aspects of a tablespace. For example, the ALTER TABLESPACE command can rename or add datafiles for the tablespace, as indicated in the following statement:

```
alter tablespace user_tabs
 rename 'o:\dbs\user.dbf' to 'o:\dbs\user1.dbf';
```

```
alter tablespace user_tabs
 add datafile 'o:\dbs\user2.dbf' size 250m autoextend off;
```

This statement changes the name of the existing user.dbf operating system file to user1.dbf and adds a second operating system file, user2.dbf, to the tablespace. In versions of Oracle prior to 7.2, the ALTER TABLESPACE command was the only way to extend the size of a tablespace. As a result, many tablespaces were built with excessively large sizes to allow for anticipated growth. The other side effect of this "problem" was that databases often ended up with too many datafiles attached to the database.

The ALTER TABLESPACE command can also change the status of a tablespace. Oracle7 supports the concept of READ ONLY tablespaces. These tablespaces can provide reference information that does not normally change. Additionally, READ ONLY tablespaces require less system overhead because rollback and transaction log information does not need to be maintained for the tablespace. To modify the tablespace to be read only, issue the following command:

```
alter tablespace user_reference
 read only;
```

You can permit write operations on the tablespace by issuing the ALTER TABLESPACE command with a READ WRITE parameter. Finally, you can take a tablespace offline by using the OFFLINE parameter with a NORMAL (default), TEMPORARY, or IMMEDIATE option. These options define how the DBA can bring the tablespace back ONLINE. Each option requires a different recovery procedure, which is beyond the scope of this book.

Removing Tablespaces

You can use the DROP TABLESPACE command to remove an existing tablespace, as shown in the next bit of code:

```
DROP TABLESPACE tablespace_name
 [INCLUDING CONTENTS]
```

DROP TABLESPACE permanently removes a tablespace from the database; the tablespace cannot be recovered. The INCLUDING CONTENTS clause is required for any tablespace that contains database objects. If the INCLUDING CONTENTS clause is not specified and the tablespace is not empty, an error message is returned. It is important to note that the DROP TABLESPACE command does not remove the database files from your storage environment. To remove these files, you must use the appropriate operating system commands.

Schema

Once the tablespaces exist, you can add objects to the database. The owner of each object is the schema under which the object is created. The concept of a schema is a subtle change to the Oracle RDBMS in Oracle7. Previously, all objects were owned by the users that created them.

By default, the schema is the same as the currently connected user, which provides compatibility with prior versions of Oracle. To create a database schema, use the following command:

```
CREATE SCHEMA AUTHORIZATION schema_name
 [CREATE TABLE commands]
 [CREATE VIEW commands]
 [GRANT commands];
```

The CREATE SCHEMA command can create several database objects in a single transaction. Rather than including a semicolon at the end of each CREATE OBJECT command, include only the final semicolon for the entire transaction. The individual commands are described later in this chapter.

Tables

The primary repository for the data in Oracle database objects is a table. A *table* represents a collection of similar data organized in one or more fields or columns. Details on how to organize table structures are explained in Chapter 21, "Creating the Initial Database Objects."

Creating Tables

To create a table, issue the following command:

```
CREATE TABLE [schema_name.]table_name
 (column_specifications)
 [table_constraints]
 [PCTFREE integer]
 [PCTUSED integer]
 [INITRANS integer]
 [MAXTRANS integer]
 [TABLESPACE tablespace_name]
 [STORAGE storage_clause]
 [RECOVERABLE¦UNRECOVERABLE]
 [CLUSTER cluster_name (cluster_columns)]
 [PARALLEL parallel_clause]
 [ENABLE enable_clause ¦ DISABLE disable_clause]
 [AS subquery]
 [CACHE ¦ NOCACHE];
```

The table name may be any valid Oracle object name (up to 30 characters) that has not already been used within the schema. If no schema is specified, the default schema will be used (this value is the same as the user's database logon ID or USERNAME). The table will be created with the columns as detailed in the column specifications. If no column specifications are defined, the CREATE TABLE command must use a subquery to define the table columns using the AS clause. The syntax of the column specifications clause is

```
column_name data_type [DEFAULT expression] [column_constraint]
```

where column_name must be a valid Oracle name and must be uniquely defined for the table. The storage format and size of each column must be defined using a valid datatype as detailed in Table 3.2.

Table 3.2. Oracle datatypes.

Datatype	Description
CHAR(n)	A fixed length character string, *n* bytes long. If no length is specified, it will be 1 byte. CHAR columns may be up to 255 characters long.
VARCHAR2(n)	A variable length character string up to *n* characters long. A VARCHAR2 column may be up to 2,000 characters long.
LONG(n)	A variable length data item up to 2GB long. LONG columns have most of the characteristics of VARCHAR2 columns, except that their use in SQL is subject to some restrictions. See the note following this table note for information about these restrictions.
DATE	DATE columns contain a structure representing date and time. In DATE columns, time is part of the value; if no time is specified, the time portion of the value defaults to midnight.
NUMBER(p,s)	NUMBER columns hold numeric data with a precision (total number of digits) equal to *p* and a scale (number of digits after the decimal point) equal to *s*. The scale can be less than zero, at which point the value will be rounded to the nearest appropriate factor of 10. For example, a scale of –2 will round the stored value to the nearest 100.
RAW and LONG RAW	These datatypes store binary data. LONG and other character datatypes will strip out noncharacter data before the column is processed.
MLSLABEL	This datatype is used with Trusted Oracle to embed an operating system security label with the data to restrict access based on user login information.

NOTE

You should use the LONG datatype to store large blocks of character data only when no data manipulation is required. LONG columns can be used only in column SELECT lists, SET clauses of UPDATE statements, or VALUES clauses of INSERT statements. Other restrictions are that a single table may have only one LONG column, and that LONG columns cannot be indexed or appear in integrity constraints. Additionally, LONG columns may not be used in the following situations:

■ As a selected column in a CREATE SNAPSHOT command

■ As part of a WHERE, GROUP BY, ORDER BY, or CONNECT BY clause or in a DISTINCT or UNIQUE clause in a SELECT statement

■ In any SQL functions or expressions

■ As a selected column in a subquery

Oracle also provides support for non–Oracle-specific column types to ensure compatibility with the ANSI standard and other SQL databases. Table 3.3 defines these datatypes.

Table 3.3. Other datatypes.

Datatype	*Oracle Equivalent*
VARCHAR(n)	VARCHAR2(n) (This compatibility may change in later releases.)
CHARACTER(n)	CHAR(n)
CHARACTER VARYING(n)	VARCHAR2(n)
CHAR VARYING(n)	VARCHAR2(n)
NUMERIC(p,s)	NUMBER(p,s)
DECIMAL(p,s)	NUMBER(p,s)
INTEGER	NUMBER(38)
INT	NUMBER(38)
SMALLINT	NUMBER(38)
FLOAT	NUMBER
DOUBLE PRECISION	NUMBER
REAL	NUMBER

You should not use the following SQL/DS and DB2 datatypes; they do not have an equivalent Oracle translation.

■ GRAPHIC

■ VARGRAPHIC

■ LONG VARGRAPHIC

■ TIME

■ TIMESTAMP

Optionally, you can specify a default value for the column using any valid Oracle expression. (Oracle expressions are described in Chapter 4, "Oracle Queries.") Finally, you can define a constraint for the column (or table), as detailed in Chapter 14, "Database Constraints, Triggers, and Procedures."

> **NOTE**
>
> Although you can define constraints as part of the table definition command, you should add table constraints through an ALTER TABLE command after all the tables and views have been created. For most constraints (other than NULL or NOT NULL constraints), dependencies exist between several tables. If the table required in the constraint does not yet exist, the table creation will fail. Whenever I build a database, I construct the objects in the following order: tables, constraints, indexes, views, sequences, procedures, and triggers. You can create other objects at any time.

Next, the PCTFREE parameter defines the percentage of a data block that is reserved for growth of individual rows. As rows are added to the table, the RDBMS examines a structure within the table called a *free list*, which maintains a list of available blocks that can receive data. If a block is found, a check is made to determine if, by adding the new row, at least PCTFREE percent of the block remains unused. If room for the new row remains, it is inserted into the block. Otherwise, the block is removed from the free list, and the next available block is checked until a valid position is found. If no valid blocks are found, Oracle will allocate an additional extent for the table. As updates are performed, the free area within the block will be used to hold the growth of the row. If the expanded row will not fit within the data block, the entire row will be moved to a new block location if possible. Thus, if a table has little or no update activity (such as audit trail tables), the PCTFREE parameter should be relatively low (0 to 5 percent). Conversely, a table with significant maintenance may have 50 percent (or more) free space.

> **NOTE**
>
> The relocation of the data row was introduced in Oracle7 to prevent *row chaining*, that is, a single row spanning multiple data blocks. Previously, only the part of the data row that did not fit within the original data block was "chained" to a secondary data block. Chaining can still occur in Oracle7, but it is usually restricted to instances when the entire row cannot fit within a single data block.

The next parameter, PCTUSED, defines the low threshold for space usage before the data block can be returned to the free list. As rows are deleted from a table, the unused space cannot be reused until the total space used within a block falls below PCTUSED. If this parameter is too low, a table may have significant wasted space. The sum of PCTFREE and PCTUSED must be 100 or less. If no values are specified, the defaults are 40 for PCTUSED and 10 for PCTFREE.

> **NOTE**
>
> The total space available within a data block is somewhat less than the total size of the block because of the overhead structures for database maintenance. Overhead typically represents about 10 percent of the total data block size.

The INITRANS and MAXTRANS parameters process transactions in the data block. As transactions are processed against a table, Oracle allocates storage space within the data block to allow for multiple concurrent transactions on the data block. As the transactions are processed, the RDBMS will dynamically allocate buffers for the transactions based on these values up to the maximum number specified by MAXTRANS. If significant data maintenance is performed on a table, the INITRANS should be set relatively high. However, if this value is too high, the overhead for the data block will result in wasted storage. Under most circumstances, the default values of 1 and 255 are acceptable.

The next optional parameter for table creation is TABLESPACE. If the tablespace is not specified, the table will be created in the DEFAULT_TABLESPACE for the current user based on the value set by the DBA when he or she created the user ID. Next, the storage parameters for the table may be specified as explained earlier in the discussion of tablespaces. The RECOVERABLE or UNRECOV-ERABLE parameters specify whether the command should be recorded in the redo log files for database recovery. If neither is specified, the table will be created with recovery on.

Next, the table may be created as part of a clustered group of tables. (Clusters are explained later in this chapter.) The PARALLEL clause defines how the table can be accessed using the PARALLEL QUERY option if your database supports it. (See Chapter 33, "Parallel Processing.") The ENABLE and DISABLE clauses apply to the constraints for the table as explained in Chapter 14.

As mentioned earlier, you can use the AS clause to construct a table based on the results of a subquery. The columns for the new table will match the names as specified in the subquery unless column specifications are provided. If the datatypes of the column specifications do not match the subquery datatypes, an error will occur and the table will not be created. Finally, you can create the table with a CACHE or NOCACHE parameter. If you use the CACHE parameter, the table will be cached in memory whenever a full table scan is performed. This technique may improve performance for small, frequently accessed reference tables.

Chapter 8, "Table Creation," contains several examples that use the CREATE TABLE command to define a usable, efficient database.

Examining Tables

To determine which tables you have access to, execute the following query against the data dictionary view, ALL_TABLES:

```
select owner,
 table_name
 from all_tables;
```

As shown in the preceding code, the query retrieves the OWNER and TABLE_NAME columns from the ALL_TABLES data dictionary view. OWNER defines the name of the user who created the table and TABLE_NAME is the name of the table. In addition to these two columns that can be returned from the ALL_TABLES view, Table 3.4 describes the information available from other columns in the view.

Table 3.4. Data dictionary information in ALL_TABLES.

Column Name	Description
CLUSTER_NAME	Name of cluster the table belongs to
PCT_FREE	PCT_FREE parameter
PCT_USED	PCT_USED parameter
INI_TRANS	Initial transactions value
MAX_TRANS	Maximum transactions value
INITIAL_EXTENT	Initial extent size in bytes
NEXT_EXTENT	Next extent size in bytes
PCT_INCREASE	Growth rate for extent allocations
BACKED_UP	Indicates whether table has been backed up using a hot backup since last change
DEGREE	Degree of parallelization for parallel option
INSTANCES	Number of parallel query instances
CACHE	Indicates whether table should be cached during full table scans
NUM_ROWS	Number of data rows in the table
BLOCKS	Number of blocks used by table data
EMPTY_BLOCKS	Number of unused table blocks
AVG_SPACE	Average amount of free space in each data block
CHAIN_CNT	Number of rows that are chained across multiple data blocks
AVG_ROW_LEN	Average number of bytes in each data row

The last six columns in this table contain information about the space utilization for the table whenever the table is analyzed. You can use that information to manage the growth and sizing of your database. Additionally, the cost-based optimizer uses information from the ANALYZE command to create an execution plan for your queries. (See Chapter 31, "Oracle's Query Optimizer," for details.)

```
ANALYZE my_table
COMPUTE STATISTICS;
```

To see the columns and their respective datatypes, use the DESC (describe) command as follows:

```
DESC owner.table_name
```

Listing 3.3 shows the results of the preceding command.

Listing 3.3. Table description.

```
SQL> desc customers
 Name                            Null?    Type
 ------------------------------- -------- ------------
 CUST_NO                         NOT NULL NUMBER(6)
 CUST_NAME                       NOT NULL VARCHAR2(35)
 CUST_ADDRESS                    NOT NULL VARCHAR2(35)
 CUST_CITY                       NOT NULL VARCHAR2(20)
 CUST_STATE                               VARCHAR2(2)
 CUST_POSTAL_CODE                         VARCHAR2(10)
 CUST_COUNTRY                             VARCHAR2(15)
 CUST_PHONE                               VARCHAR2(20)
```

As stated earlier in this chapter, when tables fill with data, they acquire new extents as needed. A general rule of thumb is that a table should optimally occupy a single contiguous extent in the database. Therefore, you need to keep track of the number of extents that the table is using. To see the number of extents that have been allocated to the CUSTOMERS table, issue the following query:

```
select extent_id,
 bytes
 from user_extents
 where segment_name = 'CUSTOMERS'
 and segment_type = 'TABLE'
 order by extent_id;
EXTENT_ID     BYTES
========= =========
        1     65536
        2     32768
        3     49152
```

Modifying Tables

As in the case of tablespaces, it is often necessary to modify the table using an ALTER TABLE command. The first use of this command is to change the storage or transaction parameters for the table. Simply include the new values after the ALTER TABLE *table_name* command. Note that changes to storage parameters affect only future allocations for the table and do not adjust currently allocated extents.

You can also use the ALTER TABLE command to add new columns or modify existing columns in the table. To add a column for the customer credit limit to the CUSTOMERS table, issue the following command:

```
ALTER TABLE CUSTOMERS
 ADD (CUST_CREDIT_LIMIT NUMBER(7,2));
```

To modify the storage size for the country name, use the following command:

```
ALTER TABLE CUSTOMERS
 MODIFY (CUST_COUNTRY VARCHAR2(25));
```

Unfortunately, Oracle does not allow you to drop columns from a table or rename them. The following example shows you how to remove the CUST_COUNTRY column from the CUS-TOMERS table. The first command creates a new table, CUSTOMERS_NEW, by copying data from the CUSTOMERS table through a subselect of all columns other than the CUST_COUNTRY column. Once the data has been copied, the existing CUSTOMERS table should be removed using the DROP TABLE command. (This command is explained later in this chapter in the section entitled, "Removing a Table.") Finally, the name of the new table should be changed to the original CUSTOMERS name to complete the removal of a column from the table. The following steps illustrate this process:

1. ```
   CREATE TABLE CUSTOMERS_NEW AS

       select CUST_NO,

       CUST_NAME,

       CUST_ADDRESS,

       CUST_CITY,

       CUST_STATE,

       CUST_POSTAL_CODE,

       CUST_PHONE

       from CUSTOMERS;
   ```
2. ```
   DROP TABLE CUSTOMERS;
   ```
3. ```
   RENAME CUSTOMERS_NEW TO CUSTOMERS;
   ```

NOTE

This series of commands will enable you to successfully drop a column from a table. However, any other objects linked to the existing table will need to be re-created. These objects include indexes, views, triggers, snapshots, and any stored procedural modules that access the original table. In addition, any privileges granted for the original table have to be reissued for the new table.
   ```

This process works if you have enough free space to hold the copy of the new table and enough rollback space to handle the transaction. However, you also must reissue all commands associated with the old CUSTOMERS table, such as INDEX, VIEW, and TRIGGER CREATION, as well as any other objects associated with the old table.

Removing a Table

Finally, to remove a table from the database, issue the DROP TABLE command, like this:

```
drop table customers;
```

Indexes

After tables, indexes are probably the most important objects in an Oracle database. An index is a tree-structured mechanism that, if properly used, can reduce the I/O operations needed to locate and retrieve the data. The query optimizer uses indexes to facilitate efficient retrieval of the database information. Another use of indexes is to ensure uniqueness of data in the table.

Creating Indexes

An index is created using the CREATE INDEX command.

```
CREATE [UNIQUE] INDEX index_name
 ON table_name (column_list [ASC¦DESC])
 [INITRANS integer]
 [MAXTRANS integer]
 [TABLESPACE tablespace_name]
 [STORAGE storage_clause]
 [PCTFREE integer]
 [NOSORT]
 [RECOVERABLE ¦ UNRECOVERABLE]
 [PARALLEL parallel_clause]
```

In this example, the index is specified as unique with the UNIQUE parameter on the CREATE INDEX statement. The index must be defined against a single table using one or more columns in the table. Creative selection of the indexed columns can result in significant performance gains in the database. Although indexes can greatly improve database performance for queries, too many indexes can severely compromise the performance of inserts and updates to a data row.

For the most part, the parameters for the CREATE INDEX command are the same as the parameters for the CREATE TABLE command. The exception is that the default INITRANS parameter value in indexes is 2 because, generally, indexes have heavier volumes of activity than tables. Additionally, you can use the NOSORT parameter to improve index creation and insertion if the data is added to the table already sorted, for example a table with a unique sequential ID that is incremented for each new row.

Modifying Indexes

After the index has been created, you can change the storage and transaction parameters for the index with the ALTER INDEX command:

```
alter index CUST_PK
 storage (NEXT 100K);
```

> **NOTE**
>
> As in the case of tables, any changes affect only new extents for the index and do not affect any existing extents.

How Indexes Are Used

As stated previously, indexes can be used by Oracle's Query Optimizer to improve the performance of data access. Oracle uses two different optimizers. The first variant, the rule-based optimizer, executes a query based on a set of hierarchical rules that define the priority for all access options. The other optimizer option is the cost-based optimizer that attempts to retrieve the data at the lowest possible cost in terms of time and resources. (For more details on the optimizers, refer to Chapter 31.)

For the cost-based optimizer to use indexes properly, statistics must be generated for all the indexes. This operation is performed whenever the ANALYZE TABLE command is executed for the associated table.

Examining Indexes

To see which indexes (and the columns for the index) are available for a particular table, execute a query such as the one that follows for the CUSTOMERS table:

```
select i.index_name,
 i.uniqueness,
 c.column_name
 from user_indexes i,
 user_ind_columns c
 where i.index_name = c.index_name
 and i.table_name = 'CUSTOMERS'
 order by i.index_name, c.column_position;
INDEX_NAME                       UNIQUENESS COLUMN_NAME
================================ ========== ===============================
CUST_PK                          UNIQUE     CUST_NO
CUST_AK1                         NONUNIQUE  CUST_NAME
CUST_AK2                         NONUNIQUE  CUST_POSTAL_CODE
CUST_AK2                         NONUNIQUE  CUST_CITY
CUST_AK2                         NONUNIQUE  CUST_ST
CUST_AK2                         NONUNIQUE  CUST_COUNTRY
```

To view how the index utilizes space in the database, execute a query against the ALL_INDEXES data dictionary view as shown:

```
select blevel,
 leaf_blocks,
 distinct_keys,
 avg_leaf_blocks_per_key,
 avg_data_blocks_per_key,
 clustering_factor
 from all_indexes
 where index_name = 'CUST_AK1';
```

Table 3.5 explains the statistics returned by the preceding query.

Table 3.5. Index statistics.

Column	Description
BLEVEL	The depth of the index. In other words, the maximum number of index blocks that must be accessed to look up any value. A level of 1 indicates a relatively flat index against a small table or an index that is not very selective.
LEAF_BLOCKS	The number of blocks that contain index pointers. An index also uses branch blocks to link the various nodes in the tree structure.
DISTINCT_KEYS	The number of distinct values in the index. For unique or primary key indexes, this value will be equal to the number of rows in the table. The best indexes generally have a high number of distinct values relative to the number of table rows.
AVG_LEAF_BLOCKS_PER_KEY	This statistic indicates the average number of leaf blocks used by each distinct key value.
AVG_DATA_BLOCKS_PER_KEY	This statistic indicates the average number of table data blocks associated with each distinct key value.
CLUSTERING_FACTOR	This statistic reflects the relative degree of table organization with respect to the index. If the value is close to the number of data blocks used by the table, then the table is relatively sorted according to the index. If the value, on the other hand, is close to the number of rows in the table, then the table is most likely unsorted.

> **NOTE**
>
> These statistics are generated by the ANALYZE TABLE command, as shown here:
>
> ```
> ANALYZE TABLE CUSTOMERS COMPUTE STATISTICS;
> ```
>
> If the table has not been analyzed, all the statistics shown in the query will be null or zero. Also, the statistics will reflect the status of the index as of the last time the ANALYZE command was executed. This is a common source of confusion. I usually include the ANALYZE command as the first line of any scripts that I write to examine the object statistics. In that way, I am always reading accurate statistics.

Removing Indexes

To remove an index from a table, use the DROP INDEX command as shown:

```
DROP INDEX index_name;
```

> **NOTE**
>
> As stated previously, the number of indexes on a table can adversely affect the performance of any inserts or updates on a table. To speed up performance of programs loading a large amount of data into the database, many Oracle shops drop all (or most) indexes on a table before running the load. After the load has finished, the indexes are rebuilt using CREATE INDEX commands. Although this technique can minimize the batch load window, I have seen several cases where the time saved by the load program is lost in the index creation step. This condition is most evident when the number of rows affected by the load is significantly less than the total number of rows in the table. Therefore, if you decide to drop the indexes and recreate them, perform extensive testing using both scenarios. Additionally, you should plan to monitor the process as your database matures and grows larger.

Sequences

Oracle uses sequences to generate a unique sequential value for table keys. The CREATE SEQUENCE command follows:

```
CREATE SEQUENCE sequence_name
 [INCREMENT BY integer]
 [START WITH integer]
 [MAXVALUE integer]
 [MINVALUE integer]
 [CYCLE ¦ NOCYCLE]
 [CACHE integer ¦ NOCACHE]
 [ORDER ¦ NOORDER]
```

When the sequence is created, it must be defined with a specific name. The sequence will be created to generate numbers between the minimum and maximum values starting with the START WITH value and incremented by the INCREMENT BY parameter. The integer values for these parameters can be any integer value (positive, negative, or zero) up to 28 digits in length and the INCREMENT BY value cannot be equal to zero. If the INCREMENT BY parameter is negative, the sequence will be decremented for each access. The default for INCREMENT BY, START WITH, and MINVALUE is 1 and the default MAXVALUE is 10^{28}.

You can specify whether the sequence should recycle after the last value occurs using the CYCLE parameter. To facilitate performance, the sequence generator will cache 20 values at a time unless you specify another value or the NOCACHE parameter. Finally, the ORDER clause specifies that numbers in the sequence will be selected in the order that they are requested. If NOORDER (the default) is specified, the values selected from the cache may not be in order, although in most cases, they will be.

To obtain the next sequence value, reference the sequence generator using the following pseudocolumn:

```
sequence_name.nextval
```

For example, to insert a new record into the CUSTOMERS table, use the following code segment:

```
insert into customers
 (cust_no,...)
 values (CUSTOMER_SEQUENCE.nextval,...);
```

To remove a sequence generator from the database, use the DROP SEQUENCE command.

> **NOTE**
>
> A sequence generator does not indicate the record number in the table. Once a sequence number is cached, you cannot retrieve it. Thus, if the database is shut down and then restarted, the first select against the sequence generator will retrieve the next set of values. Additionally, if a value is selected and not used (that is, the insert fails or doesn't occur), it will be lost forever.

Clusters

One way to improve performance for data acquisition is to organize the database tables into their master-detail relationships through the use of clusters. You should use a cluster only when the master-detail relationship always exists and the number of detail records for each master record is fairly consistent. Also, clustered tables should be fairly stable with little or no update activity. For example, you can use clustered tables in an order-entry system that has an order header record containing customer and other point-of-sale data. The detail records would represent information related to the specific items in an order. Typically, the detail records are added to the database at the same time as the order, and new items are rarely added to an order.

To create a cluster, use the CREATE CLUSTER command shown here:

```
CREATE CLUSTER [schema_name.]cluster_name
 (column_specifications)
 [PCTFREE integer]
 [PCTUSED integer]
 [INITRANS integer]
 [MAXTRANS integer]
 [SIZE integer]
 [TABLESPACE tablespace_name]
 [STORAGE storage_clause]
 [INDEX ¦ HASHKEYS expression]
 [PARALLEL parallel_clause];
```

The column specification defines the linkage information between the joined tables and represents the common data elements between the two tables. The SIZE parameter defines how much space (in bytes) each clustered group requires.

The advantage of using clusters is that they improve database performance. The downside of using clustered tables is that you must treat all tables in the cluster as a single entity and perform all operations, such as backups and recovery, on the entire cluster.

NOTE

In my opinion, clusters do not improve performance enough to offset the additional maintenance concerns of using them. However, you may find that clusters are beneficial in your specific situation.

Views

You can think of views as logical tables in the database. A view consists of a predefined query against one or more tables and can be used in Oracle queries as if it were a table. You can use a view in database INSERT and UPDATE statements if both of these two conditions exist:

1. The view is based on a single table.
2. All not null columns in the table are included in the view.

To construct a view, use the following syntax:

```
CREATE [OR REPLACE] VIEW view_name AS
 select_statement
 [WITH READ ONLY ¦ WITH CHECK OPTION];
```

The view must have a unique name (up to 30 characters); that is, no other object in the database can use the same name as a view. The OR REPLACE clause will overwrite the existing text for the view. If this option is not selected and the view already exists, an error message will be generated. If the view is created using the WITH READ ONLY parameter, inserts, updates, and deletes will not be allowed against the view. The WITH CHECK OPTION parameter validates that any rows inserted or updated through the view can subsequently be selected through the view.

The SELECT statement used in the view can be any valid Oracle query. (Oracle queries are discussed further in Chapters 4 through 7 of this book.) When views are used in Oracle, the query parser substitutes the text of the view into the SQL statement before an execution plan is generated by the query optimizer. If the view is joined to other tables or views, the entire text of the multiple views is merged into a single SQL statement before the statement is executed. As a result, the expected execution plan can change significantly depending on how the joins are merged.

You should use views in an Oracle database to force a specific query or to restrict data from a table (such as security access). Although you can use a view to select all columns and rows from a specific table, the utility of such a view is minimized by the performance loss associated with the merge step.

To view the text of the SELECT statement in a view (using SQL*Plus), first determine the size of the text block using the following query:

```
select text_length
 from user_views
 where view_name = 'MY_VIEW';
```

Now, you need to set the display size for the view text to a value greater than the TEXT_LENGTH value (in this case 5000 characters) retrieved using the following commands:

```
set long 5000
set arraysize1
```

Now you can select the text of the view using the following query:

```
select text
 from user_views
 where view_name = 'MY_VIEW';
```

To remove the view from the database, use the DROP VIEW command as follows:

```
DROP VIEW view_name;
```

Snapshots

A snapshot is similar to a view in that it is based on the results of a query. Unlike a view, however, a snapshot uses physical storage, and the data in the snapshot is static until it is refreshed. The purpose of a snapshot is to provide a point-in-time representation of data. Snapshots provide query capabilities against the data based on the last time it was refreshed; for example, snapshots can provide information from tables from the start of a day or other designated period. Maintenance can be performed on the tables without affecting the online queries. To create a snapshot, use the following command:

```
CREATE SNAPSHOT snapshot_name
 [PCTFREE integer]
 [PCTUSED integer]
 [INITRANS integer]
 [MAXTRANS integer]
 [TABLESPACE tablespace_name]
 [STORAGE storage_clause]
 [USING INDEX [PCTFREE integer]
 [INITRANS integer]
 [MAXTRANS integer]
 [STORAGE storage_clause]]
 [CLUSTER cluster_name (cluster_columns)]
 [REFRESH [FAST ¦ COMPLETE ¦ FORCE]
 START WITH date_expression NEXT date_expression]
 [AS subquery]
```

Most of the parameters for this command match the usage in other commands. The USING INDEX option creates an index based on the ROWID (a pseudocolumn defining the specific storage location for a data row) in the original master table. The REFRESH clause defines when the snapshot should be refreshed and how the refresh is to be done. The date expression should be anything that will translate to a date value such as SYSDATE + 7. (The SYSDATE value is the current system date and time. Thus the previous expression would evaluate to seven days from the current date and time.) The refresh method can be either COMPLETE or FAST depending on whether a snapshot log has been created for the master table. FORCE specifies that the RDBMS will choose a fast refresh or a complete refresh based on availability. A COMPLETE refresh executes the query each time the snapshot is refreshed, whereas a FAST refresh uses information in the snapshot log to update only the rows that have changed.

To define a snapshot log for the master table, issue the following command:

```
CREATE SNAPSHOT LOG ON table_name
 [PCTFREE integer]
 [PCTUSED integer]
 [INITRANS integer]
 [MAXTRANS integer]
 [TABLESPACE tablespace_name]
 [STORAGE storage_clause];
```

When the snapshot is created, Oracle creates a table and view that correspond to the snapshot. To determine the names of these objects, issue the following query:

```
select table_name,
 master_view
 from user_snapshots
 where name = 'new_snapshot_name';
```

Once the names of these objects are known, you can execute queries, create indexes, and perform any other functions against the new table as if it were a "normal" table. If the snapshot is no longer needed, use the DROP SNAPSHOT command to eliminate it.

Data Access SQL Commands

Thus far, this chapter has presented the syntax for Oracle's Data Definition Language (DDL) commands. Oracle also provides commands that enable other users to access your objects.

Synonyms

You can use a *synonym* to create an alias for a table or view in the Oracle database. To create a synonym, use the following command:

```
CREATE [PUBLIC] SYNONYM synonym_name FOR [schema.]object_name;
```

As the CREATE SYNONYM statement shows, a synonym may be either *private* (available only to the user who created it) or *public* (available to all users). To create a public synonym, you must have DBA authority on the database. The advantage of public synonyms is that they can be created and maintained in a single location. If the schema is specified at the time of synonym creation, users will not have to specify the schema name when executing queries against a table. One common use of synonyms is to create a public synonym for a table with the same name as the original table. The syntax is

```
create public synonym customers for demo.customers;
```

where demo is the name of the schema that owns the table.

To remove the synonym from the database, issue the DROP SYNONYM command as shown here. (Note: If the synonym was created as a public synonym, you must specify the PUBLIC keyword.)

```
DROP [PUBLIC] SYNONYM synonym_name;
```

Granting Privileges

To allow other users to access your tables, you must grant permission to use the table to individual users, a role defined for a set of users, or to all users (via the PUBLIC userid). To grant privileges, issue the following command:

```
GRANT [SELECT] [,INSERT] [,UPDATE] [,DELETE] [,INDEX]
 ON object_name
 TO [PUBLIC ¦ user_name ¦ role_name] [WITH GRANT OPTION];
```

The various options define what activities the users may perform against a table or view. The WITH GRANT OPTION parameter allows the granted user to grant any of the same privileges to any other user.

To revoke these permissions, use the REVOKE command:

```
REVOKE privilege_list
 ON object_name FROM [PUBLIC ¦ user_name ¦ role_name];
```

Data Manipulation Language Commands

Most of Part II of this book is devoted to the various commands for accessing and maintaining Oracle data. Table 3.6 lists the Data Manipulation Language (DML) commands and the chapters in which you will find in-depth discussions of them.

Table 3.6. Where to find the Oracle DML commands.

Command	Use	Chapter(s)
SELECT	Retrieve data from the database	4, 5, 6, 7
INSERT	Insert data rows on a table	9, 11
UPDATE	Modify an existing row	9, 11
DELETE	Remove an existing row	9, 11
TRUNCATE	Remove all rows from a table	9

Oracle's Procedural Extensions

Although Oracle7 is essentially an object-oriented database, you often need to write procedural program modules to follow a specific sequence of events based on a particular event. Oracle provides the PL/SQL language to facilitate these tasks. Chapter 12, "PL/SQL," covers PL/SQL in detail.

You can use PL/SQL to define triggers based on specific activities against the Oracle tables. These triggers may execute stored procedures and functions that are also written in this procedural language. Finally, you can organize these stored procedural objects into packages to improve performance when the objects are accessed. Chapter 14 will explore these objects in detail.

Summary

This chapter introduced many of the commands that make up Oracle's SQL implementation. At this point, you should be able to create your database objects based on a sound design. Part IV, "Design and Construction of an Oracle Database," can help you gain a better understanding of the criteria you can use to define the database. The remainder of Part II, "Oracle Fundamentals," shows you how to manipulate the data in your database, beginning with how to query Oracle data in the next chapter.

4

Oracle Queries

by Joe Zafian III

Retrieval and display of stored information are the primary functions of any relational database management system (RDBMS). Oracle provides this functionality through the use of the SQL SELECT statement. Data queries can range from simple single table "dumps" of information to more complex queries involving multiple tables with calculations based on the data in the tables. This chapter introduces the SELECT statement and its various component clauses. The chapter begins with several relatively simple queries, and then provides examples that demonstrate more powerful features of the SELECT statement. Subsequent chapters will introduce more complexity until you are able to formulate a data query that can retrieve virtually any set of information you may need in your application.

The Basic Query

When you need to communicate a thought, you need to place your words in a proper order or syntax. The SQL SELECT statement, like a sentence, requires the component clauses to appear in a specific order. Every SELECT statement must specify the information to be retrieved and provide instructions on where the information is stored. The simplest form of an Oracle query is shown in the following example, which selects all data from the departments table (DEPT):

```
select * from dept;

DEPT_NO DEPT_NAME              LOCATION              BUDGET
------- -------------------- -------------------- --------
     10 ACCOUNTING            NEW YORK                25000
     40 BROADCAST OPERATIONS  LOS ANGELES            412500
     30 HOSPITAL SERVICES     WASHINGTON             875000
     20 PERSONNEL             NEW YORK                14000
     50 CONSULTING SERVICES   CHICAGO               2350000
     60 SALES                 NEW YORK               650000
     70 QUALITY CONTROL       CHICAGO                500000
     80 SHIPPING              ST LOUIS                19800
```

Note that the asterisk in the query tells Oracle to retrieve all information in the selected tables. Although ANSI standard rules allow this shorthand, I advise you not to use it in any production applications. Tables change as a business evolves, and your applications may no longer work if the default is used. Therefore, you should use this shorthand only when you are trying to examine the table in an interactive mode with a tool such as SQL*Plus.

Instead of using the asterisk shorthand as shown in the preceding example, you should explicitly list all the columns that you want the query to return. Simply list the names of the columns in the column list portion of the SELECT statement. The preceding query would then be written as follows:

```
select dept_no, dept_name, location, budget from dept;
```

This first example selected all rows from the DEPT table, but you may be interested in a subset of the rows in your table. In the next example, the query selects the IDs and names of all employees who have been assigned to department 10 (accounting).

```
select emp_id,
       emp_last_name
  from emp
 where dept_no = 10;

EMP_ID EMP_LAST_NAME
------- -------------------
    17 ADAMS
   357 HERSHEY
    19 ANDERSON
   112 RACCIO
```

The conditional portion, or WHERE clause, of the SELECT statement will filter all rows from the table based on the logic specified. (The column that the condition is based on does not have to appear as a selected column.)

Another requirement for many queries is to retrieve the data in a specific order. To do so, add an ORDER BY clause to the query. The first query in this chapter displayed the results in a seemingly random order. The following query orders the results by department number:

```
select dept_no, dept_name, location
  from dept
 order by dept_no;

DEPT_NO DEPT_NAME            LOCATION
------- -------------------- --------------------
     10 ACCOUNTING           NEW YORK
     20 PERSONNEL            NEW YORK
     30 HOSPITAL SERVICES    WASHINGTON
     40 BROADCAST OPERATIONS LOS ANGELES
     50 CONSULTING SERVICES  CHICAGO
     60 SALES                NEW YORK
     70 QUALITY CONTROL      CHICAGO
     80 SHIPPING             ST LOUIS
```

You may need to sort the returned data by more than one column, for example, when you have multiple occurrences of data for the primary sort column. In such cases, you can specify a second sort key in the ORDER BY clause, as shown in the next example:

```
select dept_no,
       emp_last_name
  from emp
 where salary > 50000
 order by dept_no, emp_last_name;

DEPT_NO EMP_LAST_NAME
------- -------------------
     10 ADAMS
     10 RACCIO
     30 BROWN
     30 BRUNNER
     30 SMITH
     40 GIARDINA
     40 JONES
     40 O'BRIEN
     50 FULLER
```

```
50 LUNDY
50 NEWTON
60 FARRELL
60 MATTEO
   RUSSO
```

To sort the values from highest value to lowest (or reverse alphabetical order), use the DESC option in the ORDER BY clause, as shown here:

```
select emp_last_name,
       salary
  from emp
 where dept_no = 10
 order by salary desc;
```

```
EMP_LAST_NAME            SALARY
-------------------- --------
RACCIO                    87500
ADAMS                     72000
HERSHEY                   48000
ANDERSON                  42000
```

Using Expressions

As you develop your applications, you may need to retrieve data based on a calculation or other operation that does not specifically refer to the value in a particular column. For example, you could write the following query to compute the weekly salary for all employees in the accounting department, based on a 15 percent raise:

```
select emp_last_name,
       (salary * 1.15) / 52
  from emp
where dept_no = 10;
```

```
EMP_LAST_NAME        (SALARY*1.15)/52
-------------------- ----------------
RACCIO                    1935.09615
ADAMS                     1592.30769
HERSHEY                   1061.53846
ANDERSON                  928.846154
```

Expressions based on numerical data use conventional algebraic symbols and logic such as addition (+), subtraction (-), multiplication (*), and division (/). In addition, expressions based on a date use the addition and subtraction operators to calculate a new date that is a specific number of days before or after the original date. Finally, character fields may be concatenated with the concatenation operator (¦¦) as shown here.

```
select emp_first_name¦¦' '¦¦emp_last_name
  from emp
 where dept_no = 50;
```

```
EMP_FIRST_NAME||'' ''||EMP_LAST_NAME
----------------------------------------
FREDERICK FULLER
STEVEN NEWTON
MARK LUNDY
FRANK BEECHER
OTTO NEUMANN
BARRY MITTLER
DAVID CANNELL
JAMES ZAFIAN
```

Other types of expressions can be constants such as a numerical value or a specific character string enclosed in single quotes (for example, `'HOSPITAL SERVICES'`). Finally, an expression can be based on the result of a function such as `ABS (salary - 75000)`, which returns the absolute value of the difference between `salary` and `75000`.

NOTE

Functions will be explained in greater detail in Chapter 5, "Working with Date, Numeric, and Character Functions."

Expressions are not limited to the column select list. They can be used anywhere within the `WHERE` clause and `ORDER BY` clause, as well. The next example selects all employees whose base salary is greater than $1,000 per week:

```
select emp_last_name
  from emp
 where salary > 52000;
```

The preceding `SELECT` statement is equivalent to

```
select emp_last_name
  from emp
 where salary > 52 * 1000;
```

which is also equivalent to

```
select emp_last_name
  from emp
 where salary / 52 > 1000;
```

As you can see, standard algebraic properties will apply to any SQL expression. You can also use parentheses to explicitly enforce the order of precedence within an expression or to make the expression easier to read. In the following example, the parentheses force the calculation to follow the specified order of operation:

```
select emp_last_name, 1.05 * (salary + (commission_rate * sales_quota))
  from emp
 where emp_id = 113;

EMP_LAST_NAME      1.05*(salary+(commission_rate*sales_quota))
----------------   -------------------------------------------
MATTEO                                              435641.85
```

Using Special Pseudocolumns

A pseudocolumn is a column that is not actually a part of any table but returns a value when selected. An example of a pseudocolumn is SYSDATE, which represents the current system date and time. An expression using the SYSDATE pseudocolumn in the following example returns a date that is one week from the current date:

```
select sysdate + 7
  from dual;

SYSDATE+7
---------
15-OCT-96
```

> **NOTE**
>
> Note that this query selects its values from a special system table named dual. The dual table can provide data based on a single row, as shown in the preceding example. Typically, application modules use the dual table to get system information or to validate data values for specific formats such as date validation.

Table 4.1 lists all the pseudocolumns that may be used in Oracle applications.

Table 4.1. Oracle pseudocolumns.

Pseudocolumn	*Return Value*
sequence.CURRVAL	The last selected value from the sequence generator for the sequence named. This pseudocolumn is available only after a value has been selected initially for the sequence during the current instance session.
LEVEL	The depth of the query within a tree. LEVEL is applicable to a special type of query called a tree query. (See Chapter 5.)
sequence.NEXTVAL	Selecting this pseudocolumn will cause the sequence generator to return the next value in the sequence. Once this value has been selected, it cannot be reused, because each subsequent retrieval will return the next value.
ROWID	This pseudocolumn defines the exact storage location of a data row. The format of ROWID is a set of three groups of hexadecimal values that appears like AAAAAAAA.BBBB.CCCC, where AAAAAAAA represents the block number within the datafile containing the row, BBBB is the row number within the data block, and CCCC is the file ID within the database.

Pseudocolumn	Return Value
ROWNUM	The sequence number in which the row was retrieved.
SYSDATE	The current date and time.
UID	The unique ID for the current user.
USER	The name that the user logs in to the database with.

sequence.NEXTVAL **and** *sequence*.CURRVAL

If you need to select the next sequence number before inserting new values into a table, use the sequence generator to obtain the value from the sequence generator with a query against the dual table, as shown here:

```
select employee_sequence.nextval
  from dual;
```

Once a number has been selected, you can check for the last value selected by using the following query, also against the dual table:

```
select employee_sequence.currval
  from dual;
```

ROWID

If your application needs to select data from a table and update it at a later time, you should select the ROWID from the base table at the same time that you are selecting the data. When you update the row later, you can enhance performance by using the ROWID for your data access path. If you add a FOR UPDATE clause to the query, the data row will be locked from any other changes by other users. Locking ensures data consistency between selection and update. The following example selects a specific employee record and locks the data row for update:

```
select rowid,
       emp_last_name
       emp_first_name
       dept_no,
       salary
  from emp
 where emp_id = 73
   for update;
```

ROWID	EMP_LAST_NAME	EMP_FIRST_NAME	DEPT_NO	SALARY
00001C3A.0007.0002	ZAFIAN	JAMES	50	37500

After the row has been retrieved, you can use the returned ROWID as the condition to update the employee record, as shown in the next example. (You learn more about the UPDATE statement in Chapter 9, "Modifying Table Data.")

```
update emp
   set salary = 45000
 where rowid = '00001C3A.0007.0002';
```

ROWNUM

The ROWNUM pseudocolumn serves many purposes besides counting the rows returned. One of the most important uses of this pseudocolumn is to limit the number of rows returned by a query. The example below selects up to 10 rows from the EMP table.

```
select dept_no,
       emp_last_name
  from emp
 where rownum < 11
 order by emp_last_name;

DEPT_NO EMP_LAST_NAME
------- --------------------
     10 ADAMS
     10 ANDERSON
     30 BROWN
     30 BRUNNER
     50 FULLER
     10 HERSHEY
     40 JONES
     40 O'BRIEN
     10 RACCIO
     30 SMITH
```

> **NOTE**
>
> One thing to note about the preceding query is that the ORDER BY clause applies to the final query result and will not affect the rows returned. This query will select and sort the first 10 rows in the EMP table. However, you cannot use this query to select the first 10 rows alphabetically.

UID **and** USER

The UID and USER pseudocolumns perform many functions. For example, you can create an audit trail column to log the name or ID of any user that updates a data row. Also, one technique that I use with the UID pseudocolumn is to attach security to a data row based on a user's login ID. For example, suppose a column is added to the EMP table as SUPERVISOR_UID, which represents the user ID for an employee's supervisor. Your query can allow an employee to look up only the rows that apply to his direct subordinates, as shown in the next example:

```
select emp_id,
       emp_last_name,
       salary
```

```
  from emp
 where supervisor_uid = UID;

EMP_ID EMP_LAST_NAME            SALARY
------ -------------------- --------
   102 BRUNNER                104000
   103 GIARDINA                87000
   105 LUNDY                   78000
   111 RUSSO                   65000
   113 MATTEO                 150000
   127 GOLDSMITH               48000
```

Nonequality Query Conditions

Besides constructing queries based on a column value being equal to another value, SQL also supports logical operators, as shown in Table 4.2.

Table 4.2. SQL logical operators.

Example	Explanation
salary = 50000	salary *equal to* 50000
salary != 50000	salary *not equal to* 50000
salary ^= 50000	salary *not equal to* 50000
salary <> 50000	salary *not equal to* 50000
salary < 50000	salary *less than* 50000
salary <= 50000	salary *less than or equal to* 50000
salary > 50000	salary *greater than* 50000
salary >= 50000	salary *greater than or equal to* 50000

Additionally, a query can use the range-checking operator BETWEEN to test for all values between each end point (including the end points), as shown in the next code segment:

```
select emp_last_name
  from emp
 where hire_date BETWEEN '01-JAN-96' AND '31-MAR-96'

EMP_LAST_NAME        HIRE_DATE
-------------------- --------
SMITH                02-FEB-96
FULLER               02-JAN-96
NEWTON               01-JAN-96
ZAFIAN               31-MAR-96
```

In the preceding example, notice that the between operator includes data values that are equal to the specified end points. The BETWEEN conditional operator translates to greater than or equal to value 1 and less than or equal to value 2. If the second value specified is less than the first value, no error will be issued. The query will simply return no rows.

SQL also provides a mechanism for pattern matching in character strings. The LIKE operator uses an underscore character (_) to represent a single character position within a string and a percent sign (%) to represent any number of characters in the string. The following example demonstrates how this operator works in an Oracle query.

```
select emp_last_name
  from emp
 where emp_last_name like '%SM_TH%'
 order by emp_last_name;


EMP_NAME
==============================
GOLDSMITH
SMITH
SMOTHERS
SMYTHE
```

Working with Null Values

A null value represents a column that does not have any value, as opposed to 0 or all spaces. For example, suppose your company has an employee table and the employees in the sales department receive a commission based on performance, rather than a conventional salary. The salary column for all the sales people would be empty, or null. The problem with using a null value is that *NULL MEANS NOTHING!* I repeat, *NULL MEANS NOTHING!* You cannot use the proceeding logical operators with null values. For example, the following query will not work:

```
select emp_name
  from emp
 where salary = null;


no rows selected
```

It is very important to note that a column with a null value will never equal anything (including null). This point bears repeating. Many developers get caught because they are trying to select data from a table while using a conditional operator against a null column. Unfortunately, Oracle will not generate an error for this query (as you would hope). To test for the null condition, SQL provides the IS NULL operator (or IS NOT NULL to return all rows that have an entry), as shown in the next example:

```
select emp_last_name
  from emp
 where salary is null;

EMP_LAST_NAME
--------------------
SIM
ANNUNZIATO
```

In addition, any expression based on a null value will return a null value. For example, the next query should present the budgeted compensation for all employees in the company.

```
select emp_last_name,
       salary + sales_quota * commission_rate
  from emp
 where dept_no = 60
 order by salary + sales_quota * commission_rate;

EMP_LAST_NAME          SALARY+SALES_QUOTA*COMMISSION_RATE
--------------------   ----------------------------------
FARRELL
MATTEO                                            414897
SIM
ANNUNZIATO
```

This query returns null values for all employees except for the sales director who receives both salary and commission. Oracle's NVL function corrects this "problem" by instructing the query to substitute a value for any instance where null is found. This function requires two arguments: the column that may be null and the substitution value that should be used for all nulls. The following query may be used to return the value for each row where one of the components to the expression may have been null:

```
select emp_last_name,
       nvl (salary, 0) + nvl (sales_quota, 0) * nvl (commission_rate, 0)
  from emp
 where dept_no = 60
 order by nvl (salary, 0) + nvl (sales_quota, 0) * nvl (commission_rate, 0);

EMP_LAST_NAME          NVL(SALARY,0)+NVL(SALES_QUOTA,0)*NVL(COMMISSION_RATE,0)
--------------------   -------------------------------------------------------
SIM                                                             94362.75
ANNUNZIATO                                                     135534.15
FARRELL                                                        206412.35
MATTEO                                                            414897
```

Queries Based on Sets of Values

If you want to select data in which the value is (or is not) a member of a set of values, use the IN or NOT IN operator, as shown in the following examples:

```
select emp_name
  from emp
 where dept_no in (30, 40);
```

```
EMP_LAST_NAME
--------------------
BRUNNER
BROWN
SMITH
JONES
O'BRIEN
GIARDINA

select dept_no,
       dept_name
  from dept
 where location not in ('NEW YORK', 'CHICAGO'');

DEPT_NO DEPT_NAME
-------- --------------------
      40 BROADCAST OPERATIONS
      30 HOSPITAL SERVICES
      80 SHIPPING
```

Combining Logic

The preceding section presented several examples in which the query was based on a single query condition. However, the SQL language syntax includes three logical operators that enable you to combine logical expressions. These operators are AND, OR, and NOT. Tables 4.3, 4.4, and 4.5 show the logical result of these multiple conditions.

Table 4.3. NOT conditional logic.

Cond1	NOT Cond1
FALSE	TRUE
TRUE	FALSE
null	FALSE

Table 4.4. AND conditional logic.

Cond1	Cond2	Cond1 AND Cond2
FALSE	FALSE	FALSE
FALSE	TRUE	FALSE
FALSE	null	FALSE
TRUE	FALSE	FALSE
TRUE	TRUE	TRUE
TRUE	null	FALSE

Table 4.5. OR conditional logic.

Cond1	*Cond2*	*Cond1* OR *Cond2*
FALSE	FALSE	FALSE
FALSE	TRUE	TRUE
FALSE	null	FALSE
TRUE	FALSE	TRUE
TRUE	TRUE	TRUE
TRUE	null	TRUE

You can also combine several conditional operators to formulate a query filter. Suppose that you wanted to find all the employees in either the hospital services department (department 30) or the broadcast operations department (department 40) whose salaries are greater than $50,000. You might formulate this query:

```
select emp_last_name,
       dept_no,
       salary
  from emp
 where dept_no = 30
    or dept_no = 40
   and salary > 50000;


EMP_LAST_NAME        DEPT_NO    SALARY
-------------------- --------- --------
BRUNNER                   30    104000
BROWN                     30     57000
SMITH                     30     55000
JONES                     40     51000
O'BRIEN                   40     63000
GIARDINA                  40     87000
HEIMER                    30     47000
```

Obviously, the result is not what you hoped for. The record for Heimer appears in the output, even though the salary is below $50,000. The reason for this result is Oracle's hierarchical order of precedence for conditional logic. Here is the precedence hierarchy:

1. All resolutions of expressions (*, /, +, -)
2. All single column comparisons (for example, =, !=, >, <, between, in)
3. NOT conditions
4. AND conditions
5. OR conditions

Thus, the previous query first retrieves all rows where the department equals 40 and the salary is greater than 50000. Then all rows from department 30 are merged into the query. You can use parentheses to enforce the order of precedence, as shown in the following code:

```
select emp_last_name,
       dept_no,
       salary
  from emp
 where (dept_no = 30
    or dept_no = 40)
   and salary > 50000;

EMP_LAST_NAME         DEPT_NO    SALARY
--------------------  --------  --------
BRUNNER                    30    104000
BROWN                      30     57000
SMITH                      30     55000
JONES                      40     51000
O'BRIEN                    40     63000
GIARDINA                   40     87000
```

Using Column and Table Aliases

In order to make your queries easier to understand, Oracle allows you to specify alternative names (or aliases) for items in the column list, as well as for the tables in the FROM clause. Simply supply the alias name immediately after the object you wish to rename, as shown in the next example:

```
select e.emp_last_name EMPLOYEE,
       (e.salary * 1.15) / 52 NEW_SALARY
  from emp e
where e.dept_no = 10;

EMPLOYEE              NEW_SALARY
--------------------  ----------
ADAMS                  1592.3077
HERSHEY                1061.5385
ANDERSON               928.84615
RACCIO                 1935.0962
```

When data is returned from this query, the new column aliases, rather than the database name, will be displayed above the appropriate column. Using aliases is one way to customize SQL*Plus output to generate a fast database report. Also, note that the expression e is being used as an alias for the EMP table and that the table alias was specified for the table for each column name in the query.

Selecting Distinct Values

Sometimes you need to generate a list of all valid entries in a table, based on a set of conditions. For example, you might want to select all departments in the company that have at least one employee earning over $50,000. You could use the following query:

```
select dept_no
    from emp
 where salary > 50000
 order by dept_no;

DEPT_NO
--------
      10
      10
      30
      30
      30
      40
      40
      40
      50
      50
      50
      60
      60
```

Although this query does contain the information you need, your application will have to process nine rows of data to determine the full set of entries, rather than the four rows that are necessary. SQL provides the SELECT DISTINCT option to limit the result set to a distinct set of values. The following query selects the distinct values for the department number for departments that have employees earning over $50,000 in the EMP table:

```
select distinct dept_no
  from emp
 where salary > 50000;

DEPT_NO
--------
      10
      30
      40
      50
      60
```

NOTE

A few thoughts about using DISTINCT. First, in the current version of Oracle, SELECT DISTINCT sorts the rows in order of the columns selected; however, Oracle does not promise that this sort will work in future releases. If you need data in a specific order, use the ORDER BY clause or force the query to use the proper indexed column. Next, SELECT DISTINCT is a very inefficient SQL construct, and you can usually find other, much better ways to obtain the information you need. You should avoid SELECT DISTINCT whenever possible; use it only as a last resort.

Joining Multiple Tables in a Query

If you could always select data from a single table (as you have been able to do in the examples thus far), you would not need to read an entire book on Oracle. In most circumstances, you will need to select data from several tables in a single query. As a general rule of thumb, the fewer queries that your application needs to execute, the more efficiently the application will perform.

You can select data from multiple tables by specifying more than one table in the FROM clause and using the WHERE clause to specify the join condition, or relationship between the tables. For example, to create a report that lists all departments and their employees, use the following query:

```
select d.dept_name,
       e.emp_last_name
  from emp e,
       dept d
 where d.dept_no = e.dept_no
order by d.dept_no;

DEPT_NAME              EMP_LAST_NAME
--------------------   --------------------
ACCOUNTING             ADAMS
ACCOUNTING             HERSHEY
ACCOUNTING             ANDERSON
ACCOUNTING             RACCIO
HOSPITAL SERVICES      BRUNNER
HOSPITAL SERVICES      HEIMER
HOSPITAL SERVICES      BROWN
HOSPITAL SERVICES      SMITH
BROADCAST OPERATIONS   JONES
BROADCAST OPERATIONS   O'BRIEN
BROADCAST OPERATIONS   GIARDINA
CONSULTING SERVICES    FULLER
CONSULTING SERVICES    LUNDY
CONSULTING SERVICES    BEECHER
CONSULTING SERVICES    MITTLER
CONSULTING SERVICES    CANNELL
CONSULTING SERVICES    NEUMANN
CONSULTING SERVICES    ZAFIAN
CONSULTING SERVICES    NEWTON
SALES                  FARRELL
SALES                  MATTEO
SALES                  SIM
SALES                  ANNUNZIATO
QUALITY CONTROL        GOLDSMITH
QUALITY CONTROL        SMOTHERS
QUALITY CONTROL        SMYTHE
```

In this example, the relationship between the two tables is defined using the department number on each table. The department number is defined as the primary key for the DEPT table. By using a foreign key reference from the EMP table, the two tables may be joined. This condition represents a master-detail (or parent-child) relationship between the two tables—the most common way in which tables can be joined. The relationship condition causes the data to be tightly bound with a one-to-many relationship.

Without a join condition, the tables would be joined in a *Cartesian product*, which means that all of the rows in one table are joined to all of the rows in the other table. For example, if each of the five departments has 100 employees, the result would be 500 rows. In this case, a Cartesian product would be an undesirable result. However, in some situations a Cartesian product can produce dramatic improvements. For example, if several queries return only one row, you can formulate them to join, via a Cartesian product, to return a single row from a single query. This technique produces significant performance gains.

You can also use a Cartesian product to produce a matrix of records when you want all rows to be joined between two tables. In the following example, this type of query produces one row for every month in the calendar table for every department:

```
select d.dept_name,
       c.month_name
  from dept d,
       calendar c
 where c.start_date between '01-JAN-95' and '31-DEC-95';
```

```
DEPT_NAME            MONTH_NAM
-------------------- ---------
ACCOUNTING           JANUARY
ACCOUNTING           FEBRUARY
ACCOUNTING           MARCH
ACCOUNTING           APRIL
ACCOUNTING           MAY
ACCOUNTING           JUNE
ACCOUNTING           JULY
ACCOUNTING           AUGUST
ACCOUNTING           SEPTEMBER
ACCOUNTING           OCTOBER
ACCOUNTING           NOVEMBER
ACCOUNTING           DECEMBER
PERSONNEL            JANUARY
PERSONNEL            FEBRUARY
        .
        .
        .
```

You could even supplement this query with a financial table to define monthly budgets for each department.

Besides being able to join multiple tables within a query, you can also join a table to itself.

```
select t1.emp_last_name SUPERVISOR,
       t2.emp_last_name SUBORDINATE
  from emp t1,
       emp t2
 where t1.emp_id = t2.supervisor_emp_id
order by 1, 2;
```

```
SUPERVISOR            SUBORDINAT
--------------------  ----------
BRUNNER               BROWN
BRUNNER               HEIMER
BRUNNER               SMITH
GIARDINA              FULLER
GIARDINA              JONES
GIARDINA              NEWTON
GIARDINA              O'BRIEN
GOLDSMITH             SMOTHERS
GOLDSMITH             SMYTHE
LUNDY                 BEECHER
LUNDY                 CANNELL
LUNDY                 MITTLER
LUNDY                 NEUMANN
LUNDY                 ZAFIAN
MATTEO                ANNUNZIATO
MATTEO                FARRELL
MATTEO                SIM
RACCIO                ADAMS
RACCIO                ANDERSON
RACCIO                HERSHEY
RUSSO                 RACCIO
```

By using an alias for the table name, Oracle treats each table as if it were a separate entity. Thus the preceding query will retrieve all supervisor names for each employee. Also observe the ORDER BY clause in this query, where the ORDER BY columns are specified according to the relative position in the query, rather than by explicitly declaring the column names. Oracle has stated that this convention will be dropped in future releases of the RDBMS, so you should try to avoid using this method. Beginning with version 7.2, you can specify the column alias in the ORDER BY clause instead.

Using Subqueries

Another form of the multiple-table query is the subquery. A *subquery* is a secondary (or nested) query that returns one or more rows of data used to satisfy conditions within the primary query. You can use a subquery that returns only one row in a WHERE condition with any logical operator, such as equality. Suppose that you need to retrieve all employees that work in the accounting department, but you do not know the department number. In a series of single-table queries, you would first determine the department with this query:

```
select dept_no
  from dept
 where dept_name = 'ACCOUNTING';

  DEPT_NO
--------
      10
```

Next, you would create the query to retrieve the appropriate employees, as shown here:

```
select emp_last_name
  from emp
 where dept_no = 10;
```

As stated previously, a single query usually performs better than two separate queries. In this case, you can write a query to join the tables in a simple join condition, or you can use a subquery to attain the same result, as shown in the next example:

```
select emp_last_name
  from emp
 where dept_no = (select dept_no
                    from dept
                   where dept_name = 'ACCOUNTING');
```

```
EMP_LAST_NAME
-------------------
ADAMS
HERSHEY
ANDERSON
RACCIO
```

Note that you can enclose the subquery in parentheses and run it as an autonomous query. In this case, the query returns a single row of data. Suppose instead that you wanted to base the query on a subquery that returns more than one row, such as all employees working in departments whose headquarters are in New York. This query would fail because the subquery must return only one row of data. To accomplish the location subquery, you can specify an IN clause to handle multiple rows of data. (By the way, if a single row is returned, the query will still work.)

```
select emp_last_name
  from emp
 where dept_no IN (select dept_no
                     from dept
                    where location = 'NEW YORK');
```

```
EMP_LAST_NAME
-------------------
ADAMS
HERSHEY
ANDERSON
RACCIO
FARRELL
MATTEO
SIM
ANNUNZIATO
```

Starting with version 7.1 of the Oracle RDBMS, you can use a subquery variation called a dynamic view. *Dynamic views* specify that a subquery may be used as a table in the FROM clause of a primary query, as shown in the following example:

```
select d.department,
       e.emp_last_name,
       e.salary
  from emp e,
       (select dept_no,
               dept_name department
          from dept
         where location = 'NEW YORK') d
 where e.dept_no = d.dept_no
 order by d.department, e.emp_last_name;
```

```
DEPARTMENT               EMP_LAST_NAME           SALARY
-------------------      --------------------    --------
ACCOUNTING               ADAMS                     72000
ACCOUNTING               ANDERSON                  42000
ACCOUNTING               HERSHEY                   48000
ACCOUNTING               RACCIO                    87500
SALES                    ANNUNZIATO
SALES                    FARRELL                   95000
SALES                    MATTEO                   150000
SALES                    SIM
```

This query satisfies the subquery and "creates" a temporary table D that joins with the EMP table. Note that any references to columns in the subquery are based on the column aliases in the query, rather than on the actual column names. The biggest advantage of using a dynamic view is the flexibility it gives you to create a simpler base query. Unfortunately, by using the dynamic view for the table definition, you don't gain any potential performance benefit from any indexes from the other tables into the dynamic view. If, on the other hand, the overall query can be driven from the dynamic view, this technique can be a very efficient way to join the tables.

Unions and Other Multiple-Part Queries

Finally, you can combine multiple queries with the UNION, INTERSECT, and MINUS operators. To create a multiple-part query, you should define two or more queries, with an exact correspondence between the column data type definitions in each query. Then, depending on the operator that connects the two (or more) queries, the result sets would be combined. In a UNION, all distinct rows that are in either query appear in the result set. For example, to define a list of values for the departments and to provide an additional row to represent an unknown department, you would use the following query:

```
select dept_no,
       dept_name
  from dept
            UNION
select 99,
       'UNKNOWN'
  from dual;
```

```
DEPT_NO DEPT_NAME
------- ------------------
```

```
10 ACCOUNTING
20 PERSONNEL
30 HOSPITAL SERVICES
40 BROADCAST OPERATIONS
50 CONSULTING SERVICES
60 SALES
70 QUALITY CONTROL
80 SHIPPING
99 UNKNOWN
```

Similarly, INTERSECT returns all rows that are found in all the individual queries, and MINUS returns the rows that are found only in the first query.

Putting It All Together

Finally, I have a recommendation that you should consider when building complex Oracle applications with large, complex, multiple-table queries. Construct the query in a piecemeal fashion, adding an additional table and testing the query as it is being built. This process will help you to isolate the problem areas very quickly. Many installations have defined rules that no queries should access more than a specified number of tables or views. Although this rule may simplify understanding an application query, it does very little for improving application performance. Depending on how the query is constructed, an eight-table query may actually perform much better than a two-table query.

As an example, suppose that you need to develop a query for the staffing coordinator in the personnel department. A requirement has been defined for a consultant with at least two years' experience using Oracle Forms 4.5. This person should be an expert (level 4 out of 5) and must be available on June 1, 1997. The billing rate is $75 per hour (maximum hourly rate of $52.50 or maximum salary of $66,000).

As a start, first formulate the query to retrieve all consultants who meet the salary requirements. Use the ROWNUM pseudocolumn to limit the query for testing.

```
select e.emp_first_name||' '||e.emp_last_name EMPLOYEE,
       e.salary SALARY,
       e.hourly_rate HRLY
  from emp e,
       dept d
 where d.dept_no = e.dept_no
   and d.dept_name = 'CONSULTING SERVICES'
   and (e.salary < 66000 or e.hourly_rate < 52.50)
   and rownum < 10;
```

Next, add the skills condition to the query, as shown.

```
select e.emp_first_name||' '||e.emp_last_name EMPLOYEE,
       e.salary SALARY,
       e.hourly_rate HRLY,
       es.skill_level LEVEL,
       es.skill_months / 12 YEARS
  from emp e,
```

```
        dept d,
        employee_skills es,
        skills s
  where d.dept_no = e.dept_no
    and es.emp_id = e.emp_id
    and s.skill_code = es.skill_code
    and d.dept_name = 'CONSULTING SERVICES'
    and (e.salary < 66000 or e.hourly_rate < 52.50)
    and s.skill_name = 'ORACLE FORMS 4.5'
    and es.skill_level >= 4
    and es.skill_months >= 24
    and rownum < 10;
```

Finally, use a dynamic view to determine the consultants who will be available on June 1.

```
select e.emp_first_name¦¦' '¦¦e.emp_last_name EMPLOYEE,
       e.salary SALARY,
       e.hourly_rate HRLY,
       es.skill_level LEVEL,
       es.skill_months / 12 YEARS,
       ca.avail_date AVAIL
  from emp e,
       dept d,
       employee_skills es,
       skills s,
       (select emp_id,
               assigned_end_date + 1 AVAIL_DATE
          from current_assignments ca
         where assigned_end_date < '01-JUN-97'
               UNION
        select emp_id,
               sysdate + 1
          from emp
         where emp_id not in (select emp_id
                                from current_assignments)) ca
 where d.dept_no = e.dept_no
   and es.emp_id = e.emp_id
   and s.skill_code = es.skill_code
   and ca.emp_id = e.emp_id
   and d.dept_name = 'CONSULTING SERVICES'
   and (e.salary < 66000 or e.hourly_rate < 52.50)
   and s.skill_name = 'ORACLE FORMS 4.5'
   and es.skill_level >= 4
   and es.skill_months >= 24
   and rownum < 10;
```

This last change uses a previously built view, CURRENT_ASSIGNMENTS, that defines information related to the current consulting assignment for each consultant. The second part of the union selects all consultants who do not have a current assignment. Once you are satisfied that your query works, remove the ROWNUM condition to generate the final list.

NOTE

This last example is *not* the best way to process this query; it merely encompasses many of the examples in this chapter. Later chapters will explain how to tune this query for performance and suggest other methods that will improve the query.

Summary

This chapter presented the basic information you need to select data from an Oracle database for your applications. As you should be aware by now, Oracle usually gives you several ways to accomplish the same data query task. By learning and understanding the alternatives, you will be able to define more than one approach to any problem. By working with the examples provided and interpolating them to your specific application, you will be able to determine quickly the best solution. The following chapters build on these basics to help you develop your Oracle skills.

5

Working with Date, Numeric, and Character Functions

by Joe Zafian III

In addition to using regular expressions in SQL queries, you can also use any of the several dozen built-in functions or (since Oracle7.1) user-written stored database functions. You can use functions to perform calculations or other operations based on input arguments and to convert various data elements to a different datatype or display format. This chapter provides examples of how you can use each function in your applications.

Conversion Functions

Conversion functions convert and format Oracle data values for use with the various datatypes. For the most part, they convert dates and numbers to a specific character format or convert a character value to its valid date or numeric equivalent.

CHARTOROWID (*string*)

CHARTOROWID converts a character string in the form AAAAAAAA.BBBB.CCCC into a ROWID type. The following example selects a record from the EMP table based on the ROWID provided:

```
select emp_last_name
  from emp
 where rowid = chartorowid ('0000002A.001C.0001');
```

> **NOTE**
>
> Oracle performs default conversions of datatypes when possible. In the preceding example, if the conversion function was not specified, the RDBMS optimization parser would imply the conversion at runtime. By specifying the function, you may be able to save a very small amount of time when your application is executed. For the most part, this savings won't be noticeable.

CONVERT (*string, dest_character_set [, source_character_set]*)

CONVERT converts a character string from the specified source character set. (If no character set is specified, the default is the National Language default for your database instance.) Common uses of this function are to convert data between operating system environments. The following example converts the value of the employee name, which is stored in IBM PC 8-bit format, into its equivalent EBCDIC 7-bit values:

```
select convert (emp_last_name, 'WE8PC850', 'WE8EBCDIC500')
  from emp;
```

HEXTORAW (*string*)

HEXTORAW converts a character representation of a hexadecimal value into its equivalent byte values. The example converts the two-character hexadecimal string into its equivalent single-byte representation equal to 143.

```
select hextoraw ('8F')
  from dual;
```

RAWTOHEX (*raw_value*)

RAWTOHEX performs the inverse of HEXTORAW to convert a raw column value into its equivalent hexadecimal string. The example displays the decoding key for an encryption algorithm in an application.

```
select rawtohex (decode_key)
  from security_table
 where user_id = uid;

RAWTOHEX(DECODE_KEY)
----------------------------------------
7D856FCA11B654A7
```

ROWIDTOCHAR (*rowid*)

ROWIDTOCHAR converts a rowid pseudocolumn value into its displayed character equivalent.

```
select rowidtochar (rowid)
  from emp
 where emp_last_name = 'JOHNSON';

ROWIDTOCHAR(ROWID)
------------------
000007F1.0008.0002
```

TO_CHAR (*number [, format]*)

The first use of the overloaded TO_CHAR function is to convert a numeric value to its equivalent character representation. Without a specified format, Oracle converts the value to the simplest character representation of the value with a leading minus sign if the number is negative. In many cases, you may want to display the number in a specific format; fortunately, Oracle provides many format models for numbers. Table 5.1 lists the acceptable format model elements with an example and the resulting character string for the given number.

Table 5.1. Oracle numeric format models.

Element	Description	Example	Value	Result
9	Returns the value with the specified number of digits with leading zeroes displayed as blanks	99999	784 -578 1234567 45.885	' 784' ' -578' '######' ' 46'
.	Inserts the decimal point as applicable	9999.99	784 -578 1234567 45.885	' 748.00' '-578.00' '#######' ' 45.85'
,	Inserts the comma in the result string where specified	9,999,999	784 -587 1234567 0.44	' 784' ' -587' '1,234,567' ' 0'
$	Returns the value with a leading dollar sign	$99,999	784 -587	' $784' ' -$587'
B	Displays the integer portion of the result as a blank if it is zero	B9999.9	784 -587 0.44	' 784.0' ' -587.0' ' .4'
MI	Returns a negative value with a trailing minus sign	9999MI	784 -587	'784 ' '587-'
S	Returns the value with the appropriate negative or positive sign	S9999 9999S	784 -587 784 -587	'+784' '-587' '784+' '587-'
PR	Surrounds a negative value with angle brackets <>	9999PR	784 -587	' 784 ' '<587>'
D	Inserts a decimal point at the specified position	9999D99	784 -587 83.659	' 784.00' '-587.00' ' 83.66'
G	Inserts a group separator at the current position (see next Note)	9G999	1234 543 -2566	' 1,234' ' 543' '-2,566'

Element	Description	Example	Value	Result
C	Returns the ISO currency symbol at the specified position (see next Note)	C999	123	USD123
L	Returns the National currency symbol at the specified position (see next Note)	L9,999	1234	$1,234
EEEE	Returns a value in scientific notation	9.9EEEE	45 628 .0666	4.5E+01 6.3E+02 6.7E-02
RN	Returns a number as an uppercase Roman numeral. Value must be between 1 and 3999	RN	684	DCLXXXIV
rn	Returns a number as a lowercase Roman numeral. Value must be between 1 and 3999.	rn	684	dclxxxiv

Note: The single quotation marks used in the last column of the table have been included to show where spaces will be inserted in the output. They will not be displayed in the final result.

NOTE

The default National symbols are defined by the initialization parameter `NLS_TERRITORY`, which is defined by the DBA. Additionally, the DBA or developer may set the values using the following parameters.

Format Element	Description	Parameter
D	Decimal point	NLS_NUMERIC_CHARACTER
G	Group separator	NLS_NUMERIC_CHARACTER
C	ISO currency symbol	NLS_ISO_CURRENCY
L	Local currency symbol	NLS_CURRENCY

Suppose, for example, that you have an application for an international organization that needs to produce a report that shows account values in both American dollars and

British pounds. You can set the ISO currency symbol to $ and set the local currency symbol to £ using the following commands:

```
alter session set nls_iso_currency = '$';
alter session set nls_currency = '£';
```

TO_CHAR (*date, format*)

TO_CHAR converts a date item into its representative character format as specified in the format argument. Oracle, again, provides several different format models that you can combine to define the final output format. The only restriction is that the final format mask must be no larger than 22 characters. Table 5.2 shows the date formatting elements.

Table 5.2. Date formatting elements.

Element	*Description*
A.D. or AD	AD or BC indicator with or without periods
A.M. or AM (or P.M. or PM)	AM or PM indicator with or without periods
B.C. or BC	AD or BC indicator with or without periods
CC	Century portion of date
D	Day of week (1–7)
DAY	Name of day of week padded with blanks to nine characters
DD	Day of month (1–31)
DDD	Day of year (1–366)
DY	Abbreviated name of day (SUN–SAT)
IW	Week of year based on ISO standard
IYY, IY, or I	Last three, two, or one digits of ISO year
IYYY	ISO Year
HH or HH12	Hour of day (1–12)
HH24	Hour of day (0–23), sometimes referred to as military time
J	Julian day, equal to integer number of days since 1 January 4712 BC
MI	Minute of hour (0–59)

Element	Description
MM	Month of year (1–12)
MONTH	Name of Month
MON	Month name abbreviation (JAN–DEC)
RM	Roman numeral equivalent for month of year (I–XII)
RR	Last two digits of year
Q	Quarter of year
SS	Seconds in minute (0–59)
SSSSS	Seconds since midnight (0–86399)
W	Week of month (1–5) where week 1 starts on first of month
WW	Week of year (1–53) where week 1 starts on 1 January
Y, YY, YYY, YYYY	Last one, two, three, or all digits of the year

To retrieve a date in a specific format, you can use the TO_CHAR function.

```
select to_char (sysdate, '"The "fmDdspth" Day of "Month" in the Year "Year')
  from dual;

TO_CHAR(SYSDATE,'"THE"FMDDSPTH"DAYOF"MONTH"INTHEYEAR"YEAR')
-----------------------------------------------------------
The Twenty-Ninth Day of April in the Year Nineteen Ninety-Six
```

As the example shows, you can add text to the format by including it in double quotation marks within the format definition. (The extra text does not apply to the 22-character limit within the format mask.) Next, by preceding a format element with FM, you can strip all insignificant leading and trailing blanks and zeroes from the output value for each subsequent format element. Additional occurrences of this modifier will toggle the filtering mode. Table 5.3 shows how this mask affects various displays of the time 2:05 p.m.

Table 5.3. Effect of various format masks on retrieved value.

Format Mask	Retrieved Value
HH:MI	02:05
HH24:MI	14:05
fmHH:MI PM	2:5 PM
fmHHfmMI PM	2:05 PM

The next thing to note in this example is that the SP extension on a value returns the element spelled out in the default language for the database, and the TH extension returns the element as an ordinal number (first, second, third, and so on). Finally, capitalizing only the first letter of the mask element returns the value with only the first letter of each word capitalized. Likewise, using all uppercase or all lowercase in the mask element returns the data in that case.

In SQL*Plus, whenever you retrieve a date without the TO_CHAR function, it is displayed in the default date format for your current session, which is DD-MON-YY in most Oracle installations. You can, however, change the default format for all dates retrieved by using the following command to specify the date format you want to display:

```
alter session set NLS_DATE_FORMAT = 'MM/DD/YY  HH24:MI:SS';
```

TO_DATE (*string, format*)

TO_DATE converts a character string into an Oracle date, based on the format mask provided. Table 5.2 defined the allowable format mask elements for the TO_DATE function. The next example converts a character string into a date:

```
select to_date ('960212', 'RRMMDD') from dual;
```

Using the YY format element (rather than RR as shown in the example) returns the same result. However, you can use RR to accept dates in other centuries while allowing for the two-digit years that appear in many legacy data systems. Table 5.4 describes how the RR format mask works.

Table 5.4. Using the RR format mask.

	Current Year Is Less Than xx50	*Current Year Is Greater or Equal To xx50*
Input Date < *xx50*	Current century	Next century
Input Date >= *xx50*	Previous century	Current century

Using this code

```
select to_date ('960212', 'RRMMDD') from dual;
```

the resulting date will be February 12, 1996, if the current year is between 1950 and 2049. After 2049, this statement will return February 12, 2096. Note that this is much different than if you use an input mask of YYMMDD, which will return February 12, 2096, after the year 1999.

One of the key uses of the TO_DATE function is to validate input dates. In many other types of applications, you have to write an elaborate procedure to check whether an input date is valid. Your procedure would need to check whether the input month was less than 12 and whether the day part of the date was less than the number of days in the given month. The preceding query not only validates the date but also returns the appropriate message from the database if the input date is invalid.

TO_LABEL (*string, format*)

Trusted Oracle uses the TO_LABEL function to convert a character string to an MLSLABEL datatype, which defines the security for a given row of data. TO_LABEL will be discussed further in Chapter 35, "Trusted Oracle."

TO_MULTI_BYTE (*string*)

TO_MULTI_BYTE converts a single-byte character string to its equivalent multiple-byte string in languages that support multiple-byte character sets, such as the Japanese Katana character set.

TO_NUMBER (*number [,format]*)

The TO_NUMBER function converts a character string to its equivalent numeric equivalent. For simple string equivalents of numbers (for example, numeric digits with a decimal point), the format mask is optional. To define the format mask, use the mask elements defined in Table 5.1.

TO_SINGLE_BYTE (*string*)

The TO_SINGLE_BYTE function converts all multiple-byte characters in the input string to their respective single-byte equivalents. If no single-byte equivalent is available for the character, the multiple-byte character will be returned as input. This function is valid only if your NLS character set supports both single-byte and multiple-byte characters.

Oracle Date Functions

Date functions perform operations based on a date value. Depending on the function used, the operation returns a new date value or a numeric value.

ADD_MONTHS (*date, number*)

ADD_MONTHS adds the specified number of months to the input date to return a new date. If a negative number is given, the return value is the appropriate number of months prior to the input date. The number value should be an integer, although Oracle will not generate an error if a fractional number is provided. A positive number is truncated to the next lower integer value, and a negative number is truncated to the next higher integer. The following example returns a date that is one year prior to '29-FEB-96':

```
select add_months('29-FEB-96', -12.99)
  from dual;

ADD_MONTH
- - - - - - - -
28-FEB-95
```

LAST_DAY (*date*)

LAST_DAY returns the date of the last day of the month containing the input date. For example, the following query returns the last day of the month for an employee's first anniversary date:

```
select hire_date,
       last_day (add_months (hire_date, 12))
  from emp
 where emp_last_name = 'FARRELL';

HIRE_DATE LAST_DAY(
- - - - - - - - - - - - - - - -
13-FEB-96 28-FEB-97
```

MONTHS_BETWEEN (*date1, date2*)

MONTHS_BETWEEN returns the number of months between two dates. If the day of the month is the same for both dates (or the last day of the month for both dates), MONTHS_BETWEEN returns a whole number value. Otherwise, the fractional part of the month will be included in the return value based on $1\div31$ of a month for each day. If the second date is prior to the first date, the return value is negative. The following example retrieves all employees that have worked at least one year:

```
select emp_last_name
  from emp
 where months_between (hire_date, sysdate) >= 12;
```

NEW_TIME (*date, zone1, zone2*)

NEW_TIME returns the time in time zone *zone2* based on the input time *date* in time zone *zone1*. The valid time zones are shown in Table 5.5.

Table 5.5. Valid Oracle time zones.

Code	Description
ADT	Atlantic daylight savings time
AST	Atlantic standard time
BDT	Bering daylight savings time
BST	Bering standard time
CDT	Central daylight savings time

Code	Description
CST	Central standard time
EDT	Eastern daylight savings time
EST	Eastern standard time
GMT	Greenwich mean time
HDT	Alaska/Hawaii daylight savings time
HST	Alaska/Hawaii standard time
MDT	Mountain daylight savings time
MST	Mountain standard time
NST	Newfoundland standard time
PDT	Pacific daylight savings time
PST	Pacific standard time
YDT	Yukon daylight savings time
YST	Yukon standard time

A salesperson can use the following query to retrieve the appointment schedule (in his or her personal home time zone) when the international main office stores all appointment times in Greenwich mean time:

```
select to_char (new_time (a.appointment_date, 'GMT', p.home_zone), 'HH24:MI') TIME,
       a.appointment_contact CONTACT,
       a.appointment_phone_no PHONE
  from appointments a,
       user_preferences p
 where a.user_id = p.user_id
   and p.user_id = uid
   and trunc (a.appointment_date) = trunc (sysdate);


TIME  CONTACT             PHONE
----  ------------------- -----------
08:30 Jim Taylor          (860)555-1000
10:00 Jackie Reeves       (860)555-1234
13:45 Mark Lundy          (860)555-6111
```

NEXT_DAY (*date, day*)

The NEXT_DAY function returns the date of the next occurrence of the given day after the input date. For example, the following query returns the date of the last Friday of the current month:

```
select next_day ((last_day (sysdate) - 7), 'FRIDAY') from dual;

NEXT_DAY((LAST_DAY(SYSDATE)-7),'FRIDAY')
----------------------------------------------------------
26-APR-96
```

If the input date is on the same day of the week as the next day you are looking for, the return value will be one week after the input date. Therefore, if you need to include the input date in the search, subtract 1 from the date before applying the NEXT_DAY function.

ROUND (*date, format*)

The ROUND function rounds a date to the nearest format element. For example, if you want to round the current date (3/27/96 10:35:21) to the nearest hour, you could use the following query:

```
select round (sysdate, 'HH') from dual;

ROUND(SYSDATE,'HH'
------------------
03/27/96  11:00:00
```

Table 5.6 shows the effect of rounding the date using each of the available format elements.

Table 5.6. Rounding a date.

Format Element	Result
SS	03/27/96 10:35:21
MI	03/27/96 10:35:00
HH	03/27/96 11:00:00
DD	03/27/96 00:00:00
MM	04/01/96 00:00:00
YY	01/01/96 00:00:00
CC	01/01/00 00:00:00

TRUNC (*date, format*)

The TRUNC function is similar to the ROUND function in that it returns a date value with only the significant portion of the date, based on the format mask element specified. However, TRUNC drops the insignificant portion, whereas ROUND rounds it to the nearest value.

```
select trunc (sysdate, 'HH') from dual;

TRUNC(SYSDATE,'HH'
------------------
03/27/96  10:00:00
```

You can also use TRUNC without a format mask element, in which case the date returned reflects only the date portion of the value. Many applications store the date of an event (such as date of sale) in an Oracle table using the system date pseudocolumn, SYSDATE. If your application retrieves records based on the date only (and does not need the time for any type of retrieval), you should consider using the TRUNC function in your database maintenance commands.

Oracle Numeric Functions

Oracle's numeric functions perform mathematical computations on stored database values. These functions represent standard trigonometric and algebraic constructs with which you may be familiar.

ABS (*number*)

ABS returns the absolute value of a numeric value. The absolute value is the numeric portion of the number without a sign. For example, suppose that you wanted to know the relative difference of an employee's salary from $50,000 regardless of whether it is less or greater, you can use the following query:

```
select emp_last_name,
       salary,
       abs (salary - 50000)
  from emp
 where dept_no = 20
 order by abs (salary - 50000) desc;


EMP_LAST_NAME            SALARY ABS(SALARY-50000)
-------------------- -------- ----------------
JONES                     36000            14000
FARRELL                   57000             7000
BRUNNER                   52000             2000
ROBERTS                   50000                0
```

CEIL (*number*)

The CEIL function returns the next integer value greater than or equal to the input value. You can use this function to calculate the number of blocks required for 25,000 customers on the customer table based on the current storage requirements for the existing 8,500 customers. Write the query as follows:

```
select ceil (25000 / (num_rows / blocks)) BLOCKS
  from user_tables
 where table_name = 'CUSTOMERS';

  BLOCKS
--------
      73
```

COS (*number*)

The COS function returns the trigonometric cosine of the number of radians. To calculate the cosine of a number in degrees, multiply the input value by 0.01745 (3.1415÷180) to convert it to radians as shown here:

```
select cos (90 * 0.01745) "COSINE" from dual;

COSINE
--------
       0
```

COSH (*number*)

The COSH function returns the hyperbolic cosine of the input number:

```
select cosh (1) from dual;

COSH(1)
------
     0
```

EXP (*number*)

As shown here, EXP returns e (2.71828183...) raised to the *number* power. This function performs the inverse on the LN or natural logarithm function and is used in engineering calculations.

```
select exp(5) "e to the 5th power" from dual;

e to the 5th power
-----------------
        148.41316
```

FLOOR (*number*)

FLOOR returns the largest integer value that is less than or equal to the input number. If the input number is negative, the result will be a number with a higher negative magnitude, as shown in the following example:

```
select floor (-12.05)  FLOOR from dual;

    FLOOR
--------
      -13
```

LN (*number*)

The LN function returns the natural logarithm for the input value, as shown in the following example:

```
select ln (254) "the natural log of 254" from dual;

the natural log of 254
----------------------
             5.5373343
```

LOG (*base, number*)

This function returns the logarithm for the input base, for the input value as shown in the next example:

```
select log (2, 65536) from dual;

LOG(2,65536)
------------
          16
```

MOD (*n, m*)

The MOD function returns the modulus of a number *n*, with respect to the divisor, *m*. The result is the remainder of the integer division of *m* into *n*, as shown in the following example:

```
select mod (17, 4) from dual;

MOD(17,4)
---------
        1
```

POWER (*x, y*)

As shown here, POWER performs the inverse of the LOG function and returns *x* raised to the *y*th power:

```
select power (2, 5) from dual;

POWER(2,5)
----------
        32
```

ROUND (*number, decimal_digits*)

Earlier in this chapter, the ROUND function was presented in the section describing the date functions. The ROUND function is also available to use for numeric values. It operates in much the same way as the date function using numeric values for input. The ROUND function rounds a value to the nearest number of decimal digits. If the number of digits specified is zero, the returned value is an integer. If the decimal_digits value is negative, the returned value is rounded to the nearest power of 10.

```
select round (587.653, 1) "Nearest Tenth" from dual;

Nearest Tenth
-------------
        587.7

select round (587.653, -1) "Nearest Ten" from dual;

Nearest Ten
-----------
         590
```

SIGN (*number*)

The SIGN function returns a value of 1 if the input value is a positive number and −1 if the input value is negative. If the input value is equal to 0, SIGN returns a 0. You can use this function to compare two numbers.

```
select emp_last_name NAME,
       sign (months_between (hire_date, sysdate)  -60) VESTED
  from emp
 where dept_no = 10;

NAME                    VESTED
-------------------- --------
SMITH                        1
BROWN                        1
FARRELL                     -1
GRANT                       -1
JONES                        1
```

SIN (*number*)

SIN returns the trigonometric sine of an angle specified in radians. In the example, SIN determines the sine of 45 degrees.

```
select sin (0.7854) "Sine of 45 degrees" from dual;

Sine of 45 degrees
------------------
         0.707106
```

SINH (*number*)

The SINH function returns the hyperbolic sine for the given input value, as shown in the following example:

```
select sinh (1) from dual;

  SINH(1)
---------
1.1752012
```

SQRT (*number*)

As shown here, the SQRT function returns the square root of the input value, which must be 0 or a positive number. If a negative number is given, SQRT returns an error.

```
select sqrt (144) from dual;

SQRT(144)
---------
       12
```

TAN (*number*)

TAN returns the trigonometric tangent of an angle specified in radians. In the next example, TAN retrieves the tangent of 45 degrees:

```
select tan (45 * (3.14159265 / 180)) "Tangent" from dual;

Tangent
---------
       1
```

TANH (*number*)

As shown here, the TANH function calculates the hyperbolic tangent for the input value:

```
select tanh (1) "Hyperbolic Tangent" from dual;

Hyperbolic Tangent
------------------
        0.7615941
```

TRUNC (*number* [,*decimal_places*])

Like the date function, TRUNC, the numeric TRUNC function truncates a numerical value at the specified number of decimal places. If the precision is not specified, TRUNC assumes zero decimal places. If a negative number of decimal places is selected, the input value will be truncated at the defined power of 10. This function is illustrated in the following example:

```
select trunc (587.653, 1) "Trunc at Tenth" from dual;

Trunc at Tenth
--------------
        587.6

select trunc (587.653, -1) "Trunc at Ten" from dual;

Trunc at Ten
------------
          580
```

Oracle Character Functions

The Oracle character functions operate on character string input values and return either another character string or a numeric value depending on the respective function. These functions are typically used to retrieve information about the string or to alter the way the string is displayed.

ASCII (*character*)

The ASCII function returns the ASCII value for the specified character, as shown in this example:

```
select ascii ('Z') from dual;

ASCII('Z')
----------
        90
```

CHR (*number*)

The CHR function performs the inverse operation of the ASCII function and returns the character with the ASCII value equal to the input number. This function is typically used to add nonprinting characters to a character string, as shown in the following example:

```
Select 'This line contains embedded characters'¦¦chr(10)¦¦chr(13) TEXT
    from dual;

TEXT
----------------------------------------
This line contains embedded characters
```

CONCAT (*string1, string2*)

The CONCAT function returns a character string containing *string1* followed by *string2*. This function is equivalent to using the concatenation operator (¦¦) and has been provided for compatibility with other SQL databases and for use on platforms where the vertical pipe symbol is not available. This function is illustrated in the next example:

```
select concat ('Four score and seven years ago ',
               'our fathers set forth on this continent...')
    from dual;

CONCAT('FOURSCOREANDSEVENYEARSAGO','OURFATHERSSETFORTHONTHISCONTINENT...'
-----------------------------------------------------------------------
Four score and seven years ago our fathers set forth on this continent...
```

The same SQL statement also can be written as

```
select 'Four score and seven years ago '¦¦
               'our fathers set forth on this continent...'
    from dual;
```

The two processes are virtually identical. If possible, however, you should use the double-pipe operator.

INITCAP (*string*)

As shown in the following example, the INITCAP function returns the input character string with the first letter of each word in uppercase. All other characters appear in lowercase.

```
select initcap (emp_first_name¦¦' '¦¦emp_last_name)
  from emp
 where dept_no = 50;

EMP_FIRST_NAME¦¦''¦¦EMP_LAST_NAME
-----------------------------------------
Jessica Farrell
Robert O'Brien
Steven Jones
Michael Brown
Aaron Smith
Joseph Mcdonald
```

As you can see in the last line of the preceding output (Joseph Mcdonald), the INITCAP function does not always return the desired result. Perhaps a better way to enter the last name for that employee would be 'MC DONALD' if you want to use the INITCAP function against it.

INSTR (*input_string, search_string [,n [,m]]*)

As shown here, the INSTR function finds the *m*th occurrence of a search string embedded within the input string starting at position *n*. If the search string is not found, INSTR returns a value of 0.

```
select instr ('the quick sly fox jumped over the '¦¦
               'lazy brown dog.', 'the', 7, 2) SEARCH
  from dual;

  SEARCH
--------
       0
```

INSTRB (*input_string, search_string [,n [,m]]*)

The INSTRB function is similar to the INSTR function, but the returned value is a number of bytes, rather than a number of characters. For NLS character sets that contain only single-byte characters, the behavior of INSTRB and INSTR is identical.

LENGTH (*string*)

The LENGTH function returns the number of characters in the input string. This function can be used with the MAX function to determine how much space to allocate in a report for a particular column, as shown in the next example:

```
select max (length (emp_last_name)) from emp;

MAX(LENGTH(EMP_LAST_NAME))
- - - - - - - - - - - - - - - - - - - - - - - - -
                        16
```

LENGTHB (*string*)

LENGTHB returns the number of bytes in a character string. For character sets that contain only single-byte characters, the behavior of LENGTHB and LENGTH is identical.

LOWER (*string*)

As shown here, LOWER returns the input string in all lowercase letters. For numbers and other nonalphabetic characters, no conversion is performed.

```
select lower ('ThIs Is ThE InPUt STring in LOWER cASe.') "Convert" from dual;

Convert
- - - - - - - - - - - - - - - - - - - - - - - - - - - - - - - - - - - -
this is the input string in lower case.
```

LPAD (*string, n [,pad_chars]*)

The LPAD function pads the left side of the input string with repetitions of the pad characters to return a character string that is *n* characters long. The following example will print the employee salary with leading asterisks to make the resulting string ten characters long.

```
select emp_last_name,
       lpad (to_char(salary), 10, '*') SALARY
  from emp
 where dept_no = 10
 order by salary desc;

EMP_LAST_NAME           SALARY
- - - - - - - - - - - - - - - - - - - -   - - - - - - - - - - -
ADAMS                 **** 72000
BRUNNER               **** 52000
HERSHEY               **** 48000
ANDERSON              **** 42000
SIM                   **** 28000
```

LTRIM (*string [,set_of_chars]*)

As shown here, the LTRIM function strips all leading occurrences of all characters in a character set from the input string. If no character set is specified, LTRIM strips all leading spaces from the input string. One use of this function is to remove all leading spaces (left justify) from a user input value.

```
select ltrim ('     This is the user input.') from dual;

LTRIM('THISISTHEUSERINP
----------------------
This is the user input.
```

Note that spaces within the input string were not removed—just the leading spaces. LTRIM can also remove the sign position to convert a numeric value to a packed filename string for a personnel photo for each employee, as shown in the next example:

```
select emp_last_name,
       'emp_'¦¦ltrim (to_char (emp_id))¦¦'.jpg'
  from emp
 where dept_no = 50;

EMP_LAST_NAME          'EMP_'¦¦LTRIM(TO_CHAR(EMP_ID))¦¦'.JPG'
--------------------   -----------------------------------------------
ADAMS                  emp_17.jpg
HERSHEY                emp_357.jpg
ANDERSON               emp_19.jpg
SIM                    emp_624.jpg
BRUNNER                emp_45.jpg
```

NLSSORT (*string [,nlsparms]*)

NLSSORT returns the set of bytes used to sort the string. You can use NLSSORT to sort values based on the sequence of characters within a character set, rather than based on the strict ASCII value of each character. If no value is provided for the *nlsparms* argument, the default value for your default character set will be used.

NLS_INITCAP (*string [,nlsparms]*)

NLS_INITCAP returns the input string with the first letter of each word in uppercase. The *nlsparms* argument specifies the character set to be used for the character conversion.

NLS_LOWER (*string [,nlsparms]*)

The NLS_LOWER function returns the input string with all characters in lowercase as defined by the *nlsparms* character set.

NLS_UPPER (*string [,nlsparms]*)

The NLS_UPPER function returns the input string with all characters in uppercase as defined by the *nlsparms* character set.

REPLACE *(string, search_string [,replace_string])*

The REPLACE function replaces all occurrences of a *search_string* in the input *string* with the values in the *replace_string*. You can use this function to replace all occurrences of a tokenized command line with a valid substitution name, as shown in the next example:

```
select replace ('r25run module=%FILE%.rdf destype=file desname=%FILE%.prn',
                 '%FILE%', 'orpf002') COMMAND
   from dual;

COMMAND
------------------------------------------------------------
r25run module=orpf002.rdf destype=file desname=orpf002.prn
```

If the *replace_string* is not specified, the search string will be removed from the input string. In the following example, question marks are removed from a customer input time of day:

```
select replace ('?12:00??', '?') from dual;

REPLA
-----
12:00
```

RPAD *(string, n, [,pad_string])*

The RPAD function works like the LPAD function except that with RPAD the string is padded to the right to a length of *n* characters. If a pad string is not given, spaces will be used to pad the input string. You can use the following commands to print mailing labels. The first command, COLUMN, defines the display length for the ADDRESS column, and the SQL query retrieves the result.

```
column ADDRESS format a35
select rpad (emp_first_name¦¦' '¦¦emp_last_name, 35)¦¦
       rpad (emp_home_address, 35)¦¦
       rpad (emp_home_city¦¦', '¦¦emp_state¦¦' '¦¦emp_zip, 35) ADDRESS
  from emp
 where emp_id = 624;

ADDRESS
-----------------------------------
ROBERT SIM
123 MAIN STREET
WHARTON, NJ 07885
```

RTRIM *(string [, char_set])*

RTRIM removes all characters in the character set from the right side of the input string. One of the most common uses of RTRIM is to test for equality of two values when you don't know whether any extraneous spaces exist in either the stored value or the user input value, as shown in the next example:

```
select emp_id,
       emp_last_name,
```

```
      salary
  from emp
 where upper(rtrim (emp_last_name)) = rtrim ('BRUNNER');

EMP_ID EMP_LAST_NAME           SALARY
-------- -------------------- --------
    102 BRUNNER                104000
```

SOUNDEX (*string*)

The SOUNDEX function returns a character string based on the characters in the input string. This function is provided to return all words that sound like the example string. The rules for this function require that both words being tested begin with the same letter and follow an algorithm to assign values for the remaining letters in the word. In the next example, SOUNDEX returns the names of employees that have the same code value as 'JANICE':

```
select emp_last_name
  from emp
 where soundex (emp_last_name) = soundex ('JANICE');

emp_last_name
-------------------
JONES
JOHNS
JAMES
JONAS
```

NOTE

As the preceding example indicates, the SOUNDEX function is minimally useful at best. If the user is unsure of the first letter in a person's name, the function will not work. Therefore, I don't recommend its use. You can probably attain better results using a LIKE operator in the WHERE clause and requiring the user to enter part of the lookup name.

SUBSTR (*string, start [,length]*)

The SUBSTR function extracts a substring from the input string, starting at character number *start* for the specified length of characters. If no length is specified, SUBSTR defaults to the end of the input string. The following string extracts the date-of-birth value from a user input value:

```
select substr (ltrim (substr ('DOB:  11/08/58 (Bayonne, NJ)',
            instr ('DOB:  11/08/58 (Bayonne, NJ)', ':')+1)), 1, 8) DOB
   from dual;

DOB
--------
11/08/58
```

SUBSTRB *(string, start [,length])*

The SUBSTRB function is the byte-level equivalent of the SUBSTR function. For NLS character sets that contain only single-byte characters, SUBSTRB returns the same result as SUBSTR.

TRANSLATE *(string, search_set, replace_set)*

The TRANSLATE function translates all occurrences of the characters in the search set with the respective character in the replacement set. The following example replaces all numeric characters with a 9 and replaces all alphabetic characters with an X:

```
select translate ('GYK-87M', '0123456789ABCDEFGHIJKLMNOPQRSTUVWXYZ',
                   '9999999999XXXXXXXXXXXXXXXXXXXXXXXXXX')
    from dual;

TRANSLA
------
XXX-99X
```

> **NOTE**
>
> Here are a few points to keep in mind when using the TRANSLATE function. First, if a character in the input string is not in the search set, it will be returned from the function. Second, if the replacement set has fewer characters than the search set, any matching characters at the end of the search set will be stripped from the return value. Consequently, the TRANSLATE function can incorporate the functionality of the REPLACE function to strip out any unwanted characters.

UPPER *(string)*

As shown here, UPPER returns the input string in all uppercase letters. For numbers and other nonalphabetic characters, no conversion is performed.

```
select upper ('ThIs Is ThE InPUt STring in upper cASe.') "Convert" from dual;

Convert
-------------------------------------
THIS IS THE INPUT STRING IN UPPER CASE.
```

Other Oracle Single-Row Functions

In addition to the commands already listed that operate on a specific datatype, Oracle provides several functions that can take any of several datatypes for input.

DUMP (*expression [, format[, start[, length]]]*)

The DUMP function returns the internal representation of the input expression in the format specified. Table 5.7 shows the valid values for the format.

Table 5.7. Oracle DUMP formats.

Format Code	Description
8	Octal
10	Decimal
16	Hexadecimal
17	Single characters

The dump output will display the internal datatype code and the length of the dump output, in bytes, starting at the start position for *length* bytes, as shown in the next example:

```
select dump ('FARRELL', 16) DUMP from dual;

DUMP
-----------------------------------
Typ=96 Len=7: 46,41,52,52,45,4c,4c
```

GREATEST (*list of values*)

The GREATEST function returns the highest value among the entries in the list. For numeric lists or dates, the returned value is the largest value or latest date. If the list contains character strings, the returned value is the last item alphabetically in the list. To find the operating budget for each department with a minimum budget of $250,000, you could use the following query:

```
select dept_name,
       greatest (250000, budget)
  from dept
 order by dept_no;

DEPT_NAME              BUDGET
--------------------   --------
ACCOUNTING              250000
PERSONNEL               250000
HOSPITAL SERVICES       875000
BROADCAST OPERATIONS    412500

CONSULTING SERVICES    2350000
```

GREATEST_LB (*label [,label [,label...]]*)

The GREATEST_LB function returns the highest lower bound from a list of labels. This function is available in Trusted Oracle.

LEAST (*list of values*)

The LEAST function returns the lowest value among the entries in the list. For numeric lists or dates, the returned value is the smallest value or earliest date. If the list contains character strings, the returned value is the first item alphabetically in the list. The following example shows you how to create a call list for clients who have either not been contacted in the last 30 days or have contracts expiring within 30 days.

```
select client_name
  from clients
 where client_salesman_id = uid
   and sysdate >= least (last_contact_date+30, contract_end_date-30);

CLIENT_NAME
--------------------
XYZ CORPORATION
MEGADATA, LTD.

WHARTON ASSOCIATES
```

LEAST_UB (*label [,label [,label...]]*)

The LEAST_UB function returns the lowest upper bound from a list of labels. This function is available in Trusted Oracle.

NVL (*expression, replacement_value*)

The NVL function returns the value of the expression if it is not null. If it is null, then the replacement value is returned. The next example returns a value of 0 if the employee salary is null:

```
select emp_last_name,
       nvl (salary, 0) SALARY
  from emp
 where dept_no = 30
 order by salary;

EMP_LAST_NAME           SALARY
--------------------  --------
WASHINGTON               38000
WILLIS                   41000
HARPER                   50000
ZIGLAR                       0
LOMAN                        0
```

USERENV (*parameter*)

USERENV returns information about a user's operating environment as specified by the *parameter* argument. Table 5.8 shows the valid parameter values.

Table 5.8. Valid USERENV parameters.

Parameter	Description
OSDBA	Returns TRUE or FALSE depending on whether the user has the OSDBA role enabled.
LABEL	In Trusted Oracle, returns the user's secure operating system label.
LANGUAGE	Returns the NLS language and territory for the current user session.
TERMINAL	Returns the operating system identifier for the user terminal.
SESSIONID	Returns the current session ID.
ENTRYID	Returns the entry ID for auditing transactions.

The following example retrieves the session ID for the user. The session ID can store specific session information for auditing database transactions.

```
select userenv('SESSIONID') from dual;

USERENV('SESSIONID')
--------------------
                2437
```

VSIZE (*expression*)

The VSIZE function returns the number of bytes required to store an expression in the Oracle internal data representation. By adding up the size of all the columns in a data row, you can determine the number of bytes needed to store the row in the database.

```
select 4 + vsize (dept_no) +
       vsize (dept_name) +
       vsize (location) +
       vsize (budget) STORAGE
  from dept
 where dept_no = 10;

  STORAGE
--------
      27
```

Oracle Multiple-Row Functions

The functions presented thus far in this chapter have been based on a single row of data. Oracle also provides functions that operate on groups of rows in a single query. To calculate the values for sets of data or groups, you must use the GROUP BY clause in a query. For more information on the GROUP BY clause, refer to Chapter 7, "Innovative Techniques Using the Oracle Functions."

Group functions can also operate on either all values of the expression or on just the distinct set of values. The general syntax for the group functions is

```
function ([DISTINCT |ALL] expression)
```

If neither DISTINCT nor ALL is specified, function will operate on all rows returned in the query. You cannot combine group functions and single-row expressions in the same select column list.

AVG (expression)

The AVG function retrieves the average value for the rows returned by the query. The next example retrieves the average salary for department 10:

```
select round (avg (salary), 0) "Average Sal"
from emp
 where dept_no = 10;

Average Sal
----------
     54156
```

COUNT (expression)

COUNT counts the number of entries based on expression. To count the number of employee records in the EMP table, you can use the following query:

```
select count(*) from emp;

 COUNT(*)
--------
     157
```

Additionally, you can specify a column in the expression to retrieve the number of rows in the table that have non-null values. Thus, to count the number of employees who are paid based on a salary, you can use the following query:

```
select count(salary) from emp;

COUNT(SALARY)
-----------
     92
```

Finally, the COUNT function is commonly used to return the number of unique values in a table. The next example counts the number of departments that have at least one employee assigned to the table:

```
select (distinct dept_no)
  from emp;

COUNT(DISTINCTEMP)
------------------
                 5
```

GLB

GLB returns the greatest lower bound associated with the secure operating system label in Trusted Oracle.

LUB

LUB returns the least upper bound associated with the secure operating system label in Trusted Oracle.

MAX (expression)

The MAX function retrieves the highest value from the set of rows returned by the query. For example, to retrieve the employee(s) who receive the highest salary in the company, you can use the following query:

```
select emp_last_name,
       salary
  from emp
 where salary = (select max (salary)
                   from emp);

EMP_LAST_NAME           SALARY
--------------------    --------
ZAFIAN                   225000
```

MIN (expression)

MIN returns the lowest value from a set of rows returned by a query. For example, to retrieve the date when the first employee was hired in department 40, you can use the following SQL command:

```
select min (hire_date)
  from emp
 where dept_no = 40;

MIN(HIRE_
---------
08-AUG-90
```

STDDEV (*expression*)

The STDDEV function returns the statistical standard deviation for all rows returned by the query. The following query can calculate the standard deviation for the salary:

```
select stddev (salary) "Standard Dev."
from emp;

Standard Dev.
- - - - - - - - - - -
        7143
```

SUM (*expression*)

SUM returns the total of all non-null values returned by the query. If all returned values are null, then a null value will be returned. The following query returns the total salary for department 10:

```
select sum (salary) "Total"
from emp
 where dept_no = 10;

   Total
- - - - - - - -
   242000
```

VARIANCE (*expression*)

The VARIANCE function computes the statistical variance for all rows returned. The following query determines the variance for all salaries for the company:

```
select variance (salary) "Variance"
from emp;

 Variance
- - - - - - - -
 51022449
```

Summary

This chapter presented the Oracle functions. These functions are the power tools at your disposal when you build an Oracle application. Although a carpenter could construct a house using only a hammer and saw, the job will take much longer and the finished product won't be as sound as a house built with better tools. Likewise, you may be able to construct Oracle applications without using these functions, but the finished product will not be as good.

6

Complex Queries

by Joe Zafian III

The information you have read so far should enable you to construct Oracle applications that serve most of the needs of your end users. To maximize the performance of your applications, Oracle provides several specialized constructs for your queries. This chapter explores these complex additions to the standard query language by discussing recursive (or tree) queries, outer joins, and correlated subqueries.

Recursive Queries

In many Oracle systems, tables are constructed so that a column in the table points to the primary key in another row of the same table. For example, the employee table may have a column, SUPERVISOR_EMP_ID, that represents the supervisor of an employee. This column represents the EMP_ID for the given employee record for the supervisor. This organizational structure can be represented graphically by the organization chart shown in Figure 6.1. Using a recursive query, you can retrieve the organizational structure for the entire company. This feature is an extension to the ANSI SQL Language and is available exclusively for Oracle databases.

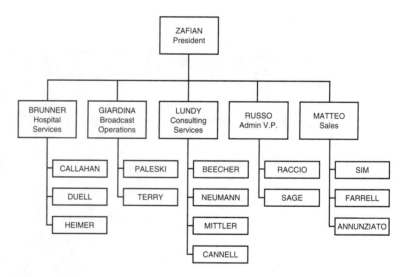

FIGURE 6.1.

Graphical representa-
tion of tree structure.

Constructing a Tree Query

A tree query is accomplished by using two new clauses in the standard SELECT statement:

■ CONNECT BY defines how individual rows in the table are related to each other.

■ START WITH defines the data row(s) that are the initial starting point for the query.

All other standard query elements can be included in a tree query to formulate the SELECT command. To display the entire company structure, you can use the following query:

```
select emp_id,
       emp_last_name,
       supervisor_emp_id
  from emp
 connect by supervisor_emp_id = prior emp_id
 start with supervisor_emp_id is null;

    EMP_ID EMP_LAST_NAME               SUPERVISOR_EMP_ID
---------- -------------------         -------------------
       101 ZAFIAN
       102 BRUNNER                                   101
       108 CALLAHAN                                  102
       109 DUELL                                     102
       110 HEIMER                                    102
       103 GIARDINA                                  101
       104 PALESKI                                   103
       117 TERRY                                     103
       105 LUNDY                                     101
       106 BEECHER                                   105
       107 NEUMANN                                   105
       118 MITTLER                                   105
       119 CANNELL                                   105
       111 RUSSO                                     101
       112 RACCIO                                    111
       116 SAGE                                      111
       113 MATTEO                                    101
       114 SIM                                       113
       115 ANNUNZIATO                                113
       120 FARRELL                                   113
```

As shown in the preceding example, the PRIOR keyword specifies that the row selected must have the SUPERVISOR_EMP_ID equal to the EMP_ID of the previously selected row. The START WITH clause specifies that the query start with any rows that have no supervisor (for example, the company president).

Embedding Structure in the Tree Query

The preceding example retrieves rows in order, but it may still be difficult to see the organizational structure. The reader must match rows to build the organizational layout. In many applications, the tree structure can be made more obvious by indenting each organizational level. To do this, leading blanks are concatenated onto the query, as shown in the next example.

```
select rpad (' ', (level-1)*3)¦¦emp_last_name employee
  from emp
 connect by supervisor_emp_id = prior emp_id
 start with supervisor_emp_id is null;

EMPLOYEE
-------------------
ZAFIAN
   BRUNNER
      CALLAHAN
      DUELL
      HEIMER
```

```
GIARDINA
    PALESKI
    TERRY
LUNDY
    BEECHER
    NEUMANN
    MITTLER
    CANNELL
RUSSO
    RACCIO
    SAGE
MATTEO
    SIM
    ANNUNZIATO
    FARRELL
```

Navigating Toward the Roots

Besides looking at the structure below a particular node in the tree, many applications need to examine the structure above a selected node. To determine the chain of command over an individual employee, use the following query:

```
select level,
       emp_last_name
  from emp
 connect by emp_id = prior supervisor_emp_id
 start with emp_last_name = 'SIM';

LEVEL      EMP_LAST_NAME
---------  --------------------
        1  SIM
        2  MATTEO
        3  ZAFIAN
```

As shown in the preceding example, the condition used in the START WITH clause can be based on any condition for the table. It does not need to be one of the columns referenced in the CONNECT BY clause, although in most cases it is.

Pruning Branches

There may be times when you need to eliminate branches from the tree query. To do this, add the pruning condition to the CONNECT BY clause, as shown in the following example:

```
select rpad (' ', (level-1)*3)||emp_last_name employee
  from emp
 connect by supervisor_emp_id = prior emp_id
   and emp_last_name not in ('RUSSO', 'MATTEO')
 start with supervisor_emp_id is null;

EMPLOYEE
--------------------
ZAFIAN
   BRUNNER
      CALLAHAN
```

```
        DUELL
        HEIMER
    GIARDINA
        PALESKI
        TERRY
    LUNDY
        BEECHER
        NEUMANN
        MITTLER
        CANNELL
```

Many developers make the mistake of specifying the exclusion criteria as part of the WHERE clause, which results in erroneous output, as shown in the next example.

```
select rpad (' ', (level-1)*3)¦¦emp_last_name employee
  from emp
 where emp_last_name not in ('RUSSO', 'MATTEO')
 connect by supervisor_emp_id = prior emp_id
 start with supervisor_emp_id is null;

EMPLOYEE
--------------------
ZAFIAN
    BRUNNER
        CALLAHAN
        DUELL
        HEIMER
    GIARDINA
        PALESKI
        TERRY
    LUNDY
        BEECHER
        NEUMANN
        MITTLER
        CANNELL
        RACCIO
        SAGE
        SIM
        ANNUNZIATO
        FARRELL
```

Joining a Tree Query with Other Tables

Oracle does not allow you to join other tables in a tree query using a simple SELECT statement. For example, suppose that for each employee record retrieved in the tree query, you also want to retrieve the department name. You can try to use the following query:

```
select rpad (' ', (level-1)*3)¦¦e.emp_last_name,
       d.dept_name
  from emp e,
       dept d
 where e.dept_no = d.dept_no
connect by e.supervisor_emp_id = prior e.emp_id
 start with e.supervisor_emp_id is null;

ORA-01437: cannot have join with CONNECT BY
```

As this example indicates, it is impossible to join another table to the tree query to obtain the additional information. However, beginning with Version 7.1 of the Oracle RDBMS, you can use a dynamic view within the FROM clause of the query to create the tree query as a separate autonomous block to facilitate the join operation. The following example can be used to retrieve information for an employee and all her subordinates:

```
select d.dept_name,
       e1.emp_last_name,
       e1.salary
   from emp e1,
       dept d,
       (select emp_id
          from emp
        connect by supervisor_emp_id = prior emp_id
         start with emp_security_uid = uid) e2
 where e1.emp_id = e2.emp_id
   and e1.dept_no = d.dept_no;

DEPT_NAME                EMP_LAST_NAME            SALARY
-------------------      --------------------     ---------
CONSULTING SERVICES      LUNDY                    95000
CONSULTING SERVICES      BEECHER                  72000
CONSULTING SERVICES      NEUMANN                  65000
CONSULTING SERVICES      MITTLER                  64000
CONSULTING SERVICES      CANNELL                  68000
```

The Outer Join

All the examples presented so far in this book that use multiple tables are based on a simple, or *inner*, join. In an inner join, only the rows that have a matching value in the joined tables are returned. In some cases, however, you may want to retrieve rows that do not have a corresponding match in the joined table. For example, suppose that you need to select all employees and their respective departments from the EMP table. As long as every employee is assigned to a department, a simple join works. Unfortunately (for the purposes of our query only), the company president does not have a department, and a simple join between the tables leaves him off the list.

The solution to this problem is to use an *outer* join. An outer join works by forcing a null row to match in the joined table. The following example illustrates the syntax of the outer join query:

```
select d.dept_name,
       e.emp_last_name
  from emp e,
       dept d
 where e.dept_no = d.dept_no (+)
 order by d.dept_name, e.emp_last_name;

DEPT_NAME                EMP_LAST_NAME
-------------------      --------------------
ACCOUNTING               SAGE
BROADCAST OPERATIONS     GIARDINA
```

```
BROADCAST OPERATIONS PALESKI
BROADCAST OPERATIONS TERRY
CONSULTING SERVICES  BEECHER
CONSULTING SERVICES  CANNELL
CONSULTING SERVICES  LUNDY
CONSULTING SERVICES  MITTLER
CONSULTING SERVICES  NEUMANN
HOSPITAL SERVICES    BRUNNER
HOSPITAL SERVICES    CALLAHAN
HOSPITAL SERVICES    DUELL
HOSPITAL SERVICES    HEIMER
PERSONNEL            RACCIO
SALES                ANNUNZIATO
SALES                FARRELL
SALES                MATTEO
SALES                SIM
                     RUSSO
                     ZAFIAN
```

The placement of the plus (+) sign specifies the table that has the null row forced on it. By changing the position of the outer join, the results of the preceding query change significantly, as shown next:

```
select d.dept_name,
       e.emp_last_name
  from emp e,
       dept d
 where e.dept_no (+) = d.dept_no
 order by d.dept_name, e.emp_last_name;
```

```
DEPT_NAME            EMP_LAST_NAME
-------------------- --------------------
ACCOUNTING           SAGE
BROADCAST OPERATIONS GIARDINA
BROADCAST OPERATIONS PALESKI
BROADCAST OPERATIONS TERRY
CONSULTING SERVICES  BEECHER
CONSULTING SERVICES  CANNELL
CONSULTING SERVICES  LUNDY
CONSULTING SERVICES  MITTLER
CONSULTING SERVICES  NEUMANN
HOSPITAL SERVICES    BRUNNER
HOSPITAL SERVICES    CALLAHAN
HOSPITAL SERVICES    DUELL
HOSPITAL SERVICES    HEIMER
PERSONNEL            RACCIO
QUALITY CONTROL
SALES                ANNUNZIATO
SALES                FARRELL
SALES                MATTEO
SALES                SIM
SHIPPING
```

In using the outer join, you must make sure that the access path into the outer-joined table is based on a single table-join condition. Suppose you want to determine all employees and clients who have no assignments by using a single query. You can try to execute the following query, which will return the error shown:

```
select e.emp_last_name,
       c.client_name
  from emp e,
       clients c,
       assignments a
 where (a.client_id (+) = c.client_id
    or a.emp_id (+) = e.emp_id)
   and a.assignment_start_date is null;
```

```
ORA-01417: a table may be outer joined to at most one other table
```

Performing Data Integrity Checks

An outer join can be used to test the integrity of data in the database. For example, the DEPT_NO value in an employee record must exist in the DEPT table. This rule can be enforced with an integrity constraint, but in many cases integrity constraints are not implemented in the database due to various maintenance issues. Also, in many cases data is loaded before any constraints are enabled. If you try to enable a constraint and there is an integrity issue, an error is generated. Using the syntax of the NOT IN condition shown earlier, you could write a query to return the bad data as follows:

```
select emp_id, dept_no
  from emp
 where dept_no not in (select dept_no
                         from dept);
```

This particular query performs poorly because the secondary query is executed once for every row in the EMP table. As a result, if the company has many employees, the query performance is significantly reduced. A much better query takes advantage of the outer join to return the same results more quickly. To do this, use the following query:

```
select e.emp_id, e.dept_no
  from emp e,
       dept d
 where e.dept_no = d.dept_no (+)
   and d.dept_no is null;
```

To use the outer join in this manner, you must ensure that the column you are checking against cannot be stored as a null value. (Typically, the primary key can be used in this manner.)

Using a Second Condition Against an Outer-Joined Table

In some circumstances, you may need to use additional conditions in the outer-joined table to further qualify the selection criteria. Suppose you need to return the total budget from the BUDGET table for all departments. If the department has no budget established, return a value of zero. This query can be written as follows:

```
select d.dept_no,
       nvl(b.budget_amount, 0)
  from dept d,
```

```
        budget b
 where d.dept_no = b.dept_no (+)
   and (b.budget_line_item = 'TOTAL BUDGET' or b.budget_line_item is null);
```

```
DEPT_NAME               BUDGET_AMOUNT
--------------------    -------------
ACCOUNTING                     285000
BROADCAST OPERATIONS          1500000
CONSULTING SERVICES           2400000
HOSPITAL SERVICES              750000
PERSONNEL                       52000
QUALITY CONTROL                     0
SALES                          850000
SHIPPING                            0
```

Correlated Subqueries

A special type of subquery called a *correlated subquery* can be used in the WHERE clause to define the selection criteria for the main query. A correlated subquery references tables in the primary query to qualify the conditions for the subquery.

Correlated Subqueries for Single-Row Conditions

The correlated subquery can be used to select a single row of data to be used in the primary query. To select all employees in the CONSULTING SERVICES department with their respective current assignment end dates, you can use the following query:

```
select e.emp_id,
       e.emp_last_name,
       nvl (to_char(a.assignment_end_date, 'DD-MON-YY'), 'UNKNOWN')
  from emp e,
       assignments a1
 where a1.emp_id (+) = e.emp_id
   and (a1.assignment_start_date is null or
        a1.assignment_start_date = (select max (a2.assignment_start_date)
                                      from assignments a2
                                     where a2.emp_id = e.emp_id))
   and e.dept_no = (select dept_no
                      from dept
                     where dept_name = 'CONSULTING SERVICES');
```

```
EMP_ID    EMP_LAST_NAME          ASSIGNMEN
---------  --------------------   ----------
     105  LUNDY                   UNKNOWN
     106  BEECHER                 31-AUG-96
     107  NEUMANN                 15-MAR-96
     118  MITTLER                 UNKNOWN
     119  CANNELL                 31-DEC-96
```

EXISTS

The EXISTS condition is used to determine whether any rows match the specified correlated criteria. For example, you can specify the query to select all employees that work for a department located in NEW YORK, as shown in the next example:

```
select e.dept_no,
       e.emp_last_name
  from emp e
 where exists (select 'x'
                 from dept d
                where e.dept_no = d.dept_no
                  and d.location = 'NEW YORK')
 order by e.emp_id;

DEPT_NO   EMP_LAST_NAME
--------- --------------------
      10  RACCIO
      60  MATTEO
      60  SIM
      60  ANNUNZIATO
      20  SAGE
      60  FARRELL
```

In this particular case, the preceding query can be written as a simple join query. The correlated subquery should not be used when a simple query can be used as shown below:

```
select e.dept_no,
       e.emp_last_name
  from emp e,
       dept d
 where e.dept_no = d.dept_no
   and d.location = 'NEW YORK'
 order by e.emp_id;
```

In general, a correlated subquery performs less efficiently when a small set of data can be returned by the subquery. If, however, the correlated subquery can return many rows for each instance of the primary query, the correlated subquery is beneficial. As a rule of thumb, if the correlated subquery is based on a primary key of the subquery table, the correlated subquery is not warranted. Suppose you needed to know the distinct set of departments that have employees assigned. You could use the following query:

```
select distinct d.dept_name
  from emp e,
       dept d
 where e.dept_no = d.dept_no;

DEPT_NAME
--------------------
ACCOUNTING
BROADCAST OPERATIONS
CONSULTING SERVICES
HOSPITAL SERVICES
PERSONNEL
SALES
```

This query selects all rows from the EMP table and collates the result set to determine the distinct set of values. By using a correlated subquery, you can select all departments, execute a subquery for each department until at least one row is found, and then return the row as follows:

```
select d.dept_name
  from dept d
 where exists (select 'x'
                 from emp e
                where e.dept_no = d.dept_no)
 order by d.dept_name;
```

> **NOTE**
>
> One advantage of using the distinct clause is that the rows are returned in alphabetic order automatically (using the most recent versions of Oracle). To achieve the same result with a correlated subquery, you *must* specify the ORDER BY clause. Please note, however, that Oracle insists that to retrieve any data in an expected order, you must specify an ORDER BY clause. Oracle makes no promises that future releases of the RDBMS will achieve the same implicit results.

NOT EXISTS

The NOT EXISTS condition is the opposite of the EXISTS condition in that it returns a TRUE result if no rows are found that match the specified criteria. To achieve maximum performance, you should use the NOT EXISTS condition instead of a NOT IN condition in any query that is based on a secondary query. The reason for this is that the NOT IN condition is translated by the optimizer as

$$z \text{ NOT IN } (c1, c2,...cx) \;\textcircled{6}\; z \mathrel{!=} c1 \text{ and } z \mathrel{!=} c2 \text{ and } z = cx$$

This does not use any indexes and forces a merge join to occur after all conditions have been tested. If the NOT EXISTS condition is used with a correlated subquery, the subquery is solved using all available indexes, and if any rows are found, a FALSE condition is returned. To retrieve all rows from the DEPT table that do not have any employees assigned to the department, you can use the following query:

```
select d.dept_name
  from dept d
 where not exists (select 'x'
                     from emp e
                    where e.dept_no = d.dept_no);

DEPT_NAME
-------------------
QUALITY CONTROL
SHIPPING
```

Summary

This chapter expanded your knowledge of Oracle queries by introducing you to three new concepts that can be used to enhance your Oracle applications. Recursive queries help you to work with database structures that represent sets of data that relate to each other within the same entity. Outer joins can be used to relate tables when there may not be a corresponding entry in the joined table. Finally, the correlated subquery shows how a subquery can be qualified by data in the primary query. As you expand your knowledge base, you can apply these concepts to enhance the usability and performance of your applications.

7

Innovative Techniques Using the Oracle Functions

by Joe Zafian III

Based on what you have read so far, you should be able to write applications that access Oracle data to retrieve any information that can be stored in the database. This chapter discusses techniques that you can use to maximize the usability of your Oracle applications. In addition, this chapter illustrates two new concepts related to Oracle queries: the DECODE function and the GROUP BY clause.

Using DECODE

The DECODE function is by far the most important function that you can use in any SQL query. You can use this function to translate data values and dynamically direct the query to operate in a particular way. The basic syntax of the DECODE function is

```
decode (expression, val1, trans1, val2, trans2, ... valn, transn, default)
```

which can be translated (in pseudocode) to

```
if expression = val1 then
     return trans1
else if expression = val2 then
     return trans2
...
else if expression = valn then
     return transn
else
     return default
```

The obvious use of this function is to translate the retrieved value of an expression into a more descriptive value, as shown in the following example:

```
select emp_last_name NAME,
       decode (employee_sex, 'M', 'Male', 'F', 'Female', 'Data Error') SEX
  from emp
 where dept_no = 60;

NAME                   SEX
--------------------   ----------
MATTEO                 Male
SIM                    Male
ANNUNZIATO             Male
JONES                  Female
FARRELL                Data Error
```

Like other functions, the DECODE function can be nested to return a translation value as shown in the next example:

```
select emp_last_name NAME,
       decode (salary, null, decode (hourly_rate, null,
                                     'COMMISSION', 'PER DIEM'),
'SALARY') "Compensation"
  from emp;
```

```
Employee                Compensation
--------------------    ------------
ZAFIAN                  SALARY
BRUNNER                 SALARY
CALLAHAN                SALARY
DUELL                   PER DIEM
HEIMER                  PER DIEM
GIARDINA                SALARY
PALESKI                 SALARY
TERRY                   SALARY
LUNDY                   SALARY
BEECHER                 PER DIEM
NEUMANN                 PER DIEM
MITTLER                 PER DIEM
CANNELL                 PER DIEM
RUSSO                   SALARY
RACCIO                  COMMISSION
SAGE                    SALARY
MATTEO                  COMMISSION
SIM                     COMMISSION
ANNUNZIATO              COMMISSION
FARRELL                 COMMISSION
JONES                   COMMISSION
```

Using DECODE to Sort Data

The DECODE function also might be used to customize the sort sequence for the data returned. Suppose that you need to sort employees according to marital status in the order: 1) Married, 2) Divorced, and 3) Single. You can define this query as shown in the next example:

```
select decode (emp_marital_status, 'M', 'Married',
                                    'D', 'Divorced',
                                    'S', 'Single', 'Unknown') "Status",
       emp_last_name "Name'
  from emp
 order by decode (emp_marital_status, 'M',1, 'D',2, 'S',3, 999);

Status   Name
-------  --------------------
Married  JOHNSON
Married  FORD
Married  SIM
Married  JACKSON
Divorced SMITH
Divorced O'BRIEN
Single   JONES
Single   FARRELL
Single   TAYLOR
```

Using DECODE for Data Ranges

The DECODE function might also be used to define ranges of data values when combined with the SIGN function. Suppose that a vacation benefit is set up as defined in Table 7.1.

Table 7.1. Weeks of vacation by length of service.

Months of Service	Weeks of Vacation
Less than 6	0
6-24	2
24-60	3
60-120	4
Greater than 120	5

The number of weeks of vacation can be defined by the following query:

```
select emp_last_name,
       hire_date,
       decode (sign (months_between (sysdate, hire_date)-6), -1, 0,
           decode (sign (months_between (sysdate, hire_date)-24), -1, 2,
           decode (sign (months_between (sysdate, hire_date)-60), -1, 3,
           decode (sign (months_between (sysdate, hire_date)-120), -1, 4,
                                                          5)))) WEEKS,
from emp
 where salary is not null;

EMP_LAST_NAME         HIRE_DATE    WEEKS
--------------------  ----------   ---------
ZAFIAN                08-NOV-58        5
BRUNNER               03-OCT-92        3
CALLAHAN              02-JAN-94        3
GIARDINA              08-AUG-90        4
PALESKI               10-JUL-95        2
TERRY                 29-APR-96        0
LUNDY                 13-DEC-93        3
RUSSO                 02-SEP-92        3
SAGE                  12-OCT-95        2
```

Using GROUP BY

Another construct that you can use in your Oracle queries is the GROUP BY clause. The GROUP BY clause directs Oracle to accumulate values based on the specified expression, as shown in this example:

```
select d.dept_name,
       count(e.emp_id)
  from emp e,
       dept d
 where e.dept_no(+) = d.dept_no
 group by d.dept_name;

DEPT_NAME             COUNT(*)
--------------------  ---------
ACCOUNTING                3
BROADCAST OPERATIONS     15
CONSULTING SERVICES      47
```

```
HOSPITAL SERVICES         22
PERSONNEL                  2
QUALITY CONTROL            0
SALES                      8
SHIPPING                   0
```

Any of the group functions from Chapter 5, "Working with Date, Numeric, and Character Functions," can be used with the GROUP BY clause. By using the outer join in this query, you also can retrieve all departments that have no employees assigned. When using a GROUP BY expression, all non-group expressions in the column select list must be specified in the GROUP BY clause. Finally, the rows returned by the query are sorted by the expressions in the GROUP BY clause.

> **NOTE**
>
> When I need to obtain a distinct list of values from a table, I prefer to use the GROUP BY clause rather than using a SELECT DISTINCT, because it is possible to obtain the additional information, such as counts or averages, for each type returned. This information is helpful to define the selectivity of a specific value for a query.

Filtering Values Using HAVING

The HAVING extension to the GROUP BY clause allows you to filter the rows returned based on the group function. For example, suppose you want to return the data only for departments with at least ten employees. This query might be written as follows:

```
select d.dept_name,
       count(e.emp_id)
  from emp e,
       dept d
 where e.dept_no(+) = d.dept_no
 group by d.dept_name having count(e.emp_id) >= 10;

DEPT_NAME               COUNT(*)
-------------------     ---------
BROADCAST OPERATIONS         15
CONSULTING SERVICES          47
HOSPITAL SERVICES            22
```

Retrieving a Data Histogram Chart

A histogram is a bar chart that indicates the relative distribution of data between various entities. Using the GROUP BY clause, you can retrieve the data and format the chart in a single query statement. The following example retrieves a histogram chart indicating the number of employees in each department.

```
select d.dept_name,
       rpad ('X', ceil (count(*) / 3), 'X') "Histogram"
  from dept d,
       emp e
 where e.dept_no = d.dept_no
 group by d.dept_name;

DEPT_NAME            Histogram
------------------   ------------------------------
ACCOUNTING           X
BROADCAST OPERATIONS XXXXX
CONSULTING SERVICES  XXXXXXXXXXXXXXX
HOSPITAL SERVICES    XXXXXXXX
PERSONNEL            X
SALES                XXX
```

Using GROUP BY in Dynamic Views

As discussed previously, you can use a subquery as a dynamic table in the FROM clause of a query. By using a GROUP BY clause in the dynamic view, you can use the group data as part of the query's selection criteria. The following query uses this technique to select all employees who make at least 20 percent less than the average salary for their department:

```
select d.dept_name,
       e.emp_last_name,
       e.salary,
       g.avg_salary
  from dept d,
       emp e,
       (select dept_no,
               avg (salary)
          from emp
         group by dept_no) g
 where e.dept_no = d.dept_no
   and e.dept_no = g.dept_no
   and e.salary <= 0.80 * g.salary;

DEPT_NAME            EMP_LAST_NAME          SALARY AVG_SALARY
------------------   --------------------   ------- ----------
BROADCAST OPERATIONS TERRY                    38000      55000
```

Retrieving a Matrix of Values

The DECODE function and the GROUP BY clause might be used together to create some useful and powerful data presentations. Users often expect to see certain types of data (such as financial reports) laid out as a matrix rather than in individual rows. For example, suppose that you want to produce a report that shows the total billing amount by client for each quarter for the entire year. The data can be retrieved using the following query:

```
select c.client_name,
       to_number(h.bill_date, 'YYQQ') SEQ,
       to_char (h.bill_date, 'Q"Q"-YY') QTR,
       sum (h.hours * cr.rate) BILL
```

```
   from clients c,
        billing_hours h,
        client_rates cr
  where h.bill_date between '01-JAN-95' and '31-DEC-95'
    and h.emp_id = cr.emp_id
    and h.client_id = cr.client_id
    and h.bill_date between cr.eff_start_date
            and nvl (cr.eff_end_date, to_date ('47121231', 'YYYYMMDD'))
    and c.client_id = cr.client_id
  group by c.client_name,
        to_number(h.bill_date, 'YYQ'),
        to_char (h.bill_date, 'Q"Q"-YY');
```

```
CLIENT_NAME                  SEQ QTR       BILL
-------------------------    ---------  ---------
AAA ENGINEERING              953 3Q-95      78000
AAA ENGINEERING              954 4Q-95      52000
DOWN EAST ADVENTURES         951 1Q-95      29000
MERIDIAN COMMUNICATIONS      952 2Q-95      46000
MERIDIAN COMMUNICATIONS      953 3Q-95      14000
PORTLAND HEALTHCARE ASSOC    953 3Q-95      21000
PORTLAND HEALTHCARE ASSOC    954 4Q-95      19000
XYZ CORPORATION              951 1Q-95     128000
XYZ CORPORATION              952 2Q-95     128000
XYZ CORPORATION              953 3Q-95     150000
XYZ CORPORATION              954 4Q-95     175000
```

After the data is retrieved, you would need to manipulate it to present it as a matrix. Using the DECODE function and GROUP BY functions together, you can retrieve the entire matrix in its final form, as shown in the next example:

```
select c.client_name,
      sum (decode (to_char (h.bill_date, 'Q'), '1',
                            h.hours*cr.rate,0) "1Q-95",
      sum (decode (to_char (h.bill_date, 'Q'), '2',
                            h.hours*cr.rate,0) "2Q-95",
      sum (decode (to_char (h.bill_date, 'Q'), '3',
                            h.hours*cr.rate,0) "3Q-95",
      sum (decode (to_char (h.bill_date, 'Q'), '4',
                            h.hours*cr.rate,0) "4Q-95"
   from clients c,
        billing_hours h,
        client_rates cr
  where h.bill_date between '01-JAN-95' and '31-DEC-95'
    and h.emp_id = cr.emp_id
    and h.client_id = cr.client_id
    and h.bill_date between cr.eff_start_date
            and nvl (cr.eff_end_date, to_date ('47121231', 'YYYYMMDD'))
    and c.client_id = cr.client_id
  group by c.client_name;
```

```
CLIENT_NAME                  1Q-95      2Q-95      3Q-95      4Q-95
-------------------------  ---------  ---------  ---------  ---------
AAA ENGINEERING                    0          0      78000      52000
DOWN EAST ADVENTURES           29000          0          0          0
MERIDIAN COMMUNICATIONS            0      46000      14000          0
PORTLAND HEALTHCARE ASSOC          0          0      21000      19000
XYZ CORPORATION               128000     128000     150000     175000
```

Joining a Table to Itself

Sometimes, a column in a table might relate to a different column in a table. By using aliasing, the same table might be specified multiple times in the FROM clause of the query. The following example retrieves the name of every employee with the name of his or her supervisor:

```
select a.emp_last_name,
       b.emp_last_name
  from emp a,
       emp b
 where a.supervisor_emp_id = b.emp_id
 order by b.emp_last_name, a.emp_last_name;
```

```
EMP_LAST_NAME          EMP_LAST_NAME
-------------------    -------------------
CALLAHAN               BRUNNER
DUELL                  BRUNNER
HEIMER                 BRUNNER
PALESKI                GIARDINA
TERRY                  GIARDINA
BEECHER                LUNDY
CANNELL                LUNDY
MITTLER                LUNDY
NEUMANN                LUNDY
ANNUNZIATO             MATTEO
FARRELL                MATTEO
SIM                    MATTEO
RACCIO                 RUSSO
SAGE                   RUSSO
BRUNNER                ZAFIAN
GIARDINA               ZAFIAN
LUNDY                  ZAFIAN
MATTEO                 ZAFIAN
RUSSO                  ZAFIAN
```

When I build a large, normalized database with static reference code information, I typically build a reference table (described in Table 7.2) for all the code translations. The entire table can be cached in memory to improve application performance.

Table 7.2. Reference codes table (REF_CODES).

Column Name	Format	Description
LOOKUP_TYPE	VARCHAR2(10)	Category for the reference code set
LOOKUP_VALUE	VARCHAR2(30)	Value to be looked up
LOOKUP_DESC	VARCHAR2(100)	Translation for the lookup value

Queries might then use this table for each code that needs to be translated in the query. For example, use the following query to attach the reference code table to the query:

```
select e.emp_last_name.
       a.lookup_desc  mstat,
       b.lookup_desc sex,
       c.lookup_desc "401K?"
  from emp e,
       ref_codes a,
       ref_codes b,
       ref_codes c
 where e.dept_no = 60
   and e.marital_status = a.lookup_value
   and a.lookup_type = 'MAR_STAT'
   and e.emp_sex = b.lookup_value
   and b.lookup_type = 'SEX'
   and e.emp_401k_participant = c.lookup_value
   and c.lookup_type = 'YES_NO';

EMP_LAST_NAME          MSTAT       SEX         401K?
- - - - - - - - - - - - - - - - - - - -  - - - - - - - - -  - - - - - - - - -  - - - - - - - - -

MATTEO                 Married     Male        Yes
SIM                    Married     Male        No
ANNUNZIATO             Married     Male        No
FARRELL                Single      Female      Yes
```

> **TIP**
>
> You should use a separate caching referencing table if the storage space for the table is relatively small (less than two blocks) and the data in the table will rarely be modified. Although this is not an absolute requirement, consider this option to improve the performance of your application.

Generating SQL from SQL

Oracle stores detailed information about the database objects in various data dictionary tables. You can examine these tables by querying against dictionary views. Besides the obvious utility of this information to examine the structure of the database, you can use these views to create SQL scripts around the database information. For example, suppose you want to allow all users to select data from all tables in your schema. You cannot grant this by using wildcards such as this:

```
grant select on * to public;
```

Each table must be specified explicitly in separate grant statements. Creating this script can become quite tedious if you have to type every grant statement. SQL can be used to create that script very easily using the following sequence of commands:

```
SQL> set heading off
SQL> set pagesize 9999
SQL> set termout off
```

```
SQL> set feedback off
SQL> set echo off
SQL> spool grants.sql
SQL> select 'grant select on '¦¦table_name¦¦' to public;'
  2>   from user_tables;
SQL> spool off
SQL> set echo on
SQL> set termout on
SQL> set feedback on
SQL> start grants
```

This series of commands (which can be stored as a `.sql` script) is a significant time-saver when your database contains many objects. The result of executing this script is that a file named `grants.sql` is created. The following example illustrates three lines of this file:

```
grant select on customer to public;
grant select on dept to public;
grant select on emp to public;
```

Another useful script, shown in the following example, determines the number of blocks that are used to store data in a table:

```
SQL> set heading off
SQL> set pagesize 9999
SQL> set termout off
SQL> set feedback off
SQL> set echo off
SQL> spool size.sql
SQL> select 'select '''¦¦table_name¦¦''', '¦¦
  2>        'count (distinct substr(rowid,1,8)¦¦substr(rowid,15)) '¦¦
  3>        'from '¦¦table_name¦¦';'
  4>   from user_tables;
SQL> spool off
SQL> set echo on
SQL> set termout on
SQL> set feedback on
SQL> start size
```

This technique is useful for many maintenance and analysis tasks for your Oracle database. Additionally, you can reverse-engineer an Oracle database by using the data dictionary views. This is helpful as a first step when you are tasked with the maintenance and enhancements for an existing database where no table creation scripts exist.

The useful data dictionary views are listed in Table 7.3.

Table 7.3. Data dictionary views.

View Name	Description
USER_CLUSTERS	Information about database clusters
USER_CLU_COLUMNS	Information linking table columns to cluster index columns
USER_COL_COMMENTS	Information about comments regarding table columns

View Name	Description
USER_COL_PRIVS	Grants on table columns where the user is owner, grantor, or grantee
USER_COL_PRIVS_MADE	Grants on table columns where the user is grantor
USER_COL_PRIVS_RECD	Grants on table columns where the user is grantee
USER_CONSTRAINTS	Constraints on user's tables
USER_CONS_COLUMNS	Information on columns in constraint definitions on user's tables
USER_DB_LINKS	Database links owned by the user
USER_EXTENTS	Extents of the segments belonging to the user
USER_FREE_SPACE	Available extents in tablespaces accessible to the user
USER_IND_COLUMNS	Information about the columns that are indexed
USER_INDEXES	Information about indexes created by the user
USER_ROLE_PRIVS	Roles granted to the user
USER_SEGMENTS	Storage allocations for the user's objects
USER_SEQUENCES	Information about the user's sequence generators
USER_SNAPSHOTS	Snapshots the user can view
USER_SNAPSHOT_LOGS	Snapshot logs owned by the user
USER_SOURCE	Information about the user's stored PL/SQL objects
USER_SYNONYMS	Information about the user's synonyms
USER_TABLES	Information about the user's tables
USER_TABLESPACES	Information about tablespaces accessible by the user
USER_TAB_COLUMNS	Information about the columns in the user's tables
USER_TAB_COMMENTS	Comments on the tables and views owned by the user
USER_TAB_PRIVS	Grants on tables where the user is owner, grantor, or grantee
USER_TAB_PRIVS_MADE	Grants on tables where the user is grantor
USER_TAB_PRIVS_RECD	Grants on tables where the user is grantee
USER_TRIGGERS	Information about the user's triggers
USER_TRIGGER_COLS	Usage of columns in triggers owned by the user
USER_USERS	Information about the current user
USER_VIEWS	Information about the user's views

You can examine the structure of these views by describing them with the DESC command.

Summary

This chapter concludes the discussion of SQL queries. The complete syntax of the query is shown in the following code example, with each of the clauses shown in its correct order:

```
select [/* optimizer_hints */]
       * ¦ expression_list
  from list_of_tables
[where conditions]
[connect by connect_conditions start with start_conditions]
[group by group_list [having group_filter] ]
[order by order_columns]
```

Optimizer hints can be added to a query to instruct the Oracle query optimizer on how the query should be executed. These hints are used to ensure the performance of the query and are discussed in detail in Chapter 30, "Performance Tuning."

Use the expression list to define the columns that should be returned from the query. An expression might be a simple constant or column name, or it might be the output of a function as applied to a simple expression. You can design your own stored functions (using PL/SQL) to use in the expression list of your query. Chapter 14, "Database Constraints, Triggers, and Procedures," explains how to create and implement stored functions.

After specifying the data to be returned by the query, you must provide the list of tables and views from which the data will be retrieved. These elements might be database tables or views. Optionally, you might define a dynamic view by using a subquery to define a "table" from which data is to be retrieved.

The WHERE clause defines the relationship between the tables in the FROM clause and specifies selection criteria for the query. The conditional expressions are used to apply logical operators against valid Oracle expressions. Without a WHERE clause, a query based on multiple tables will cause a Cartesian join to occur where every row from one table is joined with every row in the other table.

The CONNECT BY clause is used in special types of queries called *recursive*, or *tree*, queries. When using a recursive query, only one table might be used in the FROM clause of the query. Each subsequent row of data returned is based on data values from the prior row as specified in the CONNECT BY clause.

The GROUP BY clause accumulates data based on the columns or expressions listed in the clause. The columns in the GROUP BY clause do not necessarily have to be specified in the selection list; however, any single row column or expression in the selection list must be specified in the GROUP BY clause. The optional HAVING operator in the GROUP BY clause filters groups in the query based on the condition specified.

Finally, the ORDER BY clause directs the RDBMS engine to return data in the order specified by the order columns.

These clauses combine to provide a myriad of possibilities that you can use in your Oracle database applications. To understand the relationship between these clauses, you should understand the order of precedence of each of the clauses as shown in the following list:

1. Any dynamic views in the FROM clause are resolved immediately, and the text for any views used in the FROM are merged into the query text.

2. If a CONNECT BY clause is specified, the recursive join is performed.

3. The WHERE clause is applied. The order of the various segments in the WHERE clause are explained later in Chapter 30, "Performance Tuning," and Chapter 31, "Oracle's Query Optimizer."

4. As each row of data is returned, it is accumulated based on the criteria in the GROUP BY clause.

5. Finally, the rows that are returned will be sorted based on the ORDER BY criteria.

You have been supplied with an extensive tool set that you can use to retrieve and format your data as needed. As you can see, there are often many ways to achieve the same result. In Chapter 30, you learn how to formulate the optimal query based on your application needs.

8

Table Creation

by Lave Singh

The Basic CREATE TABLE Statement

The CREATE TABLE statement is used, in its basic form, to create a table in the database to be used to hold rows of data. The simple form of the CREATE TABLE statement accepts the table name, column names, and column datatypes and sizes.

In addition to the column names and descriptions, however, you can specify constraints, storage parameters, and whether or not the table is part of a cluster.

Most of the information about which tables and columns of data should exist comes from the design stage of a project, although developers typically decide to include more tables later to make a system more flexible, functional, or efficient.

Table Names

A table name can be up to 30 characters long and cannot begin with a number (although it can begin with an underscore). The table name cannot conflict with the name of another object created in the same user account, and it also cannot be the name of an Oracle reserved word. This means that the following types of objects must be uniquely named inside an Oracle account: tables, synonyms, views, sequences, procedures, functions, packages, indexes, and clusters.

Column Names

Up to 254 columns may be created for any single table (although it's unusual to have such a large number of columns for any one table). Again, most of the columns in a table are identified during the design stage of a project, but more can be added during development.

Datatypes

By specifying a datatype for a column, you specify what kind of data is to be stored in that column. Oracle checks to make sure (for numbers and dates) that only valid data is entered in each field in the column. It does not allow invalid numbers to be entered into a number column, and it automatically performs rounding to the number of decimal places specified (if any). In addition, for columns identified as date columns, Oracle ensures that only a valid date (and, if specified, time) is entered in the field.

> **NOTE**
>
> Oracle validates dates according to the Gregorian calendar. To validate against other calendars (such as the Jewish or Arabic calendars), the NLS_CALENDAR National Language Support setting can be made at the instance (in the INIT.ORA file) or session level (with the ALTER SESSION statement).

Oracle offers a number of datatypes, but only some of them are used in practice. The commonly used ones are described in the following sections.

NUMBER

The NUMBER datatype is used to declare both real numbers and integers and allows numbers up to 38 digits long—enough for most applications.

When declaring a number, the scale and precision of the number is specified—that is, the number of digits before and after the decimal point.

For example, the following statement creates a table with a column that can hold an integer of size 4.

```
SQL> CREATE TABLE mytab (mycol NUMBER(4));
```

```
Table created.
```

The maximum number that can be held in the sample column is 9999. If you attempt to insert a number with more than four digits before the decimal place, you get an error message saying that the value is larger than the specified precision allows.

```
SQL> INSERT INTO mytab VALUES (12345);
INSERT INTO mytab VALUES (12345)
                      *
ERROR at line 1:
ORA-01438: value larger than specified precision allows for this column
```

If you attempt to insert a real number into the table, the number is rounded automatically to the nearest integer (which may or may not be what you want). Oracle always rounds numbers to the nearest number of digits specified for the column after the decimal place.

```
SQL> INSERT INTO mytab VALUES (10.2354);
```

```
1 row created.
```

```
SQL> SELECT * FROM mytab;

    MYCOL
=========
       10
```

To create a real number (that is, one with decimal places specified), you first specify the total number of digits allowed and then the number of digits after the decimal point (the scale).

```
SQL> CREATE TABLE mytab (mycol NUMBER(5,2));
```

```
Table created.
```

The table created by the preceding code allows three digits before the decimal place (not five), and rounds to a scale of two after the decimal point, which means that the largest number the table can hold is 999.99. If you attempt to insert a value with more than three digits before the decimal place, you get an error.

As before, rounding occurs if you specify a number larger than the size allowed for the field.

```
SQL> INSERT INTO mytab VALUES (1234);
INSERT INTO mytab VALUES (1234)
                          *
ERROR at line 1:
ORA-01438: value larger than specified precision allows for this column
```

However, if you try to insert a number with more than two digits after the decimal point, the number is rounded automatically to the specified scale.

```
SQL> INSERT INTO mytab VALUES (123.45657);

1 row created.

SQL> SELECT * FROM mytab;

    MYCOL
=========
   123.46
```

Note that when numbers are specified in a SQL or PL/SQL statement, no quotes are required around the value.

DATE

Columns declared with the datatype DATE can store not just dates but times as well. In fact, they can store the day, month, year, century, hours, minutes, and seconds.

```
SQL> create table mytab (mydate DATE);

Table created.
```

No size is given for a date field. When a date is used in a SQL or PL/SQL statement, the date field is enclosed by single quotes.

The default Oracle date format is DD-MON-YY—that is, it shows two digits for the day, a three-letter abbreviation for the month, and two digits for the year. By default, dates must be provided in this format.

```
SQL> insert into mytab VALUES ('01-JAN-97');

1 row created.
```

If, however, you want to change the format in which dates are input or entered, you can use either the TO_CHAR or the TO_DATE function. You can also use these functions to specify that you want to see the time portion of the date; with the TO_DATE function, you can specify that you want to enter the time into a date field. If the time is omitted when a date value is entered, the default is midnight.

The following example shows a date being entered with a non-default Oracle date format. The month number is provided along with the century and the time.

```
SQL> INSERT INTO mytab VALUES(TO_DATE('31/01/1996 23:11:12','DD/MM/YYYY
➥HH24:MI:SS'));
```

```
1 row created.
```

To show the date in something other than the default format, you must use the `TO_CHAR` function.

```
SQL> SELECT TO_CHAR(mydate,'Day Month Year HH24:MI:SS') FROM mytab;
```

```
TO_CHAR(MYDATE,'DAYMONTHYEARHH24:MI:SS')
================================================
Wednesday January   Nineteen Ninety-Six 23:11:12
```

It does not matter how the date is entered into the database; the internal format of the date will always be the same.

Another way to change the default date format that Oracle uses is to use the Oracle National Language Support elements. The default date format can be set at the instance level, at the session level, or even at the statement level with the National Language Support parameters to the `TO_DATE` and `TO_CHAR` functions.

The following example shows the date format being modified for this session so that the month number is shown first and the century and time are included. All dates will be shown and input in this format.

```
SQL> ALTER SESSION SET NLS_DATE_FORMAT = 'MM/DD/YYYY HH24:MI:SS';
```

```
Session altered.
```

```
SQL> SELECT * FROM mytab;
```

```
MYDATE
===================
01/31/1996 23:11:12
```

```
SQL> INSERT INTO mytab VALUES ('12/30/1996 23:11:12');
```

```
1 row created.
```

Because date fields contain a time element, they will not match if only the date portion is compared against a character string. The Oracle functions `ROUND` and `TRUNC` are useful to round up the date to the nearest day based on the time or to ignore the time portion altogether.

The following example shows that the time portion is recorded in the date column, and by using `TRUNC` you can match on only the date and not the time element.

```
SQL> SELECT TO_CHAR(mydate,'DD-MON-YY HH24:MI:SS') FROM mytab;
```

```
TO_CHAR(MYDATE,'DD-MON-YYHH24:MI:SS')
==========================================================================
30-DEC-96 23:11:12
31-JAN-96 23:11:12
```

```
SQL> SELECT * FROM mytab WHERE mydate = '31-JAN-96';

no rows selected

SQL> SELECT * FROM mytab WHERE TRUNC(mydate) = '31-JAN-96';

MYDATE
=========
31-JAN-96
```

> **TIP**
>
> Use the TRUNC to ROUND functions to ignore the time element of a date field.

VARCHAR2

VARCHAR2 is the declaration most commonly used to declare a character column. It has a maximum size of 2000 characters. Within a column declared as VARCHAR2 you can store any kind of characters.

The following example shows a table created with a VARCHAR2 column and some data being inserted into it.

```
SQL> CREATE TABLE mytab (myvarchar2   VARCHAR2(2000));

Table created.

SQL> INSERT INTO mytab VALUES ('Kailan and some other text !@#$%^&*()');
1 row created.

SQL> SELECT * FROM mytab;

MYVARCHAR2
===============================================================================
Kailan and some other text !@#$%^&*()
```

Oracle takes up only as much storage as needed for a VARCHAR2 field; in the preceding example, only 37 bytes—the length of the data value—are needed.

VARCHAR

Columns declared as VARCHAR currently are translated to VARCHAR2 when a table is created. VARCHAR should not be used; VARCHAR2 is preferred.

The following code example shows that even though VARCHAR is used to specify a column definition, it is translated to VARCHAR2 when the table is described.

```
SQL> CREATE TABLE mytab (myvarchar   VARCHAR(10));

Table created.
```

```
SQL> DESC mytab
 Name                             Null?    Type
 ------------------------------- -------- ----
 MYVARCHAR                                VARCHAR2(10)
```

CHAR

Columns declared with the CHAR datatype, which has a maximum length of 255, are padded with spaces up to the size of the column.

The following code example shows that, when a column is declared with the CHAR datatype and a small value inserted into it, the column is padded with spaces to 255 characters.

```
SQL> CREATE TABLE mytab (mychar CHAR(255));

Table created.

SQL> INSERT INTO mytab VALUES('Amriss');

1 row created.

SQL> SELECT LENGTH(mychar) FROM mytab;

LENGTH(MYCHAR)
==============
           255
```

CHAR column definitions should be avoided in most cases because of the large amount of storage they can occupy.

LONG

A LONG datatype is similar to a VARCHAR2 datatype in that character data can be stored in a LONG column; however, up to 2 gigabytes of data can be stored in one column of one row—more than enough for most applications.

The following code example shows a LONG column being created in a table and some character data being inserted into it.

```
SQL> CREATE TABLE mytab (mylong LONG);

Table created.

SQL> INSERT INTO mytab VALUES('Harman');

1 row created.

SQL> SELECT * FROM mytab;

MYLONG
============================================================================
Harman
```

One major drawback of LONG columns is that no function can be applied to them. Other restrictions include that a LONG column cannot be used in expressions (such as the concatenation operator), and only one LONG column can be declared on any one table.

The following code example shows an attempt to use a function around a LONG column:

```
SQL> SELECT SUBSTR(mylong,1,10) FROM mytab;
SELECT SUBSTR(mylong,1,10) FROM mytab
             *
ERROR at line 1:
ORA-00932: inconsistent datatypes
```

RAW

The RAW datatype is used to hold binary data (sounds, for example). The maximum length of a RAW column is 255 bytes.

LONG RAW

A LONG RAW column can be used to hold large amounts of binary data, such as graphics, drawings, video images, sounds, and other large binary objects.

ANSI Standard and Others

Oracle allows other datatypes to be used when creating tables. This permits ANSI compatibility and compatibility with other databases. These other datatypes are translated into the data types you have already seen. Oracle datatypes are preferred because other datatypes are translated to the Oracle datatypes anyway.

The following code example shows the use of the DECIMAL and INTEGER datatypes; they are translated to numbers when the table is described:

```
SQL> CREATE TABLE mytab (mydec    DECIMAL,
  2                       myint    INTEGER);

Table created.

SQL> DESC mytab
 Name                              Null?    Type
 --------------------------------- -------- ----
 MYDEC                                      NUMBER(38)
 MYINT                                      NUMBER(38)
```

Privileges Required

Before an Oracle user can create a table, there are two things that the database administrator must give him. The first is a system privilege called CREATE TABLE, which allows you to create tables in your own user. The database administrator must also give the user privileges to use up storage either across the entire database or in individual tablespaces. The database administrator can provide this ability in a number of different ways; the most common is the GRANT RESOURCE command, which specifies which tablespace can be used for storage and how much storage the user is permitted (not just for tables but for any other objects that will use up storage in the Oracle database files).

To check whether you have the system privilege to create tables, you can issue the following command to see which system privileges are currently in effect for your session.

```
SQL> select * from session_privs;

PRIVILEGE
========================================
CREATE SESSION
ALTER SESSION
UNLIMITED TABLESPACE
CREATE TABLE
CREATE CLUSTER
CREATE SYNONYM
CREATE VIEW
CREATE SEQUENCE
CREATE DATABASE LINK
CREATE PROCEDURE
CREATE TRIGGER

11 rows selected.
```

To check whether you have the privilege required to use up storage, and on which tablespaces, you can issue the following command. It shows how much storage you're allowed to use, in which tablespace, and how much you've currently used.

```
SQL> SELECT * FROM user_ts_quotas;
```

TABLESPACE_NAME	BYTES	MAX_BYTES	BLOCKS	MAX_BLOCKS
USER_DATA	225280	0	110	0

The storage numbers are shown both in terms of bytes and the number of Oracle blocks.

Storage for Tables

When a table is created, no storage parameters have to be specified—everything will default. However, having the wrong storage parameters can cause problems to appear more often, will result in more storage being used than is actually required, and can reduce the performance of the whole system.

This section looks at storage and at other parameters that affect how the table is stored in the database.

The STORAGE Clause

At the end of the CREATE TABLE statement, you can specify a storage clause to control the amount of storage that will be allocated to the table and how the table uses storage when it needs to grow. This storage clause can also be applied to other database objects that use storage (such as indexes).

If no storage clause is specified for a table, the table uses the default storage for the tablespace in which it is created. By default, the table uses five Oracle blocks when it is first created, another five when it needs to grow, and then any additional storage it uses will be 50 percent bigger than the last extent. The table will ask for more and more storage each time it needs to grow.

Each piece of storage that the table uses is known as an *extent*. The very first extent is known as the INITIAL extent and others are known as secondary extents.

The following example shows a table being created with non-default storage parameters:

```
CREATE TABLE mytab (mycol      VARCHAR2(1))
       STORAGE (    INITIAL     100K
              NEXT        20K
               MINEXTENTS   1
              MAXEXTENTS   99
              PCTINCREASE     50);
```

The table is being created with 100KB of initial storage for the very first extent even though there is no data in the table. The number of Oracle blocks that this constitutes depends on the Oracle block size chosen when the database was first created.

When the rows are inserted into the table, the storage allocated to the table for the very first extent starts to fill with data. When the first extent is filled, the table automatically allocates another extent with the size specified in the storage clause—20KB in our case. When this second extent is filled with data, the table allocates a third extent, which will be 50 percent bigger than the second—that is, 30KB. The amount by which to increase is specified in the storage clause as the PCTINCREASE parameter. For the fourth extent, it will be 50 percent bigger still and may allocate 46KB of storage (30KB + 50 percent is 45KB, which may be the storage allocated if the Oracle block is 1KB or will be rounded up to 46KB for a 2KB block size). Each time the table needs to grow, it keeps allocating 50-percent-bigger extents each time. This can potentially cause a problem because that amount of storage may not be available and free in the database. Having either small next extent sizes or a smaller PCTINCREASE figure would help.

The MINEXTENTS parameter specifies how many extents the table is to allocate when it is first created; the default is one. If the storage parameter is to default, you don't have to specify it in the storage clause.

The MAXEXTENTS parameter specifies the maximum number of extents that this table can have. Once it reaches this maximum, the table does not allocate any more extents but instead reports an error message to the user who caused the table to attempt to allocate another extent. The maximum in the preceding example has been set to 99. In Oracle7.3, there is no absolute maximum for the number of extents a database object can obtain (prior releases had an absolute maximum based on the Oracle block size used for the database).

Once a table allocates too many extents, it's wise to re-create the table so that only one extent is allocated. This can improve performance in accessing the data in the table.

The table can be reorganized using the export and import utilities, or a copy of the table can be created with the correct storage parameters and the data copied over to it. (This is covered in a later section.)

Other Storage Parameters

This section examines some of the other storage type parameters that affect how and where storage is used for a database object.

TABLESPACE

The TABLESPACE parameter with the CREATE TABLE statement specifies which logical area of the database will be used to hold the data for the table. The table may have extents in any database file that belongs to this tablespace. The Oracle user who is to create the table must have been given resource privileges on the tablespace by the database administrator.

```
SQL> CREATE TABLE mytab (mydec    DECIMAL,
  2                       myint    INTEGER)
          TABLESPACE user_data;

Table created.
```

PCTFREE

The PCTFREE parameter specified with a table determines the amount of space to leave free in each Oracle block for the rows to grow into. The default for this parameter is 10 percent, which means that only 90 percent of each Oracle block for the table is to be used when new rows are inserted. The other 10 percent is to be reserved to allow rows that are updated in that block to use more space.

To set this parameter, you must know how the data in the table is to behave. If many columns are to be updated so that they use more storage (increasing the VARCHAR2 field values, for example), or if fields are changed from null on insert to real values, you would set this parameter to the percentage by which you think the rows will grow. If the rows are inserted and the column values do not need to use more storage, this parameter would be set to a low value (even zero).

```
SQL> CREATE TABLE mytab (mydec    DECIMAL,
  2                       myint    INTEGER)
          TABLESPACE    user_data
          PCTFREE    5;

Table created.
```

PCTUSED

This PCTUSED parameter for a table specifies the watermark level below which the amount of storage used in a block must fall (when the block starts to release space by rows being deleted or updated so that they use less storage) before new rows are allowed to be inserted into the block. This figure defaults to 40 percent so that when the amount of storage used in a block starts to fall, the block will not be used for new inserts of rows before at least 60 percent of the block's storage has been freed up.

```
SQL> CREATE TABLE mytab (mydec    DECIMAL,
  2                       myint    INTEGER)
          TABLESPACE     user_data
          PCTFREE        5
          PCTUSED        30;
Table created.
```

PARALLEL

The PARALLEL option for a table specifies the number of parallel query processes that are to be spawned to speed up full-table scans on this table. This can be used even with the parallel query option of the Oracle database.

CACHE

This parameter specifies that the table is to be regarded as a primary candidate to be left cached in the database buffer pool of the SGA. This ensures that the table, when accessed using a full-table scan, will be placed at the end of the list of Oracle blocks that will be moved out first if free blocks are required. This parameter does not guarantee that the table will always be left in the database buffer pool of the SGA.

CLUSTER

This parameter specifies that the table is to be stored as part of a cluster that has already been created (whether this be an index cluster or a hash cluster).

Estimating Storage for a Table

If you know how much storage is likely to be required for a table, you can set this as the INITIAL extent storage parameter for the table.

In practice, for small tables you should err on the side of caution by allocating more storage than is actually required. This helps you to avoid getting too many extents with small tables. With larger tables, you should make more of an effort to calculate the actual amount of storage required.

The following steps can help you arrive at a formula you can use to determine how much storage you should allocate. These steps use only the major factors affecting the amount of storage allocated for a table. No account is taken of, for example, chaining (where rows requiring more storage, usually after an update, move to another block where they can be held) or clusters. This realistic formula gives a reasonable estimate of the amount of storage you should allocate.

1. First, you must determine the Oracle block size being used for the database—usually a default of 1KB, 2KB, or 4KB, depending on the platform being used. These Oracle blocks are used to hold the table data.

2. The most important part of the formula is knowing the number of rows and the average size of each row. Each row has an additional five bytes of storage for the row header in the block. In addition, each column that contains a value has another one byte of storage for holding the length of the column. Based on this information, you know that the amount of storage required for the rows is

   Storage For Rows = Number of Rows * (Average Row Size + 5 + 1 byte for each non-null column)

3. The calculation in step 2 is used in the Oracle blocks. However, not all the Oracle blocks will be used to hold the data. Each Oracle block has some overhead bytes allocated to it. The fixed size of every data block is 57 bytes. In addition, there is overhead of 23 bytes (plus 23 for every extra INITTRANS parameter value specified for the table; this is usually left to the default value of 1).

   Bytes In Oracle block available for storage = (Oracle block size - 57 - (23 * INITTRANS))

4. Another consideration is that when a table is created, you can specify that you want to leave some of the Oracle block free to allow rows to grow in that table; this is the PCTFREE parameter at the end of the CREATE TABLE statement. So the amount of storage in an Oracle block must take this into account.

5. In addition, you need to allocate an additional amount of storage to take account of estimating errors and future growth—perhaps another 10 or 20 percent.

In summary, the following formula gives a good approximation of the amount of storage required for the very first initial extent of a table.

```
Storage Required = Oracle Block Size *
       (Number Of Bytes For Data
       / Amount Of Storage In Each Oracle Block
       )
```

Using the overhead figures for Oracle blocks, rows, and so on mentioned in the preceding few paragraphs, you can translate this to the following:

```
Storage Required = Oracle Block Size
       *(
           (Number of Rows * (Average Row Size + 5 + 1
                               byte for each non-null column))
           /
           ((Oracle Block Size - 57 - (23* INITTRANS))
           * (1-PCTFREE/100))
       )
```

The preceding formula provides the amount of storage to allocate for the initial extent of a table. You could increase this by perhaps 10 percent to give a safety margin. If the amount of storage required for a table exceeds this figure, the table automatically allocates additional extents based on the NEXT and PCTINCREASE storage parameters.

Location of Tables

The physical location of tables does not affect the SQL within the application programs, but it can improve the performance of the application system itself.

Different Tablespaces

There are many reasons for having many tablespaces (logical partitions) for your database. One reason, from the application developer's viewpoint, is that by storing tables and indexes in different tablespaces that use physical database files on different disk drives, you can use the index to improve data access. This is because you can use two disks at the same time—one to bring the table blocks into memory and the other to read the index blocks.

Another approach is to put tables that are frequently accessed together onto separate disk drives. This can also improve access speed.

Striping

For very large tables, it may be preferable to create a table across separate disk drives so that access operations on different parts of the table can be performed by many disk drives at the same time. This can be accomplished by having a large table use its own tablespace, which has a number of files across different disk drives. When you create the table, you can specify the size of the table's initial extent (using the INITIAL storage parameter, which should be the same size as the physical file for the tablespace minus one Oracle overhead block), the size of the next extent (the size of the second file for the tablespace minus, again, the overhead block), and the MINEXTENTS parameter set to 2 so that when the table is first created it will be using two extents in two different physical database files. Extending this further, you can stripe the table across as many disk drives as are available.

Reorganizing Tables

On occasions it may be necessary to re-create a table. The table may be re-created due to having allocated a large number of extents and wanting to reduce the number to 1 to speed up access to the table data. The table can be reorganized in two different ways: 1) by creating a copy table inside the database with the right storage parameters for the new amount of storage taken up by the table; 2) by using the Oracle export and import utilities, which take the table definitions and data out of the database and into an operating system file.

Reorganizing within the Database

This is the simplest way to re-create a table. A copy of the table is created with the right storage parameters and then the original is dropped and the new copy renamed to the original name.

The following example shows this being done for a table called mytab. In this example, 200KB seems to be enough to hold all the data for the data that currently exists in the table; if the table needs more storage, the next extent to be allocated will be 20KB. In fact, all further extents will be 20KB since the PCTINCREASE parameter is set to 0.

```
CREATE TABLE mytab_copy
    STORAGE (INITIAL      200K
                 NEXT       20K
           PCTINCREASE      0)
    PCTFREE 5
    PCTUSED 60
AS SELECT * FROM mytab;

DROP TABLE mytab;

RENAME mytab_copy TO mytab;
```

CAUTION

When a table is dropped, any indexes and privileges that have been created on the table are lost!

One final step is to re-create the indexes, constraints, and privileges on the table.

Before the table is dropped, you should ensure that you have a script readily available to re-create the indexes (and other constraints) that were set up on the table and that you have the required GRANT statements to reset the privileges that were given to other Oracle users or roles.

Using Export and Import

The export and import Oracle utilities can be used to unload the data and definitions not just for one table but for many tables in one run into an operating system binary Oracle file. This exported file has all that you need to create the tables again.

Using the COMPRESS EXTENTS parameter in the export file, the export program calculates the correct initial extent size that will be used when the table is (potentially) re-created when the import utility runs.

Import can re-create the table definition, if it does not already exist, and then bring the data back, too, by inserting all the rows from the exported file.

The export and import utilities can provide a more convenient method for reorganizing a large number of tables. These utilities are covered in a later chapter.

Describing Table Definitions

Once a table has been created, there are a number of ways to find out what has been set up on the table (column names, datatypes, indexes, constraints, triggers, and so on).

DESC

The DESCRIBE command can be used to see the definition of not only a table but also of other objects. The full word DESCRIBE or the abbreviation DESC can be used.

```
SQL> DESC mytab
 Name                                Null?    Type
 ----------------------------------- -------- ----
 MYCOL1                                       NUMBER(5,2)
 MYCOL2                              NOT NULL VARCHAR2(10)
 MYCOL3                                       DATE
```

What Is Shown

The DESCRIBE command shows only the name of the table, the names of the columns, the datatype and size of the columns, and whether the column value is mandatory or not (NOT NULL).

What Is Not Shown

The DESCRIBE command does not show the constraints (apart from the NOT NULL constraint), the indexes, the database triggers, or any other information about a table.

System Tables

The Oracle system tables (otherwise known as the Oracle data dictionary) must be used to gather the information that is not shown by the DESCRIBE command. There are a number of tables that can be accessed to show information about a table, such as: USER_TABLES, USER_TAB_COLUMNS, USER_CONSTRAINTS, USER_CONS_COLUMNS, USER_INDEXES, USER_TRIGGERS, and others.

Modifying Tables

Once a table has been created, the definition of the table can be modified, even when data exists in the table. The data does not have to be deleted or the table otherwise taken offline.

> **NOTE**
>
> The table structure can be modified as long as no other Oracle users have outstanding locks on the table.

Modifying Column Definitions

The ALTER TABLE command can be used to add a column to the end of the table definition (it cannot be added to the middle of the table definition) or to change the datatype or length of a column.

The size of a column datatype can be increased even when there is data in the table. If the column size is to be decreased or the datatype changed, the table must be empty.

```
SQL> select * from mytab;

    MYCOL1 MYCOL2     MYCOL3
========== ========== =========
         1 Benisha    17-APR-96
         2 Kashmir    17-APR-96
         3 Taejen     17-APR-96

SQL> DESC mytab
 Name                            Null?    Type
 ------------------------------- -------- ----
 MYCOL1                                   NUMBER(5,2)
 MYCOL2                          NOT NULL VARCHAR2(10)
 MYCOL3                                   DATE

SQL> ALTER TABLE mytab MODIFY mycol2 VARCHAR2(20);

Table altered.

SQL> DESC mytab
 Name                            Null?    Type
 ------------------------------- -------- ----
 MYCOL1                                   NUMBER(5,2)
 MYCOL2                          NOT NULL VARCHAR2(20)
 MYCOL3                                   DATE

SQL> ALTER TABLE mytab MODIFY MYCOL3 VARCHAR2(10);
ALTER TABLE mytab MODIFY MYCOL3 VARCHAR2(10)
                         *
ERROR at line 1:
ORA-01439: column to be modified must be empty to change datatype
```

CAUTION

Columns cannot be renamed. The table must be re-created.

Modifying Storage Parameters

The storage parameters for a table can be modified to change the way that the Oracle blocks and extents will be used. The INITIAL and MINEXTENTS storage parameters cannot be modified but the rest can.

```
SQL>  ALTER TABLE mytab
  2           STORAGE (NEXT        30K
  3                    MAXEXTENTS  99
  4                    PCTINCREASE 0)
  5           PCTFREE 10
  6*          PCTUSED 60
SQL>
SQL> /

Table altered.
```

These new storage parameters take effect when the Oracle blocks are next used or as the table has to allocate additional extents.

Modifying Constraints

Constraints can also be turned on and off using the ALTER TABLE command. Chapter 14, "Database Constraints, Triggers, and Procedures," describes this procedure.

Allocating an Extent

When a table is first created, the table allocates itself one extent of storage if the MINEXTENTS parameter is left to the default. The table will, once the first extent has been filled with data, automatically allocate another extent with the size specified for the NEXT extent parameter.

If you want to allocate storage for a table, even though the table is not going to use the storage for a while, the ALTER TABLE command can be used to manually allocate another extent of storage. This may be required when you know that a large amount of storage will be required for the table in the near future, that the amount of storage currently allocated is not enough, and that you want to allocate the storage for the table before it is used by another database object.

The following code example shows the allocation of another extent for a table:

```
SQL> SELECT extent_id, blocks, bytes
  2  FROM   user_extents
  3  WHERE  segment_name = 'MYTAB';

 EXTENT_ID     BLOCKS       BYTES
========== ========== ==========
         0          5       10240

SQL> ALTER TABLE mytab ALLOCATE EXTENT (SIZE 20K);

Table altered.

SQL> SELECT extent_id, blocks, bytes
  2  FROM   user_extents
  3  WHERE  segment_name = 'MYTAB';

 EXTENT_ID     BLOCKS       BYTES
========== ========== ==========
         0          5       10240
         1         10       20480
```

With the ALTER TABLE ALLOCATE EXTENT command, you can also specify the Oracle database file that will be used for this new extent, which would be useful for striping a table across different devices.

Renaming a Table

The RENAME TABLE command can be used to change the name of the table. The constraints and database triggers go with the new table. However, views and synonyms need to be re-created to refer to the new table name.

```
SQL> RENAME mytab TO mytab_old;

Table renamed.
```

Copying Another Table

Tables can be created very quickly using the CREATE TABLE command, or they can be copied to another user by using export and import (this is covered in Chapter 20, "Defining and Creating the Initial Database").

Simple Copy of Another Table

When we wish to create a new table based on the definition of another table that exists in the database (even in another Oracle account), we can use another version of the CREATE TABLE statement.

Fixing Table Storage Problems

A simple way to fix storage problems, without using export and import utilities, is shown in the following code example. This would be used to reduce a table to one extent and also to fix the migrated (chained) rows problem. To ensure that the table allocates one extent and does not allocate more extents than are actually required, the correct storage parameters would be worked out and specified when the new table is created.

```
CREATE TABLE customers_copy
    STORAGE (INITIAL         300K
             NEXT           50K
        PCTINCREASE     0)
    PCTFREE 5
    PCTUSED 60
AS SELECT * FROM customers;

DROP TABLE customers;

RENAME customers_copy TO customers;
```

Dropping a Table

You can use various options to remove the definition and data for a table. You learn about these options in this section.

Simple Drop

The DROP TABLE command can be used to remove both the data and the definition of a table. The data does not need to be removed separately. Any database triggers are removed automatically when the table is dropped.

If you want to remove only the data and keep the data definition, you can use either the DELETE command or the TRUNCATE command to remove the rows. The DELETE command can be rolled back; the TRUNCATE command cannot be rolled back.

> **CAUTION**
>
> Once a table has been dropped, it is gone—the DROP command cannot be rolled back.

```
SQL> DROP TABLE mytab;

Table dropped.
```

Dropping Tables with Constraints

If a table has other tables referring to it with foreign key constraints then you cannot simply drop the table. If you attempt to, you get an error message indicating that other tables have foreign key constraints that refer to the table.

```
SQL> DROP TABLE mytab;
DROP TABLE mytab
           *
ERROR at line 1:
ORA-02266: unique/primary keys in table referenced by enabled foreign keys
```

You can either manually remove the foreign key constraints or, by using the CASCADE CONSTRAINTS option, you can get the DROP TABLE command to remove the constraints for you as the next code example shows.

```
SQL> DROP TABLE mytab CASCADE CONSTRAINTS;

Table dropped.
```

Another way for the database administrator to drop many tables in one command is to use the DROP TABLESPACE command with the INCLUDING CONTENTS option. This can be a dangerous option.

Summary

In this chapter, you learned different ways to create a table. In its simplest form, just the table names and column names are required; this type of table may be fine for a development set of tables for aiding in testing and debugging programs. You also learned how to quickly copy an existing table—either with or without data.

For live production systems with large amounts of data, you should specify the other table and storage parameters to make optimum use of the available storage and other resources, and to ensure that access to the data is as efficient as possible. Along with constraints (which are covered in Chapter 14), the CREATE TABLE statement can take longer to write than was the case in previous versions of the Oracle database.

9

Modifying Table Data

by Lave Singh

In this chapter, you examine how the data in the database is modified using SQL language statements. The four major statements covered in this chapter are INSERT, UPDATE, DELETE, and TRUNCATE. Even though there are other ways to modify data in the Oracle database (OCI calls, for example), these four statements are used most often.

Overview of Modifying Data

When you want to change some data, you can use the INSERT, UPDATE, or DELETE statements to add new rows, update existing rows, or delete rows from a table. The TRUNCATE statement, as you see later, is really just a quick way of removing all the rows in the table.

These statements work on sets of data rather than on individual rows. This means that which-ever rows satisfy the WHERE clause of these statements will be modified. There is no need to loop through each row in the table to make changes. In addition, these statements can modify only one table at a time, unlike a SELECT statement, which can retrieve data from more than one table at a time.

These statements are issued by most of the Oracle front-end tools that modify database tables. Whether the developer writes these statements or the Oracle tool generates them, these state-ments are the primary means by which data is modified in the Oracle database. For example, with the Oracle Forms product, the base table blocks cause SELECT, INSERT, UPDATE, and DELETE statements to be generated automatically by the forms software whenever the user operates the screen program. Application developers may also decide to code extra business rules and pro-cessing in other SELECT, INSERT, UPDATE, and DELETE statements in order to work on tables other than the one on which the screen block has been based.

Whenever a set of changes are made to the database, the changes must either be saved or backed out. This is known as "commit and rollback." If you want to save changes, you issue a COMMIT statement that will save all the changes made in the current transaction. The Oracle database software ensures that either all the changes are saved permanently to the database or an error message is reported. If you get an error, you can ensure that none of the changes in the current transaction has been saved. Transactions, commit, and rollback are covered in Chapter 11, "Transactions."

INSERT Statement

The INSERT statement is used to insert brand-new rows into a database table. Two versions of the INSERT statement can be used, depending on whether you want to insert a single row or many rows into a table.

Inserting a Single Row

The INSERT command can be used to insert single rows into a table. In its simplest form, the VALUES keyword is used to provide values for each of the columns of the new row. If any column value is not known, the NULL keyword can be used to set this value to NULL (two commas can be also be used to accomplish this, but using the NULL keyword is clearer).

The following example shows a single row being inserted into a table.

```
SQL> DESC delegates
Name                              Null?     Type
--------------------------------- --------- ----
D_DELEGATE_ID                     NOT NULL  NUMBER(5)
D_LASTNAME                        NOT NULL  VARCHAR2(20)
D_FIRSTNAME                                 VARCHAR2(20)
D_ORGANISATION                              VARCHAR2(20)
D_SEX                                       VARCHAR2(1)
D_DATE_LAST_CONTACTED                       DATE

SQL> INSERT INTO DELEGATES
  2      VALUES (1,'Hayre','Mandip',NULL,'M',NULL);

1 row created.

SQL> SELECT * FROM delegates;

D_DELEGATE_ID D_LASTNAME    D_FIRSTNAME          D_ORGANISATION        D D_DATE_LA
------------- ------------- -------------------- --------------------- - ---------
            1 Hayre         Mandip                                     M

SQL>
```

Two of the columns on the table have been created as NOT NULL, which means that when a new row is inserted (or a row updated) the column value must always be known; it cannot be left undefined. If you attempt to insert a row into the table and attempt to provide a NULL value for a NOT NULL column, the following error occurs:

```
SQL> INSERT INTO delegates VALUES (NULL,NULL,'Hayre','Yasmin','F',NULL);
INSERT INTO delegates VALUES (NULL,NULL,'Hayre','Yasmin','F',NULL)
            *
ERROR at line 1:
ORA-01400: mandatory (NOT NULL) column is missing or NULL during insert

SQL>
```

This is a very common error. One obvious way to fix it is to provide all the values for the NOT NULL columns when you attempt to insert a row. Another way is to allow the database triggers to provide the value for the column automatically whenever a new row is inserted.

Specifying Column Names

In the preceding example, you had to put the NULL keyword where you wanted to leave a column value undefined.

There is another option with the single-row insert statement, and that is to mention in the INSERT part of the statement all the columns for which you will provide values. Any column names not mentioned in the INSERT part automatically default to NULL. Values must be provided for all the columns that have been declared on the table as NOT NULL, but those declared as NULLable can be left out altogether.

The following example shows another example of inserting a new row, with just the two NOT NULL columns and another of the NULLable columns populated.

```
SQL> DESC delegates
 Name                              Null?    Type
 ------------------------------- -------- ----
 D_DELEGATE_ID                    NOT NULL NUMBER(5)
 D_LASTNAME                       NOT NULL VARCHAR2(20)
 D_FIRSTNAME                               VARCHAR2(20)
 D_ORGANISATION                            VARCHAR2(20)
 D_SEX                                     VARCHAR2(1)
 D_DATE_LAST_CONTACTED                     DATE

SQL> INSERT INTO delegates
  2       (d_delegate_id,
  3        d_lastname,
  4        d_firstname)
  5     VALUES
  6       (2,
  7        'Hayre',
  8        'Parminder');

1 row created.

SQL> r
  1  SELECT d_delegate_id, d_lastname, d_firstname,d_organisation
  2  FROM    delegates
  3* WHERE   d_delegate_id = 2

D_DELEGATE_ID D_LASTNAME D_FIRSTNAM D_ORGANISA
------------- ---------- ---------- ----------
            2 Hayre      Parminder

SQL>
SQL>
```

Since only three column names are mentioned in the first part of the statement, only three values have to be provided.

TIP

With an INSERT statement, always mention the column names even though it is optional. If you do, your programs will still work even if new columns are added to the table or the table is reorganized with the columns in a different order.

Most coding standards require that column names whose values are to be provided always be mentioned in INSERT statements. This ensures that the programs will continue to work even if new columns are added to the table or the database administrator re-creates the table with the column names in a different order.

If another column is added to the table, existing INSERT statements that do not mention the column names will fail because they won't be providing enough values. The existing INSERT statements that do mention the column names will still work because they will provide the right number of values for the number of column values mentioned.

Inserting More than One Row

The preceding version of the INSERT statement allows insertion of only one row at a time. There is another version of the INSERT statement that can insert all the rows retrieved by a SELECT statement into a table. This is often used when you want to copy rows quickly from one table to another, or to provide a quick means of backing up some rows into another copy of the table.

The following code example shows two rows in the delegates table being copied to the delegates_copy table, which already exists.

```
SQL> INSERT INTO delegates_copy
  2      SELECT *
  3      FROM   delegates;

2 rows created.
```

The SELECT statement in the preceding example can be any standalone SELECT statement.

In the following code example, the SELECT statement does not return all the rows in the table (only those that match the WHERE clause), and the INSERT statement only populates some of the columns in the new rows—those that must be populated are the NOT NULL columns, as before.

```
SQL> INSERT INTO delegates_copy
  2         (d_delegate_id,
  3          d_lastname)
  4      SELECT d_delegate_id,
  5             d_lastname
```

```
    6     FROM    delegates
    7     WHERE   d_firstname LIKE '%M%';

1 row created.

SQL>
```

The number of items mentioned in the INSERT part of the statement must be returned by the SELECT statement; you cannot specify that you want to populate four columns and then have the SELECT statement return only three values.

Copying Data from Another Table

To quickly copy data from a table to another table that does not already exist, use the CREATE TABLE statement to define the table and copy rows from the results of a SELECT statement. This can be seen in the following code example:

```
SQL> CREATE TABLE delegates_copy
    2     AS
    3     SELECT *
    4     FROM    delegates;

Table created.

SQL> SELECT * FROM delegates_copy;

D_DELEGATE_ID D_LASTNAME        D_FIRSTNAME          D_ORGANISATION        D D_DATE_LA
------------- ----------------- -------------------- --------------------- - ---------
            1 Hayre             Mandip                                     M
            2 Hayre             Parminder                                  F
            3 Hayre             Jasmin                                     F
            4 Hayre             Manveer                                    M

SQL>
```

If you want to copy only some of the rows and columns from the original table, the CREATE TABLE statement can be modified so that the SELECT statement defines the columns and rows that are to be brought over to the new table.

```
SQL> CREATE TABLE delegates_copy2
    2     AS
    3     SELECT d_delegate_id,
    4            d_organisation,
    5            d_lastname
    6     FROM    delegates
    7     WHERE   d_lastname LIKE '%M%';

Table created.

SQL>
```

The order in which the columns are created is the order in which they appear in the SELECT statement. Notice that in the preceding example only one of the NOT NULL columns was created in the copy table.

UPDATE **Statement**

The SQL UPDATE statement is used to modify the columns of existing rows. As with the INSERT statement, changes made by an UPDATE statement within a transaction need to be committed or rolled back.

The UPDATE statement updates all rows that satisfy the WHERE clause of the statement. The following example shows the UPDATE statement making changes to columns in more than one row, with the values being set to constant values provided in the UPDATE statement.

```
SQL> r
  1  UPDATE delegates
  2  SET    d_organisation = 'Ascend'
  3         ,d_date_last_contacted = '01-JAN-96'
  4* WHERE d_delegate_id >= 1

2 rows updated.

SQL>
```

The values to set the column values to can be retrieved from a SELECT statement in the same way that the values for an INSERT statement can be retrieved from a SELECT statement.

The following example shows the values for one row being retrieved from a SELECT statement. The very last WHERE clause relates to the UPDATE statement and controls which rows are to be updated. The SELECT statement joins together the delegates_copy table, which has been given a table alias of DC after the table name in the UPDATE statement, and the delegates table in the SELECT statement. The innermost SELECT statement is executed once for each row that is to be updated.

```
SQL> UPDATE delegates_copy dc
  2  SET    (d_lastname
  3         ,d_firstname
  4         ,d_organisation
  5         )
  6      = (SELECT d.d_lastname
  7                ,d.d_firstname
  8                ,d.d_organisation
  9         FROM  delegates d
 10         WHERE d.d_delegate_id = dc.d_delegate_id
 11         )
 12  WHERE d_lastname LIKE 'H%';

3 rows updated.

SQL>
```

The preceding example could be rewritten using PL/SQL to simplify the code and, depending on the data, might be quicker.

DELETE Statement

The DELETE statement is used to remove rows from a table and has a WHERE clause that determines which rows are to be deleted.

The following example shows rows that satisfy the WHERE clause being deleted from the delegates table.

```
SQL> DELETE FROM delegates
  2  WHERE   d_lastname LIKE 'H%';

3 rows deleted.

SQL>
```

The WHERE clause can contain multiple conditions that must be satisfied before a row is deleted. These conditions are the same as the conditions that are entered for a SELECT statement, and can include subqueries. The following example shows a simple subquery being used to provide a list of delegate_ids, which are then matched against the delegates table to determine which rows are to be deleted.

```
SQL> DELETE FROM delegates
  2  WHERE   d_delegate_id IN (SELECT dc.d_delegate_id
  3                            FROM   delegates_copy dc);

3 rows deleted.

SQL>
```

Using Functions in Statements

In the same way that functions can be used in SELECT statements on columns, functions can be used in INSERT, UPDATE, and DELETE statements to modify the column values.

The following example shows functions being used in an UPDATE statement to modify existing rows in a table. The SYSDATE pseudocolumn is used to retrieve the current date and time, and the TRUNC function is applied against it to remove the time element. In addition, the SUBSTR (substring) function is used to update the lastname to just the first five characters of the last name, starting at position 1. The WHERE clause is again used to determine which rows are to be updated.

```
SQL> l
  1  UPDATE delegates
  2  SET    d_lastname = SUBSTR(d_lastname,1,5),
  3         d_date_last_contacted = TRUNC(SYSDATE)
  4* WHERE  d_lastname LIKE 'H%'
SQL> /

3 rows updated.

SQL>
```

The following example shows a function being used to accept a date that is not in Oracle default date format. Using the function, you can convert the date into the Oracle default format before the row is inserted into the table.

```
SQL> INSERT INTO delegates
  2      (d_delegate_id, d_lastname, d_firstname, d_organisation, d_sex,
d_date_last_contacted)
  3   VALUES
  4      (3,'Hayre','Manveer','Titanium','M',TO_DATE('31/01/1996','DD/MM/YYYY'));

1 row created.

SQL>
```

The only functions that cannot be used in standalone INSERT, UPDATE, or DELETE statements are the aggregation functions—that is, those functions that summarize data, such as SUM, MAX, MIN, COUNT, and so on. These functions can be used, however, in a SELECT statement that is within an INSERT, UPDATE, or DELETE statement.

Locking

To guard against two or more users attempting to modify the same data, Oracle automatically locks the data. In fact, Oracle also locks the definitions of the objects being used in the statements (to guard against, for example, someone dropping the table or modifying the structure of the table while it is in use). These two types of locks are known as DDL (Data Definition Language) locks and DML (Data Manipulation Language) locks, respectively.

Even if rows have been locked by one user process, other user processes can still query the data; the old version of the data is seen until the changes made by the locking user are committed to the database. This is discussed in detail in Chapter 11.

Locks are released whenever a COMMIT or a ROLLBACK statement is issued.

TRUNCATE Statement

Deleting rows from a table can take some time, because the old version of the data must be restored to the system rollback segment objects, in case you need to undelete the rows. It is not uncommon to find that deleting a large number of rows takes many hours.

Truncating Tables

A quick way to delete the rows from a table is to use the TRUNCATE command, which deletes *all* the rows from a table. This is a DDL command, and like all DDL commands it first implicitly commits any pending changes, performs its function, and then commits the changes it made to the data. Changes made by the TRUNCATE command cannot be rolled back.

CAUTION

Remember that changes made by the TRUNCATE command cannot be rolled back.

The following example shows the TRUNCATE command being used to remove all the rows from the delegates table.

```
SQL> TRUNCATE TABLE delegates;

Table truncated.

SQL>
```

There is no option with the TRUNCATE command to selectively delete rows from a table; the DELETE statement must be used if this is required.

Because all the rows in the table are to be removed, the TRUNCATE command releases any additional extents allocated to the table and only the initial extent remains.

If you want to truncate the table because you want to reload the same amount of data again, it would be wise to hold on to the storage already allocated to the table. This can be done using the REUSE STORAGE option of the TRUNCATE command, which keeps all the extents that currently exist for the table allocated.

```
SQL> TRUNCATE TABLE delegates REUSE STORAGE;

Table truncated.

SQL>
```

TIP

Use the TRUNCATE command with the REUSE STORAGE option to hold on to storage if the same amount of data is to be reinserted into the table.

The TRUNCATE command, as you might expect, manages indexes, too. All entries in the indexes for the table are removed automatically.

Modifying Data and Privileges

For any Oracle database there are a number of Oracle users set up, each of whom may have their own tables and other database objects. The owner of a database object (for example, a table) can do whatever she wants with that object, including inserting, updating, deleting, and truncating rows, and changing or removing the structure of the table.

Other Oracle users who do not own the table must be given either system-level or object-level privileges to allow them to make changes to the table.

A detailed discussion of Oracle security is covered in Chapter 16, "SQL*DBA and Server Manager."

System Privileges

There are over 80 system-level privileges that control what each Oracle user on the database can do. The database administrator controls which of these privileges are given to other Oracle users by using the GRANT SQL statement.

ANY TABLE System Privilege

The system privileges that affect what an Oracle user can do on another user's tables are DELETE ANY TABLE, UPDATE ANY TABLE, and INSERT ANY TABLE. If an Oracle user has these system-level privileges, he can insert, update, and delete into tables that he doesn't own and where the owner has not explicitly given him the rights to modify the data. The user becomes, in effect, a type of "superuser" and can modify data anywhere in the database.

> **CAUTION**
>
> System privileges with ANY in the privilege name will enable the user who has that privilege to modify the core data dictionary tables.

Normally these privileges are available only to Oracle database administrator accounts and not to developer or end user accounts.

> **TIP**
>
> Use the SESSION_PRIVS data dictionary view to see which system privileges are currently in effect for your Oracle account.

Object-Level Privileges

The more common way of allowing other Oracle users to modify data is for the owner of the table to give them the right to insert, update, and delete rows.

Granting and Revoking

The GRANT statement can be used to give other Oracle users the right to insert, update, and delete rows. The privilege can also be given to everyone (PUBLIC).

The following example shows just the insert and UPDATE object-level privileges being given on the delegates table to the TAEJEN Oracle user. This Oracle user then attempts to perform a SELECT on the table.

```
SQL> GRANT SELECT,UPDATE ON delegates TO taejen;

Grant succeeded.

SQL> CONNECT taejen/taejen
Connected.
SQL> SELECT * FROM delegates;
SELECT * FROM delegates
              *
ERROR at line 1:
ORA-00942: table or view does not exist

SQL>
```

The preceding example shows that even though the TAEJEN Oracle user has been given privileges on the delegates table, he cannot access the data simply by specifying the table name. When a table name is encountered, Oracle looks for the name in that Oracle account. If the table does not exist in that user's account, a check is made for any views or private synonyms with that user's name. If object names are still not found in that Oracle user's account, a final check is made to see whether a public synonym exists with the name referred to. Finally, if no public synonym is found, Oracle returns the table or view does not exist error message, as shown.

If you have privileges on another user's tables and you want to access a table, you must specify who owns the table, as shown by the following example:

```
SQL> SELECT * FROM ascend.delegates;

D_DELEGATE_ID D_LASTNAME           D_FIRSTNAME        D_ORGANISATION       D D_DATE_LA
------------- -------------------- ------------------ -------------------- - --------
            1 Andreas              Connirae           DSS                  F
            2 Brooks               Micheal            US Army              M
            3 Grinder              John               Sequent              M
            4 Connor               Joseph             Bellcore             M
            5 Robbins              Anthony            Compaq               M
            6 Kaur                 Kashmir            Titanium             F
            7 Kaur                 Benisha            Titanium             F
            8 Singh                Taejen             Titanium             M
            9 Samra                Karam
           10 Samra                Kailan
           11 Singh                Harman
           12 Kaur                 Amriss

12 rows selected.

SQL>
```

The table name in the preceding example has been prefixed by the Oracle user who owns the table. This is less than ideal since the owner of the tables is likely to change between the development stage and the time the code is released for production. To get around this, you can create a synonym to provide an alias for the table; that avoids having to prefix the name of the table with the owner.

The following example shows a synonym being created for the table and used in all further statements referring to the table.

```
SQL> CREATE SYNONYM delegates FOR ascend.delegates;

Synonym created.

SQL> SELECT * FROM delegates;

D_DELEGATE_ID D_LASTNAME          D_FIRSTNAME        D_ORGANISATION      D D_DATE_LA
------------- ------------------  ----------------   ------------------- - ---------
            1 Andreas             Connirae           DSS                 F
            2 Brooks              Micheal            US Army             M
            3 Grinder             John               Sequent             M
            4 Connor              Joseph             Bellcore            M
            5 Robbins             Anthony            Compaq              M
            6 Kaur                Kashmir            Titanium            F
            7 Kaur                Benisha            Titanium            F
            8 Singh               Taejen             Titanium            M
            9 Samra               Karam
           10 Samra               Kailan
           11 Singh               Harman
           12 Kaur                Amriss

12 rows selected.

SQL>
```

Using the synonym, you avoid specifying the owner. If the preceding statement were in a program, you could drop the synonym and re-create it to point to a table owned by a different Oracle user; without changing the application code, you would have it working against a different set of data.

The database administrator can create public synonyms that can be used by everyone on the Oracle database.

The following code example shows the TAEJEN user attempting to update and delete rows from the table (remember that he was given only select and update privileges).

```
SQL> UPDATE delegates
  2  SET     d_firstname = 'Fred'
  3  WHERE   d_delegate_id = 1;

1 row updated.

SQL> DELETE FROM delegates
  2  WHERE   d_delegate_id = 1;
DELETE FROM delegates
            *
ERROR at line 1:
ORA-01031: insufficient privileges

SQL>
```

The UPDATE statement works, but the DELETE statement fails. If the TAEJEN user wants to be able to delete rows from the table, the owner must give the user the DELETE object-level privilege.

If you give a user a privilege but then decide you want to stop the user from making any further changes to the tables, you can use the REVOKE command to remove a privilege.

The following example shows the UPDATE privilege being taken away from an Oracle user by the owner of the table.

```
SQL> REVOKE UPDATE on delegates FROM taejen;

Revoke succeeded.

SQL>
```

The TAEJEN Oracle user still keeps his other privileges, but cannot update any further rows.

> **TIP**
>
> Use the ALL_TAB_PRIVS and ALL_COL_PRIVS data dictionary views to check which object-level privileges have been given to your Oracle user account.

Limiting Rows and Columns

The object-level privileges discussed in the last section allow the grantee of the privilege to view or change any column in any row in the table. The INSERT and UPDATE object-level privileges can be taken down to the column level to control exactly which columns can be inserted into and which columns can be updated; however, the user will then be able to modify those columns on any rows.

If you want to control which rows and columns can be viewed or changed, you have the additional option of using a view on the data. A view is created on the table and all changes are made through the view. Using the WITH CHECK option at the end of the CREATE VIEW statement, you can ensure that modifications cannot be made if the rows would not be visible through the view after the change.

> **TIP**
>
> To control which rows and columns can be retrieved and changed, use views on the table.

Using views to enhance security privileges is discussed in further detail in Chapter 15, "Security in an Oracle Environment."

Roles

With a large number of users and a large number of tables, it can be quite cumbersome to issue GRANT statements for all users for all tables. To make the life of a database administrator easier, Oracle provides the roles facility. This facility allows named groupings of privileges to make it easier to grant and revoke the privileges from Oracle users. See Chapter 15 for more information about roles.

Using Procedural Objects to Modify Data

Another option when it comes to controlling who can perform retrievals and changes to data is to use procedures, functions, and packages.

If you write a procedure that will be called whenever changes are required on a table, you can give other users the ability to call that procedure whenever they want to change the data in the table. The procedure performs the INSERT, UPDATE, or DELETE on the table.

Oracle users with the appropriate privileges can call the procedure. However, other Oracle users do not need to have any direct privileges on the tables used by the procedure. The owner of the procedure is the only Oracle user who needs to have the requisite privileges on the tables being modified by the procedure.

The following code example shows a simple procedure being created to allow deletions on the delegates table. The EXECUTE object-level privilege is given to the TAEJEN user to allow him to call the procedure.

```
SQL> CREATE OR REPLACE PROCEDURE delete_delegate
  2                       (p_delegate_id IN delegates.d_delegate_id%TYPE)
  3  IS
  4  BEGIN
  5     DELETE FROM delegates
  6     WHERE  d_delegate_id = p_delegate_id;
  7  END;
  8  /

Procedure created.

SQL> GRANT EXECUTE ON delete_delegate TO taejen;

Grant succeeded.

SQL> CONNECT taejen/taejen
Connected.
SQL> EXECUTE ascend.delete_delegate(1);

PL/SQL procedure successfully completed.
SQL>
SQL> SHOW USER
user is "TAEJEN"
```

```
SQL> SELECT * FROM ascend.delegates;
SELECT * FROM ascend.delegates
              *
ERROR at line 1:
ORA-00942: table or view does not exist

SQL>
```

The preceding example shows that the user with the EXECUTE privilege can call the procedure (using the owner prefix before the procedure name in the same way you refer to another Oracle user's tables), but the Oracle user TAEJEN cannot directly access the tables—no direct privileges on the tables used by the procedure have been given to the TAEJEN user.

In the same way that you can create synonyms for tables, you can create a synonym for a procedure to avoid having to identify the owner of the procedure in the application code.

Indexes, Constraints, Database Triggers, and Modifying Data

INSERT, UPDATE, and DELETE statements on the table automatically cause constraints to be checked and database triggers to be fired (if they are enabled). In addition, indexes created on the table are also maintained automatically.

Indexes

Indexes are created either by setting up PRIMARY KEY or UNIQUE KEY constraints on a table (for unique indexes) or by using the CREATE INDEX SQL statement for non-unique indexes.

Once an index has been created, it is automatically maintained by any INSERT, UPDATE, and DELETE statements that modify the rows on the table. For example, if there is a unique index on delegate_id and a non-unique index on the delegate_lastname, both indexes are maintained automatically when a new delegate row is inserted into the table.

> **CAUTION**
>
> The more indexes that exist on a table, the more slowly INSERT, UPDATE, and DELETE statements will run, as more indexes need to be maintained.

Indexes can both slow down and speed up INSERT, UPDATE, and DELETE statements. If many indexes exist on a table, each row that is modified has to maintain all the indexes. However, an index can speed up statements if it can be used to quickly locate the rows to be modified (determined by the WHERE clause of the statement).

Constraints

There are five types of constraints that can be set up on a table: NOT NULL, PRIMARY KEY, UNIQUE KEY, FOREIGN KEY, and CHECK. Once these constraints have been set up and enabled, they are checked and enforced when any row is modified in the table.

If a statement affects more than one row and any row conflicts with a constraint on the table, no rows will be modified. For example, if you have an UPDATE statement affecting all the rows in a table and just one of the rows conflicts with the index, no rows will be updated.

The following code example shows an attempt to remove all the rows from the delegates table. However, some of the delegates have bookings on the bookings table. A FOREIGN KEY constraint exists between the bookings table and the delegates table to ensure that bookings are made only for valid delegate_ids. The DELETE statement does not affect any rows because one or more of the rows conflict with the FOREIGN KEY constraint (one or more of the delegate rows have bookings referring to their delegate_id).

```
SQL> DELETE FROM delegates;
DELETE FROM delegates
            *
ERROR at line 1:
ORA-02292: integrity constraint (ASCEND.FK_BOOKINGS) violated - child record found

SQL>
```

The error message that appears after a constraint violation does not indicate how many rows disobeyed the constraint. All that is reported is the name of the constraint (in brackets). You can trap the error message using PL/SQL exception handlers, and provide a more informative message for the user. The way you implement this depends on the Oracle tool from which the DELETE statement originates.

Database Triggers

In addition to any constraints that fire when an INSERT, UPDATE, or DELETE statement is issued against a table, any enable row- and statement-level database triggers also fire. These triggers might provide further checking and processing that cannot be put into constraints. However, if database triggers are disabled, there is no way for them to fire automatically after a change has been made to the table.

The following code example shows a database trigger being created for the delegates table and an UPDATE statement causing the database trigger to fail.

```
SQL> l
  1  CREATE OR REPLACE TRIGGER bir_delegates
  2  BEFORE
  3  UPDATE
  4  ON delegates
  5  FOR EACH ROW
```

```
  6  BEGIN
  7    IF :new.d_date_last_contacted > SYSDATE THEN
  8          RAISE_APPLICATION_ERROR(-20001,'ERR: Date last contacted can not be in
the future');
  9    END IF;
 10* END;
SQL> /

Trigger created.

SQL>
SQL> UPDATE delegates
  2  SET    d_date_last_contacted = SYSDATE + 1
  3  WHERE  d_delegate_id = 2;
UPDATE delegates
       *
ERROR at line 1:
ORA-20001: ERR: Date last contacted can not be in the future
ORA-06512: at line 3
ORA-04088: error during execution of trigger 'ASCEND.BIR_DELEGATES'

SQL>
```

Again, as with constraints, the way that errors from database triggers are reported is less than ideal. A front-end program could trap the database trigger error shown and report it to the user in a friendlier way.

If an INSERT, UPDATE, or DELETE statement causes the database trigger to fail, no rows are affected by the statement. These statements affect either all rows or no rows.

Oracle Tools and Modifying Data

Oracle tools modify data in database tables by using the INSERT, UPDATE, and DELETE statements. For example, with the Oracle Forms tool, which is used to produce screen programs for the end user, there is the concept of a base table block. With very little coding, a screen can query, update, delete, and insert rows into a table. The SELECT, INSERT, UPDATE, and DELETE statements are automatically generated by the Forms tool to translate the operations initiated on the screen into SQL statements that the database understands. Application developers can write much more code (including further SQL statements), in addition to these Forms-generated statements, to work with tables that are not part of the screen table. This is where much of the Forms development work comes in. Other Oracle tools use the same concept of using SQL to communicate with the database—sometimes these statements can be easily seen and at other times they are hidden from the end user and the developer.

Summary

In this chapter, you examined how data is modified in an existing table using the INSERT, UP-DATE, and DELETE statements (and the TRUNCATE statement, which is really just a quick way of deleting all the rows in a table). In addition, this chapter touched on some of the system- and object-level privileges that are required before you can make changes to data in database tables; these privileges are covered in more detail in the security part of the book.

You also learned how other database objects, such as indexes, constraints, and database triggers, are automatically maintained whenever a change is made to the table, meaning that the application developer has less code to write because the database software performs many maintenance chores.

One major drawback in the current version of Oracle is the way in which error messages from database constraints and database triggers are reported to the calling environment. They are not very informative or user-friendly. Application developers may want to trap these error messages and present them to the user in a more suitable way.

10

Other Database Objects

by Lave Singh

In this chapter, you examine some of the database objects, besides tables, that you can create on an Oracle database. Although it is possible to create only tables on a database, the other objects—views, synonyms, database links, and so on—not only help simplify the system's functionality, they also make it more efficient. You can save a great deal of time and effort by using these objects on your Oracle database.

Why Use Other Database Objects?

In theory, the only objects that must exist on an Oracle database for an application to work are tables. The tables hold the rows of data which, at the end of the day, are all that is required for any application system. The other database objects you can create on a database improve the performance of the system and make it more flexible in changing the structure of the database or make it easier to access data.

The following few sections describe some of the advantages of using the database objects you learn about in this chapter.

Performance

To improve the performance of an Oracle database, you can create indexes and clusters. These provide a quicker way of retrieving data than scanning through all the rows of a table. The actual workings of indexes and clusters are discussed in much of the rest of this chapter.

Flexibility

Use of synonyms provides a degree of flexibility in your application systems. Application programs often have statements in the programs referring to the synonym names for the other database objects instead of referring to the database objects directly. This means that if you want to change the database object that the application program works on, you do not need to change the program itself. All that you need to do is re-create the synonym to point to the new database object you want to use.

Easier Access to Data

Database links provide an easy way of referring to tables in another database—whether it be an Oracle or some other non-Oracle database. After you set up a database link, you can use the database objects on another database as though they were on your local database without any other complex coding or configuration required.

Database views allow a level of indirection in the viewing of data. Instead of viewing the data in the database tables directly, you can write a SELECT statement for a view, and the SELECT statement determines how the data appears. If application programs use views instead of the actual database object names, you can change the definition of the view to provide a different set of data without having to change the application programs themselves.

Now that you know some of the advantages of these other database objects, the next section looks at the first type of object: indexes.

Indexes

Indexes are created for two major reasons: to provide uniqueness of key values (to ensure, for example, that no duplicate delegate numbers exist) and to enhance performance. Indexes let you do a quick lookup to the table data if you know what the key values are for the database columns.

Indexes do take up storage on the database, but usually much less than a table.

An index might be based on either a single column or on more than one column on the table. If it is based on more than one column, it is known as a concatenated index. Concatenated indexes behave in much the same way as single-column indexes in the way that they are maintained and used.

After you create the indexes, they are maintained automatically by the database software every time an INSERT, UPDATE, or DELETE statement is issued against the table.

For performance, the index speeds up SELECT statements and also UPDATE, DELETE, and INSERT statements—depending on how the SQL statement has been written. For example, if the statement doesn't have a WHERE clause, no index can be used.

Storage and Usage of Indexes

Figure 10.1 shows a visual representation of the logical structure of an index.

The index entries are stored logically in a tree structure, which makes it easier to search for a particular key value. The Oracle blocks for the index contain only the column(s) that are indexed—whereas the Oracle blocks for the actual table contain the entire row with every single column value in the row.

The columns used in the index are always stored in ascending sequence and the front part of the index entry might be compressed (because it is already known as you traverse the index tree). In addition, any NULL values are not stored in the index.

CAUTION

NULL values are not stored in the index. This means that when you want to retrieve column values that are NULL from the database table, the index is not used.

FIGURE 10.1.
Index tree diagram.

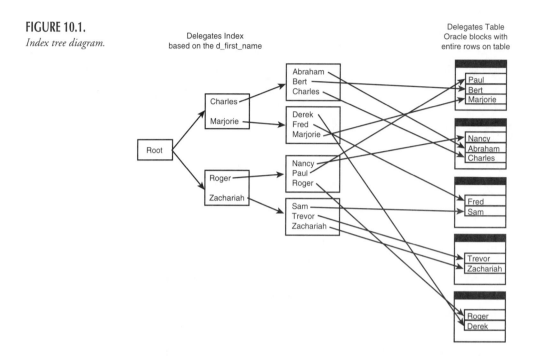

Remember that the order in which the rows are stored in a table is indeterminate—you cannot guarantee that the rows will be retrieved from the table in the same order they were inserted.

In the diagram, you can see an index created on the delegate's first name (non-unique) in order to speed up access to the record for a delegate, if you know what the first name is. By having the index stored in a tree-like structure, it's easier for the Oracle software to search through the index entries looking for a particular key value—in this case the delegate's first name.

In the diagram you can see at the lowest level of the index structure, a pointer to the actual row with the particular key value in the index. This pointer is the ROWID, which exists for every row on every table and is a unique physical address of the record.

If the index shown did exist in the table, then instead of searching through the entire list of possibly thousands of delegate records looking for a particular name, the Oracle software can use the index to quickly locate the physical address of that record from the index and then simply read that one Oracle table block containing the record, without having to read the whole table. In most cases, this significantly speeds up access to the data based on the index key column.

Index Types

There are two types of indexes that you can create on any table: unique and non-unique indexes.

Unique indexes are created when a PRIMARY KEY or UNIQUE KEY constraint is created or enabled on a table. Whichever columns make up the PRIMARY KEY or UNIQUE KEY constraint are also used in the index.

NOTE

Use PRIMARY KEY and UNIQUE KEY constraints to create unique indexes, even though the CREATE UNIQUE INDEX command can be used to create these indexes. The CREATE UNIQUE INDEX command might not be available in future releases of the Oracle RDBMS software.

Non-unique indexes are created using the CREATE INDEX command and are created primarily for speeding up access to the data when the columns used for the index are used to retrieve data from the table.

In the next section, you examine how PRIMARY and UNIQUE KEY constraints relate to indexes.

Using Constraints to Create an Index

When you first create and enable PRIMARY KEY and UNIQUE KEY constraints on a table, Oracle automatically creates an index on the columns that make up the primary key or unique key. This is how the uniqueness is determined and checked for the primary and other secondary keys for the table. It is not obvious after the constraint has been created that the indexes have been set up.

The following code shows how to add a PRIMARY KEY constraint to an index and check the system tables to see that the index has been created.

```
SQL> ALTER TABLE delegates ADD CONSTRAINT pk_delegates
  2        PRIMARY KEY (d_delegate_id);

Table altered.

SQL> SELECT index_name FROM user_indexes where table_name = 'DELEGATES';

INDEX_NAME
------------------------------
PK_DELEGATES

SQL>
```

In this example, you can see that the index is given the same name as the constraint.

CAUTION

When a PRIMARY KEY or UNIQUE KEY constraint is disabled, the index is automatically dropped.

If an index does already exist on the columns that are to be the primary key or unique key columns, the existing index is used.

The index is created when the PRIMARY KEY or UNIQUE constraint is added or enabled on a table. However, when the PRIMARY KEY or UNIQUE constraint is disabled, the index is dropped.

The next code example shows the PRIMARY KEY constraint being disabled and then enabled again, and that the index is dropped and re-created automatically.

```
SQL> ALTER TABLE delegates DISABLE CONSTRAINT pk_delegates;

Table altered.

SQL> SELECT index_name FROM user_indexes WHERE table_name = 'DELEGATES';

no rows selected

SQL> ALTER TABLE delegates ENABLE CONSTRAINT pk_delegates;

Table altered.

SQL> SELECT index_name FROM user_indexes WHERE table_name = 'DELEGATES';

INDEX_NAME
------------------------------
PK_DELEGATES

SQL>
```

The index is also dropped when you remove the constraint from the table.

The USING Clause

When an index is automatically added to a table with a constraint, you do not have the option of specifying the name of the index. However, often you want to specify the storage parameters that are to be used for creating the index. Use the USING clause when you set up or enable the constraint to specify how and where the index is to be created.

The following code shows the USING clause specifying the storage parameters for an index that is created with a constraint.

```
SQL> ALTER TABLE delegates ADD CONSTRAINT pk_delegates
  2         PRIMARY KEY (d_delegate_id)
  3         USING INDEX
  4              INITRANS 5
  5              MAXTRANS 10
  6              TABLESPACE user_data
  7              STORAGE (INITIAL 20K
  8                       NEXT    20K
  9                       MINEXTENTS 1
```

```
 10                      MAXEXTENTS 99
 11                      PCTINCREASE 0)
 12              PCTFREE 0;
```

Table altered.

SQL>

The components of the USING clause are the same as when you create a table on the database. The only major difference is that the PCTFREE figure (specified as 0) for a table is used for the rows to expand and grow, but for an index, it specifies what percentage of each Oracle block to leave free for new index entries to be slotted into the index blocks. In the preceding example, because a sequence generates the delegate_id, there are no entries between existing delegate IDs (as the sequence continues to generate higher and higher numbers for the delegate_id).

You can also use the same USING clause when a PRIMARY KEY or UNIQUE constraint is enabled— because the index is created when the constraint is enabled.

The indexes created when PRIMARY KEY and UNIQUE constraints are enabled will not only help in enforcing uniqueness in the chosen columns but also in speeding up access to the data when the key column is specified in a SQL statement.

Foreign Key Constraints

When a FOREIGN KEY or REFERENCES constraint is specified on a table, the column or column that makes up the FOREIGN KEY constraint is not automatically indexed.

In the vast majority of cases, these foreign key columns that refer to other tables should be indexed to speed up the joins between tables in SQL statements. Use the CREATE INDEX SQL command (shown in the following example) to index these columns.

This code example shows a foreign key column being indexed after the FOREIGN KEY constraint has been set up.

```
SQL> ALTER TABLE bookings ADD CONSTRAINT fk_bookings_delegates
  2      FOREIGN KEY (b_delegate_id)
  3      REFERENCES delegates(d_delegate_id);

Table altered.

SQL> SELECT index_name FROM user_indexes WHERE table_name = 'BOOKINGS';

INDEX_NAME
------------------------------
PK_BOOKINGS

SQL> CREATE INDEX bk_ind_1 ON bookings (b_delegate_id);

Index created.

SQL>
```

The index manually created in the preceding example is a non-unique index, which means that you have the same delegate ID in more than one booking record.

If you want to join the two tables together in a statement, the index created here can help to improve the performance of the two (or more) table join.

The following example shows a statement in which the index created in the preceding example would be useful.

```
SQL> l
  1  SELECT d.d_firstname, d.d_lastname, b.b_start_date
  2  FROM   delegates d
  3         ,bookings b
  4* WHERE  b.b_delegate_id = d.d_delegate_id
SQL>
```

Enabling and Disabling Constraints

As I mentioned, the indexes are created when the PRIMARY KEY or UNIQUE constraint is enabled and is dropped when the constraint is disabled. If you have large tables, the enabling and disabling of these constraints might take a very long time as the indexes are built and dropped.

The indexes created to speed up table joins for foreign keys are not affected by the enabling or disabling of the FOREIGN KEY constraints. The indexes remain even if the FOREIGN KEY constraint is dropped.

CREATE INDEX Command

You can use the CREATE INDEX command to create indexes—both unique and non-unique. However, you should create unique indexes by creating PRIMARY KEY and UNIQUE constraints on the table.

The following code example shows a non-unique index being created on a table.

```
SQL> l
  1  CREATE INDEX delegates_ind ON delegates (d_lastname)
  2       INITRANS 5
  3       MAXTRANS 10
  4       TABLESPACE user_data
  5       STORAGE (INITIAL 20K
  6               NEXT    20K
  7               MINEXTENTS 1
  8               MAXEXTENTS 99
  9               PCTINCREASE 0)
 10*      PCTFREE 10
SQL> /

Index created.

SQL>
```

The index just created can help in speeding up queries such as the one shown in the following code example:

```
SQL> l
  1  SELECT d.d_firstname, d.d_lastname, d.d_delegate_id
  2  FROM   delegates d
  3* WHERE  d.d_lastname = 'Kaur'
SQL> /

D_FIRSTNAME          D_LASTNAME           D_DELEGATE_ID
-------------------- -------------------- -------------
Kashmir              Kaur                     6
Benisha              Kaur                     7
Amriss               Kaur                    12

SQL>
```

As already mentioned, there can be a number of indexes set up on a table and they are maintained automatically whenever a change is made to rows that affect the indexes. The more indexes you have, the more index blocks Oracle updates whenever you change data—but the query statements will run more quickly. This means that the kind of statements that you want to run against the table affects the number of indexes created on a table. If most of the statements against the table are query statements, you might decide to have more indexes. If much of the activity against a table is inserts, updates, and deletes of rows, you might decide to have fewer indexes to speed up those operations.

> **TIP**
>
> As a general rule, there will be no more than five indexes on any one table—otherwise inserts, updates, and deletes on the table will be slower.

Dropping Indexes

Whenever you want to remove an index from a table, use the DROP INDEX command.

Constraint Indexes

Indexes that are currently being used to implement PRIMARY KEY and UNIQUE constraints cannot be dropped by themselves. The constraint must either be disabled or dropped (both of which automatically drop the index). In addition, if there are FOREIGN KEY constraints that refer to the PRIMARY KEY or UNIQUE constraint, the PRIMARY KEY or UNIQUE constraint cannot be dropped or disabled unless the CASCADE option is specified as well. This CASCADE option disables (or drops depending on the command used) the FOREIGN KEY constraints.

The following example shows an attempt to drop an index being used by a PRIMARY KEY constraint.

```
SQL> DROP INDEX pk_delegates;
DROP INDEX pk_delegates
*
ERROR at line 1:
ORA-02429: cannot drop index used for enforcement of unique/primary key


SQL> ALTER TABLE delegates DISABLE CONSTRAINT pk_delegates;
ALTER TABLE delegates DISABLE CONSTRAINT pk_delegates
*
ERROR at line 1:
ORA-02297: cannot disable constraint (ASCEND.PK_DELEGATES) - dependencies exist


SQL> ALTER TABLE delegates DISABLE CONSTRAINT pk_delegates CASCADE;

Table altered.

SQL> SELECT index_name FROM user_indexes WHERE table_name = 'DELEGATES';

no rows selected

SQL>
```

Dropping the index does not affect the functioning of the application system—the only thing that you might notice is that the programs might run slower (sometimes much slower).

Indexes created with the CREATE INDEX command can be dropped by themselves with the DROP INDEX statement. This is possible because there are no constraints attached to the index. This applies both for non-unique indexes and for unique indexes that do not have PRIMARY KEY or UNIQUE constraints relying on them. The next code example shows a non-unique index being dropped on the delegates table.

```
SQL> DROP INDEX delegates_ind;

Index dropped.

SQL>
```

Again, the functioning of the application system is not affected by dropping the index.

What to Index

In reality, the indexes that exist on a table will appear during the development life cycle. Many of the indexes will be created from the information gathered during the analysis and design stages. These are the indexes created by PRIMARY KEY and UNIQUE constraints, and those manually created to speed up joins between master and foreign key tables. Additionally, the analysts and designers might have identified other columns on a table, which will often be used to query the rows. Indexes should be created on these columns to speed up access to the data when those column values are used in retrieving rows from the table.

However, during the build and later on in the project life cycle, the developers and support personnel will identify cases where it would be useful to have additional indexes in order to improve the performance of the application programs.

Self-Balancing

The indexes are logically kept in a tree structure on the database. The number of levels through the tree you have to traverse for any key value will always be the same even if the key values are skewed. For example, if most of the delegates have a name beginning with A, the number of levels you have to traverse through the tree to find a name beginning with A rather than another key value would be greater (because more key values would be stored beginning with A) if the tree structure was not self-balancing.

A Word on Performance and Indexes

Indexes are useful for ensuring uniqueness (with PRIMARY KEY and UNIQUE constraints) and also for speeding up access to the data where the key value is used to retrieve rows. There are a number of performance-type considerations covered here with regard to indexes.

Indexes That Should Exist on any Table

On any table, you should have at least one unique index implemented via PRIMARY KEY or UNIQUE constraints. This is one of the fundamental rules about any relational database—that each row must be uniquely identifiable and that duplicate rows cannot exist on a table.

This index might not be used for speeding up access to data—in fact it wouldn't be a great idea for small tables, but it should always be there and enabled to guard against duplicate rows in a table.

When to Drop Indexes

For large, batch-type data loads it might be prudent to remove some of the indexes so that as data loads, the indexes do not have to be maintained on the table each time a new row is added. It would be faster to remove the indexes, run the load program, and re-create the indexes or enable the constraints again afterward than it would be to have the indexes maintained for every new row.

However, depending on how the load program has been written, it might be detrimental to the load program to have all the indexes removed. Some of the queries in the load program might run very slowly indeed with no indexes available to help locate rows quickly. Think about which indexes could be used by the statements in the load program and which ones could be disabled.

Using Indexes to Speed Up Access to Data

Indexes can significantly help in improving performance with regard to accessing data; instead of searching through the entire list of rows for a table (a full-table scan) it is, in most cases, faster to use the index to locate the rows required and then access just those blocks for the data.

This involves the performance tuning aspect of an Oracle application, and this section describes the pertinent issues with regard to indexes.

Cost-Based and Rule-Based Optimizer

The part of the Oracle RDBMS software that decides how to run your statements is known as the Oracle Optimizer. In Oracle RDBMS version 7.*x*, two Optimizers are available. The old one is known as the rule-based Optimizer, and as the name suggests, it follows a set of rules in determining the best access path. The cost-based Optimizer has more information available to help it make better decisions on how to run a statement. This extra information comes in the form of statistics that have been gathered on the tables, indexes, and clusters. With the extra information available, the cost-based Optimizer makes the best judgment for the access path in the majority of cases.

The Optimizers will decide, for example, when it is appropriate to use an index and when to do a full-table scan. If you want to access all the rows in a table, it would be faster to access the entire table than to use the index to get to all the rows.

To provide extra hints to the Optimizers (for example, to guide it not to use an index for a statement), you can specify Optimizer hints after the very first keyword of the SQL statement.

The following code example shows a hint, telling the Optimizer to ignore the use of the index and to do a full-table scan instead. The hints are specified after the first keyword of the statement.

```
SQL> l
  1  SELECT /*+ FULL(delegates) */ *
  2  FROM    delegates
  3* WHERE   d_lastname LIKE 'A%'
SQL>
```

The Oracle explain plan and the trace facilities give the full story on which Optimizer access paths are the best ones for your statement. You could then use this information to decide on the hints to give the Optimizer.

When Indexes Are Used

Sometimes, indexes are useful in retrieving data, and other times they are not. Be aware, however, that you should think about a number of other considerations when it comes to tuning your statements and programs.

Any one SQL statement can have up to five indexes (if that many exist and are useful for running the query).

The majority of the points made here assume that the rule-based Optimizer is used and that no further statistics are available to help the Optimizer make better choices.

If a statement does not have a WHERE clause, then you want to work on all the rows on the table. Instead of using the index to find the index entry for the first row and then accessing the table data and repeating these steps for each row, it would be better to perform a full-table scan to process all the rows in the table and ignore the index. As a general rule, if you want to retrieve anything more than about 10 percent of the rows (the figure varies depending on the Oracle RDBMS options chosen), it would be better to ignore the index and use a full-table scan (using Optimizer hints).

Tables that use only a small number of rows and Oracle blocks (less than 10) would usually not benefit from using the index to retrieve the rows. Instead of incurring the overhead of accessing and using the index Oracle blocks, it would be quicker to perform a full-table scan of the table and read all the Oracle blocks for the table in one pass.

In addition, full-table scans use the multiple-block read capability, which means that more than one block of the table is read from the database files in one pass, which results in faster access to the data. Index accesses read only one block at a time.

Indexes would still be left on the table to enforce uniqueness, but Optimizer hints would disable the use of the indexes for the statement.

If the column that is indexed is modified in the WHERE part of the statement, the index will not be used for the statement. This modification can be the indexed column used in an expression or with a function around the indexed column in the WHERE clause.

The following statements do not use the index on the delegate's last name column.

```
SQL>
  1  SELECT *
  2  FROM    delegates
  3* WHERE   d_lastname||' ' LIKE 'A%'
SQL>
SQL> l
  1  SELECT *
  2  FROM    delegates
  3* WHERE   NVL(d_lastname,' ') LIKE 'A%'
SQL>
```

Negation and IS NULL

If the column that is indexed is involved in a negative operator or if it's compared against NULL, the index is not used in the statement.

The following statements do not use the index on the delegate's last name.

```
SQL>
  1  SELECT *
  2  FROM    delegates
  3* WHERE   d_lastname NOT LIKE 'A%'
SQL>
```

```
SQL> l
  1   SELECT *
  2   FROM    delegates
  3*  WHERE   d_lastname IS NULL
SQL>
```

As I already mentioned, there are many other considerations that you should take into account when it comes to determining why the statements are not running as quickly as you might expect and what action you can take. The preceding code gives an indication of some of the pertinent issues relating to indexes and tuning.

The preceding sections focused on indexes, which can be set up on tables or clusters. In the next section, you examine clusters.

Clusters

Normally, when new rows are inserted into a table, all the rows being inserted into that table, by all users, are stored in the same Oracle block. After this block has been filled, any further new rows are stored in another Oracle block allocated to the same table.

Clusters provide an alternative method for storing rows. This method is based on a key value. New rows (from any user) are not all stored in the same Oracle block; instead they are stored in an Oracle block determined by the key value. Having tables clustered together does not affect the functioning of the programs (but will affect the performance of the statements).

There are two different types of clusters: index clusters and hash clusters, which I describe in the following sections.

Index Clusters

An index cluster can store data from more than one table in the same Oracle block based on a common key value (there might be up to 16 columns that make up the join between the tables). If you determine that two tables are frequently accessed together in the application, you can decide to hold the data for the two tables together in the Oracle database. If the data for the two tables is held in the same Oracle blocks, both sets of table rows can be retrieved from just one set of Oracle blocks. Reducing the number of Oracle blocks that need to be accessed will improve the performance of the application.

In order to create an index cluster, you must first create a cluster object on the database specifying the type of column and size to link the two sets of rows. Next you create an index on the cluster. Finally, you create the tables as in the preceding sections, and specify at the end of the CREATE TABLE statement that the tables are to be stored in the cluster and which column in the table is to hold the data.

The following example shows an index cluster that holds together both customer and orders table rows:

```
SQL> CREATE CLUSTER delegates_bookings_cluster
  2          (delegate_id NUMBER(5,0));

Cluster created.

SQL>
SQL>
SQL> CREATE INDEX delegates_bookings_ind ON CLUSTER delegates_bookings_cluster;

Index created.

SQL>
SQL> CREATE TABLE delegates (
  2          d_delegate_id           NUMBER(5)               NOT NULL
  3          ,d_lastname                      VARCHAR2(20)   NOT NULL
  4          ,d_firstname                     VARCHAR2(20)
  5          ,d_organization         VARCHAR2(20)
  6          ,d_sex                  VARCHAR2(1)
  7        ,d_date_last_contacted    DATE
  8        )
  9      CLUSTER delegates_bookings_cluster(d_delegate_id);

Table created.

SQL>
SQL> CREATE TABLE bookings (
  2          b_delegate_id           NUMBER(5)               NOT NULL
  3          ,b_course_code          VARCHAR2(8)             NOT NULL
  4          ,b_start_date           DATE                    NOT NULL
  5          ,b_location                      VARCHAR2(30)   NOT NULL
  6          ,b_paid                 VARCHAR2(1)
  7        )
  8      CLUSTER delegates_bookings_cluster(b_delegate_id);

Table created.

SQL>
```

Being part of a cluster does not affect the way you use the tables.

The following code example shows the previous two tables being used with the INSERT statement. The rows for the two tables have the same ROWID block, which indicates that they are in the same Oracle block physically.

```
SQL> INSERT INTO delegates (d_delegate_id, d_lastname)
  2          VALUES (1,'Permjit');

1 row created.

SQL> INSERT INTO bookings
        (b_delegate_id, b_course_code, b_start_date, b_location)
  2        VALUES (1,'TEST','01-JAN-96','Riyadh');

1 row created.

SQL> SELECT ROWID
  2  FROM    delegates;
```

```
ROWID
- - - - - - - - - - - - - - - - - -
00000E75.0000.0001

SQL> SELECT ROWID
  2  FROM   bookings;

ROWID
- - - - - - - - - - - - - - - - - -
00000E75.0000.0001

SQL>
```

Any storage, tablespace, or other parameter should be specified for the cluster.

With the preceding two tables being stored in a cluster, the following type of query would run more quickly because one Oracle block would contain both the delegates and bookings rows.

```
SQL> SELECT d.d_lastname, d.d_firstname, b.b_start_date, b.b_location
  2  FROM   delegates d
  3         ,bookings b
  4  WHERE  b.b_delegate_id = d.d_delegate_id
  5  AND    d.d_delegate_id = 25;
```

In the preceding example, it is likely that when you access details for orders, you also want to retrieve details about the customer who made the order. This would a good business case of clustering tables.

One drawback of clusters is that if you want to access just one of the tables, performance would be slower. This is because each Oracle block would contain data for the two tables, and you want to use the data for only one of the tables.

You need to know how the data will be used and in what percentage of cases the tables will be accessed together before you can decide whether to cluster the tables together.

Hash Clusters

A hash cluster is similar in nature to an indexed cluster in that the rows are stored depending on a key value. However, only one table is part of a hash cluster. The physical location of a stored row is still based on a key value, but the key value is used in a hash function that works out the physical location of the row.

The advantage of a hash cluster is that when you want to retrieve a row based on a key value, you can work out the physical location of the row from the key value without having to run a full-table scan or an indexed access to the data.

For a hash cluster you create the cluster object specifying the type of the key columns, the size of each row, and the number of different key values. This information is used to determine where the rows will be stored and the amount of storage to allocate initially to the hash cluster (if no storage clause is specified)—more storage will automatically be allocated if and when required in the same way that additional extents are allocated for other database objects.

The following example shows the creation of a hashed cluster that holds the delegates table data. You can specify that the rows with the same hash value (`mycol` which holds the customer number) will have an average size of 1KB. The number of different hash key values is 200 (the number of different customer numbers).

```
SQL> CREATE CLUSTER hashed_delegates
  2        (delegate_id NUMBER(5,0))
  3     SIZE        1K
  4     HASH IS     delegate_id
  5     HASHKEYS    200;

Cluster created.

SQL>
SQL> CREATE TABLE delegates (
  2           d_delegate_id          NUMBER(5)      NOT NULL
  3          ,d_lastname             VARCHAR2(20)   NOT NULL
  4          ,d_firstname            VARCHAR2(20)
  5          ,d_organization         VARCHAR2(20)
  6          ,d_sex                  VARCHAR2(1)
  7          ,d_date_last_contacted  DATE
  8          )
  9      CLUSTER hashed_delegates(d_delegate_id);

Table created.

SQL>
```

You can use the preceding hash cluster in the following type of query, where the key value is known:

```
SQL> SELECT *
  2  FROM    delegates
  3  WHERE   d_delegate_id = 25;
```

You can use hash clusters where an exact equality match is made on a key value. Hash clusters will not be used for key range checks or for wildcards. You can use indexes in some searches for wildcards and range checks, and you can have an index and a hash cluster on the same column to speed up both exact matches (hash clusters) and partial matches (indexes).

> **NOTE**
>
> There might be a hash cluster *and* an ordinary index set up on the same column of a table.

One drawback of hash clusters is that if the key values are not evenly distributed (for example, if you create a hash cluster on the delegate last name and you have many delegates with the same last name), you will have many rows mapping to the same physical location. The Oracle blocks can hold only so many rows (depending on how big they are), and the ones that cannot fit into the block will be stored in another block called the *overflow block.* If you then want to access all the rows with the same key value, the Oracle software will access the original block and all the overflow blocks. This leads to accessing more Oracle blocks, which results in slower performance.

Clustering the Same Table

It is possible to cluster only one table. Use this where you want to have rows in the same table with the same key value stored together. In the following example, assume that when you access the bookings table, the table will be based on the bookings for a particular delegate. So hold the bookings rows together for each different delegate ID.

```
SQL> CREATE CLUSTER bookings_cluster
  2         (delegate_id  NUMBER(5,0));

Cluster created.

SQL>
SQL>
SQL> CREATE INDEX bookings_cluster_ind ON CLUSTER bookings_cluster;

Index created.

SQL>
SQL>
SQL> CREATE TABLE bookings
  2         (b_delegate_id  NUMBER(5,0)    NOT NULL
  3         ,b_course_code  VARCHAR2(8)    NOT NULL
  4         ,b_start_date   DATE           NOT NULL
  5         ,b_location     VARCHAR2(30)   NOT NULL
  6         ,b_paid         VARCHAR2(1)
  7         )
  8         CLUSTER bookings_cluster(b_delegate_id);

Table created.

SQL>
```

The preceding indexed cluster would help improve the performance of queries where you want to retrieve the bookings for a particular delegate. This would be the case if you have master/detail-type relationship in a front-end program, such as Oracle Forms or Oracle Reports, where each delegate row is shown on the screen. You show the bookings for that particular delegate on the bottom part of the screen, with the master data (delegate details) on the top part of the screen.

The following code example shows the type of query that would benefit from having the bookings table clustered.

```
SQL> SELECT *
  2  FROM   bookings
  3  WHERE  b_delegate_id = 25;
```

Dropping Tables in a Cluster

If you create tables in a cluster, you can drop them with the ordinary DROP TABLE command. Use the DROP CLUSTER command with the INCLUDING tables option for a quick way to remove the cluster, its index, and all the tables that belong to it. This removes all trace of the cluster and any objects that belonged to it from the database, as the following example shows:

```
SQL> DROP CLUSTER delegates_bookings_cluster INCLUDING TABLES;

Cluster dropped.

SQL>
```

Privileges Required for Creating Clusters

The database administrator must give the CREATE CLUSTER or CREATE ANY CLUSTER system privilege to the Oracle account in which you create the clusters. After they're created, the security privileges on the tables that are part of the cluster are managed in the same way.

Advantages and Disadvantages of Clusters

The primary advantage of using clusters is that they reduce the number of Oracle blocks that you must access for the data.

Direct Access to Data Without an Index

Indexes do provide a quick method of locating some of the rows but indexes use their own storage in Oracle blocks, which must be read and accessed before you can get to the table data. By using hash clusters, you can avoid accessing the index blocks and go directly to the data blocks containing the data for the row with the exact key value specified. By using indexed clusters on two or more tables, you can access the data for both sets of rows by reading just the one Oracle block (with the overhead of accessing the index on the indexed cluster).

Less Storage for Key Values

Another minor advantage of using indexed clusters is that they might use less space for storing the key values. For two or more tables, the key values used to link the rows together will be stored just once because the location of the child rows depending on the key value of the master row.

Slower Full-Table Scans

One disadvantage of using indexed clusters is that full-table scans of the tables will be slower because only some of the data in the Oracle blocks is used (the data for the table on which you perform a full-table scan).

Slower Inserts

Another disadvantage of using clusters is that inserts of new rows for tables is slower because you do not insert into the same Oracle block for all new rows from all users. Instead, the key values determine the correct data blocks to store the rows.

Sequences

In many applications there will be occasions when you need a sequence number to provide a system-generated key value for a row. For example, on the delegates table, you have a `delegate_id` column, which uniquely identifies each delegate record. This `delegate_id` value is used in other tables as a foreign key to refer to a particular delegate record.

One option for generating the next number is to use a table, which has a row containing the next number to be used. To guard against two or more people requesting the next number at the same time, you ensure that the row in this table is locked when you want to generate another number. After the next number has been used (usually for the insertion of a new row), you ensure that the row for the next number increments by using an UPDATE statement.

The following code example shows a table that generates the next delegate_id for a new delegates row. A table is created (the next_delegate_number table), and a row is inserted. The next_delegate_number table is used to generate a delegate_id for a new delegates row.

```
SQL> CREATE TABLE next_delegate_number
  2      (next_delegate_id    NUMBER(10));

Table created.

SQL> INSERT INTO next_delegate_number VALUES (1);

1 row created.

SQL> DECLARE
  2      v_next_id       next_delegate_number.next_delegate_id%TYPE;
  3  BEGIN
  4      SELECT n.next_delegate_id
  5      INTO   v_next_id
  6      FROM   next_delegate_number n
  7      FOR UPDATE OF next_delegate_id;
  8  -- Now that we have the next delegate number we can use it to
  9  -- insert a new row.
 10  --
 11      INSERT INTO delegates (d_delegate_id, d_lastname, d_firstname)
 12          VALUES(v_next_id, 'Kaur','Permjit');
 13
 14  --
 15  -- Now ensure that the next number is incremented for anyone else who
 16  -- needs to insert a new row.
 17
 18      UPDATE next_delegate_number
 19      SET    next_delegate_id = next_delegate_id + 1;
 20
```

```
 21  END;
SQL> /
```

PL/SQL procedure successfully completed.

One issue with the preceding is that you must ensure that all application programs, which want to insert a new row into the delegates table, use the next_delegate_number table to get the next number and at the same time lock the row (so that the same number cannot be retrieved by more than one process). Although the row is locked on the next_delegate_number table, other processes that want to generate the next number will have to wait. A COMMIT releases the locks, and other processes can continue.

An Oracle sequence is a database object that can generate numbers very quickly and simply. With sequences, you have no waiting for locks to be released. After you create a sequence on the database, you can obtain the next number by referring to the <sequence name>.NEXTVAL, which gets the next number and increments the sequence so that any subsequent references to <sequence name>.NEXTVAL will get the next number. After you refer to the <sequence name>.NEXTVAL, you can use the <sequence name>.CURRVAL to refer to the last value that has just been generated in the session.

The following code example shows the creation of a sequence and the NEXTVAL pseudocolumn that gets the next number from the sequence. Every time the NEXTVAL pseudocolumn gets referenced the sequence returns the incremented number. The CURRVAL shows the last number generated.

```
SQL> CREATE SEQUENCE myseq;

Sequence created.

SQL> SELECT myseq.NEXTVAL FROM SYS.DUAL;

  NEXTVAL
---------
        1

SQL> /

  NEXTVAL
---------
        2

SQL> /

  NEXTVAL
---------
        3

SQL> SELECT myseq.CURRVAL FROM SYS.DUAL;

  CURRVAL
---------
        3

SQL>
```

When sequences generate numbers, you won't have to wait on locks. Two or more processes can access the next number from a sequence at the same time, and they will not retrieve the same numbers; the numbers will be unique.

If you want to use sequences to generate the delegate_ids you end up with much simpler code than you had before. The next example shows the same functionality as the preceding example but with sequences instead of a table to generate a unique number.

```
SQL> CREATE SEQUENCE delegates_seq;

Sequence created.

SQL>
SQL>
SQL> INSERT INTO delegates (d_delegate_id, d_lastname, d_firstname)
  2       VALUES(delegates_seq.NEXTVAL, 'Kaur','Permjit');

1 row created.

SQL>
SQL>  /

1 row created.

SQL>
```

As the code example shows, you do not have to store the number retrieved from the sequence in any variable. You do not have to worry about locking the sequence (it is done implicitly when you refer to NEXTVAL), and you do not have to UPDATE the sequence after a number is retrieved from it. This is all done when you use the <sequence name>.NEXTVAL.

Every time you run the preceding INSERT statement, you will have a new number for the delegate_id. This ensures that you end up with unique numbers for the key for the table.

Other Options When Creating a Sequence

When you create a sequence, as in the preceding examples, the sequence will start at 1, increment by 1, and have a maximum value of 10 to the 27th power (big enough for most applications!). You can override these defaults when you create a sequence.

The following code example creates a sequence with some of the defaults overridden. The sequence increments the numbers by 4 (instead of 1) and starts with the number 50. The maximum number that it will generate is 60, and after it goes above 60, it CYCLEs back to the minimum value (set at 50). Additionally, to ensure that the sequence numbers are generated even faster you decide to CACHE 3 sequence numbers (these numbers are pre-allocated and stored in the SGA for faster retrieval).

```
SQL> CREATE SEQUENCE new_seq
  2       INCREMENT BY 4
  3       START WITH 50
  4       MAXVALUE 60
  5       MINVALUE 50
```

```
  6        CYCLE
  7        CACHE 3;

Sequence created.

SQL> SELECT new_seq.NEXTVAL FROM SYS.DUAL;

  NEXTVAL
---------
       50

SQL> /

  NEXTVAL
---------
       54

SQL> /

  NEXTVAL
---------
       58

SQL> /

  NEXTVAL
---------
       50

SQL> /

  NEXTVAL
---------
       54

SQL>
```

Besides using sequences for incrementing, you can have the sequence decrement if you supply a negative number in the INCREMENT clause of the CREATE SEQUENCE command.

Drawbacks of Sequences

Sequences provide a very quick and simple way to generate unique numbers for a number of users at the same time without the users having to wait for locks to be released.

After a sequence number has been generated, it cannot then be rolled back. A ROLLBACK statement reverses all other changes in the transaction apart from those changes to sequences.

The following example shows a sequence inserting a new delegate row and a ROLLBACK statement that reverses the INSERT of a new row, but the sequence continues to increment.

```
SQL> INSERT INTO delegates (d_delegate_id, d_lastname, d_firstname)
  2        VALUES(delegates_seq.NEXTVAL, 'Kaur','Permjit')
  3  /

1 row created.
```

```
SQL> SELECT delegates_seq.CURRVAL FROM SYS.DUAL;

  CURRVAL
--------
       2

SQL> SELECT * FROM delegates;

D_DELEGATE_ID  D_LASTNAME    D_FIRSTNAME   D_ORGANIZATION  D  D_DATE_LA
-------------  -----------   -----------   --------------  -- --------
            2 Kaur          Permjit

SQL> ROLLBACK;

Rollback complete.

SQL> SELECT * FROM delegates;

no rows selected

SQL> SELECT delegates_seq.CURRVAL FROM SYS.DUAL;

  CURRVAL
--------
       2

SQL> SELECT delegates_seq.NEXTVAL FROM SYS.DUAL;

  NEXTVAL
--------
       3

SQL>
```

The ROLLBACK statement does not affect the sequence. For this reason, when you use sequences for generating unique numbers, there will be gaps in the sequence of numbers as various transactions are rolled back either in the program code or for other reasons due to system or process failure.

If you want to change the next number that generated from a sequence, you can either drop the sequence and re-create it starting with a new MINVALUE value, or you can use the ALTER SEQUENCE command to do the same thing.

> **TIP**
>
> Use sequences where the users will not see the number generated or where it is acceptable to have gaps in the numbers generated.

Now that you have been introduced to sequences you can use to quickly generate unique numbers, you look at another type of database object in the next section: views.

Views

A view is a stored SELECT statement that runs whenever the view name is used in a SQL statement. The view does not have a separate copy of the data and so the data shown through a view is always the latest version available. If the view is a simple view (such as performing any summary of data, modifying the columns in the SELECT part of the underlying query, or joining tables), you can perform inserts, updates, and deletes through the view.

The column names for the view will be the same as the column names being SELECTed on the underlying query. However, if the column names have functions around them or are used in expressions in the SELECT part of the query, you must use a column alias, and this alias is how you see the column information through the view.

Advantages of Views

You can use views to provide a simple means of accessing complex data. For example, if you have a SELECT statement that retrieves data from many tables using complex joins and functions, you can create a VIEW with the SELECT statement as the underlying statement for the view. Every time you want to access the complex data, you can run a simple query on the view and the underlying SELECT would be run. This example shows a view based on two tables.

```
SQL> CREATE OR REPLACE VIEW delegate_bookings AS
  2      SELECT SUBSTR(d.d_lastname,1,3)
  3                      d_lastname, d.d_firstname, b.b_start_date, b.b_location
  4      FROM    delegates d,
  5              bookings  b
  6      WHERE   d.d_delegate_id = b.b_delegate_id;

View created.

SQL>
SQL> SELECT * FROM delegate_bookings;

D_LASTNAME            D_FIRSTNAME           B_START_D B_LOCATION
-------------------- -------------------- --------- ----------
And                  Connirae              08-JAN-96 London
Gri                  John                  08-JAN-96 London
Rob                  Anthony               08-JAN-96 London
And                  Connirae              06-FEB-96 Tehran
Bro                  Micheal               05-FEB-96 Tehran
Bro                  Micheal               08-JAN-96 Riyadh
Con                  Joseph                08-JAN-96 Riyadh
Kau                  Kashmir               08-JAN-96 Riyadh

8 rows selected.

SQL>
SQL>
```

By using the view name in the SELECT statement, you end up with a simple query based on the view rather than a query where you have to join the tables yourself.

Summary Data

You also can use views to provide an up-to-date summary of the data in the application tables. This easily shows the summarized data by a simple query on the view.

The following code example creates a view on the delegates table showing the number of delegates in each of the different organizations. If the underlying data is changed, the view always reflects the most up-to-date information, as the latter part of the example shows.

```
SQL> CREATE OR REPLACE VIEW best_customers AS
  2      SELECT d_organization, COUNT(*) number_of_delegates
  3      FROM   delegates
  4      GROUP BY d_organization;

View created.

SQL> SELECT * FROM best_customers;

D_ORGANIZATION        NUMBER_OF_DELEGATES
--------------------  -------------------
Bellcore                                1
Compaq                                  1
DSS                                     1
Sequent                                 1
Titanium                                3
US Army                                 1
                                        4

7 rows selected.

SQL>
SQL> UPDATE delegates SET d_organization = 'Compaq'
        WHERE d_organization = 'Bellcore';

1 row updated.

SQL> SELECT * FROM best_customers;

D_ORGANIZATION        NUMBER_OF_DELEGATES
--------------------  -------------------
Compaq                                  2
DSS                                     1
Sequent                                 1
Titanium                                3
US Army                                 1
                                        4

6 rows selected.

SQL>
```

Even as the data changes the view, the view always reports the latest information because it always runs the underlying SELECT statement that constitutes the view. Views can be especially useful for the queries where you want to summarize data.

Extra Security

Another reason for using views is to provide extra security that is not ordinarily available in the Oracle standard software. For example, if you want to give some privileges on a table to other Oracle users, but you want to restrict which rows and columns they can access, you have to create a view and give privileges on the view.

You can make changes through the view if it is a simple view. However, you could make changes to cause the rows not to be visible through the view again (that is, the rows would not satisfy the WHERE clause of the underlying querying for the view after the changes have been made). The WITH CHECK OPTION clause at the end of the CREATE VIEW statement will ensure that the changes made through the view will still be visible through the view.

The following example shows a view created to hide some of the columns and rows from the delegates table. The WITH CHECK OPTION clause was not specified, the rows can't be updated, and they are not visible through the view.

```
SQL> l
  1  CREATE OR REPLACE VIEW male_delegates
  2     AS SELECT d_lastname, d_firstname, d_sex
  3        FROM   delegates
  4*       WHERE  d_sex = 'M'
SQL> /

View created.

SQL> GRANT SELECT,UPDATE ON male_delegates TO TAEJEN;

Grant succeeded.

SQL> CONNECT taejen/taejen
Connected.
SQL> SELECT * FROM ascend.male_Delegates;

D_LASTNAME           D_FIRSTNAME          D
-------------------- -------------------- --
Brooks               Micheal              M
Grinder              John                 M
Connor               Joseph               M
Robbins              Anthony              M
Singh                Taejen               M

SQL> UPDATE ascend.male_delegates SET d_sex = 'F';

5 rows updated.

SQL> select * From ascend.male_delegates;

no rows selected

SQL>
```

In the preceding example, you have restricted access to the table by allowing the user to query only certain columns and rows on the underlying delegates table. By giving SELECT and UPDATE privileges on the view to another Oracle user (TAEJEN), you have enforced a stricter level of security. However, the rows can be updated (to set the d_sex column to female) so that they are then not accessible through the view. You can create a synonym on the view to avoid hard-coding the owner of the view in the preceding example code.

The following example uses the WITH CHECK option clause when the view is created so that the other Oracle user cannot make changes to the data through the view if the rows would not then be visible again in the view.

```
SQL> l
  1  CREATE OR REPLACE VIEW male_delegates
  2     AS SELECT d_firstname, d_lastname, d_sex
  3        FROM   delegates
  4        WHERE  d_sex = 'M'
  5*       WITH CHECK OPTION
SQL> /

View created.

SQL> GRANT SELECT,UPDATE ON male_delegates TO taejen;

Grant succeeded.

SQL> CONNECT taejen/taejen
Connected.
SQL> UPDATE ascend.male_delegates
     SET d_firstname = 'Fred'
     WHERE d_lastname = 'Brooks';

1 row updated.

SQL> UPDATE ascend.male_delegates SET d_sex = 'F';
UPDATE ascend.male_delegates SET d_sex = 'F'
                                  *
ERROR at line 1:
ORA-01402: view WITH CHECK OPTION where-clause violation

SQL>
```

As the preceding example shows, you can still update other columns through the view but not make any changes that will stop the rows appearing through the view again.

Easier Programming

Often you create a view to make programming easier and simpler in other Oracle tools. If, for example, a query-only Oracle Forms screen program is based on a view that joins tables together, the program will not have to code master/detail block relationships because the view provides the "joined" data. Another example would be where users are using end-user querying tools, such as the Oracle Discoverer 2000 tools (for example, Data Browser), and the user wants to see data from more than one table in a simple manner. Developers could create views on the data that do the difficult joins between tables because the views support these end-user querying tools.

Data Independence

By basing your application programs on views rather than on the actual tables, you have a level of data independence but with the added drawback of having potentially more complex programming in your application programs.

The next example shows a view used in a statement; the view is then changed, and the statement using the view still works.

```
SQL> l
  1  CREATE OR REPLACE VIEW delegates_view
  2     AS SELECT *
  3*        FROM   delegates
SQL> /

View created.

SQL> UPDATE delegates_view SET d_firstname = 'Jack' WHERE d_delegate_id = 1;

1 row updated.

SQL> CREATE OR REPLACE VIEW delegates_view
  2     AS SELECT *
  3*        FROM   new_delegates_table
SQL> /

View created.

SQL> UPDATE delegates_view SET d_firstname = 'Jack' WHERE d_delegate_id = 1;

1 row updated.

SQL>
```

In this simple example, the UPDATE statement is the same in both cases, but because it's working through a view, the underlying table for the view can change (from the delegates table to the new_delegates_table) without affecting the UPDATE statement. The UPDATE statement could be an UPDATE statement in any Oracle application program.

Now that you've taken a look at views, the next section examines yet another type of database object: database links.

Database Links

Database links are aliases to other Oracle or non-Oracle databases that have a connection to the database to which your Oracle account is currently connected. With a database link, you can very simply access tables and other database objects on another database by suffixing the name of the remote table in a SQL statement with the "at" symbol (@) sign followed by the name of the database link.

You can use a synonym to provide another name for the table at the remote database so that you do not have to use the @ notation.

In order to set up a database link, you must have a way for the two databases to communicate. This involves the SQL*Net Oracle product, which interfaces to the underlying networking software and is set up by the database administrator. For the database link, you supply the name of the network protocol, the address or name of the host machine (on which the remote Oracle instance is running), and the instance identifier on the remote machine, such as `'t:big_unix_machine:main_db'`.

With SQL*Net version 2, it is easier in that you can use the name of the TNS alias for the instance on the remote machine, which would remove the physical details required on the database link command. The SQL*Net product set can set up an alias for the remote instance, and you can refer to the alias in the CREATE DATABASE LINK SQL command.

The following example shows a database link accessing tables and other objects on the SCOTT Oracle user, which exists on another database, and the database link is then used to access that table.

```
SQL> CREATE DATABASE LINK mylink
  2          CONNECT TO scott IDENTIFIED BY tiger
  3          USING 't:big_unix_machine:main_db';

Database link created.

SQL>
SQL> select * From emp@mylink;

    EMPNO ENAME      JOB            MGR    HIREDATE      SAL      COMM    DEPTNO
--------- ---------- -------------- ------ ------------ -------- -------- --------
     7369 SMITH      CLERK          7902   17-DEC-80    800                    20
     7499 ALLEN      SALESMAN       7698   20-FEB-81    1600     300           30
     7521 WARD       SALESMAN       7698   22-FEB-81    1250     500           30
     7566 JONES      MANAGER        7839   02-APR-81    2975                   20
     7654 MARTIN     SALESMAN       7698   28-SEP-81    1250     1400          30
     7698 BLAKE      MANAGER        7839   01-MAY-81    2850                   30
     7782 CLARK      MANAGER        7839   09-JUN-81    2450                   10
     7788 SCOTT      ANALYST        7566   19-APR-87    3000                   20
     7839 KING       PRESIDENT             17-NOV-81    5000                   10
     7844 TURNER     SALESMAN       7698   08-SEP-81    1500     0             30
     7876 ADAMS      CLERK          7788   23-MAY-87    1100                   20
     7900 JAMES      CLERK          7698   03-DEC-81    950                    30
     7902 FORD       ANALYST        7566   03-DEC-81    3000                   20
     7934 MILLER     CLERK          7782   23-JAN-82    1300                   10

14 rows selected.

SQL>
```

After you create the database link, you can use the name of the database link in SELECT statements as the preceding example shows.

If the distributed database option of the Oracle7 RDBMS is installed, you can make changes to tables on the local database and on remote databases in the same transaction. The Oracle 2-Phase commit mechanism then ensures that when the transaction is committed, either all databases involved in the distributed update have their changes committed, or all are rolled back. Without the Oracle distributed database option, you can make changes to only one database at a time.

The following code example, running on a database with the distributed option, makes changes to a table in the local database and also to a table on the remote database, and the COMMIT statement ensures that both sets of changes on both databases are committed.

```
SQL> DELETE FROM delegates WHERE d_delegate_id = 3;

1 row deleted.

SQL> DELETE FROM emp@mylink WHERE deptno = 10;

3 rows deleted.

SQL> COMMIT;

Commit complete.

SQL>
```

If any problems occur during the COMMIT, the changes to both sets of tables on both tables would automatically be rolled back.

Synonyms

A synonym is an alias for another database object. In some cases, perhaps you want to refer to an object owned by another Oracle user. If you code application programs to refer to the synonym names instead of the database objects directly, and if the database object changes, you can re-create the synonym for the new object without having to change the application programs. This provides a level of location transparency.

After you create a synonym you can use it in place of the real database object. Whenever the Oracle RDBMS software encounters a synonym name, it makes a translation to the real database object to be operated on. If the underlying object to which the synonym refers is dropped, the synonym will not automatically be removed. You'll get an error when you attempt to use the synonym in a SQL statement.

Private Synonyms

Private synonyms are synonyms that you create within one Oracle user and they can be used only by that Oracle user. The name of the synonym object must be a unique object name in the Oracle user in which it resides. For example, you cannot have a table and a synonym with the same name.

The following code example creates a synonym for the delegates table, and the synonym is then used in other SQL statements.

```
SQL> CREATE SYNONYM deles FOR delegates;

Synonym created.

SQL> desc deles
 Name                             Null?    Type
 ------------------------------- -------- ----
 D_DELEGATE_ID                   NOT NULL NUMBER(5)
 D_LASTNAME                      NOT NULL VARCHAR2(20)
 D_FIRSTNAME                              VARCHAR2(20)
 D_ORGANIZATION                           VARCHAR2(20)
 D_SEX                                    VARCHAR2(1)
 D_DATE_LAST_CONTACTED                    DATE

SQL> SELECT COUNT(*) FROM deles;

  COUNT(*)
 ---------
        12

SQL> UPDATE deles SET d_lastname = 'Smith' WHERE d_firstname = 'Micheal';

1 row updated.

SQL>
```

Often, you might want to use synonyms to avoid having to hard-code the owner of a database object, especially when you're developing a set of programs where on a development database, an Oracle user owns the objects, and on the production system, a different Oracle username will own the objects. If the application programs refer to the owner directly, they would not work when they are moved to the production environment.

> **CAUTION**
>
> Do not hard-code the owner of any database object in application programs—use synonyms instead.

The following example shows a synonym that avoids having to hard-code the owner of a database object.

```
SQL> GRANT SELECT, UPDATE ON delegates TO taejen;

Grant succeeded.

SQL> CONNECT taejen/taejen
Connected.
SQL> CREATE SYNONYM delegates FOR ascend.delegates;

Synonym created.

SQL> DESC delegates;
 Name                                Null?    Type
 ----------------------------------- -------- ----
 D_DELEGATE_ID                       NOT NULL NUMBER(5)
 D_LASTNAME                          NOT NULL VARCHAR2(20)
 D_FIRSTNAME                                  VARCHAR2(20)
 D_ORGANIZATION                               VARCHAR2(20)
 D_SEX                                        VARCHAR2(1)
 D_DATE_LAST_CONTACTED                        DATE

SQL> UPDATE delegates SET d_lastname = 'Smith' WHERE d_delegate_id = 5;

1 row updated.

SQL>
```

The Oracle user TAEJEN is given privileges to SELECT and UPDATE the delegates table. After you connect to the TAEJEN user, you create a private synonym with the same name as the table owned by the other Oracle user. This is possible because the Oracle user TAEJEN does not have another database object with the same name as the synonym. Any application code from this point on can refer to the synonym name rather than to the owner of the object, which makes the programs more flexible and portable. After you take the programs to the production environment, only the synonym needs to be re-created to work on the tables owned by the production user.

Public Synonyms

A private synonym can only be used by the owner who creates the private synonym. However, any Oracle user on the database can use a *public* synonym, which must be created by a database administrator who has the appropriate privileges.

The public synonyms are available only if there is no object with the same name created in the Oracle user's own account. By default, the Oracle RDBMS software will use the local definition of an object before using the public synonym.

Even though public synonyms are global in nature, in that all Oracle users of the database can refer to them, the Oracle users still need to have security privileges before they can access the object to which the synonym refers.

You create public synonyms in a manner very similar to private synonyms, except that the word PUBLIC is between the CREATE and SYNONYM keywords, as is shown in the next example.

The next example shows a public synonym and two Oracle users who attempt to use it. Only the TAEJEN Oracle user has been given privileges on the object to which the public synonym refers.

```
SQL> REVOKE ALL ON delegates FROM taejen;

Revoke succeeded.

SQL> REVOKE ALL ON delegates FROM PUBLIC;

Revoke succeeded.

SQL> GRANT SELECT, UPDATE ON delegates TO taejen;

Grant succeeded.

SQL> CREATE PUBLIC SYNONYM delegates FOR ascend.delegates;

Synonym created.

SQL> CONNECT taejen/taejen
Connected.
SQL> SELECT COUNT(*) FROM delegates;

 COUNT(*)
--------
      12

SQL>
SQL> CONNECT benisha/benisha
Connected.
SQL> SELECT COUNT(*) FROM delegates;
SELECT COUNT(*) FROM delegates
                    *
ERROR at line 1:
ORA-00942: table or view does not exist

SQL>
```

If the original grant of privileges has been made to public rather than to individual users, then all Oracle users could access the table, and all Oracle users could use the public synonym.

> **NOTE**
>
> You can create a synonym for a table, view, sequence, procedure, stored function, package, snapshot, or another synonym.

Summary

In this chapter you looked at some of the other objects you can create on an Oracle database. You do not *have* to create any of these objects, but as you have seen, your application probably will run faster, be more flexible, and be easier to maintain if you use them. You will find that the majority of application systems use a combination of the objects covered in this chapter.

11

Transactions

by Lave Singh

In this chapter, you take a look at one of the fundamental concepts of Oracle: the transaction known as the *commit-unit*.

What Is a Transaction?

With Oracle, as with many other databases, when changes have been made to the database they can either be saved permanently or backed out (rolled back). This applies to changes made in most of the Oracle tools—for example, SQL*Plus, Oracle Forms, and Oracle Reports. In some tools, however, changes can be saved automatically without issuing a COMMIT statement (as in SQL*Plus or Server Manager when the user leaves the tool).

A transaction is a logical unit of work that consists of a set of changes (inserts, updates, and deletes). Transactions must either be saved to the database or rolled back. Either all the changes in the transaction are committed or none is.

For example, a user using a screen program, such as the Oracle Forms product, may make changes to five rows on a screen. When he commits the changes to the database, the Oracle Forms program either informs the user that all five rows have been saved or that a problem occurred (meaning that none of the changes was saved). If the user manages to commit the changes successfully and starts to make changes to additional rows, the user is starting another transaction.

> **NOTE**
>
> Once a transaction has been committed to the database, it cannot be rolled back.

If the user receives a message indicating that his changes have been saved, those changes are permanent. If the database and instance have been set up correctly, work is not lost even if serious failures occur; the database can be reinstated successfully.

> **NOTE**
>
> A COMMIT statement either saves all changes in a transaction or none.

The way that the COMMIT and ROLLBACK statements are issued varies from one Oracle tool to another.

When Does a Transaction Start and End?

A transaction starts when either the user connects to the Oracle database and starts to perform work (even if only a SELECT statement) or immediately after a COMMIT or a ROLLBACK statement.

A transaction ends with the next COMMIT or ROLLBACK statement or when the process making the changes ends.

The following code example shows three transactions that have been made in the Oracle SQL*Plus tool.

```
SQL> SELECT * FROM delegates;

D_DELEGATE_ID D_LASTNAME       D_FIRSTNAME       D_ORGANIZATION        D D_DATE_LA
------------- ---------------- ----------------- --------------------- - ---------
            1 Andreas          Connirae          DSS                   F
            2 Brooks           Micheal           US Army               M
            3 Grinder          John              Sequent               M
            4 Connor           Joseph            Bellcore              M
            5 Robbins          Anthony           Compaq                M
            6 Kaur             Kashmir           Titanium              F
            7 Kaur             Benisha           Titanium              F
            8 Singh            Taejen            Titanium              M
            9 Samra            Karam
           10 Samra            Kailan
           11 Singh            Harman
           12 Kaur             Amriss

12 rows selected.

SQL> DELETE FROM bookings
  2  WHERE  b_delegate_id = 2;

2 rows deleted.

SQL> DELETE FROM delegates
  2  WHERE  d_delegate_id = 2;

1 row deleted.

SQL> COMMIT;

Commit complete.

SQL> DELETE FROM bookings;

6 rows deleted.

SQL> ROLLBACK;

Rollback complete.
SQL>
SQL>
SQL>
SQL> DELETE FROM bookings;

6 rows deleted.

SQL> EXIT
```

> **CAUTION**
>
> The SQL*Plus tool automatically commits the last transaction when you leave the tool—even when you exit using the QUIT command.

Statement Level Rollback

With Oracle there is also the concept of statement-level rollback. This means that either all changes for a particular statement are made or no changes are made. For example, if an UPDATE statement has been running for some time and fails just before updating all the rows, the UPDATE statement does not affect any of the rows.

However, other changes made in the transaction are still pending; they wait to be committed or rolled back.

The following example shows a database trigger that fails if the last row in the table is being updated. As the update runs, the rows are updated one by one, but as the update fails on the very last row (due to the database trigger forcing a failure), the changes in the other rows are rolled back.

```
SQL> select * From delegates;

D_DELEGATE_ID D_LASTNAME      D_FIRSTNAME    D_ORGANIZATION      D D_DATE_LA
------------- ------------    ------------   --------------      - ---------
            1 Andreas         Connirae       DSS                 F
            2 Brooks          Micheal        US Army             M
            3 Grinder         John           Sequent             M
            4 Connor          Joseph         Bellcore            M
            5 Robbins         Anthony        Compaq              M
            6 Kaur            Kashmir        Titanium            F
            7 Kaur            Benisha        Titanium            F
            8 Singh           Taejen         Titanium            M
            9 Samra           Karam
           10 Samra           Kailan
           11 Singh           Harman
           12 Kaur            Amriss

12 rows selected.

SQL> l
  1  CREATE OR REPLACE TRIGGER bur_delegates
  2  BEFORE
  3  UPDATE
  4  ON delegates
  5  FOR EACH ROW
  6  BEGIN
  7    IF :NEW.d_delegate_id = 12 THEN
  8        RAISE_APPLICATION_error(-20001,'Forced failure');
  9    END IF;
 10* END;
SQL> /
```

```
Trigger created.
SQL> UPDATE delegates
  2  SET    d_lastname = 'Fred';
UPDATE delegates
       *
ERROR at line 1:
ORA-20001: Forced failure
ORA-06512: at line 3
ORA-04088: error during execution of trigger 'ASCEND.BUR_DELEGATES'


SQL> SELECT * FROM delegates;

D_DELEGATE_ID D_LASTNAME       D_FIRSTNAME       D_ORGANIZATION        D D_DATE_LA
------------- ---------------- ----------------- --------------------- -- --------
            1 Andreas          Connirae          DSS                   F
            2 Brooks           Micheal           US Army               M
            3 Grinder          John              Sequent               M
            4 Connor           Joseph            Bellcore              M
            5 Robbins          Anthony           Compaq                M
            6 Kaur             Kashmir           Titanium              F
            7 Kaur             Benisha           Titanium              F
            8 Singh            Taejen            Titanium              M
            9 Samra            Karam
           10 Samra            Kailan
           11 Singh            Harman
           12 Kaur             Amriss

12 rows selected.

SQL>
```

In the preceding example, if statement-level rollback does not occur some of the rows remain updated after the failure and others do not. Obviously, statement-level rollback means less error handling is necessary on the part of the application program to take account of in terms of error handling.

When Are Rows Locked?

At times, rows are locked by transactions. This section examines those occurrences.

Default Data Locking

By default, Oracle automatically locks rows that are affected by an INSERT, an UPDATE, or a DELETE statement; no extra coding is required. Only those rows that are actually affected are locked; Oracle does not lock the entire table or the entire block of data (as some other relational database systems do). The default level of locking is adequate for most situations.

The first user to obtain the lock can continue with his or her work, and others who want to update the same data have to wait for the lock to be released before they can continue. In some of the Oracle tools (for example, SQL*Plus), by default and without any extra coding, a user process does not receive any additional messages indicating that the process is waiting for a lock. In others (such as Oracle Forms), a message appears when a user attempts to change a row that has already been locked, indicating that the row has already been locked by another user.

SELECT FOR UPDATE

In some situations, you may want to lock a row or set of rows before issuing an INSERT, UPDATE, or DELETE statement. The FOR UPDATE clause at the end of the SELECT statement can be used for this as the following example shows, causing three rows to be locked with the SELECT statement.

```
SQL> SELECT d_lastname, d_firstname
  2  FROM   delegates
  3  WHERE  d_lastname LIKE 'H%'
  4  FOR UPDATE OF d_delegate_id;

D_LASTNAME            D_FIRSTNAME
-------------------   -------------------
Hayre                 Mandip
Hayre                 Parminder
Hayre                 Manveer

SQL>
```

The FOR UPDATE clause must be followed by the names of one or more columns; at the time of writing, it does not matter which columns are mentioned after this clause. Locking is done at the record level and is not taken down to the column level.

The preceding SELECT statement locks the rows returned by the WHERE clause so that only this transaction can continue to make changes to those rows; other transactions are prevented from modifying the data.

However, if the rows that the SELECT FOR UPDATE statement tries to lock have already been locked, the SELECT FOR UPDATE statement waits for the locks to be released. In some of the Oracle tools (for example, SQL*Plus), this wait causes the tool to appear to be hanging. There is another option, NOWAIT, that you can append to the FOR UPDATE clause to let Oracle know that the SELECT FOR UPDATE statement should fail if the rows are already locked.

The following code example shows a SELECT FOR UPDATE statement failing when one of the rows it tries to lock is already locked by another process.

```
SQL> SELECT *
  2  FROM   delegates
  3  WHERE  d_lastname = 'Connor'
  4  FOR UPDATE OF d_lastname
  5  NOWAIT;
ERROR:
ORA-00054: resource busy and acquire with NOWAIT specified


no rows selected

SQL>
```

You can trap the resulting error using PL/SQL exception handlers and take appropriate action.

> **NOTE**
>
> Even if rows are locked, other transactions can always run queries against them.

LOCK TABLE **Command**

There is another way to prevent other users from making changes to tables, and that is to issue a LOCK command against the entire table. These commands can be useful especially when large batch runs are required against the data when the database is being used.

The different modes in which a table can be locked are

- LOCK TABLE IN EXCLUSIVE MODE
  Stops any other user process from locking the table in any mode or any rows in the table. This is the most drastic way of locking a table.
- LOCK TABLE IN SHARE MODE
  Allows other processes to issue the same command against the table, but stops updates to the table.
- LOCK TABLE IN ROW SHARE MODE
  Allows other processes to lock the table in the same mode. Also allows other processes to lock the entire table for exclusive mode. Changes can still be made to the rows when the table is locked in this mode.
- LOCK TABLE IN ROW EXCLUSIVE MODE
  Similar to locking the table in ROW SHARE MODE but stops any other processes from locking the table for exclusive use.
- LOCK TABLE IN SHARE ROW EXCLUSIVE
  Stops the table from being locked in SHARE mode or for any changes to be made to the rows. This means that the only thing that other user processes can do is read the table data. Alternatively, other processes can issue the same LOCK command, thereby ensuring that they are stopping any changes being made to the table data.
- LOCK TABLE IN SHARE UPDATE MODE
  Same as ROW SHARE MODE.

As with the SELECT FOR UPDATE statement, the NOWAIT clause can be specified to indicate that the LOCK statement is to fail immediately if the table cannot be locked (one or more rows are already locked by another user process).

Table locks are released when the transaction ends—that is, when a COMMIT or ROLLBACK statement is issued or when the user process fails abnormally and is rolled back automatically by the PMON background process.

What Can Be Done When Rows Are Locked?

If rows are locked by a transaction, only that transaction can make changes to those rows. Other transactions cannot UPDATE or DELETE the rows.

If another transaction attempts to modify rows that have already been locked by another user process, the INSERT, UPDATE, or DELETE statement waits until the locks have been released.

Even if the rows have been locked by one transaction, other transactions (that is, other users) can still query the data. No locks are required to query data. If a query is performed on some data while the data is being modified by another process, the query displays the old row values. Until the changes are committed, other transactions still see the old version of the rows, but after a COMMIT, all other transactions can see the changes.

This applies regardless of which Oracle or non-Oracle tool makes the changes.

The following example shows two transactions. The first transaction is making changes to data; the other transaction does not see the changes until the first transaction commits them.

Transaction 1	Transaction 2
| ```
SQL> UPDATE delegates
  2   SET    d_firstname = 'Benisha'
  3   WHERE  d_delegate_id = 6;
1 row updated.
SQL>
SQL> SELECT d_firstname
  2   FROM    delegates
  3   WHERE   d_delegate_id = 6;
D_FIRSTNAME
-------------------
Benisha
SQL>
SQL> COMMIT
  2   /
Commit complete.
SQL>
SQL> SELECT d_firstname
  2   FROM    delegates
  3   WHERE   d_delegate_id = 6;
D_FIRSTNAME
-------------------
Benisha
SQL>
``` | ```



SQL> SELECT d_firstname
  2   FROM    delegates
  3   WHERE   d_delegate_id = 6;
                        D_FIRSTNAME
                        -------------------
                                Kashmir
                                SQL>




SQL> SELECT d_firstname
  2   FROM    delegates
  3   WHERE   d_delegate_id = 6;
                        D_FIRSTNAME
                        -------------------
                                Benisha
                                SQL>
``` |

The preceding example shows that after the COMMIT, Transaction 2 sees the changes made to the data.

If the second transaction does not want to see any changes made by other transactions while it is in effect, the SET TRANSACTION READ ONLY command can be issued. This ensures that the transaction sees the same version of the data throughout the transaction, even if other transactions make changes to the data. This ensures, for example, that a report sees all rows in a table with the values they had when the report began running; subsequent changes to the data do not appear in the report.

If the SET TRANSACTION READ ONLY statement is issued, and it must be the first statement issued in the transaction, the transaction is not allowed to make changes to any tables in the database.

The ability of transactions to run queries against tables that are being modified is provided by *rollback segments*. Rollback segments are system database objects that record the old values of any changes made to database blocks; they are used automatically whenever a transaction starts to make changes to data. If old values of any changes are recorded in rollback segments, the old values can be used to provide a query-able version of the data for other transactions while the data is being modified. In addition, rollback segments can be used to back out any changes to the data and restore the old values of the Oracle blocks when a ROLLBACK statement is issued.

When Are Locks Released?

When a transaction ends, the locks that were obtained by that transaction are released. This happens when the transaction ends with a COMMIT or a ROLLBACK or even when an abnormal failure occurs. If an abnormal failure does occur, the Oracle PMON background process automatically releases any locks taken out by the transaction and, by default, rolls back any changes that were in the process of being made in the aborted transaction.

Deadlock

A problem, usually rare, can occur as two or more processes wait for each other to release locks. The reasons why this problem occurs and how it is detected are described in this section.

What Is a Deadlock?

Deadlock is a situation that can occur when two or more processes are waiting for each other to release resources, resulting in neither one of them being able to continue. This is sometimes called a "deadly embrace."

The following example shows two transactions that lock each other out when each of them waits for a lock to be released by the other.

Transaction 1	*Transaction 2*
| ```
UPDATE  bookings
SET     b_start_date = '01-OCT-97'
WHERE   b_courses_code = 'XYZ';
``` | ```
UPDATE  courses
SET     c_duration = 5
WHERE   c_code = 'ABC';
``` |
| ```
UPDATE  courses
SET     c_duration = 10
WHERE   c_code = 'ABC';
``` | ```
UPDATE  bookings
SET     b_start_date = '01-OCT-97'
WHERE   b_course_code = 'XYZ';
``` |

Each transaction is now waiting for the other transaction to release a lock—they're each waiting for the other, so they're in a deadlock situation.

How Is Deadlocking Handled?

The PMON background process detects a deadlock situation and automatically backs out one of the statements that causes the deadlock. The user process to be notified of the deadlock situation is whichever one the PMON background process detects first—this cannot be predicted very easily. The process that receives the deadlock error message must decide whether to roll back any other changes it made, which would allow the other process to continue, or to take other action (possibly asking the database administrator to find the other transaction involved in the deadlock and to kill that session).

What You Can Do to Avoid It

A deadlock situation is relatively rare in production systems where a large amount of data is being used by a large number of users. However, it cannot be eliminated entirely. One simple way of reducing the occurrence of deadlock is to ensure that, if possible, tables are locked in the same order in all transactions working against the database. If this had occurred for the preceding transaction, at least one of the transactions could have continued.

Savepoints

A savepoint is a marker that is set in a transaction so that you can roll back any changes made since that point. Any changes made before the savepoint marker still need to be committed or rolled back.

The following code example shows an example of a savepoint being used in a transaction that makes changes to a table. An UPDATE statement is issued and a savepoint marker is made after the UPDATE. Another row is then deleted, followed by a rollback to the savepoint. All changes made since the savepoint marker was made are backed out and the following COMMIT statement commits any changes still pending prior to the savepoint.

```
SQL> UPDATE delegates
  2   SET    d_lastname = 'Bandler'
  3   WHERE  d_delegate_id = 3;

1 row updated.

SQL> SAVEPOINT after_the_update;

Savepoint created.

SQL> DELETE FROM delegates WHERE d_delegate_id = 4;

1 row deleted.


SQL> ROLLBACK TO SAVEPOINT after_the_update;

Rollback complete.
```

```
SQL> COMMIT;

Commit complete.

SQL>
SQL> SELECT d_lastname
  2  FROM   delegates
  3  WHERE  d_delegate_id = 4;

D_LASTNAME
-------------------
Connor

SQL> SELECT d_lastname
  2  FROM   delegates
  3  WHERE  d_delegate_id = 3;

D_LASTNAME
-------------------
Bandler

SQL>
```

There may be a number of savepoints set in a transaction, and you may roll back to a particular savepoint. You cannot commit just part of a transaction in the same way that a rollback to a savepoint can be done.

Often it is better for an application program to use PL/SQL to determine whether a particular change should be made, rather than making the change and then backing it out by rolling back to a savepoint.

Savepoints can be useful when calling standalone subprograms. The subprogram may issue a savepoint in the program before it starts to make any changes. If it encounters any failure conditions, the subprogram can roll back any changes to the savepoint, thereby wiping out any changes that it made but still leaving the changes made by the calling program intact. The calling program can then decide whether to commit its own changes or roll them back.

TIP

Savepoints can be useful when writing subprograms that make changes.

PL/SQL and Transactions

As far as statement-level rollback is concerned, if a PL/SQL block fails, the whole set of changes in the PL/SQL block are rolled back. The PL/SQL block acts as a meta-statement and all changes made in the block are backed out if it fails.

The following code example shows a PL/SQL block making changes and failing, and all the changes it made being backed out.

```
SQL> l
  1  BEGIN
  2     DELETE FROM bookings;
  3     DELETE FROM delegates;
  4     RAISE_APPLICATION_ERROR(-20001,'Forced Error');
  5* END;
SQL> /
BEGIN
*
ERROR at line 1:
ORA-20001: Forced Error
ORA-06512: at line 4


SQL> SELECT COUNT(*) FROM bookings;

 COUNT(*)
---------
        8

SQL> SELECT COUNT(*) FROM delegates;

 COUNT(*)
---------
       12

SQL>
```

In the preceding example, even though the two DELETE statements worked and the PL/SQL block failed after the DELETEs finished, all the changes made in the PL/SQL block are backed out.

Other changes made in the transaction are still pending and need to be committed or rolled back.

DDL Statements and Transactions

A DDL (Data Definition Language) statement in a transaction automatically ends the transaction by issuing a COMMIT statement, and that causes the start of a new transaction. Remember that once committed, the changes cannot be backed out again.

The following code example shows a DDL statement that automatically issues a COMMIT statement. The ROLLBACK statement rolls back only changes made since the last commit (performed by the DDL statement).

```
SQL> DELETE FROM bookings;

8 rows deleted.

SQL> CREATE TABLE temp (first_field NUMBER);

Table created.
```

```
SQL> DELETE FROM delegates;

12 rows deleted.

SQL> ROLLBACK;

Rollback complete.

SQL> SELECT COUNT(*) FROM delegates;

 COUNT(*)
---------
       12

SQL> SELECT COUNT(*) FROM bookings;

 COUNT(*)
---------
        0

SQL>
```

In any application system, there are few, if any, DDL statements that run in the production system once it's been set up initially. However, the preceding code example shows a common mistake during the development stage of the system and for database administrators.

> **CAUTION**
>
> A DDL statement automatically commits any pending changes.

Distributed Transactions

A distributed transaction is a transaction that involves changes to more than one database. To make use of distributed transactions the Distributed Option of the Oracle RDBMS software must be installed. Once installed, distributed transactions work the same way as local transactions—either all the changes made to all the databases are committed or none of the changes are made. Synchronization of the COMMIT statements is handled automatically by the Oracle two-phase commit mechanism.

No extra coding is required to identify a distributed transaction. The Oracle synchronization mechanism is automatically activated when Oracle detects that another database is involved in the transaction.

The following code example shows a database link being created to refer to another database. The database link is used to UPDATE a table on a remote database, and the second UPDATE modifies a table on the local database. The changes are then saved.

```
SQL> CREATE DATABASE LINK big_database
  2      CONNECT TO ascend IDENTIFIED BY ascend
  3      USING 't:big_unix_machine:main_db';

Database link created.

SQL> UPDATE delegates@big_database
  2  SET    d_firstname = 'TAEJEN'
  3  WHERE  d_delegate_id = 3;

1 row updated.

SQL> UPDATE bookings
  2  SET    b_delegate_id = 2
  3  WHERE  b_delegate_id = 1;

2 rows updated.

SQL> COMMIT;

Commit complete.

SQL>
```

A synonym could have been created to refer to the remote table accessed via the database link.

As you can seen from the example, having more than one database involved in the transaction is handled automatically and invisibly in the code. The database administrator needs to get involved only if major problems occur during the committing of the distributed transaction. For minor failures, the Oracle RECO background process automatically backs out changes to all involved databases.

Summary

In this chapter, you looked at the basic concept of a transaction, which is sometimes called a commit-unit, and at how locks are obtained, how the default level of locking can be overridden, and how failures are handled. If any changes are made on an ad hoc basis or in a program, those changes should be explicitly committed or rolled back.

12

PL/SQL

by Joe Greene

PL/SQL is Oracle's programmatic language (PL) extension to the Structured Query Language (SQL). So what is a *programmatic extension*? SQL was designed to enable you to write statements that interact with the database. It is good at that job. However, if you look through the SQL standard, you will find a lot of statements missing that you would normally expect to find in a programming language. For example, how do you execute a given statement only when a certain condition is true? Another example would be a statement that allows you to perform a given action multiple times within a loop. These types of constructs are what PL/SQL provides. Together with SQL, you have the capability to write fairly complicated programs that are optimized to interact with databases.

This chapter provides you with an introduction to PL/SQL. My goal is to expose you to the major statements that you need and provide a number of examples that you can use to see how things really work. Combined with a knowledge of SQL gained in previous chapters, you should be comfortable writing database access programs. A good question at this point is where would you be using this PL/SQL language? Some examples of where you might use PL/SQL include

- Oracle stored procedures and triggers
- Oracle Forms triggers
- Scripts run from SQL*Plus to perform database processing tasks

Some of the following constructs are provided in PL/SQL and are not available in SQL, and you might need them in your programming endeavors:

- `IF...THEN` blocks
- `WHILE...DO` loops
- `FOR...NEXT` loops
- Variables used within the program
- Cursors (ability to scroll through the results of a query one row at a time with the results stored in memory variables that you can process)
- Exception handling, which enables you to take actions based on problems detected by Oracle and avoid having nasty errors displayed on the screen

Of course, there are a few limitations on PL/SQL that you need to know about. The most significant limitations include the following:

- It usually is difficult to display information to the screen within a PL/SQL loop. For example, you must select data into memory variables within PL/SQL, as opposed to having the results displayed on the screen in a SQL query in SQL*Plus. You can write the results to a holding table and then display the data after you complete the PL/SQL programming. Sometimes you can use the DBMS_OUTPUT package to display information to the screen, but there are many cases (for example, triggers) where there is not a screen available for the output.
- You cannot dynamically form SQL statements (at least until Oracle8).

Is PL/SQL the answer to all of mankind's problems and the ultimate programming language that will replace all others? It's probably not. However, if you are working in the Oracle environment, with Oracle Forms in Developer/2000 particularly, PL/SQL is definitely worth learning. It provides a reasonable amount of power, is easy to learn, and enables you to write fairly complex applications without having to resort to third-generation programming languages. All you have to do is learn the PL/SQL syntax of the commands that you are used to from other programming environments (for example, IF...THEN), and you can be up and productive in a relatively short period of time.

Setting Up PL/SQL

The good news is that PL/SQL may already be set up for you within your Oracle database. If not, all you have to do is run a single database script (catproc.sql) to have this capability. The processing of PL/SQL commands occurs at the database level for stored procedures, triggers, and functions. Therefore, the database has to understand how to process PL/SQL. Several years ago, the capability to process PL/SQL was considered to be an option that you might or might not add on to your system (you'll still see it referred to as the procedural option in some scripts). The script that is used to set up the database for PL/SQL processing is called catproc.sql. It is located under the Oracle home directory. The title of the directory is something like RDBMS/ admin (perhaps you have an RDBMSxx directory where *xx* is the version number of Oracle that you are using, such as 72 for Oracle7.2). This script has to be run by the DBA (as the SYS account) and calls a series of scripts in this directory to set up the procedural functionality.

Of course, if you are using a tool such as Oracle Forms, that tool is designed to process PL/ SQL. It processes the commands, such as IF...THEN blocks, itself. Therefore, you do not need to have the procedural option set up in the database. However, it is not a bad idea because there are some advantages to having some of the software stored in the database. The database is a centralized location where everyone can access common software routines as opposed to having to replicate the same code in multiple locations. Also, triggers are designed to function automatically, even when the user is not using one of your applications (for example, they are using MS Query to access the database tables directly).

Uses of PL/SQL

PL/SQL shows up in a number of different places. In this section, I cover some of the more common places (SQL script files, stored procedures, packages, functions, and triggers) in which you will find PL/SQL in Oracle applications. Each of these has slightly different requirements as to the structure in which you enclose your PL/SQL. But as you'll soon see, it's easy to learn these differences. Figure 12.1 shows the basic locations for these PL/SQL blocks.

FIGURE 12.1.
Locations for PL/SQL code.

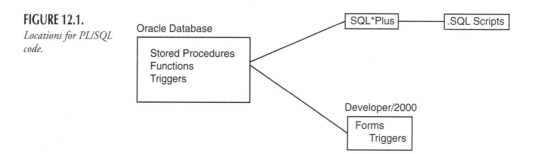

SQL Script Files

The first type of PL/SQL code that you'll encounter is in SQL files, such as those run using SQL*Plus, SQL*DBA, or Server Manager. Here, your syntax would be as simple as the following:

```
declare
. . .
(variable declarations)
begin
. . .
(SQL and PL/SQL commands)
end;
```

The commands for the preceding script file are saved as a simple ASCII text file (which you can edit using Notepad under Windows or good old vi under UNIX). To execute the script file under SQL*Plus, you would typically use the @ command followed by the filename. For example, if you have a PL/SQL script under UNIX stored in the /u/jgreene directory titled create_schema.sql, you would issue the following command at the SQL> prompt:

```
SQL> @/u/jgreene/create_schema.sql
```

Stored Procedures

The disadvantage of running SQL script files in a distributed computing environment is that you have to keep the correct version of these scripts on a large number of computers. It is much easier to store the software in the database (one location) for everyone to access. Stored procedures are becoming much more popular in Oracle environments in that they have all the security of the Oracle database in terms of being protected from alteration or review. To create a stored procedure, you wrap the SQL and PL/SQL statements in a CREATE command similar to the following:

```
create or replace procedure score_answers
as
. . .
```

```
(variable declarations)
begin
. . .
(SQL and PL/SQL commands)
end;
```

Some stored procedures perform a fixed set of actions that do not depend on where they are being used. They also are not designed to return values to the calling program. An example of such a program would be one that clears out all of the data in a series of database tables when called. However, most of the stored procedures that I have worked on require some form of input or output information. This data transfer is accomplished by a series of calling parameters that are part of the definition of the stored procedure. Each of these parameters is specified to be either an input or an output parameter along with the datatype. For example, suppose that the preceding score_answers procedure needs to have student_id and answer_key supplied to it as input parameters and returns letter_grade back to the calling program. This stored procedure would be created as follows:

```
create or replace procedure score_answers
(student_id IN number,
answer_key IN char,
letter_grade OUT char)
as
. . .
(variable declarations)
begin
. . .
(SQL and PL/SQL commands)
end;
```

I want to make one final point when it comes to passing parameters to procedures. Some procedures have a long list of parameters which may have the same value most of the time that the stored procedure is called. In a few cases, you might want to vary the inputs. You could establish a standard set used by all applications, but this is somewhat prone to error. Another alternative is to agree on a standard, such as passing -1 when the user wants to use the default values. You could then use the IF...THEN constructs (which I talk about more in the "Controlling Program Flow" section later in this chapter) to assign the standard values if -1 is passed to the stored procedure. Again, this is prone to some errors, and you might also have parameters in which -1 (or whatever value you chose to indicate using default values) may be valid. There is a construct in stored procedures that enables you to specify the default value in the calling parameters.

If users do not specify the parameter when they call the stored procedure, the default value is used automatically. It is much easier to leave something blank than it is to remember what the default value is supposed to be. Suppose you have a stored procedure that sets up tables for a new home loan account. It requires you to pass the customer ID (which must be specified) along with the term of the loan (which would default to 30 years). The format of this call would be similar to the following:

```
create or replace procedure score_answers
(customer_id IN number,
term number default 30)
as
. . .
(variable declarations)
begin
. . .
(SQL and PL/SQL commands)
end;
```

You now know the general structure for creating stored procedures within an Oracle database. I typically build a series of ASCII text files (yes, I work in UNIX and MS Windows) that contain the CREATE OR REPLACE PROCEDURE commands.

> **NOTE ·**
>
> This command construct is very convenient. With tables, you have to check to see whether the table exists already and drop it before you could issue the CREATE command. In the CREATE OR REPLACE PROCEDURE command, the database checks for you and performs the drop automatically, if needed.

After I have these ASCII text files, I modify them until I get the stored procedure working correctly. An advantage of this method is that I have operating system files that I can back up and check into software version control systems just as I would other program files.

Packages

The CREATE PROCEDURE command is good for simple applications. However, you typically would want to break larger applications down into a series of smaller software modules. The stored procedure is the lowest level of software in an Oracle database. However, you do have the option of grouping multiple procedures into a *package*. You can think of this package as an application that contains multiple software modules (procedures). Use the following format to create a package:

```
create or replace package score_all
as
. . .
(procedure and function specifications)
end;
```

The procedure and function specifications in the package are similar to those created with the CREATE PROCEDURE command. However, because they are already in a compilation package, you do not have to include the words "create or replace." For example, if the earlier example of the procedure to score answers to questions were located within a package, its specification would be

```
procedure score_answers
(customer_id IN number,
term number default 30)
is
. . .
(variable declarations)
begin
. . .
(SQL and PL/SQL commands)
end;
```

There is another interesting construct that Oracle has built into the package framework. The procedures and functions that you include as part of the package definition shown here are available to the general public (as long as they have execute privileges, of course). When you change the calling parameters in that section, you might have to recompile your applications. Similar to a lot of other programming tools, Oracle enables you to define protected (hidden) software components that are used only by the procedures and functions that are defined in the public section. For example, you might have a public function to score answers depending on a letter grade calculator. The user applications cannot call the letter grade calculator directly (because you need to have a score total first). Therefore, you can hide this procedure in what Oracle refers to as a *package body*. The format of the example would look something like this:

```
create or replace package score_all
as
procedure score_answers
(customer_id IN number,
term number default 30)
is
. . .
(variable declarations)
begin
. . .
(SQL and PL/SQL commands)
end;
create or replace package body score_all
as
procedure letter_grade
(total_score IN number,
letter_grade OUT char)
is
. . .
(variable declarations)
begin
. . .
(SQL and PL/SQL commands)
end;
end;
```

Functions

Sometimes, you want to execute a set of stored software where your only goal is to get a single number (or character string) back. You could take a variable and assign it the return value from a call to the function and then perform some calculations on it later on. However, because this is a fairly common occurrence, Oracle has come up with a better way of handling it. They created the function construct (similar to functions in many other programming languages) that enables you to make a call to stored software in the middle of a calculation. For example, suppose you want to write a function that calculates the value of y according to the formula:

$y = 3x^2 + 2x + 2$

You would then be able to use this function in places such as

$z = 2y + 47.2$

You would write a formula like the following:

$z = 2*X\_to\_Y(x) + 47.2$

The command used to create a function is similar to the one used to create a stored procedure:

```
create or replace function X_to_Y
(xin IN number) return number is
. . .
(variable declarations)
begin
. . .
(SQL and PL/SQL commands)
end;
```

Triggers

Storing software in the database is a good start. A nice extension to this concept would be configuring that software stored in the database to execute automatically if certain conditions are encountered. There are two parts to this functionality. The first is the stored software that is to be executed when the condition occurs. The second part is the ability to specify the condition that causes the software to be executed. Oracle refers to this combination of software and the event that causes it to occur as a *trigger*. The format of a trigger is similar to that for stored procedures. For example, a trigger that calculates your running total golf score when you insert a score for a particular hole might look something like this:

```
create trigger populate_total
after update of hole_score on golf_scores
for each row
begin
. . .
(statements to perform the calculations and update the database)
end;
```

An important advantage of using triggers is that you do not have to remember to execute them. This alleviates the need for each programmer to remember a series of procedures that have to be executed on every insert or update. It also provides security in client/server environments where users can use tools, such as MS Query or the Oracle Navigator, to bypass application-based security and interact directly with the database. You might, for example, check data in other tables to ensure that it matches what would be expected, based on an entry that is being made into another table.

Benefits of Stored Procedures, Functions, and Triggers

Stored procedures, functions, and triggers provide the means for you to move your software into the database as opposed to having to include it in every application that you develop. This has some side benefits as well. First, the stored PL/SQL code is stored in both raw and parsed formats. This saves time in that Oracle can grab the parsed software and save the time it would take to parse the commands within the software.

The second advantage (which can also be a problem if you are not aware of it) is that you can do things through stored procedures that you would not normally have permission to do. This comes from the fact that when you execute the commands in a stored procedure, you are not executing the commands with your normal privileges. Instead, you execute the commands as though you are the person who owns the stored procedure. This opens up some interesting possibilities.

> **CAUTION**
>
> Stored procedures have access to other database objects based on the permissions of the owner of the stored procedure, not the person who is executing it.

For example, suppose you have to allow users to write to a particularly sensitive table—but only in one rare circumstance. You could grant the users insert and update privileges for that sensitive table and hope that all of the other application developers build in the correct security scheme in their software modules and that no one gets a copy of MS Query to directly access the database. Another alternative would be to build a stored procedure that checks to see that the requirements for this special update have been met and then perform the updates or in-serts. Your common users would not have insert or update permissions to this sensitive table. You would create the stored procedure as an account that did have insert and update privileges (for example, the object owner) and then grant execute permissions on the stored procedure to the users. The stored procedure then becomes responsible for verifying that your special secu-rity requirements are met before allowing the users to write to that sensitive table.

Final Notes on PL/SQL Usage

Because I have talked about stored procedures so much, you might be curious as to how you can call a stored procedure from within another stored procedure. The process is actually quite simple. You use the name of the stored procedure along with any input or output parameters in parentheses. The parameters have to be in the exact order and have the same datatypes as those specified when the procedure was created. Let's continue with the student example, which was created with the following command and creates a procedure to score some answers to questions stored in the database:

```
create or replace procedure score_answers
(student_id IN number,
answer_key IN char,
letter_grade OUT char)
as
. . .
```

You can make a call to this procedure by entering the following in the middle of a PL/SQL block:

```
declare
grade char(1);
begin
. . .
(some SQL or PL/SQL statements)
score_answers(1234,'Hard test',grade);
. . .
(some more SQL and PL/SQL statements)
end;
```

Similar to other database objects, such as tables, every stored procedure and function has an owner and can be called using the format *owner.name*. Because it can be annoying to have to remember the owner name for each of the objects that might be in a complex database application, you have the option of using synonyms (see Chapter 10, "Other Database Objects") to provide a simpler reference to the object. You have the option to create public synonyms (which can be referenced by all database users) or private synonyms (which apply only to you). It is important to understand the hierarchy of names within Oracle when you are using synonyms (see Figure 12.2).

The most precise way to specify a stored procedure that you want to run is to use the owner.name format. This guarantees that you get to the right spot. Again, this does not enable you to take advantage of the convenience of synonyms as mentioned previously. For example, a developer may want to make up a special set of tables in his schema. If the code is written using the owner.name format, it will have to be altered in all locations to access these test data tables. However, if synonyms are set up correctly, all the developer has to do is create the tables and they will be accessed automatically over those in the main schema with the same name. If you just specify the name of the object, you will access stored procedures according to the following rules:

■ If you have a stored procedure with that name, you will access your own stored procedure.

■ If you do not have a stored procedure with that name but have a private synonym that points to an object owned by another user, you will access that other user's stored procedure.

■ If you have neither your own object with that name nor a private synonym with that name, but there is a public synonym with that name, you will access the object pointed to by the public synonym.

■ If there is neither a personal object, private synonym, nor public synonym with that name, you will get an error message.

FIGURE 12.2.

Hierarchy of references within Oracle.

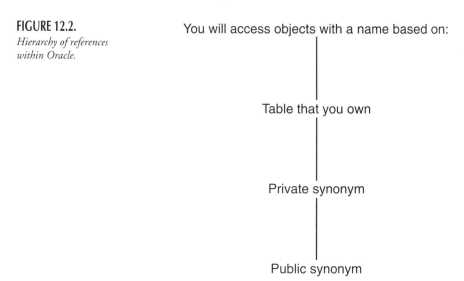

You will access objects with a name based on:

Table that you own

Private synonym

Public synonym

Those of you who work with Oracle's Developer/2000 application development tools will be familiar with the triggers that are used to control processing within applications such as Oracle Forms. These triggers are simply PL/SQL blocks that contain SQL and PL/SQL statements. They resemble database triggers in that they are executed when a specified event occurs (for example, you can specify a trigger that fires when the form is opened and another that fires when the user clicks a particular button on the screen). They are stored within the form itself and are not available to other applications. However, you can call stored procedures and functions from Oracle Forms. You might have situations where a software routine is called from many different locations, and it is easier for you to make it a stored procedure and reference it when needed.

One final caveat to end this section on different uses of PL/SQL: This language is fairly stable, but it will evolve over time. Some examples of upgrades that should be coming soon are the ability to build SQL statements programmatically (dynamic SQL) from variables within your software and the ability to call operating system utilities. Therefore, I would always recommend that you look at the PL/SQL references applicable to your particular release of the software to see which features are available to you.

PL/SQL Syntax Overview

In this section, I describe a few general notes about the syntax of PL/SQL before I go into the details of some of the statements in the following sections. Every programming language has a series of rules that govern what the statements and programs look like. The syntax of PL/SQL is relatively simple compared to most languages. The following are the rules you should know:

■ Statements in PL/SQL end with a semicolon (;).

```
X := 2*y + 1;
```

■ PL/SQL statements that begin a programming block (such as the IF... or BEGIN statements) do not have semicolons.

```
If y=7 then
. . .
(series of statements)
end if;
```

■ Text values are enclosed in tick marks (' ') as opposed to quotation marks (" ").

```
If last_name = 'SMITH' then ...
```

■ Procedures allow you only one exit at the end. The exit command takes you out of things such as WHILE loops, but it does not allow you to exit in the middle of a program. This requires a little extra care when designing your blocks in that you might have to enclose large sections of code in IF...THEN conditions to prevent them from being executed.

Block Structure

When you look at PL/SQL, you will find that there are three sections to each PL/SQL block. First, what is a *PL/SQL block*? It is any group of PL/SQL code that has a BEGIN statement and an END statement. It might or might not have a DECLARE statement just as it might or might not have an EXCEPTION statement. These blocks occur in order according to the following rules:

```
declare
. . .
(list of variable declarations)
begin
. . .
(list of SQL and PL/SQL statements to be executed)
exception
. . .
(series of exception handlers)
end;
```

The first section (DECLARE) is used to define the variables that will be used in the PL/SQL block. This is a simple format, which has the name of the variable followed by its datatype. I discuss variables and datatypes later in the section titled, "Variables in PL/SQL." Let me give some examples here to give you the general idea:

```
declare
last_name       char(20);
counter         number;
begin
. . .
(rest of the PL/SQL block)
```

The next section (BEGIN) contains the code that is executed in the PL/SQL block. This is the main purpose of PL/SQL. It can contain both SQL and PL/SQL statements along with comments. The following is an example BEGIN section:

```
declare
counter         number;
begin
select count(*)
   into counter
   from user_tables
   where table_name = 'SCORES';
if (counter > 0) then
   score_answers(1234,'Hard test',grade);
end if;
end;
```

The third section of PL/SQL is the exception handlers. Because PL/SQL does not have a user interface component, it has no good way of displaying errors to the users. Therefore, if you do not have exception handlers, you would have either success or failure for the stored procedure or other PL/SQL code section. The exception handlers enable you to deal with problems. The responses you give to errors depend on your needs. For example, if you are trying to delete an object and it does not exist, you might be unconcerned and simply want to continue processing. If, however, you are trying to insert data into a general ledger table and that table does not exist, you might want to return a value to the calling routine that indicates a serious error requiring administrator attention. A sample exception handler might look like the following:

```
exception
   when NO_DATA_FOUND then
      return_code := 99;
end;
```

The block structure in PL/SQL is relatively simple. Unlike some languages, it is pretty rigorous in terms of which statements are allowed in each of the sections. You cannot define variables in the exception handlers. You cannot have exception handlers in the BEGIN section. However, after you learn to deal with these rules, you know where everything is supposed to be and can get on with the business of writing applications.

Passing Values to or from Procedures

In the section covering the creation of stored procedures, functions, and so on, I showed the basic format used to pass data to and from procedures. The parameters passed are defined right after the procedure name. Note that the names used in the parameter definition do not have to match up with the names used when calling the procedure. Instead, PL/SQL reads the parameters in order between the calling program. In the following example, the variable x in the calling procedure maps to `xin` in the stored procedure, and y maps to `yin`. The variable `output_value` in the calling routine maps to `return_code` in the stored procedure.

Call to the stored procedure:

```
test_procedure (xin, yin, output_value);
```

Definition of the stored procedure:

```
create or replace procedure test_procedure
(xin IN number, yin IN char, return_code OUT number)
is
. . .
(stored procedure contents)
```

Considerations for Parameters

There are a few things you'll want to consider when you work with parameters being passed into or returned from a stored procedure. The first thing I try to do is validate any inputs that I receive in the stored procedure. Because you don't have an interactive component and cannot easily perform debugging in your stored procedures, you can get a number of rather confusing error codes or else call the exception handler with things such as NO_DATA_FOUND when you have bad input data.

For example, suppose that you have a program that copies data from one table to another. The user supplies a NULL for one of the key input parameters due to a lack of understanding as to what is required. When you try to execute the query on the first table, you will get a NO_DATA_FOUND condition, which could be due to a lack of data in the table, typing the wrong table name, and so forth. However, if you insert a bit of code to check for common problem conditions, you might save yourself some time. For example, the following might help:

```
create or replace procedure tester
(filter IN char,
return_code OUT number;)
is
begin
if filter is null then
   return_code = 11;
end if;
. . .
(rest of the procedure)
```

A point to gather from the preceding example is that you do not have to declare input parameters in the DECLARE section. Placing them in the parameters section of the procedure automatically defines them. Note that you do not have to specify exact sizes for the input parameters. PL/SQL adapts to handle shorter or larger parameter values.

Input parameters are not declared in the DECLARE section of the PL/SQL block. Instead, they are declared as part of the definition of the procedure itself.

Another common thing that you can do with input parameters that have the character data type is to convert them to uppercase and trim them. You might be calling procedures from a number of different environments, and people have different programming styles. PL/SQL is case sensitive when it performs comparisons, and it is also sensitive to spaces. It can be very difficult when you're debugging to figure out why the following types of comparisons do not work:

■ 'Yes' is not equal to 'YES' or 'yes'.
■ 'Yes ' is not equal to 'Yes'.

There are two functions that you can use to solve this problem. The UPPER() function converts a string to uppercase whereas RTRIM() trims spaces off the right of your string. If you expect that you might receive blank spaces on the left of the actual string, you could use the LTRIM() function. For example, if you have an input string called last_name_in that you want to convert to uppercase and trim any blanks on its left side, you would use the following command:

```
last_name_in := ltrim(upper(last_name_in));
```

Depending on your application needs, you might come up with a number of other conversions or integrity checks that you might want to apply to input parameters. It is much easier for you to add a few lines of code at the beginning of a complex procedure than it is to figure out why an INSERT or SELECT statement is failing during program execution. It typically takes a fair amount of time to figure out just which statement is failing. Exception handlers are the last line of defense in error handling. I like to catch errors in input parameters before the exception handlers have to get involved.

Variables in PL/SQL

It is difficult to conceive of a programming language that does not allow you to store and manipulate data items in the form of variables. For example, how could you have an IF...THEN construct without variables? Variables are something that SQL lacks (it was never designed for this purpose), but PL/SQL provides them. You can take the results of queries in SQL and store the results in PL/SQL variables, thereby providing your programs with access to database data.

Defining Data Types

The first thing that most programming languages have to deal with is defining what type of information is contained in the variable. Early languages often made assumptions based on such things as the first letter of the variable name to determine whether it contained integer information, and so forth. Some later languages had a default datatype (such as INTEGER), which applied unless you specifically designated a different type. However, that caused a lot of problems that were very difficult to debug in programs. A typical problem would be that you would get an error adding data to a variable called net_pay because you had forgotten to define it explicitly way back at the beginning of your program, and, therefore, it was considered to be an integer.

Most modern programming languages require explicit variable type declarations. There are no assumptions. This is done in the section before the BEGIN statement in your PL/SQL block. A *variable declaration* is the name that you want to assign to the variable followed by the datatype that you want to use. In general PL/SQL blocks, variable declaration occurs after the DECLARE statement. In stored procedures, functions, and so forth, the variable declaration occurs after the AS or IS keywords. Note that you cannot use SQL or PL/SQL reserved words (such as SELECT or CREATE) for variable names because they are already taken.

The next decision that you have to make is the datatype that you want to assign to the variable. There is a wide range of datatypes in SQL and PL/SQL. If you are using Developer/2000, additional datatypes are available to you when you use some of the built-in packages. However, in general, the following datatypes are the most common ones:

- CHAR—Stores a fixed-length, ASCII character string. This allows you to store numbers, text characters, punctuation marks, and so forth up to 255 characters.

- VARCHAR2—Stores characters in a variable-length string. Although you might still define the maximum size of the character string, the difference between CHAR and VARCHAR2 is that if you do not fill up the entire allocated size of the string, it will not store blanks to fill up the remaining allocated space. You can place up to 2,000 characters into a VARCHAR2 field.

- DATE—This actually is a fairly powerful date/time stamp to capture time information. Basically, you can store any date and time from 4,712 BC to 4,712 AD (perhaps some archeologists will have trouble with this limited range of dates, but it is good enough for my purposes). When working with date information, one of the biggest challenges is getting the format the way you want it. There are several ways to express a date (for example, 12/31/96 and 31-Dec-96) and even times (12:00 AM, 0600, and so on).

- NUMBER—Stores numeric data, both integers and floating-point. Your data can range from 1×10^{-84} power to 38×10^{127} power. Again, you have a pretty wide range of data storage.

- BOOLEAN—This is something that is most often of interest to computer types. It represents a yes/no, true/false, 1/0 type of answer. It is most useful when working with logic statements for loops and decision making. A lot of people still use single character fields in which they manually place 1s and 0s (or was it Ts and Fs or Ys and Ns...?).

You can further refine the definition of most variable types (such as NUMBER, CHAR, and VARCHAR2) by adding sizing information. This provides excellent internal checking because it is usually a fault in your logic if you try to put a very long character string into a field that is designed to be shorter. You put the size of the variable in parentheses after the type. With character data, you specify a single number, which is the number of characters. With numbers, you specify the total number of digits and, optionally, the number of digits to the right of the decimal point separated from the number of digits by a comma. If you perform a division and get an irrational result such as 78.73333333..., the data will be rounded to the number of decimal places that you specify. The following are examples of field definitions where the size is specified:

```
my_string varchar2(32);
my_integer number(8,0);
my_integer number(8);
my_hourly_wage number (4,2);
```

Before I leave this discussion of variable types, I should mention that there are other datatypes, although they are less common in PL/SQL programs. For example, you are somewhat limited in what you can do with long raw fields (which are typically used for storing things such as image data in an Oracle database) within a PL/SQL program. About all you would do is transfer the data between tables, and so forth. However, if you are creative enough to think up a way of using them, the following additional datatypes are available:

- LONG—This is a string of text longer than the 2,000 characters allowed in a varchar2 field. This field can store up to 2GB of characters. You are restricted to character information as opposed to raw binary data.

- RAW—This stores raw binary data as used by your operating system. It can be used for information such as images or sound recordings. This datatype holds up to 255 bytes of information.

- LONG RAW—This is the binary data equivalent to the long field. It holds up to 2GB of binary data.

- BINARY_INTEGER—This field stores information in the binary format that computers love—from -2^{31} to $2^{31} - 1$.

You also can build more complex datatypes in PL/SQL. The most common example of this would be an array. An *array* is a collection of similar data elements that share the same variable name and datatype. They are differentiated from one another by an *index* number. For example, you could have a five-element array of last names as follows:

```
last_name(1) := "Smith";
last_name(2) := "Jones";
last_name(3) := "Davis";
last_name(4) := "Clinton";
last_name(5) := "Dole";
```

To define an array, you use the table type definition statement. (I guess this term makes sense to database developers more than the terminology used in other programming languages.) To define the array of last names, you would use a statement similar to the following:

```
type last_name_list is table of varchar2(22)
index by binary_integer;
last_name last_name_list;
```

In this example, you define a table that is an array of datatype VARCHAR2 with a length of 22 characters. You define a BINARY_INTEGER index that maps the numbers shown in the LAST_NAME example to the values contained within the array. After this type definition is completed, all you have to do is create a variable name of this type. In some ways, this construct is more flexible than other languages where you have to define the exact size of the array in advance. (This must be an extremely challenging section of code written by the authors of the PL/SQL processor.)

Variable Scope

A concept that you need to know comfortably is that of the *scope* of a variable. In a large program, you might use several variables. These variables can take up a large amount of memory. You also can get into trouble if you want to reuse modules that you developed for other purposes within your new application. You might run into trouble when you define a variable called counter, because it might already have been defined in another part of your application.

Variable scope solves these problems for you. Most of the variables that you deal with will have *local scope*. This means that you defined them in the DECLARE section of a PL/SQL block. They exist until you reach the end of the PL/SQL block and then are released (their values are lost if you have not saved them). You are free to use those same variable names in the next block.

However, you might want to have some variables that are global (that is, their values can be seen within multiple PL/SQL blocks). This often occurs when you build a package of cooperating procedures and functions. To make a variable global, you define it outside of the individual procedures and functions within the package body. For example, to make the variable prime_rate visible to a number of procedures within the loan_calc package, you would do the following:

```
create or replace package body
loan_calc
as
prime_rate      number(4,2);
. . .
procedure
. . .
```

Operators and Variables

Now that you have defined variables, it is time to manipulate them. There are three components to this process. The first is the assignment operator (:=). It allows you to tell PL/SQL to perform some calculations on the variables and constants on the right side of the equation and store that value in the variable on left side of the equation. For example, to store a value of 6 times the variable x_in plus 2 into the variable y_out, you would type

```
y_out := 6*x_in + 2;
```

The next manipulation component that you have to get a handle on is the operations that you can perform on data. In the preceding example, I used multiplication (*) and addition (+). The common operations also include division (/) and subtraction (-). Although this covers the basic operations that you would need to work with numbers, you still need some functions for text manipulation. The main text manipulation operator is the *join* (¦¦). This takes the character string on the left and appends to it the character string on the right.

> **NOTE**
>
> Note that the join operator (¦¦) does not insert any spaces, so you have to consider that if you want words to be separated by spaces. If you want spaces, you have to add them manually with ' ' strings joined to the variable.

The following are some examples of these basic operations:

```
y := 6*x*r + 4*z;
y := x/3;
full_name := first_name ¦¦ ' ' ¦¦ last_name;
```

The final manipulation component that you will be using is the built-in functions. You *could* build algorithms in PL/SQL to perform these functions yourself. However, because they are so common, Oracle decided to build them into PL/SQL and SQL for you. There is quite a list of functions that you can find in the online help reference for SQL and PL/SQL. What I list here are some of the more common functions that I have used:

- rtrim(*char*)—Removes any blank spaces to the right of the last non-blank character in the character string
- ltrim(*char*)—Removes any blank spaces to the left of the first non-blank character in the character string
- substr(*char,start,number_of_characters*)—Selects the specified number of characters from the middle of the character string
- to_char(*number*)—Converts a number to a character string

- `to_date(char, date_format)`—Converts a character string to a date using the date format specified (for example, `'DD-MON-YY'`)
- `upper(char)`—Converts the character string or variable to uppercase
- `avg(column)`—Computes the average of the results returned in a query for the given column
- `max(column)`—Returns the maximum value of the results returned in a query for the given column
- `min(column)`—Returns the minimum value of the results returned in a query for the given column
- `sum(column)`—Returns the summation of the values returned in a query for the given column

There are more operators and functions. I could devote several pages to the list of functions alone. However, the online references are pretty good, and most of the function names make sense to users (for example, to calculate the sine of a number you would type `sin(number)`). Besides, I have a lot of other things to discuss related to PL/SQL in this chapter. Before you leave this section though, I include a sample PL/SQL program that shows some of the elements working together. This procedure shows how to call a stored procedure and capture its return code for display outside of the PL/SQL block:

```
declare

out_message varchar(255);
out_return_code varchar(2);
out_status varchar(2);

begin

pr_test_proc (90001,'END','', out_message, out_return_code, out_status);

insert into test_results
values ('R',1,'Return code= '||out_return_code||'  Status= '||out_status);

insert into test_results
values ('R',2,'Message= '||out_message);

commit;
end;
/
select * from test_results;
```

To summarize, you have a lot of computational and processing capacity thanks to variables in PL/SQL. I tend to think of SQL as a series of database commands. SQL scripts are not really full-fledged programs, in my estimation. However, when you add in the variables and program control constructs from PL/SQL (discussed in the next section), you have a fairly functional programming environment. I would not try to write operating system device drivers with it, but PL/SQL is very powerful when it comes to interacting with a database (which is what it was designed to do).

Controlling Program Flow

So far you have a number of components that you can assemble to form a *linear* program (one that executes a series of statements in order). However, common business logic patterns require you to make decisions and perform certain operations only when it is appropriate. Also, you often find yourself performing a set of operations over and over again. Although you *could* copy the set of operations multiple times to handle this situation, PL/SQL provides you with a number of loop constructs that enable you to execute the same set of code multiple times. This section covers the program control constructs that enable you to build sophisticated PL/SQL applications.

IF...THEN...ELSE

The most common program control function that I tend to use is the IF...THEN logic. What this allows you to do is make a decision. If a certain condition exists, then you execute the statements after the THEN keyword. If you want to execute an alternative set of statements when the condition is false, you include an optional ELSE keyword followed by the statements to execute if the condition is false. Finally, you end up the IF...THEN...ELSE section of code with an END IF statement.

The first trick to master is building the condition clause. Some conditions are relatively simple and intuitive (for example, if x=5). What you have is an expression on the left side, an expression on the right side, and a logical operator in the middle. The common logical operators that are available to you include

- An = condition is true if the expression on the left is equal to the expression on the right.
- A <> condition is true if the expression on the left is not equal to the expression on the right.
- A less-than operator (<) is true if the expression on the left is less than the expression on the right. This applies to both numbers and ASCII characters.

> **NOTE**
>
> In ASCII character strings, uppercase and lowercase characters have different values, so you have to understand the ASCII character set number equivalents to work with this. Otherwise, you have to use the UPPER() function to eliminate case sensitivity.

- The > statement is true if the expression on the left is greater than the expression on the right (again, either numbers of ASCII characters are compared).

■ The >= condition is true when the expression on the left is greater than or equal to the expression on the right (either numbers of ASCII characters are compared).

■ The <= condition is true if the expression on the left is less than or equal to the expression on the right (either numbers of ASCII characters are compared).

Perhaps an example will clarify any questions that might remain about IF...THEN statements:

```
declare
   counter   number(2);
   total_score number(3,0);
begin
   select count(*)
      into counter
      from golf_scores
      where last_name = 'PALMER';
   if counter <> 0 then
      select sum(round_score)
         into total_score
         from golf_scores
         where last_name = 'PALMER';
      insert into score_board (last_name, tournament_total)
         values('PALMER',total_score);
   else
      insert into score_board (last_name, notes)
         values ('PALMER','Did not play');
   end if;
end;
```

LOOP

The most basic construct for repeating a set of instructions multiple times is the LOOP statement. It is similar to some of the other forms of loop that will be shown later, except that it does not have any means to exit automatically from the loop. In the basic LOOP statement, you have to manually issue the EXIT statement when you want to exit. The format for this statement can be drawn from the following example:

```
declare
   counter   number(2,0);
begin
   counter := 0;
   loop
      insert into test_results values (2*counter);
      counter := counter + 1;
      if counter >= 8 then
         exit;
      end if;
   end loop;
end;
```

WHILE **Loop**

The basic LOOP statement discussed previously works. However, in larger programs it might take you some time to search around in the code to find out what the exit condition is, and there is always a chance that you will miss it or put it in a section of code that is not always executed. Therefore, most programming languages provide you with some loop constructs where you get to specify the condition for exit as part of the LOOP statement itself, and this condition is tested for every pass through the loop. The easiest of these constructs is the WHILE...LOOP construct. The format of this structure is shown in the following example, which is a rewrite of the previous example:

```
declare
   counter   number(2,0);
begin
   counter := 0;
   while counter < 8 loop
      insert into test_results values (2*counter);
      counter := counter + 1;
   end loop;
end;
```

FOR **Loop**

The WHILE loop allows you to exit on some pretty complicated conditions (such as gross_national_product >= 9000000000). However, in many cases, you simply want to repeat a set of operations a fixed number of times. Many other programming languages enable you to iterate through that fixed number of times while maintaining an index variable by using FOR...NEXT loops. PL/SQL has a similar construct that performs this work as shown in this example:

```
declare
   counter   number(2,0);
begin
   counter := 0;
   for counter in 1..8 loop
      insert into test_results values (2*counter);
   end loop;
end;
```

CURSOR FOR **Loop**

A final loop option that you might want to use if you use cursors (which you learn about shortly in the "Cursors" section) is the CURSOR FOR loop. Basically, it cycles through the loop as many times as you have rows in the query specified by the cursor. The format of this loop is

```
declare
cursor cursor_name is
. . .
   (SQL statement for the cursor)
begin
   for variable_name IN cursor_name LOOP
. . .
      (statements)

   end loop;
end;
```

I tend not to use this construct very much anymore. If you are familiar with BASIC and other programming languages, however, it may be the most comfortable loop construct to use.

Handling Errors

Experienced programmers know that there is an amazing number of things that can happen during the execution of a program. Hardware failures, database corruption, and overloaded processors are just a few of the things that can cause application errors, in addition to mistakes in the software. Because PL/SQL operates in a number of closed environments, such as stored procedures and database triggers, it cannot guarantee that there is a display console available to show any errors encountered. One of Oracle's basic design philosophies seems to be to err on the safe side. Therefore, by default, if a PL/SQL program encounters an error condition, it shuts down and returns the error to the program that called it.

This is good enough for many situations. However, there are some applications that can expect some errors to occur in special circumstances, and the users want the application to handle or solve the problem itself and then continue processing. Also, in large PL/SQL applications, you do not want to see an error that indicates that a SELECT statement has returned no rows. Instead, you might prefer to know which statement it is, what the values are for the variables that make up the WHERE clause, and so on.

This is where that last section of the PL/SQL block comes into play. The EXCEPTION portion of the PL/SQL block enables you to write SQL and PL/SQL statements that are automatically executed when an error condition is detected. You write a section of code after each of the conditions that you want to trap. The following example illustrates the general technique:

```
DECLARE
. . .
   (declarations)
BEGIN
. . .
   (main processing code)
EXCEPTION
   when NO_DATA_FOUND then
      out_status := 'Data not found for general ledger';
      return_code := 5;
```

```
    when TOO_MANY_ROWS then
        out_status := 'Query retrieved more than 1 row';
        return_code := 6;
END;
```

So what are the error conditions that are detected by PL/SQL? The following are the internal errors that are processed:

- CURSOR_ALREADY_OPEN
- DUP_VAL_ON_INDEX
- INVALID_CURSOR
- INVALID_NUMBER
- LOGIN_DENIED
- NO_DATA_FOUND
- NOT_LOGGED_IN
- PROGRAM_ERROR
- STORAGE_ERROR
- TIMEOUT_ON_RESOURCE
- TOO_MANY_ROWS
- TRANSACTION_BACKED_OUT
- VALUE_ERROR
- ZERO_DIVIDE

You also can make up your own exceptions if you see fit. The first thing that you have to do is define the exception in the DECLARE section of the PL/SQL block. For example, if you want to make an exception for invalid Social Security numbers, you can first define the exception similarly to this:

```
invalid_ssn  exception;
```

After it is defined, you have to raise the exception in the correct spot. When an exception is raised, you stop all processing in the normal (BEGIN) portion of the PL/SQL block and go immediately to the exception handler at the end of the block. The following example shows you how to raise this newly defined exception:

```
begin
. . .
    (some processing statements)
    if ssn > 999999999 then
        raise invalid_ssn;
    end if;
. . .
    (some more processing statements)
exception
. . .
    (some other exception handlers)
```

```
    when invalid_ssn then
       return_code := 7;
       out_status := 'Invalid SSN';
 . . .
   (any remaining exception handlers)
end;
```

Exception handling is not all that difficult to do. It can be very useful to avoid having stored procedures and other PL/SQL routines that fail under certain conditions, such as when the table from which they are querying data has been deleted. Like all other error-trapping code, it requires a little bit of planning and thinking to see where you are likely to run into errors, how to detect them, and then how to respond to them. One of the pre-defined exceptions deserves special mention. The OTHERS handler is called when all problems other than those handled in the exception section occur. For example, you could simply have an OTHERS exception handler to care for all exceptions in the same way. Using the preceding example, you could add an OTHERS clause similar to the following:

```
begin
 . . .
   (some processing statements)
   if ssn > 999999999 then
      raise invalid_ssn;
   end if;
 . . .
   (some more processing statements)
exception
 . . .
   (some other exception handlers)
   when invalid_ssn then
       return_code := 7;
       out_status := 'Invalid SSN';
   when OTHERS then
       return_code := 8;
       out_status := 'An exception without a handler occurred';
end;
```

Cursors

So far, I have covered a number of options for building loops and formatting data with functions. However, I have only discussed one way to perform one of the most important functions of a database: retrieving the data stored in tables. There is a problem with the SELECT...INTO... query statements that you use in PL/SQL to obtain data from the database. If you get more than one row from the database at a given time, you receive an exception of TOO_MANY_ROWS. The variables in PL/SQL are designed to accommodate one instance of a data item. If you need to pull back multiple rows of data from the database and work on them one at a time, you need to use *cursors*. For those of you familiar with ODBC programming, a cursor is very similar to a recordset. Multiple rows that match the query are available to the user, but only one at a time. You define the query up front and then scroll through the results and perform whatever processing you need.

The first step in the process is defining the cursor. This is accomplished by a statement similar to the following:

```
cursor good_golfers is
select last_name,first_name
from golf_scores
where score <= 80;
```

Although this describes exactly what the cursor will be like, the code has not done anything with the cursor yet. To actually execute the query and draw out the rows of interest, you open the cursor:

```
open good_golfers;
```

It is here that you will detect problems with the query you formulated. There are four checks that are built-in conditions for PL/SQL cursors:

- %NOTFOUND
- %FOUND
- %ROWCOUNT
- %ISOPEN

These come in handy when you want to know things, such as the number of rows that have been retrieved, and so forth. However, you still have not moved the data into any variables for processing. That is the next step in the process and uses the FETCH statement. The format is relatively simple:

```
fetch good_golfers
    into golfer_last_name, golfer_first_name;
```

You now have the data stored for the first row into PL/SQL variables, which you can use in calculations, IF...THEN statements, and so forth. When you want to retrieve the next row, simply issue the FETCH command again. You will often find these fetch statements nested within loops with a statement that checks for the %NOTFOUND property to see when it is time to exit the loop.

There is an important consideration before those of you used to programming languages implement all of your applications using cursors. For a cursor to work, you have to transfer information from the database to the application cursor and then from the application cursor into PL/SQL variables. If some of this transfer has to take place over computer networks or the amount of information transferred is large, this can severely slow down your programs. Therefore, you will want to consider the following speed hierarchy when devising the constructs that you use for programming in PL/SQL:

- A single SQL statement (such as an INSERT INTO...SELECT... statement) is by far the fastest way to move data.

- A PL/SQL block with decision constructs is usually an in-between design in terms of speed. You might need to use it to implement your business logic, but it will be slower.

- A PL/SQL block with a cursor processing your data on a row-by-row basis is probably the slowest option. There is just a lot of data that has to be moved around.

Comments in Your Software

By now, you probably sense that you can build some fairly complicated programs in PL/SQL. The moment a program goes from trivial to complicated, it is time to start considering comments. You can utilize these two forms of comment within PL/SQL programs:

- *Whole line comments*—Here the entire line is intended to be a comment.

- *Inline comments*—With this form, you insert comments following some executable statements to clarify specifically what the statement is doing or how it is doing it.

There are two formats for comments within PL/SQL. The first one is the double hyphen (--). PL/SQL considers the remainder of the line following the double hyphen to be a comment. The other way to indicate a comment is to enclose it between /* and */. Perhaps the following example will clarify things:

```
-- This is a comment

select * from test_results;   -- This is an inline comment

/* This is also a whole line comment*/

select * from test_results;   /* Another inline comment */

/* Finally, you can create multi-line comments
using the slash-star format */
```

That covers the syntax of comments within PL/SQL. Many of you are experienced developers who have your own opinions and styles when it comes to internal program documentation. For those of you who might be open to suggestions, I'll present some of my preferences for program commenting.

I start off all programs with a comment block that describes the function of the program, its external interface, and its revision history. The functional description is pretty obvious. I like to document the external interface (that is, what the calling and output parameters are) at the beginning to make it easy for someone who is looking to call by program (as in the case of a stored procedure or function). Finally, I like to keep a revision history because it helps me remember what I have done on a particular module (that is, which changes I made before it started to have problems). This is especially true when you have multiple developers who might be working maintenance on a program. The following is an example of my comments at the beginning of a program:

```
-- ************************************************************
--
-- Program:     sample.sql
-- Purpose:     Provide a sample for the comments discussion
--              in this book. It does not perform any processing
--              and consists of a single PL/SQL block.
-- Interface:   This simulates a SQL script called from a tool
--              such as SQL*Plus
--
-- Revisions
--
-- 12/2/96      Created (Joe Greene)
-- 12/3/96      Typographical errors removed (Joe Greene)
--
-- ************************************************************
```

You can get a lot more complicated in the header documentation, but this format is what I tend to use for most applications. I like to use a line of asterisks to provide easy visual separation between sections of the code. I typically provide separators and comments for the DECLARE, BEGIN, EXCEPTION, and END portions of a PL/SQL block. I also like to provide separators and comments between major sections of the application. This is a judgment call, but it helps me to scan through the code when I am looking for something in particular. The following example shows how I might approach documentation on a very simple scale:

```
-- ************************************************************
-- Declare variables

declare
    counter     number;
    total_rows  number;

-- ************************************************************
-- Main processing portion of the program

begin

    select count(*)
        into total_rows
        from test_results;

-- ************************************************************
-- Loop to copy every row from test results into a duplicate table

    for counter in 1..total_rows
        insert into test_results_2
            select * from test_results
                where result_number = counter;
    end loop;

-- ************************************************************
```

```
-- Exception handlers
exception
   when others
      insert into test_results_2 (result_text)
         values ('An error occurred in the PL/SQL code');
-- ************************************************************
-- End of PL/SQL block

end;


-- ************************************************************
```

Okay, I know I could have implemented the processing in the FOR loop with a single command, but I wanted to illustrate concepts with documentation, not efficient application design. I do have one other documentation standard that is close to my heart. I like to put a marker on the end of the file showing that it is the end of file. That way I can tell looking at a printout that I am truly at the end of the program, and it is not just that I am missing the last page of the output. PL/SQL has the END statement as its last line, so I can tell when I reach the end of a PL/SQL block. But, I often build scripts that contain multiple PL/SQL blocks, and I even include SQL*Plus output commands after the PL/SQL blocks to display the results for me. So, my output lines look something similar to

```
-- ************************************************************
-- END OF FILE
-- ************************************************************
```

PL/SQL Testing

I mentioned a little bit about testing PL/SQL earlier in the chapter. Let's take that discussion a little bit further. Testing and troubleshooting always seemed to be the most difficult parts about working with PL/SQL. Because you can select items only into variables and not select them from display on the screen, you have no direct output from inside some PL/SQL blocks (you can use DBMS_OUTPUT if you have a console window from which the PL/SQL block is running). If you are not using exception handling, the entire PL/SQL block or stored procedure will stop processing and return an error code to the calling program. Using exceptions prevents this total work stoppage and enables you to correct minor problems. However, you still do not have the information that would make it easy for you to find problems and fix them.

There are two primary challenges when you have a PL/SQL block that encounters an error. The first one is dealing with syntax errors and the like when you are creating stored procedures, functions, and so forth. If you are using SQL*Plus, you do not get a very clear message when you try to compile a PL/SQL block with errors. As a matter of fact, you have to issue a query to the user_errors view to get enough information to do any troubleshooting. The following is an example of a sample bug-fixing session:

```
SQL> create or replace procedure testing as
  2  return_code number;
  3  begin
```

```
4  select * from non_existent
5  where last_name = 'SMITH;
6  return_cod := -1;
7  end;
8  /
```

Warning: Procedure created with compilation errors.

SQL> select * from user_errors;

NAME	TYPE	SEQUENCE	LINE	POSITION
TEXT				

```
TESTING                PROCEDURE        1      5         19
PLS-00103: Encountered the symbol "SMITH;
return_cod := -1;
end;
" when expecting one of the following:

   ( - + all mod null <an identifier>
   <a double-quoted delimited-identifier> <a bind variable>
   <a number> <a single-quoted SQL string> any avg count max min
   prior some sql stddev sum variance
```

This is no big deal. I forgot to put the second tick mark around the name *SMITH*. I also misspelled the word *code* in *return_code*, but PL/SQL did not see that yet because it was fixated on the first error. Anyway, all I would have to do is correct those mistakes, and then I could get the program to compile. Be prepared to go through several iterations because PL/SQL is not good about catching all of the errors on the first pass.

The next problem that you will run into when working with PL/SQL blocks is figuring out what the problem is when you encounter a runtime error within the PL/SQL block. This can be a problem because, depending on the tool that you use to call the PL/SQL block, you may not get a very detailed message. You will get the type of error and probably a line number. (Of course, to find the line number if you are using stored procedures, you have to look at the user source view to see how Oracle decided to store your program.) Anyway, I have found two useful techniques you may want to consider when you are debugging inside PL/SQL blocks.

The first trick is to make a table with a name such as test_results. This table should contain a text field (for example, results varchar2(80)) and perhaps a time stamp or some other indicators that tell you more about the problem. You then write INSERT... statements in your PL/SQL source to capture key processing information, such as the value of index variables or just lines saying things such as Made it to main loop. After you are done with the PL/SQL block, you can issue a query against test_results to see what happened.

Another trick I use when I am having trouble figuring out which line caused the problems is to comment out sections of code using the /*...*/ construct. Sometimes, I have to comment out a whole section of code and add it back in, one statement at a time, to figure out the offender. This might seem like a bit of a pain, but it can help you in certain circumstances.

Summary

In this introduction to PL/SQL, I have tried to cover everything from basics, such as variables, through more advanced topics, such as cursors and exception handling. It is a lot to absorb, but if you understand the general concepts, you can always come back to it to work out the details. I hope that the examples will serve as a basis for your code. I usually start with a book example and then add features to it to match my individual application needs.

13

Embedded SQL and the Oracle Precompilers

by Renae Rogge-Hoar

The demand for collection, access, and manipulation of data has become more and more important as the industry's demand for organized, stored data has skyrocketed. Relational databases are being developed with intense forethought for normalization, integrity, and efficiency in collecting the data, but in many cases, the accessibility and retrieval of that data can be frustrating and confusing, to say the least.

Some of the databases I have inherited have been extremely complex and normalized to the best of the development team's ability, but the contortions needed to access and retrieve the data were immense. It was standard practice to have reports with five to eight table joins, extensive views, and the creation of multiple temporary tables in PL/SQL for storing incremental data and durations. All this made the database extremely difficult to maintain.

The best way I have found to get data out is the Oracle Precompiler, which offers a method to access and retrieve data in a timely manner with very few limitations. The Oracle interface between the developer's "host language" and the database is extremely powerful and flexible. Multiple queries using arrays, manipulation of that data, and dynamic SQL are only a few of the mechanisms you can use to simplify your life as an Oracle developer.

Oracle7 provides many tools for accessing and retrieving data, including the following:

SQL
PL/SQL
Oracle Browser
SQL*Forms
Oracle Data Query
Oracle Graphics
Oracle Precompiler

All of these tools can be extremely powerful in themselves; however, Oracle Precompilers using embedded SQL are the focus of this chapter. They offer a flexible interface between the host language and the database for complex data processing.

Languages Supported by the Oracle Precompiler

In Version 1.8 of Oracle Precompilers, four host languages are available for the use of embedded SQL, as shown in Table 13.1. All source code examples in this chapter use Pro*C, which interacts between the host language, C (my language of choice), and the Oracle database. Any examples of shell scripting to call the precompiler are in Bourne Shell.

Table 13.1. Available host languages.

Host Language	Precompilation Command	File Extension
C/C++	PROC	PC
FORTRAN	PROFOR	PFO
COBOL	PROCOB	PCO
ADA	PROADA	PAO

> **NOTE**
>
> PRO*PL/I and PRO*Pascal have been placed in maintenance mode and will not contain any new enhancements or features beyond the 1.6 release. Patches for correcting bugs or errors will still be released.

> **CAUTION**
>
> The Precompilers presented in Table 13.1 may not be available on all operating systems and platforms available to Oracle databases.

Description of the Oracle Precompilers

The Oracle Precompiler is a tool that enables you to embed SQL statements directly into the host language, which interfaces with the database. The Precompiler does this by translating embedded SQL and calling Oracle runtime subroutines. In most of the Oracle Precompilers, these subroutines exist in the ORACLE Runtime Library (SQLLIB). After your source code has been precompiled, your host language source code can then be compiled and linked as it always has been in the past.

Reasons for Using the Oracle Precompiler

Oracle Precompilers that use embedded SQL combine the best of procedural and nonprocedural languages. The Oracle Precompilers offer a multitude of benefits. Table 13.2 lists some of these benefits.

Table 13.2. Benefits of Oracle Precompilers.

Benefits	Description
Standardization	Oracle Precompilers version 1.8 complies fully with the ANSI/ISO and NIST standards.
Performance	PL/SQL transaction blocks. Host array manipulations. Dynamic SQL.
Flexibility	Multiple precompiler options. Alternative host languages allowed. Conditional precompilation. Automatically converts host language and Oracle internal datatypes. Highly customized source code using embedded SQL. SQL*Forms interface can be accomplished using user exits. ORACA and SQLCA provide variables for warning and error conditions. Multiple (concurrent) logons both locally and remotely.
Efficiency	Automatically converts host language and Oracle internal datatypes. Conditional precompilation. Dynamic SQL. Host array manipulations. PL/SQL transaction blocks.
Training	If staff is already comfortable with one of the supported languages, the training curve is much less than the curve for learning a new coding tool. The staff has to learn only the syntax and concepts of embedded SQL within their host language.

How This Chapter Is Organized

The best way to navigate the intrinsic details of the Oracle Precompiler is to take it in the phases that you would naturally go through when you code an application. The rest of this chapter is divided into the following sections:

- Declaration of variables, datatypes, and declarative embedded SQL statements
- Connecting to the database
- Accessing and manipulating data using embedded SQL
- Error and communication handling
- Precompiling source code
- Performance tuning

Declaration of Variables, Datatypes, and Declarative Embedded SQL Statements

When developers begin to code an application, one of the first things they have to know is how to declare and handle variables and datatypes.

Host Variables

Host variables are variables used within a host language to store input and output data. When used in conjunction with Oracle, they provide communication between Oracle and your program. When they are used with Oracle, the database tables usually store the input information, with the host variables storing the output information. To use host variables in your embedded SQL, you must declare them within the DECLARE SECTION of your program. They can then be used anywhere an expression can be used in a SQL statement, and they can be associated with an indicator variable. All host language variables declared within the DECLARE SECTION should be prefixed with a colon in SQL statements and PL/SQL blocks, as the following example shows:

```
EXEC SQL BEGIN DECLARE SECTION;
  VARCHAR oid[2];
EXEC SQL END DECLARE SECTION;
```

CAUTION

A host variable *cannot* be any of the following:

■ An Oracle reserved word, such as ALTER, CREATE, INSERT, DELETE and DROP

■ Subscripted

■ Prefixed with a colon in host language statements

■ Used to identify a column, table, or other ORACLE objects

■ Used in data definition statements such as ALTER, CREATE, and DROP

Indicator Variables

An *indicator variable* is an optional variable that is associated to a host variable and enables you to monitor the host variable when it is used in a SQL statement. A result code is stored in the associated indicator variable and can be assigned within your source code. Input host variables can be assigned the following values in the indicator variable slot within your program:

Result Code	Meaning
-1	Oracle ignores the value of the host variable and assigns a null value to the column.
>=0	Oracle assigns the value of the host variable to the column.

Output host variables can be assigned the following values within the program:

Result Code	Meaning
-1	Because the column value is null, the value of the host variable is undetermined.
0	Oracle assigns the complete column value to the host variable.
>0	Oracle assigns a truncated column value to the host variable. The integer returned by the indicator variable is the original length of the column value and SQLCODE in SQLCA is set to zero.

DECLARE SECTION

The DECLARE SECTION consists of the two statements shown in this sample syntax:

```
EXEC SQL BEGIN DECLARE SECTION;

   EXEC SQL END  DECLARE SECTION;
```

Between these two DECLARE statements, only the following declarations are allowed:

- ■ EXEC SQL INCLUDE statements
- ■ EXEC SQL VAR statements
- ■ EXEC ORACLE statements
- ■ EXEC TYPE statements
- ■ Host and indicator variable declarations
- ■ C, COBOL, FORTRAN, or ADA comments

> **CAUTION**
>
> Not all host languages allow multiple DECLARE sections within one precompiled unit.

DECLARE **Statement**

The DECLARE statement accomplishes three tasks: it defines a cursor, associates it to a query, and names it. The cursor_name is not a host variable and should not be defined in the DECLARE SECTION.

The following segment is an example of the DECLARE statement:

```
EXEC SQL DECLARE cursor_name CURSOR FOR
    select product_name
    from product_table
    where product_number = :prod_num
```

Follow these guidelines when you use the DECLARE statement:

■ The DECLARE statement must be executed first before all other SQL statements referencing the cursor are declared.

■ DECLARE, OPEN, FETCH, and CLOSE make up a logical unit of work that controls the cursor; they all must occur within the same precompiled unit.

■ DECLARE statements cannot have multiple cursors using the same name within one precompilation unit.

■ Hyphenation is not allowed in the naming of cursors.

■ Although cursor_names can be any length, for ANSI compatibility, cursor names should be no longer than 18 characters.

■ When using a cursor, the INTO clause cannot be used within the SELECT statement because the INTO clause has been separated out and is now used in the FETCH statement.

The INCLUDE Statement

The INCLUDE statement inserts a copy of the contents of the stated file in the precompiled source code. This command copies the following SQLCA data structure into the host language program and is similar to the C #INCLUDE and the COBOL COPY commands.

```
EXEC SQL INCLUDE SQLCA
```

Any file with embedded SQL must be declared in the INCLUDE statement to be recognized during precompilation.

If you want to specify a location other than the default location for INCLUDE files, the precompilation option INCLUDE=*path* must be set. The path will default to the current directory. Oracle Precompilers use the following order to search for an INCLUDE file:

■ The current directory
■ The directory specified by INCLUDE
■ The directory used for standard INCLUDE files

CAUTION

If your operating system, such as UNIX, is case-sensitive, be sure to specify the correct filename, using the same case, when you use this precompiler option.

Datatypes

Datatypes define the format that a variable will be associated with. Oracle recognizes two datatypes: *internal* and *external.*

Internal Datatypes

Internal datatypes designate the formats used by Oracle to store the values in a column in the database tables. Table 13.3 shows a list of the internal datatypes. Internal datatypes also represent the pseudocolumn values and pseudofunctions shown in Table 13.4 along with the associated conversion code and description. Pseudocolumn values return data that does not actually exist in the table. These values must be treated as true columns and selected from a table to retrieve a value. A dummy table called *dual* is commonly used for this purpose.

Table 13.3. Internal datatypes.

Code	Internal Names	Description
1	VARCHAR2	Stores variable-length character strings with a maximum length of 2,000 bytes.
2	NUMBER	Stores fixed or floating-point numbers consisting of virtually any size.
8	LONG	Stores variable-length character strings such as text, arrays of characters, or even short documents with the maximum length of 65,535 characters.
11	ROWID	Stores binary values called *rowids*, which uniquely identify the row and provides the fastest access.
12	DATE	Stores dates and times in 7-byte, fixed-length fields.
23	RAW	Stores binary data or byte strings with a maximum length of 255 characters.
24	LONG RAW	Stores binary data or byte strings with a maximum length of 65,535 characters.
96	CHAR	Stores variable-length character strings; the maximum length allowed is 255 bytes.
106	MLSLABEL	Stores variable-length binary data with a length of 2-5 bytes.

NOTE

Raw data is not interpreted by Oracle.

Table 13.4. Pseudocolumns and pseudofunctions with corresponding internal datatypes.

Code	Pseudo	Internal Datatype	Description
2	nextval	number	nextval returns the next unique number generated for that sequence.
2	currval	number	currval returns the current number existing in a specified sequence. (nextval must be used first to generate the first sequence number.)
2	level	number	level gives you the levels in a tree structure. 1—root 2—children of root 3—grandchildren and continues on
2	rownum	number	rownum returns the sequence number of that row indicating the order in which it was retrieved.
11	rowid	rowid	rowid returns a hexadecimal address of a row.
1	user	char	Returns the name of the user currently logged into Oracle.
2	uid	number	Returns the unique userid that has been assigned by Oracle to the user.
12	sysdate	date	Returns current date and time.

External Datatypes

The second datatype is called an *external* datatype, and it specifies the formats used to store values in input and output host-language variables. External datatypes include all the internal datatypes referred to in Table 13.3 combined with the external datatypes provided in Table 13.5. When host language source code is precompiled, an external datatype is assigned to each host language variable in the DECLARE section. When the source code is precompiled, compiled, and linked, the datatype *code* of every host language variable used in embedded SQL is supplied to Oracle. (Tables 13.3, 13.4, and 13.5 display the conversion code column.) This code aids Oracle in its datatype conversion. Conversion tables can be found in Oracle documentation for your precompiler.

Table 13.5. External datatypes that cannot be used as internal datatypes.

Code	External Names	Description
3	INTEGER	Stores numbers that have no fractional part.
4	FLOAT	Stores numbers that do have a fractional part or that exceed the limitations of the integer datatype.
5	STRING	Stores variable-length character strings with a maximum length of 255 and is null-terminated.
6	VARNUM	Stores fixed or floating point numbers specifying precision and scale. The maximum precision is 38. The magnitude range is 1.0E-129 to 9.99E125. Scale can range from -84 to 127.
7	DECIMAL	Stores packed decimal numbers for calculation in Pro*COBOL and Pro*PL/I.
9	VARCHAR	Stores variable-length character strings. VARCHAR variables consist of two fields: a 2-byte length field and a string field with a maximum length of 65,533 characters.
15	VARRAW	Stores binary data or byte strings. Consists of two fields: a 2-byte length field and a data field with a maximum length of 65,533 characters.
68	UNSIGNED	Stores unsigned integers with 2-4 bytes.
91	DISPLAY	Stores numeric character data and is used in Pro*COBOL referring to a COBOL DISPLAY SIGN LEADING SEPARATE number.
94	LONG VARCHAR	Stores variable-length character strings.
95	LONG VARRAW	Stores variable-length binary data.
96	CHARF	Stores a fixed-length null terminated string with a maximum length of 65,536 characters.
97	CHARZ	Stores C fixed-length, null-terminated character strings.

NOTE

When specifying a variable-length character datatype, be sure to include 2 bytes for the length field.

Connecting to the Database

Two types of logons are allowed in the Oracle interface Precompiler: external and internal.

External Logons

If the user has been set up by the DBA to be identified *externally* within the database, the system username is then used to connect to the database. For you, the developer, this means that a slash (/) must be passed into the Oracle connect statement as the userid/passwd. This makes connecting to the database fairly simple and dynamic for you; if the user is granted database accessibility, the hard-coded / works for all system users granted that database privilege. The source code shown in Listing 13.1 provides an example of connecting to Oracle using an external logon. The source code shown in bold is the focus of what's currently being discussed.

Listing 13.1. Using external logons to Oracle.

```
/* Start source code listing 13.1 */

#include <string.h>
#include <stdlib.h>

EXEC SQL BEGIN DECLARE SECTION;
  #include <stdio.h>
  VARCHAR oid[2];
EXEC SQL END DECLARE SECTION;
EXEC SQL INCLUDE SQLCA;

main()
{
/* Sets oid equal to a / to identify user externally for ORACLE      */
/* connection .                                                       */
/* Note:  Remember varchar datatype houses 2 fields, the actual data */
/*        and the length of that data                                */

    strcpy(oid.arr, "/");
    oid.len = strlen(oid.arr);

/* Connection call to the database */
    EXEC SQL CONNECT :oid;

    if (sqlca.sqlcode < 0)
    {
       printf("\n%s",sqlca.sqlerrm.sqlerrmc);
       EXEC SQL ROLLBACK WORK RELEASE;
       exit(1);
    }
    else
    {
       printf("\n Connected to Oracle...");
       EXEC SQL COMMIT WORK RELEASE;
       exit(0);
    }
 }
```

Internal Logons

If users are set up by the DBA to be identified *internally* by a specific userid/passwd, the developer needs to prompt the user for those identifiers or pass them in as arguments. The source code shown in Listing 13.2 is an example of connecting to the database using an internal logon.

Listing 13.2. Logon using internal userid/passwd.

```
#include <string.h>
#include <stdlib.h>

EXEC SQL BEGIN DECLARE SECTION;
  #include <stdio.h>
  VARCHAR username[15];
  VARCHAR password[15];
EXEC SQL END DECLARE SECTION;
EXEC SQL INCLUDE SQLCA;

main()
{
/* Prompts and reads in information into username and password array */
/* Note:   Remember varchar datatype houses 2 fields, the actual data */
/*         and the length of that data                                */
    printf("/n Enter User Name ");
    scanf("%s",username.arr);
    printf("\nEnter Password: ");
    scanf("%s",password.arr);

    username.len = strlen(username.arr);
    password.len = strlen(password.arr);

/* CONNECTS TO DATABASE */
    EXEC SQL CONNECT :username IDENTIFIED BY :password;

    if (sqlca.sqlcode < 0)
    {
       printf("\n%s",sqlca.sqlerrm.sqlerrmc);
       EXEC SQL ROLLBACK WORK RELEASE;
       exit(1);
    }
    else
    {
       printf("\nConnected to Oracle...");
       EXEC SQL COMMIT WORK RELEASE;
       exit(0);
    }
 }
```

Concurrent Logons

Oracle Precompilers using SQL*NET offer great database-connection flexibility. Oracle allows multiple, local, and remote connections to one or more databases within one single application.

Using Embedded SQL to Access and Manipulate Data

Executable, embedded SQL statements can be divided into four different categories: data definition, data control, data manipulation, and data retrieval. These categories can be further divided into two separate arenas: the declarative arena, discussed in the preceding section, and the data manipulation arena, discussed in this section. The data manipulation arena uses the executable embedded SQL statements to make calls to and return codes from the database, and to access, manipulate, and retrieve data from the database.

The *data definition* category defines Oracle data using the executable embedded SQL statements: ALTER, CREATE, DROP, and RENAME.

The *data control* category controls access to the Oracle data using the executable embedded SQL statements: CONNECT, GRANT, LOCK TABLE, and REVOKE.

The *data manipulation* category manipulates Oracle data using the executable embedded SQL statements: DELETE, INSERT, and UPDATE.

The *data retrieval* category retrieves Oracle data by using the executable embedded SQL statements: CLOSE, FETCH, OPEN, and SELECT.

Transaction processing and *dynamic* SQL are powerful methods of manipulating data using the Oracle Precompiler interface to the database. The following information briefly discusses the embedded executable SQL statements used, and some of the benefits and options allowed.

Transaction Processing

Transaction processing is a series of one or more logically related SQL statements you define to accomplish some task. The following executable embedded SQL statements are used in transaction processing. To get more extensive details on transaction processing, see Chapter 11, "Transactions."

The COMMIT Statement

The COMMIT statement is used when the transaction processing unit is complete and makes permanent all changes within the current transaction to the database. After the COMMIT statement is executed, you can see the permanent changes to the database; however, all your savepoints are erased and all row and table locks, except for your parse locks, are released.

The following is the syntax for the COMMIT statement:

```
EXEC SQL COMMIT WORK RELEASE;
```

The ROLLBACK Statement

The ROLLBACK statement is used when the transaction processing unit has been aborted or canceled. It backs out all changes made within that transaction to the database or to the most current SAVEPOINT. When this command is executed, all your savepoints are erased, all row and table locks (except for your parse locks) are released, and the transaction is ended.

The following is the syntax for the ROLLBACK statement:

```
EXEC SQL ROLLBACK WORK RELEASE;
```

The SAVEPOINT Statement

The SAVEPOINT statement marks and names the current point within a transaction process. When this statement is executed, all your savepoints following the current savepoint are erased, whereas all your savepoints preceding the current savepoint are saved. This command enables you to roll back to a set savepoint and roll back only parts of the transaction.

The following is the syntax for the SAVEPOINT statement:

```
EXEC SQL SAVEPOINT  big_update
    EXEC SQL ROLLBACK TO SAVEPOINT big_update
```

The SET TRANSACTION Statement

The SET TRANSACTION statement defines a transaction using three options: READ WRITE, READ ONLY, and USE ROLLBACK SEGMENT. The default option is READ WRITE, which enables you to access and manipulate the tables if you have been granted those database privileges. With the READ ONLY option, you cannot manipulate the database tables within the current transaction, except to read the data. This gives you read access to the table during your transaction while others may be manipulating the data. The USE ROLLBACK SEGMENT option enables you to explicitly state the rollback segment you want to use.

The following is the syntax for the SET TRANSACTION statement:

```
EXEC SQL SET TRANSACTION READ ONLY.
```

The preceding statement can be issued only once within a transaction and must be the first embedded SQL statement within the READ ONLY transaction. SELECT, COMMIT, and ROLLBACK are valid embedded SQL statements within a READ ONLY transaction; any other embedded SQL statement causes an error. The COMMIT, ROLLBACK, and declarative embedded SQL statements will end the read-only transaction.

The FOR UPDATE and LOCK TABLE Statements

The FOR UPDATE and LOCK TABLE statements override default locking within a transaction. To acquire exclusive locks, use the FOR UPDATE statement, which identifies the rows that will be updated or deleted and then locks those rows.

The following is the syntax for the FOR UPDATE statement:

```
EXEC SQL DECLARE big_update CURSOR FOR
select product_name, product_price from prod
    where prod_no = 4444
FOR UPDATE OF product_price;
```

When you use the FOR UPDATE OF statement, only one table can be referenced. Rows are locked when they are opened, not when they are fetched. When the COMMIT and ROLLBACK statements are issued, row locks are released. This is not true if the transaction is "rolling back" to a SAVEPOINT.

The LOCK TABLE statement enables the developer to set specified locks on one or more tables. An example of a specified lock is the row share lock, which locks a row, enabling other users to access that table and disallowing exclusive locks to be placed on the table.

Exclusive locks prohibit any other user from executing any data manipulation, such as UPDATE, DELETE, or INSERT, on the table.

The following is the syntax for the LOCK TABLE statement:

```
EXEC SQL LOCK TABLE PROD IN ROW SHARE MODE
```

An optional keyword NOWAIT can be placed at the end of the preceding statement to tell Oracle not to wait for a table if it has been locked by another user. It allows the developer more control to continue processing before trying again for the lock. If NOWAIT is omitted, there is no set limit for waiting for the availability of that table.

Dynamic SQL

Dynamic SQL is a complex programming technique that allows the host program to accept or build SQL statements at runtime and take explicit control over datatype conversion. Because of the possible complexities in programming dynamic SQL, it has been known to scare away the best of developers. Don't let this happen to you! If planned and done in phases, even the most complex methods can be fairly straightforward. Of course, as in all cases, a program can be as "maintainable" and simple as the developer chooses to make it, and truly understanding the methods is the key. The following SQL statements are used when using certain methods of dynamic SQL.

Dynamic SQL—Method 1

Method 1 allows the developer to build a dynamic SQL statement and immediately execute it using the EXECUTE IMMEDIATE command. This method does not use host variables within the SQL statement and has two result conditions of success or failure. Statements in method one are parsed every time they are executed and do not allow SELECTs. When you use dynamic SQL, this is the most straightforward method of all the four methods allowed and therefore, the easiest to understand and code. Listing 13.3 shows dynamic SQL using Method 1.

Listing 13.3. Example of Dynamic SQL (Method 1).

```
#include <string.h>
#include <stdlib.h>

EXEC SQL BEGIN DECLARE SECTION;
  #include <stdio.h>
  VARCHAR oid[2];
  VARCHAR  sql_statement[300];
EXEC SQL END DECLARE SECTION;
search_cond     char[40];
EXEC SQL INCLUDE SQLCA;

main()
{
/* Sets oid equal to a / to identify user externally for ORACLE        */
/* connection .                                                         */
/* Note:  Remember varchar datatype houses 2 fields, the actual data */
/*        and the length of that data                                   */

    strcpy(oid.arr, "/");
    oid.len = strlen(oid.arr);

/* Connection call to the database */
```

```
   EXEC SQL CONNECT :oid;

   if (sqlca.sqlcode < 0)
   {
      printf("\n%s",sqlca.sqlerrm.sqlerrmc);
      EXEC SQL ROLLBACK WORK RELEASE;
      exit(1);
   }
   else
   {
      printf("\n Connected to Oracle...");
      EXEC SQL COMMIT WORK RELEASE;
   }
   strcpy(sql_statement.arr,"UPDATE PROD SET PROD_PRICE = 999  WHERE ";
   printf("\nEnter a search condition for the following statement: ");
   printf("\n%s",sql_statement.arr);
   scanf("%s\n",search_cond);
   strcat(sql_statement.arr,search_cond);

EXEC SQL EXECUTE IMMEDIATE :sql_statment;
EXEC SQL COMMIT WORK RELEASE;
exit(0);
}
```

Dynamic SQL—Method 2

Method 2 of dynamic SQL also is fairly straightforward and almost identical to Method 1, except that host variables are allowed. These variables need to be known at precompile time. With Method 2, the SQL is parsed just once but can be executed many times. This method enables the user to use the USING clause. Every placeholder in the prepared dynamic SQL statement must match a corresponding host variable in the USING clause. Listing 13.4 shows a Method 2 statement.

Listing 13.4. Example of Dyamic SQL (Method 2).

```
#include <string.h>
#include <stdlib.h>

EXEC SQL BEGIN DECLARE SECTION;
  #include <stdio.h>
  VARCHAR oid[2];
  VARCHAR   sql_statement[300];
  NUMBER         prodprice;
EXEC SQL END DECLARE SECTION;
search_cond      char[40];
EXEC SQL INCLUDE SQLCA;

main()
{
/* Sets oid equal to a / to identify user externally for ORACLE       */
/* connection .                                                        */
/* Note:  Remember varchar datatype houses 2 fields, the actual data */
```

continues

Listing 13.4. continued

```
/*         and the length of that data                        */

    strcpy(oid.arr, "/");
    oid.len = strlen(oid.arr);

/* Request connection call to the database */
    EXEC SQL CONNECT :oid;

    if (sqlca.sqlcode < 0)
    {
        printf("\n%s",sqlca.sqlerrm.sqlerrmc);
        EXEC SQL ROLLBACK WORK RELEASE;
        exit(1);
    }
    else
    {
        printf("\n Connected to Oracle...");
        EXEC SQL COMMIT WORK RELEASE;
    }
    strcpy(sql_statement.arr,"UPDATE PROD SET PROD_PRICE  = :c WHERE ";
    printf("\nEnter a search condition for the following statement: ");
    printf("\n%s",sql_statement.arr);
    scanf("%s\n",search_cond);
    strcat(sql_statement.arr,search_cond);

    EXEC SQL C1 FROM :sql_statment;

    printf("\nProduct Price? : ");
    scanf("%d\n",prod_price);

    EXEC SQL EXECUTE C1 USING :prod_price;

    EXEC SQL COMMIT WORK RELEASE;
    exit(0);
}
```

Dynamic SQL—Method 3

Method 3 of dynamic SQL allows your program to accept or build a dynamic query and then process it using a PREPARE command with the DECLARE, OPEN, FETCH, and CLOSE cursor commands. At precompile time, the following needs to be known: select-list items, number of placeholders, and datatypes of host variables. Method 3 is used for dynamic SQL with a known select list, giving the developer more flexibility to build SQL statements on-the-fly. Listing 13.5 shows a Method 3 statement.

Listing 13.5. Example of Dynamic SQL (Method 3).

```c
#include <stdio.h>

EXEC SQL BEGIN DECLARE SECTION;
  VARCHAR oid[2];
  VARCHAR student_no[10];
  VARCHAR student_name[30];
  VARCHAR classes[30];
  VARCHAR sql_statement[600];
EXEC SQL END DECLARE SECTION;

/* Program Variables*/
int employee_no;

/* PROCEDURE DECLARATION */
void log_on();
void build_select();

main()
{
   char    where_clause[80];
/* Call function for request for connection to the database */
    log_on();
    build_select();
    EXEC SQL PREPARE C1 FROM :sql_statement.arr;
    EXEC SQL DECLARE C1 CURSOR FOR S1;
    sql_statement.len := length(sql_statement.arr);
    EXEC SQL OPEN C1 USING employee_no;
    EXEC SQL FETCH C1 INTO :student_name;
    if (sqlca.sqlcode < 0)
    {
       printf("\n%s",sqlca.sqlerrm.sqlerrmc);
       EXEC SQL ROLLBACK WORK RELEASE;
       exit(1);
    }
    else
       printf("\n%s\n",:student_name.arr);

       EXEC SQL CLOSE C1;
    exit(0);
}

void log_on()
{
    strcpy(oid.arr, "/");
    oid.len = strlen(oid.arr);

/* Connection call to the database */
    EXEC SQL CONNECT :oid;

    if (sqlca.sqlcode < 0)
    {
       printf("\n%s",sqlca.sqlerrm.sqlerrmc);
       EXEC SQL ROLLBACK WORK RELEASE;
       exit(1);
    }
```

continues

Listing 13.5. continued

```
    else
    {
        printf("\n Connected to Oracle...");
    }

void build_select()
{
    strcpy(sql_statement.arr,"SELECT FIRST_NAME ¦¦ ' '¦¦ LAST_NAME, ");
    strcat(sql_statement.arr,"FROM EMP ");
    strcat(sql_statement.arr,"WHERE EMPNO = ");
    printf("\nEnter employee number: ");
    scanf("%d",employee_no);
    strcat(sql_statement.arr,employee_no);
}
```

Dynamic SQL—Method 4

Method 4 is the most complex of the four methods, but it also allows the most flexibility and diversity in coding. SQLDA is used when the SQL query statement is completely unknown at development time. At precompile time, the following things are unknown: select-list items, number of placeholders, and datatypes of host variables. To process this type of dynamic query, you must be able to use the DESCRIBE SELECT LIST command and be able to declare a data structure called the SQL descriptor area (SQLDA). *Descriptors* are a segment of memory used by the computer and Oracle to hold a complete description of the variables in a dynamic SQL statement. Descriptor variables are defined as a data structure containing the following information:

- Maximum number of columns that can be evaluated
- Actual number of columns in the SELECT list
- Array of pointers to column names
- Array of maximum lengths of columns
- Array of actual column lengths
- Array of data types for each column
- Array of pointers to data values
- Array of pointers to indicator variables

To process the dynamic SQL statement, your program must issue the DESCRIBE BIND VARI-ABLES command and declare another kind of SQLDA, called a *bind descriptor*, to hold descriptions of the placeholders for input. If you have more than one method for SQL statements, each statement will require its own SQLDA(s); nonconcurrent cursors, however, can reuse SQLDAs. There is no set limit on the number of SQLDAs in a program. Table 13.6 shows the elements that make up the SQLDA structure.

Table 13.6. SQLDA structure elements.

Elements	Description
int N	Stores maximum number of returned columns (upper limit)
char **V	Points to a location to store returned columns
int *L	Points to the length of returned columns
short #T	Points to the column datatype (for example, char)
short **I	Points to the location of stored indicator variables
int F	Stores actual number of columns returned
char **S	Points to the location of column names
short *M	Points to the maximum length of each column
short *C	Points to the actual length of each column
short **X	Points to the location of indicator variable names
short *Y	Points to the maximum lengths of indicator variable
short *Z	Points to the actual lengths of indicator variable

The DESCRIBE command is useful in determining what the SQL statement contains. DESCRIBE instructs Oracle to provide the host variables for any SELECT statement. It examines the SELECT statement to determine the number of columns and type of each in the select list. Oracle must define a storage area to hold fetched rows from the database, and actual data returned from the SELECT is stored in descriptor variables.

The following are coding steps for Method 4:

1. Define a descriptor variable:

   ```
   SQLDA *descr_var
   ```

2. Place a SQL SELECT statement into a host variable:

   ```
   scanf("%[^\n",sql_statement);
   ```

3. Prepare the SQL statement:

   ```
   EXEC SQL PREPARE S1 FROM sql_statement;
   ```

4. Declare a cursor area for the SELECT statement:

   ```
   EXEC SQL DECLARE C1 CURSOR FOR S1
   ```

5. Execute the query and create an active set:

   ```
   EXEC SQL OPEN C1 USING DESCRIPTOR descr_var;
   ```

6. DESCRIBE the SELECT into the descriptor variable:

   ```
   EXEC SQL DESCRIBE SELECT LIST FOR S1 INTO desc_var
   ```

7. FETCH rows from the active set:

   ```
   EXEC SQL FETCH C1 USING DESCRIPTOR descr_var;
   ```

8. CLOSE the cursor:

   ```
   EXEC SQL CLOSE C1;
   ```

Error and Communication Handling

One of the most important steps you should use to ensure database integrity, application flow, and control is proper error handling and condition checking. When using the Oracle Precompilers, the developer has powerful tools available for anticipating and recovering from embedded SQL statement errors and warnings. The following three sections discuss different ways of handling errors, depending on the level of communication you want from Oracle.

SQLCA

SQLCA is a data structure shown in the following segment, with a brief description of each element. It is updated after every executable SQL statement.

```
struct sqlca
{
    char      sqlcaid[8];              /* "SQLCA"                      */
    long      sqlabc;                  /* Length of  SQLCA            */
    long      sqlcode;                 /* Oracle error message code   */
                                       /* 0   : Successful execution  */
                                       /* <0 : Abnormal term. w/error code */
                                       /* >0: Successful exe. w/stat code */
                                       /* +1403 NO DATA FOUND         */
    struct
    {
    unsigned short    sqlerrml;        /* Text length                 */
    char              sqlerrmc[70];    /* Text of error message       */
      }sqlerrm;                        /* Subrec for error code & message */
    char      sqlerrp[8];              /* Not Used                    */
    long      sqlerrd[6];              /* Array of 6 integer status codes */
                                       /* SQLERRD(3)  - Number of rows */
                                       /* SQLERRD(5)  - Parse error offset */
                                       /* Remaining are NOT USED      */
    char      sqlwarn[8];              /* Array of 8 warning flags    */
                                       /* SQLWARN(1)- Warning flag set */
                                       /* SQLWARN(2)- Char string trunc */
                                       /* SQLWARN(4)- Unbal SEL/INTO list */
                                       /* SQLWARN(5)- Del/Upd w/o WHERE */
                                       /* Remaining are NOT USED      */
    char      sqlext[8];               /* Not Used                    */
};
struct sqlca sqlca;
```

The developer can determine the outcome of a SQL statement by checking SQLCA return codes and can recover from each error or warning by proper action. SQLCA contains the following information:

- ■ Warning flags
- ■ Error codes
- ■ Information about events

■ Parse error offset

■ Limited diagnostics

■ Number of rows processed

There are two ways of checking the return codes: *implicit checking* (using the WHENEVER statement) and *explicit checking* (using the SQLCA variables). The source code in Listing 13.6 shows examples of explicit checking.

Listing 13.6. SQLCA example of explicit error checking.

```
#include <string.h>
#include <stdlib.h>


EXEC SQL BEGIN DECLARE SECTION;
  #include <stdio.h>
  VARCHAR oid[2];
EXEC SQL END DECLARE SECTION;

EXEC SQL INCLUDE SQLCA;

main()
{
/* Sets oid equal to a / to identify user externally for ORACLE     */
/* connection .                                                      */
/* Note:  Remember varchar datatype houses 2 fields, the actual data */
/*        and the length of that data                                */

    strcpy(oid, "/");
    strlen(oid.arr);

/* Request for connection  to the database */
    EXEC SQL CONNECT :oid;

    if (sqlca.sqlcode < 0)
    {
        printf("\n%s",sqlca.sqlerrm.sqlerrmc);
        EXEC SQL ROLLBACK WORK RELEASE;
        exit(1);
    }
    else
    {
        printf("\n Connected to Oracle...");
        EXEC SQL COMMIT WORK RELEASE;
        exit(0);
    }
  }
```

NOTE

SQLCA is not defined when it precedes a declarative statement.

SQLCODE

SQLCODE enables the developer to learn the outcome of the most recent SQL statement executed within the host language. This can be done either implicitly, by using the WHENEVER statement, or explicitly, by checking the status variables manually.

The WHENEVER Statement

The WHENEVER statement allows for automatic error, warning, and no-rows-selected situations. To trap these circumstances, you should use the following options:

- ■ SQLWARNING (traps warning information)
- ■ SQLERROR   (traps error information)
- ■ NOT FOUND   (traps NO DATA FOUND information)

When the preceding conditions exist, you should take the following actions:

- ■ DO
- ■ GOTO
- ■ STOP
- ■ CONTINUE

The following is the syntax for the WHENEVER statement:

```
EXEC SQL WHENEVER SQLERROR CONTINUE
```

> **NOTE**
>
> Pascal has no equivalent command to STOP; therefore it cannot be used.

ORACA

ORACA is a data structure that gives more Oracle-specific information than SQLCA. It is a great diagnostic tool. It monitors Oracle resources and gives much lengthier message text on errors, but it also takes up more runtime resources when enabled. See Table 13.8 in the "Precompiler Options" section to learn about enabling ORACA. The data structure is shown in the following segment, with a brief description of each element:

```
struct oraca
{
    char    oracaid[8];        /* "ORACA"                        */
    long        oracabc;       /* Length of ORACA                */
    long        oracchf;       /* Cursor Cache consistency flag  */
    long        oradbgf;       /* Master debug flag              */
```

```
    long        orahchf;                /* Heap consistency flag           */
    long        orastxtf;               /* Save SQL statement flag         */
    struct
    {
    unsigned short      orastxtl;       /* Length of current SQL statement */
char                orastxtc[70];       /* Text of current SQL statement*/
}orastxt;                               /* Sub-rec for storing SQL statement */
    struct
    {
    unsigned short      orasfnml;       /* Length of filename              */
    char            orasfnmc[70];       /* Nme of file w/current SQL statement*/
}orasfnm;                       /* Sub-rec for storing filename        */
    long    oraslnr;                    /* Line in file at or near SQL statement */
    long    orahoc;                     /* Highest MAXOPENCURSORS req.     */
    long    oramoc;                     /* Maximum open cursors required   */
    long    oracoc;                     /* Current number cursors used     */
    long    oranor;                     /* Number of cursor cache reassignments */
long        ;                   /* Number of SQL statement parses      */
    long    oranex;                     /* Number of SQL statement executions  */

};
struct oraca oraca;
```

ORACA contains the following information:

■ Option settings
■ System statistics
■ Extended diagnostics

Precompilation of Source Code

In version 1.8, four host languages are available to use with the Oracle Precompiler. The commands associated with each language to precompile code are stated in Table 13.1 of this chapter along with the extension to be applied to the source code.

You can precompile, compile, and link an embedded SQL program in several ways. Compiling multiple embedded SQL programs can become very time-consuming if each step is performed for each program. This approach of issuing individual commands can lead to inconsistency between program modules. Executing each step of the compilation process should probably be used when it doesn't matter whether standardization is met. It doesn't matter, for example, whether a common library is linked into your program, but all other programs for this system depend on it. For most situations, it is advisable to compile embedded SQL programs utilizing an executable control file. This executable will evaluate what tasks need to be accomplished while adhering to company standards. Depending on the platform on which you are working, an executable file such as a .bat, .com, .sh, or a makefile can be created to accept parameters.

After receiving the parameters to evaluate, the control file can determine what needs to be done. The control file can control precompiling, compiling, and linking host programs. Compiling using a control file can be used even if you don't have embedded SQL in your program. This keeps all applications created by your shop consistent with each other.

You can control precompiling in two more ways: *conditional precompilation* and *separate precompilation*. These two methods of precompiling your program offer flexibility, control, and efficiency.

Conditional Precompiling

Conditional precompiling enables you to write a program for several different platforms without changing your precompilation scripts. For example, you may want to include a section of your program for a UNIX platform but not for a DOS or VMS platform. Oracle precompilers recognize conditional sections of code. These sections are indicated by statements that define the environment and what actions to take. Procedural and embedded SQL statements can be used to perform platform-specific operations.

The Oracle statements in Table 13.7 are utilized when a conditional section is created.

Table 13.7. Conditional statements.

Conditional Statement	*Meaning*	*Type*
`EXEC ORACLE DEFINE symbol`	Names the symbol	Declarative
`EXEC ORACLE IFDEF symbol`	If the symbol is defined	Operational
`EXEC ORACLE IFNDEF symbol`	If the symbol isn't defined	Operational
`EXEC ORACLE ELSE`	Else/Otherwise	Operational
`EXEC ORACLE ENDIF`	Ends the control block	Operational

The first conditional Oracle statement is declarative and defines the name of the symbol to be used. The next four statements require an action to be taken under specified conditions.

Some symbols are port-specific and predefined for you when the Oracle precompilers are installed. Predefined operating-system symbols include CMS, MVS, DOS, UNIX and VMS. In Listing 13.7, conditional precompiling is shown using a predefined symbol.

Listing 13.7. Conditional precompiling example.

```
#include <stdio.h>
#include <string.h>
#include <stdlib.h>
#ifdef  UNIX
   #include <unix.h>
#endif
```

```
/* Host variable Declarations */
EXEC SQL BEGIN DECLARE SECTION;
  VARCHAR user_id[20];
  VARCHAR passwd[20]
EXEC SQL END DECLARE SECTION;

/* Include SQLCA communications area */
EXEC SQL INCLUDE SQLCA;

/* FILE Declarations */
FILE *output_file;
main()
{
    printf("/n What is your User ID: ");
    scanf("%s",user_id.arr);
    printf("\nEnter Password: ");
    scanf("%s",passwd.arr);

    user_id.len = strlen(user_id.arr);
    passwd.len = strlen(passwd.arr);

/* Request for Database Connection */
    EXEC SQL CONNECT :userid IDENTIFIED BY :passwd;

    if (sqlca.sqlcode < 0)
    {
       printf("\n%s",sqlca.sqlerrm.sqlerrmc);
       EXEC SQL ROLLBACK WORK RELEASE;
       exit(1);
    }
    else
    {
       printf("\nSuccessfully connected to Oracle.");
/* Conditional Precompilation. */
       #ifdef UNIX
          output_file = fopen("/usr/tmp/login.out","w");
          fprintf(output_file,"log in by %s",:userid);
          fclose(t_file);
       #end if;
       EXEC SQL COMMIT WORK RELEASE;
       exit(0);
    }
 }
```

Precompiler Options

Oracle Precompilers enable flexibility and efficiency in coding and offer many options in the development of your code. If you want more extensive diagnostic error handling, you could set your ORACA option to yes. If your code exceeds 80 characters maximum per line, you can set your IRECLEN option to 132. These are only two examples of the many options available. Table 13.8 shows an example of the options available as of the Oracle Precompiler 1.8 release.

Table 13.8. Precompiler options.

Options/Syntax/[Default]	Meaning
ASACC=YES/[NO]	Carriage control for listings
ASSUME_SQLCODE=YES/[NO]	Precompiler assumes SQLCODE is declared
AUTO_CONNECT=YES/[NO]	Automatic logon
CONFIG=filename	Name of user configuration file
COMMON_NAME=block_name	Name of FORTRAN common blocks
DBMS=[NATIVE]/V6/V7	Version-specific behavior of Oracle at precompile time
DEFINE=symbol	Defines symbol for conditional precompiling
*ERRORS=[YES]/NO	Errors send to the terminal
FIPS=YES/[NO]	Whether ANSI/ISO extensions are flagged
FORMAT=[ANSI]/TERMINAL	Format of COBOL/FORTRAN input line
*HOLD_CURSOR=YES/[NO]	How cursor cache handles SQL statements
HOST=C/COB74/COBOL/FORTRAN	Host language of input line
INAME=path and filename	Name of input file to be precompiled
*INCLUDE=path	Directory path for include files
IRECLEN=integer [80]	Record length of input files
LINES=YES/[NO]	C #inline directives generated
*LITDELIM=APOST/[QUOTE]	Delimiter for COBOL strings
LNAME=path and filename	Name of listing file
LRECLEN=integer [80]	Record length of listing file
LTYPE=[LONG]/SHORT/NONE	Type of listing
*MAXLITERAL=integer	Maximum length of strings
*MAXOPENCURSORS=integer [10]	Maximum number of cursors cached
MODE=[ORACLE]/ANSI/ANSI13/ ANSI14/ISO1/ISO13/ISO14	Complies with ANSI/ISO standard
MULTISUBPROG=[YES]/NO	Whether FORTRAN COMMON BLOCKS are generated
NLS_LOCAL=[YES]/NO	Blank-padding operations to be performed by SQLLIB
ONAME=path and filename	Name of output file
*ORACA=YES/[NO]	Whether ORACA error communications will be used
ORECLEN=integer [80]	Record length of output file
PAGELEN=integer [66]	Lines per page in listing

Options/Syntax/[Default]	Meaning
`*RELEASE_CURSOR=YES/[NO]`	How cursor cache handles SQL statements
`*SELECT_ERROR=[YES]/NO`	How SELECT errors are handled
`*SQLCHECK=SEMANTICS/FULL/` `[SYNTAX]/LIMITED/NONE`	Extent of syntactic/semantic checking
`UNSAFE_NULL=YES/[NO]`	Disables the ORA=1405 message
`USERID=username/password`	Valid Oracle username and password
`VARCHAR=YES/[NO]`	Recognizes implicit VARCHAR group items in COBOL
`*XREF=[YES]/NO`	Cross-reference section in listing

The above asterisks (*) represent options that can be declared on the command line and also inline with your host language source code. Declaring precompiler options within your program allows flexibility in changing the values within your program and can optimize runtime performance. The following syntax shows how the options should be declared within your program:

```
EXEC ORACLE OPTION (option=value)
```

There is only one mandatory argument: INAME. This argument tells the precompiler what the input filename is. The following statement uses the minimum requirements for any precompiler command line and will precompile the program missme.pc.

```
PROC INAME=missme.pc
```

An example of a precompiler command line using a few of the preceding options could look like the following:

```
proc iname=missme.pc include=ora_pcc: include=clib oraca=yes
```

All of these precompiler options can be accessed online. There is a help feature on most operating systems that can help you in defining the options needing to be used. Just enter the precompiler option without any argument at your operating system prompt. This help feature will display the following:

- The option name
- The syntax for using it
- The default value
- The description of each option

Entering the precompiler option with a ? succeeding it, will give you the current value of the option.

NOTE

When you precompile the program module that CONNECTs to Oracle, specify a value for MAXOPENCURSORS that is high enough for any of the program modules that will be linked together.

If you want to use just one SQLCA, you must declare it as a global in one of the program modules and as external in the other modules. In C, for example, this is done by using the external storage class, which tells the precompiler to look for the SQLCA in another program module. Unless you declare the SQLCA as external, each program module will use its own local SQLCA.

You *cannot* DECLARE a cursor in one file and reference it in another.

To speed up the precompiling function in the client/server environment, you can set the SQLCHECK parameter to NO. When SQLCHECK is set to NO, statement syntax checking will not be performed against the database. The SQLCHECK parameter must be set to NO if your precompiler program physically connects to more than one Oracle database. A precompiler program can be compiled (syntaxed) against only one of the two databases at a time. If this option is not disabled, any references to tables in the other database will be reported as the error Undefined Tables Referenced during compilations.

CAUTION

Setting the SQLCHECK parameter to NO should be a last resort; do this only if absolutely necessary to speed up program compilation times.

Performance Tuning

Performance tuning is essential in any application and database. As an application developer and DBA, I am always looking for new release tidbits or suggestions from other developers to tune my applications for better performance.

The most common area in poor performance I have found in using embedded SQL is with SQL itself. There are a few tools to help debug SQL, but I have found that EXPLAIN PLAN is the most helpful in deciphering how your SQL is being interpreted. EXPLAIN PLAN will help you find problems with full table scans, nested loops, or misused indexes.

A second cause of poor performance is high Oracle communications overhead. Oracle can process only one SQL statement at a time. In a networked environment, this can add to heavy network traffic, which could impact your application significantly.

A third cause of poor performance is poor cursor management, resulting in unnecessary parsing and binding. Parsing examines the SQL statements for correct syntax and refers to valid database objects. Binding associates host language variables with their addresses, so Oracle knows where to read and write their values.

There are many other possible reasons for poor performance; read Chapter 30, "Performance Tuning," for an in-depth discussion of performance issues.

Summary

I hope this chapter has offered some reference help for your embedded SQL adventures. Because of the complexities of some of these features in embedded SQL, development can be a little defeating at times. After you have totally grasped the concepts, however, the coding becomes tremendously easier. You will be amazed at the portability, flexibility, and efficiency your program can have.

14

Database Constraints, Triggers, and Procedures

by Joe Greene

For the most part, the tendency has been to move applications off large central computers where all processing was performed from a single set of controlled software directories. The current trend is to use a number of servers with a large number of client workstations that interact to complete the business processing needs of your organization. Although this trend has enabled us to build user interfaces that are far more powerful than could have been imagined in the old mainframe world, it has a few drawbacks that need to be addressed. One of these drawbacks is the separation of the software (on the client workstation) from the data located on the server.

This chapter covers some techniques that you can use to put part of the software logic within the database. This subject is broken into three areas, the first of which is database constraints. *Database constraints* are rules that are applied to the data in tables that match standard rules of referencing and legal values in relational database theory. You can define a set of columns that must have unique, non-null values. You can define columns that must contain values which are stored in other tables. You also can define other rules such as not allowing a column to be null. These options enable you to control the values that are placed within your database tables to help ensure data integrity.

The next technique presented in this chapter involves triggers stored in the database. Although constraints provide you with a number of options that control the data placed in tables from a general, relational database theory perspective, they cannot implement complex, customer-specific business logic, such as ensuring that a specific column is updated with a calculated value whenever the user inserts or updates data in another column. What you really need in these cases is the ability to write programs that are automatically executed whenever specific events occur. This is where database *triggers* come into play. You write software using SQL and PL/SQL and store it in the database with instructions that the software is to be executed whenever a specific event occurs. For example, whenever someone inserts data into the golf_scores table, the total score is calculated.

Finally, this chapter covers a technique that is similar to triggers but used in a different manner. *Stored procedures* (and their close relative *functions*) are PL/SQL programs that are stored within the database. They can be called by applications to perform specific processing tasks when needed. You actually can assemble collections of individual procedures into packages, which can be fairly complex applications.

My approach to presenting this material is to discuss each technique from a general perspective and then move into more details. I describe only part of the theory behind these constructs and instead focus on their actual implementation within the Oracle relational database management system. I also try to present a number of examples that you can use as templates for your own work. You should be able to adapt the concepts in these examples to the specifics of your implementation. I find this method saves time for me and hope that it helps you get your applications done more quickly.

Reasons for Software in the Database

Why put software in a database? The database management system already has enough to do when it comes to storing data. Why not have the developers spend more time on making the system faster and use fewer resources rather than try to turn it into a programming language interpreter? Those might seem like reasonable questions when you first start to think about the idea of storing software in the database. After all, we have been making applications work for decades with relatively dumb data storage systems by placing all of the smarts into software applications written in traditional programming languages.

What I suggest in this section is to challenge you to consider the alternative of putting *part* of your logic into the database. Obviously, we are nowhere near wanting to put all the software into the database. What I propose instead is that certain business logic components are applied to a number of different applications. For example, you could rewrite the code for each of these applications in each of the locations where you update a table. It would be easier, though, to implement this logic in a single location and just use it when needed. This reduces the amount of code that you need to write. It also gives you a single set of code to maintain as opposed to having multiple programs which are distributed on every user's workstation.

However, this concept of executing a single set of code has been taken a step further. Rather than merely having one set of code that could be executed when the developer remembers to put in a call to that software, why not have the software executed automatically? If a rule is really important (such as keeping totals up-to-date or making sure the data entered in a given record is valid), then it is important to have that rule followed. This is what constraints and triggers are all about. After they are put in place, everyone has to follow them.

Some people may scoff at the need for constraints and triggers. Perhaps these people are developing in a highly object-oriented development environment where they inherit a lot of functionality from a given set of base classes. They could then argue that all you have to do is change the functionality of the base class and then recompile everything. You have a software-only solution that is easy to maintain and enables the programmers to control when the functions are executed. There is one thing that you should consider though when working in a client-server environment. You might not control how the user accesses the database. Consider for a moment Figure 14.1.

Users probably will use the software you developed to get to the database. However, some might figure out that they can use tools, such as Microsoft Query or Oracle's Navigator or Discoverer/2000 products, to get to the database directly. Perhaps due to application development backlogs, you allow certain key analysts to write their own programs. In all of these cases, they will bypass any application logic that the developers write and go right to the database. They would not, however, bypass constraints and triggers that have been applied to these database objects from within the database.

FIGURE 14.1.
Client/server access issues.

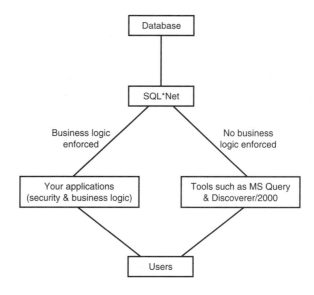

Another reason that you might consider putting some of your processing logic within the database is speed. Take the example of logic that ensures that any value put in a column is contained in a table in the database that contains a list of valid values (*foreign key*). If you are writing your applications in a highly optimized language, such as C, you could argue that you *could* do the comparisons more quickly than a PL/SQL program could. This might be true, but if you are inserting a series of records, you will be issuing a number of queries to the database. Each of these queries will have to be transmitted over the network, processed, and the results returned to you. If the validation table is small, you could simply download it at application startup. However, if you have a lot of columns to validate, you might find it quicker to have the database perform these validations.

I mentioned that you might want to use stored procedures, constraints, and triggers from a maintenance point of view. All of the benefits that I described become even more important if security is a major concern for your application. It can be quite a challenge to perform security audits on a large number of applications, some of which might have multiple versions on different client workstations on your network. However, if the security logic is located in the stored procedures and the database, it is much easier to perform a complete audit and certify the system.

Finally, I want to lobby just a little for database integrity. I know that many programmers think that they understand the schema and are therefore ready to write software that properly enforces integrity constraints. However, I have found that their true understanding varies from superb to questionable. It is much easier to have an expert implement integrity constraints in the database. Also, the people who are usually assigned to do a lot of screen creation work (where you would often want to enforce constraints) tend to be somewhat inexperienced. If your system is set up properly, it is usually easier to recover from the complete failure of a disk drive than it is to deal with a database corrupted by applications that are not filling in the data properly.

Constraint Basics

Because I ended the previous section by discussing the virtues of database integrity, I thought it appropriate to start with the solution to this integrity problem: constraints. From the term itself, you get the general idea that constraints somehow limit what the user can do, just like the data validation algorithms that you put in your software. We need to refine this definition here to correctly fit how Oracle defines constraints. In the Oracle database world, *constraints* are rules that are applied to tables during or after their creation that affect how those tables can be populated. Perhaps the following example can illustrate what I mean:

```
SQL> create table book_demo
  2  (key_field        number,
  3  last_name         varchar2(20) not null,
  4  first_name        varchar2(20),
  5  department_name   varchar2(20),
  6  employee_id       number(5) unique,
  7  constraint fk1_book_demo
  8      foreign key (department_name)
  9      references departments(department_name),
 10  constraint pk_book_demo
 11*     primary key (key_field))
SQL> /

Table created.
```

This little example shows a number of different capabilities of database table constraints. First, you can apply a constraint to individual columns as part of the column definition as I did with the last_name (not null) and employee_id (unique) columns. You also can define the constraints as separate line items as I did with the primary key and the foreign key. You also can define names for the foreign keys that you can use to later reference them. If you do not define a name for the constraint, one will be made up for you. I prefer to define my own constraint names and make the table name a part of the constraint name for easy references.

This example also covers solutions to some very common business processing rules:

■ *You need a key field in the table to uniquely reference a row from other tables that are joined in queries to this table.* As I explain in the "Primary Keys" section later in this chapter, values that are part of the primary key have the properties of being unique and not being null. This makes the key_field perfect for this reference.

■ *There are certain fields that the user must fill in.* In this case, the not null constraint on the last_name field guarantees that people will not be able to update or insert a record with the last name blank.

■ *Sometimes you have fields that are either blank or have a unique value.* The `employee_id` field's unique constraint guarantees that now two rows have identical values for this column. However, unlike a primary key, null values are permitted.

■ *You have some columns that can take on only a limited set of values.* The list of legal values will vary over time as users add or subtract them. Therefore, you want to have a table containing these valid values and ensure that the values in other tables contain only one of the values in the valid values table. This is the case with the foreign key on `department_name`.

This example does not show all the options available to you, but you should now have a general idea of what these constraints can do for you.

Creating and Modifying Constraints

The nice thing about constraints is that they enforce themselves. You do not have to make a call to a constraint. They are fully automatic. You do, however, have to create the constraint because it is your business processing rules that are being enforced (Oracle can not guess for you). This section is devoted to the subject of creating and modifying your constraints.

In the example from the previous section, I showed you the most common way to create constraints using table creation commands. Constraints should be part of your basic schema design, and you should be ready to create them when you create your tables. There are two places in which you can define a constraint as a part of a table creation command. The first way is to include the constraint on the same line as the rest of the column definition, like this:

```
create table book_example
(identifier   number  not null);
```

You also have the option of naming constraints when defining them on the same line as the column, as the following example shows:

```
create table book_example
(identifier   number   constraint book_example_1 not null);
```

There are three parts to a named constraint definition. The first is the keyword CONSTRAINT. The second is the name that you want to give the constraint. Again, I like to put the table name in as part of the constraint to make it easier to review. The final part is the description of the constraint. The preceding example has a simple NOT NULL constraint. However, you also can define more complex constraints, such as primary keys and foreign keys, on the same line that you define the columns as long as those primary and foreign keys reference only that single column. You can have combinations of columns that make up primary keys and foreign keys.

The second place that you can define a constraint is at the bottom of your list of columns, but before the parenthesis that denotes the end of the field definitions. The following is an example of this:

```
create table book_example
(identifier     number,
description_1  varchar2(20),
constraint book_example_1 primary key(identifier));
```

As you can see, the format is similar. You do have to identify the column or columns that make up the primary or foreign key in this example. Why would you want to do it this way? One reason might be that you like to have a nice, clean list of fields to review in your schema creation scripts. If you have several constraint definitions in the middle of your field list, it might be more difficult to pick out the field definitions. Another reason to do this is that it is the only way to define primary keys or foreign keys that are composed of more than one column. Other than that, it is a matter of personal preference. For reference purposes, primary and foreign keys are usually referred to as table constraints, whereas NOT NULL and UNIQUE type constraints are referred to as column constraints. I tend to prefer to list all of my primary and foreign keys as separate, named constraints at the bottom of the field list because I find it more readable. Perhaps you should try it both ways and see what makes sense to you.

Suppose that you did not catch all the constraints you wanted when you created the tables themselves. All is not lost. Thanks to the ALTER TABLE command, you can add or delete constraints as you see fit. You cannot modify constraints, but because you are not altering the data that is currently in the table, you can simply drop an incorrect constraint and add it back with the proper format.

First, let's look at dropping constraints. The format you would use for the ALTER TABLE command would be similar to the following:

```
SQL> alter table book_example
  2  drop constraint book_example_1;

Table altered.
```

This case shows where it is helpful to choose logical names for your constraints. Oracle will make up names for you, which you can obtain by querying the correct view (which I do later in this section), but it is not as easy as a well-chosen name.

Now you are ready to add a constraint with the format that you like. I will first show how to add a table constraint. I will add back in the primary key that I just deleted. The format for this command is

```
SQL> alter table book_example
  2  add (constraint book_example_1 primary key (identifier));

Table altered.
```

You use a slightly different format when modifying column constraints. Here you are merely adjusting a property on the column. Therefore, you would use the ALTER TABLE with the MODIFY clause. The format of this command is

```
SQL> alter table book_example
  2  modify (description_1 varchar2(20) not null);

Table altered.
```

If you modify the description of the column and do not include the NOT NULL column constraint, the column will start accepting null values. Still, the format of this command also is quite simple, and you can keep at it until you get all of the columns and constraints exactly the way you want them.

Which brings up a good question: How do you know when things are the way that you want them? You would typically start by issuing the DESCRIBE command similar to the following to determine the table structure:

```
SQL> desc book_example

Name                               Null?    Type
-------------------------------    -------- ----
 IDENTIFIER                        NOT NULL NUMBER
 DESCRIPTION_1                     NOT NULL VARCHAR2(20)
```

What you see here in the way of constraints is two NOT NULL constraints. Only column DESRIPTION_1 has been given the NOT NULL constraint. Oracle recognizes, however, that NOT NULL is part of the requirements for a primary key, and therefore shows this with the DESCRIBE command. So how do you know about your primary keys and foreign keys? The answer to this is a series of queries to another set of views as shown in the following example:

```
SQL> select * from user_constraints
  2  where table_name = 'BOOK_EXAMPLE';

OWNER                            CONSTRAINT_NAME                             C TABLE_NAME
-------------------------------  ------------------------------------------  - ------------
SEARCH_CONDITION
----------------------------------------------------------------------------------------
R_OWNER                          R_CONSTRAINT_NAME                           DELETE_RU STATUS
-------------------------------  ------------------------------------------  --------- ------
JGREENE                          BOOK_EXAMPLE_1                              P BOOK_EXAMPLE

                                                                                        ENABLED

JGREENE                          SYS_C00417                                  C BOOK_EXAMPLE
DESCRIPTION_1 IS NOT NULL
                                                                                        ENABLED


SQL> select * from user_cons_columns
  2  where table_name = 'BOOK_EXAMPLE';

OWNER                            CONSTRAINT_NAME                             TABLE_NAME
-------------------------------  ------------------------------------------  --------------
COLUMN_NAME                      POSITION
-------------------------------  ----------
JGREENE                          BOOK_EXAMPLE_1                              BOOK_EXAMPLE
IDENTIFIER                             1

JGREENE                          SYS_C00417                                  BOOK_EXAMPLE
DESCRIPTION_1
```

Notice a few points about this example:

- As with most things you want to observe about your Oracle database, you issue a query to one of those views that Oracle creates for you. In this case, you need to query user_constraints and user_cons_columns.

- Notice that user constraints lists the constraint name and the table name but not the columns that are involved. That is why you need to query user_cons_columns.

- user_constraints does not list the name of the table that is being referenced in a foreign key. It has only a column for the remote constraint name. This is another factor arguing in favor of putting the name of the table into its constraint names. In the case of a foreign key, it needs to reference a primary key in the referenced table because it has no way of deciding which row to choose if there are multiple occurrences of that value.

- Notice in the line for DESRIPTION_1 that you have a system-assigned constraint name. As I mentioned, they are not easy to remember.

Validating constraints takes a little bit of time, and there might be times when you want to temporarily disable the constraint but not drop it permanently. Perhaps you have a data warehouse where you are downloading a lot of information from the legacy system every night. You could save time on your processing cycle by using the following command:

```
SQL> alter table book_example
  2  disable constraint book_example_1;

Table altered.
```

Of course, you will want to know the command that reactivates your constraint after you are done. The format of this command is as follows:

```
SQL> alter table book_example
  2  enable constraint book_example_1;

Table altered.
```

Before I leave this general discussion on constraints, I have to point out that constraints can make certain tasks more difficult. For example, if you want to drop a table and then re-create it with a slightly altered format, you would simply use the drop table command. That is, unless you have foreign keys that point to that table. If you try to drop a table that is referenced by foreign keys, Oracle will tell you that you cannot do it. You can't drop the table if you *disable* the constraints that point to the table. Instead, you have to *drop* the constraints that reference the table that you want to drop, drop the table, re-create the table, and then re-create the foreign keys that reference the table. It is a bit of extra work, but it can be worth it in certain circumstances.

Primary Keys

You have already seen a couple examples of primary keys. A *primary key* is a set of one or more columns that are joined together in an index that is automatically created as part of the primary key. That index has two properties. The first is that it is unique. No two rows in that index will have the same values. The second property is that none of the columns in that index are allowed to contain null values. These properties are what you need to have if you are going to use the columns in the primary key to reference this table from other tables. It guarantees that you will have one and only one row match the criteria for linkage.

Again, primary keys can be either named (that is, you make up the name) or unnamed (in which case Oracle makes up a name for you). If you have a primary key that consists of a single column, you can define the constraint on the same line as the column. You also can define the constraint at the bottom of the list of columns if you so choose. If you want to make up a constraint containing multiple columns, use the format at the bottom of the list of columns. The following example shows the basics of creating primary keys:

```
SQL>  create table employee_addresses
  2   (employee_id     number(5),
  3   effective_date   date,
  4   street_1         varchar2(20),
  5   street_2         varchar2(20),
  6   city             varchar2(20),
  7   state            varchar2(2),
  8   zip_code         number(9),
  9   phone_number     number(10),
 10   constraint pk_employee_addresses
 11   primary key (employee_id,effective_date));

Table created.
```

> **NOTE**
>
> Raw, long, and long raw columns cannot be used in primary keys.

Note that there are a few columns that cannot be used as primary keys. Raw, long, and long raw columns will not work for this purpose. Also, you might not want to make a primary key that is too long unless it's absolutely needed for integrity. You will wind up duplicating most of the table in an index, and it takes time to maintain this index. Finally, you should remember that an index is created when you make a primary key. You should work to order the columns in the order that you are likely to use them in queries so that your queries can take advantage of this index.

Foreign Keys

Next on the list of constraints is the foreign key. The foreign key requires a bit of thought in that it is a constraint that affects more than one table. The moment you create a foreign key that references the table, you will be restricted from dropping that referenced table or truncating it. You can work around this by dropping the constraint when you need to perform these functions and then re-creating it. However, if you have dropped the contents of the referenced table, you will not have any values to use to populate your existing referencing table columns. This can get a little tricky and requires a knowledge of your overall schema.

Foreign keys are either named or unnamed. Because you might have to manipulate foreign keys more often than other constraints, I recommend naming them. There are three parts to a foreign key:

■ The constraint name which is optional

■ The column or columns in the local table, which must match a row in the referenced table or be null

■ The name of the table and column(s) in the referenced table, which serve as the matching criteria for the foreign key

Now look at some examples. In the first example, you can build a simple foreign key from a single column in this table to the employee table that you created earlier.

```
SQL> create table pension_status
  2  (employee_id          number(5),
  3  pension_start_date    date,
  4  pension_type          varchar2(1),
  5  salary_base           number(8,2),
  6  percentage            number(2),
  7  notes                 varchar2(40),
  8  status                varchar2(40),
  9  constraint fk1_pension_status
 10  foreign key (employee_id)
 11  references employees(employee_id));

Table created.
```

The next example shows off some of the more complicated features of foreign keys. First, I built a foreign key where two columns in this table are used to reference two columns in the employee_addresses table. I also have created three foreign keys for this table. Notice that two of them (`employee_id` and `manager_id`) actually reference the same columns in another table. You can place considerable control on a table. What these keys do for you is ensure that you do not get invalid employee IDs in a given record which would make the record generally useless.

```
SQL> create table employee_history
  2  (employee_id          number(5),
  3  effective_date        date,
  4  department            varchar2(20),
  5  title                 varchar2(20),
```

```
 6   manager_id              number(5),
 7   pay_grade               varchar2(10),
 8   number_of_employees number(7),
 9   constraint fk_employee_history_address
10   foreign key (employee_id,effective_date)
11   references employee_addresses (employee_id, effective_date),
12   constraint fk_employee_history_employee
13   foreign key (employee_id)
14   references employees(employee_id),
15   constraint fk_employee_history_manager
16   foreign key (manager_id)
17*  references employees(employee_id));

Table created.
```

Foreign keys are a powerful mechanism to ensure that the data placed in a table is valid. As opposed to static validation (as with the Yes/No buttons on some applications), your list of legal values is stored in a database table. This validation table can be updated to keep up with changing business demands. There is a bit of a price to be paid in that you lose some freedom to drop tables when they have foreign keys referencing them, but you would want to be very careful in this situation anyway.

Other Constraints

Several other constraints are available for your use. Typically these are applied at the column level, but also can be applied at the table level to perform a number of different validations on the data. These usually are fixed constraints that can not be changed without modifying the table definition. The following are the constraints you might want to consider:

- UNIQUE
- NOT NULL
- CHECK
- REFERENCES (FOREIGN KEYS)

The UNIQUE constraint is used to specify that the value in a column is not to be repeated in another row in this table. You also can form a table constraint where you specify that a combination of columns is not to be repeated in a given table. The following two examples apply this constraint:

```
SQL> create table pension_status
  2   (employee_id           number(5) unique,
  3    pension_start_date    date unique,
  4    pension_type          varchar2(1),
  5    salary_base           number(8,2),
  6    percentage            number(2),
  7    notes                 varchar2(40),
  8*   status                varchar2(40));

Table created.
```

```
SQL> create table pension_status
  2  (employee_id          number(5),
  3  pension_start_date    date,
  4  pension_type          varchar2(1),
  5  salary_base           number(8,2),
  6  percentage            number(2),
  7  notes                 varchar2(40),
  8  status                varchar2(40),
  9  constraint unique_pension_status
 10* unique (employee_id,pension_start_date));

Table created.
```

In the first example, the column employee_id has to be unique in all rows, as does the column pension_start_date. In the second example, you can have duplicates in either employee_id and pension_start_date, but the combination of the two fields has to be unique in every row.

The next type of constraint that you will run across is the NOT NULL constraint. What this specifies is that the user has to put some nonblank data in this column. As with other constraints, you can explicitly name the constraint or allow Oracle to make up a name for you. The following examples show both named and unnamed NOT NULL constraints:

```
SQL> create table pension_status
  2  (employee_id          number(5) not null,
  3  pension_start_date    date not null,
  4  pension_type          varchar2(1),
  5  salary_base           number(8,2),
  6  percentage            number(2),
  7  notes                 varchar2(40),
  8  status                varchar2(40));

Table created.
```

```
SQL> create table pension_status
  2  (employee_id          number(5) constraint nn_employee_id not null,
  3  pension_start_date    date constraint nn_start_date not null,
  4  pension_type          varchar2(1),
  5  salary_base           number(8,2),
  6  percentage            number(2),
  7  notes                 varchar2(40),
  8* status                varchar2(40));

Table created.
```

A very powerful form of constraint is the CHECK constraint. This can perform a fixed validation on one or more columns worth of data. What you are allowed to do here is write a short SQL comparison statement similar to those that you would use in a WHERE clause. The next two examples show what this can do for you:

```
SQL> edit
Wrote file afiedt.buf
  1  create table pension_status
  2  (employee_id          number(5),
  3  pension_start_date    date check (pension_start_date >
  4       to_date('01-JAN-1990','DD-MON-YYYY')),
```

```
    5   pension_type            varchar2(1),
    6   salary_base             number(8,2),
    7   percentage              number(2),
    8   notes                   varchar2(40),
    9*  status                  varchar2(40))
SQL> /

Table created.

SQL> create table pension_status
    2   (employee_id            number(5),
    3   pension_start_date      date,
    4   pension_type            varchar2(1),
    5   salary_base             number(8,2),
    6   percentage              number(2),
    7   notes                   varchar2(40),
    8   status                  varchar2(40),
    9   constraint check_pension_status
   10*  check (pension_type = 'Z'));

Table created.
```

As you can see, there is a lot that you can do with the referential integrity constraints provided by Oracle. After you understand what is available, you can start to factor it into your schema design. One point to remember is that you need to publish the constraints that you have applied to the tables and the names of these constraints. Otherwise, you will have a bunch of developers who are totally mystified when they keep getting error messages that refer to things such as FK_EMPLOYEES.

Stored Procedures

Next on the list of discussion topics is stored procedures. These are very much like the PL/SQL scripts that you store in text files on your operating system. The key difference is that they are stored within the database, both in parsed (somewhat like compiled) and raw text form. The following is the general format of a stored procedure:

```
procedure procedure_name
(input and output parameters)
as
. . .
(variable declarations)
begin
. . .
(SQL and PL/SQL commands)
exception
. . .
(exceptions)
end;
```

When planning your stored procedure, you need to think about four main parts:

■ *The input and output parameters*—These are how you have other applications and procedures communicate with the stored procedure. The input parameters can be used to control flow and provide data needed to run the procedure. The output parameters are used to get data back from the stored procedure.

■ *The variable declarations*—With these, you define PL/SQL variables that will be used in your stored procedure. Remember that the variables that you create have a scope limited to the block in which they are created when you are devising multiple-block, stored-procedure applications.

■ *The main body of the program*—Here is where you place the bulk of your processing code. It can contain SQL and PL/SQL statements.

■ *The exception handlers*—These help you catch error conditions and respond to them. When an exception is raised, processing in the main body of the program stops and an exception handler is sought to react to the problem. If there is no exception handler, you will get an error returned from the stored procedure. The exception handlers are the key difference between applications that are flexible and can deal with routine problems (such as when a table has not been initialized with data yet), and programs that fail, giving the rather cryptic errors so common to databases and programming languages.

For more information about the details of PL/SQL programming, please refer to Chapter 12, "PL/SQL." This chapter goes into the details of the block structure, PL/SQL variables, and the major programming commands. Look at the following example of a stored procedure:

```
SQL> create or replace procedure book_sp_example
  2  (in_employee_id IN number,
  3  return_code OUT number,
  4  return_status OUT number)
  5  as
  6  counter number;
  7  begin
  8  select count(*)
  9    into counter
 10    from employees;
 11  if counter = 0 then
 12    return_status := 'Employees table is empty';
 13    return_code := 2;
 14  else
 15    select count(*)
 16      into counter
 17      from employees
 18      where employee_id = in_employee_id;
 19    if counter = 0 then
 20      return_status := 'Employee ID not found';
 21      return_code := 3;
 22    else
 23      delete from employees
 24        where employee_id = in_employee_id;
```

```
25    end if;
26  end if;
27  return_status := 'success';
28  return_code := 0;
29  exception
30  when others then
31    return_status := 'Exception raised '||substr(sqlerrm,1,30);
32    return_code := 4;
33* end;
SQL> /
```

```
Procedure created.
```

This is not atypical of the kind of stored procedures that you might have to write. It has one input parameter—the employee ID that is to be deleted by this procedure. It has two output parameters: a numeric return code, which indicates success or the type of error found and a text return status, which can be displayed by the calling program or stored in a log file for later troubleshooting. You first validate that the employees table has been initialized with data. If it has not, you correctly flag the error message and avoid any further processing (the DELETE statement would result in only an error on an empty table).

The next part of the program is devoted to validating the input data. Here you check to see that the employee_id that has been received as input is valid. If the employee ID is not valid, you flag this specific error and avoid the deletion code. If the ID is valid, you try to delete it. There could be a number of reasons why a deletion could fail (for example, lack of delete privileges or the value is referenced as a foreign key in another table). You catch these errors and any other errors with the OTHERS exception handler, which returns its own code and status message. Note that I have included the text error message that you would see if you had issued this command at the SQL*Plus command line. I used the sqlerrm system variable to build my return status field.

You can do many things with stored procedures. The key here is that you have to make an overt call to the stored procedure to get it to execute. There are forms of software stored in the database that execute automatically when a specified condition occurs. Unlike these triggers, stored procedures have the advantage of having input and output parameters, which can control their flow and also provide output information to the calling program.

Packages

Just as applications in other programming languages are composed of multiple procedures or subroutines, PL/SQL procedures can be assembled together into stored applications. Oracle refers to these stored applications as *packages*. The simplest format for a package would look something like the following:

```
create or replace package score_all
as
procedure score_answers
(customer_id IN number,
term number default 30)
is
. . .
(variable declarations)
begin
. . .
(SQL and PL/SQL commands)
end;
create or replace package body score_all
as
procedure letter_grade
(total_score IN number,
letter_grade OUT char)
is
. . .
(variable declarations)
begin
. . .
(SQL and PL/SQL commands)
end;

end;
```

The procedures and functions that you include as part of the package definition just shown are available to the general public (as long as they have execute privileges). In line with a lot of other programming tools, Oracle enables you to define protected (hidden) software components that are used only by the procedures and functions defined in the public section. You may, for example, have a public function to score answers that relies on a letter-grade calculator. The user applications cannot call the letter-grade calculator directly (because you need to have a score total first). Therefore, you can hide this procedure in what Oracle refers to as a package body. This should make C++ and other object-oriented programmers feel somewhat at home.

Functionally, you can call any of the publicly available package procedures as you would any other stored procedure. The package is just merely a convenient grouping mechanism. Also, procedures and functions within the package can call each other, procedures and functions within other packages, or those that are stored by themselves and are not in a package.

Finally, you can use packages to create global variables that are defined within the package but outside of any of the procedures or functions. This is important because any variable defined within a procedure goes out of scope (and its value is lost) after you exit from that procedure. You could always pass information between procedures in a package using an input parameter, but that could get rather lengthy. Other programming environments support the concept of global variables, so if you are more comfortable using this technique, Oracle can support you.

Functions

Stored procedures allow you to perform operations by using code stored in the database. In many cases, all you really need is to get a single output parameter based on the input parameters received. You could, for example, write a routine that calculates the absolute value and returns it to you. A call to this procedure, which I call ABSOLUTE_IT, would look something like this:

```
declare
  x   number;
  y   number;
  z   number;
begin
  absolute_it(x,y);
  z := y * z;
end;
```

Of course, this is simply a duplication of the ABSOLUTE VALUE built-in function, but let's look at it again. The key point here is that there are many operations for which you do not need to have all the calling and return value options that are available in stored procedures. What you really want to do is supply one or more input parameters and get a single output result. You also make your code difficult to follow if you have numerous calls to stored procedures to calculate preliminary values and then link them together later in a final calculation.

Most programming languages enable you to make calls to functions in the main body of a calculation. Rewriting the preceding example where ABSOLUTE_IT is a function instead of a stored procedure would look like the following:

```
 declare
  x   number;
  y   number;
  z   number;
begin
z := absolute_it(x) * z;
end;
```

So, what does the function itself look like? Well, actually it looks very much like a stored procedure. The key difference is that you must specify a return value, and you do not have any output parameters other than the return value. The general format for functions stored within the Oracle database looks like this:

```
create or replace function X_to_Y
(xin IN number) return number
is
. . .
(variable declarations)
begin
. . .
(SQL and PL/SQL commands)
return output_value
exception
. . .
(exception handlers)
end;
```

NOTE

You can use these functions within other functions and within stored procedures.

One thing I would suggest is that you check out the functions provided by Oracle before you write your own functions. There are a number of the more common conversion, calculation, and processing functions that have been built for you. Putting it another way, ask yourself if it is likely that you are the first one to need this function. If the function is specific to your application or business, the answer might be yes. If the function is likely to be needed by a large number of programmers, Oracle has probably implemented it for you. The following are just a few examples of the functions that are built in to Oracle:

- CONCAT—Concatenates two strings together.
- INITCAP—Converts the input string so that the initial letter of each word is capitalized with all the remaining letters in lowercase.
- LENGTH—Returns the number of characters in the input string.
- LOWER—Converts the input string to all lowercase letters.
- UPPER—Converts the input string to all uppercase letters.
- RTRIM—Trims any trailing blanks from the character string.
- LTRIM—Trims any leading blanks from the character string.
- SUBSTR—Selects a substring from the character stream input. You specify the position of the first character that you want and then the number of characters to the right of it that you want to see.
- TO_CHAR—Converts numbers or dates to character strings. You can specify the format parameters that control how the string will look (such as 12/31/96 or 31 Dec 96).
- TO_DATE – Converts a character string into a date using the format parameters specified or the default format parameters for your database.
- TO_NUMBER—Converts a string into a number.
- ADD_MONTHS—Enables you to add a specified number of months to a date. This is much easier than developing the old algorithm that knows about leap years and the number of days in a month.
- LAST_DAY—Returns the last day of the month for an input month.
- NEXT_DAY—Returns the day following the day that you input. Again, this keeps track of leap years and the number of days in a month.
- SYSDATE—Returns the current system date.
- USER—Returns the current Oracle user ID.
- SIN—Returns the sine of the input angle specified in radians.

This list could go on for some time. For the details of all of the functions supported in your release of SQL and PL/SQL, check your online reference or hard copy manuals. The main point, though, is that there are a wide range of built-in functions available to you.

You can see that functions are basically the same as stored procedures in that they are sections of PL/SQL code stored in the database. The main difference is their capability to be used in the middle of various lines of calculation as opposed to being separate calls with return values that can be used later in calculations.

Triggers

Oracle has one more variation on the theme of software stored in the database that you should know. Although stored procedures can provide some nice functionality when you call them, there are situations where you might want some software executed automatically whenever a situation occurs. This is where triggers come into play. Triggers have a format similar to the following:

```
create trigger populate_total
after update of hole_score on golf_scores
for each row
begin
. . .
(statements to perform the calculations and update the database)
exception
. . .
(exception handlers)
end;
```

Notice that there are no input or output parameters on triggers. This is because you cannot call them directly. They are called by the Oracle database itself. Any inputs to your trigger processing must be derived from the tables and status variables within the database. The outputs of the trigger also need to be applied to the database as opposed to being returned to the calling program or displayed on the screen.

The unique section of the definition of a trigger is the EVENT clause. This is the section of the preceding example right after the line with the CREATE statement. In this case, it indicates that the trigger should be fired after the HOLD_SCORE column of the golf_scores table is updated. What you typically specify in the EVENT clause is the use of a privilege by a user—in this case, the update privilege. You have a little finer control in that you can specify the object and even the column for object privileges.

When do you use triggers? One common use is when you want some security constraints enforced. Another use would be when you have a lot of business processing rules that are of the format "I want to calculate a total value whenever the record is updated." Triggers ensure that the task is completed without worrying whether every programmer knows to make every function call in a complex business rules scheme.

Building Stored Procedures, Functions, and Triggers

You have three basic commands that enable you to build stored procedures, functions, and triggers in the Oracle database:

- ```
  create procedure
  ```
- ```
  create function
  ```
- ```
  create trigger
  ```

There is a slight variation on these commands that makes working with stored procedures much easier than, say, creating tables. Because tables contain data that might cause serious problems if that data is lost, Oracle takes a very strict view on creating tables. If you try to create a table whose name already exists, the CREATE command fails on you. You have to explicitly issue the DROP TABLE command and then reissue the CREATE TABLE command to get the new table built. That way, it is your fault if you drop a table that contains mission-critical company data that has not been backed up for the last five years.

However, with stored procedures, things are easier. Because they do not contain any persistent data, there is no harm in overwriting a stored procedure unless, of course, you have a software error, which is a problem in any case. Therefore, Oracle allows you to specify CREATE OR REPLACE commands as follows:

- ```
  CREATE OR REPLACE PROCEDURE
  ```
- ```
  CREATE OR REPLACE FUNCTION
  ```
- ```
  CREATE OR REPLACE TRIGGER
  ```

Other than that, the format for these stored software constructs is pretty straightforward. You concentrate on good PL/SQL and SQL program design rather than formatting the individual containers. For review, the following formats are used to create stored procedures, functions, and triggers:

For stored procedures:

```
create or replace procedure procedure_name
(input and output parameters)
as
. . .
(variable declarations)
begin
. . .
(SQL and PL/SQL commands)
exception
. . .
(exceptions)
end;
```

For functions:

```
create or replace function X_to_Y
(xin IN number) return number
is
. . .
(variable declarations)
begin
. . .
(SQL and PL/SQL commands)
return output_value
exception
. . .
(exception handlers)
end;
```

For triggers:

```
create trigger trigger_name
. . .
(event_clause)
begin
. . .
(statements to perform the calculations and update the database)
exception
. . .
(exception handlers)
end;
```

My favorite technique for building procedures is to type the creation commands in an operating system text file. That way, I have a copy to work with while I am working out errors. I use SQL*Plus to run these script files using the following format:

```
SQL> @create_trigger_1.sql
```

The actual creation and debugging process can be a little tricky. For example, if you have any errors in your code, you will get a message similar to the following:

```
SQL> create or replace procedure testing as
  2  return_code number;
  3  begin
  4  select * from non_existent
  5  where last_name = 'SMITH;
  6  return_cod := -1;
  7  end;
  8  /

Warning: Procedure created with compilation errors.
```

So what are the errors? You have to issue a query against the user_errors view to actually see what is happening:

```
SQL> select * from user_errors;

NAME                              TYPE          SEQUENCE   LINE  POSITION
--------------------------------- ------------- ---------- ----- ----------
TEXT
------------------------------------------------------------------------------
TESTING                           PROCEDURE         1        5     19
PLS-00103: Encountered the symbol "SMITH;
return_cod := -1;
end;
" when expecting one of the following:

   ( - + all mod null <an identifier>
   <a double-quoted delimited-identifier> <a bind variable>
   <a number> <a single-quoted SQL string> any avg count max min
   prior some sql stddev sum variance
```

There also are some tricks to debugging PL/SQL that I cover in Chapter 12 that you might
want to use. This definitely is not the most convenient development environment to work in,
but it is not impossible either. After you get used to what you have to do and the lack of robust
debugging facilities, you can become quite productive. There are some debugging facilities out
there, but they are not in all distributions of the database or require you to purchase third-
party tools.

One final note that, as a DBA, I have to make. When you create a stored procedure, you do
not have the option of specifying the tablespace in which you want the software to be stored.
That is because you do not have any options. Oracle stores the software in the SYSTEM tablespace.
The SYSTEM tablespace is the heart of your Oracle database, containing all the internal tables
that keep Oracle running. If you run out of space in your SYSTEM tablespace, you are in *deep*
trouble, and your instance will probably crash. Therefore, you should warn your DBA and keep
an eye on the amount of free space in the SYSTEM tablespace if you are writing a large amount
code in the form of stored procedures, functions, or triggers.

> **NOTE**
>
> Stored procedures are created in the SYSTEM tablespace. Make sure that there is enough
> room in this tablespace for your stored procedures; running out of space in this
> tablespace can cause serious problems for your database.

Accessing Stored Procedures and Functions

You cannot call stored procedures using SQL calls. They are designed to work with database
tables and other data objects. You have to be in a PL/SQL block to make a call to the functions
and procedures that you have just created or use a tool, such as Developer/2000, that

understands that it should look to the database for function calls that it does not know how to handle. The basic calling formats are simply the following:

```
absolute_it(x,y);     -- stored procedure call, x input, y output
z := absolute_it(x);  -- function call with x input
```

Stored procedures and functions have schema owners just like other database objects do. Therefore, if you are the superdev user, you could reference a stored procedure called BEST_PROC by typing:

```
best_proc
```

or

```
superdev.best_proc
```

Other users would have to use the superdev.best_proc form, unless you created a public synonym for them. In that case, they could simply call your procedure with BEST_PROC.

Stored procedures and functions are integrated into the Oracle security scheme. To execute a stored procedure or function, you need to have EXECUTE privilege on it. You can grant the execute privilege on your stored procedures to individuals or roles. You also can give everyone using the database access by using the public role:

```
grant execute on best_proc to public;
```

You do not have to grant security access to triggers because they fire automatically, regardless of the user who causes the event to occur. In effect, they are tied directly to the database tables on which they were created.

NOTE

When users execute a stored procedure, they are not using their own privilege set. They are using the privilege set of the person who owns the stored procedure or function. Therefore, if a DBA creates a stored procedure, even users with merely CREATE_SESSION privileges could be executing commands and accessing data that is normally restricted to the DBA. This creates opportunities for you to allow users to access sensitive data, but only in the controlled manner specified in your stored procedure. This prevents you from having to grant them outright access to that data. However, it also means that you have to be careful to put in appropriate controls when you are designing those procedures.

Finally, suppose that you want to know what software you have out there. Because you're using Oracle, you would use a SQL query to access a database view. The view that you would use is user_source. The following shows some examples of how to use this view:

```
SQL> select unique(name) from user_source;

NAME
-------------------------------
BOOK_SP_EXAMPLE
TESTING

SQL> select text from user_source where name = 'BOOK_SP_EXAMPLE';

TEXT
------------------------------------------------------------------
procedure book_sp_example
(in_employee_id IN number,
return_code OUT number,
return_status OUT number)
as
counter number;
begin
select count(*)
  into counter
  from employees;
if counter = 0 then
  return_status := 'Employees table is empty';
  return_code := 2;
else
  select count(*)
    into counter
    from employees
    where employee_id = in_employee_id;
  if counter = 0 then
    return_status := 'Employee ID not found';
    return_code := 3;

TEXT
------------------------------------------------------------------
  else
    delete from employees
      where employee_id = in_employee_id;
  end if;
end if;
return_status := 'success';
return_code := 0;
exception
when others then
  return_status := 'Exception raised '||substr(sqlerrm,1,30);
  return_code := 4;
end;

33 rows selected.
```

Summary

This chapter covered the concepts related to the ways in which Oracle lets you store business processing logic within the database as opposed to software written by traditional programming tools. I discussed the advantages of and the times when you would want to consider using these techniques. It's probably not a good idea to get to the point where all your software logic is stored in the database. Instead, you have to blend using database-stored software with your other programming tools to achieve a mix that makes the best use of each of the tools.

I also covered the concept of database constraints. These are rules that are applied directly to your tables to ensure that the data that is placed in the tables is "good." What is "good?" That is for your business processing rules and schema design to decide. The key is that there are a number of constraints that you can apply in the right circumstances, and they will guarantee that certain rules are enforced or else the data cannot be entered.

For more complicated algorithms, I covered the concepts of storing PL/SQL programs within the database. Depending on the calling format you desire, you can choose between stored procedures or functions. If you want software to be executed automatically by the database whenever certain database events occur (such as when a column in a particular table is updated), you also have the option of creating triggers.

All of these techniques are relatively easy to design and apply after you get the hang of PL/SQL and SQL. The facilities provided for creation and editing are not sophisticated, but they get the job done. Finally, you have some security and access considerations that you should think about as part of your design process.

15

Security in an Oracle Environment

by Lave Singh

This chapter examines the various options available for protecting the data in an Oracle database. Oracle provides a number of options, some of which may be more applicable to a particular environment than others. On a development database, security may be relatively lax because the data is not necessarily final. In a production environment, the level of security can vary depending on the type of data being held and the risk that someone might want to break into the system. For banking or military applications, obviously, a high degree of security is required. However, for a database that enables connections through the Internet (even through Web browser software such as the Oracle Power Browser), a lower level of security may be all that is required.

Oracle Users

At the core of security is the Oracle database user account—without an Oracle username there is no way (well, almost) that one can break into an Oracle database.

An Oracle database typically has a number of Oracle user accounts that were either created when the database was created (for example, the SYS and SYSTEM users) or created later by the database administrator. Before any objects on the Oracle database can be accessed, a user must make a connection to the Oracle database with a valid Oracle username and password. This is true regardless of which Oracle or non-Oracle tool is used to access the database.

Once created, an Oracle user has a number of privileges that allow him to create and modify database objects. The objects belong either to that Oracle user or to other Oracle users who explicitly permit their objects to be modified by others.

Once an Oracle user is given a username and password, he can connect to the Oracle database using any tool.

Creating, Altering, and Dropping Users

There is an old way and a new way for database administrators to create a user account. The old way, using the CONNECT, RESOURCE, and DBA roles, is described later in this chapter.

Oracle users can create their own database objects (if other requisite privileges have been given to the Oracle account) or use other Oracle users' objects (if the other users have given them this privilege).

Any further privileges given to the Oracle user account refer to the account's username.

CREATE USER

The CREATE USER command is a SQL command that can be used to define an Oracle account in the database. There are a number of additional options that can be specified when creating an Oracle user, but the only mandatory requirement is that the name of the new Oracle user be known.

Once an Oracle user account is created, it cannot be used until the user has at least one system privilege (system privileges are described in a later section). The CREATE SESSION system privilege allows the user to create a session against the Oracle database. This is the minimum level of privilege that a user account must have. Without the CREATE SESSION system privilege, the Oracle user account cannot be used.

> **NOTE**
>
> The CREATE USER command is not enough to create a functional Oracle user. The CREATE SESSION system privilege must also be given to the new user account.

In the following code example, a new Oracle user account is created and assigned the CREATE SESSION system privilege and then a valid connection is made to the database using the new username and password:

```
SQL> connect system/manager
Connected.
SQL> CREATE USER permjit IDENTIFIED BY lovely;

User created.

SQL> GRANT CREATE SESSION TO permjit;

Grant succeeded.

SQL> CONNECT permjit/lovely
Connected.
SQL> SELECT * FROM SYS.dual;

D
-
X
SQL>
```

The password for the Oracle user is held in the Oracle database in an encoded format in a hexadecimal string. You cannot decipher the text password from the hexadecimal string. If a user forgets her password, the database administrator cannot find out what the current password is but can assign a new password.

> **NOTE**
>
> Not even the database administrator can figure out the text password from its encrypted format.

The preceding example shows just the Oracle username and password being specified when the user is created. The following sections describe a number of additional options that can be specified by the database administrator.

Default Tablespace

When you first create an Oracle user, you can specify the default tablespace in which the user's objects are created. If the default tablespace is not specified, the user will have the SYSTEM tablespace assigned as the default location where his objects use storage. The DEFAULT TABLESPACE clause can be used as part of the CREATE USER statement to specify that the user's objects are to be placed in a tablespace other than SYSTEM. However, the Oracle user must also be assigned a quota that specifies how much storage the user can use in the tablespace.

The DEFAULT TABLESPACE may or may not be the location of the user's objects. For example, if the user creates a table and specifies the tablespace location of the table in the CREATE TABLE statement, the table is created in that tablespace (assuming the user has the quotas necessary in that tablespace).

> **CAUTION**
>
> In addition to specifying the DEFAULT TABLESPACE for a user, you must also give the user a quota of storage on that tablespace.

Temporary Tablespace

You can also specify the location of temporary segments that can be created by a new user. Remember that temporary segments are created when any sort-type operation requires additional space on the database.

Because temporary segments may be created and dropped frequently (depending on the nature of the application system), they can fragment the free storage in the tablespaces.

> **TIP**
>
> Temporary segments for all users should be created in a separate tablespace to avoid free space fragmentation in the other tablespaces.

Quotas

You can control how much storage can be used by each user's objects in the database. This is especially important in a development environment for preventing any one Oracle user from consuming all the free storage in the tablespaces.

With the CREATE USER command you can specify which tablespace the user has a quota for and how much storage he can use in that tablespace. The amount of storage allocated to that user can be used by any type of database object that takes up storage. If the amount of storage used exceeds the amount allocated to the user, an error message appears to explain that the user exceeded his quota. It is up to the user to either drop some objects or ask the database administrator to increase his quota on the tablespace.

If the database administrator decides that the Oracle user may use up all the free storage in the tablespace, the administrator can use the keyword UNLIMITED to indicate an infinite quota on that tablespace.

The quota may be exceeded either when the user creates an object or when an object attempts to use more storage by allocating an additional extent.

> **NOTE**
>
> Quotas are not necessary for the tablespace in which temporary segments are created.

The following code example shows an Oracle user being created with the additional options that affect the amount and location of storage available to that user:

```
CREATE USER fowler identified by alan
    DEFAULT TABLESPACE user_data
    TEMPORARY TABLESPACE temp_ts
    QUOTA 20K ON user_data
    QUOTA UNLIMITED ON scratch_area

/

User created.

SQL>
SQL> GRANT CREATE SESSION TO fowler;

Grant succeeded.

SQL>
```

The quota assigned to an Oracle user and the amount of storage currently used by an Oracle user can be seen by accessing the data dictionary view DBA_TS_QUOTAS. The following code example shows the quota currently assigned to the user fowler and the amount of storage used:

```
SQL> l
  1  SELECT *
  2  FROM   dba_ts_quotas
  3* WHERE  username = 'FOWLER'
SQL> /
```

```
TABLESPACE_NAME                 USERNAME      BYTES MAX_BYTES   BLOCKS MAX_BLOCKS
-----------------------------   ---------  -------- ---------   ------ ----------
USER_DATA                       FOWLER            0     20480        0         10
SCRATCH_AREA                    FOWLER            0        -1        0         -1

SQL>
```

The quota is shown as the number of bytes and in terms of Oracle blocks (the number of bytes divided by the Oracle block size currently in effect for the database). The bytes column shows the number of bytes currently used and the max bytes column shows the maximum number of bytes that the user can use in that tablespace. By taking the bytes away from the max bytes column, you can see how much more storage the Oracle user has in that tablespace. The -1 in the max bytes column indicates that the unlimited quota option has been used on that tablespace.

Which Oracle Users Exist

The names for user accounts can be obtained by querying the DBA_USERS data dictionary view. Other details about user account setups must be accessed from different data dictionary views (for example, DBA_TS_QUOTAS for information about the quotas on tablespaces for that user).

The following code example reveals details about an Oracle user:

```
SQL> l
  1  SELECT username, user_id, password, default_tablespace, temporary_tablespace,
  2         created
  3  FROM   dba_users
  4* WHERE  username = 'FOWLER'
SQL> /

USERNAME USER_ID PASSWORD          DEFAULT_TABLESPACE TEMPORARY_TABLESPACE CREATED
-------- ------- ---------------   ------------------ -------------------- ---------
FOWLER   16      A559F1E82BEB8C1E  USER_DATA          USER_DATA            08-MAY-96

SQL>
```

The user id column shows a sequence number that increases for each new user account; the password column shows the encrypted form of the password. The created column shows when the user was first set up.

ALTER USER

You can use the ALTER USER command to change such user settings as the password, the default and temporary tablespaces, and the storage quota.

The following code example changes the user's password and other settings:

```
SQL> ALTER USER fowler
  2  IDENTIFIED BY waterhouse
  3  DEFAULT TABLESPACE user_data
  4  TEMPORARY TABLESPACE user_data
  5  QUOTA 60K ON user_data;

User altered.

SQL>
```

If you increase a user's quota, the new maximum storage amount includes the storage already allocated for that user's own objects. It is not an additional amount of storage that he can use, but a new maximum figure that takes effect. If you decrease the quota or set it to zero, the user cannot allocate any more storage for its objects. Objects that the user has already created and the storage allocated to them are not affected.

The following code example prevents the Oracle user `fowler` from using any more storage on the database:

```
SQL> ALTER USER fowler
  2  QUOTA 0 ON user_data;

User altered.

SQL>
```

The database administrator can change any user's password. Any user can change her own password with the ALTER USER command. However, without the necessary privileges, ordinary users cannot change anyone else's password with the ALTER USER command.

The following code example shows how a user changes her own password:

```
SQL> CONNECT fowler/waterhouse
Connected.
SQL> ALTER USER fowler
  2  IDENTIFIED BY price;

User altered.

SQL>
```

In practice, an ordinary Oracle user needs access to a tool such as SQL*Plus before she can issue the preceding command. For end users, a screen program may be provided that prompts the user for the new password and then issues the ALTER USER command to the database.

DROP USER

To delete a user from the database, you use the DROP USER command to remove the user from the Oracle data dictionary; this prevents anyone else from using the account. All trace of the Oracle user is removed from the DBA_USERS data dictionary view.

If the Oracle user owns any database objects, you can either drop each of the objects before using the DROP USER command or use the CASCADE option with DROP USER to drop all objects automatically when the user account is removed.

The following code example shows an attempt to remove an Oracle user that owns some tables. The DROP USER command fails and then is retried with the CASCADE option to automatically remove all objects owned by the user.

```
SQL> SELECT user_id
  2  FROM    dba_users
  3  WHERE   username = 'PERMJIT';

  USER_ID
---------
       14

SQL> DROP USER permjit;
DROP USER permjit
*
ERROR at line 1:
ORA-01922: CASCADE must be specified to drop 'PERMJIT'


SQL> DROP USER permjit CASCADE;

User dropped.

SQL> SELECT *
  2  FROM    dba_users
  3  WHERE   username = 'PERMJIT';

no rows selected

SQL>
```

All synonyms, views, and so on created by other Oracle users on the dropped user's objects are no longer usable. They still exist, but any attempts to use them result in an error message.

CONNECT, RESOURCE, and DBA

Another way of creating an Oracle user is to grant the user the CONNECT, RESOURCE, and DBA roles (roles are discussed in more detail in a later section). Although this method is quick, it is included primarily for backwards compatibility with previous versions of the Oracle RDBMS software. The CREATE USER command is the preferred method because both quota and other settings can be performed in one command.

The following code example shows a new Oracle user being created by granting the CONNECT, RESOURCE, and DBA roles:

```
SQL> GRANT CONNECT, RESOURCE, DBA
  2  TO    kal
  3  IDENTIFIED BY kal;
```

```
Grant succeeded.

SQL> CONNECT kal/kal
Connected.
SQL>
```

CAUTION

The RESOURCE privilege gives the user the UNLIMITED TABLESPACE privilege, which enables the user to use as much storage space in whatever tablespace is desired.

The CREATE SESSION privilege does not need to be explicitly given to a new Oracle user created using this method.

Sharing Usernames and Passwords

When an Oracle user is created, no default limit exists for the number of connections that can be made with the user's name and password. Many people, possibly using different tools, can use the same username and password to connect to the database. This is fine as far as locking and database integrity is concerned; however, it's not a good idea in respect to auditing and is certainly not very secure. Locking is performed at the session level so that even if two people decide to use the same username to connect to the database, they are seen as two sessions and only one at a time can lock the same row.

On development and some production systems, you often find different people logged in under the same username at the same time. It makes the job of a database administrator a little more difficult because the administrator does not know exactly who is connecting to the database.

If you want to limit the number of connections that can be made using a particular username and password, you use Oracle *profiles*. Profiles are discussed in more detail in the "Profiles" section near the end of this chapter.

Externally Identified User

Externally identified user accounts (also known as *proxy* accounts) provide a quick way of connecting to the Oracle database. An Externally Identified account allows you to connect to the database without specifying an Oracle username and password (you use the forward slash / instead). The Oracle username to which you connect is based on the operating system username you used to log in to the machine from that you're connecting to the Oracle database. No password is needed for the Oracle account, meaning that this account is not secure. You must be logged in to the correct operating system account before you can use the forward slash to connect to the right Oracle account.

By default, an externally identified user must be prefixed by the OPS$ string, but the database administrator can change this to another string (or nothing at all) using the OS_AUTHENT_PREFIX INIT.ORA parameter file setting.

The following example shows how an externally identified Oracle user called OPS$SINGH is created, and how a database connection is then made using the forward slash. This example assumes that you are connected to the operating system (for example, UNIX) using the SINGH operating system account.

```
SQL> CREATE USER OPS$singh IDENTIFIED EXTERNALLY
  2  /

User created.

SQL> GRANT CREATE SESSION
  2  TO    ops$singh;

Grant succeeded.

SQL> SQL> CONNECT /

Connected.
SQL>
```

Once the externally identified Oracle user exists, it can issue the same commands as other Oracle users.

CAUTION

Externally identified Oracle accounts are not secure. They should not be used where security is important.

Externally identified accounts are found mostly where a dumb-terminal type of connection is made to an Oracle database (for example, where you use a dumb-terminal connection to a UNIX machine). It is uncommon to find externally identified accounts being used in a client/server environment.

Different Types of Privileges

Once you create an Oracle user, the user account isn't worth much unless it can create its own database objects or access objects created by another Oracle account. In this section, you look at system- and object-level privileges that control in fine detail what an Oracle user account can do.

System-Level Privileges

There are more than 80 different system-level privileges that control an Oracle user's ability to use some SQL commands. For example, before an Oracle user can use the CREATE PROCEDURE command to create database procedures, the user needs to have the CREATE PROCEDURE system-level privilege.

Which System Privileges Exist?

There are two major groups of system-level privileges—those that have the word ANY as part of their name and those that don't. Privileges with the word ANY in their names allow Oracle users to perform specific commands in any Oracle user account. For example, the CREATE ANY PROCEDURE system privilege allows an Oracle user to create procedures in any Oracle account as if the procedure belonged to the user's account.

If an Oracle user does not have the system privilege for a command and he attempts to run the command, the following code sequence shows the type of error message that is returned:

```
SQL> CREATE TABLE can_i_do_it(dummy NUMBER);
CREATE TABLE can_i_do_it(dummy NUMBER)
*
ERROR at line 1:
ORA-01031: insufficient privileges

SQL>
```

The preceding code example shows the error that appears if the user attempts to create a table—even if you gave the CREATE TABLE system privilege to the user, he still needs to have some quotas on tablespaces.

Granting of System Privileges

System-level privileges can be given either directly to an Oracle user or to a role that has been assigned to an Oracle user (roles are discussed later).

To give a system-level privilege directly to a user, you can use the following version of the GRANT statement:

```
SQL> GRANT CREATE TABLE,
  2        CREATE PROCEDURE,
  3        CREATE TRIGGER
  4  TO    permjit;

Grant succeeded.

SQL>
```

After the preceding code runs, the Oracle user permjit can use the CREATE TABLE (assuming quotas have been given), CREATE PROCEDURE, and CREATE TRIGGER commands to create database triggers.

If you want to give a system-level privilege to every Oracle user (including any future Oracle users that may be created), you can give the system privilege to PUBLIC, which means every Oracle user.

The last example shows the CREATE PROCEDURE system privilege being given to everyone on the database.

```
SQL> GRANT CREATE PROCEDURE
  2  TO    PUBLIC;

Grant succeeded.

SQL>
```

Once the privilege has been given to PUBLIC, individual users cannot be stopped from using it.

System-level privileges can also be given to an Oracle user by using the WITH ADMIN OPTION clause at the end of the GRANT statement. This allows the Oracle user who receives the system privilege to pass the privilege on to any other Oracle user. Essentially, she become another administrator of that system privilege.

The following code example shows a system-level privilege being given to an Oracle user through the WITH ADMIN OPTION and then shows that user passing the privilege on to another user:

```
SQL> GRANT CREATE PROCEDURE
  2  TO    permjit
  3  WITH ADMIN OPTION;

Grant succeeded.

SQL> CONNECT permjit/lovely
Connected.
SQL> GRANT CREATE PROCEDURE TO ascend;

Grant succeeded.

SQL>
```

Revoking System Privileges

To take a system-level privilege away from an Oracle user (or role, as discussed later), you use the REVOKE command. More than one system privilege and username can be specified at one time in the command.

The following command shows two system privileges being removed from two Oracle user accounts. The second example shows a system-level privilege being removed from the PUBLIC user.

```
SQL> REVOKE CREATE PROCEDURE, CREATE TRIGGER
  2  FROM   permjit, fowler;

Revoke succeeded.
```

```
SQL> REVOKE CREATE PROCEDURE
  2  FROM   PUBLIC;

Revoke succeeded.

SQL>
```

Any objects created while the system privilege was in effect are not affected when the system privilege is revoked. In addition, if the system privilege is taken away from the PUBLIC user, other users who were granted the system privilege directly are not affected.

Any Oracle user granted the system privilege through the WITH ADMIN OPTION can revoke the system privilege from other Oracle users—they are, in effect, additional administrators of the system privilege.

Checking Which System Privileges Exist

System privileges can be given either directly to users or to a role that is then given to a user. (Roles are discussed later.) If a system privilege is given directly to an Oracle user, the user can check which system privileges it has by accessing the USER_SYS_PRIVS data dictionary view. The database administrator can use the DBA_SYS_PRIVS data dictionary view to check privileges for all Oracle users in the database.

The following example shows an Oracle user checking which system privileges it has been granted:

```
SQL> SELECT *
  2  FROM   user_sys_privs;

USERNAME                         PRIVILEGE                                  ADM
-------------------------------- ------------------------------------------ ---
PERMJIT                          CREATE SESSION                             NO
PERMJIT                          CREATE TABLE                               NO

SQL>
```

The ADM column in the preceding example shows whether the user is allowed to administer the system privilege (that is, GRANT and REVOKE the privilege from other Oracle users).

Object-Level Privileges

When an Oracle user owns a database object, such as a table, other Oracle users can be allowed to use that object by granting them one or more object-level privileges. For example, if the Oracle user ascend wants to allow the Oracle user permjit to use his table, but only to INSERT or UPDATE rows, then UPDATE and INSERT privileges can be given to permjit.

Granting of Object-Level Privileges

The GRANT statement can be used to give one or more object-level privileges to one or more Oracle users. If you want to give the object-level privilege to all Oracle users in the database, you can give it to the PUBLIC user. In addition, object-level privileges can be given to a role that is then given to an Oracle user—an indirect and sometimes simpler way of giving privileges.

The following code example shows two object-level privileges being granted to the permjit Oracle user; only those two operations are allowed on the table:

```
SQL> SHOW USER
user is "ASCEND"
SQL> GRANT SELECT,UPDATE
  2  ON     delegates
  3  TO     permjit;

Grant succeeded.

SQL> CONNECT permjit/lovely
Connected.
SQL> SELECT COUNT(*)
  2  FROM   ascend.delegates;

 COUNT(*)
---------
       12

SQL> UPDATE ascend.delegates
  2  SET    d_lastname = 'Smith'
  3  WHERE  d_delegate_id = 3;

1 row updated.

SQL> DELETE FROM ascend.delegates
  2  WHERE  d_delegate_id = 3;
DELETE FROM ascend.delegates
                  *
ERROR at line 1:
ORA-01031: insufficient privileges


SQL>
```

The GRANT command is used in the same way as for system-level privileges, but object-level privileges are granted rather than system privileges.

> **TIP**
>
> To avoid having to hard-code the identity of the table owner, as in the preceding example, synonyms can be used.

Which Object-Level Privileges Exist?

The following table shows the object-level privileges that can be granted to an Oracle user, and which types of database objects they affect.

Privilege	Tables	Views	Sequences	Procedure / Function / Package	Snapshot
SELECT	x	x	x		x
INSERT	x	x			
UPDATE	x	x			
DELETE	x	x			
EXECUTE				x	
ALTER	x		x		
INDEX	x				
REFERENCES	x				

SELECT

The SELECT object-level privilege allows another Oracle user to query data in the table. If this privilege is given, the Oracle user can query any column on any row in the table.

Views can be used to restrict which columns and which rows can be queried.

INSERT

The INSERT object-level privilege enables another Oracle user to INSERT rows into the table. Database constraints and triggers are checked as if the change were made by the table owner.

With the INSERT object-level privilege, you can control which columns can be inserted; NOT NULL columns are usually included in the list of columns.

The following code example shows the INSERT object-level privilege being given to another Oracle user, but that Oracle user can only populate two columns on a new row. If the user attempts to populate columns for which they do not have the necessary privileges, an error message appears.

```
SQL> desc delegates
 Name                            Null?    Type
 ------------------------------- -------- ----
 D_DELEGATE_ID                   NOT NULL NUMBER(5)
 D_LASTNAME                      NOT NULL VARCHAR2(20)
 D_FIRSTNAME                              VARCHAR2(20)
 D_ORGANISATION                           VARCHAR2(20)
 D_SEX                                    VARCHAR2(1)
 D_DATE_LAST_CONTACTED                    DATE
```

```
SQL> l
  1* GRANT INSERT(d_delegate_id,d_lastname) ON delegates TO permjit
SQL> /

Grant succeeded.

SQL> CONNECT permjit/permjit
Connected.
SQL> INSERT INTO ascend.delegates(d_delegate_id, d_lastname, d_firstname)
  2        VALUES (999,'Disteldorf','Terry');
INSERT INTO ascend.delegates(d_delegate_id, d_lastname, d_firstname)
                       *
ERROR at line 1:
ORA-01031: insufficient privileges


SQL> l
  1  INSERT INTO ascend.delegates(d_delegate_id, d_lastname)
  2*        VALUES(999,'Disteldorf')
SQL> /

1 row created.

SQL>
```

UPDATE

The UPDATE object-level privilege allows an Oracle user to update rows in a table—whether or not those rows were originally created by the Oracle user. In fact, when the UPDATE privilege is given to an Oracle user, the user can UPDATE any row in the table. (Views can be used to restrict which rows may be modified.)

With the UPDATE privilege, you can control exactly which columns the user is allowed to populate.

The following code example shows the UPDATE privilege being granted to another Oracle user; that user is only allowed to UPDATE two columns in the table. If she attempts to UPDATE columns for which she does not have the necessary privileges, she receives an error message.

```
SQL> GRANT UPDATE(d_firstname)
  2  ON     delegates
  3  TO     permjit;

Grant succeeded.

SQL>
SQL> CONNECT permjit/permjit
Connected.
SQL> UPDATE ascend.delegates
  2  SET    d_sex = 'X'
  3  WHERE  d_delegate_id = 3;
UPDATE ascend.delegates
               *
ERROR at line 1:
ORA-01031: insufficient privileges
```

```
SQL> UPDATE ascend.delegates
  2  SET    d_firstname = 'Test'
  3  WHERE  d_delegate_id =3;

1 row updated.

SQL>
```

DELETE

The DELETE object-level privilege enables the deletion of any existing rows from the table. By using views, you can restrict which rows can be deleted.

EXECUTE

The EXCECUTE privilege enables an Oracle user who owns database procedural code (procedures, functions, or packages) to allow other Oracle users to call his procedural objects.

When called, the procedure affects and works on the tables and other objects it was created against.

The following code example shows the creation of a procedure that returns the number of bookings that currently exist in the database. Another Oracle user is allowed to call the procedure.

```
SQL> l
  1  CREATE OR REPLACE PROCEDURE num_bookings
  2          (p_total OUT NUMBER) IS
  3  BEGIN
  4     SELECT COUNT(*)
  5     INTO   p_total
  6     FROM   bookings;
  7* END;
SQL> /

Procedure created.

SQL> GRANT EXECUTE
  2  ON     num_bookings
  3  TO     permjit;

Grant succeeded.

SQL> CONNECT permjit/permjit
Connected.
SQL> SET SERVEROUT ON

SQL> DECLARE
  2     v_total    NUMBER(4);
  3  BEGIN
  4     ascend.num_bookings(v_total);
  5     DBMS_OUTPUT.PUT_LINE('Total Returned is '||v_total);
  6  END;
  7  .
SQL>/
SQL> /
Total Returned is 8
```

```
PL/SQL procedure successfully completed.

SQL> SELECT COUNT(*)
  2  FROM    ascend.bookings;
FROM    ascend.bookings
               *
ERROR at line 2:
ORA-00942: table or view does not exist

SQL>
```

As the preceding example shows, the procedure can be called, but the table that the procedure uses cannot be accessed directly by the user.

You don't have to grant any privileges on tables and other database objects used by a procedure, function, or package if you use the EXECUTE privilege to allow another Oracle user to call the procedural object.

Functions and packages are treated in the same way as procedures as far as the granting of privileges is concerned.

ALTER

The ALTER object-level privilege enables an Oracle user to alter the definition of a table or a sequence. The owner of the object does not usually allow other Oracle users to change the definition of the object. This option is not used often.

INDEX

The INDEX object-level privilege allows another Oracle user to create indexes on the owner's tables. This affects the performance of the DML statements against the table. The owner of the object does not usually allow other Oracle users to change the definition of the object. This option is not used often.

REFERENCES

The REFERENCES object-level privilege enables an Oracle user to reference another user's objects. For example, one Oracle user might need to set up some foreign key constraints on another user's table.

The following code example shows the REFERENCES privilege allowing another Oracle user to create a foreign key to a table:

```
SQL> GRANT REFERENCES
  2  ON     delegates
  3  TO     permjit;
```

```
Grant succeeded.

SQL> CONNECT permjit/permjit
Connected.
SQL> CREATE TABLE delegate_payments
  2      (dp_delegate_id     NUMBER(5) NOT NULL
  3            REFERENCES ascend.delegates(d_delegate_id)
  4      ,dp_payment_date    DATE NOT NULL
  5      ,dp_payment_amt     NUMBER(6,2)
  6      )
  7  .
SQL> /

Table created.

SQL>
```

The REFERENCES object-level privilege is more likely to be used in either development environments or large production applications where a number of different Oracle users own tables.

ALL

If you want to quickly give all object privileges to another Oracle user, you use the keyword ALL to avoid having to specify each privilege individually.

The following code example shows all the object-level privileges being given to an Oracle user:

```
SQL> GRANT ALL
  2  ON      delegates
  3  TO      permjit;

Grant succeeded.

SQL>
```

The Oracle user permjit has all the previously discussed object-level privileges available on the delegate table after the preceding command is executed.

WITH GRANT OPTION

The WITH GRANT OPTION clause can be specified at the end of the GRANT statement for an object-level privilege that allows the Oracle user who receives the privilege to pass it on to another Oracle user. This option is not used a great deal because the owner of the object loses complete control over the object.

The following code example shows the WITH GRANT OPTION clause being used with an object privilege:

```
SQL> GRANT SELECT,UPDATE
  2  ON      delegates
  3  TO      permjit
  4  WITH GRANT OPTION
  5  /

Grant succeeded.
```

```
SQL> CONNECT permjit/permjit
Connected.
SQL> GRANT SELECT,UPDATE
  2  ON     ascend.delegates
  3  TO     OPS$singh;

Grant succeeded.

SQL>
```

Revoking Object-Level Privileges

If you want to remove an object-level privilege from one or more Oracle users, use the REVOKE command.

The following code example shows the person who granted the object-level privilege revoking another Oracle user's ability to use the object:

```
SQL> REVOKE SELECT, UPDATE
  2  ON      ascend.delegates
  3  FROM    permjit;

Revoke succeeded.

SQL>
```

> **CAUTION**
>
> Once an object-level privilege has been granted to the PUBLIC user, individual users cannot be stopped from using that privilege. To revoke the privilege, it must be revoked from the PUBLIC user.

Using the REVOKE command to remove an object-level privilege prevents application programs that require the privilege from running.

Checking Which Object-Level Privileges Exist

There are a number of data dictionary views that show which object-level privileges have been given directly to a user and which privileges have been granted by another user.

The USER_TAB_PRIVS data dictionary view shows the object-level privileges that have either been granted or received by the Oracle user. The USER_COL_PRIVS data dictionary view shows the object-level privileges where granted or received by the Oracle user at the column level (INSERT, UPDATE, and REFERENCES privileges can be implemented to the column level).

The TABLE_PRIVILEGES data dictionary view shows the full list of object-level privileges associated with the user, regardless of whether the privilege is given directly to the user or is available through a role. This view changes depending on which database roles are currently enabled. In the same manner, the COLUMN_PRIVILEGES data dictionary view shows all column-level privileges currently in effect for the current user.

There are other data dictionary views beginning with ALL_ (indicating privileges for all objects to which the user has access), and DBA_ (indicating all privileges across the entire database).

Using Views with Object-Level Privileges

With the SELECT, INSERT, UPDATE, and DELETE object-level privileges you cannot restrict which rows the receiver of the privilege can work with. The columns that can be populated or updated can be controlled, but this applies to the columns in all the rows in the table.

Using views, you can restrict the privileges to certain columns and certain rows in the table. Once a view has been created on the database objects, the view can be used in GRANT statements that give object-level privileges.

The following code example shows a view being used to control columns and rows that can be affected by the delegates table:

```
SQL> CREATE OR REPLACE VIEW titanium_delegates
  2  AS
  3    SELECT d_organisation,
  4            d_firstname,
  5            d_lastname
  6    FROM    delegates
  7    WHERE   d_organisation = 'Titanium'
  8    WITH CHECK OPTION;
View created.

SQL> GRANT SELECT,UPDATE
  2  ON     titanium_delegates
  3  TO     permjit;

Grant succeeded.

SQL> CONNECT permjit/permjit
Connected.
SQL> SELECT *
  2  FROM    ascend.titanium_delegates;

D_ORGANISATION       D_FIRSTNAME           D_LASTNAME
-------------------- --------------------- --------------------
Titanium             Kashmir               Kaur
Titanium             Benisha               Kaur
Titanium             Taejen                Singh

SQL> UPDATE ascend.titanium_delegates
  2  SET    d_firstname = 'Jazz'
  3  WHERE  d_lastname = 'Singh';

SQL> /

1 row updated.
```

```
SQL> UPDATE ascend.titanium_delegates
  2  SET    d_organisation = 'Ascend';
SET    d_organisation = 'Ascend'
                            *
ERROR at line 2:
ORA-01402: view WITH CHECK OPTION where-clause violation

SQL>
```

As the preceding example shows, only some of the columns and rows are visible and can be updated through the view. The WITH CHECK OPTION clause ensures that the rows cannot be updated if they will not again be visible through the view (that is, the WHERE clause must be satisfied).

The view must be simple, not complex, before changes can be made through it.

Roles

A role is a collection of system and object-level privileges that have been grouped together under one name to make the granting and revoking of these privileges easier and simpler. Once an Oracle user has been given a role, all the privileges associated with that role are inherited by the user.

Why Roles?

As you learn in this section, roles can offer benefits such as an easier way to grant system and object-level privileges, the capability to establish security privileges even before a user exists, and a simplified method to enable and disable user privileges.

Easier Grants

One way of granting system and object-level privileges is to grant each privilege required to every single user who needs it. Running a GRANT statement for each privilege required by each user could become time-consuming when there is a large number of tables or users.

Instead, you can create a role to logically group the users and assign the privileges required to the role. You can then assign the role to the different Oracle users, resulting in fewer GRANT statements.

Set Up Security Before Users Exist

If you want to set up security privileges before creating Oracle users, you can do it by creating a role and giving the privileges to the role (for example, a manager role). When an Oracle user account has been created that requires the privileges, you assign the role to the user with one simple GRANT statement.

In addition, if the Oracle user is removed from the database with the DROP USER command, you can keep the privileges that were given to him if the privileges were assigned through a role. You can then reassign the privileges to any new user that requires the same set. If the privileges were not originally assigned through a role, all record of them is lost when the first user is dropped.

Enabling and Disabling

With roles, the set of the privileges assigned to a user can be turned off and on by enabling and disabling the roles. For example, when the user interacts with a screen program, that program turns on a particular set of privileges required for the screen. For a report program, a different set of privileges can be turned on.

Operating System Authenticated

Another benefit of database roles is that you can ensure that the Oracle user has some operating system privileges before the role is enabled. This means that some of the security can be controlled at the operating system level.

The way that this is implemented varies from one operating system to another. For example, on a UNIX platform UNIX groups are used; on a VAX VMS platform process rights are required at the operating system level.

Hierarchies of Roles

Roles can be assigned to other roles as well as to Oracle users, and to the PUBLIC predefined username. If a new role needs the same set of privileges as another, already created role, the existing role's privileges can be assigned to the other. The higher-level role inherits all the privileges of the lower-level role (that is, a role that receives a role inherits all the privileges given to the role it received). Any user given the higher-level role inherits all the privileges given to both roles. There is a limit to the number of roles that can be active at any one time, and the database administrator can configure this number using the INIT.ORA parameter file.

Password Protection

You can specify that a password must be provided before a role's privileges can be enabled.

Creating, Altering, and Dropping Roles

Before you can assign privileges to a role, the role must be created in the database.

Creating a Role

The CREATE ROLE SQL command can be used to create a database role. Roles' names must not conflict with the names of any Oracle users already created in the database.

The following example shows the creation of a role that will be assigned privileges:

```
SQL> CREATE ROLE salesperson;

Role created.

SQL>
```

The following code example shows the creation of a password-protected role:

```
SQL> CREATE ROLE manager
  2  IDENTIFIED BY secret;

Role created.

SQL>
```

A role can be protected further by ensuring that the user must have specific operating system privileges before the role can be enabled. Check the Oracle *Installation and User's Guide* for your platform to see how this feature has been implemented on your machine and operating system.

The following code example shows the creation of an operating system-protected role:

```
SQL> CREATE ROLE accountant
  2  IDENTIFIED EXTERNALLY;

Role created.

SQL>
```

Altering a Role

Once a role has been created, the role's setup can be changed, as shown in the following example:

```
SQL> ALTER ROLE manager NOT IDENTIFIED;

Role altered.

SQL> ALTER ROLE salesperson
  2  IDENTIFIED BY secret;

Role altered.

SQL>
```

Dropping a Role

To remove a role from an Oracle database, you do not need to revoke it from any Oracle users or roles to which it has been granted. This happens automatically.

The following code example shows the definition of a role being removed from the database:

```
SQL> DROP ROLE accountant;

Role dropped.

SQL>
```

If the role is re-created, you must reassign the role to the Oracle users who originally had it assigned to them.

Giving System and Object Privileges to Roles

The way that system-level and object-level privileges are granted to roles is similar to the way that these privileges are given to ordinary Oracle users: The name of the role is used where the username would have been used.

The following code example shows system- and object-level privileges being assigned to a role:

```
SQL> show user
user is "SYSTEM"
SQL> GRANT CREATE TABLE, CREATE PROCEDURE
  2  TO     manager;

Grant succeeded.

SQL> CONNECT ascend/ascend
Connected.
SQL> GRANT SELECT,UPDATE
  2  ON     delegates
  3  TO     manager;

Grant succeeded.

SQL>
```

You cannot tell by looking at the GRANT statements above whether the recipient of the privilege is an Oracle username or a role name—the syntax is the same for both.

Granting and Revoking Roles

Roles can be granted to Oracle users, to other roles, or to the PUBLIC user if you want everyone on the database to have the role.

Granting Roles

Roles are assigned using the same version of the GRANT statement that is used for giving system privileges.

The following code example shows a role being assigned to two different Oracle users:

```
SQL> GRANT salesperson
  2  TO     permjit, fowler;

Grant succeeded.

SQL>
```

Roles can be assigned with the WITH ADMIN OPTION just like system-level privileges. Whoever receives the role with the WITH ADMIN OPTION can administer the role and grant the role to other Oracle users.

The following code example shows the assignment of a role with the WITH ADMIN option; the recipient can then give the role to another Oracle user.

```
SQL> GRANT manager
  2  TO     permjit
  3  WITH ADMIN OPTION;

Grant succeeded.

SQL> CONNECT permjit/permjit
Connected.
SQL> GRANT manager
  2  TO     ops$singh;

Grant succeeded.

SQL> GRANT salesperson
  2  TO     ops$singh;
GRANT salesperson
*
ERROR at line 1:
ORA-01932: ADMIN option not granted for role 'SALESPERSON'

SQL>
```

If the Oracle user did not receive the role with the WITH ADMIN option, the user cannot give the role to other Oracle users or roles (see the salesperson role in the preceding example).

The following code example shows the creation of a another role that has the two existing roles assigned to it.

```
SQL> CREATE ROLE big_chief
  2  ;

Role created.

SQL> GRANT manager, salesperson
  2  TO     big_chief;

Grant succeeded.

SQL>
```

If the two existing roles are assigned to the new role, the new role automatically inherits all privileges for these two lower-level roles. Now you need only be concerned with any additional privileges required by the new role.

Revoking Roles

The syntax of the REVOKE command for revoking roles is very similar to the syntax for revoking system-level privileges.

The following code example shows the removal of one role from another and the removal of a role from an Oracle user:

```
SQL> REVOKE manager
  2  FROM   big_chief;

Revoke succeeded.

SQL>
SQL> REVOKE manager
  2  FROM   permjit;

Revoke succeeded.
```

Enabling and Disabling Roles

Once an Oracle user has been given a set of roles, the privileges provided by them can be turned on and off (usually by application programs) by enabling and disabling the roles. This feature allows for even more flexibility in the way that privileges are used.

From the SQL*Plus tool, you can use the SET ROLE command. From other application tools, you can call the packaged procedure dbms_session.set_role to perform the same operation from a PL/SQL block.

With the SET ROLE command, if any roles are protected by passwords, the password must be provided when the role is enabled.

The following code example shows roles being set on and off by an Oracle user:

```
SQL> GRANT manager, salesperson
  2  TO    permjit;

Grant succeeded.

SQL> CONNECT permjit/permjit
Connected.
SQL> SELECT * FROM SESSION_ROLES;

ROLE
-------------------------------
SALESPERSON
MANAGER
```

```
SQL> SET ROLE manager;

Role set.

SQL> SELECT *
  2  FROM   session_roles;

ROLE
- - - - - - - - - - - - - - - - - - - - - - - - - - - -
MANAGER

SQL> SET ROLE manager, salesperson IDENTIFIED BY secret;

Role set.

SQL> SELECT *
  2  FROM   session_roles;

ROLE
- - - - - - - - - - - - - - - - - - - - - - - - - - - -
MANAGER
SALESPERSON

SQL>
```

The preceding example shows that when the SET ROLE command is used, only the roles mentioned in the command are enabled; all others are turned off.

CAUTION

The SET ROLE command is a toggle switch—it disables all roles and then explicitly enables specific ones.

Additional options for the SET ROLE command provide other ways to quickly enable and disable the roles granted to an Oracle user. Obviously, only those roles that have already been granted to the Oracle user can be turned off and on.

The following code example shows another way of quickly enabling and disabling roles assigned to an Oracle user:

```
SQL> SET ROLE ALL
  2  EXCEPT salesperson;

Role set.

SQL> SELECT *
  2  FROM   session_roles;

ROLE
- - - - - - - - - - - - - - - - - - - - - - - - - - - -
MANAGER

SQL> SET ROLE NONE;
```

```
Role set.

SQL> SELECT *
  2  FROM   session_roles;

no rows selected

SQL>
```

O/S-Enabled Roles

A role that is identified externally can be enabled only with the SET ROLE command when the Oracle user attempting to enable it has the necessary operating system privileges (for example, the user is a member of a specific UNIX group or, on a VAX VMS platform, has the process rights).

Default Roles for a User

When an Oracle user connects to the database, all the roles that have been assigned to the user are, by default, enabled. The default roles for a user can be changed with the ALTER USER SQL command so that the non-default roles must be explicitly enabled before the privileges that they give can be used.

```
SQL> ALTER USER permjit
  2  DEFAULT ROLE salesperson;

User altered.

SQL> CONNECT permjit/permjit
Connected.
SQL> SELECT *
  2  FROM   session_roles;

ROLE
------------------------------
SALESPERSON


SQL> SET ROLE manager, salesperson IDENTIFIED BY secret;

Role set.

SQL> SELECT *
  2  FROM   session_roles;

ROLE
------------------------------
MANAGER
SALESPERSON

SQL>
```

As you can see from the preceding example, when a user connects to the database, only default roles are enabled automatically but others can be enabled manually. If the end user does not have access to a tool that allows her to manually enable roles, the enabling can be done by the application system through program code hidden from the user.

Predefined Roles

Five roles are automatically created along with a new database. They are CONNECT, RE-SOURCE, DBA, EXP_FULL_DATABASE, and IMP_FULL_DATABASE. The first three are provided for compatibility with previous versions of the Oracle RDBMS software and are not typically needed.

The EXP_FULL_DATABASE and IMP_FULL_DATABASE roles can be given to an Oracle user that is to perform a full export or import of the database, without giving the user the full set of database administrator commands. This was not possible in previous versions of Oracle.

On some operating systems there are two additional roles created—SYSOPER and SYSDBA. These roles can be given to any Oracle user that wants to administer and manage an Oracle database. They both include a subset of the set of system privileges required for a database administrator (including the ability to start up and shut down the database).

Data Dictionary Views for Roles

There are a number of different data dictionary views that show information about roles and how they have been set up in the database.

You can find out the names of all roles in the database and whether they are password protected by querying the DBA_ROLES data dictionary view, as shown in the following code example.

```
SQL> SELECT *
  2  FROM   dba_roles;

ROLE                             PASSWORD
-------------------------------- --------
CONNECT                          NO
RESOURCE                         NO
DBA                              NO
EXP_FULL_DATABASE                NO
IMP_FULL_DATABASE                NO
MANAGER                          NO
SALESPERSON                      YES
BIG_CHIEF                        NO

8 rows selected.

SQL>
```

You can find out which roles have been given to which Oracle users, whether the role can be administered by the user, and whether the role is a default role by querying the

DBA_ROLE_PRIVS data dictionary view, as shown in the following example. However, this data dictionary view shows only those roles assigned directly to users; there may be lower-level roles granted to one of these roles that the user can also use.

```
SQL> SELECT * FROM DBA_ROLE_PRIVS;

GRANTEE                          GRANTED_ROLE                     ADM DEF
-------------------------------- -------------------------------- --- ---
ASCEND                           CONNECT                          NO  YES
ASCEND                           DBA                              NO  YES
ASCEND                           RESOURCE                         NO  YES
BIG_CHIEF                        SALESPERSON                      NO  YES
DBA                              EXP_FULL_DATABASE                NO  YES
DBA                              IMP_FULL_DATABASE                NO  YES
DEMO                             CONNECT                          NO  YES
DEMO                             RESOURCE                         NO  YES
FOWLER                           SALESPERSON                      NO  YES
KAL                              CONNECT                          NO  YES
KAL                              DBA                              NO  YES
KAL                              RESOURCE                         NO  YES
OPS$SINGH                        MANAGER                          NO  YES
PERMJIT                          MANAGER                          NO  NO
PERMJIT                          SALESPERSON                      NO  YES
PO7                              DBA                              NO  YES
SCOTT                            CONNECT                          NO  YES
SCOTT                            DBA                              NO  YES
SCOTT                            RESOURCE                         NO  YES
SYS                              CONNECT                          YES YES
SYS                              DBA                              YES YES

GRANTEE                          GRANTED_ROLE                     ADM DEF
-------------------------------- -------------------------------- --- ---
SYS                              EXP_FULL_DATABASE                YES YES
SYS                              IMP_FULL_DATABASE                YES YES
SYS                              RESOURCE                         YES YES
SYSTEM                           BIG_CHIEF                        YES YES
SYSTEM                           DBA                              YES YES
SYSTEM                           MANAGER                          YES YES
SYSTEM                           SALESPERSON                      YES YES

28 rows selected.

SQL>
```

Information about which roles have been given to other roles in the database (the role hierarchy) can be queried from the ROLE_ROLE_PRIVS data dictionary view.

```
SQL> SELECT *
  2 FROM   role_role_privs;

ROLE                             GRANTED_ROLE                     ADM
-------------------------------- -------------------------------- ---
BIG_CHIEF                        SALESPERSON                      NO
DBA                              EXP_FULL_DATABASE                NO
DBA                              IMP_FULL_DATABASE                NO

SQL>
```

The set of system- and object-level privileges assigned to a role can be determined by the ROLE_SYS_PRIVS and the ROLE_TAB_PRIVS data dictionary views, as shown in the following example:

```
SQL> SELECT *
  2  FROM   role_sys_privs
  3  WHERE  role = 'MANAGER';

ROLE                            PRIVILEGE                                ADM
------------------------------- ---------------------------------------- ---
MANAGER                         CREATE PROCEDURE                         NO
MANAGER                         CREATE TABLE                             NO

SQL> SELECT *
  2  FROM   role_tab_privs
  3  WHERE  role = 'MANAGER';

ROLE                            OWNER                   TABLE_NAME
------------------------------- ----------------------- ----------------------
PRIVILEGE                                       GRA
----------------------------------------------- ---
MANAGER                         ASCEND                  DELEGATES
SELECT                                          NO

MANAGER                         ASCEND                  DELEGATES
UPDATE                                          NO

SQL>
```

If you want to find out which roles and which system- and object-level privileges are currently in effect for the user session, there are three more data dictionary views you can use: SESSION_ROLES, SESSION_PRIVS, and TABLE_PRIVILEGES.

These data dictionary views prevent you from having to check which privileges have been received through roles, those given directly to the user and those given to the PUBLIC user. They show what the user can do at the current time.

The following code fragment shows examples of these three data dictionary views:

```
SQL> SELECT *
  2  FROM   session_roles;

ROLE
------------------------------
SALESPERSON
MANAGER

SQL> SELECT *
  2  FROM   session_privs;

PRIVILEGE
----------------------------------------
CREATE SESSION
CREATE TABLE
CREATE PROCEDURE
```

```
SQL>

SQL> SELECT COUNT(*)
  2  FROM   table_privileges;

 COUNT(*)
----------
      226

SQL>
```

There are so many rows in the TABLE_PRIVILEGES view because of the number of privileges granted to the PUBLIC user.

NOTE

The privileges for an Oracle user include privileges given directly to the user, to PUBLIC, and to any roles that have been assigned to the user and enabled.

Limitations of Roles

Roles make the managing of security privileges on the database much easier, especially when large numbers of database objects or users are involved.

One limitation of roles is that a procedural database object (that is, a procedure, function, or package) cannot be created using an object if the privilege for that object was received through a role.

In the following code example, the Oracle user permjit receives privileges on the delegates table through a role and then attempts to create a procedure on that table:

```
SQL> GRANT SELECT
  2  ON     bookings
  3  TO     manager;

Grant succeeded.

SQL> CONNECT permjit/permjit
Connected.
SQL> SELECT *
  2  FROM   session_roles;

ROLE
------------------------------
SALESPERSON
MANAGER

SQL> CREATE OR REPLACE PROCEDURE test_proc
  2       (total OUT NUMBER)
  3  IS
  4  BEGIN
```

```
   5    SELECT COUNT(*)
   6    INTO   total
   7    FROM   ascend.bookings;
   8  END;
   9  /
Warning: Procedure created with compilation errors.

SQL> show errors
Errors for PROCEDURE TEST_PROC:

LINE/COL ERROR
-------- -----------------------------------------------------------------
5/3      PL/SQL: SQL Statement ignored
7/10     PLS-00201: identifier 'ASCEND.BOOKINGS' must be declared
SQL> SELECT COUNT(*)
  2  FROM   ascend.bookings;

 COUNT(*)
---------
        8

SQL>
```

As the preceding example shows, the Oracle user permjit can access the bookings table (shown by the last SELECT statement) but cannot create a procedure on the table because the privilege for the table was received through a role.

> **CAUTION**
>
> Procedural objects (that is, procedures, functions, and packages) cannot be created on objects where the privilege for the object was received through a role.

Profiles

Profiles enable you to limit the resources that an Oracle user can use. Without profiles, one user can slow down all other processes attempting to use the Oracle database. Profiles can be used to limit the resources required by a single call to the database or by the whole session. If the call-level profile limit is exceeded, the statement fails. If the session-level profile limit is exceeded, the whole session is aborted and any pending work in the current transaction is rolled back.

To enable resource limiting, a profile database object is first created and assigned to one or more users. In addition, the database administrator must switch on the resource checking capability.

The Default Profile

Every Oracle database has a profile called DEFAULT that is assigned to every existing and new user created in the database. In this profile, the limit for every resource is set to "unlimited," which essentially means that a user process can hog all the resources. If you want to limit a particular resource for all Oracle users on the database, you need only change this profile. It is used not only as the default profile for new Oracle users, but the limits it specifies act as default values where other profiles do not explicitly name a limit for a resource.

You could create one profile to restrict certain resource use for developers, another to set higher limits for database administrator accounts, and so on.

Profiles can be especially useful when end users query the database, because ad hoc queries, by nature, tend to be slow and inefficient.

Creating Profiles

To create a profile, you use the CREATE PROFILE statement to specify which resource limits you want to set. Any that are not specified by the command default to the limit in the DEFAULT profile.

You can limit a number of different resources, as described in the following section.

What Can Be Limited?

The following resources can be limited with a profile; any that are not specified when the profile is created take the limit specified in the DEFAULT profile. Resources for which the limit is set to UNLIMITED are not checked.

SESSIONS_PER_USER

This parameter limits the number of sessions that can be started with the same Oracle username. By default, the same Oracle name can be used to make multiple connections to the database. Setting this value to 1 allows only one connection to the database with the same Oracle username.

This parameter is especially important for client/server-type environments, where one client machine can make multiple connections to the database using different windows.

CPU_PER_SESSION

This parameter limits the total amount of database server CPU time (in hundredths of a second) that a user can take up for a session. If the limit is reached, the Oracle user can disconnect from the database and reconnect to work up to this CPU limit all over again.

CPU_PER_CALL

This parameter limits the total amount of database server CPU time (in hundredths of a second) that a user process can use for a single call to the database. This stops any slow and badly written SQL statements from slowing down other database users.

CONNECT_TIME

This parameter limits the total time that a user process can remain connected to the database (in minutes). If a user process exceeds the connect time, the process is not told until the next time it tries to make a call to the database. The session is terminated and any work in the current transaction is rolled back. The user can reconnect to the database and start all over again.

IDLE_TIME

This parameter limits the total amount of time (in minutes) that a user process may be idle without making a call to the database. Again, if the idle time limit is exceeded, the user is told only upon the next call to the database. A reconnection to the database starts the user process again, with all the limits.

This limit would not be especially useful in client/server-type environments because much activity might be going on in the client machine but this parameter would take no account of it. This limit concerns itself only with the amount of time since the last call to the database to work out the idle time.

LOGICAL_READS_PER_SESSION

This parameter shows the total number of Oracle blocks accessed (either physically from disk or from the database buffer pool in memory) for the whole user session. You use this parameter to stop user process sessions that run too many statements against the database that access large amounts of data.

LOGICAL_READS_PER_CALL

This parameter shows the total number of Oracle blocks that a single call to the database can request (either from disk in the database files or from the database buffer pool in the SGA area in memory). You use this parameter to prevent statements (rather than sessions) that require a large amount of data.

PRIVATE_SGA

For databases running with the MultiThreaded Server configuration, this parameter limits the amount of memory that can be taken by a user process in the SGA. It affects the number of SQL statements that a user process can run and the number of cursors that can be left open.

COMPOSITE_LIMIT

This parameter allows the database administrator to set a value for a composite limit for the other profile limits already mentioned. Only the CPU_PER_SESSION, LOGICAL_READS_PER_SESSION, CONNECT_TIME, and PRIVATE_SGA limits can be controlled with a composite limit. It allows the database administrator to set an overall limit whereby the user can use different combinations of the four limits as long the composite cost is not exceeded.

The weightings for the different limits can be controlled by the ALTER RESOURCE COST SQL command.

The following code example shows a profile being created:

```
SQL> l
  1  CREATE PROFILE low_limits LIMIT
  2     CPU_PER_SESSION 2
  3     IDLE_TIME 1
  4     CPU_PER_CALL DEFAULT
  5*    CONNECT_TIME UNLIMITED
SQL> /

Profile created.

SQL>
```

The limit for CPU_PER_CALL defaults to whatever is currently set for the DEFAULT profile on the database. The CONNNECT_TIME is unlimited, which means that the amount of time that an Oracle user remains connected to the database is not controlled.

To change any of the limits, you can use the ALTER PROFILE command; the new limits take effect for all new connections to the Oracle database.

If a profile is removed from the database using the DROP PROFILE command, all users that had been assigned to that profile are assigned the DEFAULT profile.

Assigning Profiles

Once a profile has been created it must be assigned to the different Oracle users who are going to be limited by the resources set. A profile can be assigned to an Oracle user either with the CREATE USER command when the user is created, or with the ALTER USER command later on.

The following code example shows the Oracle user permjit being assigned the low_limits profile:

```
SQL> ALTER USER permjit
  2  PROFILE    low_limits;

User altered.
```

```
SQL> SELECT profile
  2  FROM    dba_users
  3  WHERE   username = 'PERMJIT';

PROFILE
-----------------------------
LOW_LIMITS

SQL> SELECT *
  2  FROM    dba_profiles
  3  WHERE   profile = 'LOW_LIMITS';

PROFILE                       RESOURCE_NAME                    LIMIT
----------------------------- -------------------------------- ----------------
LOW_LIMITS                    COMPOSITE_LIMIT                  DEFAULT
LOW_LIMITS                    SESSIONS_PER_USER                DEFAULT
LOW_LIMITS                    CPU_PER_SESSION                  2
LOW_LIMITS                    CPU_PER_CALL                     DEFAULT
LOW_LIMITS                    LOGICAL_READS_PER_SESSION        DEFAULT
LOW_LIMITS                    LOGICAL_READS_PER_CALL           DEFAULT
LOW_LIMITS                    IDLE_TIME                        1
LOW_LIMITS                    CONNECT_TIME                     UNLIMITED
LOW_LIMITS                    PRIVATE_SGA                      DEFAULT

9 rows selected.

SQL>
```

The profiles assigned to each different Oracle user can be seen by querying DBA_USERS, and the definitions of the profiles themselves can be seen by accessing DBA_PROFILES, as shown in the preceding example.

Activating Resource Checking

Profiles do not take effect and are not checked until the database administrator either explicitly sets the RESOURCE_LIMIT parameter in the INIT.ORA file to TRUE or sets it by issuing the ALTER SYSTEM command.

The following example shows resource-limit checking being turned on and the Oracle user assigned this profile exceeding the IDLE_TIME limit:

```
SQL> ALTER SYSTEM SET RESOURCE_LIMIT = TRUE;

System altered.

SQL> CONNECT permjit/permjit
Connected.

SQL> SELECT *
  2  FROM    DUAL;

D
-
X
```

```
SQL> /
SELECT *
*
ERROR at line 1:
ORA-02396: exceeded maximum idle time, please connect again

SQL>
```

As you can see in the preceding example, the user process is left in the original Oracle tool (SQL*Plus, in this case).

Summary

In this chapter, you looked at a number of different options that are available to protect the Oracle database, all of which come as part of the base product. Another option for the RDBMS software, Trusted Oracle7, allows even more control of the Oracle database, including protecting which rows can be accessed and modified by different Oracle users without the use of views. Trusted Oracle7 is used in applications where security is of paramount performance. Trusted Oracle7 is discussed further in Chapter 35, "Trusted Oracle."

III

The Oracle Tools

16

SQL*DBA and Server Manager

by Lave Singh

In this chapter, you take a look at the Oracle SQL*DBA utility primarily from the viewpoint of a developer. The Oracle SQL*DBA utility comes as part of the database software and works in the same way on all platforms. The utility is primarily intended to be used by database administrators (as the name implies), but is also useful for development staff in monitoring database activity.

Beginning with Oracle7.3, the SQL*DBA utility has been replaced by the Server Manager program. This is essentially a newer version of the SQL*DBA utility. In the line-mode version, it works the same way, runs the same commands, and even looks like the SQL*DBA program. In the screen-mode version, the general look of the screens is a little different, and neater, but the functionality is essentially the same.

Even though the discussion here tends to name SQL*DBA, specifically, this chapter applies to both SQL*DBA and Server Manager. If you have Server Manager, the entire set of options, commands, and utilities applies to you.

The SQL*DBA utility has a number of different uses, including the following:

- Creating the database
- Starting up and shutting down the instance
- Recovering the database
- Running ad hoc queries
- Using monitor screens to monitor activity in the database

Often, database administrators use the SQL*Plus utility to perform day-to-day work, and only use the SQL*DBA utility when the function cannot be performed in another tool. This is because the SQL*Plus utility has some formatting commands for output that are not available in SQL*DBA.

Who Can Use SQL*DBA?

On most platforms, during the installation of the database software the execution privileges for the SQL*DBA utility are restricted to a subset of the Oracle users on that machine—typically only those who have extra operating system privileges (for example, on a UNIX machine you must typically be a member of the UNIX dba group to be able to execute the sqldba program; on a VMS box, you must have dba process rights).

Ordinarily, developers have to ensure that they either have the operating system privileges to run the SQL*DBA tool (which also allows them to perform other restricted database administrator operations), or they have to get the system administrator to change the privileges on the program so that developers can run it, too.

Once you have the necessary privileges, you can run the program. Before you can work with the database itself, you must have a valid Oracle username and password to connect to the database.

The Internal User

There are four commands within the SQL*DBA utility that should be used only by database administrators. These four commands are CREATE DATABASE, RECOVER DATABASE, STARTUP, and SHUTDOWN. Access to these restricted commands is protected by the use of an "internal" user for which no password is required.

Before the database administrator uses any of the four restricted commands, he or she typically first issues a connect to the database, with the string "internal" in place of the Oracle username. When "internal" is specified, Oracle checks for the necessary operating system privileges before it allows that user to connect and access the restricted commands.

If you can connect as "internal", you have access to the CREATE DATABASE, RECOVER DATABASE, STARTUP, and SHUTDOWN commands. If an instance is already running and you connect as "internal", the connection is actually made to the Oracle SYS user. This user owns the core data dictionary tables and should not be used by anyone for day-to-day maintenance of the database. No password is required for the "internal" user if it is specified in the SQL*DBA tool, but the SYS password can be specified if the "internal" user is used for connecting to the database from any other Oracle tool.

Run Modes

The SQL*DBA tool can operate in two primary modes:

- Line mode
- Screen mode

Line Mode

In line mode, a command-line prompt appears at which the user enters commands (SQL*DBA, SQL, and PL/SQL commands), and the results of the commands scroll off the top of the screen. This mode is useful for experienced personnel who know the syntax and structure of the commands and want to type them quickly and execute them.

The line mode of SQL*DBA is specified by the lmode=y command-line parameter (the default) when calling the SQL*DBA program.

Figure 16.1 shows the line mode version of SQL*DBA, which is a little more basic than the SQL*Plus tool.

FIGURE 16.1.
*Line mode SQL*DBA.*

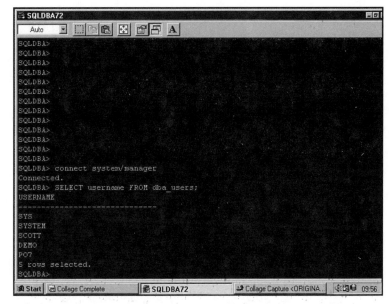

Screen Mode

In SQL*DBA screen mode, the user is presented with a different look and feel. A set of menu options appears at the top of the screen, and a window-type effect is achieved with two panes. The bottom pane, known as the input pane, is where the commands are entered; the top pane, known as the output pane, is where the output of those commands appears. A command is executed when a ; (semicolon) is entered after the command has been typed into the input pane. The user can tab between the panes and scroll backward and forward through the previous output and commands. This facility is not available in SQL*Plus, and it makes SQL*DBA more useful in terms of quick entry of commands.

The majority of the menu options just make it easier to enter the SQL and SQL*DBA commands—by filling in blanks the correct SQL*DBA or SQL command syntax is generated. The syntax generated by the menu options can be viewed; if you don't want to use the menu, you can always type the commands yourself.

The screen mode of SQL*DBA is specified by the lmode=n command-line parameter when calling the SQL*DBA program.

Figure 16.2 shows the SQL*DBA screen mode.

Among the most useful features of SQL*DBA are the monitor screens. These screens show current activity in the database as well as tuning statistics (the statistics are gathered from the time you enter the tool). All of the monitor screens can be initiated either through the Monitor menu option on the Main menu or directly through commands typed into the SQL*DBA tool.

The commands can be seen when the menu options are chosen. More than one set of monitor screens can be started at the same time, and the user can go from one screen to the next using the Rotate Window key.

FIGURE 16.2.

Screen mode SQL*DBA.

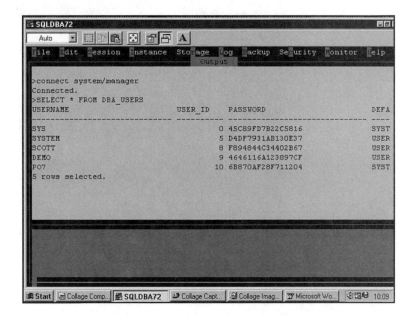

NOTE

To allow any Oracle username access to the V$ views used in the monitor screens, run the Oracle-supplied `utlmontr.sql` script in the SYS user to grant public query access to these tables.

Figure 16.3 shows a monitor screen in SQL*DBA.

You learn more about monitoring activity using SQL*DBA in Chapter 26, "Monitoring Important Database Statistics."

CAUTION

Don't rely too much on the tuning statistics shown in SQL*DBA because they only reflect information gathered since you entered the tool. Instead, access the V$ tables directly through SQL scripts to get tuning statistics gathered since the instance was last started.

FIGURE 16.3.

*A monitor screen in SQL*DBA.*

Using SQL*DBA

The major issues when running commands in SQL*DBA are described in the following sections.

Keyboard Keys

There are a number of keyboard keys available in SQL*DBA when it runs in Screen mode. These allow the user to issue the same commands available on the menus. To see which keys are available, either press the Show Keys key (often CTLR-K, but refer to the Oracle *Installation and User's Guide* for your platform) or use the menus and choose the Show Keys option from the Help menu.

Menu

If SQL*DBA is running in Screen mode, menus help you issue commands quickly without having to remember and type the correct syntax. When you fill in the blanks on the menu screens, the SQL*DBA program generates the commands for you (and they can be seen in the output pane).

> **TIP**
>
> Rather than using SQL*Plus, if you can't remember the syntax of administrator-type SQL commands, use the menus in SQL*DBA and let it generate the commands for you.

The highlighted letter of a menu option indicates that you can quickly select that choice by pressing the corresponding key on the keyboard. You don't have to navigate to the option itself.

Many menu options call screens that mimic windows-type functionality with buttons, check boxes, radio groups, and other objects, but in a character-mode environment. All of these options can be selected and deselected with keyboard keys.

Figure 16.4 shows a typical menu option screen with check boxes, buttons, and radio groups.

FIGURE 16.4.

A typical menu option screen.

Many of the options in the menu can also be initiated directly from the keyboard (for example, the Next and Previous commands).

Some interesting and not-so-obvious menu capabilities for developers include the following:

- ▪ *Cutting, copying, and pasting of commands*—Using the Select Text key (or the mouse, if it works in your version of SQL*DBA), you can copy text from the output pane and paste it into your command in the input pane. This allows you, for example, to paste long text or number strings into WHERE clauses.

■ INSTANCE, KILL SESSION *command*—This command shows the sessions currently connected to the database and, if one of the sessions is selected (using the Select Item key or the mouse, if enabled), it issues the ALTER SYSTEM KILL SESSION command for that session.

■ *Instance, Storage, Log, Backup, and Security main menu options*—These options are used primarily by the database administrator and should not be used by application developers. The options control the structure of the database, including adding more database files, controlling the structure of the redo log files, setting up new Oracle users, and performing a backup of the database.

Which Commands Can Be Used in SQL*DBA?

The SQL*DBA tool allows SQL and PL/SQL commands to be entered in the same way that commands are entered in the SQL*Plus tool. In addition, extra commands are available that can only be used in the SQL*DBA tool (for example, to start up the instance).

Some extra functionality not available in SQL*Plus is the capability to bring up previous and next commands (with the menus or the keyboard keys), and to scroll through past output in the output pane.

The number of previous statements you can retrieve in SQL*DBA is controlled by the HISTORY setting, which defaults to a value of 10 commands. To change the number of commands that can be scrolled, issue the following statement:

```
SQLDBA> SET HISTORY 100
```

The current value for the HISTORY setting can be determined by using the SHOW HISTORY command.

SQL*DBA Commands

The major SQL*DBA-specific commands (which work only in this tool) are intended specifically for the database administrator's use in controlling the entire instance and database. They control such activities as starting up and shutting down the instance, creating a new database, and backing up and recovering the database. Such commands normally are not issued by developers.

Other commands that are similar to the commands available in the SQL*Plus tool include

■ HOST—Calls an operating system command
■ DESCRIBE—Describes a table, view, or procedure
■ SPOOL—Saves the output to an operating system file
■ EXECUTE—Calls a PL/SQL procedure
■ CONNECT and DISCONNECT—Makes or releases a connection to an Oracle user account on either the local or a remote database

> **NOTE**
>
> To describe a table, view, or procedure the full word DESCRIBE must be entered; the abbreviation DESC, which works in SQL*Plus, does not work in SQL*DBA.

The rest of the SQL*DBA commands can be seen by issuing HELP while in the SQL*DBA line mode; however, they are specifically for the database administrator and normally are not issued by developers.

Help in SQL*DBA

SQL*DBA provides a basic help facility that you can access through the main Help menu when you are running in screen mode. This facility gives further information on SQL and other commands that can be entered in SQL*DBA.

If you are running in line mode, entering HELP at the command prompt provides a more basic form of help, with a list of the commands that can be entered in SQL*DBA.

COMMAND=

SQL*DBA enables you to execute a set of statements as soon as you enter the tool. The COMMAND command-line parameter specifies the name of a file containing a set of statements that are to be executed when the SQL*DBA tool is opened. After all the commands have been executed, SQL*DBA is exited.

This feature is often used to run a script that provides a set of quick reports (using the SELECT statement against the Oracle data dictionary) whenever the Oracle database is shut down or started up. These reports can include database monitoring information and early warning information about possible future problems, such as problems with free storage running out.

Summary

This chapter examined the SQL*DBA tool from a developer's perspective. The main components of the tool are used by database administrators, but the tool also can provide easier ways for developers to monitor database activity and issue administrator-type commands through menus. You should use care when you are in the SBA*DBA tool because it enables you to perform operations that can affect the entire database.

Beginning with Oracle7.3, the SQL*DBA tool has been renamed to Server Manager. All the commands and features you learned about in this chapter also apply to Server Manager. The look and feel of the Server Manager tool is the same as SQL*DBA in line mode; in screen mode, however, functionality is the same but the look is a little cleaner.

17

SQL*Plus

by Lave Singh

The SQL*Plus tool is part of the Oracle RDBMS software and works in the same manner across all machines and operating systems on which Oracle runs. This tool is a character-based tool, and although on some Windows platforms there are menu options that make it easier to run some commands, the basics of the tool remain the same across all platforms.

Other tools are available on some platforms to make command entry and database interrogation easier (for example, the Object Navigator on some Windows platforms). Everything that can be performed in these tools can also be performed in SQL*Plus.

What Is SQL*Plus?

SQL*Plus is an Oracle utility used by developers and database administrators to perform on-the-fly commands and queries against an Oracle database, often when database objects are being set up. Because knowledge of the SQL commands and of the tool itself are required, SQL*Plus is not a tool for most end users.

Developers use SQL*Plus when programs written with other tools (for example, Oracle Forms) are being tested to ensure that the correct data values are being stored on the database.

Database administrators can use SQL*Plus to enter the vast majority of queries and SQL commands available—only rarely does the database administrator need to use the Server Manager tool (which is described in Chapter 16, "SQL*DBA and Server Manager"). Prior to Oracle7.3, the Server Manager was called SQL*DBA.

Because SQL*Plus is used against an Oracle database, you need a valid Oracle username and password before you can use the tool. If you do not enter the username and password correctly the first time, you are prompted two more times before the program terminates. The username and password are validated against the Oracle data dictionary tables.

Entering and Editing

You use SQL*Plus to enter three different types of statements: SQL commands, PL/SQL blocks, and SQL*Plus commands, which control the way that this tool works. SQL*Plus commands work only in the SQL*Plus tool.

As long as the instance is up and running, the vast majority of SQL commands can be entered. Commands such as RECOVER DATABASE cannot be entered in SQL*Plus unless the instance is fully open.

There is a buffer area that can hold just one statement at a time; it can be either the last SQL statement or the last PL/SQL block. Once a new statement is entered, the previous one is removed from the buffer. If a command is already in the buffer, the statement does not have to be retyped before being run again.

When you start to enter commands, the SQL*Plus program recognizes either the very first keyword of a SQL statement or the keywords that start a PL/SQL block. Either way, once you enter a line, SQL*Plus starts to store the statement in the buffer area. If the very first keyword is not recognized, the previous statement remains in the buffer and the new one is not stored in the buffer.

SQL commands and PL/SQL blocks can be entered in a free-form format—that is, in upper-case, mixed case, or lowercase, and on one line or many lines. The lines in the buffer are numbered starting at 1. There are a number of different ways you can stop entering a command. A semicolon (;) at the end of a SQL statement terminates entry of the command and executes it. A forward slash (/) on a line by itself does the same thing for SQL commands and PL/SQL blocks. If you want to stop entering statements and return to the command prompt without executing them, press the carriage return on an empty line if you're entering a SQL command, or enter the period (.) on a line by itself if you're entering a PL/SQL block.

If a SQL command or a PL/SQL block has already been stored in the buffer, you can execute it without having to retype by typing either the forward slash (/), the word RUN (at the SQL prompt), or the abbreviation for RUN, R. Entering a semicolon at the SQL prompt causes the contents of the buffer to be listed, but does not run the command again.

The following code example shows a SQL SELECT statement being entered into the buffer, but not executed (on the dummy table, dual). The statement executes once you return to the SQL prompt. An example of a PL/SQL block is also shown.

```
SQL> SELECT *
  2  FROM    dual
  3
SQL> /

D
-
X

SQL> l
  1  SELECT *
  2* FROM    dual
SQL> RUN
  1  SELECT *
  2* FROM    dual

D
-
X

SQL> BEGIN
  2    NULL;
  3  END;
  4  .
SQL> /

PL/SQL procedure successfully completed.

SQL>
```

Editing Commands in the Buffer

There are two ways to edit the SQL or PL/SQL commands stored in the SQL*Plus buffer: using the SQL*Plus basic editing commands or using an operating system editor.

Using SQL*Plus commands

Once a SQL statement or PL/SQL block is in the buffer, it can be edited using some very basic SQL*Plus editing commands. Other SQL*Plus commands are not stored in the buffer area. They must be retyped if you want to change the statement.

> **CAUTION**
>
> The buffer in SQL*Plus can contain, at most, one SQL statement or PL/SQL block.

Each line of the SQL statement or the PL/SQL block has an associated line number that is used by the editing commands. The number is used to specify which line a command will work on. To make a line the current line, type L (or list) followed by the line number. If you type L without a line number, the last line listed becomes the current line. An asterisk appears next to the current line.

The following code example shows the current line with an asterisk next to it:

```
SQL> SELECT
  2   *
  3   FROM
  4   emp
  5
SQL> l
  1   SELECT
  2   *
  3   FROM
  4*  emp
SQL>
SQL> l3
  3*  FROM
SQL>
```

Table 17.1 shows some of the more useful commands for editing a statement in the buffer.

Table 17.1. Commands for editing a buffer statement.

Command	Function
A <text>	Appends text to the end of the current line of the buffer.
C/<old text>/<new text>	Changes the old characters on the command line to the new characters specified. If the new characters are not supplied, the old characters are removed from the line.

Command	*Function*
DEL	Deletes the current line from the buffer. If the DEL command is followed by a line number, that line number is removed even if it is not the current line in the buffer.
I	Puts SQL*Plus into Input mode so that a new line of text can be entered after the current line.
SAVE *<filename>.<filetype>*	Saves the contents of the buffer to an operating system file under the filename given. If *filetype* is omitted, a default extension of .sql is used. The full disk and directory path can also be specified in the filename in an operating system-specific manner. Once the statements have been saved to a file, an operating system editor (for example, TPU, VI, or Notepad) can be used to edit the statement.
GET *<filename>.<filetype>*	Retrieves the contents of a file into the buffer area, from which the statement can either be further edited or executed. The file can contain only one SQL statement or one PL/SQL block because only one statement may exist in the buffer. The full directory path can be specified. If the file extension is omitted, a file extension of .sql is used.
START *<filename>.<filetype>* or @*<filename>.<filetype>*	Retrieves the statements in the buffer and executes each one in turn until all the statements have been processed. This method can be used to process a file that contains more than one statement (while the GET command cannot), as the buffer contains only one statement at a time. The full directory path can be specified. If the file extension is omitted, a file extension of .sql is used.

Using an Operating System Editor

The editor that comes as part of the SQL*Plus tool is basic, but works in the same way on any platform. This trait is useful if you are using SQL*Plus on a platform where you do not know another operating system editor. However, other operating system editors probably offer more flexibility than line-by-line editing in SQL*Plus (for example, TPU for VAX VMS, vi for UNIX, or Notepad for Windows).

The operating system editor must first be defined to SQL*Plus with the DEF command. This command defines a SQL*Plus environment variable called _editor.

The following code example shows an operating system editor being defined for use in SQL*Plus.

```
SQL> def _editor=notepad.exe
```

Once the editor has been defined, you can use the EDIT command in SQL*Plus to either edit the contents of the buffer area or to initiate the editor on a specific file from within SQL*Plus (in this case you must supply the name of the file to be edited). If you enter EDIT by itself, the current contents of the buffer are copied to a file called afiedt.buf (a historical default name), and the editor is called. Once you exit the editor, the changes you made are automatically brought back into the SQL*Plus buffer.

It is faster, easier, and more convenient to use an operating system editor to edit SQL*Plus commands, although it is worth getting to know the basic SQL*Plus editing commands in case an operating system editor is not available.

Controlling the Settings in SQL*Plus

There are a number of settings that control the environment in SQL*Plus. Many of them contain default values, but the majority of those can be changed. If you are running SQL*Plus on a GUI platform, you can set these values from the Options menu without typing any commands.

Once these settings are made, they apply not just to the current statement, but to all SQL statements run in the current SQL*Plus session.

SET Command Parameters

You can use the following SET commands to control the SQL*Plus environment.

ARRAYSIZE

The ARRAYSIZE parameter controls the number of rows fetched with each call from SQL*Plus to the database. The bigger the array, the more memory you use, but the fewer the number of calls to the database. On slow systems you can see the tool pause after each array's worth of data is fetched from the database and shown on the screen.

AUTOCOMMIT

AUTOCOMMIT specifies that a COMMIT should be issued after every INSERT, UPDATE, and DELETE statement is executed in SQL*Plus. If changes are committed automatically, you do not need to manually issue the COMMIT command, but it means that you cannot roll back any work. This option is not usually set.

COMPATIBILITY

The COMPATIBILITY parameter specifies the syntax version (V5 or V6) to be used in running SQL*Plus commands. For example, in Oracle Version 5, the COMMIT and ROLLBACK statements did not require a semicolon at the end; in Version 6, constraints were named after their type was specified.

Setting the compatibility to NATIVE uses the version of the RDBMS software that SQL*Plus is currently connected to.

ECHO

The ECHO parameter causes SQL statements to be echoed back to the screen. This parameter is set to OFF for report programs when you do not want to see statements in the middle of the report output.

ESCAPE

The ESCAPE parameter is used to specify an escape character that you can use when searching for special characters used as wildcards in the data. For example, the percent sign (%) can be used as a wildcard character, but if you want to search for it in the data, you must prefix it with the escape character set here.

FEEDBACK

After a SELECT statement finishes, the number of rows it returns is displayed at the end of the output. If you do not want to see the number of rows, you can SET FEEDBACK OFF. If you want to see only the numbers of rows returned for large tables you can, for example, SET FEEDBACK 20 so that you see the number returned only if it is 20 or more.

The "No rows returned" message is not affected by this setting.

HEADING

The HEADING parameter controls whether the headings for different columns appear in the output. This parameter can be set to either ON or OFF.

LINESIZE

LINESIZE controls the size of each row of output before the text wraps to the next line.

LONG

A long column can hold up to 2GB of data in one column on one row. The LONG parameter determines how many characters of a long column should appear on the screen. The value is set higher if you want to see more information from a long column, such as some of the data dictionary views that store their information in long columns (for example, USER_TRIGGERS).

NEWPAGE

The NEWPAGE parameter determines how many blank lines to leave at the top of each logical page of output in SQL*Plus. Setting this value to 0 causes a form feed character to be issued when the screen output is saved to a file (using SPOOL), which is useful when producing basic reports.

NULL

NULL values appear by default as spaces in the output. The NULL parameter is set to a string (for example, - - - -) to make it clearer that a NULL value is present in the output.

NUMFORMAT

NUMFORMAT is the default format mask used to display number fields where the COLUMN command (described later) has not been used to format number fields in the output. For example, SET NUMFORMAT 999,999.00.

NUMWIDTH

NUMWIDTH specifies the default width to allocate on the output for number fields. If you attempt to write a number that is larger than the width allowed, a string of hash marks (#) appears in the output to indicate that the number won't fit. If NUMFORMAT is set, it overrides the setting for NUMWIDTH. In addition, the COLUMN command (described later) can be used to set the format for a particular column of output.

PAGESIZE

PAGESIZE determines the size of each logical page of output before column headings (and page titles, if set) are displayed. If the value of PAGESIZE is set to 0, column headings do not appear.

PAUSE

The PAUSE parameter causes the output to pause after each logical page (the logical page size is set by the PAGESIZE parameter). This allows the user to look at the output before it scrolls off the top of the screen, which is especially helpful when the version of SQL*Plus has no screen buffer to scroll back through.

If SET PAUSE ON is issued, SQL*Plus pauses before even the first row of output is shown, but does not display any prompt to the user. It appears as if the program has frozen. You can display a prompt by issuing the SET PAUSE command again with a character string containing the prompt to be shown to the user.

The following code example shows how PAUSE is typically used:

```
SQL> SET PAUSE ON
SQL> SET PAUSE 'Press a key to continue'
SQL> SELECT *
  2  FROM   dual;
Press a key to continue

D
-
X

SQL>
```

A SET PAUSE command is always issued in two steps: first, to set the pause to ON, and second, to set the pause to the character string prompt to be shown to the user.

SERVEROUTPUT

With the DBMS_OUTPUT.PUT_LINE packaged procedure, you can display debugging type messages from within a PL/SQL block, but those messages appear only when SERVEROUTPUT is set to ON. This means that you can, while testing, leave the debugging messages in the programs and switch the display of those messages on and off with this setting.

SPOOL <filename>.<filetype>

The SPOOL option starts saving the entire contents of whatever appears on the screen to the specified filename. You can specify the disk and directory to write to (the default is the working directory of SQL*Plus or the current directory of the user, depending on the operating system). You can omit the filetype; a default of .LST is used.

This option causes whatever appears on the screen to be written to the file until you SET SPOOL OFF, start spooling to a different file, or exit SQL*Plus.

SQLPROMPT

The SQLPROMPT parameter specifies the SQL*Plus command prompt that appears to the user. This is SQL> by default, but you can set it to the database or instance name that you are connected to.

TERMOUT

The TERMOUT parameter affects the session only if it is issued from a command file with the START command. It stops the display of any output from SQL commands to the screen. You use it when you want to run, for example, a report-type program and save the output to a file rather than display it on the screen. The amount of time saved by not showing the results on the screen can speed up execution of some SQL command files.

TIME

TIME displays the current time in front of the SQLPROMPT, as the following code example shows:

```
SQL> SET TIME ON
13:08:46 SQL> SELECT * FROM DUAL;

D
-
X

13:08:50 SQL> SET TIME OFF
SQL>
```

The time is calculated to the nearest second on the client machine and changes with each new prompt.

TIMING

The TIMING parameter can be used to tune SQL statements by showing the amount of time each statement takes to run. It is not an accurate guide, however, as it shows only the time that elapses between submitting the SQL statement to the database and getting a response back. There can be many other things that affect performance, such as a slow network, and these may affect the time a SQL statement takes to run.

A better way to tune statements is to use the EXPLAIN PLAN or the TRACE facilities.

The following code example shows TIMING being set on for a SQL statement (at the end of the output):

```
SQL> SELECT COUNT(*) FROM delegates;

 COUNT(*)
---------
       13

 real: 120
SQL>
```

The time shown is in hundredths of a second.

TTITLE and BTITLE

Each page of output can be set with a title at the top of the page (TTITLE) and a title at the bottom of the page (BTITLE). These parameters are set to a character string that can contain a number of additional formatting options. If only a character string is used, the text specified for TTITLE is centered, the date is added to the left-hand side, and the page number is added to the right-hand side.

The following code example shows examples of using TTITLE and BTITLE with a simple character string for the heading:

```
SQL> TTITLE 'Delegates Reports'
SQL> BTITLE '****Confidential ****'
SQL> i
  1  SELECT d.d_firstname, d.d_firstname
  2  FROM   delegates d
  3* ORDER BY d.d_firstname
SQL> /

Sun May 12                                                  page    1
                            Delegates Report


D_FIRSTNAME          D_FIRSTNAME
-------------------- --------------------
Amriss               Amriss
Anthony              Anthony
Disteldorf           Terry
Mudhar               Arvinder
Harman               Harman
Singh                Jazz
Samra                Kailan
Samra                Karam
Kaur                 Kashmir
Fowler               Alan



                         ****Confidential ***

13 rows selected.

SQL>TTITLE OFF
SQL>BTITLE OFF
```

TTITLE OFF and BTITLE OFF turn off the page headings for any subsequent pages of output in SQL*Plus.

Additional TTITLE and BTTITLE Options

A number of additional options are available with TTITLE and BTITLE. The major ones are described in Table 17.2.

Table 17.2. Additional options available with TTITLE and BTITLE.

Option	Function
BOLD <text>	Attempts to use boldface type for the text following this keyword in the report output. On the screen, the text is made bold by repeating it three times; when you try to print it, however, your printer may not be able to produce in a boldface type.
COLx <text>	Prints the text following this keyword in the column specified, and ensures that parts of the title appear in the exact print column specified.

continues

Table 17.2. continued

Option	Function
LEFT <text> RIGHT <text> CENTER <text>	The text following these keywords appears at the left-most, right-most, or center position on the line.
OFF	Turns off TTITLE and BTITLE so that they do not appear on any subsequent pages of output from any following queries.
<text>	The text that appears in the output of TTITLE and BTITLE, if specified.
<variable>	There are a number of SQL*Plus system variables that can be included with TTITLE. SQL.PNO is the page number of the current page of output in the current query. SQL.USER is the username of the Oracle user currently connected to Oracle.

The following code fragment shows some examples of how TTITLE and BTITLE are used:

```
SQL> TTITLE COL15 'Delegates Report' -
> RIGHT 'PAGE:' FORMAT 999 SQL.PNO SKIP 3 -
> CENTER 'Male Delegates'
SQL>
BTITLE CENTER ' ****Confidential ****'
SQL> l
  1   SELECT d_lastname, d_firstname
  2   FROM    delegates
  3* WHERE   d_sex = 'M'
SQL> /

             Delegates Report                                    PAGE:    1


                             Male Delegates
D_LASTNAME            D_FIRSTNAME
- - - - - - - - - - - - - - - - -    - - - - - - - - - - - - - - - - -
Brooks               Micheal
Smith                Test
Connor               Joseph
Robbins              Anthony
Singh                Jazz

                     ****Confidential ****
```

In the preceding example, the TTITLE option extends across more than one line, and the hyphen (-) is used to continue the option onto the next line. The COL option followed by a number starts the following text at a specific column in the output and is useful for ensuring that items line up. The RIGHT, LEFT, and CENTER options can be used to justify the text on a line; the size of the line is set by SET LINESIZE. SQL.PNO is a SQL*Plus variable that can be used to include the page number of the output in TTITLE and BTITLE. The SKIP option followed by a number specifies the number of blank lines to include in the headings.

If you want to include the date in the titles, you need to retrieve it, store it in a variable, and then use the variable name in the title parameters, as the following code example shows:

```
SQL> COLUMN todays_date NEW_VALUE title_date
SQL>
SQL> SELECT TO_CHAR(SYSDATE, 'DDth Month YY') todays_date
  2  FROM   SYS.DUAL;

14THMay96                       Delegates Report

TODAY
- - - - - - - - - - - - - - - - - - - - - - - - - - - - - - - - - - - - - - - - - - - -
14TH May       96

SQL>
SQL> TTITLE LEFT &title_date CENTER 'Delegates Report' SKIP 2
SQL>
SQL>
SQL> SELECT d_lastname, d_firstname
  2  FROM   delegates
  3  WHERE  d_sex = 'M';

14THMay96                       Delegates Report

D_LASTNAME           D_FIRSTNAME
- - - - - - - - - - - - - - - -   - - - - - - - - - - - - - - - - - -
Brooks               Micheal
Smith                Test
Connor               Joseph
Robbins              Anthony
Singh                Jazz

SQL>
SQL>
```

The COLUMN parameter in the preceding example defines a variable called title_date that is populated automatically whenever a column or alias with a name of todays_date is selected. The following SELECT statement retrieves today's date using SYSDATE and a format mask, and stores it in a column alias called todays_date, which populates the title_date variable used in the TTITLE command. The SELECT statement displays the output on the screen. The display can be turned off if you save the commands in a command file and use SET TERMOUT OFF to turn off output for any query results not required in the final report output.

UNDERLINE

UNDERLINE specifies the character used to underline characters in column headings.

VERIFY

If you use parameters in a SQL statement (for example, &delegate_name), this parameter, if set ON , displays the parameter name and the value provided for it when the SQL statement is executed. It is useful for debugging parameter problems when a SQL statement is run.

SHOW **Command**

The SHOW command can be used to list one setting or all settings, as the following code example shows:

```
SQL> show pagesize
pagesize 24
SQL>
SQL>
SQL> show all
arraysize 15
autocommit OFF
autoprint OFF
blockterminator "." (hex 2e)
btitle OFF and is the 1st few characters of the next SELECT statement
closecursor OFF
colsep " "
cmdsep OFF
compatibility version NATIVE
concat "." (hex 2e)
copycommit 0
copytypecheck is ON
crt ""
define "&" (hex 26)
echo OFF
editfile "afiedt.buf"
embedded OFF
escape OFF
feedback ON for 6 or more rows
flagger OFF
flush ON
heading ON
headsep "¦" (hex 7c)
linesize 100
lno 18
long 80
longchunksize 80
maxdata 32767
newpage 1
null ""
numformat ""
numwidth 9
pagesize 24
pause is OFF
pno 1
recsep WRAP
recsepchar " " (hex 20)
release 702020301
serveroutput OFF
showmode OFF
spool OFF
sqlcase MIXED
sqlcode 0
sqlcontinue "> "
sqlnumber ON
sqlprefix "#" (hex 23)
sqlprompt "SQL> "
sqlterminator ";" (hex 3b)
```

```
suffix "SQL"
tab ON
termout ON
time OFF
timing OFF
trimout ON
trimspool OFF
ttitle OFF and is the 1st few characters of the next SELECT statement
underline "-" (hex 2d)
user is "SCOTT"
verify ON
wrap : lines will be wrapped
SQL>
```

Windows Version

If you have a Windows version of SQL*Plus, most of the settings listed previously can also be set using the Options | Environment menu option.

Figure 17.1 shows the menu options available in SQL*Plus for controlling environment settings.

FIGURE 17.1.

Using menu options to set SQL*Plus settings.

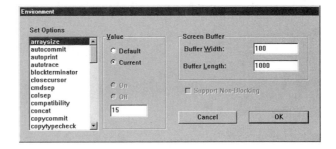

Another useful facility in the Windows version is the ability to scroll back through previous output by using scrollbars. The amount of output that can be scrolled is controlled by the Screen Buffer setting, which also appears in the preceding output.

Quick Reset

The settings described so far last only for the current SQL*Plus session and are lost when you leave the tool. If you want to quickly reset everything to their default values, exit SQL*Plus and enter it again.

If you want to keep the current settings for a future SQL*Plus session, write them to an operating system file and start the file each time you want those settings to apply. If you want the settings to apply every time you enter SQL*Plus, you can save the settings to the login.sql or the glogin.sql files that are executed automatically when you first enter the tool. These files will be found in different locations depending on the platform. The *Oracle Installation and User's Guide* for your platform can tell you where to find these files.

Miscellaneous Commands

The following sections introduce you to some of the miscellaneous commands available in SQL*Plus.

Help

There is a help facility in SQL*Plus that shows the syntax for and examples of SQL, PL/SQL, and SQL*Plus commands. The help system can be invoked by typing help at the SQL prompt in SQL*Plus and following the instructions onscreen.

In character-based environments, the help system shows the help text as characters within SQL*Plus by interrogating a set of help tables installed in the Oracle SYSTEM user by the database administrator. The way this help system is installed varies from one platform to another, but the core of the installation is a script that runs a SQL*Loader program to load the help table. In character-based environments you can go quickly to the help topic for a particular command by giving the command after the keyword HELP. For example, you can type help create table to get help on the CREATE TABLE command.

On some GUI platforms, you can type help at the SQL prompt to see the Windows help file format of the help system. You can use the available functionality to search the help system when viewing standard help files.

HOST

The HOST command in SQL*Plus enables you to run an operating system command directly from SQL*Plus (for example, ls or dir to see the directory listing). If you follow the HOST command with an operating system command, the command runs and control returns to the SQL*Plus session. If you enter the HOST command by itself without an operating system command after it, the SQL*Plus session is suspended, and you can work directly with the operating system. You return to SQL*Plus when you exit from the operating system session. On some Windows platforms, both the operating system session and SQL*Plus run at the same time.

There are other ways to issue the HOST command: The exclamation mark (!) works on some UNIX platforms and the ($) works on VAX VMS. Issuing the HOST command, however, works on UNIX, VAX, and most other platforms.

If the database administrator wants to disable the HOST command, especially if he or she wants to prevent users from going to the operating system to access objects not normally available to them, the DBA uses the PRODUCT_USER_PROFILE table in SYSTEM. With this table, the database administrator can also disable other commands in SQL*Plus. The PRODUCT_USER_PROFILE table was used in version 6 of the Oracle RDBMS software; however, system privileges are now used in Oracle7.

Formatting Columns

You can specify SELECT statement formatting options that control the appearance of output columns, settings for the SQL*Plus session (such as line and page sizes), and headings for the top and bottom of the output page. You use the COLUMN command to specify the format of a column or an alias named in any query for the rest of the session.

Table 17.3 shows the major column formatting options.

Table 17.3. Formatting options available with the COLUMN SQL*Plus statement.

Option	Function
CLEAR	Clears any formatting options that may have been specified for the column. This happens by default when you exit SQL*Plus.
FOLD_BEFORE FOLD_AFTER	Causes a carriage return before or after each value for the column, so subsequent columns in the output each appear on a new line.
FORMAT	Specifies a format string and width for the column. For example, for character and date columns A10 specifies that the column is an alphanumeric column and has a width of 10 in the output. For number fields, there are a number of format masks (for example, $999,999.99) that are similar to the format masks available in the TO_CHAR option. Columns can be formatted using the FORMAT option or the TO_CHAR option of the SELECT statement. Using COLUMN FORMAT applies the format to all subsequent statements.
HEADING <text>	Specifies the heading to be used for the column output. If you want to specify a heading that spans two lines, you can use the vertical bar (|) in the text to cause any following text to appear underneath the previous text.
JUSTIFY	Justifies the column values in the output to either LEFT, CENTER, or RIGHT. If no justification is specified, the value defaults to RIGHT for numbers and LEFT for everything else.
LIKE <column>	Causes the formatting to default to formatting already specified for another column, with the option of making some overrides in the same clause where the LIKE is specified.

continues

Table 17.3. continued

Option	Function
NEW_VALUE <variable> OLD_VALUE	Specifies the name of a variable to hold the current value for the column as the query is run. Useful in TTITLE to show the column values in the title of the page. If used in TTITLE, the TTITLE option uses the value for the current row being processed, so on the first page of the output it shows the value for the column on the first row, and on the next page it shows the value for the row about to be printed on that page, and so on for each subsequent page. OLD_VALUE is the equivalent variable used in the BTITLE option.
NOPRINT	Specifies that the column is not to appear in the output for the query. This is useful in reports where you want to retrieve the value for the column from a SELECT statement, but the results are not to be shown in the output, perhaps because the column value is being used to order the results or in the BREAK command.
NULL <text>	Determines how null values should appear in the output of a character string other than as spaces. For example, for a number field you could specify that nulls should appear as *** to make it clear that they are present in the output.
ON OFF	Specifies that the column formatting options are to be turned off or on, but not lost, which happens if the CLEAR option is specified.
WRAPPED WORD_WRAPPED TRUNCATED	Specifies the kind of wrapping to apply if the data is too large to fit into the column size specified by the FORMAT command. For example, if a character column is specified to have a format mask of A10 to allow for 10 characters in the output, a larger data value uses the wrapping style specified here.

The following code example shows the COLUMN command being used to format two columns:

```
SQL> COL d_lastname       FORMAT A6 WRAPPED HEADING 'Last¦Name'
SQL> COL alias_firstname FORMAT A6 NULL '****' JUSTIFY CENTER HEADING 'First¦Name'
SQL>
SQL> SELECT d_lastname
  2         ,d_firstname alias_firstname
  3  FROM    delegates
  4  WHERE   UPPER(d_lastname) LIKE '%A%';
```

```
Last    First
Name    Name
------  ------
Andrea  Connir
s       ae

Kaur    Kashmi
        r

Kaur    Benish
        a

Samra   Karam

Last    First
Name    Name
------  ------
Samra   Kailan
Kaur    Amriss

6 rows selected.

SQL>
SQL>
SQL> COLUMN d_lastname      CLEAR
SQL> COLUMN alias_firstname CLEAR
SQL>
SQL>
```

The COLUMN command usually specifies either the column name or alias to be formatted. However, it can take an expression that is specified in the SELECT part of a SELECT statement (for example, d_lastname¦¦d_firstname). Instead of specifying expressions as the subject of the COLUMN command, it is easier to specify an alias in the SELECT statement and then use the alias in the COLUMN command.

> **NOTE**
>
> The COLUMN command applies the formatting for the rest of the session to all columns with the specified name in any query.

Additional examples of the COLUMN command can be found throughout this chapter.

Breaks and Computes

There are two other ways of formatting output and calculating totals from our queries: BREAK and COMPUTE.

The BREAK Command

The BREAK command sets up a breakpoint in the report output. It can be used to prevent duplicate column values from appearing in the output, to cause more white space to be shown (with the SKIP option), and for calculations with the COMPUTE command.

The following code example shows how the BREAK command can be used to format a simple query's output and prevent duplicate values from appearing:

```
SQL> SELECT b_course_code
  2         ,b_start_date
  3         ,b_delegate_id
  4  FROM   bookings
  5  ORDER BY b_course_code
  6           ,b_start_date;

B_COURSE B_START_D B_DELEGATE_ID
-------- --------- -------------
OFOR4    05-FEB-96             2
OFOR4    06-FEB-96             1
OPDO     08-JAN-96             2
OPDO     08-JAN-96             4
OPDO     08-JAN-96             6
OSQL     08-JAN-96             1
OSQL     08-JAN-96             3
OSQL     08-JAN-96             5

8 rows selected.

SQL> BREAK ON b_course_code NODUPLICATES SKIP 2 ON b_start_date ON REPORT;
SQL> /

B_COURSE B_START_D B_DELEGATE_ID
-------- --------- -------------
OFOR4    05-FEB-96             2
         06-FEB-96             1


OPDO     08-JAN-96             2
                              4
                              6


OSQL     08-JAN-96             1
                              3

B_COURSE B_START_D B_DELEGATE_ID
-------- --------- -------------
OSQL     08-JAN-96             5


8 rows selected.

SQL>

SQL>
```

As the preceding example shows, without the BREAK command the values for the course code and start date are repeated in each row of the output. With the BREAK command, you can specify a breakpoint at the course code, another at the course date, and another at the end of the report. When you issue a BREAK command, duplicate values are suppressed unless you use the DUPLICATE clause; in the preceding example, the NODUPLICATES clause is used for clarity but is redundant. After the BREAK command you can specify whether you want to SKIP a number of lines when the column changes. In addition, you can use SKIP PAGE to cause a "page throw" to occur. The last option, ON REPORT, sets up a breakpoint at the end of the query and can be used with the COMPUTE command to specify calculations to be performed at the end of the report.

You can use the BREAKS command to see the currently specified breakpoints, and the CLEAR BREAKS command to clear all existing breakpoints.

CAUTION

A BREAK command overrides any previously issued BREAK commands; only one command is active at a time.

Either a column name or an alias can be specified as the subject of the BREAK command.

NOTE

The ORDER BY clause should be specified with BREAK to ensure that data is returned from the query with the BREAK order.

The COMPUTE Command

The COMPUTE command can be used to work out summaries of data at each of the breakpoints currently in effect. Many COMPUTE commands can be entered to specify different calculations to be performed with the different fields in the query.

The COMPUTE command can work out the AVG (average), COUNT, SUM, MAXIMUM, MINIMUM, STD (standard deviation), and VARIANCE of the database columns. COUNT can be specified on all column datatypes, and MAXIMUM and MINIMUM can be specified for NUMBER, CHAR, and VARCHAR2 datatypes. The rest of these options can be specified only for NUMBER datatypes.

Either a column name or an alias can be specified as the subject of the COMPUTE command.

NOTE

A breakpoint must exist for the column or alias specified for the COMPUTE command; otherwise, the COMPUTE command cannot do anything.

The following code example shows the COMPUTE command being used to work out summaries based on a simple query:

```
SQL> BREAK ON b_course_code ON b_start_date ON b_delegate_id ON REPORT
SQL> COMPUTE COUNT OF b_delegate_id ON b_course_code
SQL> COMPUTE COUNT OF b_delegate_id ON b_start_date
SQL> COMPUTE COUNT OF b_delegate_id ON REPORT
SQL> l
  1  SELECT b_course_code
  2         ,b_start_date
  3         ,b_delegate_id
  4  FROM   bookings
  5  ORDER BY b_course_code
  6*         ,b_start_date
SQL> /

B_COURSE B_START_D B_DELEGATE_ID
-------- --------- -------------
OFOR4    05-FEB-96             2
         ********* -------------
         count                1
         06-FEB-96            1
         ********* -------------
         count                1
******** -------------
count                        2
OPDO     08-JAN-96            2
                             4
                             6


B_COURSE B_START_D B_DELEGATE_ID
-------- --------- -------------
         ********* -------------
         count               -3
******** -------------
count                        3
OSQL     08-JAN-96            1
                             3
                             5
         ********* -------------
         count                3
******** -------------
count                        3

B_COURSE B_START_D B_DELEGATE_ID
-------- --------- -------------
                   -------------
count                        8

8 rows selected.

SQL>
```

In the preceding example, the number of delegates for each different breakpoint is displayed—that is, the number of delegates for each course start date, the number for each different type of course, and the total number at the end of the report.

The LABEL option of the COMPUTE command can change the label that is printed when the COMPUTE result appears in the output (for example, the text "count" that appears in the report output).

> **TIP**
>
> BREAK and COMPUTE can be used to write complex reports containing many levels of calculations without resorting to complex SQL.

When issued without any parameters, the COMPUTE command shows the COMPUTEs currently in effect. The CLEAR COMPUTE command clears the COMPUTEs and does not perform them for any further queries in the session.

BREAK commands and COMPUTE commands are cleared automatically when the SQL*Plus session is exited.

Parameters for Your Commands

To make SQL scripts more flexible, you can prompt the user for any parameters. The parameters can be provided interactively or on the command line by the user, or even set in the program code.

The Ampersand Variables

To define a variable for a SQL command, you can use the ampersand (&) followed by a name. The user is prompted for a value for that variable when the SQL statement runs. The variable is defined implicitly when first encountered in a SQL statement. Ampersand variables are often called *substitution variables*.

The following code example shows how an ampersand variable can be used to prompt for the name of the delegate to be used for the query:

```
SQL> SELECT d_firstname
  2  FROM    delegates
  3  WHERE   d_lastname = '&v_lastname';
Enter value for v_lastname: Kaur
old   3: WHERE   d_lastname = '&v_lastname'
new   3: WHERE   d_lastname = 'Kaur'

D_FIRSTNAME
------------------
Kashmir
Benisha
Amriss

SQL>
```

The value entered by the user is substituted in the statement, replacing the ampersand and the variable name. Character and date strings must be enclosed in quotes when used in a SQL statement. You can either put the ampersand variable in quotation marks within the statement (this is the preferred method), or the user can type the quotation marks when he enters the variable name.

The user prompt, by default, is always Enter value for followed by the name of the variable. In addition, the name of the variable and the value substituted for it appear when the statement runs, which can be helpful when debugging large SQL statements. If you do not want to see this substitution in the output (for example, for a report), you can use the SQL*Plus command SET VERIFY OFF.

ACCEPT and PROMPT

When an ampersand variable is used, the user prompt always defaults to Enter value for followed by the name of the variable. With the ACCEPT command you can change the prompt, specify the datatype for the variable, and hide the value typed by the user (for password-type fields).

The following code example shows the ACCEPT command being used to provide a more user-friendly prompt:

```
SQL> ACCEPT v_lastname CHAR PROMPT 'Give me the last name ' HIDE
Give me the last name ****
SQL>
SQL>
SQL> SELECT d_firstname
  2  FROM    delegates
  3  WHERE   d_lastname = '&v_lastname';
old   3: WHERE   d_lastname = '&v_lastname'
new   3: WHERE   d_lastname = 'Kaur'

D_FIRSTNAME
--------------------
Kashmir
Benisha
Amriss

SQL> PROMPT ****End Of Report ****
****End Of Report ****
SQL>
```

In the preceding example, the ACCEPT command sets up the prompt for the variable, specifying the datatype of the field, the prompt to be shown to the user, and the fact that user input should not be echoed back to the screen (instead, asterisks are to be used to represent each character typed by the user). ACCEPT command options can provide a default value for the variable if the user does not type one and specify a format string.

The PROMPT command is a separate SQL*Plus command that can be used to show a message in the output. It can be used to indicate an end-of-report message after a SQL statement finishes.

DEFINE and UNDEFINE

The DEFINE and UNDEFINE SQL*Plus commands can be used to define a variable in program code without having to prompt the user for the value. This functionality is the equivalent of constants available in other environments. Once a variable has been defined, it remains available for the rest of the session or until it is undefined.

The following code example shows the DEFINE command being used in a SQL*Plus session to show the cost of the course code with a current, though potentially changeable, sales tax rate:

```
SQL> DEFINE tax_rate = 1.175
SQL> l
  1  SELECT c_code
  2         ,c_cost
  3         ,c_cost * &tax_rate   WITH_TAX
  4  FROM   courses
  5* WHERE c_code = 'OPDO'
SQL> /
old   3:          ,c_cost * &tax_rate  WITH_TAX
new   3:          ,c_cost * 1.175  WITH_TAX

C_CODE      C_COST   WITH_TAX
--------  ---------- ----------
OPDO           200        235

SQL> UNDEF tax_rate
SQL>
```

The preceding example shows that the variable name is used without the ampersand in the DEFINE and UNDEFINE commands, but referred to with the ampersand in the SELECT statement. If the tax rate changes, you only need to change the number at the top of the program but not any of the SQL code.

The DEFINE and UNDEFINE commands are often abbreviated to DEF and UNDEF. By typing in DEF at the SQL prompt, you can see the definitions currently in effect.

Double Ampersand

In the previous example, the value of an ampersand variable is lost when the variable is used once in the statement, and the user is then prompted for the value every time the same variable name is encountered. If you use a double ampersand (&&), the value for the variable is retained for the rest of the SQL*Plus session, or until it is undefined.

The following code example shows how the double ampersand is used in a SQL statement so that it does not prompt every time it encounters the variable name. The UNDEFINE command is used to clear the variable so that the next time the statement runs, the user is prompted again for the value to be used.

```
SQL> l
  1  SELECT d_firstname, '&&v_lastname'
  2  FROM    delegates
  3* WHERE   d_lastname = '&&v_lastname'
SQL> /
Enter value for v_lastname: Singh
old   1: SELECT d_firstname, '&&v_lastname'
new   1: SELECT d_firstname, 'Singh'
old   3: WHERE   d_lastname = '&&v_lastname'
new   3: WHERE   d_lastname = 'Singh'

D_FIRSTNAME          'SING
-------------------- ----
Jazz                 Singh
Harman               Singh

SQL>
```

Ampersand with Numbers

In the preceding example, the ampersand variables have a character string name. However, a number (from 1 to 9) can be specified as the name of the variable (for example, &1). The advantage of this is that, without prompting the user, the parameters can be provided when the file containing the parameters is called.

The following example shows a command file using ampersand variables that, when called, are provided with the values to be used.

```
SQL> SELECT d_d_firstname
  3  FROM    delegates
  4  WHERE   d_delegate_id = &1
  5  AND     d_lastname = '&2'
  6
SQL>
SQL> save rept1.sql
Created file rept1.sql
SQL> start rept1 12 Kaur
old   4: WHERE   d_delegate_id = &1
new   4: WHERE   d_delegate_id = 12
old   5: AND     d_lastname = '&2'
new   5: AND     d_lastname = 'Kaur'

D_FIRSTNAME
--------------------
Amriss

SQL>
```

In all respects the ampersand variables named with a number behave in the same way as ampersand variables named with a character string.

Lexical Parameters

In the preceding examples, the parameters provided to the SQL statement are known as *bind variables* and provide individual values used in the statement. A *lexical parameter* is one that provides part of the SQL statement that is to be run. A lexical parameter can be used for any part of the statement, including table and column names. Lexical parameters are defined by the way they are used—in all other ways they are the same as other ampersand variables.

In the following code example, a lexical parameter is used to provide the field that orders the rows of output:

```
SQL> SELECT b_delegate_id
  2         ,b_start_date
  3  FROM   bookings
  4  ORDER BY &order_by_clause;
Enter value for order_by_clause: b_delegate_id
old    4: ORDER BY &order_by_clause
new    4: ORDER BY b_delegate_id

B_DELEGATE_ID B_START_D
------------- ---------
            1 06-FEB-96
            1 08-JAN-96
            2 05-FEB-96
            2 08-JAN-96
            3 08-JAN-96
            4 08-JAN-96
            5 08-JAN-96
            6 08-JAN-96

8 rows selected.

SQL> /
Enter value for order_by_clause: b_start_date
old    4: ORDER BY &order_by_clause
new    4: ORDER BY b_start_date

B_DELEGATE_ID B_START_D
------------- ---------
            1 08-JAN-96
            3 08-JAN-96
            5 08-JAN-96
            2 08-JAN-96
            6 08-JAN-96
            4 08-JAN-96
            2 05-FEB-96
            1 06-FEB-96

8 rows selected.

SQL>
```

Lexical parameters, in practice, are provided by a program rather than being entered by the user. In the preceding example, a screen program calling the SQL script would get the order to be used from the screen and then call the SQL script with a command-line parameter (for example, &1).

SQL*Plus Variables

There is another type of variable available in SQL*Plus. It is a bind variable that can be used in a PL/SQL block (but not in a SQL statement) to set a value used outside of the block. This type of variable is often used as a parameter for procedural database objects (procedures, functions, and packages) to hold the result of the procedural object. This type of variable must be created explicitly (unlike ampersand variables), and once created, it exists for the rest of the session.

To see the contents of such a variable, you use the PRINT command.

The following code example shows this type of bind variable being used to hold the result of a procedural function:

```
SQL> l
  1   CREATE OR REPLACE FUNCTION count_delegates
  2        RETURN NUMBER
  3  IS
  4    v_count NUMBER;
  5  BEGIN
  6    SELECT COUNT(*)
  7    INTO   v_count
  8    FROM   delegates;
  9    RETURN(v_count);
 10* END;
SQL> /

Function created.

SQL> VARIABLE num_delegates NUMBER
SQL> BEGIN
  2    :num_delegates := count_delegates;
  3  END;
  4  /

PL/SQL procedure successfully completed.

SQL> PRINT num_delegates

NUM_DELEGATES
- - - - - - - - - - - -
          13

SQL>
```

As the preceding example shows, these variables are referenced by prefixing a colon (:) to the name of a variable in the PL/SQL block. Outside the PL/SQL block, the variables are referenced in the normal way. Ampersand variables cannot be used to hold the results of a procedure or function call in this way.

A Complete Report

In the preceding sections of this chapter, you saw a number of commands that can be used to provide reports in SQL*Plus.

A Summary Report

The following code example shows a report being generated by many of the commands discussed earlier, and the code produces calculations on the results of a query:

```
REM Delegates Report
REM
REM File Delerep.sql
REM
REM Report showing SQL*Plus reporting capabilities
REM

SET ECHO OFF
SET FEEDBACK OFF
SET VERIFY OFF
SET PAGESIZE 40
SET LINESIZE 70
SET NEWPAGE 0

COL d_organisation FORMAT A14 HEADING 'Organisation'
COL d_lastname     FORMAT A13 HEADING 'Last¦Name' WRAPPED
COL d_firstname    FORMAT A10 HEADING 'First¦Name' TRUNC
COL b_course_code  FORMAT A6  HEADING 'Course'
COL b_start_date   FORMAT A9  HEADING 'Start¦Date'
COL b_location     FORMAT A10 HEADING 'Where'

COL sysdate        FORMAT A10 NEW_VALUE today
COL system_time    FORMAT A10 NEW_VALUE title_time

SET TERMOUT OFF
SELECT SYSDATE
      ,TO_CHAR(sysdate,'HH:MI:SS') system_time
FROM   dual;
SET TERMOUT ON

ACCEPT course_code CHAR PROMPT 'Enter the course code (Wildcards allowed) :'

TTITLE CENTER 'Delegates Report' RIGHT 'Page : ' sql.pno SKIP -
LEFT today ' ' title_time CENTER  '--------------' -
RIGHT 'Run By ' SQL.USER SKIP 2

BTITLE CENTER '***Confidential ***'

BREAK ON d_organisation SKIP 2 ON REPORT

COMPUTE COUNT LABEL 'Org Bookings ' OF d_lastname ON d_organisation
COMPUTE COUNT LABEL 'Total Bookings' OF d_lastname ON REPORT

SPOOL delerep.lis
```

```
SELECT d.d_organisation
      ,d.d_lastname
      ,d.d_firstname
      ,b.b_course_code
      ,b.b_start_date
      ,b.b_location
FROM  delegates d
     ,bookings  b
WHERE d.d_delegate_id = b.b_delegate_id
AND   b.b_course_code LIKE UPPER('&course_code')
ORDER BY d.d_organisation
        ,d.d_lastname
        ,d.d_firstname
/

SPOOL OFF

CLEAR COMPUTE
CLEAR BREAK

SET FEEDBACK ON
SET VERIFY ON
SET ECHO ON
```

The output from the preceding example looks like this:

```
Delegates Report           Page :          1
16-MAY-96 10:22:11         ---------------          Run By ASCEND
                Last            First           Start
Organisation    Name            Name        Course  Date       Where
------------    ------------    ------------ ------  ---------  ----------
Bellcore        Connor          Joseph       OPDO   08-JAN-96  Riyadh
                Robbins         Anthony      OPDO   08-JAN-96  London
**************-------------
Org Bookings                2
Sequent         Andreas         Connirae     OPDO   08-JAN-96  London
                Andreas         Connirae     OPDO   06-FEB-96  Tehran
                Brooks          Micheal      OPDO   05-FEB-96  Tehran
                Brooks          Micheal      OPDO   08-JAN-96  Riyadh
                Smith           Test         OPDO   08-JAN-96  London
**************-------------
Org Bookings                5
Titanium        Kaur            Kashmir      OPDO   08-JAN-96  Riyadh
**************-------------
Org Bookings                1
                           ------------
Total Bookings              8


                    ***Confidential ***
```

The headings for the columns, the page, and the bottom of the page would reappear if there were additional rows in the report output that caused the data to go onto a new page.

Dynamic SQL

With the reporting features available in SQL*Plus, you can use the same statements to write a SELECT statement that produces other commands.

The following example shows a file that queries the data dictionary table to produce a file that can be run standalone to describe all the tables in the current user:

```
SET TERMOUT OFF
SET ECHO OFF
SET PAGESIZE 999
SET HEADING OFF
SET FEEDBACK OFF

SPOOL desc.lis

SELECT 'DESC '||table_name
FROM   user_tables;

SPOOL OFF

SET TERMOUT ON
SET ECHO ON
SET HEADING ON
SET FEEDBACK ON
```

The resulting output looks like this:

```
DESC BOOKINGS
DESC COURSES
DESC COURSE_RUNNINGS
DESC DELEGATES
DESC DELEGATES_COPY
DESC DELEGATES_COPY2
DESC TEMP
DESC TEST
```

The next example shows a script that drops all the objects in the current user:

```
SET TERMOUT OFF
SET ECHO OFF
SET PAGESIZE 999
SET HEADING OFF
SET FEEDBACK OFF

SPOOL desc.lis

SELECT  'DROP '
        ||object_type
        ||' '
        ||object_name
        ||';'
FROM   user_objects
ORDER BY object_type;

SPOOL OFF
```

```
SET TERMOUT ON
SET ECHO ON
SET HEADING ON
SET FEEDBACK ON
```

Here is the resulting script:

```
DROP DATABASE LINK BIG_DATABASE.WORLD;
DROP FUNCTION COUNT_DELEGATES;
DROP INDEX PK_BOOKINGS;
DROP INDEX PK_COURSES;
DROP INDEX PK_COURSE_RUNNINGS;
DROP INDEX PK_DELEGATES;
DROP PROCEDURE NUM_BOOKINGS;
DROP SEQUENCE DELEGATES_SEQ;
DROP TABLE BOOKINGS;
DROP TABLE TEST;
DROP TABLE COURSES;
DROP TABLE COURSE_RUNNINGS;
DROP TABLE DELEGATES;
DROP TABLE TEMP;
DROP TABLE DELEGATES_COPY;
DROP TABLE DELEGATES_COPY2;
DROP VIEW TITANIUM_DELEGATES;
```

This same technique can be used to produce any kind of statement that can be run against the database, saving both time and effort.

Switching User IDs

Before you can use SQL*Plus, you have to provide an Oracle username and password that, if valid, determine what tables and other database objects you have access to. If you want to connect to the database with another Oracle username, you can either exit SQL*Plus completely and re-enter it, or you can use the CONNECT command to switch user IDs.

To determine which Oracle user you are currently connected to, use the SHOW USER command or use the USER pseudocolumn in a query against any table.

The DISCONNECT command can be used to break the connection from the SQL*Plus session to the database without leaving SQL*Plus. You can then use the CONNECT command to re-establish the connection.

> **NOTE**
>
> If you use the DISCONNECT command, the buffer area still contains the last SQL or PL/SQL command entered.

The following code example shows the CONNECT and DISCONNECT commands:

```
SQL> SHOW USER
user is "SYSTEM"
SQL> SELECT USER
  2  FROM    DUAL;

USER
------------------------------
SYSTEM

SQL> CONNECT ascend/ascend
Connected.
SQL> show user
user is "ASCEND"
SQL> l
  1  SELECT USER
  2* FROM    DUAL
SQL> /

USER
------------------------------
ASCEND

SQL>
```

If you disconnect from the database, the session and the transaction end, and by default any changes made in the transaction are committed. The same applies if you connect to another Oracle username with the CONNECT command.

CAUTION

The CONNECT and DISCONNECT commands commit any pending changes.

GLOGIN.SQL and LOGIN.SQL

There are two ordinary SQL files that can be set up on most platforms to contain any SQL, PL/SQL, or SQL*Plus commands to be executed automatically whenever you first enter SQL*Plus.

The glogin.sql file can be set up on a multi-user machine to contain commands to be executed for every user when they first enter SQL*Plus. In addition, each user may have his own login.sql file, which is executed after the glogin.sql file and which contains any statements that the user wants to execute automatically. The default location for the login.sql file is the directory the user is in when the command is issued to enter SQL*Plus. The locations for these files can be specified through operating system environment variables, but the way the location is specified varies from platform to platform. Refer to the *Oracle Installation and User's Guide* for your platform.

Often the `glogin.sql` and `login.sql` files contain just SQL*Plus commands, such as COLUMN to format the column output for the session and SET to control the way that the session behaves.

The following code example shows a typical `login.sql` file and the effects of having that file present when you first enter SQL*Plus:

```
COL today FORMAT a30
SELECT user
      ,TO_CHAR(SYSDATE,'fmDay Month YY') today
FROM   dual;

SET TIME ON
SET PAUSE ON
SET PAUSE 'Press a key '
SET VERIFY OFF
COL d_lastname FORMAT A15 HEADING 'Last Name'
```

These are the effects of running that file:

```
SQL*Plus: Release 3.2.2.0.1 - Production on Thu May 16 09:09:17 1996

Copyright (c) Oracle Corporation 1979, 1994.  All rights reserved.


Connected to:
Personal Oracle7 Release 7.2.2.3.1

With the distributed and replication options
PL/SQL Release 2.2.2.3.1 - Production


USER                             TODAY
-----------------------------    -----------------------------
SCOTT                            Thursday May 96

09:09:18 SQL>
```

The settings made in these files apply for the entire session but can be overridden by using the appropriate setting command.

Comparison with Server Manager

Server Manager is another Oracle tool that can be used to run queries and other commands against the database. It is often used by database administrators because of its more privileged nature. The same SQL and PL/SQL statements can be run in both SQL*Plus and Server Manager. However, SQL*Plus commands (such as SET, BREAK, COLUMN, and so on) can only be used in SQL*Plus; they do not work in Server Manager, which restricts how the output can be formatted. For this reason it is preferable to use SQL*Plus for any *ad hoc* queries against the database, because you can supply some basic formatting commands to the tool.

There are some commands that can be performed only in Server Manager, such as recovering the database and bringing the instance down and up, but in the majority of cases even database administrators prefer to use SQL*Plus.

Summary

This chapter examined the capabilities of SQL*Plus. Although basic and nonintuitive, SQL*Plus is powerful enough to produce complex reports and other queries. It is used by all developers and database administrators for the majority of *ad hoc* queries against a database. It may be used by developers and database administrators for their own reporting purposes, but often another reporting product (such as Oracle Reports) is used to produce reports destined for the end user. The technique of producing dynamic SQL using the basic SQL*Plus formatting commands saves much time and effort for developers and database administrators.

18

SQL*Loader

by Lave Singh

SQL*Loader is an Oracle utility included with the Oracle database software that allows loading of data from external files into an Oracle database.

SQL*Loader loads data from an external data source into Oracle database tables. It can accept both fixed- and variable-length records that may contain character format or binary data. It has its own programming language (called the "control" language) that can specify which fields to load, which ones to ignore, which ones to skip, and the processing to be performed on the data as it's loaded.

SQL*Loader can take one input file (which contains the external data to be loaded into the database) and load the data into more than one table in the same run. The SQL*Loader program contains a number of options and commands in the control file (the "program" written in SQL*Loader's command set), and this chapter describes the major options and additional choices you can make about how the program works. When there is much complex processing to perform on the data, you can either perform it using the SQL*Loader control file commands, or perform a basic load into a set of temporary tables and later use SQL and PL/SQL to load the data into the real tables. The choice is based on which area you have the most expertise in.

The SQL*Loader program is documented in the *Oracle7 Server Utility Manual*.

SQL*Loader Files

SQL*Loader works with a number of files, only one of which is mandatory. These files control how the SQL*Loader program is going to process the data to be loaded and how it logs the results of the run and any rejected and discarded records. Figure 18.1 shows the files involved with SQL*Loader.

FIGURE 18.1.
*File types used by SQL*Loader.*

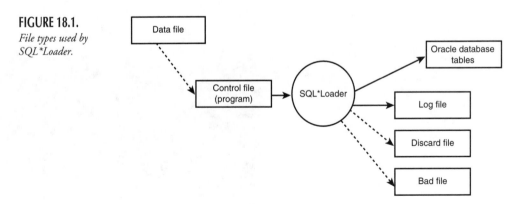

Control File

The Control File is essentially the program for SQL*Loader and specifies the format of the external data that is to be loaded into the tables and some basic processing which is to be performed on the data before it is loaded into the tables. The SQL*Loader control language offers many options, and a later section of this chapter covers some examples with some of the more commonly used options in the Control File.

The Control File is written in a free-format form; commands can be in uppercase, lowercase, on one line, or on many lines. The only time case is significant is when the SQL*Loader program runs on an operating system that is case sensitive with regard to filenames.

Some of the options specified in the Control File can be overridden at runtime by specifying parameters for the program on the command line. This is useful when you want to use the same program to process a different file that has the same structure as the files specified in the Control File. It is also useful when SQL*Loader rejects records to something called a Bad File or a Discard File. The rejected records are rows that do not satisfy the specifications of the data in the Control File, or that have been rejected due to conditions not being met in the program. You can use the same program in the Control File with the Bad File or the Discard File as input without having to rewrite the code to work on a different filename.

Log File

When the SQL*Loader program runs it always produces a Log File that records how the run performs. The Log File contains information about the load—how many records were read, how long the load took, how many records were rejected, and so on, and should always be checked after a load has been attempted. Errors do not always appear on the screen but are always reported to the Log File. Some examples of the Log File appear in a later section of this chapter.

Datafile

The datafile contains the data that is to be loaded by the SQL*Loader into the Oracle tables. The data can be stored in an external file that resides on the file system, or small amounts of data can be specified after the Control File program. Examples of both of these approaches appear later on. The data itself can take many forms: character, binary, graphics, and so on.

Bad File

When you write a SQL*Loader Control File program, you specify what the datatypes of the records are and how the data is to be loaded into tables. If any of the data in the datafile cannot be loaded because of an error condition (for example, invalid dates where a date field is expected, invalid numbers in a number field, or database trigger or constraints errors), the data record is written out to a file called the Bad File. This file has exactly the same format as the original datafile. The Bad File is a subset of the datafile that contains only the rejected records.

You can use the same SQL*Loader program to use the Bad File as input (as if it were a datafile) without having to change code. This assumes that you have fixed the program code to handle the conditions that caused the record to be rejected or fixed the data itself.

Discard File

When you write a SQL*Loader program, you can bypass processing of records in the datafile when certain conditions are not met. You do this by using the WHEN clause, which specifies the conditions under which to process or reject a row.

Any rows discarded in this manner can be written out to a Discard File that must be named explicitly in the Control File program. If the filename is omitted the Discard File cannot be produced, but the Log File shows how many records were discarded.

The Discard File contains records in the same format as the original datafile, which means that, again, you can use the same Control File program to reprocess the records once either the data has been fixed or the Control File program has been changed.

What Can SQL*Loader Load?

SQL*Loader can hold data in fixed-length and variable-length records. It can also concatenate two physical records into one logical record so that they can be treated as one record in the Control File program. In addition, SQL*Loader can handle many different datatypes, including decimal, integer, float, fixed-length character strings, binary data, and so on.

The SQL*Loader also accepts default values. For date fields, defaults for the current date and time are based on SYSDATE. Numeric field defaults are based on either an existing database sequence or on the record number (which is the order in which the record was loaded into the database tables). You can also specify constant values in the Control File program for specific database columns.

You can set additional options to say what should happen if too many errors occur or too many records are discarded or too many bad records are found. This is useful when you begin testing the programs; you don't want to wait hours to finish loading thousands of records before detecting problems. The first few rows are usually good enough indicators of most problems that may exist in the data.

Command Line and Parameters

The SQL*Loader program runs from the operating system command line. Any parameters the program should use are specified after the program name. On some platforms there is a GUI version of the SQL*Loader program that enables you to import the command-line parameters by filling in fields on a screen. In the rest of this chapter, you concentrate on the character-based version of the program so that you can clearly see which parameters are coming in. The names and values of the parameters are the same on any platform on which Oracle runs. To determine the exact name for the SQL*Loader program, however, you should check with the *Oracle Installation and User's Guide*; the name can vary from one implementation to another.

You can specify parameters on the command line, or in the Control File with the OPTIONS clause. Parameters specified in the OPTIONS clause become the default parameters; they can be overridden by specifying new parameters on the command line.

Running the Program

The following code shows an example of the SQL*Loader program.

```
c:\> sqlldr userid=ascend/ascend control=loader1.ctl
```

Table 18.1 shows the command-line parameters for SQL*Loader.

Table 18.1. Command-line parameters.

BAD	Specifies the name of the file used to hold records that could not be processed by the Control File program. This file has the same format as the original datafile and can be used as input to the Control program once the Control program or the bad data has been fixed.
BINDSIZE	Specifies the size of the array in bytes that holds the rows to be inserted into the database tables. The data from the datafile is constructed into rows in this array area using the conventional load path with SQL*Loader. Once the array area is filled, a set of INSERT commands are issued to the database. The bigger the BINDSIZE array, the faster the program runs.
CONTROL	Specifies the name of the Control File that contains the code for the SQL*Loader program. This is the only mandatory parameter that must be specified when SQL*Loader runs.
DATA	Specifies the name of the datafile to be processed by the program code in the Control File. This parameter is optional, as the data can be specified inline inside the Control File along with the program code.
DIRECT	The SQL*Loader can be run in two different ways—with the conventional load path or the Direct load path. This parameter specifies that the program is to be run in Direct mode. The Direct load path offers performance advantages and is described later on in this chapter.
DISCARD	Specifies the file that holds the records discarded by the Control File program because they did not meet the specified conditions in the WHEN clause. The Discard File is

continues

Table 18.1. continued

	produced only when the filename is given—either in the DISCARD parameter or in options within the Control File program. The Discard File is essentially a subset of the datafile. It can be used as a datafile for another SQL*Loader program run.
DISCARDMAX	Controls the maximum number of records that can be discarded by the SQL*Loader program before the program terminates. This parameter allows you to abort the run if too many records are rejected (which probably indicates that the program code needs to be changed).
ERRORS	Specifies the maximum number of records that can be rejected into the Bad File. Again, this parameter allows you to set a maximum number of errors above which the program stops running so that the program or data can be fixed.
LOAD	Specifies the maximum number of records to load into the database tables. This parameter can be used to process only the first part of a datafile.
LOG	Specifies the name of the Log File that contains information about how the load proceeded. After every run you should check the Log File for any errors that were not reported back to the screen.
PARFILE	Specifies the name of another file that holds the parameters to be used by the SQL*Loader program. The parameters can be saved to a disk file. By using the PARFILE parameter, you can set many values for the different parameters for the program.
ROWS	Specifies the number of rows that are held in the bind array. This parameter must be set to at least 1.
SILENT	Suppresses messages that otherwise would be shown. Information is still written to the Log File.
SKIP	Specifies the number of records to ignore in the datafile being loaded. This parameter is especially useful when the first part of the datafile contains header-type information that has been stored by the outside data source.
USERID	Specifies the Oracle username and password used to determine which Oracle tables the data should be loaded into. The SQL*Loader program can load records into any Oracle tables that are accessible by the Oracle username given.

On most platforms, if the SQL*Loader program is run without any parameters, a screen appears showing acceptable parameters, brief descriptions of each parameter, and any default values that exist.

You can specify a parameter by its name followed by its value or by putting all the parameters in the correct order and supplying the values for each one. If you use a combination of these methods, you must list the ones that have been specified by position first and the ones specified by keywords at the end.

TIP

Use the OPTIONS clause in the Control File to specify default parameters that can be overridden at runtime by specifying the parameters.

The Control File Program

The Control File contains the program code that is to be used to load data into the Oracle table. It can also include the data to be loaded, or the data can be held in an external file. In this section, you look at some of the choices for the Control File itself, but the reader is referred to the Oracle7 *Server Utilities Guide* for the complete syntax and other commands not covered here.

Some Control File Choices

The major parts of the Control File are covered in the following sections.

INFILE—Data in the Control File or in an External File

The INFILE clause within the Control File specifies the location of the data to be loaded into the Oracle table. The data can be stored in an external operating system file or, if only a small amount, listed at the end of the Control File. If the data is stored externally, the name of the operating system file is given. An asterisk (*) in the INFILE option indicates that data is stored at the end of the Control File. The keyword BEGINDATA appears in the Control File to indicate to SQL*Loader where the records to be inserted into the Oracle database tables begin.

Another option with the INFILE clause is to specify many INFILE statements to indicate that the data is going to be retrieved from many operating system files. For these files, the data may not have the same format but the record layouts must be the same.

INTO TABLE

The INTO TABLE clause of the Control File program specifies the database table to be populated with the incoming data. The Oracle username used when the program is run must have at least the INSERT privilege on that table in order to be able to insert records into it. If the table is not owned by the Oracle user, the table's owner can be specified before the table name in the INTO TABLE clause. Another way to accomplish this would be to create synonyms in the Oracle database for user IDs specified when the program is run.

The INTO TABLE clause can also specify the names of a number of tables to be populated by the SQL*Loader program.

Insertion Options

You can specify four options that indicate what is to happen to the existing data in the table into which new data is loaded.

The INSERT option specifies that new rows are to be inserted into the table but the table must be empty before the SQL*Loader performs the inserts. If the table is not empty, the SQL*Loader program aborts. The APPEND option adds new rows to the table whether the table is empty or not. Any existing rows are not modified. The REPLACE option removes all existing records from the table by using the SQL DELETE statement and then performs a COMMIT, followed by the loading of the new rows into the table. The TRUNCATE option uses the SQL TRUNCATE command to remove all the rows from the table and then performs the data load.

OPTIONS **Clause**

The OPTIONS clause within the SQL*Loader Control File specifies a number of parameters to be used by the SQL*Loader program only if the parameters are not overwritten on the command line. The OPTIONS clause in the Control program allows you to specify the parameters to be used during the run along with the program code itself. The parameters can be overridden at runtime by specifying new values on the command line. The following parameters can be specified in the OPTIONS clause: SKIP, LOAD, ERRORS, ROWS, BINDSIZE, SILENT, ERROR, DIRECT, and PARALLEL.

WHEN **Clause**

The WHEN clause specifies any conditions that must be true before data records are loaded into Oracle tables. You can compare values in the columns to be loaded against any conditions, and you can specify multiple conditions by using the AND clause. Rows that do not satisfy these conditions are not loaded into the table and can optionally be written out to a Discard File if it has been named in either the OPTIONS clause of the Control File or on the command line (with the DISCARD parameter).

Comments

Comments can be included in the SQL*Loader Control File program by placing two hyphens at the start of a line. Anything that appears on the line after these comment markers is ignored. If the data has been included in the Control File, however, comments cannot appear after the keyword BEGINDATA that marks the start of data records.

Example Programs

The following code samples show some typical SQL*Loader programs. Additional examples can be found with the Oracle RDBMS software.

Example 1—A Simple Load with Variable Data in the Control File

In this first example, you look at a SQL*Loader program with data specified in the same file as the Control File program.

Control File

The following code example shows a Control File with the data in line in the Control File.

```
--
-- Simple Load of Data - with data specified in the control file
--
LOAD DATA
INFILE *
INTO TABLE delegates
APPEND
FIELDS TERMINATED BY ','
(d_delegate_id, d_lastname, d_firstname,
 d_organisation, d_sex, d_date_last_contacted)
BEGINDATA
1,Powell,Cindy,Powell Assoc,F,15-MAY-96,
2,Neville,Tim,Albany,F,13-OCT-95,
3,Neville,Karen,Albany,M,25-JUN-96,
4,Brett,Sarah,City Printers,F,31-JAN-96,
5,Khoshnevisan,Hessam,Khoshn. Consulting Ltd,M,13-JAN-96,
6,Meier,Gerard,Fineview Ltd,M,21-MAR-96,
```

Explanation

Here's a line-by-line explanation of the preceding code:

- LOAD DATA—This line is usually the first line on any SQL*Loader program. It can be preceded by the OPTIONS clause, which specifies any default options that are to be used. No other SQL*Loader phrases can precede this line.

- INFILE *—Specifies the location of the data to be loaded by the SQL*Loader control program. The asterisk indicates that the data is included in line with the SQL*Loader Control program, and appears at the end of the file after the keyword BEGINDATA. If the data is to be loaded from an external operating system datafile, the name of that file appears here after the word INFILE.

- INTO TABLE—This clause names the database table that is to receive the data from the SQL*Loader program. The Oracle username specified on the command line when the SQL*Loader program is run must have INSERT privileges for this table or must be the owner of the table. If the table is owned by another Oracle user and a synonym does not exist, you can specify the owner's name followed by the table name, separated by a period.

■ APPEND—Specifies that the existing records in the table are not to be affected, and that the new records should be inserted into the table. Other options that can be used here are INSERT, REPLACE, or TRUNCATE.

■ FIELDS TERMINATED BY—Indicates that the record's fields are separated by the character specified in the Control File, in this case the comma. This means that you have variable-length records where the data fields may be of variable size. The SQL*Loader program looks for the commas in the data records to determine where one field ends and the next one begins. Notice that, in the data included at the end of the Control File, a comma appears at the end of every record to indicate the end of the record. This is not absolutely necessary, but it can make things clearer for anyone who needs to maintain the program.

■ Columns—Lists the names of the columns to be populated by the SQL*Loader program for clarity and in case the fields in the datafile do not appear in the same order as the columns in the table. By listing the columns here, you can ensure that the SQL*Loader program will work even if the underlying physical structure of the table changes (for example, new ones have been added to the table or the database administrator has re-created the table with the columns in a different order).

■ BEGINDATA—Lets SQL*Loader know that anything following this keyword is data to be loaded. There should be no white space after this keyword.

■ Data—The data in this SQL*Loader program has been included along with the Control File, and the individual fields are separated by commas. Any blank lines at the end of the program file are treated as records that do not fit the criteria for the program, and are rejected into the Bad File.

Output Files

Here is the Log File produced by the preceding example:

```
SQL*Loader: Release 7.2.2.3.1 - Production on Sat May 18 19:48:03 1996

Copyright Oracle Corporation 1979, 1994.  All rights reserved.

Control File:   loader1.ctl
datafile:       loader1.ctl
  Bad File:     loader1.bad
  Discard File: none specified

 (Allow all discards)

Number to load: ALL
Number to skip: 0
Errors allowed: 50
Bind array:     64 rows, maximum of 65024 bytes
Continuation:    none specified
Path used:      Conventional

Table DELEGATES, loaded from every logical record.
```

```
Insert option in effect for this table: APPEND

   Column Name                 Position   Len Term Encl Datatype
 -------------------------     ---------  ----- ---- ---- ----------------
D_DELEGATE_ID                   FIRST       *    ,         CHARACTER
D_LASTNAME                      NEXT        *    ,         CHARACTER
D_FIRSTNAME                     NEXT        *    ,         CHARACTER
D_ORGANISATION                  NEXT        *    ,         CHARACTER
D_SEX                           NEXT        *    ,         CHARACTER
D_DATE_LAST_CONTACTED           NEXT        *    ,         CHARACTER


Table DELEGATES:
  6 Rows successfully loaded.
  0 Rows not loaded due to data errors.
  0 Rows not loaded because all WHEN clauses were failed.
  0 Rows not loaded because all fields were null.


Space allocated for bind array:                63960 bytes(41 rows)
Space allocated for memory besides bind array:  112772 bytes

Total logical records skipped:          0
Total logical records read:             6
Total logical records rejected:         0
Total logical records discarded:        0

Run began on Sat May 18 19:48:03 1996
Run ended on Sat May 18 19:48:04 1996

Elapsed time was:      00:00:00.81
CPU time was:          00:00:00.00      (May not include ORACLE CPU time)
```

Here is the data that has been loaded into the table:

```
SQL> SELECT *
  2  FROM   delegates;

D_DELEGATE_ID D_LASTNAME      D_FIRSTNAME      D_ORGANISATION    D D_DATE_LA
------------- --------------- ---------------- ---------------- - ---------
            1 Powell          Cindy            Powell Assoc     F 15-MAY-96
            2 Neville         Tim              Albany           F 13-OCT-95
            3 Neville         Karen            Albany           M 25-JUN-96
            4 Brett           Sarah            City Printers    F 31-JAN-96
            5 Khoshnevisan    Hessam           Khoshn. Consult  M 13-JAN-96
                                               ing Ltd

            6 Meier           Gerard           Fineview Ltd     M 21-MAR-96

6 rows selected.

SQL>
```

Example 2—A Load with Fixed Data in an External Datafile

In this example, a Control File program loads data from an external file that has fixed-length data records.

Control File

Here is the Control File for the example:

```
--
-- Simple Load of Data - with fixed length data
--
LOAD DATA
INFILE 'loader2.dat'
INTO TABLE delegates
( d_delegate_id          POSITION(01:02) INTEGER EXTERNAL,
  d_lastname             POSITION(04:16) CHAR,
  d_firstname            POSITION(17:23) CHAR,
  d_organisation         POSITION(24:46) CHAR,
  d_sex                  POSITION(47:47) CHAR,
  d_date_last_contacted  POSITION(49:57) DATE
)
```

Here is the datafile used with the preceding program:

```
01 Powell       Cindy  Powell Assoc            F 15-MAY-96
02 Neville      Tim    Albany                  F 13-OCT-95
03 Neville      Karen  Albany                  M 25-JUN-96
04 Brett        Sarah  City Printers           F 31-JAN-96
05 Khoshnevisan Hessam Khoshn. Consulting Ltd  M 13-JAN-96
06 Meier        Gerard Fineview Ltd            M 21-MAR-96
```

Explanation

Here's an explanation of the preceding example:

- INFILE—In this example, the data for the program is to be loaded from an external file called loader2.dat. The datafile contains fixed-length records and identifies the fields by their beginning character positions. For example, the first field, d_delegate_id, is two characters long, starting at position 1 and including the second character of each row. The field is defined as an EXTERNAL INTEGER. Other fields are also specified by their positions and the datatype they contain.
- If any of the fields in the datafile do not match the datatype given for numeric and date fields, the rows are rejected into the Bad File.

Output Files

Here is the Log File produced by the run:

```
SQL*Loader: Release 7.2.2.3.1 - Production on Sat May 18 19:55:50 1996

Copyright Oracle Corporation 1979, 1994.  All rights reserved.

Control File:   loader2.ctl
datafile:       loader2.dat
  Bad File:     loader2.bad
  Discard File: none specified

 (Allow all discards)
```

```
Number to load: ALL
Number to skip: 0
Errors allowed: 50
Bind array:     64 rows, maximum of 65024 bytes
Continuation:   none specified
Path used:      Conventional

Table DELEGATES, loaded from every logical record.
Insert option in effect for this table: INSERT

    Column Name                 Position   Len Term Encl Datatype
-------------------------------- --------- ----- ---- ---- --------------------
D_DELEGATE_ID                          1:2    2            CHARACTER
D_LASTNAME                            4:16   13            CHARACTER
D_FIRSTNAME                          17:23    7            CHARACTER
D_ORGANISATION                       24:46   23            CHARACTER
D_SEX                                47:47    1            CHARACTER
D_DATE_LAST_CONTACTED                49:57    9            DATE DD-MON-YY


Table DELEGATES:
  6 Rows successfully loaded.
  0 Rows not loaded due to data errors.
  0 Rows not loaded because all WHEN clauses were failed.
  0 Rows not loaded because all fields were null.


Space allocated for bind array:                     4864 bytes(64 rows)
Space allocated for memory besides bind array:     57986 bytes

Total logical records skipped:          0
Total logical records read:             6
Total logical records rejected:         0
Total logical records discarded:        0

Run began on Sat May 18 19:55:50 1996
Run ended on Sat May 18 19:55:51 1996

Elapsed time was:      00:00:00.93
CPU time was:          00:00:00.00     (May not include ORACLE CPU time)
```

Here is the data that is loaded into the delegates table.

```
SQL> SELECT *
  2  FROM   delegates;

D_DELEGATE_ID D_LASTNAME       D_FIRSTNAME      D_ORGANISATION    D D_DATE_LA
------------- ---------------- ---------------- ----------------- - ---------
            1 Powell           Cindy            Powell Assoc      F 15-MAY-96
            2 Neville          Tim              Albany            F 13-OCT-95
            3 Neville          Karen            Albany            M 25-JUN-96
            4 Brett            Sarah            City Printers     F 31-JAN-96
            5 Khoshnevisan     Hessam           Khoshn. Consult   M 13-JAN-96
                                                ing Ltd

            6 Meier            Gerard           Fineview Ltd      M 21-MAR-96

6 rows selected.

SQL>
```

Example 3—A More Complex Load

In this example, you look at a Control File program that uses some more advanced commands to perform additional processing on the rows to be loaded. The data to be loaded by the Control File is included inside the Control program.

Control File

The following is a Control File for a more complex load with the data held in line in the Control File:

```
--
-- More Complex Load of Data - with data specified in the control file
--
LOAD DATA
INFILE *
BADFILE loader3.bad
DISCARDFILE loader3.dsc
DISCARDMAX 200
REPLACE
CONTINUEIF (1) = '-'
INTO TABLE delegates
WHEN d_lastname != 'Dummy Row'
FIELDS TERMINATED BY ','
TRAILING NULLCOLS
(d_delegate_id  SEQUENCE(MAX,1),
 d_lastname      "UPPER(:d_lastname)",
 d_firstname     NULLIF d_firstname='UNKNOWN',
 d_organisation TERMINATED BY '*',
 d_sex           NULLIF d_sex = BLANKS,
 d_date_last_contacted DATE(8) "MM/DD/YY" )
BEGINDATA
*** This row is not recognised - error row  ***
 Powell,Cindy,Powell Assoc*F,5/15/96,
 Neville,Tim,*M,11/13/95,
 Dummy Row,garbage data 399393dflkjsdf;sd
 Neville,UNKNOWN,Albany*M,6/25/96,
-Brett,Sarah,City Pri
nters*F,1/31/96,
-Khoshnevisan,Hessam,Khos
hn. Consulting Ltd*M,1/13/96,
 Meier,Gerard,Fineview Ltd*,3/21/96,
 Dummy Row,garbage data 904098-044809244--040348
```

Explanation

Here's a line-by-line explanation of the preceding code:

- INFILE—The asterisk in this parameter indicates that the data is included in the Control File following the BEGINDATA keyword.

- BADFILE—Specifies the name of the file to be used to hold any records that cannot be processed by the program due to formatting, database constraint, or database trigger errors.

■ DISCARDFILE—Specifies the name of the file used to hold any rows rejected because they don't match conditions in the WHEN clause in the Control File program. Records in the Discard File and the Bad File are in the same format as the original data records, which means that you can use these files as input to another SQL*Loader program without changing code.

■ DISCARDMAX—Specifies the maximum number of rows that can be discarded by the SQL*Loader program before the program aborts. In this example, if more than 200 rows are discarded, the program aborts.

■ REPLACE—Indicates that the existing records in the delegates table are to be deleted, the changes committed, and the new records from the SQL*Loader program inserted into the table. After the loader program runs, the only rows left in the database table are the ones that were successfully loaded by the SQL*Loader program.

■ CONTINUEIF—Indicates that one logical record may exist as two physical records in the datafile. If a hyphen is found at the start of any one record, the next record is to be included as the same logical record.

■ WHEN—Indicates which rows are to be discarded by the SQL*Loader program because certain conditions have been met; rows that have the character string 'Dummy Row' in the lastname column are ignored. If a DISCARDFILE name has been given, the discarded rows are written to the file; otherwise the discarded rows are reported to the Log File.

■ FIELDS TERMINATED BY—Indicates that the fields in the datafile are variable length and the comma character is used to indicate where one field ends and the next field begins.

■ TRAILING NULLCOLS—Indicates that not all the fields for the table may be present in the datafile. Any fields at the end that have not been specified are to be left as null when the rows are inserted into the table.

■ COLUMNS—Between the brackets are the names of the database columns that are to be populated by the fields in the datafile. In this example, some additional processing takes place on those fields. In the first example, d_delegate_id is to be set automatically to a unique sequence number that is calculated as the highest delegate ID that currently exists in the table, plus 1, as each row is inserted by the SQL*Loader program. This allows for unique numbers in that column of the database table. You can also use database sequences to generate this unique number.

The UPPER function is used with the d_lastname database column to indicate that the lastname field from the datafile is to be converted to uppercase before it is inserted into the database table.

With the d_sex field, the NULLIF clause sets the database column to a null value if the sex field is not present; the BLANKS keyword is used to show this.

The d_date_last_contact field is specified as a date field that is eight characters long. The field is formatted with two digits for the month, a slash, two digits for the year, another slash, and two digits for the day. You could also use the Oracle T-DATE function to provide the same functionality.

■ `BEGINDATA`—Anything after this keyword is a data record. In this example, the very first record is rejected into the `BADFILE` because the data format is not recognized. Other rows that contain the string `'Dummy Row'` are discarded by the `WHEN` clause. All other rows are loaded into the database table as shown below.

Output Files

Here is the Log File produced by the preceding example:

```
SQL*Loader: Release 7.2.2.3.1 - Production on Sat May 18 19:58:45 1996

Copyright Oracle Corporation 1979, 1994.  All rights reserved.

Control File:   loader3.ctl
datafile:       loader3.ctl
  Bad File:     loader3.bad
  Discard File: loader3.dsc
 (Allow 200 discards)

Number to load: ALL
Number to skip: 0
Errors allowed: 50
Bind array:     64 rows, maximum of 65024 bytes
Continuation:   1:1 = 0X2d(character '-'), in current physical record
Path used:      Conventional

Table DELEGATES, loaded when D_LASTNAME != 0X44756d6d7920526f77(character 'Dummy
Row')
Insert option in effect for this table: REPLACE
TRAILING NULLCOLS option in effect

    Column Name                     Position   Len Term Encl Datatype
------------------------------- --------- ----- ---- ---- --------------------
D_LASTNAME                           NEXT     *    ,       CHARACTER
D_FIRSTNAME                          NEXT     *    ,       CHARACTER
D_ORGANISATION                       NEXT     *    *       CHARACTER
D_SEX                                NEXT     *    ,       CHARACTER
D_DATE_LAST_CONTACTED                NEXT     8    ,       DATE MM/DD/YY

D_DELEGATE_ID                    SEQUENCE (MAX, 1)

Column D_LASTNAME had SQL string
"UPPER(:d_lastname)"
 applied to it.
Column D_FIRSTNAME is NULL if D_FIRSTNAME = 0X554e4b4e4f574e(character 'UNKNOWN')
Column D_SEX is NULL if D_SEX = BLANKS

Record 4: Discarded - failed all WHEN clauses.
Record 9: Discarded - failed all WHEN clauses.
Record 1: Rejected - Error on table DELEGATES.
ORA-01401: inserted value too large for column


Table DELEGATES:
  6 Rows successfully loaded.
  1 Row not loaded due to data errors.
  2 Rows not loaded because all WHEN clauses were failed.
  0 Rows not loaded because all fields were null.
```

```
Space allocated for bind array:                    64500 bytes(60 rows)
Space allocated for memory besides bind array:     117867 bytes

Total logical records skipped:          0
Total logical records read:             9
Total logical records rejected:         1
Total logical records discarded:        2

Run began on Sat May 18 19:58:45 1996
Run ended on Sat May 18 19:58:46 1996

Elapsed time was:       00:00:01.21
CPU time was:           00:00:00.00      (May not include ORACLE CPU time)
```

Some of the rows from the preceding program were rejected into the Discard File. Here are the contents of that file:

```
Dummy Row,garbage data 399393dflkjsdf;sd
Dummy Row,garbage data 904098-044809244--040348
```

Some of the rows were rejected into the following Bad File because they contained bad data:

```
*** This row is not recognised - error row   ***
```

Here are the contents of the delegates table after the load:

```
SQL> SELECT *
  2  FROM   delegates;

D_DELEGATE_ID D_LASTNAME      D_FIRSTNAME       D_ORGANISATION    D D_DATE_LA
------------- --------------  ---------------   ----------------  - ---------
            2 POWELL          Cindy             Powell Assoc      F 15-MAY-96
            3 NEVILLE         Tim                                 M 13-NOV-95
            4 NEVILLE                           Albany            M 25-JUN-96
            5 BRETT           Sarah             City Printers     F 31-JAN-96
            6 KHOSHNEVISAN    Hessam            Khoshn. Consult   M 13-JAN-96
                                                ing Ltd

            7 MEIER           Gerard            Fineview Ltd        21-MAR-96

6 rows selected.

SQL>
```

Constraints and Database Triggers

Constraints and database triggers still apply as the SQL*Loader program runs (from conventional mode rather than the Direct load path), and can be used to perform further validation and processing on the data. The database constraints automatically perform any predefined validation checks. You can use database triggers with the :NEW prefix before each column to perform additional validation on values inserted by the SQL*Loader program.

Constraints and database triggers can be used to implement complex processing instead of performing all processing in the Control File program of SQL*Loader. In addition, database triggers can call procedures, functions, and packages that may already have been written for some other parts of the system.

The Direct Load Path

When a SQL*Loader program is run, it runs by default in the conventional path. This means that the rows which are to be inserted into the database tables are first built in the bind array. Once the bind array is full, INSERT statements are issued to insert the rows into the database. As far as the database is concerned, the INSERT statements go through the same parts of the architecture as statements from any other Oracle tool. This means that changes to Oracle blocks caused by the INSERT statements are recorded in the Redo Logs and in rollback segments. For large data loads, the performance overhead of using rollback segments and the Redo Logs can be significant, causing the SQL*Loader program to run, in many cases, for many hours.

To speed up the runtime of the SQL*Loader Control File programs, the Direct load path can be used to bypass some of the architecture of the Oracle database. Oracle blocks are built by the SQL*Loader program and inserted into the database files, thereby avoiding the full use of the rollback segments. With the UNRECOVERABLE option, you can bypass the Redo Logs as well. However, if the database files are lost, the table's changes cannot be recovered using a backup of the database files and the online and archived redo log files.

To run the SQL*Loader program in Direct mode, you use the Direct = True keyword either on the command line or in the OPTIONS clause within the Control File.

There are a number of limitations with the Direct load path. The table in which the data is to be loaded cannot be used by any other Oracle user while the load is running and is locked exclusively for the SQL*Loader program. In addition, all constraints apart from the Not Null constraint are disabled along with all database triggers. Indexes are put into a special Direct Load state, and if the SQL*Loader program crashes or aborts while the data is being loaded, the indexes must be rebuilt manually by the database administrators. The status column on the DBA_INDEXES data dictionary view can be interrogated to see whether the indexes were left in this state. Also, you cannot use synonyms to refer to the table that is to receive the new rows—you must load directly into the tables themselves. Another restriction is that you cannot use functions on the data in the Control File, but you can process the records further after they have been inserted by using PL/SQL in a tool such as SQL*Plus. Refer to the Oracle7 *Server Utilities Guide* for information about additional restrictions.

If you can satisfy the restrictions of the Direct load path, it can produce significant performance advantages over the conventional load path in many cases.

Other Options in Loading Data

Another way to load data into an Oracle database is to write a 3GL program with embedded SQL and PL/SQL statements. 3GL programs are processed through Oracle precompilers that translate the SQL and PL/SQL statements into direct Oracle C function calls (calls to the Oracle OCI routines). There are currently six 3GL languages for which precompilers are available: C, COBOL, FORTRAN, Ada, Pascal, and PL/1.

3GL language statements can be used to read external file(s) and perform complex logic. The PL/SQL and SQL INSERT, UPDATE, and DELETE statements can be used to insert and manipulate rows in the Oracle tables. The SQL statements use the values stored in the host language variables. However, 3GL language programs are not as portable as Oracle SQL*Loader programs, and typically take longer to write. Oracle SQL*Loader programs can be ported to any other platform on which the same or higher version of Oracle is installed without any changes to the program—the same cannot be said of writing loading routines in 3GL languages. In addition, SQL*Loader offers the Direct load option, which can in many cases significantly reduce the amount of time taken to perform a data load.

Another way to load data from external data sources is to use the Oracle Gateway products that interface to other data sources (for example, DB2, Ingres, or Informix databases, and so on). If an Oracle Gateway product exists for the data source you're trying to load (for example, for data held in a DB2 database), instead of dumping the data from that data source out to an external file and using SQL*Loader to load it, you can access the external data directly by using SQL through the Gateway products. In this way, you can treat the data source as another table, making the loading of data much simpler. Cost is a factor when considering whether to use Gateway products—purchasing, installing, and configuring the Gateway products may not be worthwhile if you only need to load the data once.

Unloading Data from Oracle into Flat Files

In many situations, you may want to produce a flat file from the contents of an Oracle table, to be processed and loaded by another system. Oracle does not (yet) provide a quick and easy way to unload the contents of a table into a flat file (the Oracle export utility produces a binary compressed file, which can be used only by the import utility).

However, before considering how to produce a flat file, ask yourself whether there isn't a simpler and more convenient way to perform the processing. If you want to unload the Oracle table into a flat file to load into another data source, is there a way to perform a Direct load from Oracle without creating the intermediate file (an ODBC driver, perhaps, or a gateway-type product from the other database to Oracle)?

To produce a flat file from the contents of a table, you must resort to basic SQL*Plus programming, which allows you to select all the contents without any headings or other superfluous information and spool it directly into a flat file. With the basic Oracle tools, this is about as close as you can get.

The following code example shows the contents of a table being saved to a flat file with fixed-length records (which is how the output in SQL*Plus normally appears).

```
SET LINESIZE 132
SET PAGESIZE 9999
SET HEADING OFF
SET ECHO OFF
SET FEEDBACK OFF
SET VERIFY OFF

SPOOL booking.lis

SELECT *
FROM   bookings;

SPOOL OFF

SET PAGESIZE 50
SET HEADING ON
SET ECHO ON
SET FEEDBACK ON
```

These are the contents of the resulting file:

```
        1 OSQL      08-JAN-96 London
        3 OSQL      08-JAN-96 London
        5 OSQL      08-JAN-96 London
        1 OFOR4     06-FEB-96 Tehran
        2 OFOR4     05-FEB-96 Tehran
        2 OPDO      08-JAN-96 Riyadh
        4 OPDO      08-JAN-96 Riyadh
        6 OPDO      08-JAN-96 Riyadh
```

The following code example shows how to produce a comma-delimited file. The concatenation operator is used to concatenate commas between each of the field values.

```
SET LINESIZE 132
SET PAGESIZE 9999
SET HEADING OFF
SET ECHO OFF
SET FEEDBACK OFF
SET VERIFY OFF

SPOOL booking.lis

SELECT b_delegate_id
       ||','||
       b_course_code
       ||','||
       b_start_date
       ||','||
```

```
        b_location
        ||','||
        ||','||
        b_paid
FROM    bookings;

SPOOL OFF

SET PAGESIZE 50
SET HEADING ON
SET ECHO ON
SET FEEDBACK ON
```

Here's the output from the preceding code example:

```
1,OSQL,08-JAN-96,London,
3,OSQL,08-JAN-96,London,
5,OSQL,08-JAN-96,London,
1,OFOR4,06-FEB-96,Tehran,
2,OFOR4,05-FEB-96,Tehran,
2,OPDO,08-JAN-96,Riyadh,
4,OPDO,08-JAN-96,Riyadh,
6,OPDO,08-JAN-96,Riyadh,
```

Any more complex formats for the output file can always be handled by building the complexity into SQL or PL/SQL.

Summary

In this chapter, you looked at some of the primary options available for loading data from external files into an Oracle database using SQL*Loader. You can perform further processing on the loaded data by using procedural objects on the database, such as database functions, procedures, and packages. You can choose whether to perform the majority of the processing by using Control File commands (which are extensive) or by loading the data into temporary tables and using PL/SQL to perform additional processing as the records are loaded into the real database tables. Finally, you saw how you can quickly unload the contents of an Oracle table into an operating system file.

19

Export/Import

by Lave Singh

In this chapter, you examine two utilities that are part of the Oracle database software: Export and Import. These programs can be run in much the same way, regardless of the platform you are using to run Oracle. In addition, many of the parameters are similar.

What Are Export and Import?

Export is a program used to unload both the data and the definitions of the database objects into an operating system binary file. Export does not affect the database because it is a query-only process. The operating system file produced by the Export program has the full SQL statements required to create the database objects, and the data for tables, too.

Import is the opposite of Export. It takes the exported file and loads the data back into the database. In addition, Import can recreate database objects if they don't already exist—this is optional based on the parameters provided by the user of the program.

Both of these programs run from the operating system command line.

Export and Import are used for a number of different reasons, which are covered in the following sections.

Backup and Recovery

There are a number of different ways to back up and recover an Oracle7 database, and Export and Import complement these ways. The primary way to backup and recover a database after a failure is to use the operating system to back up the database files, and then use the Redo Logs in Archive mode to recover any transactions made up to the point of failure. This way, nothing is lost and you can recover the entire database without losing any committed work.

One drawback of using the Redo Logs after database files have been restored from a backup is that you cannot recover just one table or one set of tables. It is either the entire database (or tablespace) or nothing. With Export and Import, however, you can recover just one table without having to restore the entire database. But any changes made to the table since it was last exported are lost. There is no way of reapplying the changes to that table from the Redo Logs.

Sending Data Between Databases

Export and Import can also be used to transfer a database from one Oracle database to another. Using Export, you can export a table, a set of tables, or even an entire database from one machine, copy the binary export file to a disk or a tape drive, and then send the file to another machine that is running the same or a later version of the Oracle software. On the new machine, you can use the Import utility to bring the objects and data into the new database.

Bear in mind that the Export file is a binary file in Oracle's own internal format. It can be read by the Import program on any other machine. If you transfer data from one character set to another (for example, EBCDIC to ASCII), you should ensure no conversion takes place during the transfer. The Import program on the other machine handles any conversion automatically.

For example, you could export objects from an Oracle database on a PC, record the export file on a disk, transfer it to an Oracle database running on a UNIX machine, and the Import program on that machine would read the exported data. This is a quick and easy way to move data from one machine to another.

If a network link exists between the machines and the necessary software is installed, another option is to use database links to copy the data over using SQL statements.

Upgrading Oracle Software

Export and Import can also be used to migrate your database from one version of the Oracle database to another. For example, to move from Oracle Version 6 to Oracle Version 7, you could export the Version 6 database, take the export file, and load it into a new Oracle7 database. The Import program re-creates the entire data and structure of the old database automatically. It is a relatively simple operation, but it may take a very long time to run for large amounts of data. For this reason, Oracle Corporation recommends you use the migration utilities provided with the Oracle7 RDBMS software to migrate from Oracle Version 6 to Oracle Version 7. These programs, which run slightly differently on different platforms, essentially convert the Version 6 database files to the new Oracle Version 7 format without changing the entire set of data itself. Only the file headers, data dictionary, and other system objects are modified—not the user's own tables. As a result, the migration utilities run much faster than Export and Import.

All future versions of the Oracle database will include migration utilities. Export and Import will still exist, but only as a last resort option.

Tidying Up the Database

Export and Import are also used as a means of tidying up the data in the database. If database objects have been allocated more than one extent of storage, the Import program can re-create the program with one extent big enough to hold all the data (if the COMPRESS=Y option is chosen when the Export is performed). In addition, the indexes are re-created by Import (index data is not actually stored in the Export file).

Who Uses Export and Import?

Export and Import are used by developers and database administrators. Database administrators may use Export and Import as a means of ensuring that they can recover any one table in case it is accidentally dropped.

In addition, database administrators may use Export and Import to ensure that the entire set of Oracle blocks are accessed and read during the Export program. This way, if any Oracle blocks become corrupted, the Export program sends the user an error message that indicates the problem. Export and Import in this case are used in conjunction with the operating system backup of the database files. The Export program merely traps any corrupted Oracle block areas.

Developers also use Export and Import to ensure that they have a backup of the tables before testing their programs. For example, if you have a program that modifies a set of tables in the database, before running the program you would use Export to provide a quick backup of the tables, run the program that changes the data, drop the tables, and use Import to bring the tables and data back into the database so that you could retest the program.

Another major use of Export and Import is to transfer the definitions of database objects from a development environment to another environment—for example, from a development environment to user test, to system testing, or even to the production system. Export in this case is used to bring over just the definitions of the database objects and not the actual data itself.

The data on the development database is test data. Once the definitions are re-created (which can be done automatically by Import), either the users or the developers set up a new set of test data or production data in the database.

Import would be used in this manner to re-create the object definitions if the definitions have not been maintained in flat files or if the definitions have not been stored in a CASE tool such as Oracle Designer 2000.

Different Ways to Run the Programs

Export and Import can be run in four different ways, which are described in the following sections.

Interactively

Export and Import can both be run interactively—where the user of the program is prompted for most of the required parameters. The default value for each parameter, if available, is shown to the user at the prompt. If the user wants to accept the default value, she presses the carriage return to continue. The following example shows Export being run interactively. The Import program runs the same way.

```
Unix>exp

Export: Release 7.2.2.3.1 - Production on Fri May 10 17:39:37 1996

Copyright (c) Oracle Corporation 1979, 1994.  All rights reserved.


Username: system
Password:
```

```
Connected to: Oracle7 Release 7.2.2.3.1
With the distributed and replication options
PL/SQL Release 2.2.2.3.1 - Pr
Enter array fetch buffer size: 4096 >

Export file: EXPDAT.DMP >myexp.dmp

(1)E(ntire database), (2)U(sers), or (3)T(ables): (2)U >E

Export grants (yes/no): yes >

Export table data (yes/no): yes >

Compress extents (yes/no): yes >

About to export the entire database ...
. exporting tablespace definitions
. exporting profiles
. exporting user definitions
. exporting roles
. exporting resource costs
. exporting rollback segment definitions
. exporting database links
. exporting sequence numbers
. exporting snapshots
. exporting snapshot logs
. exporting job queues
. exporting refresh groups and children
. exporting cluster definitions
. about to export SYSTEM's tables ...
. . exporting table              DEF$_CALL          0 rows exported
. . exporting table          DEF$_CALLDEST          0 rows exported
. . exporting table       DEF$_DEFAULTDEST          0 rows exported
. . exporting table       DEF$_DESTINATION          0 rows exported
. . exporting table             DEF$_ERROR          0 rows exported

<etc. for the entire set of users and tables for the database>
```

GUI Interface

On some platforms, a graphical user interface version of the Export and Import programs accepts the required parameters. The GUI screens accept the same parameters as the character-based versions of the Export and Import programs.

This chapter concentrates more on the character-mode version of Export and Import, however, because that version is available on all platforms. In addition, the parameters are the same in both versions (character-mode and GUI).

Command Line

Export and Import can also be run by providing the required parameters on the command line. You only need to provide those parameters that are mandatory or for which you want to override the default.

This method is typically used by database administrators and developers who are familiar with the parameter names.

The following code example shows an Export program being run by providing the required parameters on the command line:

```
Unix>exp userid=system/manager file=myexp.dmp full=y

<export program runs as before>
```

Parameter File

Another way to run the Export and Import programs is to put the parameters into a file and provide the filename to the programs when they run.

This method is typically used when you run the Export and Import programs often with the same parameters. For example, a nightly batch export run to back up the database would always use the same parameters; you don't want someone running the program interactively in the middle of the night, typing values for the parameters. The correct parameters can be stored in a parameter file and the programs run automatically in batch mode.

The following code example shows the contents of a parameter file and the Export program that runs with the file.

```
Unix>pg mypar.par
USERID=system/manager
FILE=myexp.dmp
LOG=mylog.log
FULL=y

Unix>exp parfile=mypar.par

<export program runs as before>
```

Different Levels of Export

When the Export and Import programs run, the user can choose what is to be exported from the database. The available choices are described in the following sections.

Entire Database

It is possible to export the entire contents of a database, including the definitions and data for just about everything apart from the Oracle data dictionary (system tables). To do this, the Oracle account used when the program is run must be granted a default database role called EXP_FULL_DATABASE.

If the entire database has been exported, Import can be used to bring in either the entire database or just individual tables. This kind of export is typically used by a database administrator to ensure that he can get back a single table if it is accidentally dropped.

If you want to restore the entire database from a full database export, the Import program must have something to import into. The database administrator creates a new database with just the SYSTEM tablespace and at least one other rollback segment available (apart from the one called System that is always created on an Oracle database). If two rollback segments are on line, the Import program re-creates the entire set of user's tablespaces, all the other database objects in the database, and then brings back the data.

User-Level

Export and Import can also be run to Export and Import the contents of one Oracle user account. Only the name of the Oracle account and its password are required to run the programs in this way.

This kind of Export and Import is often used by developers to make a quick backup of their database objects in case any one of them is required again.

If the entire set of database objects is exported, you have the option of restoring just individual objects with the Import program. Import can also be used to restore the data and the definitions to a user other than the one who owned the objects when the export was performed.

Individual Tables

Export also allows you to specify individual tables to be exported rather than the entire database or everything for one user.

Again, you can import individual tables only or the entire Export file.

What Is Exported and Imported?

Table 19.1 shows the objects that are exported when the Export program is run for individual tables, for an entire Oracle user, or for the entire database.

Table 19.1. Objects exported.

Mode	What Is Exported
Table	Table data
	Table definitions including comments and audit options
	Grants on table issued by owner
	Indexes on table created by owner
	Constraint definitions
	Database triggers

continues

Table 19.1. continued

Mode	What Is Exported
User	Everything as above for Table Mode export
	Cluster definitions
	Database link definitions
	Sequences
	Snapshots
	Snapshot logs for quick refreshing
	Stored procedures, functions, and packages
	Private synonyms
	Views
Entire Database	Everything as above for User Mode export
	Public synonyms as well as private synonyms
	Profiles
	Roles
	Rollback segment definitions
	System-level auditing settings
	System privileges given to users and roles
	Tablespace definitions
	Tablespace quotas for users
	User definitions

Export Parameters

You can specify a number of parameters for the Export program. Many of them are the same for the Import program. Not all of the parameters are prompted for when the programs are run interactively; the command line or the parameter file method must be used to specify values for those parameters not prompted for.

HELP

When you specify HELP = Y, the full list of parameters and a short description of each parameter appears.

USERID

Oracle sees the Export program as another user process that needs access to the database files. Just like any other user, the program needs a valid Oracle username and password.

If the USERID assigned to the Export program has been granted the EXP_FULL_DATABASE role, the option of exporting the entire database is available.

BUFFER

The BUFFER parameter controls the amount of storage used to fetch rows from the database. The buffer holds the rows as they are fetched and before they are written to the Export file.

> **TIP**
>
> Increasing the size of the buffer can dramatically improve the runtime performance of the Export and Import programs.

FILE

The FILE parameter names the binary file to which the export data is written. By default the name of the file is expdat.dmp. The .dmp file extension is used by convention, but any file extension will do.

If a directory path is not specified for the Export file, the file is stored in the user's default operating system directory.

COMPRESS

If you specify Y for this parameter, the storage definitions of database objects in the Export file are adjusted to an amount sufficient to store all the data in one extent when the database objects are re-created by Import. The amount of storage to allocate for the INITIAL extent for the objects is calculated by summing the storage currently allocated for the database objects.

If the parameter is set to N and if the table (or other object) is re-created by Import, it is re-created with the same storage parameters that currently exist for the object. When the data is imported into the new table, the table may require additional extents and, therefore, will be fragmented again.

> **CAUTION**
>
> If you specify COMPRESS = Y, the Import program may not be able to create the database object again if the amount of storage required is not available in one contiguous set of Oracle blocks.

GRANTS

The GRANTS option prompts you to specify whether or not GRANT statements issued against the database should be exported. If you are using Export as a means of exporting data from one database to another, where the Oracle usernames are different, the GRANT statements will not work. If Export and Import are being used as a means of backing up and restoring data, you want to have the Import program run the GRANT statements again to set up the security privileges that are currently in effect.

INDEXES

The INDEXES option is used to control whether or not CREATE INDEX statements are to be exported along with the definitions of other database objects.

> **NOTE**
>
> Only the CREATE INDEX statement is exported with the INDEXES option—not the actual Oracle blocks for the indexes.

ROWS

The ROWS parameter controls whether the data is exported with the table definitions or not.

For example, if you use Export and Import to move object definitions from a development database to another environment (such as a user testing or production environment), the data from the development environment is not required. You want the Export program to take only the object definitions.

The Import program uses the same parameter to ignore rows in the exported file when the Import program runs.

CONSTRAINTS

This parameter specifies whether or not the constraints for the table are to be exported.

If this option is set, the Import program re-creates the foreign key constraints last, thereby fulfilling the requirement that PRIMARY KEY and UNIQUE KEY constraints must exist before a foreign key constraint can be set up.

LOG

The LOG option takes the name (and optionally the directory) of a file to hold the log of the Export run; everything that appears on the screen when the Export program runs is recorded in the Log file.

If the Export program runs in batch mode (perhaps during the night), the Log File helps you determine the success or failure of the program.

FULL

This option specifies whether an entire database export is to be performed or just an export of individual users. The Oracle USERID specified must have the EXP_FUL_DATABASE database role given to it.

OWNER

If a full export is not to be performed, this parameter gives the names of one or more Oracle users who are to have their objects exported.

TABLES

If you want to export individual tables, this option lets you specify the names of one or more tables.

You can export not only the tables owned by the specified Oracle USERID, but any other tables for which the user has received the SELECT privilege.

RECORD LENGTH

This option specifies the length of the export record and is usually used when you export directly to a tape drive (where this option specifies the block size on the tape).

INCTYPE

This option is used when incremental exports are to be performed. You can specify the type of incremental export: complete, cumulative, or incremental. A *complete* exports out the entire database. A *cumulative* exports out those objects that have changed since the last complete or the last cumulative. And an *incremental* exports out those objects that have changed since the last cumulative or the last incremental. These three export choices let you decide which one to run depending on your time constraints. For example, you may decide to run a cumulative or complete on weekends when more time is available and then run an incremental each day when time is more limited.

RECORD

The RECORD option is used to specify that the occurrence of an incremental export should be recorded in the SYS tables.

PARFILE

The PARFILE parameter specifies the name of a file containing the parameters to be used for an export.

Here is an example of a parameter file:

```
USERID=system/manager
FILE=Wednesday.dmp
LOG=Wednesday.log
FULL=y
```

The file must contain mandatory parameters. If you want to override default values for any parameters, you include the new values in this file. Default values are used for any parameters not specified in the file.

CONSISTENT

If the database is currently in use and tables are being changed, the export uses the version of the data that exists when the Export program is ready to copy it. This means that you get some tables before some changes have been made and other tables after changes have been committed.

By setting the CONSISTENT parameter to Y, you indicate that you want to export the version of the tables with the data that existed when the Export program started to run.

However, rollback segments are system objects that record the old values of any changes made to the database and are overwritten as required. The information required to determine which version of the data existed when the Export program started may not be available in the segments. If this problem occurs, you get an error message saying "Snapshot too old." You can then run the Export program again and hope that the data does not change or that the rollback segments do not get overwritten.

A safer way to export, especially if performing a full export, is to start the Oracle instance in "restricted" mode, which allows only Oracle users who have the "restricted session" system privilege to make a connection to the database. Starting the instance in this mode ensures that you have a consistent copy of the database data.

STATISTICS

The STATISTICS option allows the Import program to gather statistics on tables, indexes, and clusters when those objects are created. These statistics are used to gather information to help the cost-based optimizer make better decisions on how to run SQL statements.

The valid values for this option are COMPUTE, ESTIMATE, and NONE. COMPUTE may cause the ANALYZE command to take a long time when importing if the statistics are being gathered for large tables; ESTIMATE allows the import to run faster.

Import Parameters

The Import program reads and processes the binary file produced by the Export program. Import can re-create the database objects (if required) as well as bring the data back into the database.

Use the HELP = Y parameter to see a full list of the parameters for the Import program. Many of the required parameters are the same ones required for the Export program (for example, the Oracle username). Refer to their descriptions in the preceding sections.

To access the contents of an Export file that contains a full database export, the Import program needs an Oracle username that has been granted the IMP_FULL_DATABASE role. To process exports of a single Oracle user or of individual tables, any Oracle username will suffice.

SHOW

If set to Y, the SHOW parameter shows only the DDL statements stored inside the Export file. This is a read-only run of the exported file; no database objects are affected. If the FULL parameter is also set to Y, the full contents of the exported file are shown; otherwise the user specifies exactly which objects in the exported file she wants to see.

The SHOW option does not allow users to see actual data values; the tables must be imported into an Oracle database.

IGNORE

Import creates database objects and then inserts rows into tables. Often the tables are created before the Import program runs, to set the correct storage and other parameters. If the tables are created in advance, you can set the IGNORE option to Y to tell Import to continue bringing rows into the tables if the CREATE TABLE statement fails.

> **TIP**
>
> If the IGNORE option for Import is set to Y, make sure that the tables are empty before running the Import program. Otherwise, the rows may be duplicated in the tables.

> **CAUTION**
>
> If tables are created in advance, make sure that the columns are created in the same order that they were in when the Export program was run. Import assumes that the columns are in the same order when it brings in the data.

DESTROY

If you are importing a full database into a new database with just the SYSTEM tablespace, the Import program can re-create the full set of tablespaces by issuing the CREATE TABLESPACE command. If the physical database files already exist, the Import program fails unless the DESTROY option is set to Y to indicate that the physical files are to be overwritten if found.

It is safer to manually remove the physical database files before the Import program runs, and leave this parameter set to N (the default). That way, you can guard against accidentally overwriting database files for another database on the same machine. On some platforms, however, database files are created manually using an operating system command to ensure that a contiguous area of memory is allocated. The CREATE TABLESPACE command then overwrites the existing file. In such a case, the DESTROY option is set to Y.

INDEXFILE

The INDEXFILE option names a file to hold retrieved CREATE INDEX statements. The SQL commands for creating indexes on tables are stored in the file, as are the full commands for creating the tables (the commands, however, are commented out).

This option is useful where indexes were removed from database tables to allow a large load of data to run faster (for example, when using SQL*Loader), and after the load finishes, you want to re-create all the indexes on the tables.

CHARSET

The CHARSET option specifies the character set of the exported database where the character set is different for the import database.

FROMUSER

The FROMUSER parameter specifies the name of the Oracle user whose objects are in the exported file. If this Oracle user does not exist (and the TOUSER option is not specified), the objects are imported into the Oracle account name specified in the USERID option for Import.

TOUSER

The TOUSER option allows you to import objects into an Oracle user account other than the one specified as the USERID parameter for Import. This option is a more privileged option, as it allows you to modify an Oracle user's objects without specifying the password. For this reason, the IMP_FULL_DATABASE database role must have been given to the Oracle username specified in the USERID parameter.

For example, a full database export might export the objects owned by the Oracle user permjit. When you run the Import program, you specify the Oracle user system for the USERID option and you want to import the objects owned by permjit into the rashpal user with the TOUSER='rashpal' option.

```
Unix>imp userid=system/manager file=myexp.dmp fromuser=permjit touser=rashpal
```

COMMIT

When the Import program inserts data into database tables, it waits to perform a COMMIT statement until after the very last row is imported. This ensures that if any problems occur during the import (such as storage-type problems), the table will not have any rows. Once the failure is reported, the Import program continues with the next table.

If any failures occur, rows can be removed from the table the same way as in any other transactions: through rollback segments. If a large table is being imported, the rollback segments may grow to be large. In addition to the storage being used for the table, extra storage would be required for the rollback segments.

If there is not enough storage available for the rollback segments, you can set the COMMIT parameter to Y to indicate to the Import program that a COMMIT statement is to be issued after every bufferful of data. As soon as the COMMIT finishes, the transaction ends and the rollback segment can be reused. If any errors occur with the import, however, any rows that were inserted cannot be rolled back, which may mean that only some of the rows end up in the table. In this case it is up to you to delete the rows from the table, attempt to fix the source of the error, and retry the import.

Using Export and Import to "Clean Up" the Database

There are two types of storage issues that can slow down performance when accessing rows in tables. First, the table may have many extents of data allocated to it, usually because the INITIAL extent size was not set large enough when the table was created. As more rows are inserted into the table, more extents are allocated. Second, a row may migrate to another Oracle block when the row is updated if the block that the row is currently in does not have enough free space for the row to grow. This leaves behind a chain pointer used to ascertain the actual block the row is in when an attempt is made to get the block from its original row. This problem usually occurs if the PCTFREE parameter is not large enough to leave more room free in each data block for the table.

A problem that may occur with indexes is that index blocks may become fragmented as new key values are inserted into the index. These problems can be fixed by re-creating the table in the database, if there are just a few tables involved and there is enough space in the database to hold a copy of the data. Another way to fix the problem, when there is a large number of tables or even for the entire database, is to use the Export program to dump the contents of the tables or database, drop the tables, and then use Import to re-create the tables and bring the data back. If the COMPRESS option is set to Y when exporting, the Import program allocates one large extent to hold all the data. This fixes the problem of many extents for tables. In addition, because the Import program inserts rows into the table, the migrated rows problem does not occur. (This problem occurs only when rows are updated and they require more storage.)

Incremental Exports

If a full database export is being used as a means of backing up the database each night, the program may take a long time to run when there is a large amount of data—perhaps many hours.

The INCTYPE parameter for Export and Import allows you to export only those objects that have changed since the last time the program was run in incremental mode. The major reason for using this type of export is to reduce the time taken to perform an export.

The INCTYPE parameter can be set to one of the following values:

■ COMPLETE performs a complete export of the database.

■ CUMULATIVE exports those tables that have changed since the last complete or cumulative export was performed.

■ INCREMENTAL exports those tables that have changed since the last incremental or cumulative export was performed.

> **NOTE**
>
> Even if one row changes in a table, the entire table is marked as having changed and is exported by the next incremental export.

For example, at the start of the month you might perform a complete export of the database and then perform an incremental export so that only the tables changed that day are exported. Or on weekends you might perform a cumulative export of all the tables changed during the week. If you choose to perform a cumulative export, you don't need to do any incremental exports since the last cumulative or complete export.

If you want to perform an Import, the whole set of export files must be provided because the Import program runs for each one.

One problem with the incremental method of exporting and importing is the number of files created. A bigger issue is that an entire table is exported even if only some of its rows change. Incremental exports do not work at the row level. A simpler method is to "keep it simple" by performing a complete export of the entire database each night only if most tables change each day.

> **TIP**
>
> Only use incremental exports if there are many large tables in the database that do not change often.

Privileges Required

To run the Export and Import programs, you must have the privileges required to run the programs and a valid Oracle username and password.

If you want to export an entire database, the Oracle user account you use to run the Export program must have the EXP_FULL_DATABASE role. An exported file that contains a full database export can only be imported and processed by an Oracle username that has the IMP_FULL_DATABASE role.

Summary

In this chapter, you examined the Export and Import utilities, which complement the normal backup and recovery process (for example, using cold backups and archived redo log files). Export and Import utilities also provide other capabilities, such as fixing storage-related problems. The utilities have the same parameters and run the same way on all platforms.

IV

Design and Construction of an Oracle Database

20

Defining and Creating the Initial Database

*by Mohammad Asadi and
Kimbra McDonald*

In order to define and create an Oracle database system, you first must determine the required resources. The following section outlines the steps necessary to determine the system's required resources. Only after you determine these resources can you create a logical and physical design of the database.

Determining Required Resources

In order to build a system that meets the goals of the end users, the system's developer must combine the right hardware components with suitable application architectures that consider the complex functional, operational, and economic constraints. Even though this may prove to be a complicated task, ignoring it is much more costly. In order to successfully implement an Oracle database application, the user requirements must be fully documented. Only then can you properly assess the resources necessary to fulfill those requirements. We recommend performing the following steps so that you have a better understanding of the required resources. For new Oracle database systems, these steps assume some system analysis has been done. For redesigning existing systems, completion of the following documents should be even more apparent.

1. Prepare the Initial Database Sizing (DBS) document.
2. Prepare the Request for Information (RFI) document.
3. Prepare the Initial System Proposal (ISP) document.
4. Prepare the Hardware/Software (H/S) document.
5. Prepare the Service Level Agreement (SLA) document.

The Initial Database Sizing (DBS) Document

This document is the first step in determining the user requirements for a system. The DBS should answer the following questions:

- What are the estimated number of rows in the database?
- What are the length and number of the largest rows in the database?
- What is the estimated size of the database (in megabytes)?
- Is the database standalone or part of a distributed system? If it will be a distributed database, explain its relation with all the other databases in the distributed environment.
- Is the database primarily a DSS (Decision Support System), an OLTP (Online Transaction Processing) system, a Data Warehousing system, or a hybrid mixture of all?
- Where does the raw data come from?

- Is the raw data located locally or is it on a remote machine or multiple machines?
- If the raw data is located on one or more remote machines, do you need a gateway machine to download it to the local machine?
- How is the data inserted into the database? Will a bulk load be used? Will individual transactions be used to insert?
- If the data is loaded in bulk, what are the frequency and size of each load?
- How often are the largest rows in the database accessed?
- How many users plan to access the database?
- How many concurrent users plan to access the database?
- How many transactions will access the database?
- What type of transactions (such as updates or read-only) will they be?
- What is the number of concurrent transactions per minute?
- What is the expected transaction turn-around time?
- What type of client machines will access the server machine (such as DOS Client, Windows Client, OS/2 client)?
- What type of network will the clients use to access the database (TCP/IP, Novel, etc.)?
- What is the expected client-to-server network turn-around time in seconds?

You may want to add your specific questions to the preceding list. Answers to the initial database sizing document can help you get a general understanding of the user requirements. The answers to these questions should get you started in the right direction toward a good systems design. By reviewing the user responses to these questions and others you add, you should be able to prepare the Request for Information document.

The Request for Information (RFI) Document

RFI documents are sent to hardware and software vendors. The Initial Database Sizing document must be attached to the RFI document. An experienced database administrator (DBA) should be able to recommend the following to the hardware vendor:

- The size of the disks
- The number of tape drives for database backup and recovery
- Whether or not a RAID (Redundant Array of Inexpensive Disks) is needed
- If so, the types of RAID (RAID 0+1, RAID 5, and so on) recommended
- The number of CPUs
- The number of disk controllers
- The amount of memory

You should clearly state in the RFI that these are your recommendations only and that it is up to the hardware vendor to recommend the best price/performance configuration. Always request a list of references along with any available benchmark numbers from the hardware vendors. You also should state your timeline restrictions.

After you have received the RFI responses from all the hardware vendors, it is time to compare them for their price/performance ratio. This is where the fun begins! Even though DBAs might not be directly involved in the contract negotiations with the vendors, they should have a strong voice in choosing the right vendor. DBAs, use your privilege wisely. You may find that more than ten hardware vendors can satisfy your system's requirements. They might recommend system architectures ranging from Massively Parallel Processors (MPP), to Symmetric Multi-Processors (SMP), to the new SMP approach called Non-Uniform Memory Access (NUMA-Q). You may have noticed that we concentrated only on the hardware vendor. This is the most time-consuming part in preparing the RFI. In a Very Large Database (VLDB) or Very Many Databases (VMDB) system, you should prepare an RFI for Oracle as well and get Oracle's assurance on the subject. Review the RFI responses carefully and be sure to contact all the vendors' references. *When considering the hardware platform, you should also consider the level of Oracle support.* You are now ready to prepare the Initial System Proposal document.

The Initial System Proposal (ISP) Document

After thoroughly analyzing all of the RFI documents received, you should be able to narrow the candidates down to less than three possibilities. In the Initial System Proposal document, state your choice of hardware and software vendors.

> **NOTE**
>
> On the mission critical systems, we strongly recommend benchmarking with your data instead of relying solely on the vendor's references. Be prepared to revise your revision on the Initial System Proposal document.

Finalizing the Initial System Proposal is a lengthy process. On the mission critical systems, we have seen it drag on for two to three months. It might even get political. But there is light at the end of the tunnel!

The Hardware/Software (H/S) Document

This document should state the hardware and software of choice. For the hardware vendor, it should state the name, model, number of CPUs, amount of memory, number of disks, the operating system level, the system monitoring tools, the I/O bus speed, the networking configuration, and all other relative server and client data. On a high availability (HA) system, the

H/S document should include the expected failover time. The H/S document also should state the desired Oracle options (Oracle Parallel Server (OPS), Distributed Databases, Parallel Query Option, SQLNET driver option—such as TCP/IP or SPX).

When you design a database, one consideration to discuss is whether or not to use *RAID* (redundant array of inexpensive disks). The following sections describe the various RAID configurations.

What Is RAID?

RAID systems were first formally defined by researchers at the University of California at Berkeley in 1987.

The idea is to combine the power of small, inexpensive disks to achieve the performance and reliability of a single large expensive disk. The benefits of using RAID systems are that they offer better performance than non-RAID devices. In addition, they offer a higher availability of disk devices than non-RAID. Today, almost all hardware vendors offer RAID subsystems, which are currently more expensive than non-RAID systems, but still less expensive than a single large disk. Even though RAID subsystems are currently expensive, they should be thoughtfully considered because the benefits outweigh the expense.

Some software vendors also offer RAID architecture. Because RAID at the hardware level is more commonly used, we discuss that option here.

RAID technology is constantly evolving. However, most are variations of the original five defined by the Berkeley researchers. If you are considering using RAID, please contact your hardware vendor(s) for a complete explanation of their RAID technology.

There are six levels of RAID as it relates to Oracle7.3 databases. The six RAID levels are 0, 1, duplexed 1, 0+1, 3, and 5. Figures 20.1 through 20.6 show these six different levels of RAID.

The following are some terms frequently used with RAID and their definitions:

- *Disk array*—A group of disks working together to perform the same or better functionality as one large expensive disk.
- *Stripe*—To break up the data into equal-sized chunks; the sum of all the chunks make up one stripe.
- *Transfer rate*—The rate per second that megabytes of data can be transferred through a disk's controller.
- *I/O operations per second (IOPS)*—The number of simultaneous I/O requests in a constant period of time that can be handled by a disk's controller is measured by IOPS.

The following sections describe the different levels of RAID.

RAID Level 0—Striping

RAID 0 is a nonredundant disk configuration that can be striped. As defined, *striping* is the process of breaking up a data stream and placing it across multiple disks in equal-sized chunks or stripe blocks. Properly configured, striping yields excellent I/O response times for high concurrency random I/O and excellent throughput for low concurrency sequential I/O. Selection of stripe size for an array requires careful consideration of the tradeoff constraints.

RAID 0 does not take into account the reliability factor. Figure 20.1 shows an example of RAID 0 configuration. In this example, you have four disks and eight equal-sized chunks of data (denoted by C1 through C8). Chunks C1 through C4 make up one stripe, and C5 through C8 make up another. In this example, if C2 on disk two fails, the entire stripe is unavailable. In addition, systems administrators have to take special care in determining the stripe block size because performance and loss of data can occur if the size is not appropriate for the system being created and its transaction rate.

FIGURE 20.1.
RAID 0 configuration.

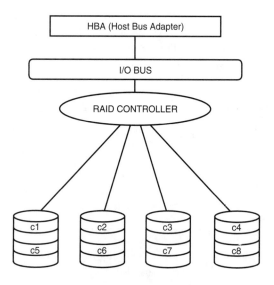

RAID 0 has excellent random read and write performance if the striping size is configured correctly. If the stripe size is not big enough, however, performance can be degraded. RAID 0 also has good sequential read and write performance if striping is done at a low enough concurrency level, or at higher concurrency levels if a striping segment can contain at least one I/O.

What RAID 0 gains in read and write performance, it costs in recovering from an outage. If a disk fails on a RAID 0 configuration, it will require any applications with data on that disk to be down while a recovery of the Oracle database is performed. **The loss of a single disk on a stripe will bring down the entire system until the disk can be replaced and recovery completed.**

The cost of RAID 0 is a benefit in that it is the least expensive of any of the RAID configurations. However, the costs of operating a RAID 0 configuration might be higher than other RAID configurations in that the cost of recovering from any outages can drive the cost of maintaining a RAID 0 configuration much higher than just the cost of purchasing a RAID 0 system. What you should also consider in the cost of RAID 0 is the cost required to increase the size of a RAID 0 configuration. This requires either buying more arrays or reworking the existing ones. The training required to optimize a RAID 0 system for better performance should also be included in the total cost of a RAID 0 system.

RAID Level 1—Mirroring

RAID 1 is a disk system that maintains two copies of data; a mirrored one is created with every write to the original disk. This failover is an important factor to consider when the requirements for your system include high availability. Also note that RAID 1 does not perform as well as RAID 0, but has the best performance of the mirrored disk configurations when writing to RAID 1.

When considering the design of your Oracle database, you should consider RAID 1 for its mirroring value, if only for redo log files, especially if the whole system can't be mirrored due to the cost.

In addition to RAID level 1, you can improve the reliability of systems by mirroring power supplies, host adapters, and I/O busses. Some production systems are triple-mirrored for even greater availability.

RAID 1 has good random read and write performance. In a RAID 1 configuration, the time required to write to all the mirrored disks is as fast as the time required for a write to the slowest disk in the mirrored configuration. Therefore, in most cases the performance of write transactions in RAID 1 is slightly worse than in independent disks. When reading mirrored disks, only one disk in the mirrored configuration is utilized. The rest are left for other transactions, giving little difference between non-mirrored and RAID 1 in read performance. However, in some mirrored systems, RAID 1 can improve IOPS performance of read operations by using the least busy drive to service requests.

RAID 1 has fair sequential read and write performance due to the same characteristics as random performance.

RAID 1 has excellent failover capabilities. RAID 1 by itself should be used only for systems where reliability is more important than performance. In the RAID 1 disk configuration the mirrored disk will take over, giving continued performance during an outage. When designing an Oracle database, we recommend using a triple-mirrored RAID 1 disk configuration for high-availability systems. In this configuration, one of the mirrors containing Oracle database files can be broken for a short time and then used as a daily backup. This process is called *resilvering* and is used in systems that are required to be constantly available.

RAID 1 configurations are expensive. In addition to purchasing more disks, you'll need to purchase more I/O controllers, adapters, and busses. Training also is a cost to consider with this configuration. Most hardware vendors provide adequate software for managing RAID 1 configurations. However, additional cost might be incurred to develop custom RAID 1 maintenance software.

Figure 20.2 shows a RAID 1 configuration. Shaded areas show the mirrored, or copied, areas of the non-shaded disks.

FIGURE 20.2.
RAID 1 configuration.

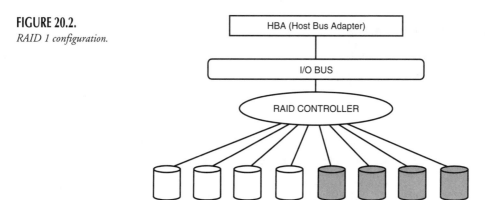

Duplexed RAID 1

Figure 20.3 shows an example of a duplexed RAID 1 configuration. In this configuration, disks, RAID controllers, I/O busses, and host bus adapters are all duplicated. This gives you an even higher availability system but, of course, at a higher cost. For example, if an I/O bus fails, the mirrored I/O bus will take over, leaving the system uninterrupted.

RAID Level 0+1—Striping and Mirroring

As its name implies, RAID 0+1 is a combination of RAID 0 and RAID 1. RAID 0+1, therefore, has the all the advantages of RAID levels 0 and 1, but at the cost of the disadvantages. In other words, it performs well but costs more.

Some argue that a duplexed mirroring configuration of striped disk arrays is a more suitable solution than RAID 0+1 for OLTP, high-availability systems, but it comes at a higher cost.

RAID 0+1 has good random read performance if each I/O request fits within a single striped segment. Otherwise, it could degrade performance. It has good random write performance, but not quite as good as RAID 0 due to the time required to write to multiple disks in the mirrored configuration.

Sequential read and write performance is excellent in a RAID 0+1 configuration for the same reasons as a random read or write. The key is that an I/O request must fit within a single striping segment. Otherwise, it will cause performance to suffer.

FIGURE 20.3.
*Duplexed RAID 1
configuration.*

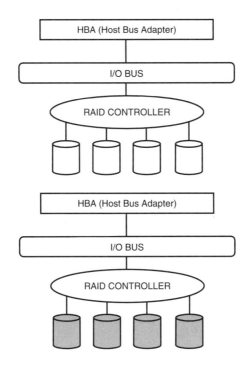

Like RAID 1, RAID 0+1 has excellent failover capabilities. RAID 0+1 should be used for systems where performance and reliability are equally important. In the RAID 0+1 disk configuration, the mirrored disk will take over, giving continued performance during an outage. In addition, striping data produces greater performance than in RAID 1 alone.

RAID 0+1 configurations are slightly more expensive than RAID 1 alone. Part of the additional cost of RAID 0+1 is that administrators of RAID 0+1 systems must be trained in determining the optimal stripe sizing and in maintaining mirrored configurations.

Figure 20.4 shows a RAID 0+1 configuration. The shaded disks represent mirrored disks.

RAID Level 3—Bit-Interleaved Parity

As opposed to RAID 1, which mirrors all disks, in a RAID 3 configuration, parity data for all other disks in an array is written to one dedicated disk. In the case of a hard drive failure, data recovery is accomplished by calculating the exclusive OR (XOR) of the information recorded in the remaining drives.

RAID 3 is not as reliable as RAID 1 or RAID 0+1. However, if cost is a significant consideration, RAID 3 might be an option—especially for those Oracle databases where most transactions are reads, particularly full-table scans and where there are few writes to the database. In other words, the database is relatively static, doesn't need to be highly available, and needs to be developed within tight monetary constraints.

FIGURE 20.4.
RAID 0+1
configuration.

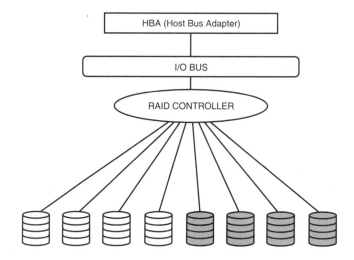

Though RAID 3 has poorer read/write performance than other RAID configurations, it does withstand an outage if only a single disk is lost. If more than one disk is lost, media recovery must be performed, and the array suffers an outage, causing the necessity for a media recovery of the Oracle database. The more disks in an array, the higher the chance RAID 3 will have a failure.

If the disk drive that has the parity information fails, the system will continue functioning as normal until the drive is replaced. If any other drive fails, performance suffers because every I/O request to the array with the failed disk drive makes the system access all other disk drives within that array.

The cost of RAID 3 is greater than RAID 0 and less than RAID 1 and RAID 0+1. Because the chance of failure in RAID 3 is greater, additional costs might be incurred to train administrators for different failure scenarios.

Figure 20.5 shows a RAID 3 configuration. The shaded disk represents the disk dedicated to parity information for the remaining four disks.

RAID Level 5—Block-Interleaved with Distributed Parity

RAID 5 is similar to RAID 3, except that RAID 5 has no dedicated parity drive. Instead, all disk drives contain data and parity information. RAID 5 allows the striping segments to be sized, with a segment containing either data or parity information. Because all drives contain data, read performance is excellent because reads can be performed simultaneously. Writes will access both the data disk drive and the drive containing that record's parity information. Therefore, in most cases, performance is better than RAID 1 because the system does not have to wait for the slowest disk write. However, a small performance degradation could be incurred if it happens that more time is needed to search and update a record's parity information. Different hardware vendors have different algorithms for updating parity information. In addition, because only the parity information is stored and not another copy of the data, RAID 5 uses less disk space than in a system that is mirroring data.

FIGURE 20.5.

RAID 3 configuration.

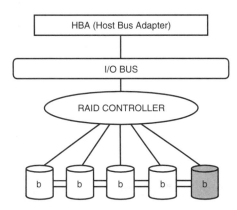

Next to RAID 0+1, RAID 5 is the most reliable RAID configuration. RAID 5 is becoming very popular for those systems that have budget constraints but require a certain degree of high availability. Similarly to RAID 3, RAID 5 does not stop processing when a single disk drive failure occurs. If two or more disk failures occur, a media recovery must be performed. Also similarly to RAID 3, if any other drive fails, performance with RAID 5 suffers because every other drive in the array must supply data to the transaction.

The cost of RAID 5 is greater than RAID 0, less than RAID 3 and can be less than RAID 1 if the number of disks in the array is greater than two. Sometimes RAID 5 also can be more expensive than RAID 0+1 if the configuration cannot deliver the performance expected and additional hardware has to be purchased to achieve the necessary performance requirements.

As in other RAID configurations, there can be costs incurred for training administrators to properly configure striping.

Figure 20.6 shows a RAID 5 configuration. The shaded areas indicate where parity information has been written to the disk drive. The non-shaded areas represent where data has been written. The diagram represents a disk binding of five disks, but it could be more or fewer disks.

In summary, when choosing a RAID configuration, consider the following options for specific types of situations:

- RAID 0 for a system requiring good performance without mirroring
- RAID 1 for high availability systems
- RAID 0+1 for high availability systems that require good performance
- Duplex RAID 1 for highest availability systems
- RAID 3 for low to moderate availability systems that require average performance at a greater cost savings
- RAID 5 for systems requiring good availability and performance at a cost savings

FIGURE 20.6.
RAID 5 configuration.

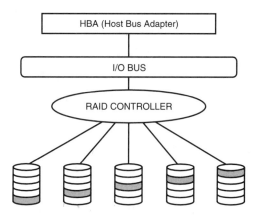

The Service Level Agreement (SLA) Document

This document should clearly define all the system's critical factors (SCFs) and endusers' expectations in precise detail for any/all SCFs. It also should specify the users' tolerance for deviation from these expectations. You must ensure that none of the users' requirements conflict with other requirements. Be objective and most of all realistic.

The SLA should have sections such as "The expected turn-around time for database recovery is 150 minutes." Furthermore, you should be more specific when the clock starts ticking in the development life cycle.

Logical Analysis and Design

Logical analysis and design is the process by which business requirements are transformed into a data model that systems developers can use to create database systems.

Normalization

Normalization of data is a procedure to ensure that a data model conforms to some useful standards. For data and entity relationship models, these standards have been defined to minimize the duplication of data, to provide the flexibility necessary to support different functional requirements, and to enable the data modeler to verify the business requirements.

Data Modeling

A *data model* is a pictorial representation of your users' requirements where business data is represented by a series of pictures of entities and the relationships between those entities. Entities are the "things" in data—such as people, places, and any other logical groupings of business data. Relationships are the logical connections between that data. For example, entities might be an airline ticket or an airline flight. The relationship between those might be that an airline ticket is used to travel on a flight, and a flight requires an airline ticket before a passenger can fly it.

In this section, let's consider a simple example: a subset of information applying to the ticketing procedure for an airline we'll call Mile High Airlines. You'll walk through the process of identifying data elements, how they are grouped together to become entities, and then how the relationships are identified. Then you'll continue with this example through the physical design process to create a physical database design.

Gathering Business Data

For the sake of this example, assume that you have been asked to develop a ticketing system for Mile High Airlines. First, gather business information, which will become the data elements. The source of the business data elements are from discussions with business analysts. After numerous sessions with the business analysts, you have a list of data elements you can logically group together into entities.

The following list of data elements is what you have gathered:

- Number of seats
- Type of airplane
- Year airplane manufactured
- Noise level of airplane
- Fuel capacity
- Schedule of flight
- Airplane identifier
- Passenger name
- Date and time of travel
- Infant indicator
- Class of seat
- Flight number
- Airport starting from
- Airport arriving to
- Seat number
- Amount of ticket
- Currency type
- Tax amount
- Number of crew on flight

■ Number of passengers on flight

■ Meal types on flight

■ Type of airplane for flight

Creating the Data Model

The next step in the database development life cycle is to develop a data model. This can be accomplished by grouping these data elements into entities. For this data model, the data elements belong in four entities: Flight, Airplane, Ticket, and Passenger. The following sections list all the data elements in their respective entities.

Flight

The following is a list of attributes associated with a flight:

■ Number of seats

■ Type of airplane

■ Schedule of flight

■ Airplane identifier

■ Passenger name 1

■ Passenger name 2

■ Passenger name 3

■ Passenger name 4 (etc., up to number of seats on that flight)

■ Number of first-class seats

■ Number of coach seats

■ Number of business seats

■ Flight number

■ Airport starting from

■ Airport arriving to

■ Number of crew on flight

■ Number of passengers on flight

■ Meal types on flight

Airplane

The following is a list of attributes associated with an airplane:

■ Number of seats

■ Type of airplane

■ Year airplane manufactured

- Noise level of airplane
- Fuel capacity
- Airplane identifier
- Miles traveled
- Number of times maintained

Ticket

The following is a list of attributes associated with a ticket:

- Ticket identifier
- Passenger name
- Date and time of travel from first city to second
- Date and time of travel from second city to third (if applies)
- Date and time of travel from third city to fourth (continue until reach desired destination)
- Infant indicator
- Class of seat
- Flight number
- Airport starting from
- Airport arriving to
- Seat number
- Amount of ticket
- Currency type
- Tax amount

Passenger

The following is a list of attributes associated with a passenger:

- Passenger's name
- Passenger's phone
- Passenger's address

After creating the desired entities, you are ready to document the entities and determine the relationships between each entity. To accomplish this, you will use the Entity Relationship (ER) Diagram.

Entity Relationship (ER) Diagram

To create an Entity Relationship (ER) Diagram, you can choose from many data modeling tools available on the market. We used System Architect by Popkin Software and Systems, Inc.

This diagram displays the entities and relationships of your data model. We have taken the data we identified, the data about each entity, or the attributes, and entered them into System Architect. In the first diagram, the attributes are not displayed in this view, giving the diagram a more global view of the business data. Figure 20.7 shows the entities and their relationships for Mile High Airlines.

FIGURE 20.7.

ER diagram for Mile High Airlines.

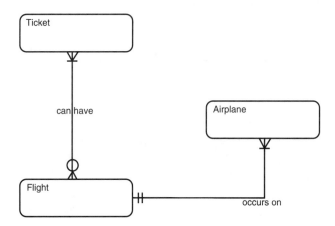

By studying this diagram, it becomes apparent that an airplane can be used on many flights, but a flight has only one airplane. In cases of flights with connecting cities, a ticket can be used for one or many of those connections. Conversely, a flight can have one or several tickets for it. The relationship between the entities Flight and Airplane is a type of relationship called *one-to-many*. The relationship between the entities Flight and Ticket is a *many-to-many* relationship. The hatched line on a relationship indicates that the relation is mandatory but can have at most one occurrence, while the circle on the relationship indicates that the relation is optional (that is, can have zero occurrences). The "crows feet" on a relationship indicates that an entity can have many occurrences in that relation.

The types of relationships depicted above are examples of relationships between entities. Figures 20.8 through 20.13 show various types of entity relationships. The first example, Figure 20.8, shows a one-to-one relationship. Only one occurrence of Entity A would be associated with only one occurrence of Entity B. This would rarely be valid because if this were a true relation between these two entities, all of the attributes in one entity would most likely belong in the other.

FIGURE 20.8.

One-to-one relationship.

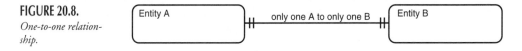

In Figure 20.9, Entity B might have either one occurrence of Entity A associated with it, or there might be zero occurrences of Entity A associated with one and only one occurrence of Entity B.

FIGURE 20.9.
Zero or one-to-one relationship.

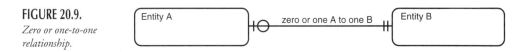

Figure 20.10 shows Entity B associated with zero, one, or many occurrences of Entity A. This is the kind of relationship most commonly depicted by a parent entity associated with zero, one, or many occurrences of a child entity.

FIGURE 20.10.
Zero, one- or many-to-one relationship.

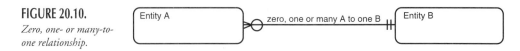

Figure 20.11 shows that this relationship is only slightly different than the previous one in that there will always be at least one (but can be many) occurrences of Entity A that are associated with one occurrence of Entity B.

FIGURE 20.11.
One- or many-to-one relationship.

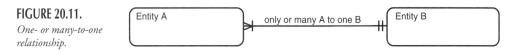

The example in Figure 20.12 shows that there must be more than one occurrence of Entity A associated with an occurrence of Entity B.

FIGURE 20.12.
Many-to-one relationship.

Lastly, this example of an ER relationship in an ER Diagram, shown in Figure 20.13, allows the data modeler to indicate that the relationship is unknown. This might be used until more analysis could flush out the actual relationship.

FIGURE 20.13.
Unknown-to-one relationship.

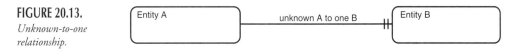

Figure 20.14 shows the data elements (attributes) related to each of the entities specific to the Mile High Airlines example. The keys for each of the entities, which are the unique identifiers for those entities, are noted in the diagram in the upper "key data" section of the entity.

Note the repeating attributes in the entities Flight and Ticket, such as passenger name and date traveled. The ER Diagram in Figure 20.15 will be the basis for the normalization process, beginning with the first normal form. In the next section, you take this diagram and break out the repeating attributes into their own entities, creating an ER Diagram in first normal form.

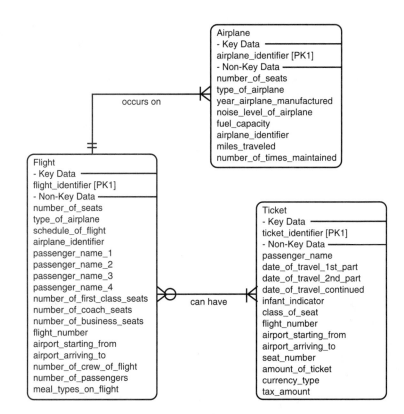

FIGURE 20.14.
Entities with their related data elements and relationships.

First Normal Form

To create an ER Diagram in first normal form, you have to remove all the repeating attributes and place them in their own entities. We created an entity, Boarding Pass, for the repeating attributes concerning flight segments; then we changed the entity, Ticket, to contain the passenger information, which can be repeated as often as the airline has passengers. An airplane is used for a flight, a flight requires a ticket, and a ticket has a boarding pass. Figure 20.15 shows an ER Diagram in first normal form.

Second Normal Form

Taking the diagram that has been normalized into first normal form, remove the attributes that are not dependent on the entire unique identifier, also called the *key*. In the airline example, suppose you were progressing in the analysis phase, but realized you missed documenting some information you wanted to capture. You want to keep information on an airplane's weight. (Believe me, this will happen—often!) You initially added AIRPLANE_WEIGHT to the Flight entity, but then realized that you needed to remove AIRPLANE_WEIGHT from the Flight entity, because it is dependent only on the AIRPLANE_IDENTIFIER and not the entire key. Figure 20.16 shows the ER Diagram in second normal form.

FIGURE 20.15.

First normal form for Mile High Airlines.

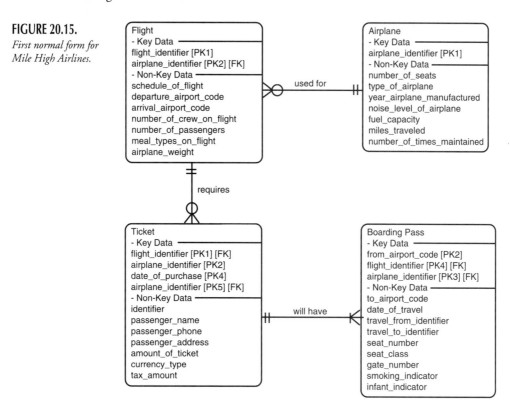

Third Normal Form

Using the diagram of second normal form, take the attributes that are dependent on something other than the unique identifier, or the key, and create a new entity for those attributes. Separate passenger information into its own entity because passenger information does not depend on the entire key of Ticket. Figure 20.17 shows the ER Diagram in third normal form.

FIGURE 20.16.

Second normal form for Mile High Airlines.

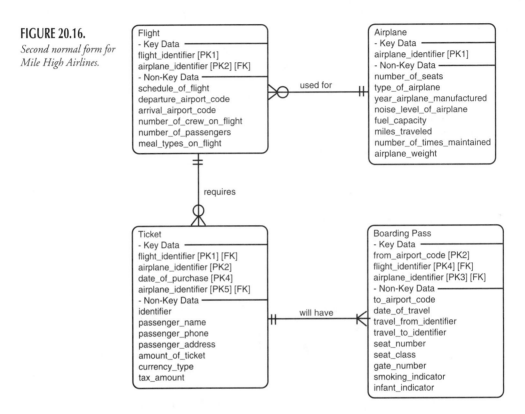

The following lists show the attributes for each of the entities in Figure 20.17.

Flight	Airplane
Flight_identifer	Airplane identifier
Airplane_identifier	Number of seats
Schedule of flight	Type of airplane
Departure airport code	Year airplane manufactured
Arrival airport code	Noise level of airplane
Number of crew on flight	Fuel capacity
Number of passengers	Miles traveled
Meal type on flight	Number of times maintained
	Airplane weight

Passenger
Passenger name
Passenger phone
Passenger address

Ticket	*Boarding Pass*
Flight identifier	From airport code
Date of purchase	Flight identifier
Passenger name	Airplane identifier
Airplane identifier	To airport code
Amount of ticket	Date of travel
Currency type	Seat number
Tax amount	Seat class
	Gate number
	Smoking indicator
	Infant indicator

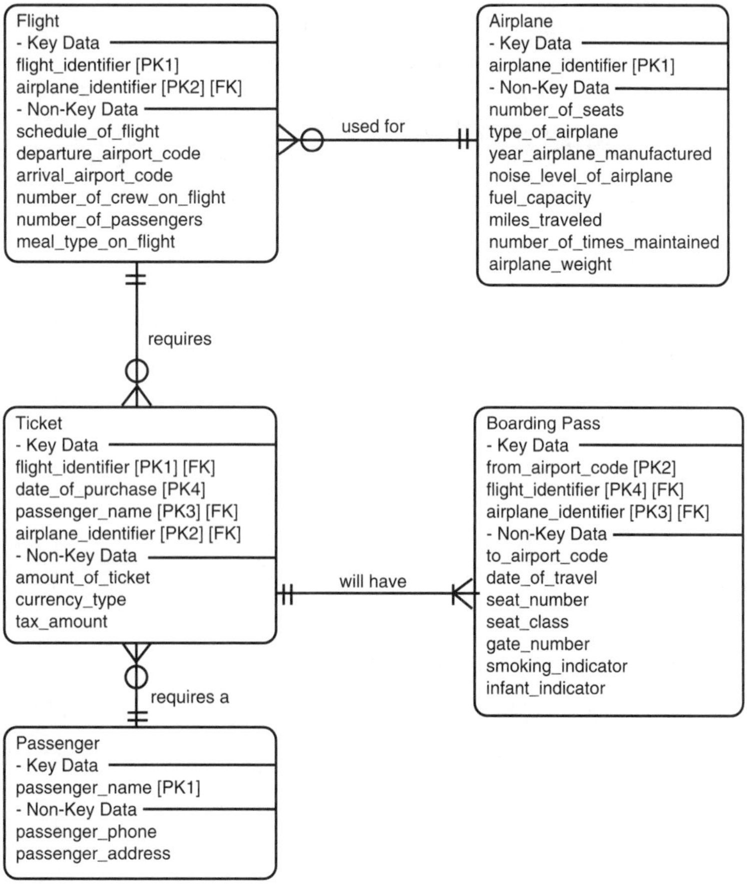

FIGURE 20.17.

Third normal form for Mile High Airlines.

Denormalization

Now that the business data model is complete, you should begin to consider the database design and performance issues related to your data model. You can denormalize the data model into a database design model, and actually reverse the normalization process to the degree necessary to enhance performance, always keeping in mind that the *meaning* of the business data model must not be altered. For example, by reviewing the third normal form diagram, you see that the ticket dates have been placed in an entity called Ticket Dates. During the denormalization process, you might decide to place those dates back into the entity Ticket in the database design diagram. As a result of this, you would use more DASD, or database storage space, but would increase performance. This denormalization process should no longer be considered a limitation of the database design due to the fact that the price of DASD has fallen so significantly in recent years.

In the airline example, you would want better performance at the expense of some increased DASD. However, in another system, where the repeating field might be so significantly large that it would cost too much in increased space usage, increasing the performance might not be justifiable at the expense of the DASD. You've added the passenger information back into the Ticket entity for performance reasons. In other words, you know that most of the queries to the database will need to have ticket and passenger information returned together, so it makes sense to duplicate passenger information in the Ticket table. Figure 20.18 shows the ER Diagram in denormalized form.

FIGURE 20.18.

ER diagram in denormalized form.

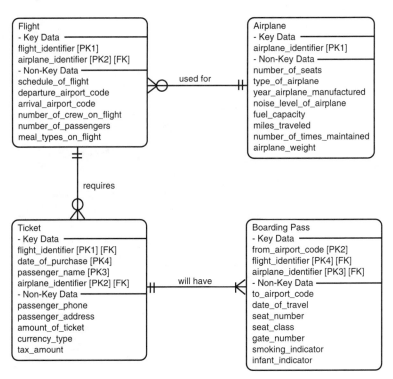

Physical Design

After denormalizing our ER model, the next step is designing the physical database. See Tables 20.1 through 20.4 for the physical layout of the tables you have identified in the physical design phase.

Table 20.1. Columns in the FLIGHT table.

Column Name	Data Type and Length
FLIGHT_ID	CHAR(10)
AIRPLANE_ID	CHAR(25)
FLIGHT_SCHED	DATE
DEP_AIRPT_CD	CHAR(3)
ARR_AIRPT_CD	CHAR(3)
NUM_CREW	NUMBER(2)
NUM_PASSGR	NUMBER(3)
MEAL_TYP	CHAR(3)

Table 20.2. Columns in the AIRPLANE table.

Column Name	Data Type and Length
AIRPLANE_ID	CHAR(25)
NUM_SEATS	NUMBER(3)
AIRPL_TYP	CHAR(10)
YR_MANUF	DATE
NOISE_LEV	CHAR(10)
FUEL_CAPAC	NUMBER(4)
MILES_TRAV	NUMBER(38)
TIMES_MAINT	NUMBER(5)
AIRPLANE_WT	NUMBER(10)

Table 20.3. Columns in the TICKET table.

Column Name	Data Type and Length
FLIGHT_ID	CHAR(10)
DATE_PURCH	DATE
PASSGR_NM	CHAR(35)
AIRPLANE_ID	CHAR(25)
PASSGR_PH	CHAR(20)
PASSGR_ADD	CHAR(100)
TICKT_AMT	NUMBER(5)
CURR_TYP	CHAR(5)
TAX_AMT	NUMBER(5)

Table 20.4. Columns in the BOARDING_PASS table.

Column Name	Data Type and Length
FLIGHT_ID	CHAR(10)
AIRPLANE_ID	CHAR(25)
DEP_AIRPT_CD	CHAR(3)
ARR_AIRPT_CD	CHAR(3)
TRAVL_DT	DATE
SEAT_NUM	CHAR(4)
SEAT_CLSS	CHAR(1)
GATE_NUM	CHAR(5)
SMOK_IND	CHAR(1)
INF_IND	CHAR(1)

Other considerations in the physical design phase of an Oracle7.3 database should be at least the following:

■ You need to estimate the size of your database tables and indexes as accurately as possible. This will help you in total operating systems disks requirements.

■ You need to decide whether or not you need to use RAID.

■ You need to estimate the operating system's memory, CPU, and I/O controllers' requirements as accurately as possible.

■ You need to have a reasonable idea of how the database will grow in the future, and how that growth will affect the preceding hardware requirements.

Database Creation

Now that you have completed your physical database design, you can take that design and begin to create a database. Before you can create an Oracle7.3 database, you need to consider the following:

■ The appropriate INIT.ORA parameters.

■ Following the Optimal Flexible Architecture (OFA) standard and deciding on the proper distribution of the Oracle7.3 data files.

■ Issuing the CREATE DATABASE statement. See the section "Creating the Physical Database."

■ Your ability to start up and shut down the database.

The INIT.ORA File

In this section, we discuss only the parameters in the INIT.ORA file that we consider to be the most important. For a complete list of INIT.ORA parameters, refer to Chapter 1 of the *Oracle7 Server Reference Manual*.

CHECKPOINT_PROCESS

Performing the checkpoint process is the responsibility of Oracle's background process, LGWR, the log writer process. At times the performance of the LGWR process is not as good as it should be. By setting this parameter to TRUE, Oracle starts another background process called CKPT. The background process CKPT relieves LGWR of the responsibility of writing a checkpoint, therefore improving performance.

COMPATIBLE

Set this parameter to the desired version number of Oracle prior to version 7.3 with which you want to remain compatible. For example, if you have programs that are working with version7.2.3, and you are migrating to version7.3, setting this parameter to 7.2.3 ensures that you are compatible with version7.2.3. However, doing so will restrict you from some features available in version7.3. You can comment out this line in the INIT.ORA file after you are comfortable with your migration to version7.3.

We recommend setting this parameter to the current release of Oracle to be able to take advantage of all the functionality available in this release (version7.3.2).

CURSOR_SPACE_FOR_TIME

This parameter should be set to TRUE to increase performance for the programs that use cursors. This parameter affects both the shared and private SQL areas.

DB_BLOCK_BUFFERS

Prior to setting this parameter, you should examine the amount of operating system memory available to your Oracle7.3 database. In Chapter 30, "Performance Tuning," you learn how to set this parameter properly. For the initial creation of your database, you can leave it set to the smallest value in the INIT.ORA file. This parameter affects the SGA (system global area) size, thereby affecting the performance of Oracle. Setting this parameter to a high value reduces the I/O time. However, setting it to a value too high consumes too much memory and might cause the SGA to swap in and out of main memory, thereby degrading performance.

DB_BLOCK_SIZE

In the INIT.ORA file, this parameter is the most important one related to creating a database. This value determines the block size of a database. After a database has been created, you cannot change this value without dropping and recreating the database. This parameter also affects the performance of the database. In Chapter 30 of this book, you learn how to determine the appropriate value for this parameter. We recommend setting this parameter to 8192 and not taking the default of 2048 in your development environment. This gives you a starting point that you can monitor and tune for best determining your database block size for your production environment.

DB_FILES

This parameter determines the maximum number of database files that is allowed to be open at runtime for the database you are about to create. Prior to creating the database, change this parameter to at least the value of MAXDATAFILES in the CREATE DATABASE statement you execute. We recommend a value of at least 100. Later in this chapter you'll learn to set the value of MAXDATAFILES.

DB_FILE_MULTIBLOCK_READ_COUNT

This parameter determines the maximum number of blocks read in one I/O operation during a sequential read. This parameter should be less than the operating system maximum I/O size. Set this parameter to the operating system maximum I/O size divided by the value of DB_BLOCK_SIZE, not to exceed the value of DB_BLOCK_BUFFERS divided by four.

DB_NAME

This is the name of the database. This name must match the name used for the database in the CREATE DATABASE statement executed to create it. Although Oracle allows you to use eight alphanumeric characters for this name, we recommend using only four. In the "Optimal

Flexible Architecture" section of this chapter, we explain the reasoning behind this recommendation. Allowed characters for database names are the following:

- All alphabetic characters
- Numbers
- Underscores (_)
- Pound sign (#)
- Dollar sign ($)

All other characters on your keyboard are not allowed.

LOG_BUFFER

This parameter determines the size of redo log buffers in the SGA. The higher this value is, the less often that a redo I/O occurs. The default is four times the database block size. If you have enough available memory, we recommend setting this parameter to 1 megabyte.

LOG_CHECKPOINT_INTERVAL

In Oracle7.3, a checkpoint always occurs when Oracle switches from one online redo log file to another. Setting this value larger than the actual redo log file size ensures that a checkpoint occurs only when Oracle switches redo logs. This will improve performance.

LOG_CHECKPOINTS_TO_ALERT

Set this parameter to YES. This causes Oracle to log the checkpoint to the ALERT.LOG file. Later, you can check the database to determine whether it is taking checkpoints too frequently.

LOG_SIMULTANEOUS_COPIES

This parameter determines the maximum number of redo buffer copy latches available to simultaneously write log entries. Set this parameter to the number of available CPUs multiplied by two on SMP machines.

LOG_SMALL_ENTRY_MAX_SIZE

Set this parameter to zero on SMP machines for performance reasons. See Chapter 30 for information on setting this value.

MTS

Here are the Multi-Threaded Server (MTS) parameters:

```
MTS_DISPATCHERS
MTS_LISTENER_ADDRESS
MTS_MAX_DISPATCHERS
MTS_MAX_SERVERS
MTS_MULTIPLE_LISTENERS
MTS_SERVICE
```

MTS (Multi-Threaded Server) is used mainly for Oracle installations that have large numbers of users using online transactions and accessing the database. MTS does not help Oracle installations that have a smaller number of users accessing Oracle with large queries or in batch processes. Refer to Chapter 30 if MTS is an important consideration for your installation. We recommend not using MTS for the initial database creation, and if MTS is appropriate for your installation, you can alter these parameters after installation.

NLS

Here are the National Language Support (NLS) parameters:

```
NLS_CALENDAR
NLS_CURRENCY
NLS_DATE_FORMAT
NLS_DATE_LANGUAGE
NLS_ISO_CURRENCY
NLS_LANGUAGE
NLS_NUMERIC_CHARACTERS
NLS_SORT
NLS_TERRITORY
```

Oracle7.3 has made considerable improvements in its support of national languages. Setting NLS_LANGUAGE to "FRENCH", for example, displays Oracle messages in French. For a complete list of supported languages, see Chapter 4 of the *Oracle7 Server Reference Manual*.

OPEN_CURSORS

This parameter determines the maximum number of open cursors within one session. The default is 50. We recommend increasing this value if your Oracle application requires more open cursors.

OPTIMIZER_MODE

This parameter determines the optimizer type that will be used. The default value is CHOOSE, which causes Oracle to use the cost-based optimizer if table statistics are present in the data dictionary and the rule-based optimizer, if statistics for at least one table in the query statement are not available. Other values are RULE, which forces Oracle to use the rule-based optimizer; FIRST_ROWS causes Oracle to select an execution plan that increases performance; and ALL_ROWS, which causes Oracle to select an execution plan that minimizes the total execution time. We recommend using the default value for this parameter (CHOOSE) and using the ANALYZE COMPUTE STATISTICS command in Oracle to create the table statistics in the catalogs. For a complete syntax of the ANALYZE command, see the *Oracle7 Server SQL Language Reference Manual*.

PARALLEL

Here are the Parallel Server parameters:

```
PARALLEL_DEFAULT_MAX_INSTANCES
PARALLEL_MAX_SERVERS
PARALLEL_MIN_PRECENT
PARALLEL_MIN_SERVERS
PARALLEL_SERVER_IDLE_TIME
```

These INIT.ORA parameters are used in parallel server configurations. This configuration is useful when you want to split the work load of Oracle7.3 database. For example, you can have two SMP machines that both access the same physical database, but they have their own separate database instances. If your Oracle7.3 server has to execute 100 transactions per second without the parallel server using a single database instance, it can execute close to 190 transactions per second with Oracle7.3 parallel server using two SMP machines. For a complete explanation and use of the PARALLEL parameters, see the *Oracle7 Parallel Server Concepts Manual* and *Oracle7 Server Administration Guide*.

PRE_PAGE_SGA

Setting this parameter to YES causes Oracle to bring all the SGA pages into memory, thereby improving performance. It also increases the time required to start the database. Because you do not anticipate creating the database and then frequently stopping and starting it, set this parameter to YES.

ROLLBACK_SEGMENTS

This parameter lists all the rollback segments that will be used in query processing. Initially, comment out this parameter. After creating the database, you must create rollback segments and list them using the ROLLBACK_SEGMENTS parameter. For example, after database creation, you might decide to have only four rollback segments and call them r1, r2, r3, and r4. This parameter would look like this: ROLLBACK_SEGMENTS= (r1,r2,r3,r4). For optimal size and number of rollback segments, see the *Oracle7.3 Server Administration Guide*.

SHARED_POOL_SIZE

The SHARED POOL buffer is an SGA area that contains the SQL shared cursors and stored procedures. Setting the SHARED_POOL_SIZE to a proper value increases the performance of queries, due to the fact that this value affects the size of the SGA. Refer to Chapter 30 in this book for determining the optimal value for this parameter. If you have an ample amount of memory, set this value to 30MB and later examine the Oracle7.3 dynamic views for the best value.

SORT_SIZE_AREA

This parameter causes Oracle to set aside the indicated bytes in Oracle's PGA (program global area) for required sort operations (such as ORDER BY). Setting this parameter to a high value increases the performance on queries that require sort operations. Refer to Chapter 30 in this book for the optimal value for this parameter. Set this parameter to 128KB (131072).

TRANSACTIONS_PER_ROLLBACK_SEGMENTS

This parameter determines the maximum number of transactions that can use one rollback segment simultaneously. Set this parameter to the value that results from this formula:

NO_OF_ACTIVE_TXNS / (NO_OF_ROLLBACK_SEGS + 1)

For all other parameters, use the values indicated in the large model in the INIT.ORA file and then alter any parameters as necessary after monitoring Oracle during benchmark runs.

Optimal Flexible Architecture

Installing Oracle and creating an Oracle database can be done using any standard desired, especially regarding the placement of Oracle files. We suggest that you use the Oracle Optimal Flexible Architecture (OFA) standard as you make these decisions. For detailed information about OFA, see Cary V. Millsap's paper called *The OFA Standard: Oracle for Open Systems*, which is part number A19308-2 from Oracle Services. OFA also is discussed in the Oracle manual called *Oracle7 for UNIX Performance Tuning Tips*.

This section describes the file system configuration that you should follow as it pertains to the OFA standard.

First, you must understand what a mount point on a UNIX file system is. UNIX file systems are made up of portions of disks called *logical volumes*, and a *mount point* is the name of the directory identifying that logical volume. Name mount points using the following convention:

/u01

/u02

/u03 (and so on)

where these logical volumes are striped across the available physical disks in order to increase performance.

The Oracle files that will be created as a result of installation and database creation will need to be distributed carefully across the available logical volumes of the file system. This is necessary for ease of maintenance, increasing performance, and supporting the stability of the database. The types of Oracle files included are the files that contain Oracle product software distributed by Oracle; files that contain information about the database (for example, administrative files such as instance parameter files or the ALERT.LOG file); files containing any software written locally for the database; and files containing the actual database (such as control files, database data files, and so forth). To follow OFA standards, all files containing Oracle software and those containing information about the database (called *administrative files* by Oracle) should be located in a subdirectory structure under the home directory of the oracle user account. A global variable called ORACLE_BASE should be set to the user account, Oracle's home directory at login to UNIX. A good standard to follow when creating home directories for an oracle user account is to create the following subdirectory under the volume /u01:

```
/u01/app/oracle
/u01/app/user1
/u01/app/user2 and so on.
```

Placing all home directories for all users on a UNIX system in a structure like this allows home directories to be located on different logical volumes but still be easily found by searching for app at the same level.

In order to have multiple versions of Oracle running on a single system, a subdirectory structure such as the following should be created. The only files that should be found under the product subdirectory should be the Oracle software files so that when new versions are installed and old ones removed, any customized files will not have to be moved or lost. In this example, you want to have both Oracle7.3 and Oracle8 running on the same machine. You would need to create the following subdirectory structures:

```
/u01/app/oracle/product/7.3.x
/u01/app/oracle/product/8.x.x
```

You would determine which version to access by setting a variable called $ORACLE_HOME to the subdirectory structure of the version you want to access. Add the subdirectory bin to the end of the preceding for attaching to the end of the global variable $PATH. In this example, if you want to access the Oracle7.3.x database, set the variable $ORACLE_HOME to /u01/app/oracle/ product/7.3.X and ensure that /u01/app/oracle/product/7.3.X/bin is attached to the end of $PATH.

To follow the OFA standard for locating database administrative files, a subdirectory called admin needs to be created under the home directory for the UNIX user account oracle, or under the directory structure found in the variable, $ORACLE_BASE. Continuing with the same example, you would create the following subdirectory: /u01/app/oracle/admin

Under this subdirectory, you will need to create the following subdirectories for the types of Oracle files indicated:

Subdirectory	Contents
arch	Any archived redo log files (if the database is operating in archive log mode)
adump	Audit files (if the audit feature is used)
bdump	Trace files created by Oracle's background processes
cdump	Core files that might be created by the database
create	Any scripts used for creating the database
ddl	Any other scripts used to create database objects, such as tablespaces, userids, and so on
exp	Any parameter files to be used in the Oracle export utility
imp	Any parameter files to be used in the Oracle import utility

continues

Subdirectory	Contents
pfile	An instance's parameter and configuration files
sql	Any scripts created to query, update, insert, and so on, the data in the database
udump	Trace files generated by users' SQL commands

We have changed the name of one of the OFA standard subdirectory names and added two others; the setup in this list works better. However, Oracle uses the subdirectory name adhoc for SQL scripts, although we like sql. We've also added ddl so that the scripts can be divided between subdirectories by function, and imp because it's missing from the OFA standards. OFA standards also include a subdirectory called logbook that we have not needed; we store any absolutely necessary log files with the script that generated them.

If your system has space constraints in the directory structure under $ORACLE_BASE, consider placing some or all of these directories in other locations and using symbolic links from the standard location of these subdirectories to where they are actually located.

If the system you are developing is on a network, some Oracle-related files can be located on other systems and be available via the network, such as locating some files on an NFS (network file system) mounted location. OFA standards allow, and encourage, the user to create a slightly different name for these mount points, such as /n01, which helps distinguish which mount points are remotely mounted. However, Oracle warns that Oracle datafiles should not be placed on an NFS mounted location, saying that the database can be corrupted by doing so. We've done this and not had any problems, but those days might be limited! In addition, any NFS can have a performance degradation, depending on the size of the table and the speed of the network.

Another subdirectory under $ORACLE_BASE can be created to hold any scripts and programs that might pertain only to this Oracle database. Oracle also documents that anyone in Oracle Consulting would use this subdirectory with any software they develop, if they happen to be called in to supply you with support.

Figure 20.19 represents an example of Oracle7.3 administrative and products file structures utilizing OFA standards. OFA places TNSNAMES.ORA, SQLNET.ORA, and LISTENER.ORA in the directory /etc. We recommend leaving these files in the $ORACLE_HOME/network/admin directory because it is easier for the database administrator to locate and maintain these files in $ORACLE_HOME/network/admin.

For detailed information about OFA, again, see Cary V. Millsap's paper called *The OFA Standard: Oracle for Open Systems*. OFA also is discussed in the Oracle manual called *Oracle7 for UNIX Performance Tuning Tips*.

By placing Oracle database files in a standard location, and using standard naming conventions, you protect those files from deletion and make them easily identifiable as database files. Under the /u01 and subsequently numbered mount points, a subdirectory called oradata should be created to house all Oracle database files. Under this directory structure, create a subdirectory for each database on this system. In the example represented in the following diagram, we show our system indicated by mhal and also show examples of other systems, namely pers and payr that might have been created for a personnel system and a payroll system.

FIGURE 20.19.

Oracle7 administrative and products file structures.

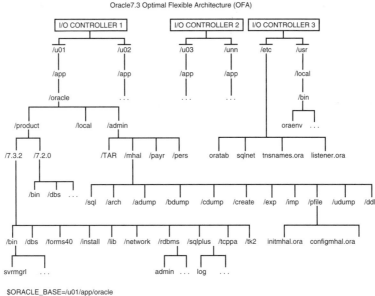

Oracle7.3 Optimal Flexible Architecture (OFA)

$ORACLE_BASE=/u01/app/oracle
$ORACLE_HOME=/u01/app/oracle/product/7.3.2

The files contained in this directory structure are all the Oracle control files, redo log files, and database data files. *Control files* are the Oracle files that contain information about the structure of the database. These files must be replicated over at least two, and we recommend three, disks with different controllers in order to maintain an acceptable failover for the database. By doing this, you ensure that even if a disk fails, you still have at least one copy of a control file to replicate. Having three control files allows for failover even if one control file is lost. Even though OFA does not suggest that you number the control files, we recommend naming the control files control01.ctl, control02.ctl, and control03.ctl.

Redo log files are the Oracle files that are continually written to as an Oracle database operates. They can be used to roll forward a database if a system crashes, either due to a disk failing or if the CPU crashes. The naming standard is to call a redo log file redo##**.log, where ## is the group that the log file belongs to, and ** is the number of the log file within that group. Figure 20.20 shows two log file groups (1 and 2). Group 1 has two members; group 2 has one member. In the example, we've named the redo logs redo0101.log, redo0102.log, and redo0201.log.

Oracle database datafiles are created to mimic the names of the tablespaces being used to contain database data. In other words, there is a set of standard tablespaces used in Oracle to contain database data, and others created to contain data specific to the system, mhal, in the current example. The standard tablespaces created for each database being created contain rollback segments, system segments, temporary segments, tools segments, and users segments. Rollback segments are contained in a tablespace called rbs, so the name of the file is rbs01.dbf through rbs##.dbf where ## is the number of data files containing rollback segments.

FIGURE 20.20.

Oracle7 database files structure.

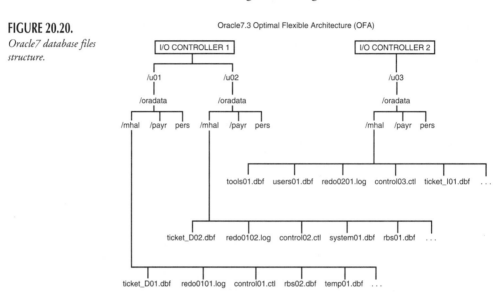

Having more than one file associated with each tablespace separates segments across disk controllers, which improves performance by reducing I/O contention. The system tablespace is contained in a series of files called system01.dbf through system##.dbf, if more than one system tablespace file is desired, where ## is a sequential number identifying the different files associated with the system tablespace. Temporary space is required to best tune an Oracle database. The standard name for the temporary tablespace is temp. Therefore, name your files associated with that tablespace temp01.dbf through temp##.dbf for the same reasons just noted. The tools and users tablespaces are likewise named tools and users, respectively. The files associated with these tablespaces are named tools01.dbf through tools##.dbf, and users01.dbf through users##.dbf, respectively, for the same reasons as noted above. For more information about tablespace naming conventions, see Cary V. Millsap's paper called *The OFA Standard: Oracle for Open Systems* (refer again to the diagram shown in Figure 20.20).

Creating the Physical Database

Now that you have the layout of your database, you can create it. The first step in creating an Oracle database is to log into SVRMGR and create an Oracle7.3 database. In the example we've been using, Mile High Airlines, we create the database by issuing the following statement from within SVRMGR:

```
CREATE DATABASE MHAL
MAXDATAFILES 200
CHARACTER SET WE8ISO8859P1
LOGFILE        group 1 ('/u01/oradata/mhal/redo0101.log',
'/u02/oradata/mhal/redo0102.log) size 15M,
group 2 ('/u03/oradata/mhal/redo0201.log',
'/u04/oradata/mhal/redo0202.log) size 15M
DATAFILE '/u02/oradata/mhal/system01.dbf' size 40M ;
```

The preceding statement creates a database called mhal, which stands for Mile High Airlines. Oracle allows the user to create a database with a name of up to eight characters in length. However, most Oracle installations use a database name of only four alphanumeric characters.

The other parameters in the CREATE DATABASE command are described in the following paragraphs.

The parameter, MAXDATAFILES, specifies that the database can consist of up to that number of database files. In this example, you can create up to 200 datafiles in mhal database.

In the statement just shown, we use the CHARSET WE88ISO8859P1, which supports all the Western European languages. For a complete description of all supported character sets for all languages, see Chapter 4, "National Language Support," in the *Oracle7 Server Reference Manual*.

The parameter LOGFILE tells Oracle where to place the redo logs and how large each should be. You created three redo log groups that each contain one redo log file member, or copy. Each is 5MB. You should try to follow the OFA (Optimal Flexible Architecture) for naming all data files for your database. See the previous section regarding the OFA standard.

```
LOGFILE    group 1 ('/u01/oradata/mhal/redo0101.log') size 15M,
                    ('/u02/oradata/mhal/redo0102.log') size 15M,
               group 2 ('/u03/oradata/mhal/redo0201.log') size 15M,
              ('/u04/oradata/mhal/redo0202.log') size 15M
```

The parameter DATAFILE indicates to the database the location of the system tablespace files. This example uses one file of 25MB for the system tablespace.

```
DATAFILE '/u02/oradata/mhal/system01.dbf' size 40M;
```

To execute the CREATE DATABASE command, you must have the authority within Oracle to execute that command. You must be part of the UNIX dba group (or the same group as the UNIX user oracle) or for backward compatibility, you must log into svrmgrl and issue a CONNECT INTERNAL statement. You can type the CREATE DATABASE command line-by-line or save it in a script file and execute it in Oracle's svrmgrl (Server Manager—line mode), with a prompt svrmgr>. For example, if you save the CREATE DATABASE command into a script with the name crtdb.sql, you can type the following at a UNIX prompt:

```
$ svrmgrl
```

The Server Manager prompt then appears.

```
svrmgrl>
```

Type the following to execute (the @ signifies "execute" to a SQL script).

```
svrmgrl> @crtdb.sql
```

The file INITMHAL.ORA, which is the INIT.ORA file used for our sample instance, mhal, is located in the following OFA standard location:

```
/u01/app/oracle/admin/mhal/pfile/initmhal.ora
```

INITMHAL.ORA

Listing 20.1 shows an example of the INIT.ORA file used for the mhal example.

Listing 20.1. The INITMHAL.ORA file.

```
#
#
# include database configuration parameters

ifile   = /u01/app/oracle/admin/mhal/pfile/configmhal.ora

#NLS_LANGUAGE = GERMAN
#NLS_TERRITORY = GERMANY
#NLS_CURRENCY = $
#NLS_ISO_CURRENCY = GERMANY
#NLS_DATE_FORMAT = DD-MON-YY
#NLS_DATE_LANGUAGE = GERMAN
#NLS_SORT =  GERMAN

rollback_segments              = (r01,r02,r03,r04)

################################################################
# Example INIT.ORA file
#
# This file is provided by Oracle Corporation to help you customize
# your ROBMS intallation for your site. Important system parameters
# are discussed, and example settings given.
#
# Some parameter settings are generic to any size installation.
# For parameters that require different values in different size
# installations, three scenarios have been provided: SMALL, MEDIUM
# and LARGE.  Any parameter that needs to be tuned according to
# installation size will have three settings, each one commented
# according to installation size.
#
# Use the following table to approximate the SGA size needed for the
# three scenarious provided in this file:
#
#                    ------Installation/Database Size------
#                    SMALL          MEDIUM          LARGE
#  Block      2K     4500K          6800K           17000K
#  Size       4K     5500K          8800K           21000K
#
# To set up a database that multiple instances will be using, place
# all instance-specific parameters in one file, and then have all
# of these files point to a master file using the IFILE command.
```

```
# This way, when you change a public
# parameter, it will automatically change on all instances.  This is
# parameters. For example, if you choose to use private rollback segments,
# these must be specified in different files, but since all gc_*
# parameters must be the same on all instances, they should be in one file.
#
# INSTRUCTIONS: Edit this file and the other INIT files it calls for
# your site, either by using the values provided here or by providing
# your own.  Then place an IFILE= line into each instance-specific
# INIT file that points at this file.
###############################################################

db_files = 200

# db_file_multiblock_read_count = 8                      # SMALL
db_file_multiblock_read_count = 16                 # MEDIUM
# db_file_multiblock_read_count = 32                 # LARGE

# db_block_buffers = 200                                 # SMALL
# db_block_buffers = 550                             # MEDIUM
# db_block_buffers = 3200                            # LARGE
db_block_buffers = 100000                       # VERY LARGE

# shared_pool_size = 3500000                             # SMALL
# shared_pool_size = 6000000                         # MEDIUM
shared_pool_size = 90000000                      # VERY LARGE

log_checkpoint_interval = 9999999
checkpoint_process = TRUE

# processes = 50                                         # SMALL
# processes = 100                                    # MEDIUM
processes = 500                                  # LARGE
sessions=500

dml_locks = 100                                        # SMALL
# dml_locks = 200                                    # MEDIUM
# dml_locks = 500                                    # LARGE

# log_buffer = 8192                                      # SMALL
# log_buffer = 32768                                 # MEDIUM
log_buffer = 1048576                             # VERY LARGE

sequence_cache_entries = 10                            # SMALL
# sequence_cache_entries = 30                        # MEDIUM
# sequence_cache_entries = 100                       # LARGE

sequence_cache_hash_buckets = 10                       # SMALL
# sequence_cache_hash_buckets = 89                   # LARGE

# audit_trail = true          # if you want auditing
# timed_statistics = true     # if you want timed statistics
max_dump_file_size = 10240    # limit trace file size to 5 Meg each

log_archive_start = true      # if you want automatic archiving

# remote_login_passwordfile = exclusive
open_cursors = 255
```

continues

Listing 20.1. continued

```
# compatible = 7.3.2
hash_join_enabled = true
always_anti_join = hash
partition_view_enabled = true
sort_direct_writes = auto
hash_multiblock_io_count = 4
sort_area_size = 2097152      # or 2M
hash_area_size = 33554432     # or 32M

global_names = TRUE

use_async_io = TRUE
pre_page_sga = TRUE

 mts_dispatchers="tcp,4"
 mts_dispatchers="ipc,4"
 mts_max_dispatchers=10
 mts_servers=3
 mts_max_servers=10
 mts_service=mhal
 mts_listener_address="(ADDRESS=(PROTOCOL=tcp)(host=hp9000)(port=1521))"
```

CONFIGMHAL.ORA

Another file you are using in the sample instance mhal is the CONFIGMHAL.ORA file. You'll find the reference to this file in INITMHAL.ORA as follows:

```
ifile   = /u01/app/oracle/admin/mhal/pfile/configmhal.ora
```

The example's CONFIGMHAL.ORA file looks like Listing 20.2.

Listing 20.2. The CONFIGMHAL.ORA file.

```
# cnfg.ora - instance configuration parameters

control_files        = (/u01/oradata/mhal/control01.ctl,
                         /u02/oradata/mhal/control02.ctl,
                         /u03/oradata/mhal/control03.ctl)
# Below for possible future use...
#init_sql_files       = (?/dbs/sql.bsq,
#                         ?/rdbms/admin/catalog.sql,
#                         ?/rdbms/admin/expvew.sql)
background_dump_dest  = /u01/app/oracle/admin/mhal/bdump
core_dump_dest        = /u02/app/oracle/admin/mhal/cdump
user_dump_dest        = /u02/app/oracle/admin/mhal/udump
log_archive_dest       = /u02/app/oracle/admin/mhal/arch/arch.log
db_block_size         = 8192
db_name               = mhal
```

LISTENER.ORA

The sample file called LISTENER.ORA is located in the following path and resembles Listing 20.3.

/u01/app/oracle/product/7.3.2/network/admin/listener.ora

Listing 20.3. The LISTENER.ORA file.

```
LISTENER=
 (ADDRESS_LIST=
  (ADDRESS=
   (PROTOCOL=IPC)
   (KEY=hp9000mhal)
  )
(ADDRESS=
    (PROTOCOL=TCP)
    (HOST=hp9000)
    (PORT=1521)
  )
 )
STARTUP_WAIT_TIME_LISTENER = 0
CONNECT_TIMEOUT_LISTENER = 60
SID_LIST_LISTENER=
 (SID_LIST=
  (SID_DESC=
   (SID_NAME=mhal)
   (ORACLE_HOME=/u01/app/oracle/product/7.3.2)
  )
 )
#TRACE_LEVEL_LISTENER = ADMIN
```

TNSNAMES.ORA

Our example TNSNAMES.ORA file is located in the following path and resembles Listing 20.4.

/u01/app/oracle/product/7.3.2/network/admin/tnsnames.ora

Listing 20.4. The TNSNAMES.ORA file.

```
hp9000mhal=
 (description=
  (address_list=
    (address=
     (community=TCP)
     (protocol=TCP)
     (host=hp9000)
     (port=1521)
    )
  )
  (connect_data=
   (SID=mhal)
  )
 )
```

Database Startup and Shutdown

One of your post-Oracle installation steps is to run a script called root.sh. This script asks you for a valid ORACLE_SID and a path for the local bin directory. The default for the local bin directory is /usr/local/bin. You must ensure that this bin directory is part of the value of your operating system path. This script also updates the /etc/oratab file with the correct ORACLE_HOME value and ORACLE_SID values. The following assumes that these steps have been completed before you proceed.

If you have multiple Oracle instances, you might find it confusing to know which instance of the Oracle database you are using. To help reduce this confusion, try the following options:

Set the ORAENV_ASK operating system environment parameter to YES. ORAENV is a script supplied by Oracle that sets the necessary environment variables for Oracle so that users can connect to the database(s). For example, if you execute ORAENV when ORAENV_ASK is set to YES, ORAENV prompts you for the value of ORACLE_SID, the instance ID you want to connect to. ORAENV validates the value you give for ORACLE_SID against the values in /etc/oratab.

Write some scripts for starting and shutting down the proper instance.

For the mhal database, you could write the following scripts for starting the database and name the script startmhal. Locate the file as follows:

/u01/app/oracle/admin/mhal/startmhal

The startmhal file contains the following lines:

```
export ORACLE_SID=mhal
. oraenv
svrmgrl < startmhal.parms
```

To execute the startmhal script, enter the following at a UNIX prompt, assuming that startmhal has been set up as a UNIX executable:

```
$ startmhal
```

This script uses a file called

/u01/app/oracle/admin/mhal/startmhal.parms

which contains the following two lines:

```
connect internal
startup pfile=$ORACLE_BASE/admin/mhal/pfile/initmhal.ora
```

The script for shutting down the database could resemble the following:

/u01/app/oracle/admin/mhal/shutmhal

where shutmhal would contain the following lines:

```
export ORACLE_SID=mhal
. oraenv
svrmgrl < shutmhal.parms
```

The file `shutmhal.parms` would be found in

```
/u01/app/oracle/admin/mhal/shutmhal.parms
```

and would consist of the following lines:

```
connect internal
shutdown immediate
```

Summary

In this chapter, you learned how to determine the required resources for building a database system and how to work through the logical analysis and design of that database system. Designing and developing an Oracle database system can be a long and complicated procedure, but the steps in this chapter will help guide you through that process.

21

Creating the Initial Database Objects

by Mohammad Asadi and Kimbra McDonald

By understanding Oracle's physical data structures, you can optimize disk storage requirements and performance. In this chapter, you examine Oracle's physical data structures and learn how to create database objects including tablespaces, tables, and indexes.

Creating the Physical Objects

After creating the mhal database, you are now ready to create other objects within the database. All objects within an Oracle database use a common space allocation algorithm. Before any object is created, you must tell Oracle how many data blocks and extents to allocate to the object. As previously mentioned, when you create a database you tell Oracle what block size to use. In the mhal database example, you made the database block size 8,192 (8KB) bytes. The database block size is an important factor in both database performance and disk storage. Special care should be taken in determining the correct value for the database block size. Because I/O requests are ultimately performed by the operating system, the database block size should be a multiple of the operating system block size. An Oracle extent is a continuous set of data blocks. In Oracle, extents can be grouped together to create a segment. Every object within an Oracle database has its own segments. Some people use objects and segments synonymously. The following list summarizes Oracle's data storage structure:

- Each Oracle database has a certain number of logical storage areas, called tablespaces.
- Each tablespace consists of one or more segments (objects).
- Each Oracle segment has one or more database extents.
- Each database extent has one or more contiguous database blocks.

Oracle Tablespaces

All Oracle objects are created within their specific tablespaces. You can take an Oracle tablespace offline. If you do so, all the objects within that tablespace become unavailable. Some DBAs use this technique for database maintenance. For example, you might want to take a tablespace offline to perform a tablespace backup. Later, you might use that tablespace backup to perform a tablespace recovery. As mentioned earlier, tablespaces are logical units within the Oracle database, and they must be related to physical locations and their operating system's datafiles. When you create an Oracle tablespace, you specify the physical name, location, and sizes of all the datafiles that can be used by the tablespace. An operating system datafile can be used by one and only one tablespace, but a tablespace can have one or more datafiles. Oracle stores the names of the datafiles in the control file. The following is the syntax for creating an Oracle tablespace:

```
CREATE TABLESPACE  tablespace_name
    DATAFILE file-specification
        AUTOEXTENT (ON /OFF)
        NEXT integer
        MAXSIZE (ULTIMATE/integer)
```

```
DEFAULT STORAGE storage_clause
ONLINE/OFFLINE
PERMANENT/TEMPORARY ;
```

The following paragraphs describe the CREATE TABLESPACE parameters in more detail.

CREATE TABLESPACE *tablespace_name*

The name you assign to the tablespace is represented here by *tablespace_name*. Oracle runs on a multitude of operating systems, ranging from MVS (mainframes), to UNIX, to PC systems. So, for portability reasons, it is a good idea to keep tablespace names to under eight characters. In the mhal database, you decided to create a tablespace called TICKET_D for storing the data portion of the Ticket table, and another tablespace called TICKET_I, for storing the index portion of the Ticket table.

DATAFILE *file-specification*

The operating system datafiles and their corresponding sizes are referred to as the *file-specification* names. When creating a new tablespace, the datafiles must not exist unless the REUSE option is specified; otherwise, Oracle returns an error saying that the file already exists. As you will see shortly, in Listing 21.2, the tablespace TICKET_D has two operating system datafiles named /u01/oradata/mhal/ticket_D01.dbf and /u02/oradata/mhal/ticket_D02.dbf. Tablespace TICKET_I has one operating system datafile, /u03/oradata/mhal/ticket_I01.dbf.

AUTOEXTENT (ON /OFF)

Whenever a tablespace in Oracle fills up, it automatically grabs another extent, unless otherwise specified by the AUTOEXTENT OFF parameter. Prior to Oracle7.3, there was a limit to the number of extents that a tablespace could "acquire"; this limit depended on the database block size. For example, prior to Oracle7.3, if the database block size was 2KB, the maximum extents that a tablespace could acquire was 121. If the limit, MAXEXTENTS, was encountered, an Oracle error was returned. That limit has been removed with Oracle7.3 if the parameter AUTOEXTENT is set to ON.

NEXT *integer*

When Oracle needs to allocate more disk space for the datafile, it uses this *integer* value to do so.

MAXSIZE (ULTIMATE/*integer*)

This is the maximum space allocation permitted for datafiles. ULTIMATE indicates no limit to the maximum space allocation for the datafile.

DEFAULT STORAGE *storage_clause*

When creating an Oracle tablespace, you can assign default storage parameters to it. If a table that uses this tablespace does not specify its storage parameters, Oracle7.3 uses the tablespace default storage parameter for the user instead, which may or may not be the same. The storage clause has the following format:

```
STORAGE (INITIAL integer
        NEXT integer
        MINEXTENTS integer
        MAXEXTENTS integer/UNLIMITED
        PCTINCREASE integer)
```

where:

- INITIAL specifies the tablespace's first extent size in bytes.

- NEXT specifies the tablespace's next extent size in bytes.

- MINEXTENTS specifies the number of extents allocated to the tablespace when it is first created.

- MAXEXTENTS specifies the maximum number of extents that the tablespace can grow to.

- PCTINCREASE specifies the percentage increase that occurs every time a new extent is allocated to the tablespace. For performance reasons, set this parameter to zero in versions of Oracle prior to version 7.3. In Oracle7.3, this parameter should be a value other than zero in order for Oracle to perform tablespace defragmentation.

ONLINE/OFFLINE

When you create Oracle tablespaces, specifying the ONLINE parameter makes the tablespace immediately available for use. Specifying OFFLINE makes the tablespace unavailable for use.

PERMANENT/TEMPORARY

Most of the tablespaces that you create are permanent ones. This is the default. Objects in permanent tablespaces are kept. In some special circumstances, you may need to create objects in tablespaces that you do not want to keep permanently. For example, tablespaces that are used in sort operations are no longer needed after the sort operation finishes. In these cases, you may want to use the TEMPORARY option. If the TEMPORARY option is specified, the object in the tablespace is deleted after the SQL statement finishes.

After database creation, but before you create specific user tablespaces (per OFA standards), the following system-dependent tablespaces should be created:

- The Rollback tablespace (RBS)
- The Temp tablespace (TEMP)
- The Users tablespace (USERS)
- The Tools tablespace (TOOLS)

Rollback Tablespace (RBS)

When a database is created, Oracle uses the SYSTEM tablespace to store rollback segment information. Immediately after database creation, you should create a specific tablespace to place the rollback segments in. The SYSTEM tablespace is not designed to handle the rollback segments. You should pay special attention to the size and operating system physical location of the ROLLBACK tablespace. The following is an example of CREATE TABLESPACE for RBS, the ROLLBACK SEGMENTS tablespace.

```
CREATE TABLESPACE rbs
    DATAFILE       '/u01/oradata/mhal/rbs01.dbf' SIZE 258M,
             '/u02/oradata/mhal/rbs02.dbf' SIZE 258M
    DEFAULT STOTAGE (    INITIAL 8M
Next 8M
MINEXTENTS 1
MAXEXTENTS 240
PCTINCREASE 0    )  ;
```

Rollback Segments

Rollback segments in Oracle contain information about the transaction updates to the database. This information is needed in case those transactions have to be rolled back or undone. For example, when a row in a table is updated, even before a COMMIT is issued, the updated row might be written to the disk. If for some reason a system crash occurs before a COMMIT command is issued (explicitly or implicitly), Oracle uses the rollback segment information to undo the changes at startup time, performing a crash recovery.

There are two types of rollback segments, private and public. A private rollback segment is the one explicitly obtained when a database is first opened. A public rollback segment is the one that may be used by any transaction with no restrictions. If you are not using the Parallel Server Option of Oracle7.3, private and public rollback segments are the same.

Depending on the nature of the Oracle transaction, rollback segments may expand and/or shrink. The size and number of rollback segments affect the database performance. For database applications that have many small transactions, many small rollback segments are needed, whereas applications with long-running batch transactions require large rollback segments. Most applications are a mixture of both small and large transactions. For the typical application you should create small, medium, and large rollback segments and use the following command for setting the transaction to a particular rollback segment, either small, medium, or large:

```
SET TRANSACTION USE ROLLBACK SEGMENT rbs_name
```

You can create a rollback segment with the OPTIMAL parameter for its size. The optimal size is the size of the rollback segment that you would like to maintain after the rollback segment expands and/or shrinks. The OPTIMAL size may be monitored for proper value by using Server Manager (svrmgrm).

It is a good idea to have the INITIAL and NEXT sizes of each rollback segment the same and set the MAXEXTENTS parameter to a high value for possible rollback expansion. PCTINCREASE does not apply to rollback segments, and its value is 0. At the initial stages of your application development, if you are not sure about the nature of the transactions (small, medium, or large), set the INITIAL and NEXT sizes of the rollback segments to about 15 percent of the size of the largest table within your database. Later, when you have a better feel about all of the transactions after monitoring the rollback segments, you can improve the size and the number of the rollback segments.

Here are some parameters in the `init.ora` file relevant to rollback segments:

■ `TRANSACTIONS`

■ `TRANSACTIONS_PER_ROLL_BACK_SEGMENT`

■ `ROLLBACK_SEGMENTS=(rbs1, rbs2, ... and so on.)`

`TRANSACTIONS` indicates the number of transactions that can be executed simultaneously in the database. `TRANSACTIONS_PER_ROLL_BACK_SEGMENT` indicates the number of transactions that each rollback segment can handle. Therefore, the number of rollback segments (denoted by N) should be

`N = TRANSACTIONS / TRANSACTIONS_PER_ROLL_BACK_SEGMENT`

`ROLLBACK_SEGMENTS` names the rollback segments that are brought online at startup time. If the number of rollback segments in `ROLLBACK_SEGMENTS` is greater than N, Oracle still acquires all of them. For example if

```
TRANSACTIONS=64
TRANSACTIONS_PER_ROLL_BACK_SEGMENT=32
N = 64 / 32 = 2
```

In this example, Oracle allocated two rollback segments. If there is a line in the `init.ora` file such as `ROLLBACK_SEGMENTS=(rbs1, rbs2, rbs3)`, Oracle7.3 ignores the calculated value and allocates three rollback segments to all the transactions, thereby overwriting the value of N.

In the example, you decided to create four rollback segments. The shell script called `rollback.sql` is located in the following directory:

`/u01/app/oracle/admin/mhal/create/rollback.sql`

ROLLBACK.SQL

Listing 21.1 shows the contents of an SQL*Plus script called `rollback.sql`.

Listing 21.1. Creating rollback segments.

```
CREATE PUBLIC ROLLBACK SEGMENT r01
 TABLESPACE rbs
    STORAGE (INITIAL 8M NEXT 8M OPTIMAL 80M MAXEXTENTS 240) ;

CREATE PUBLIC ROLLBACK SEGMENT r02
 TABLESPACE rbs
 STORAGE (INITIAL 8M NEXT 8M OPTIMAL 80M MAXEXTENTS 240) ;

CREATE PUBLIC ROLLBACK SEGMENT r03
 TABLESPACE rbs
 STORAGE (INITIAL 8M NEXT 8M OPTIMAL 80M MAXEXTENTS 240) ;

CREATE PUBLIC ROLLBACK SEGMENT r04
 TABLESPACE rbs
 STORAGE (INITIAL 8M NEXT 8M OPTIMAL 80M MAXEXTENTS 240) ;
```

Temp Tablespace (TEMP)

Some user queries require a temporary segment. Temporary segments are created in the temporary tablespace. Each user can have only one temporary tablespace. The temporary tablespace is assigned to the user when the USERID is created. The default name for the user's temporary tablespace is SYSTEM, but should be changed to some other tablespace, such as TEMP. It can be changed with the ALTER USER TEMPORARY TABLESPACE tablespace_name statement. The following is an example of creating a temporary tablespace called TEMP.

```
CREATE TABLESPACE temp
    DATAFILE '/u01/oradata/mhal/temp01.dbf' SIZE 242M
DEFAULT STOTAGE (    INITIAL 4M
Next 4M
MINEXTENTS 1
MAXEXTENTS 240
PCTINCREASE 0    ) ;
```

Users Tablespace (USERS)

When creating a user, you can specify a default USER tablespace. If you do not specify a USER tablespace, the default Oracle uses is the tablespace called SYSTEM; however, you should change it to some other tablespace name, such as USERS. To further clarify this, let's go through an example of creating a user. Let's create a user such as the following:

```
CREATE USER john IDENTIFIED BY passwd
    TEMPORARY TABLESPACE  j_temp
    DEFAULT TABLESPACE john_d ;
```

In the preceding example, the temporary tablespace for the user john is j_temp, and the default tablespace for him is john_d. Had you not specified the values for the TEMPORARY TABLESPACE and the DEFAULT TABLESPACE, their values would be TEMP and USERS, respectively. In that case, our CREATE USER statement would be

```
CREATE USER john IDENTIFIED BY passwd ;
```

Every time that a user creates an object that requires a tablespace, and the tablespace is not explicitly specified in the CREATE TABLESPACE statement, the user's default tablespace is used. The following is an example of creating a USERS tablespace:

```
CREATE TABLESPACE users
    DATAFILE '/u03/oradata/mhal/users01.dbf' SIZE 5M
DEFAULT STOTAGE (    INITIAL 50K
Next 50K
MINEXTENTS 1
MAXEXTENTS 240
PCTINCREASE 0    ) ;
```

We recommend that you create a small tablespace called USERS. When creating any object that requires a tablespace, always explicitly specify the tablespace name for both data and indexes. This is true even for imports. When importing tables that have indexes, always import the tables first (using the default tablespace for data) without importing the indexes and then run the scripts to create the indexes. This allows you to separate the data portion of tables from their indexes.

Tools Tablespace (TOOLS)

The TOOLS tablespace is used by some Oracle tools products, such as Oracle Financials. If you are using any Oracle tools, refer to their installations and user guides to properly size this tablespace. The following is an example of creating a TOOLS tablespace.

```
CREATE TABLESPACE tools
    DATAFILE '/u03/oradata/mhal/tools01.dbf' SIZE 5M
DEFAULT STOTAGE (    INITIAL 10K
Next 10K
MINEXTENTS 1
MAXEXTENTS 240
PCTINCREASE 0    ) ;
```

Other Tablespaces

In addition to the system-dependent tablespaces already described, you decided to create the following eight tablespaces for the mhal database:

- ■ TICKET_D-Used to store the data portion of the ticket table.
- ■ TICKET_I—Used to store the index portion of the ticket table.
- ■ BPASS_D—Used to store the data portion of the boarding pass table.
- ■ BPASS_I—Used to store the index portion of the boarding pass table.
- ■ PLANE_D—Used to store the data portion of the airplane table.
- ■ PLANE_I—Used to store the index portion of the airplane table.
- ■ FLIGHT_D—Used to store the data portion of the flight table.
- ■ FLIGHT_I—Used to store the index portion of the flight table.

Listing 21.2 provides the CREATE TABLESPACE statements for the preceding tablespaces.

Listing 21.2. Creating the mhal tablespaces.

```
CREATE TABLESPACE ticket_d
    DATAFILE '/u01/oradata/mhal/ticket_D01.dbf' SIZE 1000M,
            '/u05/oradata/mhal/ticket_D02.dbf' SIZE 1000M,
            '/u09/oradata/mhal/ticket_D03.dbf' SIZE 1000M,
            '/u13/oradata/mhal/ticket_D04.dbf' SIZE 1000M,
            '/u17/oradata/mhal/ticket_D05.dbf' SIZE 1000M
DEFAULT STORAGE (    INITIAL 10M
Next 10M
MINEXTENTS 1
MAXEXTENTS 490
PCTINCREASE 0    ) ;

CREATE TABLESPACE ticket_i
    DATAFILE '/u21/oradata/mhal/ticket_I01.dbf' SIZE 500M,
```

```
                    '/u25/oradata/mhal/ticket_I02.dbf' SIZE 500M,
                    '/u29/oradata/mhal/ticket_I03.dbf' SIZE 500M,
                    '/u33/oradata/mhal/ticket_I04.dbf' SIZE 500M,
                    '/u37/oradata/mhal/ticket_I05.dbf' SIZE 500M
DEFAULT STORAGE (    INITIAL 5M
Next 5M
MINEXTENTS 1
MAXEXTENTS 490
PCTINCREASE 0      ) ;


CREATE TABLESPACE bpass_d
    DATAFILE '/u02/oradata/mhal/bpass_D01.dbf' SIZE 1000M,
             '/u06/oradata/mhal/bpass_D02.dbf' SIZE 1000M,
             '/u10/oradata/mhal/bpass_D03.dbf' SIZE 1000M,
             '/u14/oradata/mhal/bpass_D04.dbf' SIZE 1000M.
             '/u18/oradata/mhal/bpass_D05.dbf' SIZE 1000M
DEFAULT STORAGE (    INITIAL 10M
Next 10M
MINEXTENTS 1
MAXEXTENTS 490
PCTINCREASE 0      ) ;


CREATE TABLESPACE bpass_i
    DATAFILE '/u22/oradata/mhal/bpass_I01.dbf' SIZE 400M,
             '/u26/oradata/mhal/bpass_I02.dbf' SIZE 400M,
             '/u30/oradata/mhal/bpass_I03.dbf' SIZE 400M,
             '/u34/oradata/mhal/bpass_I04.dbf' SIZE 400M,
             '/u38/oradata/mhal/bpass_I05.dbf' SIZE 400M
DEFAULT STORAGE (    INITIAL 4M
Next 4M
MINEXTENTS 1
MAXEXTENTS 490
PCTINCREASE 0      ) ;


CREATE TABLESPACE plane_d
    DATAFILE '/u03/oradata/mhal/plane_D01.dbf' SIZE 50M,
             '/u07/oradata/mhal/plane_D02.dbf' SIZE 50M,
             '/u11/oradata/mhal/plane_D03.dbf' SIZE 50M,
             '/u15/oradata/mhal/plane_D04.dbf' SIZE 50M,
'/u19/oradata/mhal/plane_D05.dbf' SIZE 50M

DEFAULT STORAGE (    INITIAL 1M
Next 1M
MINEXTENTS 1
MAXEXTENTS 240
PCTINCREASE 0      ) ;


CREATE TABLESPACE plane_i
    DATAFILE '/u23/oradata/mhal/plane_I01.dbf' SIZE 10M,
             '/u27/oradata/mhal/plane_I02.dbf' SIZE 10M,
             '/u31/oradata/mhal/plane_I03.dbf' SIZE 10M,
             '/u35/oradata/mhal/plane_I04.dbf' SIZE 10M,
             '/u39/oradata/mhal/plane_I05.dbf' SIZE 10M
DEFAULT STORAGE (    INITIAL 100K
Next 100K
MINEXTENTS 1
MAXEXTENTS 450
```

continues

Listing 21.2. continued

```
PCTINCREASE 0     ) ;

CREATE TABLESPACE flight_d
    DATAFILE '/u04/oradata/mhal/flight_D01.dbf' SIZE 100M,
             '/u08/oradata/mhal/flight_D02.dbf' SIZE 100M,
             '/u12/oradata/mhal/flight_D03.dbf' SIZE 100M,
             '/u16/oradata/mhal/flight_D04.dbf' SIZE 100M,
             '/u20/oradata/mhal/flight_D05.dbf' SIZE 100M
DEFAULT STORAGE (    INITIAL 2M
Next 2M
MINEXTENTS 1
MAXEXTENTS 240
PCTINCREASE 0     ) ;

CREATE TABLESPACE flight_i
    DATAFILE '/u24/oradata/mhal/flight_I01.dbf' SIZE 50M,
             '/u28/oradata/mhal/flight_I02.dbf' SIZE 50M,
             '/u32/oradata/mhal/flight_I03.dbf' SIZE 50M,
             '/u36/oradata/mhal/flight_I04.dbf' SIZE 50M,
             '/u40/oradata/mhal/flight_I05.dbf' SIZE 50M
DEFAULT STORAGE (    INITIAL 1M
Next 1M
MINEXTENTS 1
MAXEXTENTS 240
PCTINCREASE 0     ) ;
```

Tables

To create a table in Oracle, you use the following syntax:

```
CREATE TABLE   owner.table_name
    COLUMN     datatype    DEFAULT column_value     column constraints
table_constraints
PCTFREE     integer value
PCTUSED     integer value
INITRANS    integer value
MAXTRANS    integer value
TABLESPACE    tablespace_name that this table resides in
STORAGE    storage_clause
RECOVERABLE/UNRECOVERABLE
    CLUSTER        cluster_name (column(s))
    PARALLEL        parallel_clause
    ENABLE/DISABLE    enable_clause/disable_clause
    AS            subquery
    CACHE/NOCACHE ;
```

The following paragraphs describe this code in more detail.

```
CREATE TABLE   owner.table_name
```

The Oracle user ID that will contain the table is *owner*, and *table_name* is the name you assign to the table. That name can be up to 30 characters in length.

```
COLUMN    datatype    DEFAULT column_value     column constraints
```

The name of the table's attribute is COLUMN. The maximum number of columns in a table is 254, and column names can be 30 characters. The keyword DEFAULT can be used to give a column a default value. A column also can have an INTEGRITY constraint associated with it that can be used to restrict the values of that column. You can choose your column constraint name or let Oracle assign one for you. For example, if you create a column and you specify a NOT NULL constraint, the database will require that you enter a value for the column when you insert a row. Other examples of column constraints are UNIQUE, which prevents column duplication, the REFERENCES constraint, which establishes referential integrity between tables, and the CHECK constraint, which identifies a condition that must be met for a column.

table_constraints

The *table_constraints* are restrictions imposed by the database on the entire table. Examples of constraints are a FOREIGN KEY constraint, which relates one table to another, a PRIMARY KEY constraint, which uniquely identifies a row in a table, and a CHECK constraint, which validates a column's value or format.

PCTFREE   *integer value*

The keyword PCTFREE identifies the percentage of a database block that will remain free for updates.

PCTUSED   *integer value*

The keyword PCTUSED refers to the percentage of a database block that Oracle uses for row insertion. For example, a PCTUSED of 90 will cause Oracle to use 90 percent of the database block. Oracle will not use the block for row insertion unless less than 90 percent of the block is used. The default is 40 percent.

INITRANS   *integer value*

The value of INITRANS refers to the initial number of transaction entries within each data block. The default is one transaction per block.

MAXTRANS   *integer value*

The value of MAXTRANS refers to the maximum number of transaction entries within each data block. The default depends on the database block size. For example, for a database created with a 4KB block size, the default value of MAXTRANS is 255.

TABLESPACE   *tablespace_name that this table resides in*

The TABLESPACE refers to the name of the tablespace that the table will be created and stored in.

STORAGE   *storage_clause*

The STORAGE clause was discussed earlier in this chapter when the CREATE TABLESPACE command was described in detail.

RECOVERABLE/UNRECOVERABLE

The keyword RECOVERABLE means that the creation of the table will be logged in Oracle's online redo logs that can be used later in the case of recovery due to media failure. The default is RECOVERABLE.

CLUSTER   *cluster_name (column(s))*

The CLUSTER keyword indicates that the columns listed from this table are part of a cluster.

PARALLEL   *parallel_clause*

The keyword PARALLEL refers to the degree of parallelism. This option is used with Oracle's Parallel Query. This option is useful only if you have more than one CPU, such as on Symmetric Multi-Processor (SMP) machines.

ENABLE/DISABLE   *enable_clause/disable_clause*

The keyword ENABLE indicates that the constraint referenced will be enabled.

AS   *subquery*

The AS keyword refers to a subquery that is executed in the creation of the table.

CACHE/NOCACHE ;

The keyword CACHE means that Oracle puts the database block at the bottom of Oracle's least recently used list. This means that if Oracle needs to flush some blocks from its block buffers, it will flush others before flushing those marked as CACHE. This option is used only for full table scans. The default is NOCACHE, which says that if Oracle needs to flush buffers, the blocks marked NOCACHE will be flushed first.

For a complete description of the CREATE TABLE parameters, see the *Oracle7.3 Server SQL Reference Manual*.

Next, you must create the tables that will reside in the tablespaces defined in the preceding example (see Listing 21.3).

> **NOTE**
>
> Do not be overly concerned about making the INITIAL and NEXT extent sizes small. Having too many tablespace extents does not necessary degrade your database performance. Refer to the *Oracle7 Server Administrator's Guide* for setting the proper values for INITIAL and NEXT sizes suited to your database.

Listing 21.3. Creating the mhal tables.

```
CREATE TABLE FLIGHT
(FLIGHT_ID      CHAR(10)       ,
AIRPLANE_ID    CHAR(25)       CONSTRAINT FLT_AIR_FK REFERENCES
```

```
AIRPLANE(AIRPLANE_ID),
FLIGHT_SCHED    DATE           CONSTRAINT FLSCH_NN NOT NULL,
DEP_AIRPT_CD    CHAR(3)    CONSTRAINT DEPAR_NN NOT NULL,
ARR_AIRPT_CD    CHAR(3)    CONSTRAINT ARRAR_NN NOT NULL,
NUM_CREW        NUMBER(2)   CONSTRAINT NUMCR_NN NOT NULL,
NUM_PASSGR    NUMBER(3),
MEAL_TYP        CHAR(3))
         TABLESPACE FLIGHT_D
STORAGE INITIAL 10475274
NEXT 10475274
MINEXTENTS 2
MAXEXTENTS 45
PCTINCREASE 0 ;

CREATE TABLE AIRPLANE
(AIRPLANE_ID    CHAR(25)         ,
NUM_SEATS     NUMBER(3)      ,
AIRPL_TYP       CHAR(10)         CONSTRAINT AIRPL_NN NOT NULL,
YR_MANUF        DATE           ,
NOISE_LEV       CHAR(10)         CONSTRAINT NOISE_NN NOT NULL,
FUEL_CAPAC    NUMBER(4)      CONSTRAINT FUELC_NN NOT NULL,
MILES_TRAV    NUMBER(38)    CONSTRAINT MILEST_NN NOT NULL,
TIMES_MAINT    NUMBER(5)       CONSTRAINT TIMESM_NN NOT
NULL,
AIRPLANE_WT    NUMBER(10)    CONSTRAINT AIRPL_NN NOT NULL)
         TABLESPACE PLANE_D
STORAGE INITIAL 5232394
NEXT 5232394
MINEXTENTS 2
MAXEXTENTS 45
PCTINCREASE 0 ;

CREATE TABLE TICKET
(FLIGHT_ID        CHAR(10)    CONSTRAINT TKT_FLT_FK REFERENCES
FLIGHT(FLIGHT_ID),
DATE_PURCH    DATE        ,
PASSGR_NM    CHAR(35)     ,
AIRPLANE_ID    CHAR(25)     CONSTRAINT TKT_AIR_FK REFERENCES
AIRPLANE(AIRPLANE_ID),
PASSGR_PH     CHAR(20)      ,
PASSGR_ADD    CHAR(100)     ,
TICKT_AMT       NUMBER(5)      CONSTRAINT TICKA_NN NOT NULL,
CURR_TYP        CHAR(5)     CONSTRAINT CURRT_NN NOT NULL,
TAX_AMT         NUMBER(5)    CONSTRAINT TAXAM_NN NOT NULL)
         TABLESPACE TICKET_D
STORAGE INITIAL 10475274
NEXT 10475274
MINEXTENTS 2
MAXEXTENTS 450
PCTINCREASE 0 ;

CREATE TABLE BOARDING_PASS
(FLIGHT_ID        CHAR(10)    CONSTRAINT BRDP_FLT_FK REFERENCES
FLIGHT(FLIGHT_ID),
AIRPLANE_ID    CHAR(25)    CONSTRAINT BRDP_AIR_FK REFERENCES
AIRPLANE(AIRPLANE_ID),
DEP_AIRPT_CD    CHAR(3)     ,
```

continues

Listing 21.3. continued

```
ARR_AIRPT_CD     CHAR(3)     CONSTRAINT ARRAR_NN NOT NULL,
TRAVL_DT         DATE         CONSTRAINT TRAVD_NN NOT NULL,
SEAT_NUM         CHAR(4)     CONSTRAINT SEATN_NN NOT NULL,
SEAT_CLSS        CHAR(1)      CONSTRAINT SEATC_NN NOT NULL,
GATE_NUM         CHAR(5)     CONSTRAINT GATEN_NN NOT NULL,
SMOK_IND         CHAR(1),
INF_IND          CHAR(1) )
        TABLESPACE BPASS_D
STORAGE INITIAL 10475274
NEXT 10475274
MINEXTENTS 2
MAXEXTENTS 450
PCTINCREASE 0 ;
```

> **NOTE**
>
> Because you have one table per tablespace, you selected large values for the INITIAL and NEXT extent sizes. However, if you have multiple tables per tablespace, you should revisit these values.

Indexes

You use the following syntax to create an index in Oracle.

```
CREATE UNIQUE     (default is non-unique)     INDEX    owner.index_name
    ON     owner.table_name
    (table_column_name(s))     ASC/DESC
    CLUSTER     owner.cluster_name
    INITRANS         integer value
    MAXTRANS         integer value
    TABLESPACE     tablespace_name that this index resides in
    STORAGE         storage_clause
    PCTFREE         integer_value
    NOSORT
    RECOVERABLE/UNRECOVERABLE
    PARALLEL         parallel_clause
```

The following paragraphs describe this code in more detail.

```
CREATE UNIQUE     (default is non-unique)     INDEX    owner.index_name
```

The Oracle user ID that will contain the index is owner, and index_name is the name you assign to the index. That name can be up to 30 characters in length.

```
ON     owner.table_name
```

The ON keyword refers to the owner and table_name that the index will be created against.

```
(table_column_name(s))     ASC/DESC
```

The table's column names that are a part of the index are listed. The keywords ASC and DESC indicate whether the index is created in ascending or descending order. The default is ascending.

CLUSTER   *owner.cluster_name*

The keyword CLUSTER indicates whether the columns in the index are part of a cluster and what that cluster's name is.

INITRANS   *integer value*

The value of INITRANS refers to the initial number of transaction entries within each data block. The default is one transaction per block.

MAXTRANS   /   *integer value*

The value of MAXTRANS refers to the maximum number of transaction entries within each data block. The default depends on the database block size. For example, for a database created with a 4KB block size, the default value of MAXTRANS is 255.

TABLESPACE   *tablespace_name* that this index resides in

The TABLESPACE refers to the name of the tablespace that the table will be created and stored in.

STORAGE   *storage_clause*

The STORAGE clause was discussed earlier in this chapter when the CREATE TABLESPACE command was described in detail.

PCTFREE   *integer_value*

The keyword PCTFREE identifies the percentage of a database block that will remain free for updates.

NOSORT

When creating an index, the NOSORT option says to Oracle that the column(s) that will be in the index are already in ascending order. This indicates to Oracle not to sort before creating the index. Using this parameter decreases the index creation time.

RECOVERABLE/UNRECOVERABLE

The keyword RECOVERABLE means that the creation of the table will be logged in Oracle's online redo logs, which could be used later in the case of recovery due to media failure. The default is RECOVERABLE.

PARALLEL   parallel_clause

The keyword PARALLEL refers to the degree of parallelism. This option is used with Oracle's Parallel Query. This option is useful only if you have more than one CPU, such as on Symmetric Multi-Processor (SMP) machines. With this option you can create indexes in parallel.

Non-unique indexes (that is, those with syntax similar to the preceding but without the UNIQUE keyword) are used for enhancing performance. For a complete description of the CREATE INDEX parameters, see the *Oracle7 Server SQL Language Reference Manual*.

TIP

You should create the indexes after creating and loading the tables.

The following DDL (Data Definition Language) is necessary to create your indexes:

```
CREATE UNIQUE INDEX FLIGHT_PK ON FLIGHT (FLIGHT_ID,
AIRPLANE_ID)
            TABLESPACE FLIGHT_I
STORAGE     INITIAL 5232394
NEXT 5232394
MINEXTENTS 2
MAXEXTENTS 45
PCTINCREASE 0 ;

CREATE UNIQUE INDEX AIRPLANE_PK ON AIRPLANE (AIRPLANE_ID)
            TABLESPACE PLANE_I
STORAGE INITIAL 5232394
NEXT 5232394
MINEXTENTS 2
MAXEXTENTS 45
PCTINCREASE 0 ;

CREATE UNIQUE INDEX TICKET_PK ON TICKET (FLIGHT_ID,
DATE_PURCH, PASSGR_NM, AIRPLANE_ID)
            TABLESPACE TICKET_I
STORAGE INITIAL 5232394
NEXT 5232394
MINEXTENTS 2
MAXEXTENTS 450
PCTINCREASE 0 ;

CREATE UNIQUE INDEX BOARDING_PASS_PK ON BOARDING_PASS (FLIGHT_ID, AIRPLANE_ID,
DEP_AIRPT_CD, ARR_AIRPT_CD)
            TABLESPACE BPASS_I
STORAGE INITIAL 4183818
NEXT 4183818
MINEXTENTS 2
MAXEXTENTS 450
PCTINCREASE 0 ;
```

Summary

In this chapter, you learned how to create some of the most commonly used Oracle objects. This chapter does not cover the creation of all Oracle objects, nor does it explain all the options for the objects described. For complete descriptions of all the object-creation syntax, see the *Oracle7 Server SQL Language Reference Manual*.

22

Loading Data to Oracle from DB2/MVS

*by Mohammad Asadi and
Kimbra McDonald*

After you have created the physical database objects, one of your next steps is to load the database objects. If you are loading data from another Oracle database, you can use the Oracle utilities Export and Import. You also can use the Oracle utility SQL*Loader to load your newly created Oracle database. (For more information on how to use these utilities, see Chapter 18, "SQL*Loader," and Chapter 19, "Export/Import.")

In this chapter, you learn how to load data from an existing DB2 database on an MVS system, to an Oracle database on an RS/6000 UNIX machine.

Loading Reference Tables

Before you can load any target table, you must consider the source of the data. Input data could come from a variety of sources. In the simplest case, you copy data from another similar Oracle table. If the column types and length of the target table are all identical to the source table, you can perform a simple export of the source table and import it to the target table. However, in the heterogeneous environment today, this is less likely. For example, assume that the source tables are located on a DB2/MVS (mainframe) database and the target tables reside on an Oracle/UNIX machine. The following are the tasks that you need to perform:

- Dump the source tables on DB2/MVS.
- Transfer the source data from MVS to a UNIX platform.
- Convert the source data from EBCDIC to ASCII.
- Load the data to Oracle7.3 tables.

Dumping the Source Tables on DB2/MVS

Currently, you can use any of these three ways to get the data out of DB2/MVS and make it usable for Oracle7.3:

- Oracle Transparent Gateway
- DB2 UNLOAD utility
- Custom programs

These three methods are explained in the following sections.

Oracle Transparent Gateway

Oracle provides a series of gateway products that enable other databases to communicate with Oracle. The other databases don't even have to be relational. For example, Oracle Open Gateway allows IMS (IBM's hierarchical database) to communicate with Oracle, and Oracle

Transparent Gateway (OTG) allows DB2 (IBM's relational database) to communicate with Oracle. Figure 22.1 shows an example of an OTG configuration.

FIGURE 22.1.
Oracle Transparent Gateway Configuration.

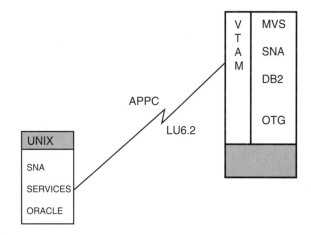

In this example, a UNIX machine (RS/6000) is used both as an Oracle7.3 RDBMS server and as a gateway server. You might have the Oracle7.3 RDBMS server on a separate machine from the gateway server machine. In either case, the gateway machine must be able to communicate with VTAM (Virtual Telecommunication Access method) on MVS using SNA (System Network Architecture). RS/6000 provides the SNA/6000 services software. SNA/6000 uses LU (logical unit) type 6.2 to communicate with DB2 on MVS. Sun MicroSystems provides a product called SunLink Peer-to-Peer software to communicate with DB2 on MVS. Other UNIX vendors have their own versions of SNA.

SNA services must be installed and properly configured before OTG can communicate with DB2 on MVS. The SNA/6000 also works with SQL/DS and AS/400 databases.

When you install SNA, it creates default SNA parameters that can be exported using an SNA configuration utility to a UNIX system file. This export utility is part of the System Management Interface Tool (SMIT) on an RS/6000 UNIX machine. The file created with the SNA export utility may be modified to suit your environment. Once this file has been modified, you may use the import utility provided in SMIT to update the new SNA parameters.

Listing 22.1 is a sample of a modified SNA configuration file we called SNA.CONFIG.INPUT and located in the directory /usr. You can modify this file to suit your requirements. (For a complete explanation of these parameters, refer to the IBM manuals called *Using AIX SNA Services/6000* and *AIX SNA Services/6000 Reference*.)

Listing 22.1. Sample of the SNA configuration file SNA.CONFIG.INPUT.

```
sna:
    prof_name                                       = "sna"
    max_sessions                                    = 200
    max_conversations                               = 200
    restart_action                                  = once
    rrm_enabled                                     = no
    dynamic_inbound_partner_lu_definitions_allowed = yes
    standard_output_device                          = "/dev/console"
    standard_error_device                           = "/dev/console"
    nmvt_action_when_no_nmvt_process                = reject
    trusted_group_ids                               = {system}
    comments                                        = ""

control_pt:
    prof_name                                       = "node_cp"
    xid_node_id                                     = "*"
    network_name                                    = "NETMHA"
    control_pt_name_alias                           = "SC0001CP"
    control_pt_name                                 = "SC0001CP"
    control_pt_node_type                            = appn_end_node
    max_cached_trees                                = 500
    max_nodes_in_topology_database                  = 500
    route_addition_resistance                       = 128
    comments                                        = ""

local_lu_lu6.2:
    prof_name                                       = "ORALU"
    local_lu_name                                   = "SC0001P1"
    local_lu_alias                                  = "SC0001P1"
    local_lu_dependent                              = no
    local_lu_address                                = 1
    sscp_id                                         = *
    link_station_prof_name                          = "otglnk"
    conversation_security_list_profile_name         = ""
    comments                                        = "Transparent Gateway LU"

partner_lu6.2:
    prof_name                                       = "ORAPART"
    fq_partner_lu_name                              = "NETMHA.LUDSN0"
    partner_lu_alias                                = "LUDSN0"
    session_security_supp                           = no
    parallel_session_supp                           = yes
    conversation_security_level                     = none
    comments                                        = "Transparent Gateway"

partner_lu6.2_location:
    prof_name                                       = "ORALOC"
    fq_partner_lu_name                              = "NETMHA.LUDSN0"
    partner_location_method                         = link_station
    fq_partner_owning_cp_name                       = ""
    local_node_is_network_server_for_len_node       = no
    fq_node_server_name                             = ""
    local_lu_name                                   = "SC0001P1"
    link_station_profile_name                       = "otglnk"
    comments                                        = ""
```

```
side_info:
    prof_name                                   = "ORACPIC"
    local_lu_or_control_pt_alias                = "SC0001P1"
    partner_lu_alias                            = ""
    fq_partner_lu_name                          = "NETMHA.LUDSN0"
    mode_name                                   = "IBMRDB"
    remote_tp_name_in_hex                       = yes
    remote_tp_name                              = "07F6C4C2"
    comments                                    = ""

link_station_token_ring:
    prof_name                                   = "otglnk"
    use_control_pt_xid                          = no
    xid_node_id                                 = 0x05dc0001
    sna_dlc_profile_name                        = "otgdlc"
    stop_on_inactivity                          = no
    time_out_value                              = 0
    LU_registration_supported                   = no
    LU_registration_profile_name                = ""
    link_tracing                                = no
    trace_format                                = short
    access_routing_type                         = link_address
    remote_link_name                            = ""
    remote_link_address                         = 0x400000918292
    remote_sap                                  = 0x04
    call_out_on_activation                      = yes
    verify_adjacent_node                        = no
    net_id_of_adjacent_node                     = ""
    cp_name_of_adjacent_node                    = ""
    xid_node_id_of_adjacent_node                = "*"
    node_type_of_adjacent_node                  = learn
    solicit_sscp_sessions                       = yes
    activate_link_during_system_init            = no
    activate_link_on_demand                     = no
    cp_cp_sessions_supported                    = no
    cp_cp_session_support_required              = no
    adjacent_node_is_preferred_server           = no
    initial_tg_number                           = 0
    restart_on_normal_deactivation              = no
    restart_on_abnormal_deactivation            = no
    restart_on_activation                       = no
    TG_effective_capacity                       = 4300800
    TG_connect_cost_per_time                    = 0
    TG_cost_per_byte                            = 0
    TG_security                                 = nonsecure
    TG_propagation_delay                        = lan
    TG_user_defined_1                           = 128
    TG_user_defined_2                           = 128
    TG_user_defined_3                           = 128
    comments                                    = ""

sna_dlc_token_ring:
    prof_name                                   = "otgdlc"
    datalink_device_name                        = "tok0"
    force_timeout                               = 120
    user_defined_max_i_field                    = no
    max_i_field_length                          = 30729
```

continues

Listing 22.1. continued

```
        max_active_link_stations                    = 32
        num_reserved_inbound_activation             = 0
        num_reserved_outbound_activation            = 0
        transmit_window_count                       = 16
        dynamic_window_increment                    = 1
        retransmit_count                            = 8
        receive_window_count                        = 8
        priority                                    = 0
        inact_timeout                               = 48
        response_timeout                            = 4
        acknowledgement_timeout                     = 1
link_name                                      = " "
        local_sap                                   = 0x04
        retry_interval                              = 60
        retry_limit                                 = 20
        dynamic_link_station_supported              = yes
        trace_base_listen_link_station              = no
        trace_base_listen_link_station_format       = long
        dynamic_lnk_solicit_sscp_sessions           = yes
        dynamic_lnk_cp_cp_sessions_supported        = yes
        dynamic_lnk_cp_cp_session_support_required  = no
        dynamic_lnk_TG_effective_capacity           = 4300800
        dynamic_lnk_TG_connect_cost_per_time        = 0
        dynamic_lnk_TG_cost_per_byte                = 0
        dynamic_lnk_TG_security                     = nonsecure
        dynamic_lnk_TG_propagation_delay            = lan
        dynamic_lnk_TG_user_defined_1               = 128
        dynamic_lnk_TG_user_defined_2               = 128
        dynamic_lnk_TG_user_defined_3               = 128
        comments                                    = " "

mode:
        prof_name                                   = "IBMRDB"
        mode_name                                   = "IBMRDB"
        max_sessions                                = 20
        min_conwinner_sessions                      = 10
        min_conloser_sessions                       = 10
        auto_activate_limit                         = 0
        max_adaptive_receive_pacing_window          = 16
        receive_pacing_window                       = 7
        max_ru_size                                 = 3840
        min_ru_size                                 = 256
        class_of_service_name                       = "#CONNECT"
        comments                                    = " "

lu_reg:
        prof_name                                   = "LRegmvs"
        lu_address_registered_list                  = {1,2,3,4,5,6,7,8,9}
        comments                                    = " "
```

The following screen shots will show you how to configure SNA for Oracle Transparent Gateway.

After modifying the SNA configuration file for your environment, you need to import it into SNA. To do this, you must login to the UNIX system as userid `root` and follow these steps.

1. From the UNIX prompt as the userid `root` type

   `# smit`

   Your screen should resemble Figure 22.2.

FIGURE 22.2.

The SMIT *main menu.*

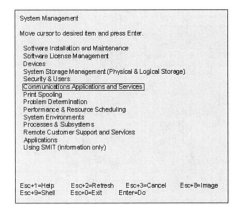

2. Select Communications Applications and Services. You should see the screen shown in Figure 22.3.

FIGURE 22.3.

The Communications Applications and Services screen.

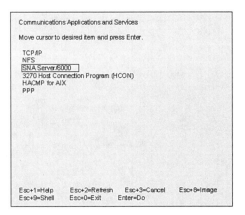

3. Select SNA Server/6000. Your screen should now resemble Figure 22.4.

4. Select Configure SNA Profiles, and the screen shown in Figure 22.5 should now be displayed.

FIGURE 22.4.

The SNA Server/6000 screen.

FIGURE 22.5.

The Configure SNA Profiles screen.

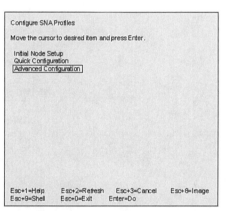

5. Select Advanced Configuration. You should now see the screen shown in Figure 22.6.

FIGURE 22.6.

The Advanced Configuration screen.

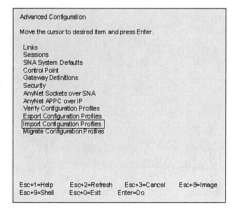

6. Select Import Configuration Profiles, and your screen should resemble the one shown in Figure 22.7. From earlier in the chapter, the location and name of the SNA configuration file is /usr/sna.config.input

FIGURE 22.7.

The Import Configuration Profiles screen.

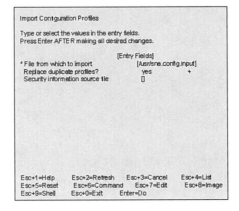

```
Import Configuration Profiles

Type or select the values in the entry fields.
Press Enter AFTER making all desired changes.

                                          [Entry Fields]
* File from which to import               [/usr/sna.config.input]
  Replace duplicate profiles?             yes            +
  Security information source file        []

Esc+1=Help      Esc+2=Refresh    Esc+3=Cancel    Esc+4=List
Esc+5=Reset     Esc+6=Command    Esc+7=Edit      Esc+8=Image
Esc+9=Shell     Esc+0=Exit       Enter=Do
```

After configuring SNA, you should be able to start the SNA link. Once again, you can use SMIT and follow these steps:

1. Enter the following at a UNIX prompt:

   # smit

   Your screen should resemble Figure 22.8.

FIGURE 22.8.

The SMIT *main menu.*

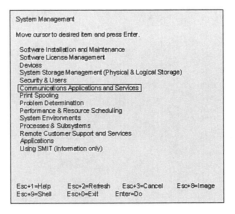

```
System Management

Move cursor to desired item and press Enter.

  Software Installation and Maintenance
  Software License Management
  Devices
  System Storage Management (Physical & Logical Storage)
  Security & Users
  [Communications Applications and Services]
  Print Spooling
  Problem Determination
  Performance & Resource Scheduling
  System Environments
  Processes & Subsystems
  Remote Customer Support and Services
  Applications
  Using SMIT (information only)

Esc+1=Help      Esc+2=Refresh    Esc+3=Cancel    Esc+8=Image
Esc+9=Shell     Esc+0=Exit       Enter=Do
```

2. Select Communications Applications and Services, and your screen should look like Figure 22.9.

FIGURE 22.9.

The Communications Applications and Services screen.

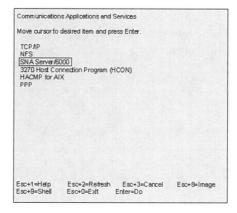

3. Select SNA Server/6000, and the screen shown in Figure 22.10 should be displayed.

FIGURE 22.10.

The SNA Server/6000 screen.

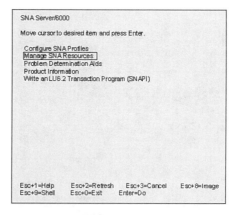

4. Select Manage SNA Resources. Your screen should now resemble Figure 22.11.

FIGURE 22.11.

The Manage SNA Resources screen.

5. Select Start SNA Resources. The screen shown in Figure 22.12 should be displayed.

FIGURE 22.12.

The Start SNA Resources screen.

6. Select Start SNA, and your screen should resemble Figure 22.13.

FIGURE 22.13.

The status of SNA.

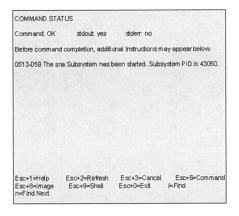

7. After verifying that the status of SNA is active, press F3 to go back to the Manage SNA Resources screen shown in Figure 22.11. To check whether the SNA link called otglnk is active, select Display SNA Resources, which displays the screen shown in Figure 22.14.

8. Select Display Active Link Information; your screen should now resemble the one shown in Figure 22.15.

9. Without changing anything on this screen, press Enter. You should see the screen shown in Figure 22.16. Notice that the SNA link, otglnk, is active.

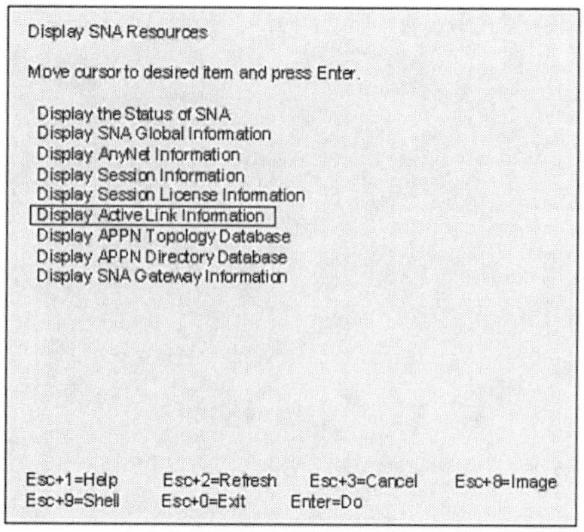

FIGURE 22.14.

The Display SNA Resources screen.

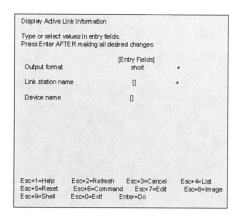

FIGURE 22.15.

The Display Active Link Information screen.

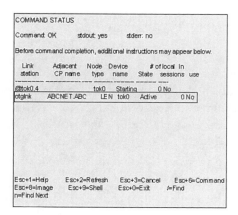

FIGURE 22.16.

The status of active link stations.

After configuring the SNA, you must perform some other tasks on the MVS side. You must define a userid and password for the owner of the program (package). The userid and password will be used by Oracle7.3 on the UNIX server. In the example, you defined ORADRDA as the userid and ORADRDA as the password. You also put the user ORADRDA as part of the RACF group that can access DB2 on MVS. Another userid and password must be defined on MVS for recovery situations, such as when a distributed transaction fails, when the network fails, or when DB2/MVS suddenly abends. You used ORADRDA for both the userid and password.

Use userid and password to set the init.ora parameters DRDA_RECOVERY_USERID and DRDA_RECOVERY_PASSWORD. Some other init.ora parameters on this sample Transparent Gateway UNIX machine are shown in the following listing:

```
LANGUAGE='US'
GATEWAY_SID=drd1
# The following setting of the generic NLS_DATE_FORMAT parameter
#  is required by Transparent Gateway for IBM DRDA.
NLS_DATE_FORMAT=YYYY-MM-DD
RESOLVE_BINDS=FALSE
RETRY=0, 1
OPTIMIZE_FILE_OPEN=FALSE
MAX_LOG_SIZE=0
ERRORTAG=ALL
OPEN_CURSORS=50
INIT_CURSORS=5
INCREMENT_CURSORS=2
TRIM_CURSORS=TRUE
D_OPEN_CURSORS=50
D_INIT_CURSORS=3
D_INCREMENT_CURSORS=1
D_TRIM_CURSORS=TRUE
TRACE_LEVEL=255
DB_NAME=DRD1
# The following parameters are specifically for Transparent Gateway
#  for IBM DRDA.
# DRDA gateway parms to access DB2 (instance DSN0)
DRDA_RDBMS_TYPE=DSN
DRDA_CONNECT_PARM=ORACPIC
DRDA_REMOTE_DB_NAME=USNETMHADSN0
DRDA_PACKAGE_COLLID=DRDA1
DRDA_PACKAGE_NAME=G2DRSQL
DRDA_PACKAGE_CONSTOKEN=A92617CB3FE54701
DRDA_RECOVERY_USERID=ORADRDA
DRDA_RECOVERY_PASSWORD=ORADRDA
#
# Be careful changing the DRDA_ISOLATION_LEVEL.
# It will affect ALL DB2 users !
DRDA_ISOLATION_LEVEL=CS
#
# DRDA_PACKAGE_OWNER allows you to assign the package owner to be someone
# other than the userid connected when the g4drutl utility is run.
# THIS USER MUST ALSO OWN THE ORACLE2PC table.
# See the Installation Guide for more
#information.
DRDA_PACKAGE_OWNER=ORADRDA
```

The following list provides descriptions of some of the important parameters:

DB_NAME—This is the instance name on the OTG UNIX machine.

DRDA_CONNECT_PARM—This is the side_info profile_name from the OTG UNIX SNA configuration parameter.

DRDA_REMOTE_DB_NAME—This parameter can be obtained by issuing the command, SELECT CURRENT SERVER FROM <table_name on DB2/MVS> (table_name is any valid table on MVS that has at least one row).

DRDA_PACKAGE_COLLID—This parameter is the collection identifier part of the package name. On DB2/MVS a package name consists of location.collection_id.package_name.

DRDA_PACKAGE_NAME—This parameter is the name you gave to the package on DB2/MVS that Oracle7.3 will be able to access.

DRDA_RECOVERY_USERID—This refers to the userid on MVS. This userid must be part of the RACF group that has access to DB2 (for example, a DB2 user).

DRDA_RECOVERY_PASSWORD—This is the password of DRDA_RECOVERY_USERID on MVS.

DRDA_PACKAGE_OWNER—This parameter is the userid on DB2 that owns the package accessed by Oracle7.3.

Another task that needs to be performed on DB2/MVS is to update the communication database (CDB). CDB stores the inbound Distributed Relational Database Architecture (DRDA) session security. There are two important tables that must have valid rows. They are the SYSIBM.SYSLUNAMES table, which must have the valid entries for the OTG logical unit (in this case, SC0001P1) and the SYSIBM.SYSUSERNAMES table, which must have valid entries for the OTG users (in this case, ORADRDA). Contact your DB2/MVS DBA for a complete explanation of the tables SYSIBM.SYSLUNAMES and SYSIBM.SYSUSERNAMES.

Installing Oracle Transparent Gateway

Oracle Transparent Gateway comes in three different media, CD-ROM, 8mm tape, and 1/4-inch tape. If you are installing the Oracle Transparent Gateway from a tape medium on a server on which you have already installed the Oracle7.3 server code, you must issue the following commands from the UNIX prompt:

```
$ cd $ORACLE_HOME
$ mkdir otg_temp
$ cd otg_temp
$ cpio -iucvdb < /dev/rmt0
```

The preceding commands are necessary because the Oracle installer on tape does not work with the Oracle Installer from the CD-ROM.

To install Oracle Transparent Gateway from the Oracle Installer prompt, select the desired installer action, choose Install | Upgrade | Patch Software Only and from the Oracle Installer prompt, select a product from the list of the products available in the staging area; choose Transparent Gateway for IBM DRDA.

When prompted for the instance ID (or SID), enter DRD1 or any other SID you chose earlier.

After installing the Oracle Transparent Gateway, follow these steps:

1. Update the /etc/oratab and add the following line to the bottom:

   ```
   DRD1:/u01/app/oracle/product/7.3.2:N
   ```

   where DRD1 is the instance ID, or SID, and /u01/app/oracle/product/7.3.2 is the value of $ORACLE_HOME.

2. Add the following lines to the file LISTENER.ORA:

   ```
   (SID_DESC=
   (SID_NAME=DRD1)
   (ORACLE_HOME=/u01/app/oracle/product/7.2.3)
   (PROGRAM=G2DRSQL)
   )
   ```

3. Add the following lines to the file TNSNAMES.ORA:

   ```
   db2dsn0 = (DESCRIPTION =
       (ADDRESS =
           (PROTOCOL = TCP)
           (PORT = 1521)
           (HOST = hostname)
       )
   )
   ```

The remaining tasks for configuring the Oracle Transparent Gateway are outlined in these steps:

1. Create the package on DB2/MVS to be used by the Oracle7.3 server. This is accomplished by running the g4drutl utility located on the OTG UNIX server as follows:

   ```
   $ g4drutl mode=bind userid=ORADRDA password=ORADRDA
   ```

   This statement creates a package called USNETMHADSN0.DRDA1.G2DRSQL. It gets its values from the following init.ora parameters:

   ```
   REMOTE_DB_NAME = USNETMHADSN0
   DRDA_PACKAGE_COLLID = DRDA1
   DRDA_PACKAGE_NAME = G2DRSQL
   ```

2. Execute the script to create the Oracle data dictionary translation capability.

   ```
   $ g4drutl mode=EXECSQL userid=ORADATA password=ORADATA
       script=$ORACLE_HOME/tg4drda/install/db2/g4ddtab.sql
   ```

3. Create ORACLE2PC (for two-phase commit) distributed tables and grant the proper permissions to them by running the following script:

   ```
   $ g4drutl mode=EXECSQL userid=ORADATA password=ORADATA
       script=$ORACLE_HOME/tg4drda/install/db2/o2pc.sql
   ```

4. Create a database link by running the following command while logged into svrmgrl:

   ```
   svrmgr > CREATE PUBLIC DATABASE LINK DRDA ;
   ```

Now you are ready to use the Oracle Transparent Gateway. To connect to DB2/MVS from the Oracle7.3 server, enter the following command at an svrmgrl prompt:

```
svrmgr > CONNECT to ORADRDA IDENTIFIED BY ORADATA
    USING 'P:DRDA';
```

Then you can access any table on DB2/MVS for which you have permissions. For example, to select all the rows from a table called TABLE_A whose owner is JOHN on DB2/MVS, you can issue the following:

```
SQL > SELECT * FROM john.table_a@DRDA ;
```

To create and load a table called TICKET owned by FRED on Oracle7.3 from DB2/MVS, you can issue the following command while logged into svrmgrl:

```
svrmgr > CREATE TABLE TICKET
         AS SELECT * FROM fred.ticket@DRDA;
```

This will create a table called TICKET on your Oracle7.3 server machine and load it with all the rows contained in the table in DB2/MVS. Oracle Transparent Gateway automatically converts the column types from DB2/MVS to Oracle7.3.

> **NOTE**
>
> IBM has recently announced TCP/IP support on its next release of the DB2 family, called DB2 Universal Database. Because configuring TCP/IP is much simpler than SNA, we expect that Oracle will implement TCP/IP support in its next release of Gateway products (Oracle Transparent Gateway, Oracle Open Gateway, and so on). In addition to Oracle Transparent Gateway, IBM's Data Joiner can work with DB2 and Oracle Databases. For a detailed explanation of Data Joiner, contact your local IBM sales representative.

Using the DB2/MVS REORG Utility to Download DB2 Data

The second method that you can use to dump the source tables on DB2/MVS is the DB2 REORG (UNLOAD) utility.

The DB2 REORG utility is a program that reorganizes DB2/MVS tables. DB2 DBAs run this utility to clean up the chained pointers and data fragmentation on DB2. The DB2 REORG utility can be broken into three sections:

- Section one unloads the data from DB2 tablespaces to an MVS flat file.
- Section two is used by DBAs to delete and define DB2 VSAM files.
- Section three loads the data back from the MVS flat files to all the tables in a particular tablespace.

You can run just the first section of the DB2 REORG utility (using the UNLOAD ONLY option) to dump the DB2 Data into an MVS flat file. After running the DB2 REORG utility, if you browse the dump file, you will see that all the columns of the tables are preceded by a column length. In addition, each record has a record header (6 bytes) that includes the row length. Knowing that, you can write a simple program to pull out only the columns that you need to load to an Oracle7.3 database. The following is an example of a DB2 REORG utility. This Job Control Language (JCL) unloads all the rows from the TICKET tablespace and creates a physical sequential (PS) file called DB2.UNLOAD.TICKET.

```
//JOBNAME   JOB ,MSGCLASS=X,NOTIFY=USERID
  //STEP1    EXEC PGM=DSNUTILB,REGION=0M,
  //              PARM='DSN0,REORGUT1'
  //STEPLIB  DD  DSN=DB2.SDSNLOAD,DISP=SHR
  //SORTOUT  DD UNIT=SYSDA,SPACE=(4000,(20,20),,,ROUND)
  //SORTWK01 DD UNIT=SYSDA,SPACE=(4000,(20,20),,,ROUND)
  //UNLD     DD DSN=DB2.UNLOAD.TICKET,
  //            UNIT=SYSDA,VOL=SER=DB2VL7,
  //            SPACE=(CYL,(10,1),RLSE),DISP=(NEW,CATLG,DELETE)
  //WORK     DD UNIT=SYSDA,SPACE=(4000,(20,20),,,ROUND)
  //SYSUT1   DD UNIT=SYSDA,SPACE=(4000,(20,20),,,ROUND)
  //SYSPRINT DD SYSOUT=*
  //UTPRINT  DD SYSOUT=*
  //SYSIN    DD  *
    REORG TABLESPACE (DB2DSN0.TICKET)
        UNLOAD ONLY
        UNLDDN (UNLD)   WORKDDN (WORK)
  /*
  //*
```

For a complete explanation of the DB2 REORG utility, refer to IBM's *DB2 for MVS/ESA Utility Guide and Reference.*

Writing Custom Programs to Download DB2/MVS Data

The third method of dumping the source tables on DB2/MVS is to write your own custom programs. These programs can be written easily by using C, COBOL, PL/I, FORTRAN, or any other language that you are familiar with. We recommend that the output of these programs be placed in one MVS flat file per DB2 table.

Transferring the Source Data from MVS to UNIX Platform (Data Conversion)

If you are not using the Oracle Transparent Gateway to get the DB2 data from MVS to the Oracle7.3 Server, you must somehow get the data, which is in the form of MVS flat files, to the Oracle7.3 Server machine. The data on MVS is in EBCDIC-type characters that must be converted to ASCII format before it can be used by the UNIX operating system. Unless you take the time to write a series of the programs that do the conversions, we recommend shopping around for them. For example, by using a program called FTP, you can both transfer and convert the data from EBCDIC on MVS to ASCII on UNIX operating systems.

Load the Data to Oracle7.3 Database (Initial Load)

If you are not using the Oracle Transparent Gateway product to download the data from DB2/MVS to Oracle7.3, you must create the Oracle7.3 tables in a way that their column types and lengths match the DB2 tables. In order to create Oracle7.3 tables, the Data Definition Language (DDL) from DB2 must be altered to be acceptable in Oracle7.3. The following section explains some of the important differences between Oracle7.3 and DB2 4.1 datatypes.

- **Oracle7.3 CHAR(*n*) datatype**—This is a fixed-length character string. The maximum column length is 255 characters.

- **DB2 4.1 CHAR(*n*) datatype**—This is identical to Oracle7.3.

- **Oracle7.3 VARCHAR2(*n*) datatype**—This is a variable-length character string. You must specify the value of *n*. The maximum value for *n* is 2000.

- **DB2 4.1 VARCHAR(*n*) datatype**—This is a variable-length character string. You must specify the value of *n*. The maximum value for *n* is dependent on the page size of the tablespace. If the tablespace page size is 4KB, the maximum value for *n* is 4,046; if the tablespace page size is 32KB, the maximum value for *n* is 32,704.

  The size limits of 4,049, or 32,704 for VARCHAR datatypes are valid only if VARCHAR is the only column in that row. Otherwise, the size of the VARCHAR datatype is limited to 4,049, or 32,704 minus the total length of all other columns within the same row.

- **Oracle7.3 LONG datatype**—This is a variable-length character string. Its maximum value is 2GB.

- **DB2 4.1 LONG VARCHAR datatype**—This is a variable-length character string. The maximum length is calculated by DB2. To see how DB2 calculates the length of LONG VARCHAR columns, refer to the CREATE TABLE statement in IBM's *DB2 for MVS/ESA Version 4 SQL Reference* (page 288).

- **Oracle7.3 RAW(*n*) datatype**—This is a fixed-length binary datatype. The maximum column length is 255 characters. You must specify the value of *n*.

- **Oracle7.3 LONG RAW(*n*) datatype**—This is a variable-length binary datatype. Its maximum value is 2GB.

- **DB2 4.1 LONG VARCHAR FOR BIT DATA datatype**—This is a variable-length binary data. The maximum length is calculated by DB2. To see how DB2 calculates the length of the LONG VARCHAR FOR BIT DATA columns, refer to the CREATE TABLE statement of IBM's *DB2 for MVS/ESA Version 4 SQL Reference* (page 288).

- **Oracle7.3 NUMBER(*p*,*s*) datatype**—This is a number with precision *p* and scale *s*. The *p* must be in the range of $1 < p > 38$, and the s must be in the range of $-84 < s > 127$.

- **DB2 4.1 DECIMAL(*p*,*s*) datatype**—This is a packed decimal number with precision *p* and scale *s*. The precision *p* must be in the range of $0 < p > 32$, and scale *s* must be in the range of $0 < s > p$.

- **Oracle7.3 NUMBER(38) datatype**—This is a number with precision 38 and scale 0. It can store positive and negative fixed and floating-point numbers ranging from 1.0×10 to the -130th power to 9.9×10 to the 125th power. An Oracle NUMBER without any precision correlates to DB2 4.1 DOUBLE.

■ **DB2 4.1 INTEGER/SMALLINT datatype**—This INTEGER is a full-word binary datatype of 32 bits ranging from -2,147,483,648 to 2,147,483,647. SMALLINT is a half-word binary datatype of 16 bits ranging from -32,768 to 32,767.

■ **DB2 4.1 DOUBLE datatype**—This is a double-precision, floating-point number of 64 bits ranging from 5.4E-79 to 7.2E+75.

NOTE

The preceding explanation does not cover all the DB2 datatypes. The explanations are for the datatypes that relate to Oracle7.3. Some other DB2 4.1 datatypes are GRAPHIC(*n*), VARGRAPHIC(*n*), LONG VARGRAPHIC(*n*), BIT, SBCS, MIXED, and REAL. For a complete description of these datatypes and their limitations, refer to Appendix A of IBM's *DB2 for MVS/ESA Version 4 SQL Reference*.

The following is an example of column datatypes in Oracle7.3 and in DB2 4.1.

Table 22.1. Comparing Oracle7.3 with IBM's DB2 4.1 datatypes.

Oracle 7.3	*DB2 4.1*
CHAR(10)	CHAR(10)
VARCHAR2(254)	VARCHAR2(254)
NUMBER	DOUBLE
NUMBER(6)	INTEGER
LONG RAW	LONG VARCHAR FOR BIT DATA

Summary

In this chapter, you learned the steps required to copy data from DB2/MVS to an Oracle7 Server database. If your system conversion process requires copying data from a source different from DB2/MVS, review Chapter 18 for loading data from an ASCII data file using Oracle's SQL*Loader, or Chapter 19 for loading data from another Oracle database using Oracle's Export and Import utilities.

23

Testing the Usability of the Database

*by Mohammad Asadi and
Kimbra McDonald*

The term *database usability* has different meanings to different developers. In this chapter, *usability* means verifying that all the Oracle options implemented in a database system are functioning properly based on the design requirements. For example, if you implemented a system using Oracle's Multi-Threaded Server (MTS), you would need to test and prove that MTS was performing as you expected, in regard to the design specifications.

In order to test a database's options, you could write your own custom scripts, or you can take advantage of the various analysis tools offered by Oracle or by third-party vendors. Testing an Oracle database system is a continual effort, as well as a potentially evolving effort, based on changes to user requirements.

This chapter discusses various ways to test Oracle database options common to many Oracle database systems. The chapter begins with the simplest form of testing the usability of a database, executing queries, and continues through some of the most commonly used Oracle database options available.

Executing Queries

The simplest form of checking for the validity of business data in an Oracle database is to issue an unqualified SELECT statement against a table. For example, you can execute the following statement

```
SQL> spool table_results
SQL> SELECT * FROM table_a ;
SQL> spool off
```

in Oracle's SQL*Plus and save the output to a spool file for viewing. The preceding example would create a file called TABLE_RESULTS.LST on a UNIX system.

However, this SELECT statement might not be a proper way of checking the data. If TABLE_A has millions of rows, the query would continue writing results to the file, TABLE_RESULTS.LST, until it would fill up a file system with results. In addition, columns with raw data cannot be displayed using the SQL*Plus program. We recommend that you look into purchasing an Oracle browsing tool, such as Oracle Browser or SQL*Forms, or other third-party vendor tools for browsing the database.

Using Analysis Tools

A number of vendors today offer database tools. These can be tools that enable the user to alter the database (such as changing a table), or tools that enable the user to monitor the activity in the database. Before you invest in a database tool, the prospective users should come to an agreement as to the desired capabilities of the database tool.

This section introduces some guidelines for selecting a database tool so that you can manage your databases more effectively. Database tools are constantly changing and improving; for that reason, we don't recommend one tool over another tool.

For a good sampling of database tools, and a brief description of each, check out DBMS Magazine Online's Web site at `www.dbmsmag.com/pcdba.html` and BMC's Web site at `www.bmc.com`.

Some tools offer only monitoring capability, but others offer database problem alert and prevention capabilities. For example, if your database is mission-critical, the cost savings generated from a tool that monitors the database and notifies the users might be justified by the increased stability and up-time of the database. You also should keep in mind that the database tool market is rapidly changing, and that new releases of different vendors' tools might have new functionality that could be of great benefit to you. Be prepared to revisit your database tool decision, depending on the mission-critical level of your database. Keep in regular contact with the database tool vendors so that you will always have a fair analysis of the DBA tool you've chosen. It would be cost-prohibitive to jump from one database tool vendor to another, but having a broad working knowledge of all the vendors puts you in a better negotiating position for insisting that your vendor add missing functionality if another vendor has already added it.

If it's time-prohibitive to keep in physical contact with the vendor's sales representative, consider accessing the vendor's information on its Web page.

When choosing a database tool, you should keep the following factors (discussed in detail shortly) in mind:

■ The tool should be user-friendly.

■ The tool should be as independent as possible from the operating system and database.

■ The tool should have monitoring, alert, and database object-management capabilities.

■ The tool should help maximize both availability and reliability.

■ The tool should be easy to install and configure.

■ The tool should have a good documentation rating.

■ The tool should be robust and should not compromise database integrity.

■ The tool should have a minimal impact on the database.

■ The tool should have user interface capability so that you can write your own scripts.

■ The tool and the tool vendor should keep up with the functionality of new releases of Oracle.

■ The tool should have a competitive price/performance ratio.

Is the Tool User-Friendly?

Choosing a database tool that is user-friendly allows database administrators (DBAs) and other technical users to use the tool. No matter how sophisticated a DBA tool is, if it's not easy to use, it does not serve the purpose for which it was intended. We have come across database tools so complicated that sales representatives even had a hard time explaining them to me.

Is the Tool Independent of the OS and Database?

In today's computing environment, most data centers have a multitude of hardware, and their associated operating systems range from mainframe to UNIX to PCs with Windows operating systems. Even each vendor offering a UNIX operating system has its own flavor, each being slightly different from the others. For example, Sun Solaris is different from Hewlett-Packard's HP/UX, which is different from IBM's AIX on an RS/6000. Sun even has two versions of UNIX—Sun O/S and Solaris. Further complicating this environment is the dilemma created by having multiple versions of the same operating system. Keep this tool-independence in mind when you choose a database tool so that if your operating system and/or database change later, you won't be faced with extensive changes to your database tool. Also remember that, even though your environment might seem simplistic at this time, changing application requirements might force you to go to a different, or additional, operating environment(s).

Does the Tool Have Monitoring, Alert, and Database Object-Management Capabilities?

Some database tools offer only monitoring capability. However, this does you little good if your database is about to run out of space in a tablespace in the middle of the night, and the monitoring-only tool doesn't have the capability to page you, so that you can correct the problem.

Another option in a tool that has monitoring capability might be that you could set up the tool to detect the problem and alter the tablespace and add space automatically. Ideally, the tool also should enable you to alter a table, an index, or permissions as needed. It's also important for the tool to have the capability to manage database object changes, so that different versions of an application or a database can be tracked over time.

If it's necessary, for example, for you to track the changes in your database over time (such as when the database is changed from one version of your application to the next), you would be able to identify those changes definitively with a database tool that ensures change management capabilities. This is a common problem in development shops where quality assurance procedures are compromised due to application deadlines, and applications are moved into production, have a problem, and then are removed from production. If the database has changed, and you don't have a way of tracking the changes, you won't know how to alter the database back to the way it should be.

Does the Tool Maximize Both Availability and Reliability?

Database tools should be designed so that they can help maximize both the availability and reliability of a system. Today, various database tool vendors define system availability and system reliability differently. *Availability* refers to the period of time that the system is accessible. For example, some critical systems such as hospital patient medical records systems must be available seven days a week, 24 hours a day, or 24×7. Some other systems, such as a payroll system, might be required to be available only eight hours a day, from Monday through Friday, or 8×5.

However, *reliability* refers to the degree to which the database is guaranteed to be up-and-running, and data integrity is guaranteed. This guarantee of reliability is referred to with a percentage. For example, you might have a requirement from users that their system must be available eight hours a day, Monday through Friday. However, within that operational period, they require 100 percent reliability.

Database tools should be able to maximize both the availability and the reliability of a system by monitoring object control functionalities. For example, a database tool should be able to monitor the system and determine that, even though the database is up, by analyzing the Oracle dynamic performance table called v$wait, more server processes need to be added. Another example would be that if more rollback segments are needed to improve performance, the tool would add those automatically.

Is the Tool Easy to Install and Configure?

The database tool should be relatively easy to install and should not require any custom modifications in order to configure it. After all, the database tool should save you time, not eat up your time. For example, some database tools require access to the root userid (on a UNIX system). That means that at installation time, you'll need the system administrator for the UNIX system to be available to you to even get the tool installed. Even though the tool itself might not take very much time to install, it could take much longer to schedule the time with the system administrator, therefore delaying your time schedule.

Does the Tool Have a Good Documentation Rating?

You should be able to use the documentation for the database tool and follow it step-by-step through a successful installation the first time. The first pages of the documentation should explain the system prerequisites clearly so that if, for example, you are required to be at a certain level of the operating system, there are no surprises. All the known problems with the tool should be documented. If none are listed, be careful, you don't know of any software that doesn't have at least one bug!

Is the Tool Robust and Does It Ensure Database Integrity?

Due to time limitations, you might not discover all the problems caused by a database tool during the evaluation. This does not necessarily mean that the database tool is bug-free. Even after extensive testing of a database tool, especially those that offer database object management, you should contact all the references provided by the vendor for known undocumented problems.

Does the Tool Have Minimal Impact on the Database?

Almost all database tools have some minor impact on the performance of the database they monitor. However, their benefits outweigh their performance costs. You should compare database tool vendors for those that perform the best with the least impact on the database.

Does the Tool Have User Interface Capability?

You should always search for a database tool that has the most functionality suited to your environment already built-in. However, it also should be flexible enough to allow you to add your own customized scripts. In addition, the tool should be flexible enough to allow other tools to coexist, such as networking tools. So often the person taking a support call receives a message such as "My terminal is not responding."

The support person should be able to easily distinguish from the monitoring tool whether the issue has been caused by a database problem or a network problem. If you already have installed a network monitoring tool, such as Sun Net Manager or Netview 6000, try to find a database tool that could be easily incorporated into your network tools. That way the support person will not have to open multiple windows searching for a resolution to the user's problem, therefore minimizing the user's downtime.

Does the Tool Stay In-Sync with Oracle's Functionality?

Each release of Oracle has new enhancements and functionality. A good database tool should keep up with these enhancements within a timely fashion. For example, when Oracle released the Parallel Query option, a good database tool would have allowed the user to quickly analyze whether or not the Parallel option was being utilized by the users' queries. Another example would be that the tool should tell you whether or not the users' query utilized the index.

Does the Tool Have a Competitive Price/Performance Ratio?

Even though the price of a database tool is important, and can't be ignored, the price alone should not be the determining factor in choosing any software, and especially not in determining the proper database tool. In determining the price of a database tool, you need to consider more than the direct cost. You also need to consider the indirect costs.

The direct costs are the initial purchase price of the product, maintenance and upgrade costs, training costs, and support costs. Don't forget to verify the license costs that might be added to the price of the product. The indirect costs are the cost of lost business due to the unavailability of the system. Direct costs are much easier to measure; however, you should not forget the indirect costs and should try to place monetary values on those as well.

> **NOTE**
>
> For an evaluation of various database tools, refer to the white paper by Bonnie O'Neil, *In Comparison of GUI DBA Monitoring Tools.*

Without knowing your specific system requirements, we cannot recommend any of these database tools over another. In addition, these and other tool vendors are constantly enhancing their database tools. You should contact the sales representative for any that you want to evaluate so that you can perform an in-depth evaluation specific to your requirements.

Examining Functional Reliability and Performance

The User's Requirement (UR) document, Service Level agreement (SLA), and Physical Analysis and Design should have a complete list of all the users' requirements including the initial requirements and all the updates. These documents are discussed in detail in Chapter 20, "Defining and Creating the Initial Database." The primary goal of any systems development team, including the DBA's, is to fulfill as many users' requirements as possible. However, due to budgetary and time constraints, it might not always be possible to meet all of the users' requirements. Personnel changes in the user community and development team could be another reason for the deviation from the original users' requirements. You may have heard the phrase, "We started building a bus, but ended up with two motorcycles." Who is ultimately right, the user who requested the bus or the development team that delivered two motorcycles? This could be a subject of frequent debates among the members of the user community and development team.

Another factor to consider is that the users' level of education is rapidly increasing. Ten years ago, about 10 percent of users had some idea about what databases are and do. Today, almost all users not only have heard about databases, they also know a great many technical details about them. For example, 10 years ago, users would merely have required some type of database backup and recovery as part of a system. Today, users demand the types of database backup (offline or hot), the type and duration of recovery, and even have a pretty good idea of which databases can fulfill these requirements.

Users now make recommendations about disaster recovery procedures, high availability machines, CPU, memory, the I/O bus, disk space, and other hardware and software platforms and products. Some users get involved in so much of the technical side of the application development cycle that they pursue DBA opportunities. (This is usually fun! A user who used to be so particular about requirements becomes the person who has to deliver them!) All of this is the primary reason for a detailed Service Level agreement (SLA) and Hardware/Software (HS) documents.

Examining the functionality of a system starts in the very early stages of development. However, the bulk of requirements testing begins when somewhere around 75 percent of the system has been developed, and continues on until all the requirements have been met, or have been postponed for the next phase of the application's development. Once again, you should document what requirements have been delivered, what have been postponed, and what requirements have been rejected together with the reasons they have been rejected.

In this section, we assume the database and its objects such as tables, indexes, views, stored procedures, triggers, referential integrity (RI), relationships, and so on have been created, and initial data has been loaded into the database. The first simple task is to make sure that you can access the data. We recommend using Oracle's SQL*Plus to read and update test tables you have created and those Oracle provides in demo tables (owned by the userid SCOTT with a password of TIGER). After the initial test of connectivity, we recommend changing the password of the userid, SCOTT, as this user is created with DBA privileges.

After performing the initial local connection test to the database, the next step is to test the networking connectivity to the database. The product you are using in this test is Oracle's SQL*Net. We are assuming that SQL*Net is installed. To configure and check that the SQL*Net listener (background) process is up-and-running, you will need to perform what is called a *loopback test* to the database. To perform this test, enter the following:

```
$ sqlplus scott/tiger@boston
```

where BOSTON is the service name found in the file called tnsnames.ora. Listing 23.1 is an example of what that file might look like.

Listing 23.1. The tnsnames.ora file.

```
boston=
  (description=
    (address_list=
      (address=
        (community=TCP)
        (protocol=TCP)
        (host=hostname)
        (port=1521)
      )
    )
    (connect_data=
      (SID=mhal)
    )
  )
```

Oracle's SQL*Net uses this file to resolve service names, which establish the connection to the desired database on the desired server, or HOSTNAME, as shown in Listing 23.1. This service name needs to match the service name in the file, listener.ora, used by SQL*Net to establish the database and server that the listener process listens on for incoming connection requests. The file is shown in Listing 23.2.

Listing 23.2. The listener.ora file.

```
LISTENER=
 (ADDRESS_LIST=
  (ADDRESS=
   (PROTOCOL=IPC)
   (KEY=boston)
  )
  (ADDRESS=
    (PROTOCOL=TCP)
    (HOST=hostname)
    (PORT=1521)
  )
 )
STARTUP_WAIT_TIME_LISTENER = 0
CONNECT_TIMEOUT_LISTENER = 60

SID_LIST_LISTENER=
 (SID_LIST=
  (SID_DESC=
   (SID_NAME=mhal)
   (ORACLE_HOME=/u01/app/oracle/product/7.3.2)
  )
)

#TRACE_LEVEL_LISTENER = ADMIN
#PASSWORD_LISTENER = (DE78D6871581F9B7)
```

For a complete description of how to set up and configure SQL*Net, refer to Oracle's *Understanding SQL*Net* in their online documentation for version 7.3.

On UNIX systems, check whether a background process called TNSLSNR exists. To check for the background process, enter the following at a UNIX prompt:

```
$ ps -ef ¦ grep tnslsnr
```

If this background process exists, it returns results similar to the following:

```
oracle 13702   1 0   Nov 25 ?   0:40 /u01/app/oracle/product/7.3.2/bin/tnslsnr\
     LISTENER -inherit
```

> **NOTE**
>
> This assumes that two files are located in the $ORACLE_HOME/network/admin subdirectory called listener.ora and tnsnames.ora. Both files are required and are required to be in this location for SQL*Net to function properly. If they do not reside in this location or are not set up properly (even to the point of requiring the exact number of matching parentheses!), SQL*Net will not function properly.

To check the status of the listener, enter the following (from the UNIX userid oracle):

```
$ lsnrctl stat
```

If the listener is not running, start the listener by entering the following (from the oracle userid):

```
$ lsnrctl start
```

If you are accessing different databases on other machines, you have to make sure that the database links are set properly, and you can access the other distributed database(s). Test this connection by issuing a SQL*Plus command, such as this:

```
$ sqlplus scott/tiger@database_link
```

Keep in mind that if you are trying to use Oracle's Distributed option, you have to ensure that it is installed on all the machines that are participating in the distributed database environment. You learn more information on the Distributed option later in this chapter, in the "Testing the Distributed Databases" section.

In application development environments where users are trying to isolate applications from the databases they access by using ODBC, you'll need to test those connections by ensuring that SQL*Net is installed on the server as well as each client. Follow the instructions for configuring your ODBC drivers, which typically includes running the ODBC administrator and adding a data source for the database you want to connect to. The ODBC administrator asks for the service name (also known as the Oracle *connect string*) for the desired database. This service name is the same as that name mentioned above found in the tnsnames.ora file. Then from the client machine, use the ODBC test ping utility, if it is included with the ODBC driver you're using. Otherwise, you can run ODBC, issue a connect to the database, and try to select data from a test table.

Checking Multi-Threaded Servers

Prior to Oracle7, the only option available to users was for the application to connect to a database through a dedicated server process. Figure 23.1 shows a dedicated server configuration. Notice that this figure shows one server process per user process. Dedicated server processes are suitable if your system doesn't have many concurrent users accessing the database. For example, if you have a batch job that runs for a long period of time with only one connection to the database, dedicated server connections will serve you adequately.

FIGURE 23.1.
Dedicated server configuration.

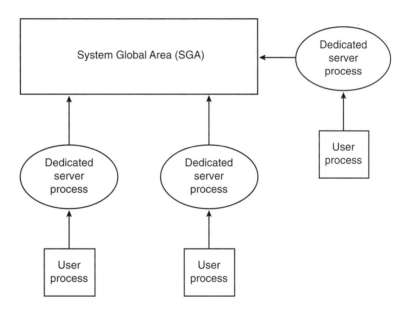

With an application that has large numbers of concurrent users accessing the database simultaneously, however, you need to consider using the option called Multi-Threaded Server (MTS), which is a feature of Oracle7 and above. MTS is depicted in Figure 23.2, which shows that multiple-user processes are serviced by one or more shared server processes.

FIGURE 23.2.
Multi-Threaded Server configuration.

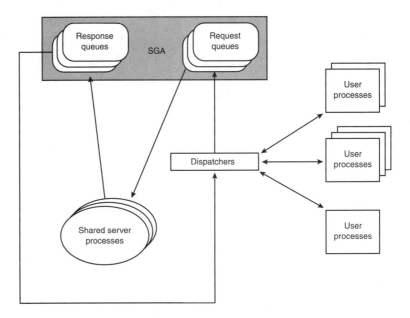

Testing the Table Column Integrity Constraints

In order to maintain the integrity of the data within your database tables, you must set certain guidelines and rules. These rules can be enforced either by your application program or by Oracle RDBMS code. Unless you can guarantee that you control all access to the database only through your application programs, you should let Oracle RDMS code enforce these rules. This is because all access to the Oracle database goes through the common Oracle RDBMS code. These rules or constraints are divided into three categories:

- ■ UNIQUE or PRIMARY KEY constraint
- ■ VALIDATION or CHECK constraints
- ■ FOREIGN KEY constraints

UNIQUE Constraint

By creating a UNIQUE constraint, you ensure that you have no duplicate rows for the column or columns involved in the UNIQUE constraint. Name each constraint, because if you don't and you allow Oracle to name the constraint for you, it will choose a name that is more difficult to relate to the actual column for which it was created. In naming the UNIQUE constraints, it's a good idea to use a naming standard for all constraints for the entire database.

VALIDATION or CHECK **Constraints**

On some columns, you might find it necessary to do either format or value validation. This can be done programmatically or by using VALIDATION or CHECK constraints in the database. Use the database wherever possible. For example, a column called GREAT_CITIES in a table might have a CHECK constraint that checks a list of values, such as (DENVER, SAN FRANCISCO, SEATTLE, BOSTON). Another column within your table might be CREDIT_RATING, which might have a CHECK constraint that verifies that the value of the column is in the range of one to nine. No other values outside that range would be allowed.

FOREIGN KEY **Constraints**

A FOREIGN KEY constraint, also called a *referential integrity* constraint, refers to a column or columns that exist in two tables, one table referencing another. The table containing the foreign key is called the *child table*, and the table containing the referenced key is called the *parent table*. In other words, a table's column such as, course_number, in a child table called Student, might reference a column, course_number, in a parent table called Course. A FOREIGN KEY constraint would be created in the Student table that would point the referential integrity to the same column in the Course table. This would cause the database to validate the value entered into course_number in Student as a valid value in course_number in Course.

When defining referential integrity constraints, you have an option to specify the delete rules to ON DELETE CASCADE, which tells the database to automatically delete dependent rows from the child table if the referenced row in the parent table is deleted. If this option is not specified, Oracle does not allow deletion of referenced rows in the parent table that have associated dependent rows in the child table.

In testing the constraints in your database, try writing some scripts that will verify that all the constraints are in place and perform properly.

Checking National Language Support

Today, in a diverse global economy, users often want their database systems implemented in their native language. This is especially true for software industries, transportation companies (especially airlines), government agencies (such as INS), international trades, and many others. Fortunately, Oracle7.3 and most operating systems support a vast variety of languages besides English. These languages are supported though single-byte (for European languages) and multiple-byte character sets (for Asian languages). A single-byte, 7-bit character set, which is primarily used for English, supports only 128 characters, while a single-byte, 8-bit character set supports most Western European languages (such as French, German, Italian, and Spanish).

A single-byte, 8-bit character set supports 256 characters, but a double-byte character set supports up to 65,536 characters. Oracle7.3 also supports a new UNICODE encoding scheme (UTF2). UTF2 supports both single-byte and multiple-byte character sets. When you install Oracle7.3, the installer asks you what languages you want to use. If you specify All, Oracle installs all the error and informational messages in the directory under $ORACLE_HOME/rdbms/ mesg. All the files have a suffix of either *.msg or *.msb. To see all the files pertaining to the English language type ls *us.* at a UNIX prompt. When you install all the supported Oracle7.3 language messages, you can change the National Language Support (NLS) parameters either dynamically or in the INIT.ORA parameters, which will set it to your desired language. Some of the most important NLS parameters are NLS_LANGUAGE, NLS_TERRITORY, NLS_CURRENCY, NLS_ISO_CURRENCY, NLS_DATE_FORMAT, NLS_DATE_LANGUAGE, and NLS_SORT. For example, you can sign on to Oracle SQL*Plus and issue the following command to set the language to German:

```
SQLPLUS> set NLS_LANGUAGE=GERMAN ;
```

From this point on, all the messages will be displayed in German. This statement remains in effect until another NLS_LANGUAGE statement is issued or you exit from SQL*Plus. For complete details on these and other NLS parameters, refer to the *Oracle7 Server Reference Manual*.

You must test all the user required languages (character sets) on your Oracle7.3 database server and all client machines. The language set for client machines does not have to match the ones set for the Oracle7.3 Server machine. For example, you might have user requirements for French, German, Italian, Japanese, and Spanish Windows NT clients, while the Oracle7.3 database server can have English as the default language. This way all the users can understand the Oracle messages in their native language, and as a DBA, you can administer the Oracle database using English language, if you choose.

Testing the Replication Databases

Sometimes user requirements dictate that one full copy (master copy) of the database be kept in a centrally located area and one or more full copies or subsets (*snapshots*) of the database be kept in remote locations. This is referred to as a *replicated database*. A replicated database environment can be configured using one of the following options, each of which will be discussed in detail shortly:

- ■ Single master with multiple read-only snapshot sites
- ■ Multiple-master replication
- ■ Single master with multiple updatable snapshot sites
- ■ A combination of the above

Single Master with Multiple Read-Only Snapshot Sites

Read-only snapshots are for querying purposes only. They can be a subset of a single master table or many master tables. Figure 23.3 shows an example of a single master database with read-only snapshot databases associated with it.

FIGURE 23.3.
Single master with multiple read-only snapshot sites.

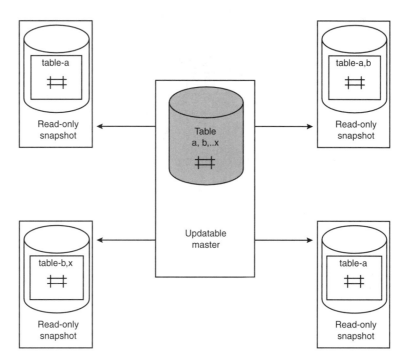

Multiple-Master Replication

In a multiple-master replication environment, copies of tables can be updated at any master site. Figure 23.4 shows an example of multiple updatable master databases.

Single Master with Multiple Updatable Snapshot Sites

The updatable snapshots can be used for queries or updates. The snapshots must be a subset of a single master table. Figure 23.5 shows an example of a single master database with multiple updatable snapshot databases associated with it.

FIGURE 23.4.
*Multiple updatable
masters site.*

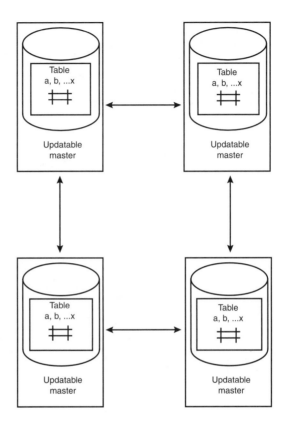

Mixture of All Replication Environments

A mixture of all the replication environments discussed to this point can be implemented.

Synchronous or Asynchronous Updates

After a replication configuration has been finalized, the next step is to decide how often the replicated database(s) need to be synchronized. Replication to updatable masters or to snapshots are done either synchronously or asynchronously. An *asynchronous* update is performed at specified intervals of time; a *synchronous* update is performed immediately. Unless you have users' requirements that all the updatable databases in the replication environment be in sync immediately, you should consider asynchronous updates. Asynchronous updates are usually less expensive than synchronous due to such considerations as peak-time network traffic.

Snapshot sites can have a subset of a table (for example, only the first two columns of TABLE-A), but the master side must have a full copy of a table. Each master must have a master definition site, which can be on the same physical machine or on a different one. Information about the replication environment is stored in Oracle7.3 catalogs. You may use Oracle's Replication Manager to configure and diagnose problems concerning the replication environment. Replication Manager updates pertinent information in Oracle7.3 replication catalogs. For a complete discussion of Oracle's Replication Manager, see Oracle's *Oracle7 Server Distributed Systems Manual*, Volumes I and II.

FIGURE 23.5.

Single master with multiple updatable snapshots.

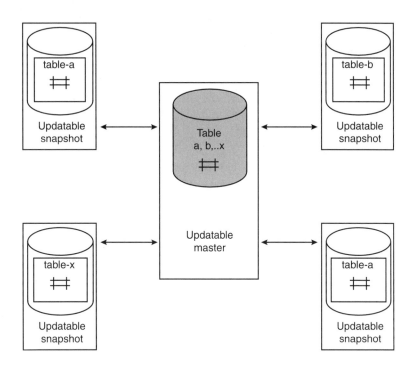

Testing the Distributed Databases

In some cases, the database that you are implementing can be one of many databases that are utilized in a user application. For example, a personnel application might need data from both the Personnel and Payroll databases. Even though in the application all the tables appear to come from one database, behind the scene, they are coming from one or more databases that participate in a distributed environment. In a distributed environment, an application can update any of the rows in any of the tables from one or all participating databases, even though distributed databases are located on separate machines in remote locations. Therefore, network performance is especially important in a distributed environment.

Be sure to consider the performance and reliability of the network that will participate in the distributed environment before designing the database in the distributed environment. Performance refers to *network bandwidth*, which is the rate that data can be transferred between two nodes in the network. To ensure network reliability, most sites implement a backup system that allows the packet to travel down an alternate route and still reach its destination.

In writing the network requirements section of the SLA (Service Level agreement), you must always detail the expected network throughput and reliability all the way from the source of the data to the user's workstation. Unfortunately, network reliability and performance are typically the parts of the development cycle that might get overlooked until late in the cycle. Instead, this issue should be addressed in the very early stages of the application development life cycle. This entire process typically requires a good deal of cooperation between the database administrators and network administrators to ensure optimal performance.

Network administrators may use network tools from various network vendors to detect and describe networking problems. An example of one of the network tool providers is Network General. You can find products and descriptions at their Web site at www.ngc.com. A list of other network tool vendors can be found at asylum.sf.ca.us/zonker/Networks/vendor.html.

It's a good idea to ensure that these tools are flexible enough to work with database tools. See the section, "Using Analysis Tools," earlier in this chapter for further information.

Because the individual databases that participate in a distributed environment might be located on two or more separate servers located in various cities, the database availability, backup, and recovery procedures must be coordinated among all the database administrators.

To keep all the databases consistent in a distributed environment, you must either complete the transaction to all the databases or roll that transaction back on the entire unit of work. Figure 23.6 shows an example of two servers (with a database on each) in a distributed environment. Database 1 could reside in Denver, and you are the database administrator for that database. Database 2 could reside in New York with another database administrator responsible for that database. If your application is running locally on a machine called DENVER and issues an explicit or implicit COMMIT statement, the database server becomes the global coordinator. This makes your database server, DENVER, responsible for ensuring that the transaction is either completed and committed, or rolled back. Every database server in a distributed environment should be tested for its ability to perform as a successful global coordinator.

There are some parameters placed in the INIT.ORA file that affect the distributed Oracle environment. These are DISTRIBUTED_LOCK_TIMEOUT, DISTRIBUTED_RECOVERY_CONNECTION_HOLD_TIME, and DISTRIBUTED_TRANSACTIONS.

■ DISTRIBUTED_LOCK_TIMEOUT controls the number of seconds that a distributed transaction would wait for the required resources to become available.

■ DISTRIBUTED_RECOVERY_CONNECTION_HOLD_TIME specifies the number of seconds that an application transaction will hold the remote connection open. This is because the application expects the communication to the remote database to be restored in a shorter amount of time than it would take to reconnect with a new connection. The background process called *reco*, which controls the recovery of transactions, executes every 30 minutes, whether or not a distributed transaction has failed. To keep the connection open indefinitely, which helps performance by not having to reestablish a new connection, set this parameter to a value greater than 1,800.

■ DISTRIBUTED_TRANSACTIONS specifies the upper limit of distributed transactions that a database can execute simultaneously.

FIGURE 23.6.

A distributed database configuration.

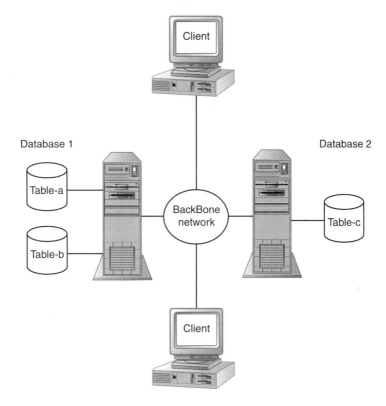

Another INIT.ORA parameter to consider in a distributed environment is COMPATIBLE. You need to ensure that all the databases in the distributed environment are either at the same release of Oracle or have this parameter set to the same release number.

Testing the Application with the Cost-Based Optimizer: The ANALYZE Statement

One of the most important functionalities of relational database management systems is being able to determine the transaction's access path. This is accomplished by using the database's optimizer. Even though the cost-based optimizers have been a feature of relational database management systems since their inception, they continue to be enhanced.

The two different types of optimizers offered in Oracle7 are *rule-based* and *cost-based*. In a rule-based optimizer, the Oracle kernel follows certain rules when choosing the most efficient execution plan for a SQL statement. In the cost-based optimizer, the Oracle kernel uses available statistics to determine the best possible access path. The more recent the available statistics, the better the optimizer performs in choosing an access path. Therefore, it is important to provide Oracle with the most up-to-date statistics—as frequently as possible.

You can use the ANALYZE statement to provide Oracle with statistics. The ANALYZE statement can be executed in either compute or estimate mode. Issuing the ANALYZE statement in the compute mode takes longer than in the estimate mode. There is a growing consensus in the Oracle database administration community that using the ANALYZE statement in the estimate mode with a 20–30% factor will yield the same result as using the ANALYZE statement in the compute mode, thereby saving execution time.

This leads to the question as to how often the ANALYZE statement should be executed. ANALYZE statements are optimally run after a large number of updates to the database have been performed. If you have a small- to medium-sized database that is loaded daily, you might be able to afford to run the ANALYZE statement immediately after each load. However, for large databases, we recommend running the ANALYZE statement either bi-weekly or monthly.

The Oracle7.3 cost-based optimizer offers a number of ways to enhance the time required to execute your SQL statement. Prior to Oracle7.3, the Oracle cost-based optimizer used nested loop and sort merge joins for joining two or more tables. Now, in Oracle7.3, the optimizer uses hash joins. To take advantage of this feature, you should leave the INIT.ORA parameter, HASH_JOIN_ENABLED, set to a value of TRUE, which is the default. Another parameter that has an effect on this optimizer is called HASH_AREA_SIZE. This parameter sets the maximum size of memory that hash join operations can use. HASH_MULTIBLOCK_IO_COUNT specifies the number of blocks that can be read and written in a hash join operation. For an 8KB database block size, set this value to something less than or equal to 8, because the block size multiplied by this value should not exceed 64KB. If you are using a MTS (Multi-Threaded Server), set this value to 1.

> **NOTE**
>
> If you are using STAR queries in your data warehousing application, be sure to use the cost-based optimizer to optimize your access paths. STAR queries are not recognized by the rule-based optimizer.

The Oracle7.3 cost-based optimizer has come a long way. As mentioned earlier, the Oracle cost-based optimizer is being constantly enhanced. However, there are some features of the cost-based optimizer that are not being utilized as a result of setting an INIT.ORA parameter or any other database global parameter. These features can be invoked only by using what Oracle calls *hints*. For example, to invoke the Oracle7.3 anti-join SQL operation, use `HASH_AJ` or `MERGE_AJ` in the hints part of the SQL statement. Because Oracle hints are used in application code, you do not have the ability to embed hints in the code if you are using third-party software that does not allow you to do so. In this instance, we recommend specifying hints in the views being used by the application. Refer to Chapter 31, "Oracle's Query Optimizer," for more information about using hints.

There are other situations where the cost-based optimizer is more suitable for the application than the rule-based optimizer. One example is in a SQL statement like the following:

```
SQL > SELECT * FROM TAB-A WHERE COL-A < 0 OR COL-A = 0 ;
```

The cost-based optimizer recognizes that the preceding line is the same as this:

```
SQL > SELECT * FROM TAB-A WHERE COL-A <= 0 ;
```

The rule-based optimizer does not have this intelligence.

Therefore, use the cost-based optimizer in Oracle7.3. Run the `ANALYZE` statement with the estimate set to 20–30% as frequently as is practical after a bulk data load. For special circumstances where `EXPLAIN PLAN` shows a different SQL access path than you desire, provide hints to enhance its performance. Refer to Chapter 31 to learn more about `EXPLAIN PLAN`.

Testing the Application Using Parallel Queries

If you are developing a large data warehousing-type database, we recommend using the parallel query option of Oracle7.3. Oracle7.3 not only allows you to execute your application queries in parallel, it also allows you to create, load, and scan tables, create indexes, sort and join (hash) data, aggregate data, group by data, order by data, and so on in parallel. You can determine whether your query is running in sequential or parallel mode by examining the cost, cardinality, other_tag, and bytes columns in the `EXPLAIN PLAN` results. For example, if the other_tag column is blank, the statement is running in serial mode, and the parallel query option is not being used. Other columns to look at are serial_to_parallel, parallel_to_serial, parallel_to_parallel, parallel_combined_with_child, and parallel_combined_with_parent.

You can set the following Oracle parameters to take advantage of the Oracle parallel query option:

- `HASH_JOIN_ENABLED` should be set to `TRUE`.
- `ALWAYS_ANTI_JOIN` should be set to `HASH`.
- `PARTITION_VIEW_ENABLED` should be `TRUE`.
- `DB_BLOCK_SIZE` should be 8KB or 16KB.
- `DB_FILE_MULTIBLOCK_READ_COUNT` should be 8 or more.
- `SORT_DIRECT_WRITES` should be set to `AUTO`.
- `HASH_MULTIBLOCK_IO_COUNT` should be set to 4 or more.

- USE_ASYNC_IO should be set to TRUE.
- SHARED_POOL_SIZE should be set to a value high enough to allow for sorting and hash join operations.
- SORT_AREA_SIZE should be set from 500KB to 4MB.
- HASH_AREA_SIZE should be set to at least 32MB.
- PARALLEL_MAX_SERVERS should be set to at least twice the number of CPUs multiplied by the estimated number of parallel queries running concurrently.

> **NOTE**
>
> Please note that the INIT.ORA parameters PARALLEL_DEFAULT_MAX_SCANS and PARALLEL_DEFAULT_SCANSIZE are no longer used in Oracle7.3.

In order to fully utilize the Oracle parallel query option, you must stripe the database data files as much as possible. As mentioned in Chapter 20, striping minimizes I/O bottlenecks. When running a query in parallel mode, multiple processes access the same Oracle data file. Therefore, it becomes even more important to stripe your Oracle data files for using the parallel query option. If you have decided to use RAID devices, be sure to include the RAID 0 configuration, or striping.

If you have a table with information that can be divided into multiple tables, create a partitioning view over all the tables by using the UNION ALL option in the view. By doing this, the partitioned view allows Oracle parallel query to access the data faster than it would if the data were in one huge table.

You should query the Oracle dynamic performance tables that pertain to the parallel query option. These are v$parameter, v$filestat, vpq_slave, vpq_sesstat, v$pq_tqstat, and v$pq_sysstat.

Checking the Database Locks

Database administrators usually check the object locks and latches in the application development life cycle step commonly known as *system stress testing*. However, these tests might not be adequately reflected in the production environment because the stress tests might not be performed with an accurate estimate of the number of concurrent users. You should simulate the number of users you expect to have in your production environment in this stress-testing stage. Doing so can give you a more realistic view of where your database locking problems might occur.

You should view the following dynamic performance tables for information regarding locks:

■ v$lock

■ v$session

■ v$objects

Refer to Chapter 30, "Performance Tuning," for more information on locks.

Testing the Backup and Recovery Procedures

Historically, backup and recovery procedures have been one of the most important responsibilities of a database administrator. Backup and recovery procedures should be clearly stated in the (SLA) Service Level agreement. For example, you should state in the SLA how long, and to what point in time it would take you to recover a specific table in case of a media failure. In some cases, the user might be happy just to go back to the backup taken the night before. Therefore, you can use the database in NO ARCHIVE log mode. However, depending on the requirements for recovery time, you might have to keep the archive logs on disk; that is, having them on tape does not even meet the requirement for a fast enough recovery.

You should completely test and retest your backup and recovery procedures so that you are assured that you are meeting your users' requirements, which are the requirements laid out in the SLA.

Refer to Chapter 29, "Developing a Backup and Recovery Plan," for more information regarding backup and recovery subjects.

Testing the Disaster Recovery Procedure

Another area that should be clearly described in the SLA is the database disaster recovery procedures. In some procedures, database files are written to tape and stored in an off-site vault to safeguard against a variety of possible disasters. However, for a company's mission-critical data, you will need more sophisticated database disaster recovery procedures. Oracle7.3 supports what it calls a *standby recovery database*, which is used for disaster recovery purposes. Basically, a standby database is a copy of the primary database, which is left in the recovery mode. Every day at a certain time, logs are taken from the primary database and applied to the standby database.

> **TIP**
>
> In addition to disaster recovery, standby databases can be used for running long-running reports, thereby relieving the primary database from the performance degradation of such a large batch-type application.

If you are using a standby database for disaster recovery, there are a few considerations to keep in mind:

- A standby database might not be in sync with its primary database because, if any alterations have been made to the structure of the primary database, they are not reflected in the standby database. In other words, put any DDL (Data Definition Language, such as altering a table or a data file) in a script and apply (that is, run) that script to both the primary and standby databases.

- If you increase the size of any object in the primary database, you must alter the standby database in the same manner before applying any logs.

A standby database requires manual database administrator intervention. To make these interventions simpler, use identical data file structures on both the primary and standby databases and always capture any database alterations in script files for applying to the standby database. Also, after applying the newest set of logs, validate that the number of rows in the standby database matches the number in the primary database to verify that all the logs have indeed been applied.

Ensuring High Availability

In some database applications, such as medical records, catalog ordering, airline reservations, and many others, it is extremely important to keep the Oracle databases available 24 hours a day, 7 days a week, or 24×7. For example, an Oracle database that holds the national organ transferring information can be a major deciding factor in a patient's life. In this type of situation, the database has to be up and available all the time. No exceptions are allowed.

In response to the growing demand for highly available (HA) systems, hardware and database vendors have been working together to establish a highly available system that is extremely fault-tolerant. In case of failure, HA systems must be able to perform the takeover automatically. The failover process must be transparent to the end user and must occur in a reasonable amount of time. The amount of time required by HA systems to complete an automatic takeover must be clearly stated in the SLA. Figure 23.7 illustrates an HA system.

As you can see in the figure, Node 1 has its own set of disks, network, and Oracle database instance. In normal operations, clients access the database on Node 1. When a failure occurs, all the operations required by the client's application may be shifted automatically to Node 2. In that case, Node 2 becomes the primary database server until the problems with Node 1 are resolved. At that time, the control can again be shifted back to Node 1.

Most hardware vendors provide tools to monitor and manage the availability of both networks and databases. The actions taken after a failure has been detected depend on the administrator of the HA system. The HA monitoring tool constantly checks the Oracle7.3 logs for errors. If an error is detected, the HA tool can issue its own internal test to be sure that the error is real and not a false alarm. If the HA tool decides that the detected error is real, it can take one of the following actions:

- *Ignore the error*—For certain Oracle errors, you might want to just log it and continue processing.
- *Restart*—The HA tools can be instructed to simply perform crash recovery on the same node without migrating to the backup (failover) node.
- *Take over*—This is when the HA starts transferring the database services from the failed node (Node 1) to the backup (failover) node.
- *Stop the database*—In some cases, you might instruct the HA tool to simply stop the database services and not perform any other failover process. For example, you might use the stop mode for a routine database release upgrade.

It's important to choose an HA system that covers both databases and networks. Then be sure to perform a thorough test of all the components that could possibly fail and compare your findings with the HA requirements stated in the SLA document. See Chapter 20 for more information about the SLA document.

FIGURE 23.7.

A highly available database system configuration.

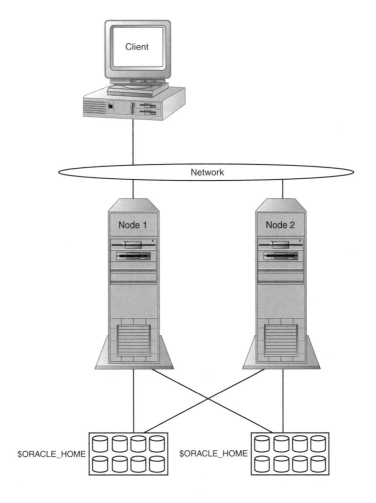

Checking Security

Depending on the sensitivity of the data in your database, testing security could be one of your most important steps in the development of your database. In most application development environments, security typically is one of the last steps to be completed. Allow enough time in your development schedule for extensive database security testing. Consider having other members of your technical development community test your database security system by telling them you want them to try to "break" your security system. Allow enough time in the schedule for testing the system's security. You might find people in your technical community who can break your security system. However, this does not mean that your security system might not be sufficient for the general user community; the latter group may not be technically sophisticated enough to break your system. You have to make a judgment call at this time and decide whether you consider your database security sophisticated enough to meet your end users' requirements.

One of the common problems that occurs in database security is that the person (or persons) responsible for setting up the security forgets the passwords. To avoid this situation, centralize the administration of userids and passwords that have database administration authority to the database.

After you've established all the database administration userids and passwords, consider placing a file containing the Oracle userids used in running an Oracle database (such as SYSTEM, SYS, and other database administration users) in a location that only DBAs can access.

For example, create a subdirectory in the OFA directory structure located in $ORACLE_BASE/admin/ <ORACLE_SID>/ called security, where security is only accessible by userids in the DBA group. You can set the permission of the security directory by issuing the UNIX command chmod 740 security. Then, within the security directory, create a file called .ORAPWDFILE. You should create .ORAPWDFILE as a hidden file that can be seen and read only by members of the DBA team. On a UNIX system, this would mean that the file .ORAPWDFILE would have the permissions of 740. This means that the UNIX oracle userid has all permissions to this file, the DBA group has read permissions, and the rest of the UNIX community has no privileges to do anything with this file—they can't even see it.

Summary

In this chapter, you learned about the testing process for some of the most important aspects of an Oracle database. Even though testing your database system may require additional time and research, this chapter should give you a solid starting point to begin testing Oracle database systems.

V

Developing Oracle Applications

24

Project Development Methodologies

by Joe Greene

In the words of the Monty Python troupe, "and now for something completely different." Most of the chapters in this book have focused on technical details such as how to build an application using PL/SQL stored procedures or using SQL*Loader. This chapter challenges you to step back a little and look at your overall approach to developing applications. Although many things about application development are absolutely right or absolutely wrong (for example, you have to set up a particular Open Database Connection (ODBC) driver in a particular manner for it to work with an Oracle database), the overall development methodology that you choose is a bit more subjective. It is influenced by personal preferences, customer requirements, organizational preferences, the development tools selected, and sometimes a fear of change.

For most projects, any one of a number of methodologies can get the job done. You may find at the start of a project, however, that consultants, product vendors, and even local staff will argue for the adoption of the one and *only* methodology that any sensible human being with even a marginal IQ would consider. For some people, a development methodology is almost like a religion. I tend to focus more on getting the job done correctly and collecting a paycheck; consequently, I use whatever methodology the customer will approve (although I am always willing to offer suggestions).

This "get the job done" attitude forms the basis of this chapter. My goal is to cover the more common development methodologies from a somewhat objective point of view. Before jumping into the current methodologies, however, I discuss the evolution of development methodologies. Finally, this chapter ends with several of my favorite topics. I refer to the first as "whole system integration," which brings up issues involved in actually deploying the system, as opposed to just writing software. The second topic is a discussion of the appropriate uses of the various development methodologies.

Evolution of Development Methodologies

A good starting point in the discussion of development methodologies is to consider *why* a development methodology is necessary. After all, a highly trained and experienced computer programmer should know what to do and how to do it, right? In a one-person development effort where the software will never have to be modified, the trained programmer is the simplest answer. However, when you have a development team or know that other programmers will maintain your software in the future, using a development methodology that is standardized across the development group or the entire software development organization can be beneficial. Here are some of the benefits that you might realize:

- Everyone understands which pieces of a complex application they are responsible for. You don't waste time and negatively affect tight development schedules by having two programmers develop the same functionality.

- You have planned for (and put into the cost estimates) all the functionality you need.

- You can accurately determine the cost of a project by understanding the productivity of a given programmer using a fixed methodology.

- You can provide documentation in a standard format that everyone who is or will be working on or with the software can understand.

- You can increase group productivity by ensuring that everyone uses a sound, compatible development methodology on which they have proper training.

This list could go on and on, with a number of points specific to individual projects or individual methodologies. However, you probably get the idea.

Early Methodologies

I would guess that the first development methodology came about soon after the first development project involving a large group of people was organized. When the group members tried to integrate the various pieces of code, they learned a few lessons about where the problems were and developed a methodology (that they probably just called "rules" or "guidelines") to facilitate their next project or the next iteration of the current software.

Some groups developed better guidelines than other groups. Companies with larger groups or multiple groups started to combine the lessons learned from multiple projects into a common methodology. This methodology enabled new groups to learn from the mistakes of others and also supported moving people among groups without having to retrain these individuals on a new methodology. Organizations published documents containing their coding and development standards. Some organizations formed standards groups that published the standards and then reviewed various projects for compliance with these standards. So what should be covered in a standard (that ultimately may become the basis for a development methodology)? Here are a few topics that you might expect to see in a standard:

- How to divide projects into a series of modules that can then be subdivided into a series of smaller modules. Once an appropriate level of complexity is reached, the project can be assigned to a programmer for development.

- How to determine which functions will be performed by the application and where, within the various modules, these functions will be implemented.

- How the data associated with the application will be divided into a series of tables, files, and so on that the software modules can use in a controlled fashion.

- How the design will be documented for both the developers and the users. One subset of the documentation forms the basis for users' agreeing that the application functions as desired (these are typically called "specifications" or "requirements"), and another subset serves as documentation that tells the users how to use the application.

- How to process changes to the design that come up during the development process.

- How to test the application to ensure that it meets the design specifications and functions correctly.

■ How to deploy the application to the user community. For example, how is the application installed on the computer(s) and what kind of training is provided?

You could go on for some time listing the items you might want to see covered in a methodology. Some people have actually spent a lot of time thinking up detailed methodologies. Perhaps you have worked under an especially complicated set of programming standards that caused more work than they saved. Wasting time following overly complicated standards is one of the things that you have to be careful about when developing these standards.

Before working in the computer field, I worked in the Navy, running the propulsion plant and reactor on nuclear submarines. Old-timers in the program spoke of the day when submarine reactors were still new and the entire operations manual fit into a couple of binders. However, every time anyone made even the slightest mistake, upper management took it as a need for additional training and therefore they wrote another chapter for the operations manual. By the time I got into the program, the manuals for the propulsion plant filled a small bookcase (and that did not count the really technical maintenance manuals).

Many organizations have applied the same logic to their computer development policies and procedures. Adding new regulations is a tempting way to cope with a problem. Eventually, however, the system can become so complicated that employees spend more time going through the motions and filling out forms than they spend doing the actual work. In the case of nuclear reactors, it is appropriate to have a good deal of control. However, if you are just trying to implement a financial report for your internal audit department, extremely complicated procedures can cause the process to bog down and lead to user dissatisfaction. Many IS shops are unpopular with their users because they are unable to turn around anything quickly. The trick is finding that balance between tyrannical, oppressive methodologies and a bunch of hackers running amuck.

Methodology Evolution

Numerous consultants, product vendors, and academic types have stepped forward with solutions to this great dilemma. Now, instead of inventing software development methodologies for themselves, companies could purchase advice and/or software to help them develop their software. At this point, advocates of various methodologies began to publicize their opinions. Consultants obtained copyrights for their techniques, and software development tool vendors supported a particular methodology. The race was on to win the loyalty of the computer industry and to have one's pet methodology become the "standard" that everyone would follow.

A lot of energy and talent was applied by consultants and vendors to this problem. It generated some of the best buzzwords in the computer industry including computer-aided software engineering (CASE) and business process reengineering. The unfortunate thing about computer buzzwords is that they get published in management magazines and advocated by tool vendors who promise almost God-like powers. People rush into areas with which they are not familiar and often wind up disappointed when the glorious claims of these tools fail to come true.

However, in the time in which I have been developing software, the general level of knowledge related to software development techniques has increased radically. So even if any one given tool or methodology is not the end-all, be-all tool, it does foster discussion and keeps pushing computer types to expand their horizons and think about new possibilities.

"New possibilities" is an excellent way to describe the evolution of software development techniques over the years. It seems to me that as soon as we come up with a sound set of tools and techniques to handle development in our current computer environment, someone comes along with applications requiring functionality beyond current capabilities, which pushes the industry to develop new tools. And these new requirements often require new, specially optimized development methodologies.

One of the biggest changes to development techniques has been the recent change from traditional computer languages, such as FORTRAN and COBOL, to fourth-generation development tools, such as Visual Basic and Oracle Developer/2000. These new tools enable programmers to generate reports and forms much more quickly than they could using traditional languages. Developers, therefore, have had to streamline portions of the design process without compromising application quality in order to keep up with the timelines for modern development projects. Another way to look at this is to see that it now costs less to correct mistakes and make minor changes; the developer, therefore, only has to focus on getting the basics right. Another feature of fourth-generation tools is that they are much more graphically oriented than traditional computer languages. Therefore, you now have to focus on the layout, fonts, and colors of the screen during the design stage. (Perhaps you even have organizational standards for these factors.) In the old days, users were usually content just to find all the data fields on the form in the correct order.

Before this major evolution in development techniques to support fourth-generation tools, most data centers changed from using simple file management systems toward sophisticated database management systems. Although I have run across a number of people who design databases exactly the way they designed flat files, I do not recommend this practice. Instead, you have to understand the basics of relational theory (in the case of the most popular database management systems such as Oracle) and know how to divide data into tables to optimize space utilization versus speed.

Developers who use the old flat file techniques without changing their methods for database management systems will probably have a system that works, but not very efficiently. Most of the popular techniques and tools on the market take into account the needs of relational databases and some even provide sophisticated reengineering technologies to help you evolve from older systems. By the way, when you are comfortable using relational database technology and build it into your methodology, you may want to start reading up on the newer object-oriented technologies that are coming down the road for Oracle and other major relational databases.

Everyone in the computer industry seems to be working hard to help their existing products evolve into something a little bit better so that they can compete in the marketplace. This trend encompasses everything from development tools such as compilers to database management systems. Also, organizations are being reengineered (another one of those hot buzzwords); the way in which people do their jobs continues to change even if organizations continue to use their existing COBOL compiler and DB2 database.

With these changes in mind, I would argue that if you have not reviewed your software development methodology for several years, it may be a little out-of-date and less efficient than it should be. Once again, there is a balancing act between jumping on all the new technologies that are published in popular computer management magazines (thereby never having the time to get good at any given technology) and staying in the Stone Age (relatively speaking for the computer environment). My one definite recommendation is that you review your software development methodology whenever your make a significant change in the development tools or supporting products (database management systems or transaction processing systems) that you use to build your applications.

Data or Application Based?

One of the topics that comes up when people discuss development methodologies is whether the methodology is based around the data or around the business processes. I believe that you really have to cover both topics to have a complete application. However, you have to start somewhere when developing an application. Most of the database systems that I have worked on run along parallel paths of data planning and functionality planning, with the two intersecting in a complete design. However, you may be using a methodology that focuses on one area or the other, so I want to cover this subject briefly.

A lot of the early CASE tools were based on data planning as the foundation of application development. You usually start out with a series of graphical design tools that let you define the types of information being stored and how they are related to one another. These tools help you to eliminate redundancy in data and ensure that you have a good set of keys to link the data together along with proper data integrity constraints. Once the data is laid out, you start to map the use of this data to various application modules. You can often design the functionality of these modules to specify what is done with the data and even how the various forms and reports are going to look.

Other methodologies are based more on function. You tend to detail the requirements for the application, assign them to modules, and divide the system into a logical series of functions. One of the common functions of the module is to get and give data to a central repository (that is, a database). Therefore, you derive the data requirements as part of the functions of the application. Just as you do with the data-oriented techniques, you may go on to specify look-and-feel requirements for the application (for example, a standard button bar in a standard location for all forms) to ensure that the users see a common interface that suits their needs.

An interesting extension of this discussion is some of the object-oriented design techniques being used today. One of the most interesting aspects of the object-oriented philosophy is the joining of data and processes (methods) to form an object that matches up closely with real-world objects. For example, your checking account could be considered an object that has data elements, such as an account number, a balance, and a series of debits and credits. Also associated with these data elements are some defined actions that can be taken on this account, such as cashing a check (which debits the account by the amount of the check) or making a deposit (which increases the balance of the account once the deposit clears). A checking account without data is just as incomplete as a checking account that cannot be debited. The data and methods are usually designed into the object at the same time. Figure 24.1 illustrates the differences between the three methodologies that I have discussed in this section.

FIGURE 24.1.

Data-centric, application-centric, and object-oriented methodologies.

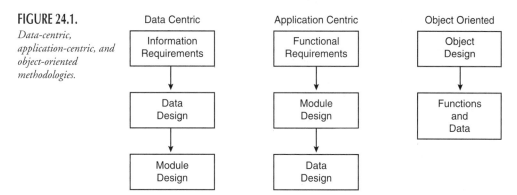

Computer-Aided Software Engineering

Not all that many years ago, computer-aided software engineering (CASE) was the hot buzzword spoken by information systems executives. As with most of these buzzwords, it was supposed to completely reform all software development, lead to enormous productivity gains, eliminate hunger, and cure all diseases known to mankind. Well, people are still hungry and suffering from diseases, and they are still struggling to improve the software development process. This is not to say that CASE technologies have not improved the software development process. The fact that CASE technologies can formalize a methodology and produce graphics that help us analyze the design for common problems can be a great help—especially in larger projects. I have observed, though, that designs produced by CASE tools are highly dependent on the skill of the person using them. A little investment in training can make a big difference in the quality of the finished product.

Most of the CASE tools in use today are based on a graphical user interface to allow the analyst to input the design requirements. Their outputs also tend to be highly graphical. Trust me, this graphical approach is much better than when a design specification was all text that read like a legal document and filled several large volumes. The problem with such large tomes was that a change to one section often affected many other sections of the application. You had no easy way to predict these effects, so you often had application modules that were out of synch.

Keeping these specifications up-to-date was a nightmare and reacting quickly to user needs was nearly impossible.

The CASE tools typically use a database to store design. When you look at a particular view of this database (such as the functional specs for a particular software module), you are drawing the information from this repository that understands the linkages to other portions of the application. When you make changes, the CASE tool automatically reflects these changes to affected modules. Developers still have to look at the design repository on a routine basis so that they pick up these changes, but some systems even send out notifications automatically.

So, what are the common graphical tools used to input the design of an application? Advocates for each methodology and every CASE tool vendor seem to have slightly different versions of the basic tools used to construct an application design. For the purpose of this discussion, I settled on the following tools:

■ Data flow diagram
■ Entity relationship diagram
■ State transition diagram
■ Pseudocode
■ Class hierarchy

Data Flow Diagram

One of the first diagramming techniques used for applications was the data flow diagram as shown in Figure 24.2. Its basic purpose is to show processes and the flow of information. This type of diagram can also be used on noncomputer systems. Figure 24.2 is actually an extension of the basic data flow diagram concept to show information repositories as elements in the figure along with the processing elements. As with all of the diagrams discussed in this chapter, you will find a number of variations on the symbols used (for example, rectangle, rounded rectangle) and rules on how the diagram is drawn (do you put a verb showing the relationship on each line?).

Here are the fundamental concepts you should understand from this diagram:

■ Processing entities are the centers around which information flows and typically are the most visible symbols on the diagram.

■ Data repositories and processing entities are shown by symbols. Data repositories may correspond to databases on high-level diagrams and tables or even individual fields and records on lower-level diagrams.

■ Information flows are shown using lines with arrows that convey starting point, ending point, and direction of flow.

FIGURE 24.2.
Data flow diagram.

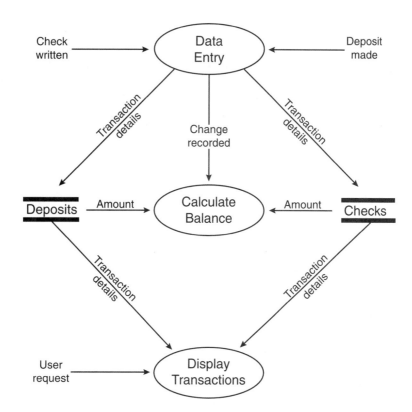

Your diagrams will have varying levels of detail. You may start off with a single diagram showing the major processing flows for the entire application. Next, you may divide this high-level picture into subsystems that have their own data flow diagrams. This process continues until you reach a level of detail that enables the developers to adequately understand the needs of the application. Knowing when you have reached the point of adequate design information without wasting time going into excessive detail requires a great deal of skill and experience.

Entity Relationship Diagram

The next diagram—the entity relationship diagram—shows the relationships between data objects (see Figure 24.3). This diagram is an ideal tool for use with relational database management systems such as Oracle.

Once again, a variety of symbols and drawing conventions have been used. Here are the basic components of this diagram:

■ Entities that represent related data objects.

■ Attributes that represent characteristics of those entities. For example, thickness (number of pages) is an attribute of this book.

■ Relationships between the entities that show how they link to one another. For example, chapter number is a link between this chapter and the corresponding table of contents entry.

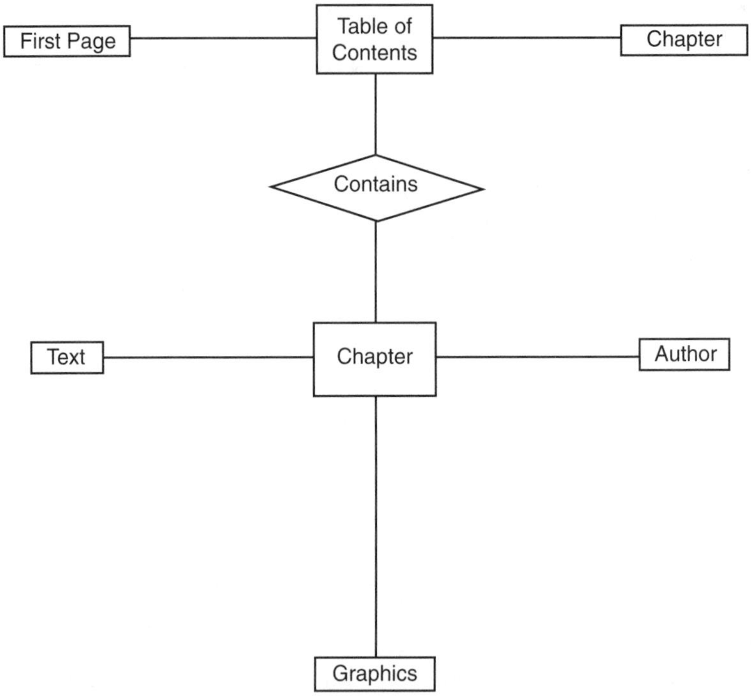

FIGURE 24.3.

Entity relationship diagram.

```
┌────────────┐        ┌──────────────┐        ┌────────────┐
│ First Page │────────│  Table of    │────────│  Chapter   │
└────────────┘        │  Contents    │        └────────────┘
                      └──────────────┘
                              │
                       ◁───────────▷
                       │  Contains  │
                       ◁───────────▷
                              │
┌──────┐        ┌──────────────┐        ┌──────────┐
│ Text │────────│   Chapter    │────────│  Author  │
└──────┘        └──────────────┘        └──────────┘
                              │
                      ┌──────────────┐
                      │   Graphics   │
                      └──────────────┘
```

The entity relationship diagram is also used at various levels of detail. For example, the attributes on one diagram may represent an entire table or series of columns within a table. On a lower-level diagram, the attributes may map to individual columns. On a higher-level database, the attributes may represent an entire database. The key to using this decomposition process is to keep track of the level on which you are operating and the relationship among the diagrams.

State Transition Diagram

The next type of diagram—state transition diagrams (see Figure 24.4)—most frequently appear in object-oriented designs in which what you are allowed to do depends on other events. In a hospital, for example, you have to be an admitted patient to undergo a certain type of surgery or to be discharged. Likewise, users want the application system to enforce certain rules, and you have to model your code accordingly.

FIGURE 24.4.
State transition diagram.

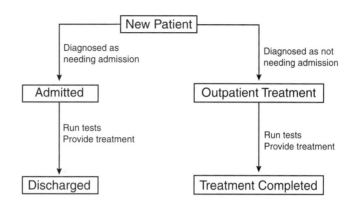

The state transition diagram is designed to capture what can happen based on the current state. Here are the basic elements of this diagram:

■ States that are defined for the system

■ Actions that can happen for the various states

■ State changes that occur in the system depending on these actions

Pseudocode

Next on my list of diagramming techniques is pseudocode. This is a tool that is not actually a picture, but is designed to fill in the blanks between the pictures. It is a technique that has been used by programmers for a long time. (Actually, it always has seemed natural to me.) This tool enables you to describe the programming steps that are to be accomplished at a higher level than the actual programming code itself. The following listing shows an example of some pseudocode. Once again, this tool can be used at an extremely high level or a very low level. Pseudocode can save you a great deal of time because you can use it to quickly express something that would take hours of diagramming to emulate.

```
Input check information
Store check transaction in database
Recalculate checking account balance
Display updated checking register
Wait for next command
```

Class Hierarchy Diagram

Once you get into object-oriented development, you may want to group objects with similar properties into *classes*. You can derive one class from a parent class. The derived child class will have the properties of the parent class (inheritance). You can then add to or override those properties to build the correct behavior for the child class. This inheritance allows you to use a hierarchy of functionality and to avoid building the same functions and data into multiple similar classes on a class-by-class basis. The class hierarchy diagram, shown in Figure 24.5, reveals the lineage of your classes so that you can see what functions are available from the parent classes.

FIGURE 24.5.
Class hierarchy diagram.

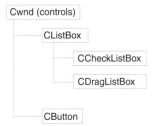

Microsoft Foundation Classes (C++)

Other CASE Features

You will run into a number of other diagramming tools and techniques, depending on the CASE tool that you choose. Remember that you can also use these techniques for your analysis even if you are not using a CASE tool. However, one of the real advantages of modern CASE tools is that they enable you to analyze the data once you have gotten it into the design repository. You can run a number of common analytical reports, including the following:

■ Detects when you repeat the same data elements in multiple tables as opposed to linking them together by joining the tables.

■ Detects when you have some data elements you are not using in any functional modules or that you have no way of populating or updating (a common problem with reference data tables in the first release of many applications).

■ Detects when you are inconsistent in the way you define data elements in different tables. (For example, sometimes you use a number, and sometimes you use a character.)

The details behind these diagrams are also important. For example, when you define a field within a table on the diagram, you might be asked to define the datatype and format specifications. You might also input a range of legal values or table storage parameters applicable to the database management system that you are using. Typically these data inputs take the form of property pages that you access from a menu or by clicking the object. These little details allow you to define the application to the level of detail needed for implementation.

Another common feature of modern CASE tools is the ability to generate software and databases from the data that is input as part of the design process. The process of building a table creation command in the SQL language is fairly straightforward once you have completely designed the table. Also, applications can make a good guess at the way the forms and reports are to be laid out and then allow you to modify the first cut generated by the CASE tool. This feature is perhaps one of the most interesting benefits of CASE tools when you are building new applications and time is especially critical.

Another thing that you have to consider with CASE tools is each of the many products on the market has a slightly different feature set. I would not dream of trying to compare the various products in this chapter. First, I do not have the space. Second, the feature sets are changing all the time. Finally, so many new vendors and tools are entering the market that this text would soon become dated. Instead, I suggest that you perform a feature comparison as it relates to the development tool set that you have chosen. For example, Oracle's Designer/2000 product is designed to work closely with Oracle's Developer/2000 tool set. However, other products are optimized to work with certain COBOL compilers, and still others have an object-oriented flavor that is better suited to C++ and other object-oriented development tools.

One final point that I want to touch on in the area of computer-aided software engineering concerns project management and version control systems. Traditional CASE tools focus on capturing the design of the application; however, that is not the complete development methodology. Other tasks are typically automated by computer software that aid the development process. The following items are two of the most common examples:

- *Software version control systems.* These packages provide formal check-out procedures for people who want to modify software modules. They also keep track of previous versions of the software in case you want to undo your changes. They implement much of the quality assurance and development control functions that are typical in a complete software development methodology.

- *Project management systems.* You may have divided the application into the component modules and know what needs to be done. The next task is to figure out who is going to do the work, when it is going to be done, and how much it is going to cost. Project management software packages are typically used to figure out this information. They are also good for tracking progress so that you can know when you are behind and need to adjust your schedules and/or costs.

This concludes my brief overview of computer-aided software engineering. Entire books have been devoted to this topic, but this introduction should suffice for now. I tried to stress the basics of how CASE tools are used to enter the design information and what they can do for you once you have completed your design. I took a broader view than most authors because I included the project management and software version control systems that usually are part of most development methodologies. Finally, I avoided discussing particular products because they change so rapidly and because different packages are suited to different tool sets and methodologies. I strongly suggest that you evaluate products based on your needs as opposed to accepting a magazine's generic recommendation.

Waterfall Methodology

Now that the basics are out of the way, I want to discuss some of the more common methodologies that I have worked with. The first one is usually called the *waterfall methodology*. This name refers to the way that the output of one phase in the development process flows down to the next phase (see Figure 24.6). This methodology was designed in the era of second- and third-generation computer languages (COBOL, FORTRAN, and so on). It is a very structured approach that starts with high-level requirements and designs and works to flesh them out into documented, detailed designs that can be implemented.

FIGURE 24.6.
Waterfall methodology.

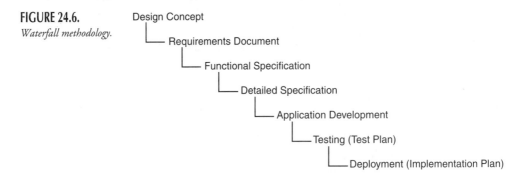

The waterfall methodology can be implemented in various ways. One of the most traditional paths appears in U.S. government contracts; the specifications are determined in great detail, and changes to these specifications are associated with cost changes. Change control is a formal interaction between the customer and the contractors. This version has very little interaction between the developers and the end users. Analysts typically prepare specifications based on meetings with key users and contracting staff. Sometimes a separate company is hired to prepare a detailed set of specifications that can be sent out for bids.

One of the elements that varies most among customers who use this methodology is the terms and definitions of the phases in the process. For example, one customer might refer to the specifications prepared as an A spec, a B spec, and a C spec. Another might call them requirements document, functional specification, and detailed specification. The level of detail can vary from fairly flexible to extremely detailed. Therefore, you must understand the development life cycle that is being used so that you can be sure of what is required and accurately determine the costs and time frames involved. By the way, one of the things that I found most unusual in this process is that some customers use the word *shall* and others use *will*. One is contractually binding; the other is a general intention. Again, you really have to understand the system before you can work in this environment.

The waterfall methodology is a very formal method that has been used for a number of years. Using this method, you might have trouble responding to business needs for getting applications into production quickly at a minimum cost. The waterfall method is also not suited to organizations that are constantly evolving and need their information systems to change with them. The methodologies that I discuss next have been designed to meet these needs.

Iterative Methodologies

One observation I have made when computer systems are first implemented in a given business unit is that people often resist the changes at first. Once they begin using them, they come to you with suggestions for how the applications can be made even more powerful. Perhaps it's a good sign of acceptance when people start to see the benefits of your labor and want to expand what they can do. The downside is that many organizations do not budget for enhancements and expect you to make it perfect the first time around.

A few developers have seen this pattern enough times to build a development methodology that accepts this behavior as natural and uses it to improve the development process. The fundamental argument is that you cannot expect users to know everything that is possible when they have not used computerized business processing systems before. Also, because technology continues to evolve, things that were impossible last year may be very doable now. Therefore, an iterative approach to development—in which you build something and then enhance it based on feedback by users and the input of new technologies—may be the best approach for some situations (see Figure 24.7).

FIGURE 24.7.

Iterative methodologies.

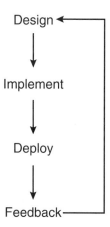

The iterative approach comes in two main flavors. The first tackles a complex application by dividing it into pieces, delivering the core technologies first, and then adding other functional components in an iterative fashion. The other approach is to deliver portions of all functional components and add reports and functions during later deliveries. Both approaches allow you to improve the later deliveries based on early feedback. Figure 24.8 illustrates the differences between these two approaches.

FIGURE 24.8.
Different iterative approaches.

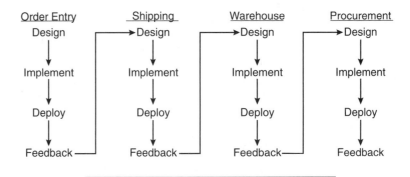

Add Subsystems

Perhaps some examples will help explain the differences, starting with the first approach. Many of today's applications are designed to enable multiple departments to work together—groups who may never have worked together before. This scenario is a good opportunity for delivering different functions at different times. For example, if you are building a new order-processing system that integrates your company, you may want to build the order-entry portion of the system first. You can print out hard copies of the orders for order fulfillment until you add them to the automated system. Later, you may include the procurement department and manage the entire inventory through this growing system. This approach has the following advantages:

■ It can spread the costs of a complex system over several fiscal periods and level out staffing requirements. Although you could hire many programmers and get the application done in several months, you may not wish to spend all of the money at once.

■ It can lower the support burden to a tolerable level. Users often require a good bit of support when a new application comes online, which can overwhelm your support group on the day when you roll out an all-encompassing application.

■ You can learn from feedback from the first few groups to make things better for them and the people who will be using modules that you will develop later in the cycle.

■ It can level the capital requirements for computer hardware and network systems, enabling you to grow at a more reasonable pace.

■ It can make the users feel good because they are participating in the development process. Some users may even begin to feel ownership in the application and will work to make it better.

■ It enables developers to learn the business area over time. A smaller development staff that works on the various iterations of the project builds experience in the business area, learns who to contact, and so on, which can make them more productive when working on the later modules.

Add Functions

However, you may not be able to live with half a system using the previous approach. Perhaps you are moving off of a legacy system that is no longer useful or merging several systems as part of a business merger, and you need a functional system as soon as possible. Most applications I have worked on include absolute requirements and nice-to-have requirements. For example, a checkbook program that does not calculate your balance is nearly useless. However, you may not need all 27 checkbook reports on the wish list to implement the application. You could, at least in most organizations, propose a system that does the basic functions and skimps on some of the reports or some of the nicer processing functions, such as the business calculator that pops up in every number field or the capability to look up all your transactions since the dawn of time. This iterative approach lets you get a functional system out first and then add the bells and whistles. Here are some of the benefits of this approach:

■ You get the core requirements out quickly.

■ You do not waste time developing less important features and then wind up being late because a critical function falls behind schedule. For a given iteration, all the features are fairly equal in importance.

■ If budgets are cut later on, you lose the less-important features of your working application instead of losing entire sections of your overall application architecture.

From a requirements point of view, one of the great simplifications in the waterfall methodology is that you wound up with a simple design model or document that told you everything that was going to be in your single delivery. If later deliveries were involved, each was typically covered by a separate design document. In iterative methodologies, you not only have to manage what the application is going to do but also when it is going to do it. Fortunately, CASE tools usually support multiple versions of the system and allow you to evolve your design.

One final note on iterative methodologies. If you use these techniques, I seriously recommend that you implement a robust version control system. You may find a really obscure little bug in your latest release of an application that makes it impossible to use in production. You may have to go back to the previous version of the product until you can work out the bugs. A good version control system can make this "retreat" relatively easy. Of course, you should also plan back-out options as part of your installation plans, just in case.

Rapid Application Development

"More for less, and I want it now." This type of request is becoming quite common. It may not be technologically possible to comply with such an expectation, but try explaining that to your users or management. Since such requests are becoming more frequent, especially in businesses that are rapidly changing as their environment changes, techniques have been developed to accommodate them. I am grouping the plethora of buzzwords that describe this process under the umbrella of rapid application development.

So what does that mean? Well, conscientious programmers always work hard and try to avoid being wasteful. Therefore, they should be working as fast as they can, right? Perhaps so, but sometimes they just need to understand the emphasis on timing that certain projects demand. They can then adjust their schedules to make sure that they meet their deadlines. Some examples of changes they would make include the following:

- Consideration of an iterative approach in which the core functions are delivered first and then nice-to-have features come in later.
- Testing that ensures correct functionality but de-emphasizes cosmetics.
- Frequent reviews of project status that enable managers to detect tasks that are falling behind and acquire additional resources to get the project back on schedules.
- Budget reserves enabling managers to acquire additional resources to shore up problems that arise.
- A closer working relationship with users who are available to answer developers' questions and review early versions of the software to ensure that the developers are on the right track.
- A conscious effort during the design process to keep the application simple so that it is doable within the time frame; that is, asking whether each proposed requirement is really necessary.

Some vendors and techniques consultants would like you to believe that they have a special methodology that is uniquely suited to rapid application development. I believe that you can optimize your existing methodologies with the goal of getting a working system in as little time as possible. The key is that you have to make some compromises to achieve this goal. It might take the form of a little extra budget to augment staff or a little harder line when determining which requirements will be implemented in this version of the application.

Prototyping

What do you do when you don't know what to do? Perhaps prototyping is the answer. Prototyping is a good technique to use to speed application development and also help get requirements out of users who cannot specify exactly what they want. The basic premise is simple.

You build a less-than-complete version of the system and then show it to the users. They give you feedback based on what they see before you have wasted time implementing functions that they may not really want.

The prototype can take many forms. For example, I show the users a drawing of the screens that I am building. We then review what buttons they would have to press and what would be displayed when they use this form. This process is especially useful if you can run through the entire business process with the users so that you don't miss or assume anything.

Another form of prototype that is relatively easy to implement with GUI-builder tools commonly found in fourth-generation application development tools is to mock up the actual screen but not implement any of the functionality behind it. Perhaps you populate the fields with simulated, hard-coded data. Another approach is that when a user presses a button, a message box pops up that explains what is going to happen next.

The key to prototyping is that changes become more expensive as you move along in the development process. A change that is relatively easy to make in the paper design stage can waste days of effort if it isn't caught until testing; it can cost weeks of effort if the problem is found after the system is in production. Prototyping short circuits this process by having the users test less-than-complete versions of the application to ensure that what you are implementing is actually what they were asking for.

You can also implement multiple phases of prototyping, each representing another iteration of your development. For example, you might ask users to review your paper designs on forms and reports. Next, you might let them review the forms and reports as they have been implemented using the GUI-design tool before you write the functional code. You might even let them review some of the basic processing modules after they are functional but before you build the remaining modules that depend on the basic modules. The number of iterations, the content provided in each of the iterations, and whether you use prototyping at all depend on the complexity of the application, how well it has been conceived and defined by the user, and also whether the users are willing to spend the time to review the prototypes. However, prototyping is a technique that you might want to keep in your bag of tricks to use when the occasion arises.

Here are a few things that I have observed about the use of prototyping:

■ *You need to have a process in place for deciding whether the prototype is good or not.* You do not want to be caught in the middle of an argument between someone who has been on the job for 30 years and another person who actually works on the function that is in question. The users should be forced to give you a unified customer decision so that you can proceed.

■ *You need to control the number of iterations in your process.* Theoretically, you could iterate forever as users think up new ways of doing things. Also, if business processes are changing rapidly, you may wind up never being able to close on the final design because the requirements change after each iteration of your prototype. One to three iterations are usually good enough for most of the projects that I have worked on.

■ *You need to clarify the success criteria for your prototype.* Although the little details, such as which font you use and what each button does, are valid areas for feedback, you must make it clear that the general requirements for the project are not open for increase. Users often try to convince you to add just one more report or some special lookup feature that was not in the application when you developed your project plan. You therefore have to set some limits up front to prevent users from justifying "scope creep" as "clarifications."

Whole System Integration

Kindly permit me to get up on my soap box for a moment. One of the biggest problems that I have run across in development projects (other than development tools not living up to the vendor's grand claims) is the lack of a *whole system approach* to the development process. What is a whole system approach? The following list provides some examples of problems I have encountered resulting from a development methodology that didn't include the whole system:

■ A wonderful application is destined for a host that is grossly overloaded and cannot possibly keep up with the demands that the application places on it. The end users cannot tell the difference between a poorly written application and an overloaded server. (The application just seems to run like a dog to them.) No one bothered to check with the system administrators or look at loading data to see if the system was adequate.

■ Another magnificent PC application is designed to run in a client/server environment. The developers build the application and get great response times when testing the application. It is sent out to the users who have great difficulty even loading it. (The developers had fast Pentium computers with 32MB of memory, but the end users had a mixture of 386 and 486 computers with only 12MB of memory.) An emergency procurement is needed to get extra memory and a few faster computers to allow the users to run this application.

■ A new application runs fine at the headquarters building, but the users in the field find it unbearably slow. An analysis reveals that even though all buildings are running with 10 million-bits-per-second Ethernet networks, the buildings are connected with relatively slow 56,000-bit-per-second lines.

■ An application is developed that is designed to interface with the existing personnel system. However, soon after the application is installed, a planned change to the personnel system database prevents the other application from accessing personnel data.

Computer systems these days continue to increase in complexity. This increase in complexity has led to specialization, which itself is the cause of many problems. In the days of central computers and terminals, you had to deal with only a few people when fielding a new application.

Today, however, you might have to talk to a relatively large cast of characters including

- System administrators for the servers
- Database administrators
- Data administrators
- Network server administrators
- Network engineers
- PC support staff
- Security administrators
- Quality assurance staff
- Server hardware support staff
- Help desk staff

At this point, your experience comes into play. You need to think through your development and implementation process. Think of everyone who is required to give you some help or whose systems (such as servers, networks, PCs) you will be using or interfacing with. Also think of those people from whom your organization requires you to obtain reviews or approvals as part of the development and implementation process. You now need to figure out the best way to give these people the access to your system that they need without taking up too much of their time or yours.

Now let me suggest a technique that will paralyze your organization and make a lot of people unhappy with you. You play it safe and make a representative from every group in the building attend every one of your design meetings. If people miss a meeting, you blame any problems that arise on them. If you take a good look at most design meetings, however, you will find that only a few people are really needed for the topics that are being discussed. It is a waste of time to bring all of these people into meetings in which you discuss font changes on the forms that you are building.

Some more useful and popular techniques that you can use to get these people involved include e-mail and invitations to special meetings devoted to specific topics that are published in advance. If a simple question comes up in one of your meetings, make a note of it and send an e-mail message to the appropriate group. Include the response as part of your project documentation. If you have to meet with these individuals to discuss topics that are probably of little interest to the majority of your design group (for example, the logon security banner for this application), call a separate meeting with only the appropriate players. This plan may seem really simple and obvious to some of you, but I have found far too many organizations that do not understand these principles.

My recommending that you distribute documentation to a wide audience is another one of my views of the development process. Obviously, you do not need to distribute the detailed database schema to the end users, but if you think a document might be useful to someone, send it. I have found that far too often people hesitate to distribute documentation because they don't believe the recipients will read it. However, some recipients might notice something useful while they scan the sections that are of interest to them. Of course, many organizations send copies of everything to everyone, which is just a waste of paper; you do have to show some judgment.

My final thought on this subject is that you have to make the whole system approach part of your basic development methodology—not just an afterthought. Most of the developers I have dealt with are so busy working out details with the users, managing scope creep, and losing software developers in the middle of the project, that they never have time to think about how to improve the development process. Also, the people who are supporting you might be too busy coping with current crises to talk to a developer working on an application that will be installed two months down the road. Many organizations make the formal sign off of the support groups part of the design process, often in the form of design reviews. The support organizations have an incentive to complete the reviews by the scheduled date because they do not want to be responsible for other projects slipping and running over budget. Consequently, I believe that if you do not incorporate a whole system engineering approach into your design methodology, you probably will not find the time to get around to thinking about the whole system, as opposed to the individual pieces.

Choosing Your Methodology

If I have done my job, none of the methodologies described in this chapter should stand out as the only possible solution for every project. I think that they all have a place in application development. Problems arise when you use the wrong methodology for a project. For example, rapid prototyping is rarely appropriate in a COBOL environment when you are doing maintenance upgrades to a large existing system. Also, the waterfall methodology is usually difficult to apply in environments where you are trying to provide rapid delivery for applications whose requirements are poorly understood by users and developers.

I want to leave you with a few items to consider when you are choosing a methodology for your next project.

- Your methodology should be compatible with your chosen development tools. Either change the tools or change the methodology; but there are some tool/methodology combinations that are highly incompatible.

- Your methodology has to be compatible with the processes of your organization. It may be important to deliver applications quickly. Conversely, it may be more important to accept less than optimal applications but have precise control over budget and schedule.

- You need to have enough experience and training to be able to run the methodology correctly.

■ Your methodology needs a plan for dealing with all possible development and implementation considerations, including how you will work with the relevant support organizations.

■ Don't be afraid to experiment. Vendors are happy to provide demonstration equipment and referrals to other companies that have implemented the vendor's solutions to meet needs similar to yours. A lot of software products have demonstration versions or white papers that you can download from the Internet. If you are moving to a totally new environment or building an especially complex system, you might want to build a miniature hardware and operating system prototype to work out all of the bugs. You can work out an amazing number of software version and hardware incompatibility problems before the development process begins in earnest.

Summary

The goal of this chapter was to provide you with a solid understanding of the concepts behind the various development methodologies. I hope I provided enough information so that you are not influenced by a vendor's sales pitch for any one technique. I personally have used many methodologies with good results. I hope you can use my suggestions and recommendations to avoid some of the problems associated with the development process. Finally, if you are unhappy with the methodologies that you find on the market today, just wait a while. Vendors and consultants are devising new schemes all the time. Eventually, someone will come up with the tools and techniques that will make your job a little easier.

25

Quality Assurance for Oracle Projects

by Joe Zafian III

Cost overrides and production delays are too often reality in large Oracle systems implementations. This chapter discusses the basic concepts of Total Quality Management (TQM) and how to apply this strategy to your Oracle application development projects throughout their life cycle. By uncovering various traps and pitfalls that can occur, this chapter focuses on the conflicts between performance, functionality, timeliness, and other quality attributes inherent in any large systems development. TQM can enable you to resolve or, at the very least, minimize these conflicts by providing a structure that enables you to construct useful applications that endure as your business grows and changes.

The Importance of Quality

In the 1950s, American electronics product manufacturers steadily lost market share to overseas competition, which came primarily from firms in Japan and the other Pacific Rim countries. More recently, the American automobile giants of General Motors, Ford, and Chrysler began to lose sales to companies such as Toyota, Nissan, and Honda. Initially, industry analysts attributed this trend to cheaper labor, better gas mileage, and lower price. It was generally assumed that after labor in these countries matured to the level of the more "advanced" American work force and the American companies re-engineered their cars to use less expensive materials (while improving fuel efficiency and cutting labor costs), "The Big Three Automakers" would once again dominate the domestic market.

Instead of improving their market share, American companies suffered further degradation of their competitive position. The reason for this, which took too long for the business analysts to recognize, was the comparative lack of quality found in American cars. By cutting costs, the American manufacturers reduced the quality of an already inferior product. In recent years, the automakers have shifted their production and design emphasis to focus on quality and, as a result, the profitability of these companies is growing at an unprecedented rate.

So, what does all this have to do with Oracle project development? Your database and the applications built around it are products that are used by end users to better accomplish their tasks and are intended to contribute to the profitability of the organization as a whole. One of the principle tenets of quality assurance is that in order to produce quality, you must begin with high-quality materials and tools. If the database application that you deliver is of poor quality, then users will become frustrated to the point where they might not use your system as intended.

Perhaps the most compelling reason for needing quality is the fact that in the long run, it costs much less to deliver high-quality products than inferior ones. It is true that careful attention to detail, thorough testing, and innovation might initially take longer and bear higher initial costs. However, a high quality system will have lower maintenance costs and will more readily accept future enhancements as needed. Marketing studies have indicated that satisfied customers will, on average, tell about eight others how much they like a product. Conversely, unhappy customers will complain to about twenty. Therefore, it is imperative that you work to achieve the highest quality applications possible. Doing so will generate cooperative end users rather than adversarial relationships that benefit no one. As stated by W. Edwards Deming, the father of TQM, "The goal must be to deliver to customers what they want and need, on time, the first time, 100 percent of the time."

What Is Quality?

The first step in determining how to ensure that you deliver a quality product is to define the parameters within which you can achieve quality. Many manufacturers believe that a quality product can be delivered by providing various mechanisms that will enable the product to operate even if one component fails. Such a design is known as *fail-safe redundancy*. I contend that a system that has been developed with fail-safe redundancy is *not* a quality product. It is a product designed to fail. Quality can be defined by eight attributes: performance, reliability, features, conformity, durability, serviceability, aesthetics, and perceived quality. When monitored carefully, these attributes ensure high-quality development.

Performance

The first attribute of quality measures how efficiently the product utilizes its available resources, such as the fuel efficiency of a car or how quickly it accelerates. In the case of an Oracle database system, performance relates to the speed at which the applications retrieve data or the amount of time necessary to process a transaction. Additionally, the efficiency of data storage and memory utilization are factors that also define the performance of the database system. Chapter 30, "Performance Tuning," covers specific details on how to recover performance from an inferior quality application.

Reliability

The next factor determining quality is related to the accuracy and completeness of the data retrieved and processed. Just as a car would be expected to start when the ignition key is turned, an Oracle application should process transactions correctly and retrieve the data when requested. Oracle provides triggers and constraints that can be used to ensure data integrity and adherence to business rules. These structures are described in detail in Chapter 14, "Database Constraints, Triggers, and Procedures."

Features

Features can either enhance or detract from the quality of a product. Although most users want as many features as can possibly be implemented in an application, each new feature could detract from the performance or some other aspect of quality in the system. Proper definition of database functionality helps to keep your project on schedule without seriously affecting the quality of the system.

Conformity

The Oracle applications that you develop must adhere to a standard that is acceptable to the end users. The application should be similar to other applications with which the user is familiar. Additionally, especially in large multideveloper systems, a set of standards should be defined so that all developers use the same guidelines for development. Various standards may include naming conventions, screen and field dimensions, colors, user-interface, or the degree of client/server partitioning.

Durability

The Oracle application must be designed to last throughout the evolution of the business. When designing a system, you should try to look ahead to determine how the business and use of the data may change in the future. Plan ahead and eliminate as many future obstacles as possible. (This attribute makes me think about all those legacy systems that exist with a two-digit year for dates that will require massive modification in the near future.) Many times databases are designed to accommodate the initial volume of data, but they fall short when the system is used in production for a short while.

Serviceability

Serviceability in a quality product defines how easily routine maintenance can be performed on a product and how easily it accepts modifications. If it were difficult to change the oil on a particular car, the time involved in this process would be unacceptably high, resulting in higher costs and dissatisfied customers. Likewise, an Oracle application must be easily maintained to allow for changes in a company's business rules or to implement enhancements to the production system.

Aesthetics

Although the aesthetic qualities of the Oracle application have very little to do with how it performs, this is a very important factor in customer satisfaction. By creating a well thought-out, aesthetically pleasing user interface, you can provide an application that your customer will enjoy learning to use.

Perceived Quality

This last attribute is somewhat nebulous in that it really isn't an attribute at all. This concept is based on the fact that users have certain expectations based on past experience and their use of other tools. As a result, if a new system is being developed to replace an existing system, users expect it to perform as well and be as easy to use as the original system, in spite of the new features that also might have been added.

These eight factors determine the overall quality of the end product. Although each is important, it is often not possible to deliver a system that will achieve maximum scores on every attribute. It is your job as the developer of the application to direct the effort toward the quality assets that most adequately address the desires and requirements of your end users. Each project is different and the emphasis must be based on the requirements of your end users. You must remember that the overall quality of your application depends on its acceptance by end users.

Achieving Quality

The starting point for any discussion of quality methods must examine the successes of the Japanese manufacturers. After the Second World War, Japan needed to rebuild its industry to compete in a peace-time world. The man who was commissioned to help establish operating procedures for the Japanese companies was an American physicist named Dr. W. Edwards Deming. Deming's philosophy was that quality is built into a product through an established process based on direction from top management. Deming felt that for a product to be manufactured of the highest quality, the process must be in place to eliminate variances in development. Additionally, quality is achieved through the use of the highest quality materials and tools used by a confident, highly trained work force. Finally, Dr. Deming believed that all barriers to quality, such as fear to innovate and lack of pride in workmanship, contribute to poor quality and must be eliminated.

A contemporary of Dr. Deming's, Joseph Juran believed that in order to achieve quality, companies have to plan for quality goals to deliver the products that meet the need of the customers. After the goals have been established, a system must be in place to measure the true quality levels being achieved and to analyze where the quality goals are not being met. Finally, after the problem areas are identified, the company needs to find the causes of the lack of quality and needs to take corrective action to ensure that the problems are fixed.

Finally, Philip Crosby, Vice President for Quality at ITT in the 1970s, defined the concept of *Zero Defects Tolerance*, which has been the quality standard for the Department of Defense. Unlike Deming and Juran, who believed that mistakes were inevitable and must be corrected, Crosby believes that mistakes are absolutely preventable. In the Zero Defects standard, the level of acceptable errors is no errors. This is done through a policy of empowered employees who can work together as a team to deliver the quality necessary.

Quality in an Oracle Environment

As discussed in the preceding section, the best way to achieve quality in any production environment is through the establishment of standards and procedures. The first step in this process is to use a well thought-out project development methodology, such as the one discussed in the Chapter 24, "Project Development Methodologies." By using this methodology through-out the project development, you can focus on the various quality attributes to develop a high-quality system. In each phase of the life cycle, you can work to achieve your quality goals as outlined in this section. It is important to note that not all attributes of quality apply to the work done in each phase. By applying most of the suggestions found in this section to your project, you *will* deliver a high quality final product.

Strategy Phase

The purpose of this phase is to define the "ground rules" for the development of your Oracle application. The most important things that must be accomplished at the earliest stage of the project is to define who the users will be and to establish the development procedures to be followed by all developers. The following list offers some guidelines for the strategy phase.

General Quality

Establish who the customers are. You should try to see how the customer performs a particular task related to the application you are developing. Try to identify the problems that are associated with the old system and think of how you might make improvements in the new system.

Conduct a thorough examination of the development tools that may be used. Determine the capabilities of the tool so that it might be used efficiently when needed.

Gain an understanding of the "big picture." Understand where your application fits into the overall scheme of all the related applications in the organization. Try to look ahead to expected changes in the company in the near future.

Performance

Establish the performance goals you want to achieve. Define a performance service agreement that is acceptable to the users. This statement should

- Say something such as "Average query response time = 3-5 seconds and no queries should exceed 30 seconds."
- Be defined based on current system parameters and user definition.

Reliability

Establish the procedures for process development. By following an established set of procedures, you eliminate any variation in the development process and, thus, ensure quality.

Conformity

Examine the existing systems and other software used by the end users to determine what should be replicated. Users expect the new system to be familiar and comfortable.

Develop a standard "look and feel" for your applications. If possible, create screen templates and library functions that can be reused by all modules as the system is developed.

Durability

Conduct system load estimates. Make sure that the hardware being used will be able to handle the necessary load. If it cannot handle the load, notify the necessary people to make sure that a new system will be in place for production.

Serviceability

Learn to use the tools. Work with the tools so that you are comfortable and can confidently develop the system based on the estimates you will be required to provide.

Define the development teams to include all resources necessary to deliver the product on time. Try to include customers in the development team as early as possible. If customers are satisfied that they play a vital role in the definition of the application, their satisfaction will be easier to achieve.

Develop the procedures and requirements for documentation. Although some communications can be conducted verbally, it is essential that key information be recorded so that when changes are made at a later date, you will be able to remember how and why you did some particular task.

Aesthetics

Develop the standard "look and feel." You should define all aspects for the user interface including

- Screen size
- Field dimensions
- Screen colors
- Operational standards
- Standard formats
- Help formats

Perceived Quality

If possible, provide education to the customer. If customers are aware of the capabilities of the system, they might be less apt to ask for impossible features. Also, users can better understand what features are available and actually might request a system that is far superior to their original expectations. Adopt the philosophy (used by a New York clothing retailer) that "an educated consumer is our best customer."

Analysis Phase

The purpose of this phase is to finalize user requirements. In this phase, you must establish the current system conditions and identify the changes that are expected to be delivered in the new system. The following list offers guidelines for the analysis phase.

Performance

Create benchmarks of the existing systems to determine the current performance. Remember that this is a starting point for user expectations.

Reliability

Begin to identify the data entities and business rules for the system. Establish the database methods for how the rules will be enforced.

Features

Examine any existing systems to determine the features that are to be re-engineered.

Conduct interviews with end users to define all new requirements. Attempt to discern the difference between absolute requirements and potential desires. Work with the customer to establish which features will be implemented in the new system.

Durability

Define the usage levels and approximate entity sizes (number of rows). Try to determine the expected transaction load levels for data maintenance.

Serviceability

Establish the process by which the scope of work might be changed. As stated in Chapter 24, the methodology must accommodate feedback to prior phases so that the system will be delivered when expected. Without a proper feedback process, the project can run over deadline or the design might not accommodate necessary changes.

Perceived Quality

Establish the trust and confidence of the end users. This is accomplished through good communication and integration of the customer in the development process.

Design Phase

In the design phase, you define the structure of the database and establish the programmer guidelines to be followed during the build phase. As the application design begins to emerge, it is important to get your customers to confirm that the design meets their needs. If your end users have been an integral part of the project team, they should understand the design and can provide direction if necessary. The following list offers some guidelines for the design phase.

General Quality

Convert the entity and functional requirements into database objects. Validate that all objects have been created without errors. Load reference and static data into the necessary tables so that the data might be used in the later stages.

Performance

As the data entities are designed, identify the expected data access paths so that indexes might be defined as needed.

Define the partition for the application code between the database server and the client system to enhance throughput.

Reliability

At this point, establish all the test criteria to validate that all applications adhere to the established data integrity and business rules. Test data must encompass all conditions, including usage of invalid data throughout the process. Too often, systems are tested only with "good" data and fail when they encounter real-world errors in early production.

Conformity

As you design database objects, make sure that they are named according to your established conventions. For example, if two columns are related in separate tables, the names should be the same except for perhaps a prefix or suffix. Additionally, if a standard abbreviation is used for one column, make sure that it is used the same throughout the database. Do not use names interchangeably, such as the suffix _NO, NUM, and NUMBER on different columns.

Durability

Make sure that the design can accommodate future growth. Generally, when I construct a database, I plan for the initial extent of a table to hold about six months worth of data. Subsequent extents are then set up to hold an additional two months of data. When the fourth extent is almost full, I usually compress the extents for the first extent to hold approximately a year's data.

Aesthetics

Create prototype screens for each system module. Work with the customers to establish these screens before adding navigational and procedural functionality.

Perceived Quality

Make sure that the design is easily understood by all users. Walk the users through the database structure to ensure that all of their data requirements are met.

Build Phase

In this phase, you develop the actual application. This phase should include an iterative approach that enables developers to establish a prototype and refine it based on the input of end users. In this way, surprises are minimized and the final system should match user expectations. The most important task in this phase is to make sure that thorough testing is carried out for every element and module in the system. The following list offers some guidelines for the build phase.

Performance

Use tools such as TKPROF or EXPLAIN PLAN to evaluate performance. Before implementing a SQL statement in application code, test it autonomously in SQL*Plus to ensure that it operates correctly. Examine the execution plan and tune the statement by itself before implementing it. These tools are described in Chapter 30.

Reliability

Make sure that code is efficient and complete. Create a checklist for all business rules and validate that each program module utilizes the rules as necessary. Create the rules at the database level if at all possible to ensure that an application cannot bypass it.

Test the application completely. (Enough said.)

Conduct peer-level departmental code walkthroughs. This process accomplishes several tasks. First, if there are any design flaws, you should try to recognize them here. Second, if a module does something that conflicts with a module developed by another developer, the conflict can be corrected before it becomes a production problem. Lastly, the walkthroughs help to communicate innovation throughout the development team. If one developer finds something new, other developers might also utilize the same concept.

Conformity

Ensure that code is written in conformity to the established standards. Validate that required comments and self-documentation within the code exist. This is helpful later with enhancements, especially if a different developer works on the enhancements.

Aesthetics

Ensure that all screens within the application look similar and are aesthetically pleasing to the customer.

Perceived Quality

As the application is being developed, create the modules in prototype mode with the customer to ensure that the requirements are being met and that the system is evolving in the direction that the customer wants.

User Documentation Phase

This phase is the least enjoyable phase for most programmers and developers because, in many cases, documentation has been neglected until this point in the project life cycle. If you have followed the structure that has been established up to this point in the chapter, this phase will consist of compiling and collating the various bits of documentation that have already been generated during project development. The following list offers some guidelines for the user documentation phase.

Reliability

Create a business rules document that can be updated as the rules change. This document should be complete at all times and should be the standard for all application development used to access or manipulate the database.

Features

Create an operator's manual, which explains how to use all the system features. This manual might be in the form of online help.

Conformity

Document the test results. Include the performance statistics and all results. Future tests should be able to generate identical results with the same data.

Durability

Define the standard operating procedures to be used to monitor database growth and the procedures to be followed if the database needs to expand.

Serviceability

Create complete program documentation. The bane of developer's everywhere, this step is essential if the application is to allow future enhancements.

Perceived Quality

Be sure that all documented and programmed features are consistent with the user documentation. Nothing erodes customer satisfaction more quickly than attempting to do something that the manual says has been implemented, and it doesn't work.

Transition Phase

In this phase, you are getting ready to release the system to your end users. This is your last chance to verify that the system has been built to provide all user requirements. It is most important that all final tests are performed before the system is released. The following list offers some guidelines for the transition phase.

Performance

Conduct a full system test with a large volume of data to determine the effects of future growth. Many systems that are developed on small development databases appear to perform very well until they are ported to the production machine. It is important that you create as much volume data as possible to validate that the performance goals have been met.

Conformity

Create the online help system if necessary.

Work with users to ensure that the new application conforms to other related processes. If possible, for re-engineering projects, try to test the systems in parallel to ensure that the results are as expected.

Durability

Conduct tests with a very large number of concurrent users. This ensures that the system can handle the load as the company grows.

Serviceability

Gather feedback and take corrective action if possible. This step allows for any changes that might be necessary prior to final production implementation.

Aesthetics

Make sure that all screens are consistent.

Perceived Quality

Ensure that customer expectations are met. At this point, you want customers to agree that the system you've delivered meets or exceeds their expectations. If there are any problems, they should be worked out prior to the Production Phase.

Production Phase

This phase occurs when the application has been released to customers. In this phase, you should be proactively monitoring the database and applications to ensure that they are continuing to meet customer needs. As the business evolves, you will need to modify the system in order to ensure that it fulfills all requirements. The following list offers some guidelines for the production phase.

Performance

Conduct regular periodic tests to ensure performance. Do not wait for users to complain that performance is degrading. Define a set of queries to test the system response time; then use them periodically to make sure that you are fulfilling the service agreement. If performance begins to degrade, take corrective action immediately.

Reliability

Make sure that the system continues to operate reliably. Document all database outages or data integrity issues. Determine causes of these problems and take steps to eliminate them.

Durability

Periodically examine the database to determine if any database objects have outgrown the design. Just as business rules are subject to change, assumptions regarding data volumes and relative relationships also might change.

Serviceability

Establish enhancement and change control procedures. Any changes to the system should flow completely through the life-cycle model to ensure that the system continues to be of the highest quality.

Perceived Quality

Constantly gather user feedback. This is your primary source of information about the system.

If you use this section as a guideline for your life-cycle project development, you will naturally deliver a high-quality application that will continue to meet user needs for a long time. Neglecting a number of these recommendations can lead to significant problems during development and after users have been using the system for a long time. Although it may seem that it will take longer to develop a system using these guidelines, the truth is—in the long run—you will be saving a great deal of time that would be lost in problem resolution. In addition, your end users will be satisfied, and you will be free to provide enhancements and to develop other new applications.

Quality in Action

As a developer, I have encountered varying degrees of quality in the various projects in which I have participated. I can state without reservation that the most successful projects have focused on delivering high-quality results. In some cases, the quality concepts were implemented quite by accident; in others, a strong methodology was followed. In this section, I describe a couple of my experiences in order to emphasize the importance of TQM.

> **NOTE**
>
> Due to confidentiality agreements (and in some cases, to protect the innocent), I do not provide company names or project specifics.

Enterprise Data Warehouse

In this project, we were attempting to create a database containing detailed information regarding all the enterprise's operations. One task involved the conversion of all legacy data into an Oracle database. Quality was nonexistent in this project, and as far as I know, the system still has not been delivered to end users.

What went wrong here? First of all, the entire concept was defined by a high-level manager who had heard of a competitor with a similar system, and he thought it would be a good idea to have such a system. Financial support was obtained from administration, and the project was a "go." The one-person development team was assigned to develop the database. When I became involved in the project, the developer had already spent several frustrating months trying to implement the system.

I immediately recognized several problems; in its current environment, however, little could be done to rectify the problems. The project was doomed from the start. We were told not to speak with any end users, and in order to get support from other departments, we were required to send all requests up and down the chain of command. This resulted in long delays in getting the information we needed. Additionally, no thought had been given to what front-end tools would be used to access the database. Management assumed that they would be able to simply "plug something in" once the database was established.

As developers, we had no idea who would be using the system or, for that matter, how many people would be accessing the information. Additionally, we did not know whether the data would be used for online access or batch reporting. Our only direction was that all legacy data needed to be in the database regardless of its "correctness." And the only acceptable tool we were allowed to use was a loader program purchased from a vendor. Finally, we were told to complete the conversion by a certain date without regard for any input from us regarding feasibility.

Needless to say, the project was mired in politics and was destined never to reach completion. As I mentioned earlier, the database has still not been implemented. Data did get converted and some reports were generated, but performance and data inconsistencies have rendered the database virtually unusable. The problems with this project can be traced to a failure to implement quality standards from the beginning.

The Sales and Marketing Database

At the opposite end of the spectrum is another project that I worked on. This project followed a very specific methodology that enabled the development team to deliver one of the first 500GB Oracle databases in the world. This system was built by empowered development teams that utilized constant customer input throughout the project life cycle.

Each aspect of the system followed the complete development methodology. Before any subproject was started, a meeting was held with the developers and customers as well as any necessary support staff. Each module was examined against the overall enterprise needs, and adjustments were made before any subproject was started. Periodic training and technical information exchange meetings were held so that all developers were performing at the highest level. Standards were established for screen layouts and various templates were created.

People were assigned to review all database changes in order to validate that any new change would not impact existing or concurrently developed applications. Users were allowed to define the application requirements; after these requirements were documented by the development staff, users agreed to the scope of work.

As the application modules were being developed, users were involved in the day-to-day acceptance of the development path. In this way, if a developer started to deviate from what the user wanted, corrective action could be taken immediately. This prevented delivery of a system that did not satisfy user requirements.

In the final phase, all modules were thoroughly tested. It was found that between 50% and 125% of the time spent developing an application was spent on unit testing. This testing was directed by the analyst for the project and validated that every line of logic was exercised. After all unit testing was performed, the module was integrated into the enterprise application in a staging environment. Then further testing was performed to determine whether it would affect any other applications.

Such thorough adherence to quality standards resulted in an Oracle database application that rarely required error correction. Even when quality approaches are taken, errors can still occur—there will always be something you didn't think of up-front. With adequate quality standards in place, however, these errors should be rare.

As these two examples illustrate, a vast difference usually exists between a project with a strict adherence to Total Quality Management and one in which quality is an afterthought, if that. In order to deliver high-quality systems, you must concentrate on quality throughout the entire project. Without TQM, projects can suffer greatly in your capability to deliver usable systems within the time required. By implementing TQM, on the other hand, you can deliver dependable systems that will satisfy your customers.

Summary

As this chapter has established, quality is not something you can add at the end of a project. It must be built-in by empowered developers who are aware of all aspects of their application and the processes that they must use. By following an established process, you can achieve consistent, high-quality results every time. Quality is the most significant factor in enhancing a company's profitability and market share. The only way to establish quality is through an absolute commitment to quality throughout the entire development team.

VI

The Care and Feeding of a Production Oracle System

26

Monitoring Important Database Statistics

by Joe Greene

To many users who first start working with an Oracle database, it might seem like a mysterious black box that is impossible for anyone but the database administrator to understand. Developers simply hope that it accepts the SQL commands that they give it and does not send back one of those Oracle numbered error messages that are sometimes a challenge to understand. Well this chapter is devoted to teaching you how to get into that black box of the database. After you are inside, you can ask the database how it is doing in order to understand whether your applications are performing correctly or you need to make some adjustments.

First, this is not the database administrator's guide to monitoring the Oracle database. If you were interested in the intricacies of Oracle database administration, you would have bought a book on that subject. I will, however, try to cover the basic monitoring functions that a developer might want to know, just in case you wind up without a database administrator or have a DBA who is exceptionally busy. Remember, it is usually easier to do it yourself rather than find someone else to do it.

The second key point is that you need to understand the important statistics that have to be monitored. After you get the hang of collecting statistics from the database, you will come to realize that there are a large number of factors that you can look at. The key here is to weed out the ones that have little chance of being a problem and the ones that duplicate others when it comes to monitoring. This chapter will propose a basic subset that should be more than adequate for developer purposes.

Finally, you need to be familiar with the tools that allow you to see these statistics. There are a few tricks that I use to get the data in an easily readable format. Also, there are some scripts that are included on the accompanying CD-ROM, and they can save you from having to type out the SQL queries that are used to obtain the key statistics. The section on SQL*DBA, Server Manager, and SQL*Plus will provide you with what you need to use these tools.

Seeing Inside the Database

For many developers, the database is a black box that contains database tables, views, and perhaps some stored procedures. These developers interact with the database using the Structured Query Language (SQL) or some higher-level query tools. Chapter 2, "The Oracle Database Architecture," should have offered you some insight into the mysteries of the database management system. It would seem logical for Oracle to build some capabilities into the database to allow users and administrators to see what is happening inside of the database. As it turns out, Oracle has built quite a respectable monitoring capability into the RDBMS. You only need to learn a few tricks to get at this information.

The first concept that you need to understand is that of a counter. It is difficult to know in what format the users will want to see their end results (such as the number of megabytes read per minute or number of megabytes read per second). It also is a bit of a burden on operating systems and database management systems to have to calculate the statistics in their final form when, for the most part, people do not access them. Therefore, Oracle has chosen to gather statistics using a series of counters, as shown in Figure 26.1. The application code associated with the database management system has been designed to increment a series of counters when certain events occur during operation.

FIGURE 26.1.

Counters for monitoring database statistics.

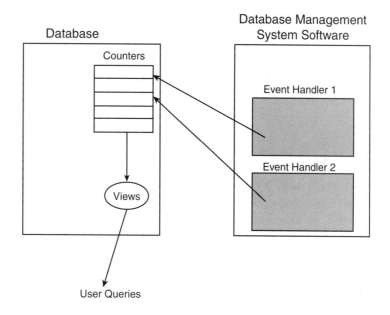

So, now we have a number of counters sitting out there somewhere within those Oracle database background processes that are running on the server. The next logical question is how do you access this data. Oracle could have built a highly proprietary interface that could be accessed only by a special Oracle monitoring program, which it could sell to customers as a separate package. However, it chose instead to implement an open interface to these counters. Not only is the interface an open one, it uses a format that is familiar to Oracle developers and DBAs. You access these counters using SQL statements issued against a series of views that are designed to access specific sets of counters.

There is one slight problem in the way that this has been implemented. To really see what is going on, you need to access some views that are normally only available to DBAs. I have experimented with some of the views that are similar but available to general users; however, they do not provide the same level of information. For example, DBA_EXTENTS view shows all database blocks that are consumed by any user, whereas the USER_EXTENTS view shows only the blocks that are consumed by the current user when it is run by a common user (it shows all extents when run by a DBA). This is probably necessary when Oracle is implemented in very high security environments. However, most environments can allow read access to these views without any problems at all. Therefore, I have built a script, titled vw_grant.sql, which appears on the

CD-ROM accompanying this book. This script is designed to grant read-only access to the database statistics views for those of you who do not have DBA privileges. You need to have your DBA review the script and run it for you if you are going to do your own monitoring and tuning.

With this preliminary action out of the way, you can now proceed to some of the basic concepts that you will need for monitoring. The first thing that you have to understand is when these counters are reset. They are reset every time you start the Oracle database instance. Therefore, if you want to measure data for a specific period of time, you have to take data points at the start and end of the period. Otherwise, your data will reflect totals since the last startup.

This can be very significant to database performance measurement. Most systems have periods of relatively light usage. For example, it is common for applications to be very active first thing in the morning, right after lunch, and then right before the end of the work day. If you take an average over the entire business day, your numbers might look satisfactory, when actually the system is overloaded during the peak periods and lightly used during the rest of the time. The solution could be as simple as suggesting to users that if they shift some of their work to less busy periods, they will get better response times.

Now, let's proceed with a simple example showing access to a key parameter that applications designers might want to view. One of the more common problems that arises in production Oracle systems is that the tablespaces fill up and additional disk space needs to be allocated for the database. To find out how many bytes of data are being used in a given tablespace, you would issue the following query:

```
SQL> select tablespace_name,sum(bytes) Bytes
  2  from dba_extents
  3  group by tablespace_name;

TABLESPACE_NAME                        BYTES
------------------------------    ---------
ROLLBACK_DATA                        1638400
SYSTEM                               7542784
USER_DATA                             133120
SQL>
```

Your next task is to evaluate whether or not this is a problem. What about the bytes being consumed in the SYSTEM tablespace—is this a problem? That depends on the total storage capacity of the SYSTEM tablespace. Therefore, you would have to issue another query to see what the total capacity of these tablespaces are. Here's an example:

```
SQL> select tablespace_name,sum(bytes) Bytes
  2  from dba_data_files
  3  group by tablespace_name;

TABLESPACE_NAME                        BYTES
------------------------------    ---------
ROLLBACK_DATA                        5242880
SYSTEM                              10485760
TEMPORARY_DATA                       2097152
USER_DATA                            3145728
SQL>
```

Now you know the capacity and amount used. You still have to answer the question as to whether this is a problem. Here is where a bit of experience and knowledge of how your database is being used come into play. You can see that you have 250MB of storage left in the system tablespace. If you are using an application that places all of its data in the USER_DATA tablespace, then you would have plenty of room to spare. If you are used to UNIX versions of Oracle, you may notice that the tablespace names are slightly different in this listing from the Windows NT version. If, however, your application stores a lot of information in the SYSTEM tablespace, then you might have to add space. I would strongly recommend keeping application information out of the SYSTEM tablespace since running out of space in this tablespace can cause your instance to crash. Of course, stored procedures must be placed in the SYSTEM tablespace, so you need to ensure there is room for growth if you use a lot of stored procedures.

With this example out of the way, I'll point out a few things that you need to think about when trying to monitor the performance of your database:

■ You need to know what each of the views contains in the way of information. Most of the names are fairly descriptive; however, as mentioned earlier, many of the better views are available only to database administrators. To see which views you can access, try the following SQL query:

```
select view_name from all_views;
```

■ You need to know which parameters are likely to indicate problems. If you look at all of the views and parameters that are available, you would spend hours going through them all looking for problems. That is not really necessary in that most of the problems show up by reviewing a handful of these monitored statistics.

■ You need to know what makes a measurement meaningful. This is based on a knowledge of what the parameter is measuring and therefore knowing when a value indicates a problem. It also means knowing over what timeframe your statistics have been gathered.

■ You need to know how to format the data in an easy-to-read manner. The sample output that I showed for tablespaces is workable, but it is hardly easy to read. For one thing, there are a lot of numbers strung together without any commas to separate them. You have to work to make sense of the numbers. Also, when you have two separate queries, you have to compare numbers on two different lists as opposed to comparing two numbers on a single line.

Before going on, let me take this opportunity to summarize the points in this chapter that I consider to be important. First, Oracle captures information about activities that are going on within the database by using counters that are reset on system start up. To access the data in these counters, you issue SQL queries against a series of views, many of which are available only to database administrators. Your challenge is to know which of the many statistics that are available can indicate common problems and know what values for these statistics are normal and which are cause for concern.

Which Statistics Are Important?

You need to understand the limitations over which you have no control. Examples of this would include operating system–specific limits on the number of files that can be associated with a database or the maximum number of extents that a given database object can consume. Since these limitations cannot be altered, they are especially important to monitor on a routine basis. It is important to note that when you reach one of these limits, you usually encounter an error message that causes your applications to terminate.

Next on the list of parameters of interest are the resources that are consumed by and within the database. The most common of these is the amount of disk space consumed by the various tables and the tablespaces themselves. It also includes space for temporary storage of transactions and query results in progress, which is a little bit tricky in that developers and users rarely see these resources being used. The errors encountered when these parameters exceed the normal range of processing vary from performance degradation to application failure or even database failure.

Finally, there are a number of parameters that will not cause errors when they go out of the desired range, but they do have a serious impact on performance. These require perhaps the greatest knowledge of how Oracle works internally to know what is acceptable and important. You might not recognize what these parameters are unless you have read about the internals of the Oracle database. You have two options if you do not understand a given parameter that I discuss in this chapter.

First, you could get out a reference book and become more familiar with the intricacies of Oracle's internal processing structures. Or, if you already have enough reading to do, you could simply trust the values that I will quote for you in this section. Actually, I did not even make up most of these values. Instead, I read through the Oracle tuning references that are put out with the database and did some research of resources on CompuServe and the Internet. Either way, it is most important to understand that you are dealing with tunable parameters in the database, and they are used to increase the performance of the application, not to prevent instance or application crashes.

One final set of information you need to access in order to evaluate your situation is the values of database configuration parameters so you can know whether certain limits are being exceeded. This seems simple enough, but it is not as easy as you might think, unless you know the right views to query. Oracle has designed a database management system that runs on platforms from PCs to the largest mainframes and supercomputers. It supports transaction processing, data warehouses, and everything in between. Oracle is already beginning to support complex multimedia datatypes that are completely different from those found in your normal relational tables.

To accomplish this daunting task, the designers have built a number of tunable configuration parameters into the database to allow the database to reconfigure itself to meet different needs.

Also, some of the parameters can be adjusted at startup, while others are adjusted during operation. Finally, by default, not all the parameters actually are set by the database administrator. Instead, Oracle provides default values for these parameters, which are optimized toward each operating system under which the database is operating. Therefore, you really have to ask the database what the values of its parameters are. You can accomplish this by a series of queries to views such as v$parameter.

Now on to the actual statistics that you will want to monitor. For purposes of my discussion here, I have broken the parameters into three areas:

- Utilization statistics
- Tuning statistics
- Current activity

I group certain things into each of these categories. The first of the three is the utilization statistics. These queries monitor consumable system resources such as disk space. There are a few fine points related to this, such as the fact that tables and other objects have several different limits, such as the total disk space and the number of extents that the object can consume. The parameters that I typically monitor for the database are

- Bytes used within each of the tablespaces against the total number of bytes available in that tablespace
- Datafiles and their sizes for the tablespaces
- The number of bytes consumed by each of the tables in the database
- The number of bytes consumed by each of the indexes in the database
- The views that are part of the database
- The number of extents that are consumed by each of the database objects that occupy more than one extent
- The size of the segments that are free within a tablespace

The next set of statistics are those related to tuning the database for better performance. Some relate mostly to the overall configuration of the database; however, others are geared more for individual applications and their data. Again, if you are not familiar with what these items are yet, do not worry too much about it. I routinely monitor the following statistics:

- Library cache
- Data dictionary cache
- Shared pool
- Multithreaded server memory
- Buffer cache

- Disk activity
- Rollback segment contention (two users trying to access the same rollback segment)
- Latch contention
- Multithreaded server dispatcher contention
- Shared server processes contention
- Redo log buffer contention
- Sort memory contention
- Free list contention
- CPU utilization
- Disk drive usage
- Computer memory utilization

Finally, there are a series of current activities that you might want to monitor. As opposed to the statistics in this list, which are gathered from the startup of the database, the current activities show such things as which users are currently logged on and what type of activities they are performing. This can be most useful when a database application is performing well, except during brief periods. Your goal is then to figure out which activities are occurring during slow periods that are not occurring during normal periods.

 There also are other parameters that you might need to know in special situations. Typically, you would get the recommendation from Oracle or a vendor, which would let you know that these parameters are important in your situation. Some of these are not documented in any of the common literature and might not be supported in future releases of the database. I ran across these parameters when working with a very large (135GB or more) Oracle data warehouse. Anyway, be aware that someone might suggest that you monitor these items. You can add them to the end of the tuning script (`27_dbtune.sql`) that is on the enclosed CD.

SQL*DBA, Server Manager, and SQL*Plus

The first thing you need to do is refer back to some other chapters for detailed information on the operation of these tools: Chapter 16, "SQL*DBA and Server Manager" and Chapter 17, "SQL*Plus." These chapters offer more than enough detail for the purposes of monitoring. Now for a bit of history for those who are new to Oracle. Server Manager and SQL*DBA perform basically the same functions. For purposes of my discussions here, they are interchangeable. This chapter provides some of the specifics of when you would want to use each of these tools when probing your database for important information.

When it comes to running the utilization and tuning monitoring scripts that I discuss in the following two sections, I would recommend SQL*Plus. As a matter of fact, the formatting commands that I put in the script make the output a little more readable, but they are designed for SQL*Plus and will not work in SQL*DBA. SQL*Plus is a much more friendly interface for issuing normal SQL commands. It has the option of spooling the output to an operating system file or printer for future reference. What I like most is the ability to use SQL*Plus on my PC and connect via SQL*Net to remote servers to run monitoring scripts. That way I get the convenience of the Windows (95 or NT) operating system user interface and do not have to deal with differences between the many operating systems on which Oracle databases are used. In Figure 26.2, I have included a sample of SQL*Plus as used for my monitoring scripts.

FIGURE 26.2.

*SQL*Plus used for monitoring queries.*

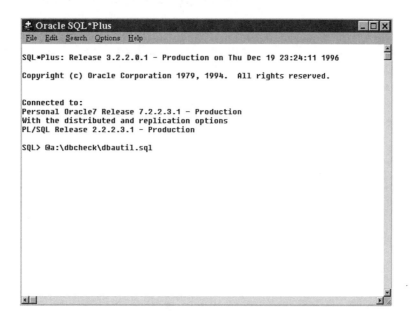

However, SQL*DBA (and its successor Server Manager) are the only tools that effectively allow you to get at the current activity. You could pull down the monitor menu and select the item you want to monitor. Some of the more common items you might monitor include users who are connected to Oracle (you also can kill the session if they disconnect improperly and leave a session hanging) and activity in hard-to-see areas such as rollback segments. Figure 26.3 shows a sample monitoring session in SQL*DBA.

FIGURE 26.3.

SQL*DBA used to monitor current activity.

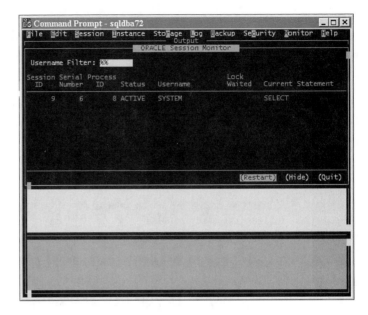

Utilization Statistics

Now let's move on to the real work. The queries in this section are stored in a file called dbutil.sql on the accompanying CD-ROM. Remember you will need to have your DBA run the vw_grant.sql file as the SYS user if you have an account that does not have DBA access to some of the internal monitoring views that are used. Finally, you need to run the script dbviews.sql to create a couple of views that are used by the scripts. What these views do is aggregate the utilization data on a tablespace-by-tablespace basis so that your queries are simpler.

The first thing I do in the dbutil.sql script is spool the output to a file in the default directory called dbcheck.out. I have actually implemented shell scripts that automatically print the output or automatically run the reports on a routine basis and send the output to me via electronic mail. (The latter is my preference.) However, these scripts are very operating system dependent, so I'll stick to the basics of getting the monitoring data.

At the top of the output file, I like to put a header that identifies the report (SQL script) being run, the date, and time that it was run, and the instance against which it was run. You might wind up maintaining multiple Oracle instances and therefore need to know the instance that you are working with. You might also like to have the date and time in case you save these reports for a while. This allows me to look for trends that can be used to calculate such things as when I might have to add disk drives to a server based on database growth. The following is a sample of this header output (again, SQL*Plus commands are used to make the heading a little more readable).

```
######################################################################
#               Oracle Database Utilization Report                   #
######################################################################
Instance Name:
oracle
Date Of This Report:
02 December  1996  22:03
######################################################################
```

After this is done, start into the first query, which is designed to capture one of the most common problems in an Oracle database. All of these queries are in the `27_dbutil.sql` script on the enclosed CD. Yes, people love using database systems so much that they just keep filling them with more and more information. Because the DBA has to allocate data files to certain fixed sizes and associate them with a single tablespace, you can run out of space to store your data if you do not keep an eye on it. Note that Oracle has started to allow autoextend mode for tables that will automatically extend the size of your objects. You need to be very careful when using this, or else one user's table could fill up an entire tablespace. The query that I use to monitor extents is

```
select alloc.tablespace_name,
     sum(free.bytes) freespace,
     sum(alloc.bytes) totlbytes,
     sum(used.bytes) / sum(alloc.bytes) * 100 pct
  from sys.tablespace_free free,
     sys.tablespace_alloc alloc,
     sys.tablespace_used used
  where free.tablespace_name = alloc.tablespace_name
     and alloc.tablespace_name = used.tablespace_name(+)
  group by alloc.tablespace_name
  order by alloc.tablespace_name
```

I use a few of the SQL*Plus formatting commands in the script file to make the output more readable. Therefore, when the above command is issued, you get output that looks like the following:

```
######################################################################
Tablespace Utilization
Table_Space              Free_Bytes      Total_Bytes  %Used
-----------------------  --------------- ------------ ------
ROLLBACK_DATA              3,604,480       5,242,880   31.3
SYSTEM                     2,922,496      10,485,760   72.1
TEMPORARY_DATA             2,097,152       2,097,152
USER_DATA                  3,012,608       3,145,728    4.2
######################################################################
```

Notice that with a little bit of work, you can make the output a good bit clearer than the earlier example. The commas really help when you are dealing with numbers that are more than three digits long. Also, it is not all that difficult to display a "percentage used" calculation, which prevents you from having to do it in your head when you are reviewing the output. So when is a tablespace too full? The answer depends on several factors:

■ Which tablespaces are your concern? Running out of space in the SYSTEM tablespace is extremely dangerous because this is the heart of the database management system. If you run out of space in this tablespace, your database will usually crash.

■ How do you use the tablespace? Having a low amount of space in the ROLLBACK (or ROLLBACK_DATA) tablespace might not be a problem because these areas are reused by multiple applications and might be full by design. You also need to get a feel for how quickly the tablespace is filling up in order to allow you sufficient time to react.

■ How quickly can you make changes? If you have spare disk space just waiting for you and can get the DBA and system administrators to add datafiles to your tablespaces in a day or so, you can let your tablespaces become fuller before you take action. However, if you have to procure new disks, and it takes several weeks or months to add space, you will have to react more quickly.

The next query that I run as part of my report lists the data files that are part of the database. It can sometimes be useful when I want to see where the files are and see the space available on a disk (as determined by operating utilities, such as df in UNIX or the Windows Explorer in Windows NT or 95), if I need to add a datafile to a tablespace. Here's the query and formatted output from my SQL*Plus script:

```
select tablespace_name,file_name,bytes
    from sys.dba_data_files
    order by tablespace_name
```

```
######################################################################
Data File Listing Report
Table Space            File Name                            BYTES
-------------------    ------------------------------       ---------------
ROLLBACK_DATA          F:\ORAWIN95\DATABASE\rbs1orcl.ora     5,242,880
SYSTEM                 F:\ORAWIN95\DATABASE\sys1orcl.ora    10,485,760
TEMPORARY_DATA         F:\ORAWIN95\DATABASE\tmp1orcl.ora     2,097,152
USER_DATA              F:\ORAWIN95\DATABASE\usr1orcl.ora     3,145,728
######################################################################
```

The next two queries that I frequently run show me the sizes of the various tables and indexes in my system that do not belong to the database management system itself (such as the SYS and SYSTEM accounts). These are the most common storage problems, so they are the ones that you typically will want to keep and eye on most. This tells you which objects within a tablespace are growing rapidly. Who knows, you might have some test tables in a development instance that are no longer needed or test tables that can be reduced in size to prevent you from having to allocate additional storage space. The queries that you issue to determine what these objects are and how much space they are taking up would be

```
select tablespace_name,segment_name,owner,sum(bytes) Bytes
    from sys.dba_extents
    where owner not in ('SYS','SYSTEM') and segment_type='TABLE'
    group by tablespace_name,owner,segment_name
    order by tablespace_name,bytes desc
select tablespace_name,segment_name,owner,sum(bytes) Bytes
    from sys.dba_extents
    where owner not in ('SYS','SYSTEM') and segment_type='INDEX'
    group by tablespace_name,owner,segment_name
    order by tablespace_name,bytes desc
```

The output will look something like the following. Note that I have chosen to order the output in descending order by size after ordering it by tablespace. That way you can quickly scan to see the large objects that are taking up most of your space.

```
######################################################################
Table Sizes Report
Tablespace Name            Table Name                  Owner          Bytes
- - - - - - - - - - - -    - - - - - - - - - - - - -   - - - - - -    - - - - - - -
SYSTEM                     DOPEY                       DOPEY          20,480
SYSTEM                     CARRIER_CODE                JGREENE        20,480
SYSTEM                     CARRIER_FREIGHT_RATES       JGREENE        10,240
SYSTEM                     CUSTOMER_CARRIER_PREFS      JGREENE        10,240
SYSTEM                     DISPATCH_SCHEDULES          JGREENE        10,240
SYSTEM                     DISPATCH_SCHEDULES_HISTORY  JGREENE        10,240
SYSTEM                     DISPATCH_SYSTEM_STATUS      JGREENE        10,240
SYSTEM                     DISPATCH_USER_ACCESS        JGREENE        10,240
SYSTEM                     PREFERRED_CARRIERS          JGREENE        10,240
SYSTEM                     SHIPPING_DISTANCES          JGREENE        10,240
SYSTEM                     STATE_NAMES                 JGREENE        10,240
SYSTEM                     TRUCKS_AVAILABLE            JGREENE        10,240
SYSTEM                     TRUCKS_AVAILABLE_HISTORY    JGREENE        10,240
SYSTEM                     TRUCK_DESTINATION_PREFS     JGREENE        10,240
SYSTEM                     TRUCK_DEST_PREFS_HISTORY    JGREENE        10,240
USER_DATA                  DOPEY                       JGREENE        10,240
######################################################################
Index Sizes Report
Tablespace Name            Index Name                  Owner          Bytes
- - - - - - - - - - - -    - - - - - - - - - - - - -   - - - - - -    - - - - - - -
SYSTEM                     PK_CARRIER_CODE             JGREENE        10,240
SYSTEM                     PK_DISPATCH_SCHEDULES       JGREENE        10,240
SYSTEM                     PK_DISPATCH_SCHEDULES_HIST  JGREENE        10,240
SYSTEM                     PK_DISPATCH_SYSTEM_STATUS   JGREENE        10,240
SYSTEM                     PK_TRUCKS_AVAILABLE         JGREENE        10,240
SYSTEM                     PK_TRUCKS_AVAILABLE_HIST    JGREENE        10,240
######################################################################
```

In my scripts, I next run two scripts that list the stored procedures (triggers, functions, and so on) that are used within the database and also the views. The views do not consume a significant amount of storage space, but I like to see which ones exist because they usually map back to one of my user tables. The stored procedures do consume space within the SYSTEM tablespace, but not very much. However, because the SYSTEM tablespace probably is your most critical resource, you want to keep an eye on it. If you see several new stored procedures appearing, you might want to check into making sure that you have enough space for them. I don't show any examples of this because, by now, you should be getting the idea of SQL script leading to formatted output.

The next query covers something that might not be obvious to folks who have not worked with the way Oracle allocates segments internally within its tablespaces. Just as you pre-allocate Oracle datafiles in fixed-size chunks, Oracle internally allocates fixed-size units inside the tablespace for individual tables, indexes, and so forth. When one unit fills up, Oracle tries to allocate another extent.

The table fragmentation monitoring query has two purposes. First, there is a database limit as to the number of extents that an object can occupy (for example, 512 for many operating systems). When this limit is reached, any statement that tries to add more data to that object will fail and cause an application error. Even before you reach this failure point though, you should be concerned about limiting the number of extents used for an object.

If you have too many extents that are scattered across a disk drive or even across multiple disk drives, it will take longer to access information on many of your queries. This is caused by having to move the relatively slow heads of the disk drive to multiple locations, issue multiple read operations, and so on. Ideally, therefore, you should keep an object in one extent or at least as few extents as possible (some tables are so large that they occupy multiple disk drives). The query and associated formatted output from my utilization script is as follows. Here, I intentionally make one table occupy a fairly large number of segments for sample purposes. I would probably want to use the export utility to export the data from this table with the compress extents option, re-create the table with a large enough extent that it could fit into one extent, and then re-import its data.

```
select owner,segment_name,segment_type,sum(bytes),count(*) frags
from sys.dba_extents
where owner not in ('SYS','SYSTEM')
having count(*) > 1
group by owner,segment_name,segment_type
order by frags desc
```

```
#####################################################################
Table Fragmentation Report
Table                                                      Bytes
Owner      Object Name                    Index             Used      FRAGS
---------- ------------------------------ ------- ----------------- ---------
JGREENE    DOPEY                          TABLE              53,248        21
#####################################################################
```

An issue closely related to fragmentation is that of free extents. When you first create a tablespace, it is completely empty, which represents a single, large, free extent. As you add objects, you will typically start from the beginning of the free extent and use space as needed, again leaving a single chunk of free space at the end of the datafiles. However, as objects are created and deleted, you might run into a situation where you have gaps between the allocated extents. Because Oracle allocates extents that occupy contiguous bytes on the storage medium, you might get into a situation where the gaps between allocated extents are too small to meet the needs of the extents that you are trying to allocate.

Even though you have more than enough room in the datafile to accommodate your new extent, Oracle cannot allocate contiguous space, and your request for additional space will fail. The solution would be to export the entire tablespace and re-import the data (which will be done in contiguous extents starting from the beginning again). The query that I use to detect this condition and the sample output are as follows. Note in this example that every tablespace except USER_DATA is in one nice free extent, and even USER_DATA has only two extents. This is where you would like to be, although you will rarely be able to have things this orderly in production databases.

```
select free.tablespace_name,free.bytes
   from sys.dba_free_space free
   order by free.tablespace_name,free.bytes

##################################################################
Tablespace Free Segments Report
Table Space                        Bytes
- - - - - - - - - - - - - - - -  - - - - - - - - - - - - -
ROLLBACK_DATA                  3,602,432
SYSTEM                         2,920,448
TEMPORARY_DATA                 2,095,104
USER_DATA                        276,480
USER_DATA                      2,734,080
##################################################################
#                          END OF REPORT
##################################################################
```

This discussion on utilization statistics has been rather ambitious for those who have never delved into the internals of an Oracle database before, but I hope the learning curve has not been too painful. What you can take from this is a series of queries that you can use to help you figure out what the problems are within your database. Some of the fixes might require support from your DBA. For example, you might not have import/export privileges to a production database. The main use of these queries is that, even when you cannot fix the problem, they will help you pinpoint the problem for others to fix. Most problem reports come in with an error of failed to allocate extent…, which does not make sense to the users or the help desk. You cannot be sure whether it is a problem with the software or with the database until you get some data. That is what these queries will help you find out.

Tuning Statistics

For purposes of brevity, I will not go into the same level of detail for the queries in the 27_dbtune.sql file on the attached CD-ROM. Most of these tuning parameters are very technical internal features that a DBA would use. I include the query so that you can have something to help you find out why an application is running poorly. These queries run in conjunction with operating system utilities (the dbcheck.sh file on the CD-ROM is a Korn shell script for UNIX that also executes some operating system utilities to determine CPU, disk, and memory utilization) to try to pinpoint what is causing the slowdown.

Think of this as a "divide and conquer" approach. If you find out that the CPU, computer memory, and disk drive utilization are moderate, then something inside Oracle or your application is causing the slowdown. You then look at the common bottlenecks within the database. If everything is normal, you have to look within your application. Here is where the tuning discussions in Chapter 30, "Performance Tuning," will come in handy. If everything is fine with your tuning, it might just be that the application is complicated and will take a while unless you buy faster computers and networks. However, most places will not let you get away with the "buy me a faster computer" answer unless you have some data to back it up. The queries in dbtune.sql will help you (or your DBA) support your suggestions.

I have written this script to be fairly straightforward to analyze. Associated with each of the queries is a goal (this indicates the range of values that you would like to see). I also print out the corrective action (usually taken by a DBA) if this goal is not met. Then I give you the actual value measured in your database. The following output shows you the results for a healthy and lightly used test instance to give you an idea of what this report looks like. To see the actual code behind this report, look at the 27_dbtune.sql file on the enclosed CD-ROM.

```
##################################################################
Memory Allocation Checks
##################################################################
Library Cache Check
Goal:                              <1%
Corrective Action:                 Increase shared_pool_size
.    Write identical SQL statements
Library Cache Miss Ratio (%)
---------------------------
                 1.09
##################################################################
Data Dictionary Cache Check
Goal:                              <10%
Corrective Actions:                Increase shared_pool_size
Data Dictionary Cache Miss Ratio (%)
------------------------------------
                 4.48
##################################################################
Multi-Threaded Server Session Memory
Goal:              Shared_pool_size at lease equal to maximum
.                  session memory
Corrective Action:     Increase shared_pool_size
Session Memory (Bytes)
----------------------
Shared_Pool_Size (Bytes)
------------------------
            3,500,000
##################################################################
Buffer Cache Hit Ratio
Goal:              Above 60 to 70 percent
Corrective Action:     Increase db_block_buffers
Hit Ratio (%)
-------------
       83.3
##################################################################
Disk I/O Checks
##################################################################
##################################################################
Disk Activity Check
Goal:              Balance Load Between Disks
Corrective Action:     Transfer files, reduce other loads to disks,
.                      striping disks, separating data files and redo
.                      logs
Data File                                  Reads        Writes
------------------------------------- -------------  ------------
F:\ORAWIN95\DATABASE\sys1orcl.ora          2,064         345
F:\ORAWIN95\DATABASE\usr1orcl.ora              2           1
F:\ORAWIN95\DATABASE\rbs1orcl.ora             14         204
F:\ORAWIN95\DATABASE\tmp1orcl.ora              0           0
```

```
######################################################################
Oracle Contention Checks
######################################################################
######################################################################
Rollback Segment Contention
Goal:                       Measured Counts < 1% of total gets
.                           (the choice of Oracle column names makes it
.                           impossible to do this calculation for you)
Corrective Action:          Add more rollback segments
      Total Gets
   ---------------
         55,954
Class                    Counts
--------------------    ------------
system undo header          0
system undo block           0
undo header                 0
undo block                  0
######################################################################
Latch Contention Analysis
Goal:                       < 1% miss/get for redo allocation
.                           < 1% immediate miss/get for redo copy
Corrective Action:          Redo allocation-  decrease log_small_entry_
.                           max_size
.                           Redo copyIncrease log_simultaneous_copies
Latch Type               Misses/Gets (%) Immediate Misses/Gets (%)
--------------------    ----------------  -------------------------
redo allocation              .03213                  .00000
redo copy                    .00000                  .00000
######################################################################
MTS Dispatcher Contention
Goal:                       < 50%
Corrective Action:          Add dispatcher processes
######################################################################
Shared Server Process Contention
Goal:                       Shared processes less that MTS_MAX_SERVERS
Corrective Action:          Alter MTS_MAX_SERVERS
Shared Server Processes
-----------------------
                    0
Latch Type               MTS_MAX_SERVERS
--------------------    ----------------
mts_max_servers                  0
######################################################################
Redo Log Buffer Space Contention
Goal:                       Near 0
Corrective Action:          Increase size of redo log buffer
     Requests
   -----------
         2
######################################################################
Sort Memory Contention
Goal:                       Mimimize sorts to disk
Corrective Action:          Increase sort-area-size
Type                 Number
--------------       ------------
sorts (memory)        1,018
sorts (disk)              0
```

```
############################################################################
Free List Contention
Goal:                          Number of counts less that 1% of total gets
Corrective Action:             Increase free lists (per table)
      Total Gets
----------------
         55,954
Class                    Counts
--------------------  -----------
free list                      0
############################################################################
```

> **NOTE**
>
> Some items in this query are not applicable to all systems and therefore show up as blanks on the preceding report when run on those systems. For example, Oracle supports a multithreaded server architecture that helps systems with a lot of users save memory on the server. The multithreaded server is an option that your DBA can implement. You do not run into it very often on smaller systems and therefore should not be alarmed if you do not see results in this section of the tuning report.

Summary

I hope this chapter struck a good balance between providing too little information to be helpful and overwhelming you with database internals. You do not have to understand the intricacies of the Oracle shared memory areas to run the reports discussed in this section, but it never hurts to learn about them in other references. If you do need to see inside the database, the queries discussed here will allow you to look for all of the common problems and point you in the right direction toward solving them.

27

Defining an Ongoing Maintenance Plan

by Joe Greene

Very few applications these days are thrown out the door to awaiting audiences who consider them to be the absolute solution to their software needs and who therefore never want any changes. In almost all cases, compromises have been made during the development process where certain features have been deferred until a future release of the product. As a result, just as you are recovering from that last-minute frenzy of getting the product into production, someone wants to talk to you about the next release, which has that feature that he or she desperately needs. Sometimes these clients will notice your blank stare and give you a few days to recover, but don't count on it.

Besides this, there is the evolution in computer technology that is taking place all around us. People such as Bill Gates and Larry Ellison seem to talk about nothing else but the future. In their versions of the future, you usually see hardware and software platforms that make today's systems look rather pitiful. How many people are willing to go out and buy PC/XT computers and VisiCalc spreadsheets any more? Whether you like it or not, the industry is moving forward, and therefore, the standards by which your applications are being judged will continue to move higher and higher.

A final push that you will be facing after you get your application out the door is the fact that things might not be absolutely perfect. Oh, I know, you never make mistakes, but perhaps some of the people who you work with are mere mortals, or perhaps the users did not convey their requirements clearly. Your users have a simple set of requirements. Whenever they find something to change, you do it immediately and send out a fix—simple—except that they also want it to be tested to work perfectly and perhaps even want updated documentation. Your help desk also would have problems if you were sending out daily upgrades that they had to install on multiple computers and support. For these reasons, you have to plan the process of fixing problems with an eye towards controlled upgrades that have been properly tested.

This chapter discusses some of the issues related to maintaining the wonderful Oracle applications that you have just developed. There is not, unfortunately, a single simple answer that applies throughout the universe for all computer applications. What I intend to do is present the considerations and alternatives that will allow you to build your own maintenance plans. A single simple answer would be nice, but why should maintenance be any different than the other phases in the application life cycle? I cover the following topics in this chapter:

- Planning upgrades
- The total system perspective
- The healthy database application
- Monitoring
- Auditing
- Capacity planning

Planning Upgrades

Many veteran developers might think that a section such as this will contain the obvious "test your upgrades thoroughly" lectures that are old hat and not worth reading by experienced developers. Okay, I do mention that in this section, but I also go a little deeper. What I hope to bring out are some of the points that you have to consider when developing centralized databases, client/server applications, and some of the other concepts that you might not have considered when building COBOL applications on the mainframe. The Oracle development environments present some unique opportunities as well as some unique problems and challenges.

The first consideration that I would like to bring up is a fairly traditional one—grouping changes together for controlled testing and deployment. Some environments are fairly freeform, and developers can simply make the changes and send them directly to their users. However, most production environments require some formal testing before changes are implemented. Some bug fixes cause more problems than they solve. This is especially important in production databases because a bug in your application can corrupt the database and thus cause larger problems. This can even ripple to other applications taking down multiple systems. For example, general ledger problems can affect the ability of accounts payable and accounts receivable systems to correctly perform their tasks.

With this in mind, you might now agree that formal testing is necessary. The problem is that a good test takes a fair amount of time, and you need to do *regression testing* (testing of other modules to make sure that they have not been affected by your new changes). This leads to the desire to group your bug fixes into controlled releases. You make up a list of which bug fixes are in the controlled release, and then when those fixes are completed, you test your software system with those fixes applied. When this new software version passes testing (again, it needs to be a complete test to ensure that other modules still work correctly), you get to the release point.

In larger applications, you usually need to be sensitive to the capabilities of your support organizations when preparing your upgrades and releases. Therefore, you will usually need to coordinate with these support teams before designing an upgrade release schedule. Examples of support groups that you typically would have to contact include system administration, database administration, help desk, and training. This might seem trivial to some people because they exist in environments where the development groups own all of these functions. However, in most organizations, development groups have to work with other groups within their company or with outside contractors to obtain this support. In these cases, this coordination becomes extremely important.

A topic related to this is planning the level of the various upgrades. What I mean by this is that some upgrades are relatively minor and cosmetic, but others are complete rewrites. You usually can perform the minor changes more often and with less support from outside organizations than you can with the major upgrades. Also, bug fixes usually are more critical to implement than enhancements. Therefore, you have to weigh your application needs to determine what level of change should be included with each release of the product. The following list describes some examples of release levels that you might consider:

■ Maintenance: You fix only bugs in the existing application. There is no significant upgrade in functionality. This usually requires little support from training and other support organizations (because they were probably teaching users how it was really supposed to work).

■ Minor upgrade: You add a few minor features, such as an automated calculation or a drop-down list box to replace a text entry field, but nothing that requires a major re-training of the users or serious infrastructure changes such as a database upgrade.

■ Major release: You make significant changes that would be obvious to anyone using the system. Perhaps you add entire modules or rewrite the application. This usually requires a lot of support from training and help desk functions. It also requires thorough testing and a well thought-out upgrade plan.

So far, I have not mentioned anything related to product upgrades that is really mystical. I find the concepts behind the whole process to be relatively easy to understand. It is the actual implementation that gets a bit tricky as you balance user demands against your staff resources and time constraints. I include this material for people who have not worked in formal software development organizations. (There are a lot of places that grow up from one or two people hacking code into large companies in this industry.) I also like to think about these things every time I plan out a new project just to make sure that I am not falling into habits that might have made sense a few years ago but are outdated today. To conclude this section on maintenance upgrades, here are a few observations that you might consider when developing your upgrade plans.

When is the most likely time that a maintenance release will be required? From my experience, it is usually right after the initial release or a significant upgrade of your application. This is important because some companies like to set absolute standards for when they release upgrades. For example, some software producers might say that they *only* release upgrades every six months. However, when they release their products, the users find a series of bugs that are very severe. This is natural in some regards. Your testing can cover only a finite group of scenarios that you would consider to be common. Also, different customers might use your product in ways that are slightly different from what you expected. If you want to make sales or have a good rapport with internal customers, you usually will be expected to quickly fix the problems that they find in your new application. Therefore, always consider planning for a maintenance release within a couple of months of a major release no matter what you consider to be your normal release cycle.

Finally, you might need some tools to properly plan these upgrade release cycles. Many people still use paper to keep track of problems. However, a number of tools support bug tracking, feature control, and so forth, and they are not really all that expensive. Combined with common

PC project management tools, you can effectively plan (and change the plans for) your upgrades. One tool that should not be left out of this list is a reliable version control system that keeps the source code for your various releases. I have often found cases where I wanted to back out changes that I had made because they caused more problems than they fixed. You could rely on people making backup disks, but it is not that difficult or expensive to set up a network server with a software repository that can keep things straight for you.

The Total System Perspective

Anothermajor concept that I would argue for when doing maintenance planning is the need to take a total system perspective. Actually this is one of my pet peeves when it comes to the computer world. There are a number of specialists out there who see a very narrow section of the overall system very well, but who see little else. This narrow perspective can become a problem, though, when you implement distributed applications. The problem comes because there are a lot of components that have to work well together to make the application work correctly, as illustrated in Figure 27.1.

FIGURE 27.1.
Components in a distributed application environment.

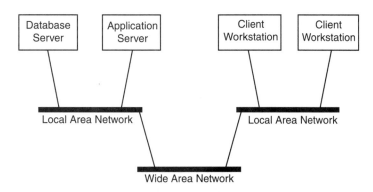

Once upon a time, you had just one computer to worry about and a bunch of dumb terminals that depended on that central computer for just about everything except electricity. Here you had the system manager for the central computer who took care of the processing and storage capacities of this system and the applications group who wrote applications to meet user needs. As long as these individuals did their jobs, you did not have to worry much about fielding an application. Many sites even carried excess capacity just to accommodate growth and handle things such as disk drive failures. The information needed to understand what was happening in this computer environment was centralized and easy for members of the central support staff to access.

However, the modern computer environment tends to be a bit different. One factor that comes into play is the constant budget pressures that have driven many organizations to implement these less expensive distributed computer environments. It seems as though every expenditure has to be thoroughly researched and justified. The result is that you often are not allowed to carry the large pool of excess processing and storage capacity that you once did. Add to this the pressures to field applications quickly, and you get an environment with little in the way of reserves and rapidly changing loads.

This is where many of the most avoidable problems surface when implementing and maintaining applications. Each generation of an application seems to need more in the way of resources than previous applications. Also, people are using more in the way of supporting products, such as the Oracle database management system or ODBC drivers. This means that when upgrading, you have to be careful to ensure that the supporting products are compatible with one another. For example, if you upgrade one supporting product, will it still work with the previous version of another supporting product? You might think that this is obvious to the most casual observer, but I have run into a large number of driver and product incompatibility problems that have delayed development and deployment.

You also need to be very careful about ensuring that the target computer environment keeps pace with application needs. Many development environments feature fairly high-powered computers that speed the development process. Compilers and other development tools are certainly far more demanding than most of the other applications that are run on PCs. This can be a problem in that an application that is developed and tested on these high-speed, high-memory computers might run very slowly or not at all on the lower-grade computers that are typically found on users' desks.

This concern extends into your entire computer infrastructure. Just because your application runs well in your test environment on your test server does not guarantee that it will work in the production environment. Figure 27.2 shows some of the more common real-world problems that I have run into, which include

- Overloaded servers—As database management systems, applications, and user demands increase, you might find that your servers need to be upgraded.

- Overloaded support applications—You might find that your database management system, transaction processing system, or other support tool needs to be upgraded or tuned to support increased demands as your applications evolve.

- Overloaded networks—One of the most often overlooked resources when fielding client/server or distributed applications is the network transmission capacity. This is tricky because you can have a network that is generally robust, but if there are just a few overloaded segments or weak links between network segments, you will have users suffering from extremely poor performance.

- Inadequate disk storage capacity—One of the more common problems experienced with applications that people like is that they start storing more and more of their data online. This can lead to rapid increases in the need for disk drives and their associated controllers.

■ Inability to back up data—This is a tricky one, but one that larger installations will have to manage. I have seen facilities that have an abundance of disk drives and processing capacity, but lack the ability to keep up with backup needs due to the sheer volume of data. These locations usually have to implement additional backup systems (such as tape drives) or go to more sophisticated backup systems to ensure that they can provide data recovery services. This is one point that very few designers would consider when designing an application.

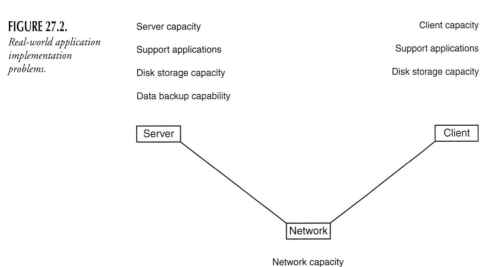

FIGURE 27.2.
Real-world application implementation problems.

To summarize this section, consider all of the elements in the computer system when laying out your maintenance plans. Perhaps disk drives or network capacity is not your problem in the design group because there are other groups to deal with these problems. I would suggest, though, that you talk to these people before you field your new applications. Remember, users have no way of knowing where the problem lies. All they know is that the application is bombing out or performing horribly. Odds are that they will come complaining to you as the developer first, so it is best to try to avoid these problems with a little bit of planning for your applications as they evolve.

The Healthy Database Application

So far I have covered some pretty routine topics in application maintenance. Almost all programmers have gone through the cycle of development followed by upgrade at some point in their careers. In the preceding section though, I discussed some concerns about the functioning of your new application and challenged you to consider the overall system picture. In the old days, there would be entire groups devoted to the subjects of application installation and operation who would worry about these details. However, in the modern environment, smaller, more tightly integrated teams are becoming responsible for the overall functioning of software systems. Developers actually are getting involved with users (or might even be part of the user's functional organization). As such, they often assume responsibility for a number of functions that used to be performed by a dedicated group of individuals in the old data center world.

I like to use the term *healthy application* to describe the condition where your application is functioning correctly and providing adequate performance. It seems to be a natural term that most users and developers can understand. There are many components to a healthy database that I briefly discuss in this section (see Figure 27.3). After you understand the components, I cover what some of the events and indicators associated with the component are so that you can measure your component's state of health. The remaining sections of this chapter are then devoted to monitoring these indicators and taking corrective maintenance actions to improve your application.

FIGURE 27.3.

Components in a healthy database application.

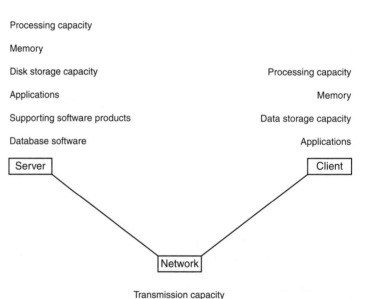

Let's start with a brief discussion of the components of an application and how they contribute to correct processing and adequate performance:

▪ Server processing capacity—If you are using the servers only to store your application files, then your processing load will be light. However, if you have a number of users running applications on the server or rely on a server-based relational database management system, such as Oracle, you can quite easily overload the processing capacity of smaller servers. A sign of this is slow overall application response time during busy periods of the day with good performance when there are few concurrent users working on the application. Of course, it is best to detect overloaded servers during routine measurement of server processing load, which is discussed in the next section.

■ Server memory—Only a few applications can eat up server memory as quickly as a relational database management system that has been optimized for performance. The reason is simple: Random access memory is orders of magnitude faster to access than magnetic disks. Database developers put everything they can into memory. Therefore, as you add users or tune your database, you need to ensure that you are not running low on memory. Most server operating systems use *virtual memory* (disk space that stores the overflow from physical memory), which is much slower to access than real memory. Server operating systems allow you to monitor this swapping activity, which will show up as severe performance degradation from the user perspective.

■ Server data storage capacity—Very few databases require the same amount of disk storage or shrink over time. As people look to perform trend analyses and start to use data effectively for planning (as opposed to just sending out bills), more data is being accessed over longer periods of time. This translates into enormous increases in disk storage space.

Although the good news is that disk storage prices have plummeted recently, it still takes time to order additional disks, and you might eventually reach limits for your computer on the number of disk drives that can be attached to it. Therefore, it is important to monitor disk utilization and perform some long-term planning of your own.

■ Client processing capacity—A common solution to increasing performance in business applications is to distribute more of the logic to the client workstations. They might not individually be as powerful as the server, but there are a large number of them. You have to be careful, though, when you upgrade your applications, to test new releases on workstations that mimic your average (and low end) client workstations to ensure that you are not asking too much from these machines.

■ Client memory—As PC client applications (and operating systems) become more complex, they demand more memory to help keep up the speed. Just as you need to test computers that have the same speed as your users, you also should test compatible memory configurations.

■ Client data storage capacity—Very few applications designed to run against Oracle databases require much in the way of local disk storage capacity, but you at least should consider this and make sure that your client workstations have sufficient disk space.

■ Network transmission capacity—This is probably the trickiest item to keep up with in my experience. The wires are in the walls and the hardware is locked away in closets to which you probably do not have the key. It is often a great challenge to get a drawing that documents the current configuration of your network. If your network is currently supporting only a little bit of printing and some electronic mail, you should take a hard look at it before you implement large client/server applications. You need to look for low bandwidth sections in the network, which could severely affect the performance of your applications when run by clients on the far side. Also, you should review network loading as you field new network applications and upgrade existing ones.

■ Client applications—These are the applications that you write to implement business processing needs. What you are searching for here is efficiency in getting the job done. I could easily write a very simple application that overloads the CPU, memory, and disk storage capabilities of most client workstations. Your challenge is to ensure that you teach your applications to make efficient use of resources. This could be a phase in the development process where you try alternative algorithms and application designs to see which produces efficient code. In your maintenance plan, you might often find that this is one of your major tasks in the second release of any application.

■ Server applications—Although your server is usually much more powerful than your client workstation, it has to support a larger number of users and demanding applications such as a database management system. Therefore, you usually will want to spend extra effort ensuring that your server-based applications are as efficient as possible.

■ Server supporting software products—So far, I have discussed things that you can do that affect loading and performance. However, you can get changes in loading with software that you purchase. Perhaps your vendors have optimized their code a little bit more, and as a result, your loading will be reduced. However, when you are planning your maintenance releases, you also should plan your upgrades of supporting applications such as the Oracle RDBMS. Running a test on a similar server (perhaps a separate development server) can give you an idea as to how your upgraded, purchased application will affect system loading and therefore the performance of your applications.

■ Database software components—This is a tricky issue that is starting to creep up more often in recent months. Most organizations have formal procedures to install and test application software that is stored in operating system files. However, the Oracle database can execute software in the form of stored procedures that are often not supported by the standard installation and testing methodology. Because these applications can be quite complex and, in the case of triggers, can be activated automatically by system events, they can place quite a load on your system if they are not optimized and tested for both functionality and loading impacts before being transitioned into production. If you use stored procedures, triggers, and so forth, you should factor these steps into your development and maintenance processes.

With these general concepts of database health behind us, let's move on to measuring the health of the database. Going along with the logic that you cannot manage something that you cannot measure, it's a good idea to spend some time on the concepts of measurement. My observation on the process or measurement for purposes of maintenance and tuning would be that you get both too much data and too little data from built-in monitoring utilities. This might seem like a riddle, but I'll clarify what I mean.

There are a large number of things that the Oracle database and most operating systems measure that are related to loading and performance. However, only a handful of these measurements are useful when assessing overall loading for the system. The first challenge that you face is to isolate which of the many indicators available to you are the most important. Although this will vary somewhat between operating systems, I suggest the following list of measurements as a starting point:

- CPU utilization (percentage of total)
- Physical memory utilization (percentage of total)
- Virtual memory swapping activity (how often this occurs)
- Read/write activity to each disk drive (how much data is transferred per unit of time)
- Usage of various database memory areas (when more is needed to keep up the speed of your application)
- Contention for database resources (how often users have to wait until another user frees up resources)

In Chapter 26, "Monitoring Important Database Statistics," you learn about monitoring these resources in more detail. You'll find a series of SQL queries that you can use to look inside the database to see what is going on. What do I mean by looking inside the database? The Oracle RDBMS stores its statistics in a series of internal counters. To access this information, you issue queries to a series of DBA_ views. The purpose of Chapter 26 is to go over those queries and explain what each of the results means to you as a developer.

The operating system monitoring utilities are not standardized as in the Oracle RDBMS monitoring utilities. Instead, you have to become familiar with the tools provided with your operating system. This can be tricky. For example, some versions of UNIX have slightly internal configurations and the same result from a sar command (for example, the swapping activity function) might not have exactly the same meaning. This is where a good book on your particular operating system can come in handy. It would be nice to have a simple, single answer, but that would allow anyone to work as a computer expert and therefore lower our salaries.

When you are finished wading through the large number of operating system and database management system results to find the true indicators, you might find that you do not have enough information. For example, you know that the CPU is overloaded, but you do not know which of the many software modules installed on the host computer is causing the problem. You might find that the system is not overloaded, but the application is taking forever to respond to certain queries. These could be indications of lockups within your application that are tough to find during testing. The following are just some of the problems that you could run across:

- A table is locked for exclusive access by one user and the other user has to wait until that table is freed.
- Your application is running fine, but you have an SQL*Net version 1 process that has lost connection with its user and starts taking up massive amounts of CPU time.
- One of your supporting applications (for example, one that cleans out a processing queue table for your application) is running with a very low priority. When the system gets busy, your queue table fills up because the cleanup application is not getting enough CPU time, thereby slowing down your other applications.

The problem is that each application has a slightly different set of potential internal problems. Although the database management system can provide some basic help monitoring things, such as locks, when you are seeing application slowdowns, many of the other things that can go wrong are completely internal to the application. Therefore, you should look at your application to see whether it has processing queues or other functions for which you might want to build monitoring routines. Your goal during design is to put in the mechanisms that allow you to count important events. After that, you can build a few quick applications to get out the results in a nice format.

Monitoring

The focus of this section is how all these monitoring concepts fit into an overall maintenance plan. I see this as a third input into the changes and upgrades that you plan for your system. The first two are pretty straightforward. The first is the enhancement list that your users and management work out for the application. There might be a lot of politics and confusion to manage as part of this process, but in the end you wind up with a list of requirements that have to be added to your next version of the software. The second input to your maintenance plan is the list of bugs that are found by your users. You have to go through the traditional game of filtering out those bugs that are actually enhancements (I guess you can't blame them for trying). You also have to prioritize the list of bug fixes and enhancements and break them down into one or more release versions.

These first two processes are all that many organizations use to determine the work required for maintenance and upgrade of their applications. What bothers me about these two techniques is that they are reactive. Very few users would think of infrastructure upgrades or algorithm changes as part of their Christmas wish list of features. However, these are the things that the computer types have to worry about and factor into their plans. The trouble is that you have to argue for infrastructure upgrades and the time to complete them, which reduces the number of bug fixes and user enhancements that can be made.

To make sound arguments, you need some data. The problem is that applications face a variety of business cycles, and therefore, you have to collect data over a period of time in order to make sense of what it is telling you. For example, your loading curve might look something like Figure 27.4. This is generic so that it could represent CPU, memory, or even disk utilization. The key here is to understand what the trends are telling you.

If you were to take a single data point at point A, you might conclude that everything is going along well and that you can implement that major upgrade to the system. If you looked at only point B, you might conclude that it is already vastly overloaded and therefore you should drop everything and buy more computer power to get the system operational. When I look at this curve, I see a system that is subject to wide variations in load (for example, financial systems around the quarterly and annual closing times). It also seems to be growing in usage and for this reason merits close monitoring.

FIGURE 27.4.

Sample loading curve.

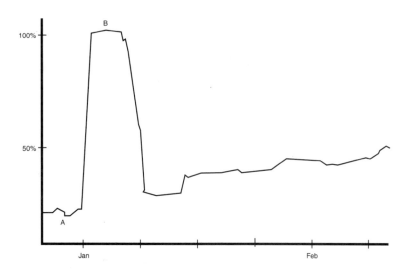

So what actions are available when you see a resource growing in usage to the point of over-load? A surprising number of computer types think that the only solution is to buy more of whatever resource you are running low on. Although it is true that computer hardware costs have fallen to the point where it is often more cost effective to purchase more hardware rather than expend expensive software talent, you should at least consider the alternatives before cutting the purchase order. Some of the things that you might consider include

- Purging old data.
- Verifying that you still need all of the processes that are running on your system.
- Verifying that your Oracle database has neither too much nor too little in the way of tunable resources. There is no way to detect that you have too much of a resource, such as one of the Oracle shared-memory areas, other than to reduce them and see if your system is still functioning well.
- Verifying that your applications are efficient. For example, have you tried alternative algorithms or performed a code review where other programmers can look at the various sections of code to see if they can come up with alternative solutions?

Before you move on, be particularly aware of the need to measure the data over time. You can see from Figure 27.4 that time variations can mean a significant difference when measured over days or months. However, there are also smaller variations in usage over time that you might want to note. For example, one of the classic patterns relates to electronic mail systems. You might have a very reasonable daily average load for your system. However, your response time might be horrible first thing in the morning, just after lunch, and right before everyone goes home. You have done nothing to change your tuning, and you are not running any special jobs during that period. What you are seeing is a natural daily pattern of how people use electronic mail—check for messages when they get in and then get on with the day's work; check it after lunch and then right before going home. You might try shifting batch jobs or letting the users know about the slow periods so that some will start checking their mail at other times.

Remember the main thing about monitoring is the real end goal—adequate user response time. Even after you have a thick stack of graphs and charts on CPU utilization and Oracle SGA sizing growth, you might want to add a quick check, such as measuring how long it takes to log into your application and run a couple of the modules. This will take care of those internal application problems or show response problems that result from the combination of a number of operating system or database factors. Besides, this is how the end users actually will judge your application.

Auditing

Auditing is a concept similar to monitoring. Actually, people like me would probably lump auditing in with monitoring, but the rest of the computer industry separates it, so I do that here as well. Auditing started when computer system security started to become a real concern. One of the goals of most security systems is to document when certain sensitive files or other resources have been accessed so that you could at least *detect* problems if not *prevent* them. As security systems continued to improve, it was also important to capture events that were failures (such as several attempts to log in to a particular account with the wrong password).

Auditing has been broadened in the Oracle database world to include a fairly robust set of features that can be monitored. Among the things that you can capture are

- Actions normally restricted to the DBA (such as `create tablespace`)
- Actions related to adding, removing, or modifying database objects
- Actions changing the privileges associated with database objects (such as `grant select` privileges followed by a `revoke select`)
- Connections and disconnects from the database
- Execution of specific, stored procedures
- Access to specific database tables and views

You have two options as to where you store this auditing information. You can send it to an operating system text file or store the auditing information within the database. The advantage to the operating system text file is that you can move it further away from the database hackers that you are trying to catch. The advantage to the database audit trail tables is that you can write standard SQL reports to display the results and monitor activity.

Of course, you might use the auditing features for purposes other than security. Perhaps you want to monitor the number of connections over the course of the day or look for users who connect to the database and do not log out, even though they are not accessing data. You could work with your DBA (only the DBA has the permissions by default to control auditing) to activate monitoring for those specific events and to provide you with access to the audit data (a grant of select on the AUDIT_ACTIONS, ALL_DEF_AUDIT_OPTS, DBA_AUDIT_TRAIL, DBA_AUDIT_SESSSION, DBA_AUDIT_STATEMENT, DBA_AUDIT_OBJECT, and DBA_AUDIT_EXISTS views).

Using these facilities, you can get to key activities that you might want to monitor within your application, as I discussed in the previous section. For example, suppose you have a table called work_queue that is used to insert jobs for processing by a background process on the server. You could capture when jobs are inserted and who inserts them into this table by having someone (such as the DBA) issue the following command:

```
audit insert on work_queue;
```

Now, I realize that, as application developers, many of you will not be involved with auditing. You might not see exactly how this fits into your maintenance plan. However, it's important that you know that this tool is available. It lets you capture a record of how people are using your application and database. You can tell which statements have been executed against which tables, when people connect and disconnect. In short, you can store for future analysis a high level of detail of the activities of the database. You might not need this today, but keep it in mind when you are having nasty performance problems that you cannot track down. It could come in handy.

For those of you who like to be proactive, you also should consider an ongoing auditing plan. You have to be careful because you could generate a mountain of data that you do not have time to wade through. If you start out auditing only for general items, such as access to key tables and things such as connections, you should be able to keep this to a manageable level. You might even build a few mini applications that reduce this data into a nice format for your reference. As such, you will be able to look for common problems before they happen and also have data indicating what was going on when a problem came up (for example, 700 people logged in at the same time just before your server crashed). Anyway, as with all other tools, you have to play with it a little to get used to it and know how to use it properly.

Capacity Planning

I have talked all around the idea of capacity planning when discussing healthy databases, monitoring, and auditing. What I do in this section is discuss the ideas behind capacity planning and provide a few thoughts for you to consider when you are devising your plans for application maintenance. *Capacity planning* is the combination of the monitoring techniques discussed in this chapter with the application planning process to ensure that you have adequate resources to meet user and application demands.

In its simplest form, capacity planning is just writing down the numbers you get during your monitoring activities and taking a look at them every now and again to see if there are any trends or problems coming up. Of course, some places use fancy statistical packages and do a lot of work to produce multicolor charts. However much work you put into the process, the general ideas are the same; get enough data to make accurate judgments regarding your ability to provide adequate services to your users.

One of the areas that I often find lacking is the estimation of the impact of application upgrades on the production environment. You might have a lot of data as to how the demand is growing with new users or how it shrank after the latest upgrade, which optimized a major portion of the software. But what about the future? Figure 27.5 shows a graph that represents the demand for computer resources that might appear on your capacity planning charts.

FIGURE 27.5.

Sample capacity planning chart.

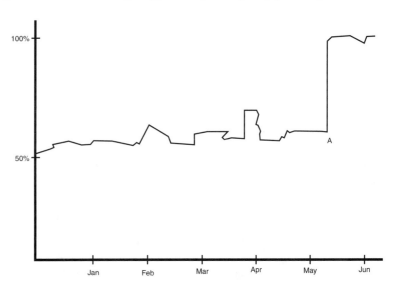

Everything seems fine up until the point labeled A. This could well represent a new release of the application that does a number of wonderful things for the users that they want. However, it also might overload your computer resources and cause massive performance problems. The trick is to know whether your application is going to impact performance before it goes into production. It is not a simple task, but consider these thoughts on the subject:

■ The first big problem is being able to simulate a measurable load on the system. For batch applications, you can queue up a number of jobs that provide a scale model of the production environment. You can then calculate the effects on production by factoring in the size differences between production and test. For online applications, you might want to schedule time when all your development team members sit at their terminals and simulate a simultaneous user load. It is not perfect, but it is better than nothing.

■ You could build a special load simulator program that sends a batch of responses that allows you to measure a fixed load. It would take some time to build but could help in environments where loading is a critical problem.

■ Know when it is worth measuring performance statistics. If your application is known to be insignificant in its load, you do not have to measure it.

Summary

This chapter took a very broad perspective on the topic of maintenance plans. I started out with some of the traditional topics such as building incremental release plans. However, I tried to broaden your horizons to include proactive maintenance planning techniques, such as monitoring, auditing, and capacity planning. You might not need to be proactive and spend a lot of time measuring loads for some applications. However, these techniques also can be applied to problem solving (such as auditing to see what is going on when a problem occurs), so they are worth having in your arsenal.

28

Enhancing an Existing Production System

by Gigi Wadley

Enhancing a production system can be a very difficult undertaking if a developer or development team makes hasty decisions. Therefore, planning becomes a very important tool in the success of the enhancement. The topics in this chapter focus on providing guidelines to help develop a comprehensive plan for enhancing a production system. Topics in this chapter include serviceability of code, approaches to adding enhancements, and testing requirements. The primary objective of this chapter is to give a developer or development team a starting point in developing a project life cycle plan. Even though the range of enhancements varies, planning for those changes should not be taken lightly and should always be considered. Therefore, the first step in making the enhancement go smoothly is to keep everything organized. This usually is driven by having standards in place for the serviceability of code.

Serviceability of Code

For code to be at the highest level of serviceability, it should be simple. Although it might be impressive to some developers to make code so difficult to understand that no one can maintain it, in a production environment, difficult code becomes the tormentor. No one will want to maintain or enhance the module, therefore leaving a weak area in the system. One proactive approach is to establish coding standards. Having standards in place leaves the challenges to creativity, not interpretation, when coding.

Standards

Standards cover a wide spectrum. They should be developed and implemented throughout the entire system and usually take a large amount of time for you or your team to determine what they should be. Standards usually focus around naming conventions, look and feel of applications, functionality, and building common routines. When creating standards, be sure to make them easy to understand and use. Standards should make a developer's job easier, not harder, and should promote serviceability. Naming conventions become a starting point for most standards.

Naming Conventions

Naming standards for physical files typically have some type of pattern to help identify the subsystem that the module belongs to, the module types, what the base table is, and a sequential position. For example, the table script for a customer table might be coded as `cst001a.sql`. The first two positions would indicate to which subsystem the module belongs. Here are some examples:

- ■ `cs` = Customer
- ■ `oe` = Order entry
- ■ `ff` = Fulfillment

The third position would indicate module type.

- f = Form
- t = Table
- r = Report

The fourth through sixth positions would be the associated table number, and the last position would indicate the sequence of modules in this unit. This type of naming standard can be used throughout the entire system. A level of serviceability is added when anyone on the development team can identify a module within the system. If naming conventions are not used, identification can become difficult because of various developers' ideas on what a file should be named.

Naming conventions also should be established for ease of identification within the module. The following list gives some ideas on what you should consider when developing internal naming conventions:

- Production table names should be distinguishable from validation table names. For example, a table script for the customer data table could be `custt.sql`, whereas the validation table would be `custv.sql`.

- Index names should be sequentially numbered in cases of multiple indexes.

- Synonym names should coincide with the table name. For example, the synonym for the customer table would be `customer`.

- Trigger names should include the action being taken. For example, if a trigger has been designed to fire when a record is inserted, `ins` should appear at the beginning of the trigger name. The following code demonstrates this style of naming convention.
  ```
  create trigger ins_time_stamp
  before insert on as_comm_customer
  for each row
  begin
    :new.insert_user := user;
    :new.insert_date := sysdate;
  end ins_time_stamp;
  ```

- Form names should follow the naming conventions established for filenames.

- Block naming within an Oracle form should be determined by the main function of the block and should be named appropriately. For example, a block that stores information about a customer should be named `customer` or `cust`.

- When establishing naming conventions for procedures or functions within an Oracle form, you have to consider the action being taken and parameters being passed into the process. Serviceability is enhanced when a developer can quickly identify what the procedure or function is doing. For example, if a procedure's purpose is to validate a customer, you could use the procedure name `validate_customer`. This type of naming convention can save a developer a great deal of time and effort.

Naming conventions also should be established for parameters being passed into programs, procedures, or functions. For example, in the following code, note how the customer's identification number is passed into the function by using the naming convention in_customer_num.

```
function  get_customer_name(in_customer_num number) return char is
            name char(32) := null;
            first char(40);
            last char(40);
      cursor c1 is select customer_first_name,
                     customer_last_name
                from customer
                where customer_num = in_customer_num;
         begin
           open c1;
           fetch c1 into first, last;
           if (c1%NOTFOUND) then
             name := 'Invalid customer';
             close c1;
             return name;
           end if;
           close c1;
           if first is not null then
             name := substr(first¦¦' '¦¦last,1,32);
           else
             name := substr(last,1,32);
           end if;
           return name;
         end;
```

This naming convention will aide the developer in identifying external and internal variables to the procedure or function.

Determining return codes for error checking should be standardized. For example, if the developer wants to capture when an user aborted an application, a custom return code could be set and reported on.

Internal Documentation

Internal documenting standards become beneficial to a developer when enhancing a module. Internal documentation could include a variety of information. The following is a list of recommended topics to include in internal documentation:

- Description and purpose of the module.
- The developer's name and when the module was created.
- Who initiated the call to the module.
- What modules does it call in return.
- What input or inputs are expected of the module.
- What return codes could be returned and their meaning.
- What source code changes have occurred. The following modification log shows how internal documentation could be presented for source change tracking.

```
/**********************************************************************/
/*    SQL   Name   : labels.sql                                     */
/*                                                                  */
/*    Created      : 05/24/96   John Doe                            */
/*                                                                  */
/*    Description: Creates package labels for all completed orders  */
/*                 (shipments and cancellations) that included      */
/*                 photo products.                                  */
/*    Assumptions: * One label generated for the entire order       */
/*                                                                  */
/*    Parameters : None                                             */
/*                                                                  */
/*    Output       : Name                                           */
/*                   Company                                        */
/*                   Address 1 and 2                                */
/*                   City, State Zip-Zip4                           */
/*      Sorted    : Zipcode                                         */
/**********************************************************************/
```

NOTE

Other module types, such as report and PL/SQL scripts, can very easily use the same naming standards.

The structure of code is another area that can provide enhanced serviceability.

Coding Standards

Establishing coding standards is a good start toward providing serviceability, but one of the simplest rules in coding is to keep functions and procedures to having one purpose and being readable. Both concepts help in debugging applications. In the following example, the function satisfies the "one purpose" rule because it receives a customer number, builds the customer name, and then returns it. It has only one purpose and that is to find and construct the customer's name. Readability is provided by utilizing indentations to align specific areas of code, such as conditional, iterative, and looping statements.

```
function  get_customer_name(in_customer_num number) return char is
            name char(32) := null;
            first char(40);
            last char(40);
    cursor c1 is select customer_first_name,
                        customer_last_name
                from customer
                where customer_num = in_customer_num;
        begin
          open c1;
          fetch c1 into first, last;
          if (c1%NOTFOUND) then
            name := 'Invalid customer';
            close c1;
            return name;
          end if;
```

```
           close c1;
           if first is not null then
             name := substr(first||' '||last,1,32);
           else
             name := substr(last,1,32);
           end if;
           return name;
         end;
```

Another structure standard that enhances serviceability is to have one entry and exit point in a procedure or function. This eliminates inadvertently branching into other lines of code. Although standards provide a beginning level of serviceability, the true challenge comes in the reusability of code.

Creating Reusable Code

Being able to create pieces of code that can be used in several applications is the ultimate goal of serviceability. This approach allows the developer to make changes in code in only one place, yet affect many applications. This level of planning provides consistency throughout the entire system. There are several means of achieving the reusability of code.

One of the most efficient means is to establish a library of common routines that can be used by several applications. Third-language programs utilize libraries, just as Oracle Forms 4.5 does. These libraries consist of generic routines that commonly are used in a production environment. But if these libraries do not exist, another approach to serviceability is to make the routines within the application generic enough to be used by different portions of the application module. In either case, the key word is *generic*. The desired level of serviceability is to make the procedure or function independent of any outside information. The following example is a check digit routine that is independent of any application. This shows how a PL/SQL function takes in a value, processes it, and returns a specific value while remaining independent of the application.

```
function check_digit (in_image_num char) return number is
      x_image_num_len number := 0;
      x_image_num          char(10);
      x_counter               number := 1;
      temp                       number := 0;
      tw                           number := 0;
      rtw                          number := 0;
      ckd                          number := 0;
      ckd_char                char(3);
      x_ckd_orig              char(3);
      x_return                    number := 0;
   begin
      x_image_num_len := length(in_image_num);
      x_ckd_orig        := substr(in_image_num,x_image_num_len,1);
      x_image_num       := substr(in_image_num,1,x_image_num_len - 1);
      x_image_num_len := length(x_image_num);
      x_image_num       := substr(x_image_num,2,x_image_num_len);
```

```
      x_image_num_len := length(x_image_num);
      while (x_counter < x_image_num_len + 1) loop
        temp       := to_number(substr(x_image_num,x_counter,1));
        tw         := tw + (temp * 2);
        x_counter  := x_counter + 1;
      end loop;
      rtw := mod(tw,11);
      if (rtw = 0) then
        rtw := 11;
      end if;
      ckd := 11 - rtw;
      if (ckd = 0) then
        ckd := 5;
      end if;
      ckd_char := to_char(ckd);
      if (ckd_char != x_ckd_orig) then
        x_return := 1;
      else
        x_return := 0;
      end if;
      return(x_return);
    end;
```

Increasing serviceability by following standards and creating code that can be used by several applications creates an atmosphere conducive to enhancing a production system. Taking the right approach becomes important to be successful.

Proper Approaches to Adding Enhancements

There are many different approaches to enhancing a production system. This section of the chapter discusses what should be included in whatever approach you select. The backbone of being successful in enhancing a production system is careful planning.

Controls are necessary because they provide assurance that standards of completeness and accuracy are enforced for each individual record or group of business transactions. Therefore, quality assurance in a production system highly depends on controls. There are a wide range of controls that can be built into any system. The following are some of the more notable controls that should be addressed during any enhancements:

- System and data security
- Input/output control
- Processing dependencies
- Design and source code control
- User training and documentation

Each area is of equal importance; therefore, attention should be given to all portions to ensure the success of the enhancement.

To properly enhance a production system, a development team should treat the enhancement as a new project to ensure that controls are implemented. Typically, major enhancements go through the project life cycle. The cycle's phases are as follows:

1. Analysis
2. Design
3. Development
4. Implementation
5. Testing

Going through this cycle will ensure data integrity, adherence to standards, and completeness. Understanding what is required from the enhancement and how it impacts the system are important in the first phase.

Analysis

Typically, a developer's involvement in the analysis phase is limited, but that's not true in every case. The analysis phase of enhancing a production system is to evaluate whether the enhancement is feasible. If the analyst does a poor job of determining whether the enhancement will work in the production system, the end result will be failure. Another area that could cause problems if not planned well is the scope and timeline for the project. The analyst should pay close attention to limiting the scope of the project and setting realistic timelines for completion. Therefore, during the analysis phase, include anyone who might be able to contribute to the success of the enhancement. This includes many meetings and discussions on the needs of the enhancement. After everyone has agreed on the scope of the enhancement, review what has been agreed upon and have the user or users sign the agreement. This helps the development team keep the project in a manageable unit. Also, don't be afraid to narrow the scope of the project and possibly break it into several parts.

> **NOTE**
>
> It is much more important to have several small successful enhancements than to try for a large enhancement and have it fail.

After the scope has been determined, the analyst should then provide the development team with the enhancement requirements. This document should outline specifically what is expected of the new enhancement. The more information that the development team has, the easier the next phase of the project life cycle will be. So before starting into the design phase, make sure everyone on the development team understands the requirements document and that any questions have been answered.

Design

This phase is where success is built. Experience has shown that if an enhancement has a solid design, coding, implementation, and maintenance become effortless phases.

> **NOTE**
>
> Do not confuse fixing a bug with an enhancement. Remember, a bug is associated with a subsystem that already has a design; however, an enhancement is something new.

A developer should insist on including the following topics in the design, no matter how insignificant the enhancement may seem. A basic design has the following sections:

- Data flow diagrams
- Entity relationship diagrams
- Database issues
- Input
- Output

The first place that a development team should start is understanding how data flows through the system, how the data relates to each other, and how the enhancement will affect the system. To graphically represent how data flows through a system and how it relates to each other, developers should consider creating data flow diagrams and entity relationship diagrams, which are the next two topics.

Data Flow Diagrams

It is very important for a developer to understand how data is flowing through a production system so that enhancements can be made successfully. Data flow diagrams (DFD) are the primary tool in assisting in this understanding. Typically, you can use CASE tools, such as Oracle's Designer 2000, to visually incorporate the enhancement into the production system. Production enhancements can involve creating and modifying existing tables; therefore, most CASE tools offer the capability to dynamically build and modify data flow diagrams, table definitions, and table scripts. What the developer is looking for from these diagrams, however, is what effect the enhancement will have on data as it goes through the processes. DFDs also provide information to the developer on what tables will be queried on or written to. Figure 28.1 is an example of a simple DFD diagram for an order fulfillment system.

Reading a DFD is fairly simple. The circles represent processes that the data will encounter. For example, validating a customer would occur in process one (P1). If a process is too complicated, it might be divided into smaller units or levels, such as enter order processing (P2).

FIGURE 28.1.

A data flow diagram for an application.

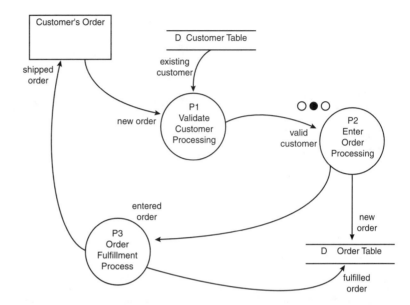

NOTE

Depending on which CASE tool is used, if a process has children, it might have some type of indicator, such as the three small circles above process P2.

Remember that inputs into a child process must match the inputs into the parent diagram, and the same applies to outputs. The arrows demonstrate the direction that the data travels and the type of data it is carrying. After establishing how the data is going to flow through the system, the developer should understand the relationship between the different types of data structures.

Entity Relationship Diagrams

The entity relationship diagram (ERD) provides information on the type of relationship, if any, that the tables have to one another. It might be possible to define the primary keys depending on which CASE tool is being used. Figure 28.2 is an example of a simple ERD, which shows how the tables in the DFD diagram in Figure 28.1 would relate to each other.

FIGURE 28.2.

An entity relationship diagram (ERD) for an application.

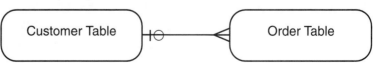

This ERD is a very simple one, but it has all the components that the developer needs to understand. To read these diagrams, start with the table in question and follow the line to the associated table. The type of symbol that connects to the other table indicates the relationship. For example, to determine how the customer table is associated with the order table, the developer would evaluate the line connecting to the order table. This connection displays a "crows feet" connection, which indicates that the customer can have many orders. However, the connection from the order table to the customer table is a "one and only one" connection, indicating that the order can have only one customer. This type of information aids in data integrity issues. After creating the DFD and ERD, the next step is to establish all of the database issues that are presented by the new enhancement.

Database Issues

Determining all the issues that affect the database is an essential part of a successful enhancement. A developer needs to be aware of all changes that might occur in order to ensure that both existing and new code will work properly. This section of the design should include the following items:

- New tables
- Modified tables
- Database triggers
- Database constraints

Providing a design on new tables furnishes the developer with information on how the data will be stored. The design should include information such as datatype, which columns are indexed, the primary keys, foreign keys, required or optional columns, and anything else that would be beneficial to a developer. Table 28.1 is an example of how a new table layout might look.

Table 28.1. Oracle table layout.

Column Name	Description	Type	Len	Req	Indexed
IMAGE_NUM	Unique number	VARCHAR2	8	Y	Y
image_text1	Manufacturing instructions	VARCHAR2	60	N	N
image_text2	Manufacturing instructions	VARCHAR2	60	N	N
image_text3	Manufacturing instructions	VARCHAR2	60	N	N
image_text4	Manufacturing instructions	VARCHAR2	60	N	N
image_product_num	Product number	VARCHAR2	10	Y	N
image_status	Status of image	VARCHAR2	1	Y	N
image_ret	Has photo been returned?	VARCHAR2	1	Y	N

continues

Table 28.1. continued

Column Name	Description	Type	Len	Req	Indexed
insert_date	Date the image was inserted	DATE		Y	N
insert_user	Who inserted the record	VARCHAR2	8	Y	N
update_date	Date the image was updated	DATE		Y	N
update_user	Who updated the record	VARCHAR2	8	Y	N

Along with providing table structure, the design should include any constraints or database triggers that may need to be placed on each table. Both types of controls help provide service-ability within the application. For example, if a column in a table can store only a Y or N, a constraint can be placed on the table to allow only these values to be inserted into the column. Constraints also are valuable in maintaining data integrity. For example, if a record cannot be deleted without deleting associated records, a constraint ensures this action. Additionally, database triggers allow the developer to force some of the processing onto the database instead of the application. This type of process is very attractive because it is application-independent and fires only when a specific action is taking place on the table. Database triggers ensure data consistency. The design should include any database triggers so that the developer will not include this type of processing into his or her application. Remember that you do not want to duplicate code. The following code shows how to set up a database trigger to date stamp a record and store who changed the record.

```
create trigger upd_time_stamp
before update on customer
for each row
begin
  :new.update_user := user;
  :new.update_date := sysdate;
end upd_time_stamp;
```

All this information will prove to be invaluable when you are debugging applications or creating a table. Modifying a table should be documented similarly to creating a new table; however, including the additional column in the table will be necessary. Designing for inputs will be the next topic discussed.

Input

Being able to control the functionality of a user interface can be difficult if the design is not specific in nature. This discussion focuses on an Oracle Forms 4.5 module as input. Developers should receive the following information about a forms module they are developing:

- The name of the form
- The filename of the form

■ The purpose of the form
■ The version of SQL*Forms in which the module is being developed
■ Any general requirements
■ Detailed requirements
■ A logic flow chart
■ Screen layout
■ Field specifications
■ Cursor movement

Providing a developer with this level of information ensures that few assumptions are made and that accurate data will be available for reporting purposes. The document illustrated in Figure 28.3 shows the level of detail that should be forwarded to a developer.

Output

The design of your output is essential because business decisions are typically made using the information provided in reports. You should create program specifications for reports, just as you do for form development. Figure 28.4 shows an example of program specifications for a report.

After designing the major components of the enhancement, you should give some thought to areas such as the security of the application and data, source control, file control, programming reviews, and user acceptance.

Security

Security controls range from possession of data resources to facilities security. Facilities security is a specialized area that usually is controlled by a system administrator, but it should be included in designing any enhancement. Allowing access to data resources is accomplished through roles and privileges and usually is controlled by the database administrator. For more information on this topic refer to Chapter 15, "Security in an Oracle Environment." It is important to include what type of access the user will have to the enhancement.

Source Control

In order to be successful at enhancing a production system, you need to have in place a plan to revert to the previous version of the software and yet still be able to promote a newer version. This process can incorporate custom-developed software or third-party software. No matter what the choice of plan, the main objective is to keep older versions of code available to the developer while promoting the new version. The capability to revert back to the previous version of software is your only safety net.

Name: **Image Scanning Form**
Filename: `asci220a.fmb`
Purpose: This PC-based application will be used on the scan stations to access Oracle and assign unique tracking numbers to
                    each image that is scanned. The form should be designed to minimize user intervention as much as possible.
Type: Oracle Forms 4.5
Tables: IMAGE

General Requirements
Follow any established development standards.

Detailed Requirements
The following are the detailed requirements for this module:

- Create a user interface to activate the scanning software, store the file, and automatically retrieve it into a graphics
  design application.
- The image tracking number should be constructed in the following way:
  - First digit assigned according to the `scan_station` number.
  - The second to seventh digits are a unique sequence number.
  - The eighth digit will be a check digit calculated by application.
- Four buttons must be created; these four buttons have
  six different functions based on the systems status.

Clear	Clears the form
Query	Sets the form in enter query mode
Execute Query	Executes the query
Print Labels	Commits the image information and prints labels
Acquire Image	Activates the interface to photoshop application
Exit	Asks about saving upon exiting

Logic Flow Chart
The following illustration is an example of a logic flow diagram for a photo processing application.

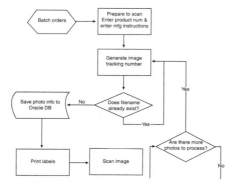

Screen Layout
Here is an example of how the screen should be laid out.

Field Specifications
Image Tracking Number

- Database name: `IMAGE.image_num`
- Required
- Queryable
- System generated
- No triggers

Each field should be addressed in the same manner. Sections for form-level and block-level triggers also should be created.

FIGURE 28.3.

*Program specifications
for a Forms 4.5
module.*

Name:	**Label Report**
Filename:	`ascr216b.sql`
Purpose:	Produce package labels for all completed photo orders.
Type:	SQL script
Tables:	IMAGE
	IMAGE_SUBSET
	ORDER
	LINE
	CUSTOMER

General Requirements

Follow any established development standards.

Detailed Requirements

This module requires the following considerations:

- The only photos that might be returned are ones that are attached to orders that have been shipped.
- Only one label should be generated for the entire order.
- Sort by customer zip code

Clear	Clears the form
Query	Sets the form in enter query mode
Execute Query	Executes the query
Print Labels	Commits the image information and prints labels
Acquire Image	Activates the interface to photoshop application
Exit	Asks about saving upon exiting

Report Layout

The following illustration shows how the label should be formatted. You should use laser label stock that provides three labels across, and five labels down on each sheet. the following example shows the layout for a single label. Replicating the label to fill the sheet should be accomplished within the module's code

```
Company Name
Company Address, City, State ZIP


John Doe
Company XYZ
123 N. Somewhere Pl.
Nowhere, XX 12345-1234
```

FIGURE 28.4.

Program specifications
for a report.

File Control

Data files, in effect, are the tools and the means by which a company continues to operate.

There have been actual cases in which a loss of data files has led to business failures. Therefore, there should be no compromising in establishing and applying controls over the handling and use of data resources.

Physical controls are the responsibility of the computer operations group. These controls are typically governed by the database administrator and rarely are a concern for the analyst when enhancing a production system. But what *will* involve the analyst is developing the tables that reside in the datafiles.

Programming Reviews

Programming reviews are advisable from the standpoint that errors might be detected by someone who is not closely involved in the project. This process also should include ensuring that standards have been met, any logic errors have been detected, and the proper documentation has been completed. After all the development staff has agreed on the design, the user will need to approve the design.

User Acceptance

User acceptance is typically at a conceptual level, whereas programming reviews are at a technical level. This acceptance stage will focus on meeting the needs of the user. You don't need to cover detailed programming steps, but you do need to show the users how their needs will be met. After users have agreed that the design will meet their processing needs, program specifications can be handed to developers to start the development phase of the project life cycle.

Development

Developers should not deviate from the program specifications created during the design phase unless they detect an error. If an error is found, it should be discussed with the project manager and development team. Determining the severity of the error will drive how, when, and who should resolve it. It may be that the severity of the error is insignificant and will not cause processing problems; therefore, it can be scheduled to be corrected while others will require immediate attention. In either case, it should be documented. After all development has been completed and tested, the enhancement should be implemented. The implementation process could become the stumbling block if not given enough attention.

Implementation

Implementing the enhancement requires careful planning. The best scenario is to avoid interrupting production. Therefore, factors such as when to implement, how to implement, who should implement, what to implement, and what the recovery plan is should all be outlined so that everyone involved, from upper management to developers, is aware of what is going to happen.

Deciding when to implement an enhancement into production is dependent on the nature of the business. Most systems have a period of time where activity is slower than normal, and this would be the target time. It is advisable to set a specific time for the implementation, including how long the implementation will take and when it will occur.

How to implement the enhancement also depends on the production environment. Having code promotion scripts is one way to ensure that executables are put into production, while some development teams use third-party software to manage promotions. There are many means of accomplishing this, but it should still be outlined in the implementation plan.

One person, typically the project manager, should control implementation. This eliminates any confusion on who is performing the implementation or what source code is being implemented. Some implementation of enhancements is dependent on other subsystem enhancements. Therefore, having one person controlling the implementation allows for implementation exceptions.

Having a recovery plan is probably the most important part of the implementation plan. If for some reason the enhancement is not successful, being able to restore production becomes very critical. It is much better to have a plan in place and not use it than to cause a company money by not preparing.

After creating an implementation plan, the developer or development team should test it, just as they would test any application within the enhancement.

Testing

One of the most important steps in the project life cycle is testing. Often, the time devoted to this phase is encroached on by previous phases and therefore is hastened. If done correctly, writing a test plan can save an enormous amount of time.

A complete test plan should include testing each individual application, combining all units into a system/integration test, performing a user-acceptance test, and, finally, an implementation test. The test plan should be in a format that the testing team and the development staff easily understand and which covers all the requirements outlined during the analysis phase. You also need a consistent and easy-to-use method by which testers can provide information on errors to the development staff. The test plan also should take into consideration the naming conventions and standards that have been established. If the testers are not familiar with these conventions, they should receive a document of these conventions.

The following steps are involved in testing a production enhancement:

1. Unit testing
2. System testing
3. User-acceptance testing

Taking a top-down approach, the first step is unit testing. If developers want to ensure that the code they have written is flawless, they will spend considerable effort focusing on testing every line they have written during this phase. There are some general guidelines to accomplishing this task.

Unit Testing

Testing should be taken to the smallest level of the subsystem first. Therefore, unit testing becomes the first step of ensuring the success of enhancing a production system. Unit testing should focus on testing procedures and functions for efficiency, logic errors, and data integrity problems. The types of Oracle units that can alter production data typically are forms, third-language programs, or a PL/SQL package. Each unit type should be tested differently, based on its requirements, but the unit test plan should test every possible option that could occur in an application. The following topics in this section provide a starting point for building a unit test plan. The focus is on tuning SQL statements, user interface testing tools, unit test plans, and test data. Because each of the programming units uses SQL, SQL statements can create huge performance issues if they are not analyzed. Oracle has provided a tool that analyzes SQL statements in the form of an explain plan.

Explain Plans

Explain plans ensure developers that their queries are properly tuned and running efficiently. This type of tool becomes very important when time means money. If a business decision is being based on a report that takes 4–5 hours to run, for example, money is being lost because information is not provided in a timely manner. By *explaining* a SQL statement, modifications can be made to better utilize indexes and decrease the runtime of any SQL-based module. Explain plans show the developer how Oracle executes a SELECT, INSERT, UPDATE, or DELETE statement. It also determines which indexes the Optimizer chooses to use and in what order the statement will be processed. The next topics show how to create explain plans, how to read them, and how to manipulate the SQL statements.

The Oracle RDBMS uses the explain plan by storing information about how SQL statements are executed in a table. The table must exist before an explain plan can work.

> **NOTE**
>
> Where the explain plan table is created depends on who is creating it. For example, :scott.plan_table would belong to the user scott/tiger.

The table name is :[user].plan_table and stores the following information:

■ Operation

■ Options

■ Object name
■ ID
■ Parent ID
■ Position

Oracle has provided a script to create this table. It can be found in $ORACLE_HOME/rdbms/admin/ utlxplan.sql. After you create the table, you can generate an explain plan by including the command to perform an explain plan. The following code shows this inclusion:

```
explain plan
set statement_id = 'query'
for
select a.prodid,
        a.qty,
        b.descrip,
        c.stdprice
  from item a,
        product b,
        price c
where a.prodid = b.prodid
    and b.prodid = c.prodid
/
```

The SET STATEMENT in the code makes the table entry unique; it can be any string up to 30 characters. The STATEMENT_ID uniquely identifies the data in the PLAN_TABLE. Running the SQL statement loads information into the PLAN_TABLE, which can then easily be queried back for interpretation. You can use several ways to retrieve the data. The first, more simplistic approach is a regular query. The following code is an example:

```
select operation,
        options,
        object_name,
        id,
        parent_id,
        position
  from plan_table;
```

The results from this query would appear as follows:

operation	options	object_name	id	parent_id	position
Merge	Join		1	0	1
Sort	Join		2	1	1
Nested Loops			3	2	1
Table Access	Full	Price	3	3	1
Table Access	By ROWID	Product	4	3	1

The more common means of retrieving data is the following SELECT statement:

```
select lpad(' ',2*level) ||operation|| ' '||options|| '
```

```
      ||object_name  query_plan
  from plan_table where statement_id = '&&1'
  connect by prior id = parent_id and statement_id='&1'
  start with id = 1;
```

When this statement is executed, it prompts the user for the STATEMENT_ID. The results of this select should resemble the following:

```
query_plan

merge join
    sort  join
      nested loops
        table access  full  price
        table access  by rowid  product
          index  unique scan  product_primary_key
      sort  join
        table access  full  item
```

The innermost level within each branch is evaluated first. The table from which Oracle retrieves the first value (*driving table*) is the most deeply nested table accessed, and when more than one operation occurs at the same level, the order of execution is from top to bottom. Because there is a "full table" scan indicated on the table price, it becomes the driving table.

When interpreting the explain plan, it is important to remember that the explain plan is based on operation/option combinations. The *operation* portion of the combination indicates what action was being performed; the *option* portion shows the type of action that occurred to achieve the operation. For example, if a query was being performed on a table without using any indexed columns, the explain plan table would show TABLE ACCESS/FULL. It would be nearly impossible to interpret all the combinations, but the following table shows the most common combinations.

Operation/Option	*Description*
Filter	Restrictions were placed on retrieved rows by using the WHERE clause.
For update	Row locks where placed on retrieved rows.
Index/range scan	Information was retrieved by a non-unique index. Typically, using the BETWEEN operator will result in this operation/option combination.
Index/unique	Information has been retrieved by using a unique index.
Merge join	Two sets of fetched records are combined into a single list. This is typically used on multiple-table queries.
Sort/full	A full table scan has been done.
Sort/group by	A sort has been done per GROUP BY clause.
Sort/join	A sort has been done on two sets of records and then joined.
Sort/order by	Rows have been sorted to satisfy the ORDER BY clause.

Operation/Option	Description
Sort/unique	A sort has been done and duplicate rows have been eliminated.
Table access/full	A full database scan has been performed.
Table access/rowid	Records have been returned using a unique ROWID.
View	Records have been returned from a temporary view.

In some cases, the Oracle Optimizer does not use an index properly. There are methods of forcing indexes to be utilized. In the following code example, the TO_CHAR function has been used on the product.prodid column to invalidate the index attached to it; this forces the optimizer to use an alternative index. Remember, Oracle doesn't always know what is best. Therefore, when using this type of manipulation, the developer needs to be able to interpret the explain plan very well. The following example demonstrates how you would force an index so that it will not be used.

```
. explain plan
set statement_id = 'query'
for
select a.prodid,
        a.qty,
        b.descrip,
        c.stdprice
  from item a,
        product b,
        price c
where a.prodid = b.prodid
   and b.prodid = to_char(c.prodid)
/
```

It is always wise when manipulating indexes to re-explain the SQL statement to ensure that the Optimizer is going to interpret the statement in the same manner.

> **NOTE**
>
> Indexes become nullified when IS NULL is used in the WHERE clause, when a column in the WHERE clause is modified by using a function such as TO_CHAR on a character column, or when a numeric column is multiplied by 1.

Because most Oracle applications are based on SQL statements, it is important for you to ensure that any new SQL statements are as efficient as possible. It is a step in development and unit testing that can save hours of searching for performance problems. Performance problems can be seen easily in user interface units such as Oracle Forms 4.5. Testing Forms 4.5 can be very time-consuming, but Oracle has provided some assistance in the Performance Event Collection System.

Forms: Performance Event Collection System

Testing Oracle Forms 4.5 is slightly more difficult than most applications because of the unlimited number of objects that require testing. Sometimes, not even the best test plans can ensure thorough testing, but Oracle's Performance Event Collection System (PECS) may help. PECS is an add-on to the old-trace and TKPROF utilities. It has significantly improved the way statistical information is collected and presented to the developer.

The PECS system consists of three main parts: PECS built-ins, PECS assistant, and the PECS reports. The PECS built-ins are used to gather information about the application. This information consists of measuring resource usage (CPU time per event) of Oracle forms or a specific event, locating performance problems, measuring object coverage, and measuring line-by-line coverage for PL/SQL triggers and procedures. All this information is stored in a binary file that is loaded into several tables. For personal computer systems, the filename is the module name with a `.dat` extension and resides in the `c:\temp` directory.

The PECS assistant is a form that aids in managing the loading of the `.DAT` file into tables, querying the data, and reporting it. Then the PECS reports generate additional reports showing results of the testing. To clarify the discussion on PECS, a brief mention of some of the model is useful. Summarizing many runs into a group is referred to as an *experiment*. A *run* is one pass through the application from start to finish. A *class* is a group of related events. An *event* might be the firing of a specific trigger. Understanding the various parts of PECS is probably as confusing as getting it to run. The following paragraphs provide guidelines to getting PECS to run properly.

Oracle has provided a script to set up the tables and synonyms needed for PECS. This script is located under the ORACLE_HOME directory in FORMS45/PECS. The script name is PECSBILD.SQL.

NOTE

The PECS_SUMMARY and PECS_DATA tables have numeric fields whose precision is not large enough to store results from the running of the summarize script. To avoid this problem, modify the columns in the PECS_SUMMARY table. They are initially set at 9,4; increase them to 11,4.

To gather statistics on forms, follow these steps:

1. Save the form to the database.

NOTE

If you are looking for line coverage, the form must be saved to the database, as well as saving it as a file. Remember that if any changes are made to the file, resave it to the database; otherwise, results will be wrong.

2. Generate the form; if you are looking for line coverage results, generate the form with the Debug option on.

3. Run the form. If you are looking only for statistic and object coverage information, set PECS = ON; if you are looking for statistic, object, and line coverage information, set PECS = FULL. This step creates a binary file that stores the statistics gathered. This file will be loaded into the database for analysis.

> **NOTE**
>
> To run the form from a command prompt, type the following:
> `f45run module=mymodule  debug=YES statistices=YES PECS=YES`

The PECS assistant easily manages the loading, querying, and reporting of the PECS data.

> **NOTE**
>
> The load portion of the assistant sometimes causes general protection fault locks. To avoid this, do not use underscores in the experiment name, do not use an experiment number for the first load, unload any captures, and do not open the .DAT file.

The first screen for the PECS utility is shown in Figure 28.5.

Loading the binary .DAT file into the PECS tables is as simple as pressing the Load button on the PECS assistant form. The load form will be displayed, and information about the experiment can be entered, as shown in Figure 28.6.

Enter the experiment name, filename, and connect string. Then decide what options should be selected. The options are as follows:

- Load PECS Data into the database—Select this only to summarize after loading multiple runs.

- Prepare for Line Coverage—Select this option only if a form has been generated with the Debug option on.

- Summarize data—Select this option to gain the averages for all the runs in the experiment.

- Delete details after summary—This should be selected only if you want the detail records to be destroyed.

After completing all the information in this screen, click the Start button. A Continue prompt will appear before each option: Load, Prepare, and Summarize.

FIGURE 28.5.

The first screen shown when using PECS.

FIGURE 28.6.

The screen used to load data into the PECS tables.

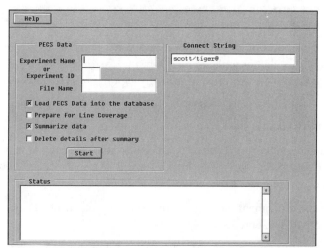

NOTE

If the Load, Prepare, and Summarize screens do not appear, it could be that other applications have taken up too much of the system's resources and these screens are unable to execute. Shut down some of the processes and try again.

When the screen in Figure 28.7 appears, the data has been successfully loaded, and reports can be generated from the tables.

FIGURE 28.7.
The PECS screen that shows a successful load.

Each time the form is run and performance data is collected, it can be saved and referred to as experiments in the PECS assistant form. This screen is shown in Figure 28.8 and displays the experiments and the runs that were executed.

FIGURE 28.8.
This screen shows experiment information and what runs were included.

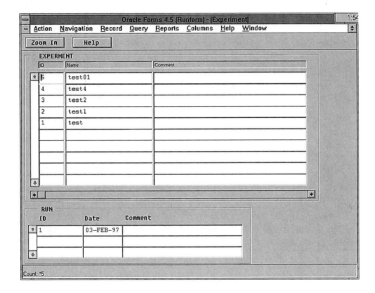

If you click the Zoom In button, the performance information is provided. This is where you can determine elapsed average time, CPU average, and the Sum Counter. All these variables are important in determining how proficient the form is from a system's resource point of view.

PECS offers a variety of analytical tools through the reports options. I recommend that you run each report and evaluate the results. You can derive a lot of helpful information from these reports, but they should not be the only means of testing an input module.

After determining that the form is running efficiently by using the PECS tool, you need to determine whether all the requirements have been satisfied as outlined in the design document. You should have a written test plan to ensure that all the requirements have been satisfied. The items in this test plan need to be specific in what the tester is to do and what reaction is expected from that action. Any deviation from the described result should be deemed a failure, and the tester should write up how to duplicate the error and what actually happened.

A test plan for a user interface should accomplish or consider the following issues:

- Test all required fields
- Test all fields in insert, query, and modify mode
- Test fields for datatypes
- Test field dependencies
- Test for record dependencies
- Test for data integrity
- Test navigation
- Standards

The following test plan shows one approach to unit testing for Oracle Forms 4.5.

```
    Testing Instructions     P/F
1   When the form is first brought up the buttons should be labeled as follows:
2   Starting cursor position should be in the product number field.
3   Enter a valid product and press enter or tab the cursor should advance to the
    first field in the manufacturing instructions. The field next to the product
    number should display the product description and the max images field should
    display a number greater than zero.
4   Enter an valid product number, then press the "Clear Form" button. The form
    should clear and the cursor should go to the product number field.
5   Enter an valid product number, then press the "Enter Query" button an alert box
    should appear which will state "The form must be cleared or finish processing
    the image before a query can be done." OK will need to be pressed in order for
    the user to continue. The cursor should return to the product number field.
6   Enter an valid product number,  then press the "Exit" button.  The form will
    clear and the user will exit.
```

It is wise for the developer to go through this plan and then have a codeveloper also go through the plan. This will help to catch anything that may have been overlooked.

In some applications, it is necessary for a developer to have access to data that is derived for every scenario that could be encountered. This type of data is test data. Test data can be beneficial when testing output from a production system. This will allow for a controlled environment to test conditional and iterative scenarios within the application. Typically, the test data is provided by the project manager so that the developer does not create data arbitrarily to fit the application. This approach ensures reporting accuracy.

After all the unit test plans have been completed and bugs have been corrected, the units must be integrated into the system. This type of planning requires a great deal of attention to detail.

System Testing

After all the units have been tested, the enhancement must be integrated into the production system. It is advisable to create a system test plan and run it through a testing environment first. The system test plan should cover the implementation plan, individual unit test plans, and then actual test cases that will use actual data. This level of testing should be done in a special environment.

Testing Environments

Generally, the best way to set up the testing environment is to have a scaled-down copy of your production environment. The environment should definitely be structured identically to production but with limited data. Most production shops have an Oracle instance dedicated to development, one for testing, and then the production instance. Ideally, a systems and database administrator ensures that the development and testing instances are similar to the production instance. Although development areas tend to become more corrupt as new ideas are experimented with, the testing instance should not be manipulated for experimental use, but for testing purposes only. The test instance is also an area in which volume testing should occur. The final effort before implementing the enhancement is to give the end-user the opportunity to approve the enhancement.

User Acceptance Testing

The user acceptance testing should be the final step of testing and be more conceptual then technical. This test should mirror what actually happens during production processes. The participants in this test include users who will actually be using the enhancement and interpreting the data derived from it. During this phase of testing, departmental procedures and training efforts can be finalized; typically, this is not a function of the development team, but it is wise to include it in the implementation plan.

Upon completion of the user acceptance test, users will make the final decision whether or not the enhancement meets their expectations. Remember that it is important not to let users change the scope of the enhancement. If there are areas they want changed, evaluate the change and determine if it is included in the requirements from which you have been working. Most likely, the change request can be targeted for a future enhancement. This keeps the focus on what was agreed to in previous phases.

Summary

There are many variables in the success of enhancing a production system. When a user's request for a system change is entertained, the analyst should evaluate the feasibility of the enhancement. Understanding what the user wants and if it can be incorporated into the production environment is a difficult job; only mission-critical requests should be considered. For this reason, the requirements document must be extremely detailed.

Translating the requirements document into a detailed design document gives you more of a technical view of the enhancement. As a designer, you are expected to translate what the analyst has requested into technical terms. This translation, giving consideration to serviceability issues, expedites the coding effort.

Bringing an enhancement to production under the time allotted is always an ideal situation to be in. To help achieve this, remember to include standards such as naming conventions and internal documentation. These two elements can greatly reduce the time required for enhancing and maintaining existing source code because they provide a communication tool. Another aide in the ease of enhancing a system is to keep all procedures/functions simple with one entry. This greatly simplifies debugging.

The testing phase of most enhancements gets reduced into a micro-minute; but this is actually the most important phase. Remember to be very detailed in this phase—testing each field, each cursor movement, your data, and so on. Prepare a well-defined plan on how, who, when, and what will be tested. Write this plan for unit, system, and user-acceptance testing. During system testing, be sure to provide test data in order to track how the enhancement is affecting the data. Also be sure to involve several different groups of people to ensure that all error possibilities have been explored. Spending substantial time in this phase can bring rewards in the end.

The actual enhancement implementation should also be subjected to a testing phase. Typically, promotion scripts are written to move source code and executables to their correct location for the production environment. To ensure that nothing has been forgotten, it is always advisable to test how you will implement your enhancement.

Enhancing a production system can vary in scope and complexity. If you pay attention to the details and document thoroughly, however, you will be successful.

29

Developing a Backup and Recovery Plan

by Ken Rogge

Assets of most corporations are usually quoted in terms of property, holdings, dollars, and cents. But the truth of the matter is that the very existence of any corporation is dependent on its most important asset: its data. Software development, operator services, customer service, and decision management are all irrelevant to the success of a business if critical corporate data is lost or grossly inaccurate. Management of any organization is dependent on reliable and accurate data stores, and how quickly you can recover that data to an accurate state in the event of data loss. The question will never be whether a backup and recovery plan is necessary. When data loss occurs, the question will always be whether backups of the data have been faithfully and methodically completed in a safe and timely manner. The second and equally important issue is whether the individuals charged with data management and stewardship have properly planned for an adequate recovery of its contents. This chapter focuses on the latter. Although entire books have been written on backup and recovery strategies, this chapter helps you review all the "must know" options that you need to address and research as you focus on building a complete backup and recovery plan.

What Is a Backup and Recovery Plan?

The backup and recovery plan itself is normally a document that is authored by advanced DBAs and system administrators at a given site. It serves as a reference as to how the people charged with data protection plan to keep the data at a given site readily accessible. The audience for the document can be management, other DBAs and/or SAs at the site, as well as the author of the plan itself. It can and will also serve as a continuity tool for the corporation when personnel turnover occurs in the data department. It is a vital part of any corporation's disaster recovery plan. The following represents a description of a backup and recovery plan as it relates to content. For the purposes of this chapter, I divide the plan into four primary parts, each with its own unique advantages.

Risk Management

This portion of the plan is designed to make the author of the plan (as well as the corporation) aware of the current risks that have a potentially damaging effect on the organization's data. The idea is that by identifying these risks, the organization can work to help eliminate many scenarios that can cause a data loss/recovery event. Any portion of the development or user environment that has the potential for data loss is a candidate for inclusion in this section. This portion of a backup and recovery plan also should provide suggested solutions for each type of risk it identifies. This chapter describes the normal review procedures for the risk management portion of your plan and suggests solutions if any of these risks apply at your site.

Runtime Strategies

After appropriately addressing risk potential, the DBA must decide what runtime strategy to implement for the corporate database. How the database is managed by the Oracle database engine at runtime has a large impact on available remedies in backup and recovery scenarios. This decision basically revolves around two distinctly different modes of operation that should be established early on in the creation of the database. The modes referred to are archivelog or nonarchivelog. Because each mode can dictate the possible backup strategies available to your site, these modes actually dictate the best possible state to which your database could be recovered in the event of a data loss occurrence. Both the advantages and disadvantages of archivelog and nonarchivelog modes are explained and discussed later in this chapter.

Backup Methodologies

Oracle7 backup strategies are many, and each has its own advantages and disadvantages. This part of the backup and recovery plan identifies which backup plan(s) the DBA has decided to implement, what types of failures the backup(s) are intended to resolve, potential backup types (what backup procedure(s) have been chosen and why), and how frequently and at what times backups actually will be run. This chapter runs through the various backup types and strategies available for Oracle and explains how each can protect your data.

Recovery Types

This part of your backup and recovery plan should explain what recovery types are available to you (your choices are pretty much tied to the type of backups you have implemented) and what recovery methodology should be used for each type of failure. This chapter reveals recovery strategies for several different data loss scenarios and should also aid you in your decisions depending on what backup strategy or strategies you want to employ.

Part I: Risk Management

Before documenting any backup and recovery plan, the individual(s) charged with managing and protecting the data must understand the most likely circumstances under which data can be lost at a particular site. Covering for the most likely data loss situations for a given site will help determine the frequency and type of backups and will give the most options for a timely and accurate recovery should a data loss event actually occur. Simply getting the database up and running again should be the *least* of the DBA's worries. Unless you are not doing any kind of backup at all (if that's the case, what are you doing in this business?), getting an Oracle database up and running should represent no significant problem, even for the least experienced administrator.

Your primary concern when planning for backup and recovery is the *state* to which you will be able to recover your database. The success of your backup and recovery plan will be measured by how closely a newly revived database resembles what management views as acceptable. As a result, significant effort must be put forth to acquire an understanding of what data recovery results would be acceptable to all concerned. It is equally imperative to understand that without knowing the different types of failures that are likely to occur, the aforementioned success measurement will be largely unknown until a data crisis arises. Obviously, the DBA needs to review the risks adequately enough to know immediately what to do in the event a particular risk comes to fruition. As a result, before we move into a variety of backup and recovery scenarios, you need to review some of the reasons for data loss or failure in the first place. By reducing your site's risk of potential data loss events, your level of success at your site will inevitably move upward.

Another reason for incorporating risk management procedures into your plan is simply that backup and recovery plans that neglect reduction of risk are prone to overuse. Your perceived success in the workplace, even if you are consistently able to return data to an acceptable state, will be diminished if you are forced to use recovery methods too frequently. All types of backups require some user inconvenience and production requirements. Recovery of almost all types halt user productivity altogether, while the DBA recovers and restarts the damaged database. Meanwhile, the company, which depends on those users for information that calculates to dollars and cents on the bottom line, waits. If a potential data loss that might cause risk goes on unaddressed or unidentified by the author(s) of the backup and recovery plan, the perceived success measurement will be largely diminished when the risk eventually identifies itself by producing data loss and a subsequent recovery scenario. The following represents some types of risks that are the most prevalent at any given site. Please take some time to prioritize which (if any) of the following risks are occurring or can occur at your place of business. This will help you decide which backup/recovery scenario (discussed later) best fits your corporation's risk exposure.

Information Gathering

The risk management portion of the backup and recovery plan requires a fair amount of information gathering (especially if you're new to your site), and also can be politically charged at larger corporations. However, your plan can easily include and successfully identify potential data loss risks by simply working *with* those people and having *them* suggest areas of possible improvement. Although later in this chapter I discuss a few items that you need to review for data risk management purposes, the personnel at your site might have some ideas of their *own* that might cause problems for your data. After they understand what you need and what you are looking for, it will be relatively easy for people in those areas to provide information that can prove to be helpful. No one knows a corporation's strengths and/or weaknesses better than the people who are employed there.

At any rate, taking the approach that you are working *with* the people in the suspect areas will greatly reduce the number of politically charged situations you have to face. It also will more often than not provide additional information that will enable you to proactively prevent data loss/recovery occurrences even further. Naturally, in smaller companies, the task is more difficult because some high risk areas are not covered by a department or group of people. In these situations, the only information you can gather regarding data risk will be what you can obtain yourself. Although this can be time-consuming, these efforts practically guarantee that you will prevent data loss/recovery occurrences at your site in the future. Of course, the more data loss/recovery scenarios that you can prevent, the more you will be sleeping at night rather than trudging your way back to the office to recover or restart your database.

The following sections describe a few basic risk management categories that need to be addressed as a part of the backup and recovery plan. Although the following list of categories is not meant to be all inclusive, it should give the author(s) of a backup and recovery plan sufficient basis from which to start a risk management assessment.

Natural Disasters/Climate/Electrical Power Supply

Simply put, this category within your plan covers all failures related to acts of God, as well as the more "human types" that are responsible for supplying climate and electrical power to your hardware. Anything that causes hardware or media to fail other than the hardware or media itself should be considered a risk in this category.

Some examples of risk indicators in this category are frequent and severe electrical storms, ice storms, earthquakes, floods, or regular power outages. "Frequent" in this context is defined as more than three of these events per year that have the *potential* to disrupt hardware operations. Depending on severity, however, even once per year might be sufficient to identify risk (for example, if you average only one earthquake a year but its severity regularly shuts down hardware or your site for extended lengths of time, you should assess your risk accordingly).

Some suggested solutions to the problems caused by natural disasters and unstable electrical power or climate supplies are listed in the next few sections.

Hardware/Data Replication

The most expensive and coordination-intensive option, this risk management decision requires researching any and all options for replicating data and machines *off-site*. If you feel your site is prone to any of the above-mentioned events and the data you've been entrusted with would cause significant operating damage to your company if made inaccessible for extended lengths of time, this option might be required. Every effort should be made to research the most economical means for replicating hardware and data stores at a site located in another location in your city, or possibly even another state. Business operations related to your database under this option could resume, therefore, even before the external problem to your current site has been corrected.

Uninterrupted Power Supply

Make sure that all power supplies to vital machinery are governed and protected with an uninterrupted power supply (UPS). This is probably the cheapest insurance you'll ever purchase for an unexpected power outage. Electrical power is so fragile that even the utility companies themselves never guarantee a continuous and consistent power feed to an electrical outlet. A UPS gives all concerned time to close down all data stores gracefully in the event of an extended power outage.

UPSs are not only helpful during power outages, but can also provide adequate power during a period of frequent and dangerous power surges and spikes. With a UPS, the DBA and other individuals charged with the protection of corporate data can simply unplug the UPS from the wall during large electrical disturbances and proceed with shutdown procedures in an orderly fashion.

Surge Protection

In the absence of an uninterrupted power supply, use power surge/spike protectors between electrical outlets and the hardware they serve. Although surge protectors represent an often futile attempt to avoid lightning spike damage, they are quite effective for "normal" surges and spikes, such as those caused by major electrical loads (such as large electric motors) and other "load hogs" residing on the same circuit.

Circuit Protection

It is best to insist that vital equipment have its own dedicated electrical circuit, especially in shops that include large electrical loads. The greatest culprits in this area are electrical motors that draw a lot of amps at startup, and then often cause a significant surge after startup has been completed. By requiring a dedicated circuit to the machines that manage the data, the DBA can provide further insurance that surges caused by large electrical loads will not have detrimental effects on the machines that house the data and therefore can cause data loss.

User-Oriented Risks

Users have and always will be given some ability to manipulate or delete data. Although many a DBA might find this rather sad, it's a fact of life, and we all might as well get used to it! After all, at the beginning of every data audit trail, there usually is a piece of paper and an individual charged with placing its contents correctly into the database. However, although errors are a part of being human, you can help a great deal in reducing your risk exposure by addressing the following user-oriented risk management items.

Delete/Insert/Update Limits

It is always best that any transactions that deal with deleting or updating large amounts of data have some limit placed on the number of them that can be done by any given user. If this is not possible, be sure that these transactions are covered by some kind of security level, as suggested in the next paragraph. The object here is to prevent a confused user from committing a large amount of errant and extremely damaging transactions without some kind of review point by another individual. After all, there is no difference between a large amount of errant transactions and an actual data loss event. Both require recovery procedures (most likely in emergency mode!) to be executed. Always be on the lookout for certain transactions from specific users or software packages within the corporation that seem to cause a disproportionate amount of data rollback or recovery procedures. If one of these "hot spots" is identified, it would behoove the DBA to request some guidelines limiting the number of transactions that a user can submit before a review is made of the entries themselves. You will probably find that certain transactions available to users are more prone to errors than others. Readily identify them in the risk management portion of your plan and suggest that some control measures be placed on them.

Security

Your plan should include a risk management section requiring that users receive different levels of access to data, proportionate to the sensitivity of certain types of data that can be updated or deleted. For instance, it makes no sense that an inexperienced user should get the same rights to sensitive data that an experienced user has. By having the most experienced or trained personnel entering or deleting data into sensitive data tables, the DBA is more certain that a data loss/recovery scenario will not develop. Although it is most often not the DBA's place or responsibility to formulate a security plan, user-oriented risks to your data must be addressed, and your plan should include recommendations regarding security in this area.

Developed Software Validation and Error Detection

Ensure that all the users' software incorporates appropriate data validation and error detection. A large number of user errors could then be detected and corrected before the transaction is even submitted. Without necessary software validation and error detection, it is entirely possible that a user could work an entire day or number of days entering inaccurate/errant transactions. Depending on the severity of the errors and sensitivity of the data, it is inevitable that the DBA would need to restore the database(s) to a given state or point in time. The fact is, an unbridled flurry of errant transactions can cause a recovery scenario every bit as involved as a media failure or hardware crash. Again, although it is usually not the responsibility of the DBA to actually develop the necessary software validations, it is very much within the domain of the DBA to require it. Other measures, such as standard use of DBA-reviewed and -accepted stored procedures for all delete, insert, update, and other transactions also can control the amount and severity of changes to a given database.

Audit Controls for Sensitive Data

Although they are rare, certain transactions granted to the user areas might be so sensitive and detrimental if submitted accidentally or errantly that the DBA might need to suggest an additional "sign-off" be required every time that transaction is requested for execution.

Data Recovery Verification Procedures (Users)

Although this point happens to be submitted last, it should certainly not be considered least important. The risk management portion of your plan should require that all users know and have documented instructions on what procedures must be followed after a data loss and recovery event has occurred. In almost all data loss/recovery scenarios, data can be recovered only to a certain point in time. Many transactions might have been entered after this point in time and left uncommitted to the database. After recovery and startup of a database, the best that the DBA can do is to inform management and the user area of what state the revived database is in (what data has been recovered and to what estimated point in time it was recovered). Because the DBA has no reference whatsoever as to what transactions were lost (other than from a point in time), the user area will need to decipher exactly what transactions were committed before the data loss event occurred, and what transactions need to be re-entered.

In summary, there are many data loss scenarios that even the best backup and recovery plans cannot completely cover. It is important that, after a recovery from a data loss event, the users have some documented procedures to help detect what transactions were recovered. Even more importantly, you need to have procedures that clearly point out to the user which transactions need to be resubmitted and committed to the database.

OS/Software Malfunctions

Even if your users provide consistently perfect transaction submissions, the operating system and developed software they use will often make up the difference!! As much as we all depend on flawless operating system performance, the fact is that there aren't any perfect OSs, and if a particular stream of processes hangs one up, your database is, by default, hung, and probably corrupted as well. Usually, a few interviews with users and QA personnel will reveal whether the configuration of the OS used by your organization has caused more than its share of problems. Unfortunately, these types of errors, although most of the time are easy to identify, the following sections represent one of very few items that might be addressed to resolve OS problems.

Review of OS configuration

With the advent of modern, sophisticated operating systems and OS overlays such as Windows 3.11, Windows 95, NT, and so on, the number of configurations and their effect on operations seems infinite. However, if OS-oriented errors occur frequently enough to have a detrimental impact on your database in regards to rollbacks and general maintenance, a review with an "expert" on your particular environment might be necessary. Usually, these reviews deal with the examination of how the OS is set up versus what the OS is being expected to accomplish. Some companies wade through years of data loss and recovery events, only to find that a simple switch or setting within an OS configuration file would have alleviated many, if not all, of the consistent problems they were having.

Examples of OS–related problems include consistent and fatal memory management errors, frequent software hang-ups requiring a cold boot and restart of the OS, or problems navigating between applications running simultaneously.

Review of Latest Version of OS

Without a doubt, many bugs that cause data loss events within an OS package can be alleviated by simply using the latest version of the product. Countless software and data problems occur by simply not taking advantage of the latest and greatest products of a given environment. If outdated OS problems consistently cause data loss/recovery events at your site, suggesting that the corporation review its OS upgrade policy is well within the scope of a DBA and the risk management section of a backup and recovery plan.

Developed Software Errors

Software bugs can easily corrupt or hang your database, especially if the bug resides within transaction creation or commit features built into the particular development tool or language being used. The following sections represent some ideas as to what can help protect your data against developed software errors.

Usage of Stored Procedures

DBAs can help shield their databases through the standard use and review of stored procedures. Stored procedures actually are a part of the database they manipulate, and they execute on the server on which the database resides. Stored procedures offer significant stability to the database they serve because they require data manipulations to be done exactly the same way each time. They also often represent tried-and-true procedures that all concerned are comfortable with. This is a significant improvement over allowing developers to write embedded SQL that accesses the database directly from the desktop. Different developers might access and update a database a myriad of different ways, some causing database problems, others not. This can necessitate significant troubleshooting effort while producing an inordinate amount of recovery events.

The DBA can ensure that the stored procedures behave correctly by writing, testing, and then limiting "write" access to all resulting routines. Although stored procedures offer predictable results for a DBA, most developers are unhappy with a database environment that completely excludes any "direct calls" to write to the database. As a result, decisions on stored procedure standards can range from requiring that *all* changes to a given database be made by calling and executing one of several approved stored procedures to allowing developers to write embedded SQL into their applications at will.

Use Latest Version of Software

As with operating system problems, many data-oriented software errors can be solved by simply requesting that the users be provided with the latest versions of any given software package.

Review Language and Tools Used by Developers

Another rarely noticed portion of a risk management assessment is whether or not the software developers are using the latest version of the development language or tools they have been charged to use. A flaw in the data transaction processing portion of a language can cause consistent data problems that are not only difficult to fix but difficult to trace. Simply asking whether an upgrade plan is in place for the primary development tool is sufficient. Again, the DBA's responsibility is not to actually "do" the needed improvement, but rather to identify how *not* doing them can cause an unnecessary data risk to the organization.

Hardware Errors or Failure

Sooner or later a hard drive, controller card, CPU, or memory chip will fail, causing your database to hang or shut down abnormally. Hardware stability is therefore an important item from which to ascertain risk as you move forward to create your backup and recovery plan. The following sections represent a few precautions that you can take to help minimize the problems that can be caused by hardware-oriented failures.

Disk Mirroring

RAID technology allows certain or all information to be mirrored on separate media, which allows prompt recovery in the event of a given device failure. There are some drawbacks to disk mirroring which will be discussed later.

On-Site Spare Parts

Simply having a small inventory of quality (new or nearly new) spare parts can be a big help in gaining access to data on a given piece of failed hardware. It is important that you have spare parts for all brands and types of hardware employed at your site. Depending on the type and nature of a given failure, spare parts for a given piece of hardware can take hours, even days, to locate. In the meantime, the data for which you are responsible and the company dependent on such data wait in limbo for someone to save them.

Replication Servers

A relatively new concept to the relational database world is the notion of creating an exact copy of a given database on separate media in *real time*. Oracle7 makes a good attempt at resolving some of the replication server issues through log file grouping. Although this sounds good, it is quite intensive administratively. Also representing a significant expense resulting at times in purchasing additional hardware, this option can produce an environment where you have near-zero downtime because log files become interchangeable.

Configuration

A DBA can set up each and every Oracle database a myriad of different ways. However, other than security complications, there are a few items that seem to cause problems for the DBA more often than any other. These items usually relate to how much disk space is allotted for a particular tablespace, how many database files are allotted per tablespace, and whether or not to incorporate manual or automatic archiving of a given database. All too often, user production is adversely affected by a too-stringent runtime framework. Mastering database configuration is based primarily on the amount of training and practice of the DBA. How to configure your database has a lot to do with how well you have been or are willing to be trained. Configuration and tuning of a database requires much outside information, followed closely by a lot of practice. Information reference resources, such as the one you're holding in your hand, are a great way to get the upper hand regarding configuration management and consequently how to avoid many potential data-loss events.

Part II: Oracle7 Runtime Strategy

Ha0ving considered all the risks mentioned in Part I in this chapter, the DBA also must look at the risks inherent at runtime. Runtime decisions dictate what risks a backup manages and what risks it doesn't. Of course, a company's data is only as good as its last backup. If that backup does not contain enough data to adequately bring business operations back up in an acceptable manner, the backup has failed. In short, what is being backed up is every bit as important as doing the backup itself. What is available for the backup is actually largely dictated at runtime. Although it might seem that there are an infinite number of configurations for a backup and recovery plan, most revolve around an initial decision that should be made before an Oracle database is even up and running. This decision is whether or not to run your Oracle database in archivelog or nonarchivelog mode. If the DBA inherits a database that someone else created and configured, the DBA can check to see which of the two modes the database is running in by using the Oracle Server Manager as follows:

```
SVRMGR>connect internal
Connected
SVRMGR>archive log list

Database Log mode            No Archive Mode
Automatic Archival           Disabled
Automatic Destination        $IT/DOESNT/MATTER/IM/DISABLED/ANYWAY
Oldest Online Log Sequence   234234
Current Log Sequence         234345
```

As you can see by the preceding lines, this particular instance is running in noarchivelog mode.

Both archivelog mode and noarchivelog mode have distinct advantages and disadvantages. To help you make your decision, I've included a summary of both modes and their importance to your backup and recovery plan in the next few paragraphs.

Archivelog Mode

An instance of an Oracle database running in archivelog mode automatically keeps log files (called *redo logs*) of any and all transactions that are committed to your database. The log file and database both contain sequences of numbers, otherwise known as System Commit Numbers (SCN), that allow Oracle to interpret, in the case of abnormal shutdown, what transactions need to be "rolled forward" from the log file into the database to make it accurate and current. For the purpose of clarification, a brief description of the two primary types of redo logs follows.

Online Redo Log Files

These files represent a current picture of what has happened to the relevant database via transactions submitted. They are used during recovery procedures to bring the database back up to speed after a data loss event occurs. Oracle uses the files to submit transactions to the database in the event that they were not committed prior to the failure that caused the recovery event to be executed.

Archived Redo Log Files

When operating in archivelog mode, online redo logs are either automatically or manually copied to separate disk media as they become full. As a result, archived redo log files represent a much more complete and historical image of database transactions. Archived redo logs can therefore be used to roll a damaged database back to a specific point in time or forward to recover everything lost up to the point of failure.

Obviously, no real advantage is wrought if both the database and its corresponding log files reside on the same media device. By putting the two files on separate disks, for example, if the disk on which the database resides crashes, the disk can be replaced followed by a restoration of the database from the last backup. Because the disk on which the redo logs has remained unaffected, Oracle would note the differences between the redo logs and the recovered database. The Oracle database engine can then "roll forward" the transactions found in the logs, bringing the database back to the state it was in just prior to the time of the crash.

You can enable the archivelog mode for a given database by using the Oracle Server Manager to mount the database instance and then applying the following statements:

```
SVRMGR>alter database archivelog;
Statement Processed
SVRMGR>alter database open;
Statement Processed
```

> **NOTE**
>
> The last statement opens the database in archivelog mode. Of course, this requires that you close the database prior to entering these lines.

Advantages

Because all transactions are kept in the redo log files, when you successfully complete recovery of a database file, the transactions that are missing from the recovered database can be "re-submitted" via the redo logs. After you commit these transactions, the database is brought back to the state it was in just prior to the data-loss occurrence.

You can perform backups while the database is up and running. These types of backups are known as *hot* backups. Because the online redo logs continue to be updated as the users work, the state of the database during backup is less of a factor. The log files will record anything that happens to the database between the time the database is backed up and the time the log files are backed up. Oracle can automatically update the database via the online and archived redo logs during crash recovery procedures.

In those instances where interdependent database files are being updated in different locations and on separate media, the redo log files for both locations could be used to roll forward both databases, allowing them to synchronize in a distributed fashion.

Disadvantages

When incorporating the archivelog mode, the DBA must ensure that there is sufficient disk space to hold the archive redo log files. The database will hang and might require abnormal shutdown if any write-oriented problems become apparent to the Oracle engine as it writes to log files. In this particular case, no work can be accomplished on the database until the DBA corrects the problem.

This option creates significantly more administration for the DBA. The log files and their database file counterparts must be kept in sync during and after backup. For example, a recovered database file that is actually newer than the recovered log file has very little use for the log file and a complete recovery is therefore impossible.

Backing up of archived log files also is an additional administrative burden for the DBA. Back-ups must be clearly marked, and as is the case at runtime, log files and their corresponding database files should be placed on separate backup media. This should ensure that the backed-up database *and* archive logs are not destroyed in case the backup media is defective or is destroyed. This also therefore requires the DBA to incorporate procedures that ensure that the online and archived redo logs, as well as the database to which they belong, are properly identified as belonging together.

Automatic Versus Manual Archivelog

You can configure Oracle to run in archivelog mode in two different ways, automatic archiving and manual archiving. The DBA can look to see how an existing Oracle instance is running by using the Oracle Server Manager and executing the following statements:

```
SVRADMIN>connect internal
Connected
SVRADMIN>archive log list

Database Log mode          Archive Mode
Automatic Archival         Enabled
Automatic Destination      $IT/admin/archlogs
Oldest Online Log Sequence 234234
Current Log Sequence       234345
```

Automatic Archiving

Automatic archiving basically means that as online redo logs become full, the Oracle engine will automatically archive the information contained in the last redo log, erase the contents of the current online redo log, and then proceed writing new information to the current log file. Because all this is done automatically, the DBA need not worry about monitoring the state of the current log files. However, the DBA must always ensure that adequate media space is available at the destination for the archivelog file. The database will hang and all accesses will be stalled if Oracle finds that there is no place to archive the current online redo logs.

Enabling Automatic Archivelog Mode

To force your database instance to open in automatic archivelog mode, you must enable this feature through modification of the INIT.ORA parameter file for that instance. Simply use any line editor you have available and set the LOG_ARCHIVE_START parameter within the file to True and you're set.

Manual archiving accomplishes the same thing as automatic archiving. The difference is that the DBA makes the call as to when and where the current online redo logs are archived. Therefore, it also is the responsibility of the DBA to configure the logs (size, number, and so forth) in such a way that manual management of archiving is feasible. As you can see, this option puts significantly more responsibility on the DBA because the database will hang and all accesses will stall if the DBA misses the queue and allows the online redo logs to fill to capacity without initiating the archive process.

Manual archiving is used primarily when a site has a very small and predictable transaction load. It also might be possible that archiving very large redo logs would require more planning than automatic archiving can provide, such as making sure that a suitable destination exists for the archive. As you can see, although manual archiving places more of a burden on the DBA, it also presents more control and options at the DBA's fingertips during runtime.

Enabling Manual Archivelog Mode

To force your database instance to open in manual archivelog mode, you must enable this feature through modification of the INIT.ORA parameter file for that instance. Simply use any line editor at your disposal and set the LOG_ARCHIVE_START in the file to False.

Noarchivelog Mode

The noarchivelog mode simply means that no logs are kept to allow a historical recovery of a given database. Although this might sound risky, there are actually several scenarios under which this mode works fine. For example, an extremely low-frequency, transaction-oriented database at a site where regular OS cold backups are regularly performed might be a candidate for the noarchivelog mode runtime option. If users can easily do the necessary "catch-up" required to resubmit all lost transactions within a specific period of time, the additional administration to manage log files within the archivelog framework might not be worth the company's (or the DBA's) time to execute.

You can force your database to operate in noarchivelog mode by using the Oracle Server Manager as follows:

```
SVRADMIN>alter database noarchivelog;
Statement Processed
SVRADMIN>alter database open;
Statement Processed
```

> **NOTE**
>
> The last statement opens the database in noarchivelog mode. Of course, this requires that you close the database prior to using any of the preceding commands.

Advantages of Noarchivelog Mode

The DBA doesn't need to obtain and manage extra disk space to serve as the destination for the archived log files.

Backups also are smaller and simpler to administer, because no "in-sync" implications relative to the log files, the control file, and the database exist. Because all connections need to be terminated and the database is shut down completely, continued transactions against the database are halted, and an image of the current state of the database is placed on backup media. The only thing to back up are the database and control file(s).

Disadvantages of Noarchivelog mode

Recovery can only be obtained from the point of the last backup. No logs can be used to roll forward log transactions that are newer than the database. By default, this requires that the user areas perform database status verification procedures to ascertain exactly at what point they must begin re-entering their transactions. The users must then bring the database to a current state by re-entering old transactions plus any backlog of work that piled up while they did so. The latter is what the DBA should take into account before making a decision to run the Oracle database in noarchivelog mode. In other words, the adequacy of experiencing data loss to the point of the last backup should be measured by how successfully users can catch up to the work demand (and the subsequent data entry lag) without damaging the operations of the corporation.

Only operating system or cold backups can be used when operating in noarchivelog mode. Both of these backups require that the database be shut down during their processing, which halts all data input until the backups are completed. This usually means that all backups must be done in a *batch mode* after hours or at times when the least amount of transaction submittals are occurring against a given database.

Part III: Backup Methodologies

As you probably guessed, a backup represents the one and only picture a DBA has of any *recovery* options. Obviously, recovery procedures will never be able to offer data other than what has been backed up. As a result, knowing what needs to be backed up becomes an imperative factor in any backup and recovery plan. Relative to Oracle, there are three types of files that must be backed up in any backup methodology. Missing any one of these three types of files not only might make your future recovery less effective, it might render it useless. The following paragraphs represent a brief explanation of each type of file that must be addressed in your backup plan.

Database Files

Database files are the heart and soul of what makes or breaks any RDBMS. They are actually the data that is contained within every tablespace. All data fields, tables, indexes, and relationships reside within a database file. Database files, because of all the information they contain, also are prone to corruptions of many kinds. Many different system and environmental culprits can cause these corruptions. More often than not, your database files will be the reason for implementing and executing a recovery event.

Control Files

Control files basically are flat files that contain imperative information the Oracle RDBMS engine needs to place data within the database. In fact, without a perfect and functional control file, Oracle will not even allow the opening of a given database. Although exactly what is contained in an Oracle control file is not made available to the general public, its "published" contents include the actual name of the database, the name of all tables in the database, what redo logs are to be used, and the latest sequence number Oracle needs to roll forward transactions on a recovered database. In other words, if you don't have a working control file, you don't have a working database.

Oracle provides several methods for ensuring that proper backups of the *control file* exist.

BACKUP TO TRACE **Command**

The BACKUP TO TRACE type of backup basically requests the Oracle database engine to generate a SQL script that will re-make the control file if necessary. Remember, this type of backup does not actually produce a copy of the control file. It simply produces a SQL script that contains all of the correct parameters for producing a *new* control file. You can then use this SQL script to alter the original control file or to help create a replacement for the corrupted one. The location of the resulting script is whatever you have set the USER_DUMP_DEST value to in the INIT.ORA file. You can execute a BACKUP TO TRACE command with the database up and running using the Oracle Server Manager as follows:

```
svrmgrl<<EOF
connect internal
connected
alter database backup control file to trace
statement processed
exit
EOF
```

After executing the preceding statement, the SQL script will be located on the media location prescribed by the USER_DUMP_DEST parameter in the INIT.ORA file. Because you can edit this SQL script file using any line editor, you can tweak and mold it however you need to. This is especially helpful in an event where global system space allocations have been exceeded, causing a complete rebuild of the control file.

Control File Replication

The Oracle RDBMS provides this type of backup through a simple request to write to two control files in real time. Simply name two locations for two control files, respectively. These names and locations are placed in the CONTROL_FILES parameter located in the INIT.ORA parameter file. For example, set this parameter (via a line editor) as follows:

```
control_files = (/put/control1/here/control.ctl, put/control2/here/control.ctl)
```

> **NOTE**
>
> It is important to remember that, because Oracle reads most of the INIT.ORA parameters only one time per startup of a given instance, you will need to shut down the instance and restart it in order to ensure that your modifications have taken effect.

Log Files

Log files are categorized into two types: online and offline. Offline log files, or *archive* logs, represent the only link the Oracle database engine has between a past instance of the DBA's database and the current or *online* log files. As a result, any chance of a complete database recovery is lost if either one of these types of log files is lost or not backed up.

Operating System

The simplest of all backups to implement is the backup facility that is packaged with your operating system as its own backup utility. This type of backup requires you to terminate all accesses to the database and completely shut it down. You can shut down an Oracle database instance in one of the following three ways.

SHUTDOWN (Normal Mode)

This particular SHUTDOWN command assumes that you have terminated all accesses to the database instance before you issued the SHUTDOWN command. In fact, if you haven't done so, it will wait until all users have actually ended their sessions. This can be somewhat dangerous if the DBA leaves the process overnight, only to find the next morning that a user had left the night before without logging out. Hence, nothing happened at all the night before—no shutdown and no backup. To shut down in normal mode, use the Oracle Server Manager as follows:

```
SVRMGR>connect internal
Connected
SVRMGR>shutdown
Database closed
Database dismounted
ORACLE instance shut down
```

SHUTDOWN IMMEDIATE

The SHUTDOWN IMMEDIATE command shuts down all of the accesses to the database, whether or not the users have logged out. Rollbacks are automatically done on all uncommitted transactions, and the database is shut down. This ensures that no background processing can destroy the DBA's OS or cold backup, but it might also terminate a critical process that happened to be running a long time. Before issuing the SHUTDOWN IMMEDIATE command, the DBA should ensure that the remaining connections are not busily sending large transactions to the database. Use a SHUTDOWN IMMEDIATE command as follows:

```
SVRMGR>connect internal

Connected

SVRMGR>shutdown immediate

Database closed
Database dismounted
ORACLE instance shut down
```

SHUTDOWN ABORT

The SHUTDOWN ABORT command should be used only after all other methods for freeing the database for backup have failed. The SHUTDOWN ABORT command does not roll back all pending transactions. It simply moves quickly to shut down the database instance without allowing any further background processing. Because of this, the database is left in somewhat of an unknown state. What transactions were "in the queue" before the database was abruptly terminated is largely unknown. This type of shutdown thus also brings what you are backing up into question; the conditions of the control files, log files, and data files are unknown. You should consider starting up the database again in "restricted mode" (to protect against any surprise connections), and then shut it down again in normal mode. When you restart the database (in restricted mode), the Oracle engine cleans up any loose ends through several maintenance procedures that are fired automatically in the background. This ensures that the control, log, and data files are all synchronized and behaving properly at the time of your backup. You can execute SHUTDOWN ABORT via the Oracle Server Manager as follows:

```
SVRMGR>connect internal

Connected

SVRMGR>shutdown abort

Database closed
Database dismounted
ORACLE instance shut down
```

To accomplish an OS backup, always use the normal mode shutdown unless all other attempts for ending connections have failed. However, if there are any doubts at all whether connections have been terminated, the DBA should use the SHUTDOWN IMMEDIATE or the SHUTDOWN ABORT/ RESTART/SHUTDOWN options before beginning the backup. The DBA can then proceed to back up all files on a given server, and then restart the database. Although some might argue that the entire server need not be backed up, discovering exactly which Oracle files need to be backed up can be somewhat tedious and error-prone. The best possible scenario at recovery time would be to include a few extra files in the final recovery result, rather than be a few short. At any rate, this type of backup usually includes all necessary files (discussed in this section) plus the entire Oracle database engine, including its executables, DLLs, and related files.

Advantages of an OS Backup

OS backups are extremely simple to incorporate. Most OS backups are completely automated and need only to be started (or scheduled) by the SA.

OS backups are usually tried and true and offer a well-tested backup, but most importantly, *recovery* also is quite stable and predictable.

Disadvantages of an OS Backup

All database access must be terminated, and the database must be shut down completely.

> **WARNING**
>
> *Never* attempt an OS backup while a database is up and running.

A huge amount of background processing takes place on almost all hot databases. Therefore, the chance that the control files, log files, and data files will all be synchronized during the entire length of time an OS backup takes to finish is near to, if not completely, zero.

Complete recovery is not possible with an OS backup. Recovery can only be completed to the time the last OS backup was executed. Users must therefore follow database verification procedures to find the point in time from which transactions must be re-entered into the database.

Cold Backup

This backup very closely resembles the operating system backup, but this method seeks to back up only the Oracle databases and all Oracle-associated files. As with the OS backup, all connections to the database must be terminated, and the database itself must be shut down. The backup is then begun for all database and log files (both online and archived) of Oracle's executables, configuration files, and control files. After the backup is completed, Oracle can then be restarted in normal mode.

Advantages of Cold Backup

Because cold backups also are accomplished through backup facilities supplied by your particular operating system, they are extremely simple to incorporate. Most cold backups can therefore be completely automated and need only to be started by the operator.

Cold backups use operating system facilities, which are usually well-tested and stable, and offer a well-tested backup and recovery option.

Disadvantages of Cold Backup

All database access must be terminated and the database must be shut down completely. Never attempt a cold backup while the database is up and running. As with straight OS backups, too much background processing is taking place to ensure that the control files, log files, and data files are synchronized for the entire duration of the backup. This, of course, requires that no work can be performed by users until after the backup has been completed and the database is brought back up.

Complete recovery is not possible with a cold backup. Recovery can be completed only to the point in time that the last OS backup was executed. Users must follow database verification procedures to find the point in time from which transactions must be re-entered into the database.

Hot Backup

This backup is the most convenient for users and operations in general, but it also is the most painful if it is not done properly. The database *must be running in archivelog mode*. It would be best if the hot backup was executed during a low-usage or off-peak time in order to lower the amount of redo, should recovery be required. From here you can do an online backup of the entire database and all tablespaces, online and archived log files, and finally a backup of the control file. Because the recovery event for this type of backup is extremely dependent on the online and archived log files, I recommend that the log file be backed up *last* in order to ensure that the latest possible transactions are included in the backup.

Export

This type of backup requests Oracle to simply unload the data contained within all or specific tablespaces within the Oracle database. The data actually is saved in binary format and can offer a variety of options during recovery (import). Online and current archive logs are not used in this type of backup and recovery. It is important to remember that an exported file contains only the data for a given database, and does not include any information relative to a historical transaction listing for the database (log files). As a result, the recovery (or import) side of this backup/recovery method requires the use of a newly created database or tablespace with an identical structure. The DBA can then import the information from the binary file created by the export into the new database. Because the affected database/tablespace is newly created, none of the log files related to the database being backed up are useful to the Oracle engine in any way.

One of the biggest advantages regarding the export backup is that it represents the only backup option that prevents corrupted, but unnoticed, tablespaces and/or blocks from being backed up also. For instance, because a complete export of a database requires a read on every field in every table within allocated tablespaces, a corrupted tablespace will cause the export to fail and give the appropriate error message. All other types of backup methods mentioned in this chapter back up the database regardless of present corruption problems and have no facility for advising the DBA that corrupted data is being backed up.

> **TIP**
>
> Executing an export backup on an entire database intermittently and at convenient intervals, regardless of your primary methodology, is a great idea from a data integrity standpoint. It ensures that your backups do not include corrupted tables within allocated tablespaces.

Backup Frequency and Automation

Backups should be performed at times and frequencies that provide the most benefit to a given organization. Unfortunately, these requirements almost always coincide with off-peak times, (especially if OS or cold backup methodologies are incorporated). In short, this means that the best time to back up is probably going to be about the same time everyone (including you) is either going or wants to go home. Setting up scripts or scheduling backup processing events for your environment will inevitably help alleviate the inconveniences of having to sit around and wait for a backup to occur. Writing scripts that are scheduled to run at off-peak hours are completely acceptable in any database environment. However, there are some pitfalls that you can avoid by using the following rules:

1. Make sure the backup procedures are fired during a time when users make the least number of hits on the database. This ensures that the least number of redo changes (either from users or via log files) will be necessary.

2. Use SQL against the system tablespace to ascertain the most current picture of the database. Then automatically use this information to dynamically write your backup scripts.

> **TIP**
>
> *Never* hard code Oracle database object names into your backup scripts. It will be increasingly difficult for you to manage these as your database is modified or grows and will diminish prospects for future recovery success.

3. Make sure to write "success" flags into your backup script so that you can see that your backups are proceeding successfully in your absence. Incorporation of time stamps for each major script line executed is one way to track the success or failure of your scheduled backup scripts.

Part IV: Recovery

Sooner or later the time will come when some sort of recovery will be required. As is the case with backup methodologies, Oracle offers a myriad of recovery options and each one has its own advantages and disadvantages. As with the backup, the method for recovery has a lot to do with how much data is actually lost and what types of backups you have at your disposal.

The following sections show some scenarios that should help you decide not only what type of recovery to use for certain situations, but which backup methods best fit your particular needs.

Scenario #1 (User Error)

A user accidentally deletes 300 rows of information from a tablespace. The data lost affects only the table from which the data was deleted. The data represents several days of work and must be recovered at the earliest possible time.

Risk Management Assessment

The following are some risk management considerations for this scenario:

- Was security properly employed by software the user used to delete rows?
- If security was employed, was the user's security level appropriate?
- Does sensitivity of data require the re-evaluation of the security policy for that table?

Solution #1: (Export Backup/Import Recovery)

A logical backup (export) had been performed the night before.

Administration Impact

The DBA can take the affected table offline, allowing other parts of the database to be accessed or updated. The DBA then imports data from the prior night's export backup and then puts the repaired table back online. The DBA informs the users of the point in time to which the table has been recovered.

User Impact

The user must follow data verification procedures as discussed earlier in this chapter (see "Data Recovery Verification Procedures (Users)") to determine at which point transaction data re-entering must begin. The user must then re-enter transactions *affecting the repaired table only* between the point in time that the deletions occurred and the present.

Corporate Impact

The corporation must wait to get access to or gain information from the table while the table is being repaired.

Data Prognosis: Incomplete recovery is the only option. Success is dependent on a satisfactory length of time for the DBA to recover/restart the database and the users to catch up from the point of recovery to the present. No damage was done to control or log files, making this export/import scenario a viable approach.

Solution #2: (OS Backup/OS Restore)

An operating system backup was performed the night before.

Administrative Impact

The DBA must terminate all accesses to the database and then shut down the database in normal mode. The DBA can then restore the prior night's database, log file and control file backups, placing the entire database at its state at the time the backup was performed. The DBA can then restart the database.

User Impact

Users must re-enter all transactions from the time the backup was performed (the night before) and the time the deletions were committed, even those that have no relationship to the affected and repaired table. The users should follow data verification procedures to determine the exact point at which data transactions need to be resubmitted.

Corporate Impact

The corporation must wait for the DBA to properly recover the prior night's backup and then for the users to re-enter lost transactions as well as enter current transactions.

Data Prognosis: Incomplete recovery is the only option. All files will be restored to the point of the last OS backup. Success depends on whether the amount of time required for users to catch up lost transaction submittals is acceptable and adequate to maintain operations for the corporation.

Solution #3: (Cold Backup/Restore)

A cold backup was performed the night before. (Refer to Solution #2.)

Administrative Impact

The DBA must terminate all accesses to the database and then shut down the database in normal mode. The DBA can then restore the prior night's database, log file, and control file backups, which would then recover the entire database to the state it was in at the time the backup was performed. The DBA can then restart the database.

User Impact

Users would then be required to re-enter all transactions from the time the backup was performed (the night before) and the time the deletions were committed, even if some of the transactions in question have no relationship to the tablespace affected by the inadvertent deletions. Data verification procedures would need to be executed by users as discussed earlier in this chapter (see "Data Recovery Verification Procedures (Users)") to determine the exact point at which data transactions need to be resubmitted.

Corporate Impact

The corporation must wait for the DBA to recover and restart the database and then must wait for the user to re-enter lost data transactions from the point of the last backup to the present.

Data Prognosis: Incomplete recovery is the only option. All files will be restored to the point of the last cold backup. Success depends on whether the amount of time required for the DBA to restore the database and the users to catch up lost transactions is acceptable to the corporation.

Solution #4 (Hot Backup/Restore/Roll Forward)

A hot backup was performed the night before.

Administrative Impact

The DBA must terminate all accesses to the database. The database file needs to be recovered from the night before. No damage was done to the control or log files, so no recovery procedures are necessary for either. The DBA then restarts the database and commands the Oracle7 database engine to roll transactions forward to the approximate point that the deletions took place. The Oracle7 engine then rolls forward all transactions to the point of the user error. Because roll-forward procedures can be performed only on the entire database (not just the damaged table), the DBA can recover only to the point that the deletions were submitted.

User Impact

Users would then be required to re-enter all transactions from the time the deletions occurred to the present. This would include transactions that had no relationship to the affected table. Data verification procedures would need to be executed by users to determine the exact point at which data transactions need to be resubmitted.

Corporate Impact

The corporation must wait for the DBA to recover and restart the database, and then must wait for the user to re-enter lost data transactions from the point of the errant deletions to the present.

Data Prognosis: Because log files were unharmed in this data loss event, the hot backup would provide the option for the DBA to perform an "incomplete" recovery by rolling transactions forward to the point of the error.

Scenario #2 (Media Failure)

The hard drive on which the Oracle Database resides crashes. All outstanding instances/threads are left incomplete.

Risk Management Assessment

The following are some risk management considerations for this scenario:

■ Are adequate spare parts/machines available in the corporation's inventory?

■ If spare parts are available, are the obvious parts available? In this case, do you have a spare controller card or hard drive readily available from this spare parts inventory?

(The following solutions assume that the hardware problem has been resolved.)

Solution #1 (Export Backup)

A logical backup (export) was performed the night before. The DBA creates a new database and structure using available structure and tablespace information. The DBA then imports data from the prior night's export backup. If running in archivelog mode prior to the crash, logs are now useless. If the DBA chooses to run in archivelog mode from here, new logs must be created/attached to the database.

Data Prognosis: Although the DBA could probably recreate the database and import all data exported the night before, log files would no longer recognize the newly created database (SCN numbers would become incompatible). If the control files or log files were damaged in this scenario, there would be significant questions as to whether the database would function properly even after their recreation by the DBA. In any event, the amount of time to get the database back online would probably be unacceptable in most instances.

Solution #2 (OS Backup)

An operating system backup was performed the night before. The DBA can then restore the prior night's backup placing the entire database in the state it was in at the time the backup was performed. The DBA can then start up the database. Users would then be required to re-enter all transactions from the time the backup was performed (the night before). Some user area auditing would need to be done to assure all lost transactions were re-entered.

Data Prognosis: Incomplete recovery is the only option. All files will be restored to the point of the last OS backup. Success depends on whether or not the amount of time required for users to catch up lost transactions is acceptable to the corporation.

Solution #3 (Cold Backup)

A cold backup was performed the night before. The DBA will need to restore all Oracle-related files from the backup. This would include the database, log files, and the control file. The database could then be started and would be in the state it was in at the point of the last cold backup. Some user-area auditing would need to be done to ensure that all lost transactions were re-entered. (Refer to Solution #2.)

Data Prognosis: All files will be restored to the point of the last OS backup. Success depends on whether the amount of time required for users to catch up lost transactions is acceptable or not to the corporation.

Solution #4 (Hot Backup)

A hot backup was performed the night before. The database and all relevant log files need to be restored to the new hard drive. The DBA can then start Oracle and request crash recovery procedures to make sure the log files and the database are synchronized. Oracle can then be commanded to roll forward all transactions to the point of the user error. The DBA can then make the database accessible, but all transactions entered after the point of the user error will need to be re-entered.

Data Prognosis: Success is probable and largely depends on log and control files not being damaged. Because log files (if located on a separate disk) were probably unharmed in this data loss event, the hot backup would provide the option for the DBA to perform a "complete" recovery by rolling all transactions forward to the point of the error.

Recovery Scenario #3 (SQL Command Failure)

The user fills a data screen and submits the data to the database. No tablespace is available for the new transaction, and the SQL update statement therefore fails.

Risk Management Assessment

The following is a risk management consideration for this scenario:

Is available tablespace reviewed regularly for all databases being administered?

Solution #1

SQL statement failures result in Oracle automatically rolling back the transaction that failed. An error-message prompt advises the user of the problem. After the problem is corrected, the user can then simply resubmit the transaction.

Administration Impact

The DBA will create more tablespace to accommodate more transactions. This can be done by creating a new or modified control file via use of a control file creation SQL Script, available if a BACKUP TO TRACE command was performed on the database instance recently. If the SQL script was not available, the DBA would need to create or modify a control file that would accomplish the additional tablespace recognition required.

User Impact

The user must wait to enter transactions until the DBA has completed the tablespace maintenance required.

Corporate Impact

Depending on the amount of time for the DBA to resolve the problem, little or no impact will be felt by the corporation.

Recovery Scenario #4 (Processing Interruption)

The user submits a transaction that abnormally aborts for no apparent reason.

Risk Management Assessment

The following are some risk management considerations for this scenario:

- Is the latest version of the user software being used?
- Is the latest version of the OS being used?
- Has the latest Oracle database engine been installed?

Solution #1

The process monitor will clean up disrupted, orphaned transactions caused by the server, an application, or the user. This type of cleanup is all done through background processing and is invisible to the user.

User Impact

The user will be notified via an error message or screen state that the transaction submitted abnormally stalled. Solutions for the user range from re-submitting the transaction to re-starting the desktop application in use. After the application is back up and running, the user will then re-submit the transactions involved in the process disruption.

Administration Impact

The DBA will have little or no responsibility (other than to find out what caused the processing interruption).

Corporate Impact

Usually the corporation will feel little or no impact because down-time is minimal.

Solution #2

In the event that Oracle itself terminated the process through the failure of one of its background processing modules, the database will need to be cleared of all accesses, brought down, and then restarted. Oracle will then automatically execute crash recovery procedures via log files.

Administration Impact

The DBA must coordinate the termination of all connections to the database and initiate total shutdown of the database. The DBA can then restart the database and allow access.

User Impact

The user must wait until the DBA has restarted the database. After the database has been recovered, the users will need to implement data verification procedures to identify which transactions have been committed to the database and are readily visible. The users will then need to re-enter any and all transactions from the point of the recovery to the present.

Corporate Impact

The corporation must wait until the DBA and users have completed their tasks before normal operations can resume.

Recovery Scenario #5 (Distributed Processing Failure)

The user submits a large transaction just as the client/server network goes down.

Risk Management Assessment

The following is a risk management consideration for this scenario:

Is the latest version of the networking OS being used?

Solution #1

When the OS is restarted, the DBA simply restarts the database. Between PMON, the RECO background processing module, and normal crash recovery procedures, these conflicts (even those that are distributed in nature) are usually completely and automatically resolved by Oracle.

Administration Impact

The DBA must wait until the OS or hardware communications facilities are again functional. The DBA can then restart the database, allow Oracle to resolve outstanding conflict, and then open all appropriate accesses to the database.

User Impact

The user must wait until all communications problems have been resolved and the DBA has re-started the database. The user will then need to perform standard data verification procedures to verify what transactions were committed to the database. The user will then need to re-enter any and all transactions from the point of the recovery to the present.

Corporate Impact

The corporation will lose the time the OS is down, the time it takes the DBA to restart the database, the time for the Oracle engine to clean up errant or partially submitted transactions, and the time it takes user areas to catch up transactions that were not submitted while the OS, and therefore the database, were down.

Summary

As you can see, building a backup and recovery plan is more about *understanding* the risks involved in typical data loss occurrences and understanding the backup/recovery capabilities of your Oracle7 database. Actually doing the backups and performing recovery procedures can result in successful data recovery depending on how well you plan for both within *the context of your corporation or site*. I hope you found this chapter helpful in your understanding of each of these areas and that it helps you become successful in both the backup *and* recovery management of the databases in your care.

VII

What to Do When It Doesn't Work

30

Performance Tuning

by Kelly Leigh

Performance tuning is an extremely important part of development. Some developers do performance tuning at the end of the development process, just before promoting software and/or databases into production. However, the earlier the performance tuning efforts start, the greater the benefits to the overall project. You should set performance goals at the start of a project and then constantly and consistently monitor progress against those goals.

Introduction

Setting goals may seem like a simple task, but sometimes that's not the case. As a simple exercise, try ranking the following items in order of importance for one of your current projects or one that you recently completed:

- Response time
- System availability
- 100-percent uptime
- Data concurrency
- Performance to the desktop
- System performance
- System/data recoverability
- Multiple-user access
- Network traffic

For many projects—especially banking and order-processing applications—these goals are all important. On the other hand, a nightly reporting system may not need to be tuned for best performance or for multiple-user access. And if processes are run against the database at night, 100-percent uptime also may not be a factor. In addition, your project may have other goals not on this list. With so many options, deciding which ones are worth striving for is important.

Many times the question is, "Who is responsible for performance tuning?" The answer is not always simple. In general, four groups have primary responsibility for performance tuning:

- Systems administrators
- Database administrators
- Application developers
- Network administrators

Network administrators may not sound like an appropriate entry for the list, but usually they are more qualified than a database administrator, system administrator, or developer in identifying performance bottlenecks on the network side and suggest alternatives. These alternatives can range from bridges, routers, and multiple subnets to a possible application redesign.

When performance tuning, all options should be discussed and all resources examined. A unique suggestion may provide a much-needed solution.

Because Oracle requires so many different resources, such as networks, disk space, CPU usage, there is much crossover in the roles of performance tuning. For example, systems administrators must work with database administrators to determine what system resources are needed and in what quantity. Also, database administrators may need to work with network administrators to ensure network connectivity to the database. Oracle can be a very memory-intensive application, so if the database administrator sets the size of the system global area (SGA) too high, system performance can suffer greatly. On the other hand, if the SGA is too small, the system may perform well, but database performance will suffer. If all groups responsible for performance tuning work closely together, they can ensure that all aspects of the database and its resources are working as well as possible.

The System Administrator's Role

The system administrator is generally responsible for all hardware and software setup for larger server platforms. The system administrator is also responsible for creating users and giving adequate permissions to allow the users of the system access to files, directories, and programs. When adding disk space to a system, the system administrator is also responsible for configuring this hardware in the most efficient way.

The system administrator must tune the system as well as possible before beginning the Oracle installation phase of a project. If the system is not performing as well as possible, downtime could result later in the project before all system-related issues are cleared up. Once Oracle is installed, even smaller issues such as disk contention can grow to an enormous proportion.

The Database Administrator's Role

The database administrator is primarily responsible for the installation, upgrade, maintenance, tuning, daily operations, and backup of the Oracle database. Part of the tuning efforts should include working with the systems administrator to determine which disks Oracle and its data will reside on. Making this decision at system installation means that the hardware can be configured for more efficient throughput to and from disk storage.

Once the system administrator has tuned the system, the database administrator must work with the system administrators to ensure that all necessary resources are available. Likewise, disks with enough storage to hold rollback segments, database files, backup files, and so on must be identified to avoid contention between database and system operations. Memory requirements are also another area that must be discussed. After the database has been created, the database and systems administrators should continue to work together to monitor the performance of the databases and systems and fine-tune any areas requiring attention.

The Application Developer's Role

Creation, maintenance, and bug fixing are some of the tasks that application developers perform. They also identify the needs of the users, tune the application to run in the most efficient manner, and work with the database administrator to define alternatives to various types of code in order to provide better database and application performance.

As the application is being developed, the developer should communicate the needs and requirements of the application to the database administrator. This may include the tables being accessed, the memory required to run efficiently, and possibly the length of time a process may run to complete a long-running job. The database administrator cannot effectively tune the database until he or she is familiar with all objects and resources that the application requires. In addition, the database administrator can probably provide feedback on more efficient means of ensuring data integrity or updating database tables.

The Network Administrator's Role

The role of the network administrator is usually fairly small in the development process. However, administrators generally have the tools that can monitor network traffic to detect performance problems. Many administrators and developers have wasted precious time trying to tune a system or application when the network is responsible for those mysterious slowdowns. If the application is client/server and very network-intensive, the network administrator may be able to subnet this particular traffic or at least be able to determine the exact origin of the network traffic and provide a suitable solution.

Determining Performance Bottlenecks

Performance bottlenecks are areas within the network, system, database, or application that cause the greatest slowdown. A bottle of soda may be several inches in diameter, for example, but because the opening in the neck is so much smaller, soda flows out of the bottle at a slow speed. The opening in the top is considered the bottleneck.

Because a performance bottleneck can have multiple symptoms, developers can waste many hours by tuning in the wrong areas or by not uncovering the true problem. The best place to begin performance tuning, in order to identify the bottleneck, is with the list of goals for the project, starting with the number one priority. However, remember that problems can show multiple symptoms.

Performance bottlenecks exist in one or more of three generic categories:

- System
- Database
- Network

Sometimes you have to solve the first problem before you can even determine whether further problems exist. At first glance, for example, a system may appear to be having a serious problem with disk I/O. Possibly, though, the system is extremely low on memory, which is forcing it to swap memory contents to disk in order to load other items into memory. You could spend a lot of time trying to find out why the system is so disk-intensive and learn later that the system really has a memory problem. By taking a sample of many different areas, you can avoid this type of situation.

Performance tuning takes time and energy, and the best teachers are intuition and experience. To start with, however, you can follow a general formula to locate performance bottlenecks. This formula consists of three steps:

- Tune the system.
- Tune the database.
- Tune the network.

Tune the System

Because the system hardware/software/operating system is the driving force that makes access to the Oracle database possible, you should examine that system first. The main problem areas are

- CPU time
- Memory use
- Disk I/O
- Operating system

Tuning each of these areas is generally the system administrator's job. Although third-party tools are in wide use and ease the effort of tuning a system, most platforms come with some sort of tool to assist in reporting system resource usage.

NT platforms come with a performance monitor that allows administrators to graph the use of system resources such as disk I/O, CPU utilization, and memory use. Many books cover the subject of tuning NT to work more efficiently. The performance monitor has options for saving the output of the program to files for later playback. This technique is very helpful for determining the peak hours of operation for production systems.

UNIX platforms generally come with a utility called sar, which is extremely helpful for monitoring CPU, memory, disk, network, and terminal traffic. Like the NT performance monitor, sar also has options for saving the output to files for later playback.

Usually, tuning the system can be accomplished by following these guidelines:

1. Begin tuning efforts with the system running all applications it normally runs (Oracle, and so on).

2. Attempt to solve memory problems first because they can contribute to CPU and disk problems. Make sure you have enough physical and virtual memory (swap space) for the system and its applications.

3. Identify and fix any disk I/O contention problems. If possible, set aside a disk for the operating system and Oracle executables and store Oracle datafiles across multiple disks. Disk problems can also lead to excess CPU usage because it must juggle the processes that must read and write from disk.

4. Determine which programs are taking up so much CPU time. Can you run them at another time or at off-peak hours? Can you limit their resource usage or lower their processing priority? If possible, run production Oracle databases on dedicated servers.

5. After all other problems have been resolved, check with Oracle or the platform vendor to see if you can change specific operating system parameters to improve Oracle performance.

NOTE

It is important to note that hardware and software vendors regularly provide patches to their operating systems or applications. Usually it's a good idea to make a phone call to the hardware or software vendors inquiring about patches that are currently available. Some of these patches may be strictly for addressing a performance problem.

Tuning the system hardware is a very platform-dependent process. If possible, consult with the system administrator or a hardware vendor for additional assistance.

Tune the Database

Once the system is tuned properly, you should focus on the database. Although you may encounter many problems, the biggest user complaint is about slow response time. These problems usually fall within four major categories. Some of these categories are similar to those mentioned in the section "Tune the System," but at this point, the problems probably exist within the Oracle database and its setup, not with the hardware platform.

The four major categories of database problems are

■ Memory (SGA) contention
■ Disk access
■ CPU time
■ Database resources (locks, latches, tables, indexes, and so on)

Many problems can cause these symptoms, and determining the culprit can be a very time-consuming process. Fortunately, products such as Oracle Server Manager and other third-party products designed for problem determination make your job easier.

You will spend most of your time in the problem-determination phase examining specific areas of the database, either looking for causes to problems or just trying to maximize performance. Either way, looking at specific goals and areas of the database is an efficient way of locating problems. Problem determination for these areas is discussed in some depth in the "Tuning the Database" section later in this chapter.

Server Manager

Oracle's Server Manager program, which is distributed with the database software, is a valuable tool to assist in uncovering problems in a database. Server Manager provides two interfaces: graphical mode and line mode. Their capabilities, unfortunately, are not the same. The biggest difference is that only graphical mode supports the following monitor features:

- Circuit monitor
- Dispatcher monitor
- File I/O monitor
- Latch monitor
- Library-cache monitor
- Lock monitor
- Process monitor
- Queue monitor
- Rollback monitor
- Session monitor
- Shared-server monitor
- SQL Area monitor
- System I/O monitor
- System-statistics monitor
- Table-access monitor
- Tablespace monitor

The options for monitoring include logging to a file, sampling at intervals, on-demand sampling, and filtering results. Using these monitors is fairly straightforward. Because the process for starting all the monitors is nearly identical, except for selecting monitor criteria, a single example—file I/O—should suffice.

> **NOTE**
>
> For the UNIX version of Server Manager, the utility names are svrmgrl for line mode and svrmgrm for graphical mode. For NT platforms, the program name is SVRMGR.EXE and automatically starts in graphical mode.

To start monitoring file I/O, start Server Manager and then select the following items from each menu as it is displayed:

1. FILE
2. MONITOR
3. FILE I/O

The monitoring screen should appear and list the database files on the left with associated file statistics (physical reads, physical writes, and so on) on the right side. The monitor starts sampling at 15-second intervals. You can change this interval by modifying the interval rate at the top of the screen. At this point, looking for the file(s) with the highest I/O rate should be your first priority; they are good candidates for relocation. These statistics tell you whether a datafile is read- or write-intensive, how much data is really being transferred per second, and whether the disk contains several very busy datafiles. Read the section "Tuning the Database" for more information on tuning file I/O.

Tune the Network

Although you cannot do much to tune the network, it is a valid place to look for response problems. If the network is consistently near maximum bandwidth capabilities, the system and database may show perfect performance, yet users will complain about poor response time. Checking the overall health of a network is usually a quick and fairly simple process and one, unfortunately, that many development teams ignore.

Three general areas to examine on a network are

- Bandwidth
- Path redundancy
- Network hardware reliability

Like tuning the system, tuning the network depends on the hardware and network layout. Consult with a network administrator or vendor for more information about locating problems and finding their resolutions.

Tuning the Database

Tuning the database can be an extremely lengthy process because of the number of options that are available and interactions that take place. You should monitor the database during peak hours or for 24-hour intervals to get an overall feeling for where problems are occurring. Once the characteristics of the problems are identified, tuning efforts can begin.

Although no cookie-cutter approach is going to assist everyone in performance tuning, some areas of the database are likely contributors to the problem(s). The following sections examine some of the problems of these database areas:

- Disk I/O and file layout
- Tuning rollback segments
- Tuning redo logs
- The System Global Area

You can use many tools to monitor a database and determine its problems. Oracle provides a tool called Oracle Server Manager. Oracle also provides several SQL scripts that can produce reports giving database statistics relating to datafile usage, SGA statistics, latch and lock contention, and many other options.

To help isolate problems, the Oracle database contains a set of dynamic performance tables, or V$ tables. One table is particularly helpful for analyzing problems and suggesting where to start looking for solutions. The V$SESSION_WAIT table contains information that will help to track problems to CPU, memory, disk, data, or database resource contention issues.

> **NOTE**
>
> For those who are familiar with Oracle versions 7.2 and earlier, SQL*DBA's functionality has been moved to Server Manager. Although the SQL*DBA program still exists, Oracle will soon discontinue its support. It is provided strictly for backward compatibility.

Tuning Database Disk I/O

Tuning disk I/O is a constant task. Unexpected growth and promotion of new production applications can create new areas of disk contention. As always, careful tuning should continue throughout the development process, but here are a few guidelines to use in setting up and tuning database files:

- Create separate tablespaces for tables and indexes.
- Locate table and index tablespaces on different physical disks.

- Store redo logs and rollback segments on different disks.
- Place Oracle executables and database datafiles on separate disks.
- Identify the most accessed tables, indexes, and their tablespaces and place them on separate physical disks.
- If possible, split physical disks between multiple disk controllers for better disk I/O throughput.
- Never install other third-party software packages onto the Oracle data disks.

By nature, a database is very disk I/O intensive because most operations must read from and write to the disks in order to store and retrieve data. Disk storage, therefore, can become an extreme bottleneck. The preceding guidelines can help you reduce or eliminate most I/O problems. However, this list is not exhaustive, and sometimes you may not be able to follow these guidelines. In these situations your best approach is to simply limit, as opposed to eliminate, the amount of disk contention between applications (database and nondatabase). Although it generally will take downtime to fix disk contention problems, in the long run, it is well worth the effort it takes to solve them.

You can monitor datafile I/O by querying the V$DATAFILE table. This table accumulates statistics from the time the database was last started and contains information such as physical reads and physical writes. You can use the V$FILESTAT table to get the name of the datafile, instead of the datafile number. By default, the V$DATAFILE and V$FILESTAT tables are accessible only to SYS, the owner, and any users granted SELECT ANY TABLE privileges.

Use a query similar to the following to get tablespace I/O activity:

```
SELECT name, phrds, phywrts
  FROM v$datafile, v$filestat
  WHERE v$datafile.file# = v$filestat.file#;
```

Output should resemble the following:

```
NAME                            PHYRDS    PHYWRTS
- - - -                         - - - - - -   - - - - - - -
/u01/oradata/orcl/system01.dbf    9812       3517
/u03/oradata/orcl/temp01.dbf        45        612
/u03/oradata/orcl/users01.dbf      193        298
```

The sum of phyrds and phywrts is the total I/O for the datafile. All datafiles should be ranked by this sum. If possible, separate all highly active datafiles on different physical disks. This step will help to alleviate disk contention.

Tuning Rollback Segments

Rollback segments have the important role of storing all information necessary to undo a transaction before all updates have been applied to disk. Because the rollback segments must hold this information, they must be sized according to the typical transactions that take place in the database. Rollback segments constitute a large portion of the file I/O for the database and should be mentioned separately from the typical file I/O section.

CAUTION

Just a reminder that rollback segments store only undo information for data manipulation language (DML) statements. Data definition language (DDL) statements, such as CREATE, DROP and TRUNCATE, cannot be rolled back.

Monitoring Rollback Segment Contention

You can monitor contention for rollback segments through the V$WAITSTAT table. Two columns within this table provide information about these segments:

◼ Class   The class of the statistic within the table
◼ Count   The value associated with the Class column

The values for Class that relate to rollback segments are listed in Table 30.1.

Table 30.1. Class descriptions for rollback segments.

Class Value	Class Description
undo header	The number of waits for buffers containing header blocks for user rollback segments
undo block	The number of waits for requests of nonheader blocks for user rollback segments
system undo header	The number of waits for buffers containing header blocks for the SYSTEM rollback segment
system undo block	The number of waits for requests of nonheader blocks for the SYSTEM rollback segment

The following is a sample SQL script to retrieve these values:

```
SELECT class, count
  FROM v$waitstat
  WHERE class in ('undo header', 'undo block', 'system undo header', 'system undo
block');
```

The output from the SQL script should appear similar to the following:

```
CLASS               COUNT
- - - - -           - - - - -
undo header           965
undo block            319
system undo header   1631
system undo block    1021
```

The Count values from the V$WAITSTAT table should be compared to the total number of read requests to generate a ratio. You can find the total number of reads with this query:

```
SELECT SUM(value)
  FROM v$sysstat
  WHERE name IN ('consistent gets', 'db block gets');
```

Output should resemble

```
VALUE
-----
29164
```

which is the total number of reads. Calculate the ratio of waits to reads by using these formulas:

> SYSTEM header waits = system undo header ÷ total reads
> SYSTEM block waits = system block ÷ total reads
> rollback header waits = undo header ÷ total reads
> rollback block waits = undo block ÷ total reads

If the value of any of these calculated wait ratios is greater than 1 percent, Oracle suggests that you create more rollback segments. Table 30.2 lists Oracle's suggestion for the number of rollback segments in a database.

Table 30.2. Suggested number of rollback segments.

Concurrent Transactions	Rollback Segments
1–16	4
17–32	8
33 or more	Concurrent Transactions ÷ 4, but no more than 50

NOTE

Both the V$WAITSTAT and V$SYSSTAT tables are cumulative. When the database is started, the values in these tables are reset and counting begins from zero. When sampling data from either table for the purpose of calculating rollback segment contention, be sure to sample both sets of values at the same time. The results will not be accurate if a significant amount of time has passed between gathering samples for both tables.

Avoiding Dynamic Space Allocation

Dynamic space allocation is a powerful feature of Oracle. By allowing database objects to grow as needed, much of the work of a database administrator becomes analytical instead of reactive. One problem with dynamic space allocation, however, is that it requires a certain amount of system overhead to manage. This overhead translates to a performance loss when it happens on a continuous basis.

If rollback segments are sized too small, the database must continue to extend the segments until it reaches the necessary size or encounters an error (lack of disk space, for example). If the rollback segment can be extended to the proper size, the only serious problem is the performance loss while the database extends the segments. Transactions will fail, though, if Oracle cannot give the rollback segment the space it requires.

One of the problems that a developer or database administrator encounters concerns the correct sizing of rollback segments and other database objects. If the size is too small, error messages and failed transactions result. If the object has too much space, disk space becomes scarce and other database objects may suffer. The best way to avoid this problem, in relationship to rollback segments, is to follow these rules:

1. Make each rollback segment large enough to handle an entire transaction.
2. Separate the rollback segments into separate tablespaces from other Oracle data.
3. Separate the rollback segments into two separate tablespaces and two physical disks if possible. This step will decrease disk contention.
4. Experiment with the `optimal` storage parameter. You can use this parameter to keep the rollback segments at a desired size, without stopping them from dynamically growing if necessary.
5. Monitor the size and growth of the rollback segments through the DBA_EXTENTS and V$ROLLBACK_SEGS tables.

Large Transactions

Applications such as reporting tools, or simply processing jobs can require large rollback segments to process all the required information. Although the database administrator is responsible for setting up this large rollback segment, it is necessary for the applications or reports to issue the proper commands so that they will use that rollback segment. If the normal rollback segments are used for this type of processing, either dynamic space allocation can occur, or the processes could produce an error because Oracle is unable to extend the rollback segment to the required length. You can avoid these kinds of errors by using an especially large rollback segment for processing large transactions.

To use a specific rollback segment, issue the SQL command `SET TRANSACTION USE ROLLBACK SEGMENT rollback segment name`. This will force the current transaction to use the specified rollback segment for all SQL commands within the transaction.

NOTE

Transactions are completed by using COMMIT or ROLLBACK commands, by exiting a session, or by issuing a DML statement. These methods are just a few of the situations that complete a transaction.

Once a transaction has been finished, you must reissue the SET TRANSACTION command to use the large rollback segment again.

Tuning Redo Logs

Redo logs, like rollback segments, are an extremely important part of the database. They are responsible for maintaining a record of data changes which are used to recover the database if it or the system should crash. In the case of a system or database crash, the SMON process is responsible for identifying any committed transactions that were not written to the database files and reapplying them. If the database is running in ARCHIVE_LOG mode, once a redo log is filled, it is written to disk in a sequentially named file. If the database ever needs to be restored from backup, these log files are used to apply transactions to the database until it has reached the most recent consistent precrash state.

It is unusual for contention for the redo logs to cause any serious performance loss, but the possibility exists. In order for a process to write to the redo log buffers, it must acquire a *latch*, which is a short-lived placeholder in memory. Although not identical to a lock, a latch is used as a way for a process to acquire and hold a resource in memory. Once the latch is acquired, the SQL statement the process is executing is written to the redo log and then executed. If the transaction is completed successfully, the redo log buffer is written to disk. If a process cannot obtain a latch, it must wait. However, the space required for storing a SQL statement in the redo log buffer is minimal, so the wait is rarely long.

Monitoring Redo Log Buffer Latch Requests

Requests for latches are recorded in the V$SYSSTAT table with the name 'redo log space requests'. The value associated with this name is the total number of requests that have resulted in a wait for a redo log buffer to become available. To obtain this value, query the V$SYSSTAT table with the following SQL statement:

```
SELECT name, value
  FROM v$sysstat
  WHERE name = 'redo log space requests';
```

The output should appear similar to

```
NAME                    VALUE
----                    -----
redo log space requests   2
```

The value returned by the query should be as close to 0 as possible. The value shown is cumulative since the database was started. If the value continually rises or is a large value, you need to increase the size of the redo log buffer. The size of the buffer is determined by DB_BLOCK_SIZE × LOG_BUFFER. Both values are in bytes, not blocks. Because the only way to change the DB_BLOCK_SIZE parameter is to recreate the database, increase the LOG_BUFFER value instead.

Reducing Redo Log Archive I/O Contention

An Oracle database must have two or more redo logs. As the redo log buffer fills, it is written out to one of the redo log files. Once a redo log file is filled, the log buffer begins to write to the other log file. When that log is filled, the redo log buffer switches back to the first log to begin writing. This process continues in a cyclic fashion. If three or more log files exist, the database will cycle through each one before returning to the first redo log file.

A database running in ARCHIVE_LOG mode, once a redo log file is filled, must go through a series of steps before it can be written to again.

1. The redo log file is marked unavailable.
2. The data from the redo log is archived to disk, in a sequentially numbered file.
3. The redo log file is marked available.

Most sites realize file I/O contention at step 2. Once the database begins archiving a redo log file, a great deal of file I/O is generated as the database copies all the data from the redo log file to the archive log file. This process creates contention as the database continues to write redo log buffer entries to the now active redo log file.

The best scenario to prevent this kind of contention is to spread the redo log files across two separate disks, if possible, which do not contain other database files, and to write the archive logs to a third, unused disk. It is important to be careful not to cause more contention between the redo logs and actual datafiles. In this type of setup, shown in Table 30.3, the database writes redo log buffer entries to a disk with little I/O activity while the disks containing the archive log files and the currently archiving redo log file are doing pure reads and writes.

Table 30.3. Optimal redo log disk locations.

Disk ID	Redo Log/File Type
1	Redo log #1
2	Redo log #2
3	Archive log destination

Obviously, not all sites have the resources for this best-case situation. At the very least, attempt to split the redo log files among separate disks where only one redo log file (or set of redo log files) shares a physical disk with the archive log files. This technique minimizes file I/O contention.

NOTE

Because the redo log files are cycled through by the database and you can see file I/O contention while the redo log files are being archived, you should keep these points in mind:

■ Never store two sequential redo log files on the same disk.

■ When adding redo log files to the database, create them in multiples of the number of disks used to store them. This step will even out the file I/O among these disks.

The System Global Area

The System Global Area, or SGA, is composed of four distinct pieces:

■ Database buffer cache
■ Redo log buffer
■ Shared pool
■ Cursors

The purpose of the SGA is to store needed and recently accessed data in memory for very quick access. If the entire SGA cannot fit in the system's physical memory, part of the SGA will be swapped to disk and the database will not perform as efficiently as possible. Regardless of whether the system must read data from datafiles or from virtual memory, swapping can greatly slow down the read steps.

NOTE

One good way to start tuning the SGA is to restart the system and bring up all normally executing software and processes except the Oracle databases. Using the available tools, find out how much physical (not virtual) memory is available. This number is probably the largest-size SGA the system can accommodate.

In reality, the SGA should be smaller than this number. As users and processes begin running on this system, they will use more memory. As that memory is used, the available physical memory continues to decrease until the normal workload of the system is reached. At this point, the SGA should still be completely in physical memory to provide optimum performance.

When the database starts, it reads into memory only the information necessary to bring up the database. As users or applications access the database, more information is read into memory until the database has stored all necessary information in the SGA. The database does not reach maximum efficiency until this time.

By setting the INIT.ORA parameter PRE_PAGE_SGA = YES, you can force the database to read the entire SGA into memory at database startup. Although the database may require more time to start with this parameter turned on, it will reach its maximum efficiency much quicker. In addition, although the SGA is loaded when the database is started, the operating system is still able to swap it to disk. The only way to prevent this swapping is to reduce the memory requirements on the system, reduce the size of the SGA (though this may decrease performance), or add more physical memory.

To see how much memory the SGA has been allocated, use this server manager command:

```
SVRMGR> SHOW SGA
```

Output from this command should resemble the following:

```
Total System Global Area    2457600 bytes
          Fixed Size          23212 bytes
       Variable Size        3378380 bytes
    Database Buffers         243760 bytes
        Redo Buffers          32768 bytes
```

NOTE

Some IBM systems have a feature called expanded storage. This feature allows the operating system to swap contents of physical memory to this location, which is much quicker than swapping to disk. In some instances, swapping the SGA might provide better performance than decreasing its size. Consult the hardware documentation for more information on this topic.

Tuning the Database Buffer Cache

The database buffer cache is responsible for storing the most recently accessed data blocks that have been read from disk. It also stores modifications that have not yet been written to disk. The INIT.ORA parameter DB_BLOCK_SIZE determines the size of the database buffers when the database is created. Generally the block size default is 2K or 4K. The only way to change this size is to recreate the database. You can use Oracle's backup tools to export and import the data in the buffers.

The INIT.ORA parameter DB_BLOCK_BUFFERS determines the number of database buffers. To determine the amount of SGA space these buffers take, multiply the value of DB_BLOCK_SIZE × DB_BLOCK_BUFFERS. The product is the total amount of memory associated with the database buffer cache.

Developers and database administrators should be familiar with the following terms associated with the buffer cache:

LRU (least recently used): A list of buffers that is organized by age, oldest first. It contains a list of blocks that have not been accessed recently and are the first candidates to be written to disk or to be cleared from memory when their space is needed.

MRU (most recently used): This term describes the LRU list, but starting with the most recently accessed buffer. When a buffer has been accessed by any process, it is placed at the end of the LRU list and is considered the most recently used buffer. Basically, the MRU is the LRU in reverse order.

Cache hit: A statistic that counts the number of times a request for data has been fulfilled by reading from the LRU list, instead of reading from disk.

Cache miss: The opposite of cache hit, this statistic counts the number of times a request for data had to be fulfilled by reading from disk, instead of from memory.

If the buffer cache is set too low, a large number of cache misses will appear. This condition is normal at the startup of a database, as no disk blocks are initially read into memory until requested. However, the ratio of cache misses to cache hits should be very low once the database goes into operation. The value for the ratio is dependent on the environment, but as a rule, the more misses, the greater the number of physical reads from disk and the slower the performance in fulfilling the user's request.

You can calculate the cache hit by selecting values from the V$SYSSTAT table. To get the values for the calculation, use the following SQL statement:

```
SELECT name, value
   FROM v$sysstat
   WHERE name IN ('db block gets', 'consistent gets', 'physical reads');
```

This is a sample of the output.

NAME	VALUE
db block gets	6184
consistent gets	173189
physical reads	7189

To calculate the hit ratio with these values, use this formula:

Hit Ratio = 1 − (physical reads ÷ (db block gets + consistent gets))

This example has about a 96 percent hit ratio, which is very good. This value should be as high as possible. Because an acceptable value depends on the tuning goals and environment characteristics, the DBA and developers need to decide what is acceptable.

Redo Log Buffer

The redo log buffer is the memory area that stores all redo information before it is written to the redo log files. The value of the INIT.ORA parameter LOG_BUFFER controls the size, which is specified in bytes, and must be a multiple of DB_BLOCK_SIZE. The default value for this parameter depends on the platform but is generally four times the size of the platform's block size.

LGWR is the process responsible for writing this information from the log buffers to the redo logs. If the log buffer is full, processes must wait until the LGWR process clears out this buffer (by writing to disk) before allowing more information to be written to this buffer. Performance decreases when users must wait for this event.

SYS.V$SYSSTAT is the performance table that contains statistics on this and other events. To find the number of requests for space in the log buffer, use the following query:

```
SELECT name, value
  FROM v$sysstat
  WHERE name = 'redo log space requests';
```

NOTE

Access to this view and other V$ views is restricted to SYS and users who have been granted the SELECT ANY TABLE privilege.

The value from the above query should be as close to zero as possible. Monitor this statistic over one or more days. If this value consistently grows, you may need to increase the size of LOG_BUFFER in the INIT.ORA file to alleviate the contention for the log buffer. However, contention for the log buffer does not usually decrease database performance.

Shared Pool

The shared pool is an area of memory in the SGA set aside for SQL areas; PL/SQL packages and procedures; and locking, data dictionary, and library cache information. It has three areas:

■ Library-cache information

■ Dictionary-cache information

■ Session information

The shared-pool size is determined by the INIT.ORA parameter SHARED_POOL_SIZE and is measured in bytes. Tuning efforts are directed to the three parts of the shared pool.

The Library Cache

The library cache contains SQL and PL/SQL information for the private and public SQL areas, as well as session information. Specifically, the SQL information contains parse data, execution plans, and statistics on all SQL statements that have been executed. Like the buffer cache, the library cache information is based on an LRU rule, in which items at the head of the LRU list are purged from memory on an as-needed basis. When items are purged and then reloaded, the statements must be reparsed.

The terms *pins* and *reloads* are important in this discussion of the library cache.

Pins refers to the number of times SQL and PL/SQL statements were found in the shared SQL area and executed without being reparsed.

Reloads refers to the number of times SQL and PL/SQL statements were reparsed and stored into the shared SQL area.

Because reloading statements requires sending the statement through the optimizer and generating execution plans, retrieving the execution plan from memory and executing it without having to reparse is a much faster process. In environments where many users are running the same application, this method can result in a significant performance benefit.

To find the pin/hit ratio, query the V$LIBRARYCACHE table as follows:

```
SELECT
  SUM(pins) "Pinned", SUM(reloads) "Reloaded"
  FROM v$librarycache;
```

The output of this query might look like this:

```
Pinned    Reloaded
------    --------
163948       1921
```

The following formula calculates the pin/hit ratio:

Pin/Hit ratio = Pinned ÷ Reloaded

The preceding value evaluates to about 1 percent. The target value for reloads should be as close to zero as possible. You can take two steps to decrease this value. First and foremost, write identical SQL statements whenever possible. Because the parser considers uppercase and lowercase letters to be different, two identical SQL statements that differ in case will be parsed separately. The second option is to increase the value of SHARED_POOL_SIZE in the INIT.ORA file to accommodate differing SQL statements. However, you must be careful to ensure that the new size does not force the system to swap part of the SGA to disk. Instead of increasing performance, it will have a negative effect.

DBMS_SHARED_POOL

Oracle provides several SQL scripts that create a package called DBMS_SHARED_POOL. This package provides a way to pin, or force, SQL, PL/SQL packages, and database triggers to stay resident in memory. Consequently, the pinned item is no longer susceptible to the LRU aging mechanism. This procedure can prevent the unexpected slowdowns that users may encounter when a statement or set of items has been aged out of memory and must be reloaded and parsed.

In order to enable this option, you must run two SQL scripts: DBMSPOOL.SQL and PRVTPOOL.SQL. These SQL scripts create the specification and package body for DBMS_SHARED_POOL. The location of these files is installation-specific. Please refer to the Oracle installation documentation for further information on where to locate these files and how to use the features of the package.

Please refer to the section "Tuning Database Objects" later in this chapter for a complete overview of how to use this option.

Data Dictionary Cache

The data dictionary is a very important part of the SGA. The data dictionary is responsible for loading and keeping track of the information pertaining to the database, such as

- Oracle users
- User roles and privileges
- Names of database objects (triggers, packages, indexes, and so on)
- Auditing information
- Space allocation and usage

The data dictionary is subject to the LRU aging mechanism, as are most other portions of the SGA. Failure to cache enough information in the data dictionary can result in premature aging of information to make room for currently needed data.

You can use the dynamic performance table V$ROWCACHE to check the activity of the data dictionary. This table contains quite a few columns, but two are of particular interest: GETS and GETMISSES. The following query can approximate the effectiveness of the data dictionary:

```
SELECT SUM(gets) "Read Requests"
  SUM(getmisses) "Reads Not in Memory"
  FROM v$rowcache;
```

The output should look like the following:

```
Read Requests      Reads Not in Memory
-------------      -------------------
        19374                      612
```

The following formula calculates the percentage of hits:

Hits = 100 × (Read Requests ÷ Reads Not in Memory)

The above value evaluates to about 3.5 percent misses. Oracle suggests this value be no more than 10–15 percent. If this value continues to increase, you should make more memory available to the data dictionary by increasing the value of SHARED_POOL_SIZE.

Cursors

Cursors are handles or pointers to a private SQL area in the SGA. The more cursors open for a session, the greater the memory requirements for the session, which in turn means greater memory requirements for the application. When working with cursor tuning, a trade-off occurs between performance of the cursor and its SQL statements, and performance of the database.

If too many cursors are open, Oracle may begin to swap out information from the shared pool in an attempt to make more room for the cursors. If cursors are closed and then reused, both Oracle and the application must reopen them, causing delays in execution. You also achieve a performance gain when explicitly opening a cursor, as opposed to allowing Oracle to implicitly open a cursor. The following guidelines may help in measuring these trade-offs:

- When possible, explicitly open a cursor.
- Unless memory is a concern, do not close the cursor if it will be used again.
- Explicitly close a cursor when completely finished with it.
- Limit the number of concurrently open cursors to limit memory requirements.

Here are some INIT.ORA parameters that you can use to increase performance:

Parameter	Values	Description
CLOSE_CACHED_OPEN_CURSORS	TRUE/FALSE	Tells Oracle whether to explicitly close all cursors associated with a call of a PL/SQL block when a COMMIT or ROLLBACK statement has been issued. If cursors are frequently reused, setting this value to FALSE increases subsequent executions of the cursor. Setting the value to TRUE decreases overall memory utilization by freeing memory after each COMMIT or ROLLBACK.
CURSOR_SPACE_FOR_TIME	TRUE/FALSE	This parameter tells Oracle to keep shared SQL areas in the shared pool as long as there is an open cursor against the shared area. Setting it to FALSE allows Oracle to age out the shared area when the space is not in use, though cursors are still open. Set this value to TRUE only if the shared pool has enough room to hold all open cursors.
OPEN CURSORS	1-platform specific	Sets the maximum number of cursors a session can have at one time. If the value is 25, the 26th attempt to open a new cursor will result in an error.

The V$SESSION_CURSOR_CACHE and V$SYSTEM_CURSOR_CACHE provide information about session and system-wide cursor statistics, respectively. Just like the shared pool, the ratio of hits to misses is a very good indication of whether cursors are being opened and then closed efficiently. The HITS_RATIO should be as high as possible.

Tuning Database Objects

Developing applications and databases requires flexibility. Because creating an object that is useful in all situations or whose use does not change in time is difficult, Oracle allows you to specify a great many options when creating database objects. As a table or index grows or its purpose in the database changes, options that were once useful can become obsolete, and options that once provided great performance benefits can become performance issues.

Therefore, you should always consider current and future uses of the database objects you create. Some issues to consider are

- The initial size of the object
- The object's growth on a regular basis
- The object's function

Although a database administrator's job is to maintain a database, a developer usually designs new objects that are added to the database. These objects include PL/SQL blocks, triggers, constraints, and possibly even tables, indexes, and clusters. Consequently, the developer needs to understand at least some of the options that can be specified when creating these objects.

Tuning Table Storage Parameters

Performance can be increased in SQL statements, in part, by some of the storage parameters used in creating the associated tables. If the database objects are not well-planned, dynamic storage allocation (allocating new storage when necessary, which slows performance) and chained rows (where a single row of data is stored across multiple data blocks, causing extra disk I/O) can occur, which in turn can hurt overall application performance. You need to plan the following items with care:

- Average row size
- Current block size
- Number of rows per block
- How dynamic the data is
- The rate of growth for the table

These items can affect the overall performance. If the data is static, you can save quite a bit of space by setting the values of PCTFREE and PCTUSED to appropriate values. Likewise, if the data is very dynamic, you can avoid chained rows and dynamic storage allocation by planning ahead.

Two values that directly affect how data is stored in the tablespace are explained in Table 30.4.

Table 30.4. CREATE TABLE storage parameters.

Parameter	Description
PCTFREE	The percentage of the data block reserved for updates to the block's rows
PCTUSED	The minimum percentage of space used in a data block before new rows can be added to the block's contents

If the value of PCTFREE is 15, 15 percent of each data block allocated to the table is set aside for growth of the table's rows. If the value of DB_BLOCK_SIZE is 4096 bytes (4K), then approximately 614 bytes of each block are set aside for updates to the rows within that block. The default value for PCTFREE is 10.

As rows are deleted from a table, the database monitors the calculated value of PCTUSED. If PCTUSED is set to 50 and the DB_BLOCK_SIZE is 4096, then the database will wait until 50 percent of the block is unused, or 2K is free, before inserting new rows into that data block. The default for PCTUSED is 40.

For large tables that are rarely updated to or deleted from, setting storage parameters to PCTFREE=0 and PCTUSED=99 saves quite a bit of space. The opposite is true if the table is consistently updated. Values of PCTFREE=15 and PCTUSED=60 might be appropriate. These values are explicitly tied to the data that will be stored in the table.

Estimating the correct values for these storage parameters is not an entirely easy process. No set of values works for every table or for every row within a table. One way to find values that will work for most rows in the table is to use the ANALYZE TABLE COMPUTE STATISTICS command against a preliminary version of the table and then retrieve the average row length from USER_TABLES.

Next, you must estimate the typical growth of each row. This percentage of growth to average size will determine the PCTFREE value.

Estimating the value for PCTUSED is a bit easier. Divide the DB_BLOCK_SIZE by the average row length to estimate the average number of rows per block. (The number will most likely be a bit less if rows larger than the average are taken into account.) The next step is to estimate the number of rows that will be deleted from the table before the database is allowed to insert new rows. Multiply the average row length by this estimate, divide it by the DB_BLOCK_SIZE to get the value for PCTUSED. This is only a beginning, however. Only time and testing will decide whether this value is too high or too low.

Enabling Parallel Queries

In Oracle7 you can increase the performance of many queries by using the parallel query option. This option allows a number of processes to divide the query among themselves to perform the query simultaneously. Once they are finished, they pass the results to a single process that completes any specific calculations or selections based on the original query.

Using the parallel option can be accomplished in two ways. First, you can add a SQL hint to the query to allow it to perform in parallel. Second, when the table is created, you can add a PARALLEL clause, which affects all queries against the specified table. For more information on the parallel query option see Appendix A, "Annotated SQL Commands," or the section "Tuning SQL" later in this chapter.

Managing Dynamic Storage Allocation on Tables

Tables can suffer performance losses on SQL commands such as INSERT and UPDATE when the storage parameters INITIAL and NEXT have been set too low. INITIAL is the size of the first extent that is allocated to a table. Once the database has filled this initial extent, it allocates a new extent to the table according to the value of NEXT. (See Appendix A for more information on the use of these options.)

If the values of INITIAL and NEXT are too small, the database is forced to continually add new extents to the table. This results in two types of performance losses. First, the transaction that forced the recursive call to add a new segment must wait until the database has completely allocated the extent. This process is fairly quick, but if done too many times, it creates a measurable performance loss.

Second, for applications that must perform a full table scan, additional waits occur because the new extents are rarely adjacent to the previous table's data blocks. This searching for the next extent forces additional waiting time while the database searches for the location of the next extent's location and reads new data blocks.

By estimating the growth of a table, you can set the INITIAL and NEXT values appropriately and minimize both types of performance loss. Estimating these sizes means taking into account the number of rows per block, the number of initial rows in the table, and the estimated growth rate per day or week. Once these values are estimated, the last step is deciding how much space to allocate for storage. Ideally, the values for INITIAL and NEXT should be large enough to give the database administrator enough time to measure the growth over a period of several weeks or months and then plan a time to reset the values to a more appropriate size.

Avoiding Chained Rows

When a table's row grows too big to fit in the current data block, Oracle attempts to *migrate the row*. If possible, the row is moved to a data block with enough free space to hold the entire row. If no block has enough free space to hold the entire row, Oracle will store the row in several data blocks; this process is called *chaining*.

Both migrating and chaining create performance problems because they require additional I/O to read and write. Queries that read these rows generally perform poorly because extra I/O is associated with reading the data.

You can use the ANALYZE TABLE command to count chained rows and then query the USER_TABLES view. The only way to fix chained rows is by exporting, dropping, and then reimporting the table with the chained rows. More information is available for these procedures in Appendix A and in Chapter 19, "Export/Import."

Tuning Index Storage Parameters

Tuning index storage parameters is usually more important than tuning the table parameters. Stated simply, if the database is for high-performance access, indexes will be used for unique and full scans, whereas tables will be accessed by ROWID, instead of by full scans. Therefore tuning the index storage parameters is usually a higher priority.

Tuning index storage is identical to tuning table storage, so follow the same rules for PCTFREE and PCTUSED settings. If unsure about the proper settings, estimate on the high side. A higher value will prevent chained index rows when you must keep the I/O count as tuned as possible.

Tuning SQL

Tuning SQL can lead to a fairly significant increase in performance, depending on the application using those statements. A common problem is the lack of SQL programming standards. Other problems include poorly written SQL statements and statements that do not make use of available indexes.

Making Use of Available Indexes

In order for Oracle to make use of indexes, you must specify a WHERE clause in the SQL statement. In addition, the columns in the WHERE clause must be part of the index. Conditions for using the indexes vary with the SQL command, how it is written, and how the index is stored. Here are some basic guidelines for using an index:

- Specify indexed columns in the WHERE clause. If the key is composite, use the AND operation between indexed columns.
- On single-column indexes, use the column name in a WHERE clause with an equality condition.
- If you are using a single columns in a WHERE clause and multiple indexes start with this column, use SQL hints to force the most logical choice for that index.

> **NOTE**
>
> Although Oracle does an excellent job of optimizing SQL statements for execution, a developer has a more complete knowledge of the data than the kernel does. The optimizer makes every attempt to choose wisely, but sometimes a developer will know more about how the data is distributed and which index is more likely to speed the retrieval of data.

Using SQL Hints

To override any index the optimizer might choose, use a hint within the SQL command. Options for using indexes are discussed in Appendix A.

The following example illustrates one use of SQL hints:

- The employees table has four columns: LAST_NAME, FIRST_NAME, EMPID, SECID.

- The employees table has two indexes: EMPLOYEES_EMPID_NAME: EMPID, LAST_NAME, FIRST_NAME (composite primary key)and EMPLOYEES_EMPID: EMPID (simple primary key).

By executing the SQL statement

```
SELECT /*+ INDEX(employees, employees_empid) */ employee, empid
  FROM employees
 WHERE empid = 74199;
```

the optimizer may decide to choose the EMPLOYEES_EMPID_NAME index, depending on the situation. There is an index on the EMPID column only, however, so the index may produce quicker results because there is less data that must be retrieved from disk (providing it is not already in memory). The hint specifying the EMPLOYEES_EMPID index guarantees that the smaller index will be used.

Standardizing SQL Statements

Although the Oracle kernel is advanced enough to know whether a SQL statement has already been parsed, and then skip to executing the parsed version, it is not smart enough to understand the difference between identical statements that differ in spacing or to distinguish between uppercase and lowercase SQL statements.

For example:

```
SELECT employee, secid FROM employees
```

is not the same as

```
SELECT EMPLOYEE, secid from EMPLOYEES
```

or

```
SELECT   employee, secid FROM employees
```

Because either case or spacing is different in each statement, the Oracle kernel parses each one, causing more time to pass before actually executing the statement. If the statements were identical, after the statement was parsed the first time, Oracle would store that information in the shared SQL area; the next time it was called, Oracle would use the parsed version. Avoiding that extra parse can be extremely valuable in environments in which the same SQL statements are executed many times for many different users.

Overriding the Optimizer Goal

As a general rule, Oracle databases should run in cost-based optimization. In this condition all SQL commands will be optimized for best throughput (the least amount of time to retrieve all rows from the database). If you need to retrieve the first set of rows from the database as quickly as possible, the optimizer goal can be altered in two ways:

- Override the optimizer goal with a hint.
- Use the ALTER SESSION command and change the value of OPTIMIZER_MODE.

For further explanation of these options, refer to Chapter 31,"Oracle's Query Optimizer."

Using EXPLAIN PLAN

You can use the SQL command EXPLAIN PLAN to view how the optimizer has optimized a SQL statement. The questions to ask are

- Are full table scans necessary?
- Can I create an index on the table(s) to better performance?
- Are the SQL commands making use of indexes?
- Is there a better choice for the index being used?

Chapter 31 and Chapter 32 describe how to use EXPLAIN PLAN.

Using TKPROF

TKPROF is another excellent tool for tuning SQL statements. Unlike EXPLAIN PLAN, TKPROF provides useful execution information, including

- Parse calls
- CPU time

■ Elapsed time
■ Disk I/O

This information can help to efficiently tune the SQL statements to minimize system resource usage while still providing the required information. Chapters 31 and 32 contain more information on using this utility. Below is a sample of the type of output TKPROF can provide.

```
***************************************************************************
SELECT COUNT(*)
FROM employees
WHERE username > 'GW0470' AND username < 'KL2501'
AND
empid < 70000 AND empid > 35000
call     count     cpu     elapsed     disk     query     current     rows
----     -----     ----    -------     ----     -----     -------     ----
Parse        9     0.00        0.00        0         0           0        0
Execute      8     0.00        0.00        0         0           0        0
Fetch        9     0.00        0.00      474       504           0        9
----     -----     ----    -------     ----     -----     -------     ----
total       27     0.00        0.00      474       504           0        9
Misses in library cche during parse:  9
Optimizer goal:  CHOOSE
Parsing user id:   17 (KELLY)
Rows    Execution Plan
----    ------------------------
0       SELECT STATEMENT   GOAL:  ALL_ROWS
0          SORT (AGGREGATE)
6822          INDEX  GOAL:  ANALYZA (RANGE SCAN) OF 'USERNAME_EMPID'
           (NON-UNIQUE)
***************************************************************************
```

Other Resources

As mentioned, tuning SQL statements before an application goes into production can provide some of the best performance gains. Writing efficient SQL statements requires, at the very least, a general understanding of Oracle and its internal workings. Please review the following chapters for additional information on tuning SQL:

■ Chapter 3, "The Elements of the SQL Language"
■ Chapter 4, "Oracle Queries"
■ Chapter 5, "Working with Date, Numeric, and Character Functions"
■ Chapter 6, "Complex Queries"
■ Chapter 7, "Innovative Techniques Using the Oracle Functions"
■ Chapter 12, "PL/SQL"
■ Chapter 13, "Embedded SQL and the Oracle Precompilers"
■ Chapter 31, "Oracle's Query Optimizer"
■ Chapter 32, "Debugging Tools"
■ Appendix A, "Annotated SQL Commands"

Tuning Applications

One of the most critical parts of tuning database applications is writing efficient SQL statements. At the development stage of a project, following a rigid set of guidelines can provide better performance gain than tuning can, especially once the application has been completed. (See the section "Tuning SQL" for a more complete list of guidelines.)

Unfortunately, you do not always have the opportunity to tune the SQL part of an application. When this is the case, your only choice is to minimize the effects of untuned SQL statements. Still, several options can help the application performance.

Part of tuning an application is understanding the application's resource usage. Once the application's performance has been logged, you can examine the statistics and decide on a course of action. One feature of Oracle is application registration. By registering an application with the Oracle database, you can track its resource usage and performance.

Registering an Application

You can register applications in the database to help track resource usage by using a module name and an action name. Resource usage is tracked via the V$SESSION and V$SQLAREA tables under the SYS account. Users with access to the SYS account or those that have been granted the SELECT ANY TABLE privilege can view the data in these tables.

The application, unfortunately, must be coded to use these Oracle features, but the benefits far outweigh the special coding necessities. Oracle provides a PL/SQL package called DBMS_APPLICATION_INFO, which is created by the DBMSUTL.SQL script. Because the location of this script is platform- and installation-specific, please check the Oracle documentation for further information on where to find it.

The DBMSUTL.SQL script creates the DBMS_APPLICATION_INFO package and makes available five procedures that can be called from an application. These function calls are used strictly to associate the code with an application and module to help track the application's resource usage; they are listed in Table 30.5.

Table 30.5. DBMS_APPLICATION_INFO procedures.

Function	Description
SET_MODULE	Sets the module and action names for the executing source. This procedure should be used for the first call of an application.
SET_ACTION	Sets the action name for the application. This procedure sets only the action name, unlike SET_MODULE that sets both the module and action names.
SET_CLIENT_INFO	Sets a 64-byte field with information that can be used to track the client that executed the application calls.

Function	Description
READ_MODULE	Reads the module and action information from the V$SESSION and V$SQLAREA tables. This function can be used to retrieve information on the specified module and the actions recorded.
READ_CLIENT_INFO	Reads the client information from the V$SESSION tables based on the client name specified.

Here are some guidelines for registering applications:

- When setting the module name, give it either the application name, a stored procedure name, or some other unique name to help track its use.

- When using an action name, be as specific as possible to describe the action that is taking place.

- It is a good idea to null out, or set to a null value, the module, action, and client information after each call. This step guarantees that the information is not being carried over from previous calls.

- Because the V$ tables are dynamic and contain information about applications and statistics for current and recent executions only, collection of the performance data should be recovered by the application or right after the application has run by a program written to gather those statistics. If they are not, the database will reset that information when it is restarted.

TIP

Module names are 48 characters or less. Anything longer than 48 characters will be truncated. If two module names are identical for the first 48 characters, they will be truncated at execution time. You may have difficulty deciding exactly where the SET_MODULE call originated.

Action names are 32 characters or less. Just like the module name, any action name longer than 32 characters will be truncated. Your results can have duplicate action names if you forget to pay close attention to this rule.

Examples of the DBMS_APPLICATION_INFO Procedures

Below are sample code statements using the procedures in the DBMS_APPLICATION_INFO package. The calls pertain to PL/SQL blocks.

Use the following syntax to call the SET_MODULE procedure:

```
CREATE PROCEDURE add_app_user(
    name        VARCHAR2(30),
    id          NUMBER(8),
    dept        VARCHAR2(30),
    role        VARCHAR2(15))
AS
BEGIN
   DBMS_APPLICATION_INFO.SET_MODULE(
       module_name = 'add_app_user',
       action_name = 'insert user into apps users table');
   INSERT INTO app_users
      (username, userid, department, role_name)
      VALUES (name, id, dept, role);
   DBMS_APPLICATION_INFO.SET_MODULE('','');
END;
```

Calling the SET_ACTION procedure requires syntax similar to the following:

```
CREATE PROCEDURE delete_app_user(
    name        VARCHAR2(30),
    id          NUMBER(8))
AS
BEGIN
  DBMS_APPLICATION_INFO.SET_ACTION(
    action_name = 'delete user from apps users table');
  DELETE FROM app_users
    WHERE app_users.username = name
    AND app_users.userid = id;
  DBMS_APPLICATION_INFO.SET_ACTION('');
END;
```

You can find additional examples in Oracle's *Server Tuning Guide* for version 7.3.

Using Triggers, PL/SQL and Constraints

Because part of application tuning is examining other options when a current scheme is not working, here is a group of alternatives to application programming. Not all application development necessarily uses a programming language as opposed to database objects, but sometimes it is easy to get into that mindset.

Many times an application developer will overlook the use of triggers, PL/SQL, and database constraints in favor of coding those types of functions directly into the application. In many ways, this makes sense because the application then removes some processing overhead from the server. In many other cases, though, coding the constraint enforcement into the application can increase the amount of network traffic generated in order to provide referential integrity. This can easily decrease the performance of the overall application.

You can use constraints in the database to guarantee various rules, including unique table entries and ensuring that values for a column fall within a specified range. Because these constraints are stored directly in the database and require no network traffic, unless they are associated to a view or link, they can be enforced more efficiently in the database.

You can store triggers directly in the database and use them to ensure certain data rules or auditing functions. Triggers can be coded to run before or after an action against a table's data has occurred, which makes them more powerful than constraints. Triggers are also much more flexible than constraints because triggers can be coded with PL/SQL commands. Consequently, they can do statements like SELECT, INSERT, UPDATE, DELETE, and so on, just like applications do. Unlike applications, though, they do not need to set up special communication channels with the database or incur network traffic to accomplish their checking and other tasks.

In functionality, PL/SQL can provide the same types of functionality that constraints and triggers do. However, it offers much more in the way of programming. PL/SQL blocks are stored in the database like other objects, but unlike others, they are compiled, which provides better performance. You should use PL/SQL when the scope of a task is large and when the size of a trigger would become excessively large. Oracle recommends a maximum of 60 lines in a trigger statement. If the trigger becomes larger than 60 lines, Oracle suggests using a PL/SQL procedure instead of a trigger.

Although I can't offer strict rules on how, when, or where to use these database objects, here are a few simple guidelines that can help you decide. Ask these questions when designing or tuning an application:

- Is network traffic a consideration?
- Will using constraint, triggers, and PL/SQL packages reduce database contention?
- Does the application need to enforce specific business rules?
- Will performance increase or decrease if the rules are enforced in the database?

Tuning Client/Server Applications

A client/server environment is very network-reliant because the database and application are generally not running on the same computer. In order to make this kind of configuration as efficient as possible, network traffic should be tuned to communicate only when necessary.

Limiting Network Traffic with ARRAYSIZE

Every programming language has some tool that limits the number of fetches returned for a single transfer. Oracle generally refers to this variable as ARRAYSIZE. (SQL*Plus, for example, uses this parameter.) The default for ARRAYSIZE is 20. For every packet sent across the network, 20 fetches, or rows, will be returned. If this value is set too low, many more packets will be required to return the same amount of data that might be sent with a single packet.

Generally speaking, limiting the number of packets transferred is more important than keeping the packet size small. Because each packet has a header, trailer, source and destination information, and data, the recipient must read each packet, decode the information, and then deliver the data to the intended application. It stands to reason, then, that a larger packet with more information will take nearly the same amount of time to decode as a smaller one will take, since the data is only forwarded, not decoded.

For environments in which many rows are returned for each query, setting ARRAYSIZE to values as high as 200 or more can drastically increase network performance by decreasing the number of packets sent out. Please check your programming language documentation for its specific way of increasing this size.

Using Explicit Cursors

Additional network calls are needed each time a SQL SELECT statement is issued using an implicit cursor. For a single execution of a select statement, there is little performance gained by using the implicit cursor. But if the SELECT statement is called 50 times, 50 additional packets are sent to re-execute the SELECT statement. This is in addition to the rest of the network traffic associated with the statement. Explicit cursors avoid this unneeded network overhead by not having to send additional packets to reopen the cursor.

Summary

This chapter has discussed many options and their benefits for performance tuning, but by no means is this chapter extensive. Many tricks of the trade are learned by experimentation and time. Entire books have been dedicated to the topic of performance tuning. Database administrators as well as application developers would find it well worth their time and efforts to seek out these books. It is also a great idea to search through the files on the Internet, its discussion groups, and mailing lists.

31

Oracle's Query Optimizer

by Kelly Leigh

Oracle's query optimizer is a critical part in the execution of a transaction. The optimizer is responsible for breaking down Data Manipulation Language (DML) statements, such as SELECT, INSERT, UPDATE, or DELETE, identifying the most efficient way of executing the statement based on the chosen optimizer mode, and then returning the requested data. Because a SQL statement can usually be executed in more than one way, the optimizer is responsible for identifying the most efficient means of executing the statement.

Optimization can take many steps to complete, depending on the SQL statement. The steps used to execute the statement make up the execution plan, which the database follows to provide the desired results (updated or returned data). Each step in the execution plan (except the last step) has a single goal: to return a set of rows for its successor to use. The function of the last step is to return data to the user or application that issued the SQL statement.

Optimization Modes

Many factors govern how the optimizer creates an execution plan. These factors are based on the type of optimization method the database uses. At the database level, three choices for optimization modes are available. The database parameter OPTIMIZER_MODE, which is located in the INIT.ORA parameter file, determines which default type of optimization mode the instance will use. The types of optimization modes are

- Rule: Uses rule-based optimization.
- Cost: Uses cost-based optimization.
- Choose: Allows the kernel to choose between cost or rule but is not a true optimization mode.

CAUTION

Here are three points of wisdom to consider:

First, each new version of Oracle may modify the method by which the optimizer makes a statement more efficient. Consequently, the optimizer in a given version may function differently than other optimizers, and the performance of each statement passed to the optimizer may vary according to the version of Oracle being used.

Second, although the optimizer makes every attempt to create an execution plan that is optimal in performance, the developer has the true knowledge of the data and its purpose. In some situations, the developer may be able to choose a more efficient means of executing the statement than the optimizer can. Whenever possible, the developer should use the EXPLAIN PLAN option of the database to examine the execution plan provided by the optimizer. If a better method of optimization exists, such as using an index different than what the optimizer has chosen, the developer can use SQL hints to force the index's use.

Finally, when working with the optimizer and the EXPLAIN PLAN option, the results may be very different when you are in a single-user database environment or using small amounts of data than they will be in a production environment. If possible, use as close to a production environment as possible when making final adjustments to any code. If you can't control your environment, consider keeping a very close eye on all code once it is promoted into production.

Rule-Based Query Optimization

Rule-based optimization rates the execution plans according to the access paths available and the information in Table 31.1. The rule-based approach uses those rankings to provide an overall rating on the execution plan and uses the plan with the lowest ranking. Generally speaking, the lower the rating, the shorter the execution time, although this is not always the case. If the optimizer finds more than one way to execute a block of code, it will use the operation with the lowest ranking.

Table 31.1. Access type ratings.

Ranking	Type of Access
1	Single row by ROWID
2	Single row by cluster join
3	Single row by cluster key with unique or primary key
4	Single row by unique or primary key
5	Cluster join
6	Hash cluster key
7	Indexed cluster key
8	Composite index
9	Single-column index
10	Bounded range search on indexed columns
11	Unbounded range search on indexed columns
12	Sort-merge join
13	MAX() or MIN() of indexed column
14	ORDER BY on indexed columns
15	Full table scan

> **CAUTION**
>
> Rule-based optimization is currently being provided for backwards support. Future versions of Oracle will not support this method of optimization. If at all possible, use cost-based optimization for the database instance, as opposed to using hints from within SQL statements. With the improvements in cost-based optimization since version 6, the optimizer can choose an equally good, and usually better, optimization over the old rule-based optimization.

Cost-Based Query Optimization

Cost-based query optimization is an optimization mode that the database kernel uses to analyze SQL statements in order to provide the most efficient way of executing the statement. When the optimizer is running in cost-based mode, it follows these steps to decide which plan is the best way to execute the statement:

1. Generate a set of execution plans based on available access paths.
2. Rank each plan based on data generated by the ANALYZE command.
3. Choose the plan with the lowest ranking (using the least estimated amount of computer resources).

Cost-based optimization uses statistics generated by the ANALYZE command for tables, indexes, and clusters to estimate the total I/O, CPU, and memory requirements required to run each execution plan. Because the goal of the cost-based approach is to provide maximum throughput, the execution plan with the lowest ranking, or lowest estimated I/O, CPU, and memory requirements, will be used.

> **CAUTION**
>
> If using cost-based optimization, be sure to analyze all tables, indexes, and clusters that the queries access. If these objects do not have any analysis data, the Oracle kernel is forced to use rule-based optimization. This execution plan, almost surely, will not be as efficient as a cost-based optimization plan created using actual data created by the ANALYZE command.

The optimization used to provide the final cost of an execution plan is based on the following data dictionary views:

- USER_TABLES
- USER_TAB_COLUMNS
- USER_INDEXES

- USER_CLUSTERS
- ALL_TABLES
- ALL_TAB_COLUMNS
- ALL_INDEXES
- ALL_CLUSTERS
- DBA_TABLES
- DBA_TAB_COLUMNS
- DBA_INDEXES
- DBA_CLUSTERS

When a table, index, or cluster is first created, the statistics within the associated data dictionary views are set to default values. These values depend on how the database and tablespaces were initially set up. Tables 31.3, 31.4, 31.5, and 31.6 (at the end of this chapter) contain descriptions of these tables. Explanations of the table values and the data that changes as a result of using the ANALYZE command also appear later in this chapter.

TIP

If performance is a major consideration for the operation of a database, determining which tables have the fastest growth rate in storage and disk location is important. Once these tables have been determined, they should be analyzed by the database administrator on a regular basis to ensure the optimum performance of all queries and applications. Be careful, however, if you decide to run these commands during peak production hours. The use of the ANALYZE command can temporarily prevent any SELECT, INSERT, UPDATE, and DELETE statements from running until after the ANALYZE command has completed its operation.

When using cost-based optimization in the INIT.ORA parameter file, the instance defaults to an optimization mode based on maximum throughput. When using the cost-based optimization mode, you have a choice of two goals. The goal you choose depends on the application you are running and the overall performance you are seeking. You need to examine each goal carefully to determine which is better for your particular need. These two goals are

- ALL_ROWS
- FIRST_ROWS

Cost-Based Optimization: ALL_ROWS

ALL_ROWS is a means of optimizing the query to provide the overall best throughput for the query. Best throughput means that Oracle will attempt to return all rows that the query accesses in the shortest amount of time. The drawback to the ALL_ROWS goal is that the optimizer is more likely to perform a full table scan rather than an index scan. This is partly a result of the slight overhead caused by scanning an index and the fact that, depending on the data and the size of the tables and indexes, doing an index scan before selecting from the table could actually take longer. Using ALL_ROWS is also more likely to perform a sort-merge join rather than a nested-loops join. Again, this is due to the possibility that the sort-merge join could return all rows faster than the nested-loops join could.

Specific uses of the ALL_ROWS goal include the following:

- Reports running in the background
- Nightly processes
- Batch jobs
- Interactive programs needing access to all affected data before continuing operation
- Applications such as SQL*ReportWriter

> **NOTE**
>
> By default, when setting the Oracle instance to cost-based optimization, the instance optimizes for best throughput (ALL_ROWS). You can override the default setting, however, by adding hints to a SQL statement or by using the ALTER SESSION command. See the section "Changing Optimization Modes" later in this chapter for further explanation.

Cost-Based Optimization: FIRST_ROWS

You should use the FIRST_ROWS goal when you are trying to achieve the fastest response time, or the minimum time to retrieve the first rows retrieved by the query. The drawback of using this goal is that although it may be faster than other optimization methods when retrieving the first set of rows requested, it may take longer to retrieve all the data the query returns. However, this goal also makes more effective use of indexes than the ALL_ROWS goal does.

The FIRST_ROWS goal can play a very important part in

- Telemarketing or interactive order-processing software
- Applications in which users need immediate access to initial results
- Interactive applications in which response time is critical
- Applications like SQL*Forms or SQL*Plus queries

When using the FIRST_ROWS goal, the optimizer follows these rules:

■ If possible, choose an index scan over a full table scan.

■ If using an index scan, always choose a nested-loops join over a sort-merge join as long as the associated table can function as an inner table for the nested loop.

■ If using an ORDER BY clause, use any available indexes to avoid a sort operation.

NOTE

The FIRST_ROWS mode is ignored when executing any DELETE and UPDATE statements. It is also ignored in SELECT statements that contain any UNION, INTERSECT, MINUS, UNION ALL, GROUP BY, and other grouping functions and DISTINCT operations. These types of statements cannot be optimized for best response time because all rows that the statement accesses must be retrieved before the operation can return the first row. These statements will be optimized for best throughput.

Histograms

With previous versions of Oracle, the cost-based optimizer could only assume that the distribution of column data was even throughout the table. Unfortunately, if the data were skewed the estimation was not accurate and the optimization suffered for it.

With Oracle 7.3, Oracle introduces the use of data value histograms, which provide accurate estimates of column data distribution for tables with skewed data. Because most data is skewed, histograms can be very helpful.

For example, a table with even data distribution would have a histogram that looks something like this:

```
+   +   +   +   +   +   +   +   +   +
1   2   3   4   5   6   7   8   9   10
```

A table with uneven distribution might have a histogram that looks like this:

```
+   +   +   +   +   +   +   +   +   +
1   1   4   6   6   6   6   9   9   9
```

Because the data has a large percentage of values 6 and 9, the data is skewed. Using the ANALYZE command with the options that create histograms should help improve performance.

Histograms can be viewed in the following data dictionary views:

■ USER_HISTOGRAM

■ ALL_HISTOGRAMS

■ DBA_HISTOGRAMS

■ TAB_COLUMNS

You can use the ANALYZE command to create histograms. Just like the other data tables that ANALYZE affects, the ANALYZE data is useful only if it reflects the current data distribution. If the table's data is static, you should run ANALYZE on a periodic basis only. However, if the table data is highly dynamic, you should run the ANALYZE command on a regular basis, which will ensure optimum performance of the Oracle database.

Because histograms improve performance for tables with skewed data, you should do a bit of experimenting before deciding when and where to use histograms.

TIP

Histograms are not useful for columns that
- Are predicated with bind variables
- Have even data distribution
- Are not used in a WHERE clause of a SQL statement
- Are unique and used only with equality operands

Choose Mode

The choose mode of optimization option allows the Oracle kernel to make a choice between rule-based optimization and cost-based optimization. The rules for choosing are simple:

- Use cost mode if data dictionary statistics exist for the objects accessed by the query.
- Use rule mode if no data exists for the objects or if data exists only for some objects.

CAUTION

When deciding to use this mode, be sure to pay very close attention to users with access to the ANALYZE command. When a group of objects has been analyzed, the Oracle kernel immediately changes the optimization mode used to execute a SQL statement. This action can drastically change the performance of any affected SQL statements. Though unlikely, the performance of a previously tuned block of SQL code could deteriorate.

How the Query Optimizer Works

In order for the optimizer to do its job, it must first break a SQL statement into discrete steps. These steps all perform a simple function: return data to the parent step. Ultimately each step will either return a row through a physical read from memory or disk or return a row by a comparison of data that was passed to it by a child step. The steps that physically retrieve data from an object in the database are called *access paths*.

Steps to Optimizing a Query

When creating an execution plan, the optimizer uses a specific set of steps to break the query into the explain plan steps. During each step, the optimizer takes into account the various ways the step can be executed. In the event of multiple choices for execution, the optimizer chooses the step that most closely follows the selected optimizer mode. When the optimizer finishes the final step, the execution plan is complete.

The optimizer follows this sequence of steps to complete the explain plan. Each step is listed once, but after the optimizer modifies the original SQL statement, it may attempt to optimize it again. This second optimization ensures great flexibility in making a SQL statement more efficient.

Step 1: Evaluate Expressions and Conditions

Because there are many ways to accomplish the same goal, Oracle evaluates the SQL statement and translates equivalent syntactic constructs to preferred constructs. Oracle can usually operate more efficiently on the translated construct than on the original. Table 31.2 lists typical operations for this step. As the optimizer works, it may repeat a step several times before reaching its actual goal.

Table 31.2. Evaluation of expressions and conditions.

Expression	Operation
Constants	The optimizer computes a constant only once. When possible, all constants—including mathematical operations—are simplified.
LIKE	If no wildcard is specified with this operation, the optimizer translates the original statement to an equality condition. This is possible only when the comparison involves variable-length datatypes.
IN	These conditions are translated to equality and OR expressions.
ANY/SOME	If followed by a list of parenthesized values, these expressions will be translated into equality and OR expressions. If a subquery follows, the optimizer replaces the original query with an equivalent EXISTS statement.

continues

Table 31.2. continued

Expression	*Operation*
ALL	This operation is translated into an equivalent equality or AND expression when followed by a list of values. When followed by a subquery, the statement is re-created using the ANY option with the correct operands (for example, AND) to keep the original intent of the query.
BETWEEN	When the BETWEEN statement is specified, the optimizer replaces it with an equivalent statement that uses the <= and >= operands.
NOT	This condition is simplified to an equivalent expression that does not use the NOT comparison.
Transitivity	A statement like WHERE A = constant AND A = C can be rewritten as WHERE A = C. When this rewrite is possible without affecting the correct operation of the query, the optimizer will choose this option. Transitivity is used only when comparing a column (A) to a constant and can be used only with the cost-based optimization mode.

Step 2: Transform Statements

The transform statements step involves transforming the given statement into an equivalent, more efficient statement. The more efficient statement might use additional indexes that were not available to the original statement. These changes include

- ■ Changing ORs to UNION ALL operations
- ■ Transforming complex statements into joins

Step 3: Merge Views

If the original query accesses one or more database views, the optimizer examines the view's SQL statement and attempts to combine it with the original SQL statement it is optimizing. The optimizer can use two methods for merging the two statements.

Use the view's base table(s). The optimizer can modify the original SQL statement to access the view's base table(s) instead of the view itself. The optimizer either merges the view's query to the original query or merges the original query to the view's query. Both options produce the same effect.

Issue the view's query. Instead of merging the two SQL statements, the optimizer adds a subquery to return the data that the view is accessing. Once the data is returned, the original statement accesses those rows as if the data were a table.

Step 4: Select Access Paths

Selecting access paths is probably the most important step of the optimizer. The access path is critical in determining how quickly the data can be retrieved from memory or disk. (Table 31.1 shows the types of access and their relative speed of access.) Generally, the lower the ranking, the quicker the execution.

Here are the basic types of access paths:

Full table scans. Scans the entire table to read all rows. If a WHERE clause exists, each row is examined to determine whether it satisfies the condition. Although a full table scan is a very slow form of access, Oracle improves its overall performance by reading each data block once and performing multiple-block reads.

Table access by ROWID. By combining the datafile and data block containing the desired row with the location of the row from within the block, Oracle can quickly and efficiently read only the data it needs to retrieve the row. This method is the quickest way to access a single row.

Cluster scans. For tables that are stored in indexed clusters, the cluster key is retrieved by a cluster scan. Because all rows with the same cluster key value are stored in the same data blocks, Oracle can obtain the ROWID of one of the selected rows from the cluster index and then retrieve the rows based on the ROWID.

Hash scans. Like indexed clusters, all rows with the same hash key value are stored in the same data blocks. Oracle applies a hash function to a cluster key value from the statement and then scans the data blocks containing rows that match the hash value.

Index scans. Retrieves data from the index based on the values of the columns within the index. Oracle searches the index for values that satisfy the SQL statement. If the index contains all the data that is requested, the data is retrieved directly from the index and no table access is necessary. If more data is required to satisfy the statement, Oracle retrieves the ROWID and then performs a table access by ROWID to retrieve the remaining data. An index scan can be either a unique scan, meaning it returns only a single ROWID or set of data, or a range scan, which returns zero or more ROWIDs, depending on how many rows satisfy the statement.

Fast full index scans. This scan is an alternative to a full table scan when the index contains all the columns that the query has requested. It is normal for a full index scan to be used because it uses multiple-block I/O and can be parallelized like a table scan. The primary difference between a fast full index scan and a regular index scan is that the former cannot use keys. In addition, with a fast full index scan, the rows may not be returned in sorted order.

Step 5: Select Join Order

For all join statements that join three tables, the optimizer first chooses the tables to be joined, then chooses the table to be joined to that result, and so on. Oracle can choose from four join operations.

Nested-loop join. To perform a nested-loop join, Oracle follows these steps:

1. The optimizer chooses an outer, or driving, table and an inner table.

2. Using each row in the outer table, the optimizer retrieves all rows from the inner table, one by one, that satisfy the join condition.

3. The optimizer combines each pair of rows from step 2 and returns the pairs that meet the join condition.

Sort-merge join. If the row sources have not already been sorted, they are sorted according to the values of the columns in the join operation. Once the two sources have been sorted, all rows that satisfy the join condition are merged and returned. This type of operation can be performed only on equi-joins.

Cluster join. This join works only on an equi-join on two tables that have been clustered together. If the tables satisfy this first condition, the outer table is accessed with a full table scan. Each row returned from the full table scan is used to find the matching rows from the inner table by using a cluster scan.

Hash join. Like other joins, this join works only on an equi-join. To perform a hash join, Oracle follows these steps:

1. Oracle performs a full table scan on each table. Based on available memory, Oracle splits each table into as many partitions as possible and pairs them so that the partitions from the first table correspond to the partitions from the second.

2. Oracle uses one of the partitions created in step 1 to build a hash table.

3. Oracle uses the corresponding partition from the second table, which relates to the hash table in step 2, to probe the hash table. In other words, Oracle uses the smaller partition to build the hash table and uses the larger partition to probe that hash table.

4. Oracle repeats these steps for each pair of partitions created in step 1.

Viewing the Execution Plan

You can view the final execution plan by using the EXPLAIN PLAN SQL command or the TKPROF program with the EXPLAIN= option. The use of TKPROF requires turning on the SQL_TRACE option from within the current transaction or turning on SQL_TRACE from within the INIT.ORA parameter file.

> **CAUTION**
>
> Turning on the SQL_TRACE option from within the INIT.ORA file logs each session to a file on the database server. This process can use significant overhead, depending on the platform. The location of these trace files is derived from the USER_DUMP_DEST parameter in the INIT.ORA. Because of the performance overhead due to running a database with SQL_TRACE turned on, you should disable this option in all production databases.

Using the EXPLAIN PLAN Command

The EXPLAIN PLAN command is an interactive method of viewing the plan the optimizer uses to execute SQL statements. It is an invaluable tool for developing and also for debugging. In order to use EXPLAIN PLAN, though, a table called PLAN_TABLE must exist in the current schema.

To create the PLAN_TABLE, execute the utlxplan.sql file. This filename and location are platform-specific. Although the file generally resides in the rdbms/admin subdirectory, you may need to refer to the platform-specific Oracle documentation for detailed information on the file's location—or try a disk search of *plan.sql.

You can begin to debug SQL statements as soon as you create the PLAN_TABLE. To use the EXPLAIN PLAN command, add the SQL code to the following command:

```
EXPLAIN PLAN SET STATEMENT_ID = 'unique identifier'
  FOR sql statement;
```

Once the statement is explained (the statement is not actually executed), the PLAN_TABLE contains the explain plan that the optimizer created and would have followed. You can view this plan with the very simple SQL statement shown here:

```
SELECT operation, options, object_name FROM PLAN_TABLE
  WHERE statement_id = 'unique identifier'
  ORDER BY id;
```

This command lists each step that the optimizer used to execute a query. To learn more about the EXPLAIN PLAN command and how to interpret the information returned by the command, please refer to Chapter 30, "Performance Tuning," for further information.

Using TKPROF

Although EXPLAIN PLAN is a very useful way to find out exactly how Oracle is executing a SQL statement, it does not give any information, such as elapsed time, rows accessed, or rows returned. If you need this information, the TKPROF is infinitely more valuable. The basic difference in this command, however, is that the SQL statements will be executed!

The TKPROF program is dependent on the SQL trace files generated by the SQL_TRACE option. In this discussion, the ALTER SESSION command creates the trace files.

> **CAUTION**
>
> The DBA in the development group should be consulted before modifying the INIT.ORA parameters to provide tracing for all transactions. Enabling the tracing functions from the INIT.ORA parameter file can have a negative impact on database performance.

To start SQL tracing, use the command ALTER SESSION SET SQL_TRACE = TRUE;

Once tracing is started, execute all the SQL statements to generate their trace data. When finished, exit the SQL session and go to the directory in which the trace files are being generated. This location is specified in the INIT.ORA parameter file as USER_DUMP_DEST. To generate the explain plan from the SQL trace file, use the command:

```
tkprof (sql trace file) (output file) EXPLAIN=userid/password.
```

For example:

```
tkprof sql_12134.trc kelly.tkp EXPLAIN=kelly/kelly
```

When the command finishes, edit the file and search for unique strings embedded in the SQL query. Finding error messages such as ORA-01031: insufficient privileges is not uncommon, but should not have caused a problem with the execution of the SQL statements. The section that is of most help is

```
*****************************************************************************
SELECT COUNT(*)
FROM employees
  WHERE salary > 45000
  AND department in ('HR', 'IT', 'DEV')

call     count     cpu     elapsed     disk     query     current     rows
----     -----     ----    --------     ----     -----     -------     ----
Parse      16      0.02      0.01         0         0          0          0
Execute    15      0.01      0.00         0         0          0          0
Fetch      16      0.01      0.00       981       882          0         83
----     -----     ----    --------     ----     -----     -------     ----
total      47      0.04      0.01       981       882          0         83
Misses in library cche during parse:   16
Optimizer goal:  CHOOSE
Parsing user id:   17 (KELLY)
Rows    Execution Plan
----    -------------------------------------------------
0     SELECT STATEMENT  GOAL:  ALL_ROWS
0       SORT (AGGREGATE)
6822        INDEX  GOAL:  ANALYZE (RANGE SCAN) OF EMP_SAL_PK'
        (UNIQUE)
*****************************************************************************
```

This information is very helpful in performance tuning. The execution plan is probably the first area of concern. Once the plan looks as optimized as possible (accessing the proper indexes, limiting full table scans whenever possible, and so on) begin examining the other details such as CPU and elapsed time, as well as library cache misses. The information which TKPROF provides about disk access, CPU use, and so on, can be used to fine-tune any database operation.

> **TIP**
>
> SQL trace files are generally created with a process ID embedded in the filename. The best way to locate a trace file is to keep track of the start and end times of the SQL session. The time the session was exited should be the final modification date of the file.

Changing Optimization Modes

Sometimes a developer can choose the optimization mode more effectively than the optimizer can, so Oracle gives you three ways to enable the different types of optimization modes and goals. As described earlier in the chapter, each optimizer mode and goal has a specific purpose. Obviously, not all modes work equally well with all code. Likewise, not all methods of enabling these modes work equally well for different types of code. The three ways to change optimization modes are

■ SQL hints
■ The `ALTER SESSION` command
■ The `INIT.ORA` parameter file

Generally, Oracle7 databases run under cost-based optimization. Therefore, you should test your code to determine whether it will run better under another optimization mode.

SQL Hints

Specifying hints in the SQL statements works at the statement level from within the transaction and affects only the current statement. Therefore, it does not affect any subsequent SQL calls, nor does it affect any PL/SQL blocks, triggers, or procedures called by the SQL statement.

This chapter is concerned with only three of Oracle's numerous SQL hint options:

■ ALL_ROWS
■ FIRST_ROWS
■ RULE

The first way to specify a hint in a SQL statement is to use the /*+ */ string where the hint is placed between the + and the last *. Another option is to use the - -+ string, where the hint follows the +, which is then followed by the remaining part of the SQL statement.

Here is an example of how to specify hints:

```
SELECT /*+ ALL_ROWS */ table_name, tablespace_name
  FROM user_tables
  WHERE table_name = 'KELLY';

SELECT --+ FIRST_ROWS  employee_id, salary, job_title
  FROM kelly
  WHERE dept = 'Human Resources'
  AND employee_id = 71432;
```

The ALTER SESSION Command

You can use the ALTER SESSION SET OPTIMIZER_GOAL SQL command to affect all statements at the transaction level. This command overrides the OPTIMIZER_MODE initialization parameter and forces all statements within the current transaction to be optimized according to the new value. The ALTER SESSION SET OPTIMIZER_GOAL command has four possible values:

- CHOOSE—Tells the optimizer to search the data dictionary views for data on at least one related table (referenced in the SQL statement). If the data exists, the optimizer will optimize the statement according to the cost-based approach. If no data exists for any tables being referenced, the optimizer will use rule-based optimization.

- ALL_ROWS—Chooses cost-based optimization with the goal of best throughput.

- FIRST_ROWS—Chooses cost-based optimization with the goal of best response time.

- RULE—Chooses rule-based optimization regardless of the presence of data in the data dictionary views related to the tables being referenced.

The ALTER SESSION SET OPTIMIZER_MODE command affects all SQL statements issued from within the transaction, including any functions and stored procedures that are called. However, the value of OPTIMIZER_MODE from the INIT.ORA parameter file is still used for any recursive SQL calls that Oracle issues on behalf of the transaction.

Examples of the ALTER SESSION command follow.

```
ALTER SESSION
  SET OPTIMIZER_GOAL = FIRST_ROWS;

ALTER SESSION
  SET OPTIMIZER_GOAL = CHOOSE;
```

These settings remain in effect until the transaction ends.

The `INIT.ORA` File

The `OPTIMIZER_MODE` initialization parameter tells the Oracle instance which default optimization mode to use. This mode will be used unless a SQL hint or `ALTER SESSION OPTIMIZER_GOAL` is specified. This option has only three valid values: `COST`, `RULE`, or `CHOOSE`. By default, the database will optimize for throughput when using `COST`.

The entry in the `INIT.ORA` file should look like one of the following:

```
OPTIMIZER_MODE = RULE

OPTIMIZER_MODE = COST
```

You can change this entry at any time, but you must stop and restart the database to effect the change.

> **CAUTION**
>
> You should take great care when changing this value, especially when changing from `RULE` to `COST` or `CHOOSE` mode. Unpredictable results may follow. Some queries that were performing perfectly under `RULE` mode may become drastically slower, and some may become faster. If migrating from an Oracle6 database and minimizing the amount of time the migration takes is very important, consider setting `OPTIMIZER_MODE = RULE` until you have time to examine and optimize the software's performance.

Using the `ANALYZE` Command

`ANALYZE` enables the query optimizer to fine-tune its execution plans. By gathering statistics on the tables, indexes, and clusters specified, the Oracle kernel can easily calculate the most efficient means of executing all SQL statements, accessing them based on the mode and/or goal being used. As mentioned previously, the `ANALYZE` command modifies a specific set of tables/views. You should be concerned specifically with the following views:

- USER_TABLES
- USER_TAB_COLUMNS
- USER_INDEXES
- USER_CLUSTERS
- USER_HISTOGRAMS
- TAB_COLUMNS

Please refer to Chapter 30 for a more in-depth discussion about using the `ANALYZE` command to tune SQL statements and improve database performance.

Data Modified by the ANALYZE Command

When creating an object (table, index, or cluster), the database adds entries to the appropriate tables using default information based on how the table was created. Other values added to these tables are unique to how the table was created and the parameters used in their creation. The modifications to these tables are listed below, in Tables 31.3 through 31.6.

Table 31.3. USER_TABLES.

Column Name	Description
NUM_ROWS	Number of rows in the table
BLOCKS	Number of data blocks used by the table
EMPTY_BLOCKS	Number of blocks that are free, generally freed by deletion from the table
AVG_SPACE	Average number of data blocks taken up by rows
CHAIN_CNT	Number of rows chained across data blocks
AVG_ROW_LEN	Average size of each row in the table

Table 31.4. USER_TAB_COLUMNS.

Column Name	Description
NUM_DISTINCT	Number of distinct values for each column

Table 31.5. USER_INDEXES.

Column Name	Description
BLEVEL	Number of levels to the b-tree index
LEAF_BLOCKS	Number of leafs at the end of the b-tree
DISTINCT_KEYS	Number of unique keys in the index
AVG_LEAF_BLOCKS_PER_KEY	Average number of leaf blocks for each key in the index
AVG_DATA_BLOCKS_PER_KEY	Average number of data blocks used by each key in the index

Table 31.6. USER_CLUSTERS.

Column Name	Description
AVG_BLOCKS_PER_KEY	Average number of data blocks used per key

Summary

Although Oracle provides the various optimization methods illustrated throughout this chapter, it is important to stress that the developer and database administrator usually have the best knowledge of the applications being run and the data within the database. They can use that knowledge, along with the understanding of Oracle's optimization methods, to tune the applications and the database for best performance.

Optimization modes are an important, and sometimes first, step in performance tuning. After you have used the best possible optimization mode for the database or query, you should follow additional tuning steps to achieve the best application and database performance.

32

Debugging Tools

by Kelly Leigh

"…OK. Something's not right here. It worked in development, didn't it? Everything seemed fine…response time was GREAT! So what's going on?"

First, don't panic. Take a deep breath; then close your eyes and count to 10. Done that? OK, open your eyes again and ponder these next sections.

Problems Generally Found

The situation above is not all that uncommon. Most problems in this area occur from a few simple oversights. The sections within this chapter discuss those oversights, and present some tools to help get to the root of the problem and find a good solution.

First off, common problems can include:

■ Gradual query slowdown over time
■ Extremely poor performance
■ Lengthy wait times
■ Timed-out sessions
■ Unexpected slowdowns or stops

Notice that each of the problems listed ultimately deals with performance. Quite honestly, that is not very strange. By the time a piece of code has reached a production machine, 99 percent of all problems (unexpected query results, major slowdowns, and so on) have already been taken care of. Now it is time to focus attention on the other 1 percent, or the unexpected problems.

Why Problems Occur

Most of the time, problems dealing with response time are caused by miscommunication, changes in the development environment never made to production, oversights during the development process, and testing against insufficient amounts of data.

Most development environments are separate database instances from the production environments, and contain only a portion of the data that production does, or will, contain. Keeping the development environment separate from production is almost a requirement. However, so is having similar amounts of data.

Many queries that run against just a few thousand rows perform flawlessly. The SQL statement is tuned; the statistics, if checked, look good. But what happens if you increase from 1,000 to 1,000,000 rows? Will the query perform in the same way?

What about storage allocation? A common problem associated with query slowdowns is an incorrect estimation of storage parameters on the tables and indexes. Chained rows, where a row's data is stored across more than one data block, at the very least require double the I/O of a single row that is not chained.

What are the initialization parameters of the production database instance? Are they identical to the development instance? Should they be? It's very possible that the production database will need added SGA and redo log buffers to handle the increased workload.

Identifying Problems

Overall, many of the problems seen in a production database can include:

- Increased data volume
- `INIT.ORA` parameters
- `OPTIMIZER_GOAL` is the same as in the development instance
- Unanalyzed tables
- Insufficient storage parameters on tables and indexes
- Lock contention between users

Increased Data Volume

Increased amounts of data in tables can cause a multitude of problems. These problems can greatly affect the performance of a query, which, in turn, can affect other users and their queries. If one query performs poorly, the performance of the entire database suffers. The trick lies in identifying where the problem started.

`INIT.ORA` Parameters

To set up a performance environment, many sites start with a copy of the development environment, or at the very least, a full export of tables, indexes, and the `INIT.ORA` parameter file. The export is an excellent place to start, but copying the `INIT.ORA` file can lead to some frustrating slowdowns, if not done carefully. If copying the `INIT.ORA` file, be sure to check the following:

- `SQL_TRACE` is set to FALSE.
- `OPTIMIZER_GOAL` is the same as what is set in development.
- `TIMED_STATISTICS` is set to FALSE.
- The SGA parameters are set at the appropriate levels.
- That there are enough rollback segments for the workload.
- `LOG_BUFFERS` are set high enough to prevent contention.

OPTIMIZER_GOAL

While the OPTIMIZER_GOAL parameter is part of the INIT.ORA file, it is worth mentioning on its own. If the OPTIMIZER_GOAL is set differently from the value used in the development environment, the instance is probably optimizing all of the SQL statements in a different way than they were optimized under development.

Some queries may even perform better, but overall, the OPTIMIZER_GOAL parameter is one of many that should not be changed from development to production. One exception to this rule is if the ALTER SESSION SET OPTIMIZER_GOAL command is used in every session created by the application. This overrides the session's default setting and uses the one specified in the ALTER SESSION command.

Unanalyzed Tables

Tied directly to the OPTIMIZER_GOAL parameter, if CHOOSE- or COST-based optimization is in use, the database instance attempts to use statistics generated by the analyze command. If no statistics exist, the instance either uses RULE-based optimization (if in CHOOSE mode), or estimates statistics for the table and then optimizes the query.

If the tables were analyzed in the development database, it was probably for the purpose of optimizing a query. In such a case, it is not surprising that the database chooses an execution plan that is not as good as it was in the development database, if that analysis data does not exist.

To verify whether a table has been analyzed or not, use the following command:

```
SELECT table_name, num_rows
  FROM user_tables
  WHERE table_name = 'USERS';

TABLE_NAME    NUM_ROWS
----------    --------
USERS
```

If the output for NUM_ROWS is NULL, the table has not been analyzed. Using ANALYZE TABLE *tablename* COMPUTE STATISTICS gathers the statistics for the table.

> **NOTE**
>
> Analyzing a table, whether in COMPUTE or ESTIMATE mode, makes the table unavailable for inserts or updates until the ANALYZE command finishes. You should not typically run this command against a production database during business hours.

Storage Allocation

Changing business and application needs, and wrongly predicted storage parameters, can cause the allocation of tables, indexes, and clusters in the database to be a performance impediment, instead of an asset. It is important to periodically analyze tables in the database to verify that the initial storage parameters set on the objects still remain effective. Items to watch out for are:

- Average row size
- Average rows per block
- Chained rows
- Number of extents

Two big hitters on the list are chained rows and extents.

Chained Rows

Chained rows are rows in the database object that are stored across two (or more) data blocks on disk. This requires the instance to read at least two blocks of data to retrieve the entire row. Since reading from disk is immensely slower than reading from memory, disk I/O should be as minimal as possible.

One or two chained rows are not a problem, but a percentage as high as 20 or more may be a sign of insufficient storage allocation. To check the value on the table, examine the statistics in USER_TABLES or DBA_TABLES with the following command:

```
SELECT table_name, chain_cnt
  FROM user_tables
  WHERE table_name = 'USERS';


TABLE_NAME    CHAIN_CNT
----------    ---------
USERS                 0
```

If the value is 0, or a low percentage of the total number of rows (NUM_ROWS), storage is probably sufficient. The idea behind storage allocation is to store the most common size rows without wasting disk space by allocating space for the largest row to be stored.

If storage allocation has been set too low, the table must be exported, the allocation on the table changed, and then the table reimported. There is no way to dynamically change some of the important storage parameters on a table or index.

Multiple Extents

An extent is a physical block of disk space used to store a database object (table, index, and so on). When a table or index runs out of space in an extent, the instance automatically allocates a new extent to the object. This continues until the value of MAX_EXTENTS (a storage parameter) is reached, or forever, if UNLIMITED is specified as the value of MAX_EXTENTS. Multiple extents require additional disk I/O and waits before retrieval of the object's data can begin again.

If indexes are used efficiently, multiple extents in a table are not a great concern, although they do slow down full table scans. Full table scans should be kept to a minimum, but sometimes they are impossible to eliminate.

Multiple extents on an index, on the other hand, almost always can be a cause for slowdowns. They may not be significant for one or two users, but if the multiple extents exist on an index used heavily by 400 or 500 users, and the index does not remain in memory, more and more time is spent doing disk I/O.

To identify the number of extents for a database object, use the following command:

```
SELECT segment_name, COUNT(*) "Extents", SUM(bytes)  "Bytes"
  FROM user_extents
  WHERE segment_name = 'USERS'
  GROUP BY segment_name;

Object    Extents    Bytes
------    -------    ------
USERS          1     512000
```

The number of extents should be as low as possible, but their number depends on the object type and environment. Again, as a general rule, the lower the number of extents, the better the performance of full table and index scans.

To compress extents on a table, the table must be exported, dropped, and imported. There is an option for the Import program called COMPRESS. The option defaults to YES. To compress extents on an index, simply drop and re-create the index.

Lock Contention

Some application developers use the FOR UPDATE clause on a SELECT statement, or a LOCK TABLE command before beginning updates. In some instances this is necessary, but at other times it can cause other users to wait for locks. To the database this appears as a process waiting for resources, but to a user it appears as poor response time.

Locking problems can be fixed by avoiding the unnecessary use of FOR UPDATE and LOCK TABLE statements, as well as by analyzing the current SQL statements and making sure they are not selecting too many rows in the FOR UPDATE clause.

Finding the Problem

At this point, the focus of this chapter is the debugging tools that can help to find where problems lie. Some of the same tools used for performance tuning can be used for debugging these various problems. They are mentioned elsewhere in this book, but not in as much depth.

Data Dictionary Performance Views

The data dictionary contains quite a few tables to help assist in analyzing performance and identifying where problems exist. Detailed descriptions can be found in the Oracle7 *Server Reference Manual.* The views listed below focus mainly, but not solely, on session statistics. Data dictionary views exist for instance-wide statistics, as well, but generally these are used for administration as opposed to debugging.

V$ACCESS

Used for tracking locking problems, this view contains information on all objects that are currently locked, the session IDs that have locked them, and the object being locked. This table can be used when tracing unexpected slowdowns and a locking issue is expected.

Column	Datatype	Description
SID	NUMBER	Session ID of the user/process accessing the object
OWNER	VARCHAR2	The object owner
OBJECT	VARCHAR2	The object name
OB_TYP	NUMBER	Numeric identifier of the object type

V$EVENT_NAME

This data dictionary view can be used as a lookup table for all of the event types, including parameters for the event.

Column	Datatype	Description
EVENT#	NUMBER	The wait event identifier
NAME	VARCHAR2(64)	The wait event name
PARAMETER1	VARCHAR2(64)	The first parameter of the wait event
PARAMETER2	VARCHAR2(64)	The second parameter of the wait event
PARAMETER3	VARCHAR2(64)	The third parameter of the wait event

V$LOCK

This is another instance-wide table, but this one lists all locks that are currently being held, the session IDs holding them, and the types of locks held and waited for. This can be one of the most important views for tracking locking problems.

Column	Datatype	Description
ADDR	RAW(4)	The address of the lock state object
KADDR	RAW(4)	The address of the lock
SID	NUMBER	The session ID of the user or session with the lock
TYPE	VARCHAR2(2)	The type of lock
ID1	NUMBER	The first lock-specific identifier
ID2	NUMBER	The second lock-specific identifier
LMODE	NUMBER	The current locking mode of the lock
REQUEST	NUMBER	The requested locking mode of the lock
CTIME	NUMBER	Cumulative time since lock was granted
BLOCK	NUMBER	Is this lock blocking another lock (0/1)?

V$SESSION_EVENT

Based on session ID and wait event, this view lists the statistics for this session/wait. TIME_WAITED and AVERAGE_WAIT contain values of 0, unless TIMED_STATISTICS is set to TRUE within the instance INIT.ORA file. Setting TIMED_STATISTICS to TRUE may cause a small percentage of performance loss; it should not be left in the TRUE state if performance is an issue.

Column	Datatype	Description
SID	NUMBER	The session ID
EVENT	VARCHAR2(64)	The wait event name
TOTAL_WAITS	NUMBER	Cumulative waits for this event name, per session
TOTAL_TIMEOUTS	NUMBER	The cumulative number of timeouts for this event, per session
TIME_WAITED	NUMBER	The cumulative amount of time, in hundredths of a second, spent waiting for this event
AVERAGE_WAIT	NUMBER	The average wait time for this event (in hundredths of a second)

V$SESSION_WAIT

Like V$EVENT_NAME, this view tracks wait events, but is based on the session statistics, as opposed to wait summaries. If a user seems to be locked up, and it is a common occurrence, this table can be queried to find the reason the session has frozen.

Column	Datatype	Description
SID	NUMBER	Session ID
SEQ#	NUMBER	The sequence number of this wait
EVENT	VARCHAR2	Event being waited for
P1TEXT	VARCHAR2	Description of parameter 1
P1	NUMBER	First parameter
P1RAW	RAW(4)	First parameter in hex
P2TEXT	VARCHAR2	Description of parameter 2
P2	NUMBER	Second parameter
P2RAW	RAW(4)	Second parameter in hex
P3TEXT	VARCHAR2	Description of parameter 3
P3	NUMBER	Third parameter
P3RAW	RAW(4)	Third parameter in hex
WAIT_TIME	NUMBER	0 if waiting, otherwise the last wait time
STATE	VARCHAR2	The current wait state

V$SQLTEXT

This view displays all SQL statements that belong to a shared cursor currently in the SGA. The V$SESSION and V$SQLTEXT views are linked by the SQL_ADDRESS and ADDRESS columns, respectively.

Column	Datatype	Description
ADDRESS	RAW	The memory address of the SQL command. Used with HASH_VALUE, it uniquely represents a cached cursor
HASH_VALUE	NUMBER	Uniquely identifies a cached cursor when combined with ADDRESS
PIECE	NUMBER	The sequence number used to piece the entire SQL statement back together in the proper order
SQL_TEXT	VARCHAR2	The piece(s) of the SQL command
COMMAND_TYPE	NUMBER	The unique ID of the type of SQL statement

Using the Dynamic Performance Views

Suppose there is a user, KCLOSE, who seems to be having a problem with performance. Currently he seems stuck and is getting no response from his terminal. One option is to break the current session and start it over, but that does not find the problem; it only circumvents it.

From another terminal, a developer with access to the performance views could use the following SQL commands to find more information on why KCLOSE is having problems.

Identifying Problems Using V$SESSION_WAIT

By querying the V$SESSION_WAIT view, it is possible to examine the most common events being waited on, and their wait times. This can point all problem resolution efforts in the right direction.

```
SELECT sid, event, wait_time
  FROM v$session_wait
  ORDER BY wait_time, event;

SID   EVENT                       WAIT_TIME
---   -----                       ---------
8     Null event                          0
71    enqueue                             0
2     rdbms ipc message                   0
3     rdbms ipc message                   0
5     rdbms ipc message                   0
6     SQL*Net message from client         1
22    SQL*Net message from client         1
8     SQL*Net message from client         2
18    SQL*Net message from client         4
25    db file sequential read             5
74    db file sequential read             6
12    db file sequential read             6
1     pmon timer                        200
4     smon timer                          0
14 rows selected.
```

Examining the output from the earlier query, it seems there are three possible problems. First, the sessions waiting for SQL*Net messages could indicate a network problem. Because the instance is waiting on the client, it is safe to assume the error is not caused by the instance being overly busy. The second possible problem is the wait time for sessions 25, 74, and 12. The event is db file sequential read, which could indicate an extremely busy database file.

Finally, SID 71 has an enqueue event that it is waiting on. Since WAIT_TIME is 0, the session is still waiting on this event. If you continue this query for a short period of time, and the value of WAIT_TIME never changes, it is possible that there is a locking problem. Let's assume that the locking problem does indeed exist. If values of WAIT_TIME are extremely large, such as the value 4294967295, it signifies that the wait time was less than one one-hundreth of a second. It is a representation of the value -1, in unsigned integer notation.

It is important to examine the V$SESSION_WAIT view at regular intervals to get an overall idea of how the database is performing. From the initial output just shown, it does seem that there is a network issue, a busy data file, and a locking problem, but there could be reasons for this. For instance, the four sessions with the SQL*Net event might have extremely busy PCs and the instance is only temporarily waiting for a response. It is also possible that the sessions with the db file sequential read wait are all running a similar report that normally is not run at this time of day, and is extremely I/O intensive.

Each problem has its unique characteristics and they cannot all be listed here. Knowing where to look for the start of problems is the beginning of the debugging process. How to carry on after that is a combination of knowledge and intuition. As an example, let's debug the enqueue wait from the previous SQL output.

Solving a Locking Problem

After querying the V$SESSION_WAIT for a few minutes, it turns out that session 71 is still waiting. Let's also say that a call was placed by KCLOSE stating that his application is locked and he cannot get any response from it. To find out exactly where the issue is, you can use a combination of performance views to see what is happening internally in the instance.

To find the SID for KCLOSE, query the V$SESSION view, which contains unique session information on a user. Providing KCLOSE is logged in to the database instance only once, the following query works. (The formatting of some of the following code has been changed so that the lines fit within the margins of the book).

```
SELECT sid, serial#, username, command, lockwait,
  status, server, schemaname, osuser, process,
  machine, terminal
  FROM v$session
  WHERE sid = 71;
```

SID	SERIAL#	USERNAME	COMMAND	LOCKWAIT	STATUS	SERVER
71	12696	KCLOSE	3	C15C3108	ACTIVE	DEDICATED

SCHEMANAME	OSUSER	PROCESS	SQL_ADDRESS	MACHINE	TERMINAL
KCLOSE	KELLYC	26721	C19F1488	wildfire	ttypb

This output shows that KCLOSE has a SID of 71, which is also the session that was waiting on a lock. Looking at LOCKWAIT, the lock ID is C15C3108 and KCLOSE is probably attempting to perform some INSERT or UPDATE function, since SELECT statements are usually not locked out from table selects. To find out who is holding the lock, you can search through the V$LOCK table for the lock ID:

```
SELECT *
  FROM v$lock
  WHERE kaddr = 'C15C3108';
```

ADDR	KADDR	SID	TYPE	ID1	ID2	LMODE	REQUEST	CTIME	BLOCK
C15C30F4	C15C3108	9	TM	1006	0	0	3	823	1

Here you can tell that SID 9 is holding the lock, and because of the value of BLOCK (1), there are other users waiting on this lock. KCLOSE, for example. By querying the V$SESSION table again, on SID 9, the value of SQL_ADDRESS can be used to find out exactly which SQL command is being run by SID 9, and then determine what the course of action should be.

```
SELECT sid, serial#, username, command, lockwait,
  status, server, schemaname, osuser, sql_address,
  process, machine, terminal
  FROM v$session
  WHERE sid = 9;
```

SID	SERIAL#	USERNAME	COMMAND	LOCKWAIT	STATUS	SERVER
71	12696	KURTH	3	C15C3108	ACTIVE	DEDICATED

SCHEMANAME	OSUSER	PROCESS	SQL_ADDRESS	MACHINE	TERMINAL
KURTH	KHOLZ	22411	C1B17858	wildfire	ttypb

Now you know that KURTH is holding the lock, he is not waiting on another lock, and that the SQL_ADDRESS of the command that caused the lock is C1B17858. By using a query against the V$SQLTEXT view to find the SQL command holding the lock, you can identify the SQL statement that caused the lock:

```
SELECT *
  FROM v$sqltext
  WHERE sql_address = 'C1B17858'
  ORDER BY piece;
```

ADDRESS	HASH_VALUE	COMMAND_TYPE	PIECE	SQL_TEXT
C1B17858	1697304552	3	1	LOCK TABLE station1 IN
EXCLUSIVE MODE				

Now you know that the user KHOLZ has locked the table in EXCLUSIVE mode. This person can either be contacted to request a release on the lock, or the administrator can use the ALTER SYSTEM KILL SESSION command to disconnect the user's session. At the time the session is terminated, all locks held by that user are relinquished, and processing should continue.

Data Dictionary Lock Views

Oracle provides a SQL command file that creates database tables and views to help in debugging and monitoring locking problems. While the name and location are operating system specific, the file can generally be found under `rdbms/admin`, and is called `catblock.sql`. When run, it provides the following tables/views:

- DBA_KGLLOCK
- DB_LOCK
- DBA_LOCKS
- DBA_LOCK_INTERNAL
- DBA_DML_LOCKS
- DBA_DDL_LOCKS
- DBA_WAITERS
- DBA_BLOCKERS

These tables are described in greater detail in the *Oracle7 Administrator's Guide*.

EXPLAIN PLAN

While EXPLAIN PLAN is an excellent command for performance tuning of SQL commands, it is also an excellent debugging tool. Since many sites keep separate development and production instances, there is always a chance a SQL command will perform differently in the production instance. This is a common cause of performance problems.

Using EXPLAIN PLAN when in the production instance shows how the query is actually performing. At this point the main concerns are:

- Are the indexes being used properly?
- Are there full table scans where there were none previously?
- Is there a better choice for the index use?
- Are the tables and indexes identical to those in development?

Creating PLAN_TABLE

Before using the EXPLAIN PLAN command, a specific table format must be used. The table name is generally PLAN_TABLE, but can be any name, so long as the columns and datatypes are the same.

The table can be created using the SQL command script UTLXPLAN.SQL, which usually resides in the `rdbms/admin` directory. The table can also be created using the following SQL command:

```
create table PLAN_TABLE (
statement_id      varchar2(30),
timestamp         date,
```

```
remarks           varchar2(80),
operation         varchar2(30),
options           varchar2(30),
object_node       varchar2(128),
object_owner      varchar2(30),
object_name       varchar2(30),
object_instance   numeric,
object_type       varchar2(30),
optimizer         varchar2(255),
search_columns    numeric,
id                numeric,
parent_id         numeric,
position          numeric,
cost              numeric,
cardinality       numeric,
bytes             numeric,
other_tag         varchar2(255),
other             long);
```

CAUTION

Although the PLAN_TABLE can be created using this script, the format of the table is dependent on the version of Oracle being run. It is highly recommended that the UTLXPLAN.SQL script be used.

The column descriptions in the PLAN_TABLE table are

STATEMENT_ID	A unique identifier given to the statement being explained
TIMESTAMP	The time and date that the EXPLAIN PLAN command was issued
REMARKS	A comment added to each line of the STATEMENT_ID
OPERATION	The operation being performed
OPTIONS	Options on the operation (such as GROUP BY)
OBNECT_NODE	The database link used, if any
OBJECT_OWNER	The owner of the object being accessed
OBJECT_NAME	The name of the object
OBJECT_INSTANCE	Where this object appears in the original statement
OBJECT_TYPE	The type of object (such as NON-UNIQUE)
OPTIMIZER	The optimizer goal used
SEARCH_COLUMNS	(Not implemented in V7.3)
ID	The step number for the entire statement

PARENT_ID	The predecessor of the current line (for ordering purposes)
POSITION	The ordering of all steps that have the same ID and PARENT_ID
OTHER	Miscellaneous information
OTHER_TAG	Describes the contents of OTHER
COST	The cost assigned to this step by the optimizer
CARDINALITY	The cost estimate used by the cost-based optimizer
BYTES	The cost-based optimizer's estimate of the number of bytes accessed by the step

Using the EXPLAIN PLAN Command

To use the EXPLAIN PLAN command, append the following SQL command to the beginning of the query:

```
EXPLAIN PLAN
  SET STATEMENT_ID = 'unique identifier'
  FOR
    (subquery);
```

where the subquery is the query to be explained. As an example, let's explain a selection from a table that contains a list of usernames. The output for this operation is as follows:

```
EXPLAIN PLAN
  SET STATEMENT_ID = 'username search'
  FOR
    SELECT username, first_name, last_name, location
    FROM users
    WHERE username = 'KCLOSE';
```

```
Explained
```

The statement has now been optimized, parsed, and the results of the optimizer's execution plan placed in the PLAN_TABLE table. To place the output into a table name other than PLAN_TABLE, use the INTO table clause and place it before the FOR clause.

> **NOTE**
>
> EXPLAIN PLAN is a non-destructive command. This means that when using EXPLAIN PLAN, the instance does not actually execute the SQL command. Instead it parses it, creates the execution plan, inserts the results into the PLAN_TABLE table, and then stops execution. No rows are inserted, updated, or deleted by the execution of EXPLAIN PLAN, with the exception of the data inserted into the PLAN_TABLE.

Interpreting the Execution Plan

Now that the execution plan has been placed in the PLAN_TABLE, the results can be displayed. To do this, another SQL command can be used. The output in the PLAN_TABLE table is ordered by ID and PARENT_ID, so a bit of ordering is necessary to display it in the proper order.

A plain SELECT statement can be used, but the display may not show the execution plan in the order the steps were executed by the instance.

```
SELECT LPAD(' ', 2*(LEVEL-1)) || operation || ' ' ||
    options || ' ' || object_name || ' ' || optimizer || ' ' ||
  DECODE(id, 0, 'Cost = '|| position) "Execution Plan"
  FROM plan_table
  START WITH id = 0
    AND statement_id = 'username search'
  CONNECT BY prior id = parent_id
    AND statement_id = 'username search';

Execution Plan
- - - - - - - - - - - - - - - - - - - - - - - - - - - - - - - - - - - - - - - - - - - - - - - - - - - - - - -
SELECT STATEMENT    CHOOSE Cost = 8
  TABLE ACCESS FULL USERS
  INDEX RANGE SCAN USERS_1

3 rows selected.
```

Depending on the output here, various actions should be taken. Most importantly, you should re-verify that the performance of this query is acceptable. Looking at the output above, there's a very good chance that the USERS_1 index is not defined properly; otherwise the query would have used the supposedly unique index USERS_1. Instead it did a range scan and then a full table scan.

Since this table is based on USERNAME, and a full table scan still resulted, the index is probably not unique, and there may even be duplicate values in the table. Further investigation shows that it is not a unique index. At this point, the index should be dropped and re-created; then EXPLAIN PLAN should be used again to verify that the query is now working properly.

As in performance tuning, several items that developers should watch for include

- Unnecessary full table scans
- The use of correct indexes
- The value of COST should be low
- The use of hints to override the optimizer's choices, if necessary

Using SQL Trace

Using the trace options creates a trace, or record, file of a session run against a database instance. Trace files can be generated at the session level or the instance level. If working with query problems in the production instance of a database, tracing should be done from the session level, to avoid unnecessary database down time and the performance hit that tracing each SQL statement can cause.

There are three INIT.ORA parameters that affect the trace facility and how the output is generated.

USER_DUMP_DEST

This parameter sets the destination for all trace files. Usually this destination is the udump directory beneath the instance's home directory (if using Oracle's OFA standards). This value can be any valid directory path and name on the database system.

MAX_DUMP_FILE_SIZE

This INIT.ORA parameter limits the maximum size of the dump files. By default, the value of this parameter is 500, which is specified in data blocks. The size of the data block is operating system dependent, but is generally 512K or 1024K. This makes the default value between 2.5MB and 5MB. This size is usually large enough for most applications, but any application with a long-running session containing many transactions may need to have this size increased. It is usually a good idea to limit a trace file to one or two transactions, providing they can be logically grouped that way.

TIMED_STATISTICS

In order to collect the timing on statistics, like elapsed CPU and parse time, the value of this parameter must be set to TRUE. Setting this value to TRUE causes the Oracle instance to make extra calls to timing functions, thereby slowing down the performance of the database. It should be turned on during tuning and debugging efforts, but turned off when those efforts are completed.

Starting a Trace Session

To start a trace session, the command ALTER SESSION SET SQL_TRACE = TRUE must be sent. This command can either be entered interactively, if the commands will be entered interactively, or added to the SQL command file or application, if the commands will be entered through either of these methods.

When this command is entered, all SQL commands that are entered, both directly and indirectly called, are added to the trace file. This includes startup commands, instance queries to NLS (National Language Support) features, and so on. The value of SQL_TRACE lasts until the session is disconnected, no matter how many transactions are completed.

Setting SQL_TRACE for Other Users

Oracle provides a PL/SQL package that allows an administrator to turn on SQL_TRACE for sessions already connected to the instance. This can alleviate the problems of having to modify applications or SQL command files to add the ALTER SESSION command.

To enable tracing for other sessions, the session ID and serial number must be found.

To find the SID and SERIAL#:

```
SELECT sid, serial#, username
  FROM v$session
  WHERE username = 'KCLOSE';

SID    SERIAL#    USERNAME
- - -  - - - - - - -  - - - - - - - -
 71        49    KCLOSE
```

To set the value of SQL_TRACE for KCLOSE,

```
EXECUTE dbms_system.set_sql_trace_in_session(71,49,TRUE);
```

where 71 is the SID, 49 is the SERIAL#, and TRUE is the value of SQL_TRACE to set.

Enabling SQL_TRACE for the Instance

To enable SQL_TRACE for all sessions that run against an instance, modify the INIT.ORA parameter and add/modify the following line:

```
SQL_TRACE = TRUE
```

> **NOTE**
>
> Setting this value to TRUE can have a negative impact on performance. For sites with very large databases and many uses, the performance loss can be extreme. Creating trace files also causes disk overhead by forcing trace files to be written for every session and SQL command issued against the instance. Use caution when enabling SQL_TRACE for an entire instance.

Viewing the Trace File

Once the session is completed, the trace file can be checked. The file is usually named in some form of ora_pid.trc, where pid is the process ID that started the session. The file, in its natural form, looks like this:

```
Dump file /u01/oracle/admin/v73/udump/ora_28325.trc
Oracle7 Server Release 7.3.2.2.0 - Production Release
With the distributed and parallel query options
PL/SQL Release 2.3.2.2.0 - Production
```

```
ORACLE_HOME = /oracle/product/7.3.2
System name:    HP-UX
Node name:      wildfire
Release:        B.10.20
Version:        A
Machine:        9000/869
Instance name: v73
Redo thread mounted by this instance: 1
Oracle process number: 9
Unix process pid: 28325, image: oraclev73


Sat Dec 14 15:42:25 1996
*** SESSION ID:(7.3343) 1996.12.14.15.42.25.952
APPNAME mod='SQL*Plus' mh=3375793674 act='' ah=403088694
=====================
PARSING IN CURSOR #1 len=33 dep=0 uid=19 oct=42 lid=19 tim=0 hv=2233225943 ad='c

17250f0'
alter session set SQL_TRACE=TRUE
END OF STMT
EXEC #1:c=0,e=0,p=0,cr=0,cu=0,mis=1,r=0,dep=0,og=4,tim=0
=====================
PARSING IN CURSOR #2 len=242 dep=0 uid=19 oct=3 lid=19 tim=0 hv=3931001927
ad='c1da5708' where (upper(parameter) in select parameter, value from
v$nls_parameters
('NLS_SORT','NLS_CURRENCY','NLS_ISO_CURRENCY', 'NLS_DATE_LANGUAGE',
'NLS_NUMERIC_CHARACTERS', 'NLS_LANGUAGE','NLS_TERRITORY'))
END OF STMT

PARSE #2:c=0,e=0,p=0,cr=0,cu=0,mis=0,r=0,dep=0,og=4,tim=0
EXEC #2:c=0,e=0,p=0,cr=0,cu=0,mis=0,r=0,dep=0,og=4,tim=0
FETCH #2:c=0,e=0,p=0,cr=0,cu=0,mis=0,r=7,dep=0,og=4,tim=0
STAT #2 id=1 cnt=9
=====================from v$nls_parameters        where (upper(parameter) = 'N
PARSING IN CURSOR #2 len=97 dep=0 uid=19 oct=3 lid=19 tim=0 hv=3370652249 ad='c1
LS_DATE_FORMAT')
END OF STMT
PARSE #2:c=0,e=0,p=0,cr=0,cu=0,mis=0,r=0,dep=0,og=4,tim=0
EXEC #2:c=0,e=0,p=0,cr=0,cu=0,mis=0,r=0,dep=0,og=4,tim=0
FETCH #2:c=0,e=0,p=0,cr=0,cu=0,mis=0,r=1,dep=0,og=4,tim=0
STAT #2 id=1 cnt=6
=====================
PARSING IN CURSOR #1 len=28 dep=0 uid=19 oct=3 lid=19 tim=0 hv=2648527759 ad='c1

724648'
select count(*) from users
END OF STMT
PARSE #1:c=0,e=0,p=0,cr=0,cu=0,mis=1,r=0,dep=0,og=4,tim=0
EXEC #1:c=0,e=0,p=0,cr=0,cu=0,mis=0,r=0,dep=0,og=4,tim=0
FETCH #1:c=0,e=0,p=0,cr=35,cu=2,mis=0,r=1,dep=0,og=4,tim=0
STAT #1 id=1 cnt=0
STAT #1 id=2 cnt=591
XCTEND rlbk=0, rd_only=1
XCTEND rlbk=0, rd_only=1
```

Unfortunately, the output is fairly useless in this format. To interpret the SQL trace files, a utility called TKPROF can be used.

Using TKPROF

TKPROF is an excellent tool not only for SQL performance tuning, but also for debugging. At times when EXPLAIN PLAN fails to give enough information, TKPROF can give total execution time, number of rows returned selected by the query, and so on. It is a very powerful and underutilized tool.

TKPROF is an executable as opposed to a SQL command. Usually located in the bin directory under the directory Oracle was installed in, it is typically named `tkprof73.exe` or `tkprof`. Location and name are platform dependent, so check the Oracle platform-specific manuals for the location and naming conventions.

TKPROF Syntax

The syntax of TKPROF is fairly simple to follow. In short, specify an input file and an output file. Other options can be added based on the output desired. If the program is executed without parameters, a summary of options is provided, and the output looks like the following:

```
Usage: tkprof tracefile outputfile [explain= ] [table= ]
             [print= ] [insert= ] [sys= ] [sort= ]
  table=schema.tablename    Use 'schema.tablename' with 'explain=' option.
  explain=user/password     Connect to ORACLE and issue EXPLAIN PLAIN.
  print=integer    List only the first 'integer' SQL statements.
  aggregate=yes¦no
  insert=filename     List SQL statements and data inside INSERT statements.
  sys=no    TKPROF does not list SQL statements run as user SYS.
  record=filename     Record non-recursive statements found in the trace file.
  sort=option    'Set of zero or more of the following sort options:
    prscnt      number of times parse was called
    prscpu      cpu time parsing
    prsela      elapsed time parsing
    prsdsk      number of disk reads during parse
    prsqry      number of buffers for consistent read during parse
    prscu       number of buffers for current read during parse
    prsmais     number of misses in library cache during parse
    execnt      number of execute was called
    execpu      cpu time spent executing
    exeela      elapsed time executing
    exedsk      number of disk reads during execute
    exeqry      number of buffers for consistent read during execute
    execu       number of buffers for current read during execute
    exerow      number of rows processed during execute
    exemis      number of library cache misses during execute
    fchcnt      number of times fetch was called
    fchcpu      cpu time spent fetching
    fchela      elapsed time fetching
    fchdsk      number of disk reads during fetch
    fchqry      number of buffers for consistent read during fetch
    fchcu       number of buffers for current read during fetch
    fchrow      number of rows fetched
    userid      userid of user that parsed the cursor
```

As an example, the file ora_121.trc was generated by the following commands:

```
ALTER SESSION SET SQL_TRACE = TRUE;

SELECT count(*)
  FROM station_location
  WHERE location IN
    (SELECT location FROM regions);

EXIT;
```

After the session ended, the trace file was closed. That places it in the format listed above, which is still unreadable. Using TKPROF, the file can be placed into a useful format. Using the EXPLAIN= option an EXPLAIN PLAN can also be generated to be added to the output of the TKPROF command.

The most typical options are EXPLAIN=*userid*/*password* and SYS=*NO*. This lists the EXPLAIN PLAN in the output file, as well as removes any statements executed by SYS (such as checking NLS parameters and other startup routines).

To create a readable file of the ora_121.trc file, let's use the following command:

```
TKPROF ora_121.trc ora_121.tkp EXPLAIN=kleigh/tiger SYS=NO
```

Once control is returned to the command prompt, the file ora_121.tkp should now exist. Editing the file should produce the following output:

```
TKPROF: Release 7.3.2.2.0 - Production on Sat Dec 14 16:04:35 1996

Copyright (c) Oracle Corporation 1979, 1994.  All rights reserved.

Trace file: ora_121.trc
Sort options: default

********************************************************************************
count    = number of times OCI procedure was executed
cpu      = cpu time in seconds executing
elapsed  = elapsed time in seconds executing
disk     = number of physical reads of buffers from disk
query    = number of buffers gotten for consistent read
current  = number of buffers gotten in current mode (usually for update)
rows     = number of rows processed by the fetch or execute call
********************************************************************************
select parameter, value
from
 v$nls_parameters     where (upper(parameter) in ('NLS_SORT','NLS_CURRENCY',
   'NLS_ISO_CURRENCY',                'NLS_DATE_LANGUAGE',
   'NLS_NUMERIC_CHARACTERS',                'NLS_LANGUAGE','NLS_TERRITORY'))

call     count      cpu     elapsed      disk      query    current      rows
------  -------  -------  ----------  --------  ---------  ---------  ---------
Parse         1     0.00        0.00         0          0          0          0
Execute       1     0.00        0.00         0          0          0          0
Fetch         1     0.00        0.00         0          0          0          7
------  -------  -------  ----------  --------  ---------  ---------  ---------
total         3     0.00        0.00         0          0          0          7
```

```
Misses in library cache during parse: 0
Optimizer goal: CHOOSE
Parsing user id: 19  (KLEIGH)
error during parse of EXPLAIN PLAN statement
ORA-01039: insufficient privileges on underlying objects of the view

parse error offset: 102
*********************************************************************************
SELECT count(*)
  FROM station_location
  WHERE location IN
    (SELECT location FROM regions);

call      count      cpu    elapsed       disk      query    current       rows
------    ------   ------   --------   --------   --------   --------   --------
Parse         1     0.00       0.00          0          0          0          0
Execute       1     0.00       0.00          0          0          0          0
Fetch         1     0.00       0.00         46         66          4          1
------    ------   ------   --------   --------   --------   --------   --------
total         3     0.00       0.00         46         66          4          1

Misses in library cache during parse: 1
Optimizer goal: CHOOSE
Parsing user id: 19  (KLEIGH)

Rows      Execution Plan
------    -----------------------------------------------------
     0    SELECT STATEMENT    GOAL: CHOOSE
     0     SORT (AGGREGATE)
   465      MERGE JOIN
  1054       SORT (JOIN)
  1054        TABLE ACCESS (FULL) OF 'STATION'
     3       SORT (JOIN)
     3        VIEW
  1054         SORT (UNIQUE)
  1054          TABLE ACCESS (FULL) OF 'REGION'


*********************************************************************************

OVERALL TOTALS FOR ALL NON-RECURSIVE STATEMENTS

call      count      cpu    elapsed       disk      query    current       rows
------    ------   ------   --------   --------   --------   --------   --------
Parse         5     0.00       0.00          0          0          0          0
Execute       6     0.00       0.00         13        642        618        589
Fetch         3     0.00       0.00         46         66          4          9
------    ------   ------   --------   --------   --------   --------   --------
total        14     0.00       0.00         59        708        622        598

Misses in library cache during parse: 2
Misses in library cache during execute: 1
```

```
OVERALL TOTALS FOR ALL RECURSIVE STATEMENTS
```

call	count	cpu	elapsed	disk	query	current	rows
Parse	0	0.00	0.00	0	0	0	0
Execute	0	0.00	0.00	0	0	0	0
Fetch	0	0.00	0.00	0	0	0	0
total	0	0.00	0.00	0	0	0	0

```
Misses in library cache during parse: 0

    6  user  SQL statements in session.
    0  internal SQL statements in session.
    6  SQL statements in session.
    2  statements EXPLAINed in this session.
**************************************************************************
Trace file: ora_121.trc
Trace file compatibility: 7.03.02
Sort options: default

    0  session in tracefile.
    6  user  SQL statements in trace file.
    0  internal SQL statements in trace file.
    6  SQL statements in trace file.
    6  unique SQL statements in trace file.
    2  SQL statements EXPLAINed using schema:
       KLEIGH.prof$plan_table
         Default table was used.
         Table was created.
         Table was dropped.
   75  lines in trace file.
```

> **NOTE**
>
> Notice that the values for columns like cpu and elapsed are empty? This is a good indication that the INIT.ORA parameter TIMED_STATISTICS is not set. (The default value is FALSE.) If the value should be set to TRUE, the instance must be stopped, the INIT.ORA file modified, and the instance started again. The parameter can also be enabled through SVRMGR interactively. See the *Oracle7 Server Administration Guide* for more information.

SVRMGR

Server manager, without going into great detail, is one final utility that can greatly help with debugging problems. While it is designed with performance tuning and analysis in mind, there are areas within its monitoring tools that can assist developers, too.

In brief, its monitoring capabilities include the following:

Circuits	Monitors MultiThreaded Server circuits
Dispatcher	Monitors the shared server processes of MultiThreaded Server
File I/O	Displays the I/O activity for each database file
Latch	Monitors latch usage within the SGA
Library Cache	Monitors the activity of the library cache
Lock	Lists all locks held within the database
Process	Shows all processes accessing the current instance
Queue	Monitors the MultiThreaded Server queues
Rollback	Displays the status of rollback segments and their usage
Session	Displays current session information
Shared Server	Shows statistics for the shared server processes of MultiThreaded Server
SQL Area	Monitors memory usage of SQL commands being executed or in cache
System I/O	Displays background process I/O information
System Statistics	Shows system runtime statistics
Table Access	Monitors table access by session
Tablespace	Displays tablespace information

Specifically, monitoring sessions, locks, and SQL areas can be an immense help in tracking down lock problems and session statistics. Oracle's *Server Manager Guide* is an excellent starting place to find out more about SVRMGR.

Summary

The commands and suggestions listed here are based on common problems. However, it could take an entire book to just begin to cover all problems, techniques, and tools available to developers for finding and fixing problems. There are many third-party packages that can assist in problem tracking and resolution and can be an immense help.

VIII

Other Oracle Concepts

33

Parallel Processing

by Kelly Leigh

Daily we are confronted with tasks that we must perform. Sometimes we can do them sequentially, but at other times they are all simple tasks that can be done in any order. If these tasks are time-consuming, we can spend an entire day working on them. If they are nonsequential, meaning that they can be done in any order, we can sometimes save quite a bit of time by enlisting the help of others.

Having help with those tasks is what Oracle Parallel Server is all about. Instead of the standard linear-processing model in which each task is performed one step at a time, Parallel Server can split a task into multiple, independent pieces and execute all the pieces simultaneously. Therefore, by using a parallel-processing model, the task is completed, usually, in just a fraction of the time it would have normally taken to finish the task.

Processing Models

A task can be performed either sequentially or in parallel. Sequential processing is sometimes necessary, but when a task is composed of multiple, individual tasks, parallel processing is usually the fastest method.

Response Time

Response time is the sum of the time required for the CPU to recognize a process and then execute the given task. If a process must wait in the queue for 2 seconds and then takes 3 seconds to process, its response time is 5 seconds. Tables 33.1 and 33.2 show the respective response times for sequential and parallel processing modes.

The Sequential Processing Model

Sequential processing, also called *linear processing*, involves processing a list of tasks in order. Step 1 must be completed first, step 2 waits for step 1 to finish, step 3 waits for step 2, and so on. Only when the final step is completed can another task begin. Table 33.1 shows an example of wait and elapsed times for sequential processing.

Table 33.1. Sequential processing response times.

Process	Executing on Processor #	Wait Time	Execution Time	Response Time	Description
Task A	0	0 sec.	2 sec.	2 sec.	Currently running on processor 0
Task B	0	2 sec.	1 sec.	3 sec.	Waiting for task A to complete

Process	Executing on Processor #	Wait Time	Execution Time	Response Time	Description
Task C	0	3 sec.	4 sec.	7 sec.	Waiting for task B to begin and complete
Task D	0	7 sec.	9 sec.	16 sec.	Waiting for task C to begin and complete

A trip to the grocery store is a good basic model of sequential processing. Suppose that Kurt thinks only sequentially. If he must go to the store for bread, mayonnaise, sliced turkey, lettuce, tomatoes, and soft drinks, he would have to search through each aisle for bread, for mayonnaise, and then stop at the deli for the turkey, and so on. Only after he has completed the first task will he go on to the next.

The total time it takes him to shop, or the elapsed time, could be as much as, say, 30 minutes, depending on how long he searches for each item.

The Parallel Processing Model

In *parallel processing*, a task is divided into individual steps that are processed concurrently, without waiting for a specific step to finish before starting the next. Once again, not all tasks can be processed in parallel, but those that can usually see an incredible increase in performance. Table 33.2 shows how parallel processing can speed up the processing of individual tasks.

Table 33.2. Parallel processing response times.

Process	Executing on Processor #	Wait Time	Execution Time	Response Time	Description
Task A	0	0 sec.	2 sec.	2 sec.	Currently running on processor 0
Task B	1	0 sec.	1 sec.	1 sec.	Currently running on processor 1
Task C	2	0 sec.	4 sec.	4 sec.	Currently running on processor 2
Task D	2	4 sec.	7 sec.	11 sec.	Waiting for task C to begin and complete

Using the grocery store as a model again, suppose that Kurt brings a few friends to help with the shopping: Jud, to find the bread; Byron, to look for the mayonnaise and soft drinks; and Chris, to wait in the deli line for sliced turkey, while Kurt searches for the lettuce and tomatoes. In just a fraction of the time Kurt needed to do the job alone, each person can finish his task and they can all meet at the checkout line to pay.

Waiting in the checkout line is an example of one task that cannot be completed in parallel. Kurt would still have to wait in line until the cashier was able to total his bill. However, the checkout line is another good example of linear versus parallel processing. If a second cashier came on duty, two customers could check out at the same time, instead of just one at a time.

Parallel Processing Goals

Parallel processing has two specific performance goals:

- Speedup
- Scaleup

Each goal can be measured, thereby proving how effective the parallel server is.

Speedup

Speedup is the measure of how fast a given task can be performed, or more important, how much the response time improves. Improving response time is generally done by adding more hardware (memory, processors, faster disks) to the system so that it performs faster.

To calculate speedup, divide the time it took to perform a given set of tasks before the upgrade by the time it took to perform the same set of tasks after the upgrade. This result is the speedup. The ideal speedup is where x times more hardware can do the task in $1 \div x$ the original time. The formula to calculate speedup is

$$\text{Speedup} = \frac{\text{Original Processing Time}}{\text{New Processing Time}}$$

For example, if the time to perform a set of tasks was originally 90 seconds, and it's now 45 seconds, the speedup is

$$\text{Speedup} = \frac{90}{45}$$

which equals 2. Because this effectively means that performance has doubled, this speedup is ideal.

> **NOTE**
>
> Additional hardware will not produce improved performance for all applications. For instance, applications that are extremely I/O intensive generally will not perform faster with additional hardware unless you also install a much quicker form of disk access, or a disk cache. Many Online Transaction Processing (OLTP) applications fall into this category.

Scaleup

Scaleup is the capability to keep response time consistent in the face of growing performance needs and system utilization. Just like speedup, scaleup is accomplished by adding hardware (processors, memory, disks) and its measure is determined by upgrading a system to x times larger in order to perform a task x times larger. The formula looks almost identical to speedup:

$$\text{Scaleup} = \frac{\text{New Volume}}{\text{Original Volume}}$$

Processing time remains consistent.

As an example, consider a system that is upgraded from two to four processors. If it originally took 90 seconds to perform 500 transactions and now the system can perform 1,000 transactions in the same amount of time, the scaleup is

$$\text{Scaleup} = \frac{1000}{500}$$

or 2. Like speedup, 2 is the ideal value for scaleup because doubling the hardware would cut the processing time in half.

Parallel Processing Obstacles

Parallel processing involves the breakdown of a task into smaller, independent parts that are sent to multiple processors to be executed. Oracle must overcome the following difficulties:

- Task breakdown
- Synchronization
- Locking
- Messaging

This simple math equation will be used to illustrate the steps in parallel processing:

```
x = (9 + 7) * (9 / 3) - (27 + 7) + 49 - 2
```

Task Breakdown

Breaking down a task into multiple parts is the first step in enabling a parallel database server to increase performance. Each task has specific parts that either can or cannot be separated. Breaking down the equation involves isolating each step that can be completed independently from the steps that depend on the results from the other steps. Once those individual steps are finished, they can be brought back to the initial equation, have their resulting values substituted into the equation, and then the final steps to the task can be completed.

The steps for processing the equation are similar to those listed in Table 33.3.

Table 33.3. Sample task breakdown.

StepZ	Task
1:	(9 + 7)
2:	(9 ÷ 3)
3:	(27 + 7)
4:	(step 1) × (step 2)
5:	49 – 2
6:	(step 4) – (step 3) + (step 5)

If we have a system with six processors, each step can go to a different CPU for processing, but steps 4 and 6 cannot be processed correctly until steps 1, 2, 3, and 5 have been completed and returned. Ensuring that each step is done in the correct order is called *synchronization*.

Synchronization

Synchronizing concurrently executing tasks is a very important task. It ensures that the proper values are returned to the query initiator. Unfortunately, though, synchronization can slow down overall processing. One of the goals of breaking down a task is to keep synchronization to a minimum. The example in Table 33.3 does not correctly illustrate the need to minimize synchronization, but can be used to show the effects of poor synchronization.

If all steps are synchronized properly, the value 61 should be returned. However, if the task is not synchronized properly, another value might be returned instead. This occurrence is not likely in this example, but if you are working with several queries that use joins, one query joined before the other could produce some unique, incorrect results.

Locking

Locking can play a very important part in synchronization. Certain queries may need to be performed after an update is done, or several processes may need to update the same table. Locking prevents those processes from updating the same records at the same time and also provides a way for the processes to synchronize themselves. Only after the first process is finished updating can the second process begin to update.

Internal locking in the database is not the only form of locking that takes place. Parallel databases, which are described in the section "Parallel Processing Architecture," use multiple instances to access the same database. When multiple instances access the same database file, an external program called the Distributed Lock Manager (DLM) reinforces the database locking scheme at the operating system level.

The DLM is responsible for coordinating the use of resources among multiple instances of a parallel database. Using the DLM, Oracle processes communicate with each other to perform SELECT, INSERT, UPDATE, and DELETE commands on shared database files and other resources.

Overall, the DLM is responsible for

- Tracking the ownership and use of a database resource
- Handling all lock requests for resources
- Notifying application processes when a resource has been unlocked and is available
- Attaining access to a database resource for a process

The DLM works in conjunction with Oracle Parallel Server to perform seamless handling of all system resources that the database and parallel instances must access. Because the DLM is an operating system program, it must start at system start time and is separate from the Oracle database kernel.

Messaging

In order for all nodes, or groups of processors, within a parallel system or parallel processing environment to work efficiently and synchronize concurrent processes, they must be able to communicate. This communication is called *messaging*.

Messaging usually takes place over a specialized interconnect, or bus, to connect all nodes. This interconnect is generally able to communicate quickly, with a high bandwidth and low latency. *Bandwidth* is the amount of data that can be communicated at the same time, and *latency* is the delay in sending a message. Ideally, the interconnect should have a high bandwidth and low latency. Interconnects can be ethernet networks or specialized cables connecting processing boards of multiple systems together.

Parallel Processing Architecture

The architecture behind parallel processing is two-fold: hardware and software. The software is the database software, and the hardware is a system with memory, disks, output devices, and multiple processors. Working together, the hardware and software can provide a tremendous increase in performance.

Hardware Platforms

Oracle Parallel Server can be installed only on a system that supports parallel processing. Hardware platforms that support parallel processing are called *parallel systems* and can be configured in various ways. All parallel systems have the following components:

- Main memory
- Disk storage
- Tape backup
- Multiple, independent processors

Although this list makes a parallel system sound like a typical multiprocessor system, the distinguishing feature of a parallel system is its ability to run tasks concurrently. The nodes (groups of processors) in the machine do not need to share processing time with the other nodes, and they don't have to wait for the scheduler in order to complete a task. Instead, each node is completely independent of the other nodes and can usually access disks, memory, and so on without their help.

The two main categories of parallel systems are

- Symmetrical multiprocessing (SMP)
- Massively parallel processing (MPP)

SMP systems have one main memory pool from which all nodes read and write. This provides very quick memory access and shared memory that can be accessed and managed by all nodes. In some cases it can speed up processing because all nodes communicate through shared memory. However, depending on the speed of the bus connecting each node, this type of processing can be costly.

MPP systems generally have several separate memory groupings that are independently owned by each node. This configuration separates the overall memory in the system into separate pools but gives each node quicker memory access because the node is responsible for reading and writing its own memory segment, instead of managing multiple node accesses.

Software

All parallel servers have two pieces of software in common: Oracle Parallel Server and the DLM. These two pieces of software, combined with the hardware, provide the entire support for an Oracle Parallel Server installation.

Parallel Server Configurations

Oracle Parallel Server can run on many hardware configurations, including Oracle Parallel Server running on a single node machine, multiple node machine, and multiple nodes across multiple machines.

The hardware configurations are named according to how each node is configured in a given system. The names are based on the type of resources shared across the nodes within a machine. The configuration names are

- Shared nothing
- Shared memory
- Shared disk

> **NOTE**
>
> Oracle runs across all the named configurations, but the ability to set up the system in a specific hardware configuration is platform dependent. You should contact both the hardware vendor and Oracle to verify that they support your desired configuration.
>
> Oracle also notes that running Oracle Parallel Server on a single node machine provides no benefit and incurs unnecessary overhead through the DLM processes.

In addition to the hardware configuration names, two additional terms describe categories of implementations: tightly coupled and loosely coupled. These terms refer to how the nodes of a system or group of systems are connected. *Tightly coupled* refers to a high bandwidth and low latency connection between nodes. *Loosely coupled* systems generally have a lower bandwidth and higher latency rating than tightly coupled systems.

Tightly coupled systems generally include MPP and SMP systems, whereas loosely coupled systems generally are clusters.

Shared Nothing Systems

A *shared nothing system* refers to the availability of a node's memory and disk on a system in relation to other nodes in the same system. In shared nothing systems, a one-to-one correlation exists between a node, its memory, and the disk (or disks) that the node owns. The database is configured so that specific data resides on the node's disk and all access to its disk (queries, updates, and so on) is routed specifically through the owning node. In many cases, each node has its own Oracle Parallel Server instance running on it. MPP systems, which are loosely coupled, generally are shared nothing systems, though they do not have to be. Shared nothing systems appear in Figure 33.1.

FIGURE 33.1.

Shared nothing systems with four nodes.

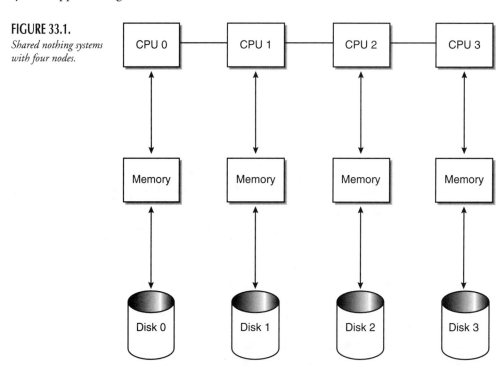

Each node is a separate entity with its own memory and disk access. To synchronize concurrent processes among nodes, a high-speed interconnect is used for messaging.

Several problems are inherent in this configuration. The most important problem is that if a node should fail and become unusable, all data on that disk is also unavailable. However, Oracle Parallel Server can continue to access the data on that disk as long as the operating system provides a transparent access across nodes, and the operating system and the database files were configured properly. This type of access has a very high latency and, in terms of Oracle, can be very costly. If the node is the only available node on a system, then in all probability the system is down and transparent data access will not be available.

Shared nothing systems, compared to the other shared configurations, require a bit more administrative work to maintain. Since each node runs its own database, database administration is compounded by the introduction of each new shared nothing system. Also, when introducing new systems into the environment, database and file reconfiguration may be necessary. This process can entail reconfiguration of the entire database. One other disadvantage of shared nothing systems is that cache consistency must be maintained across all nodes to ensure data consistency and integrity.

Although the disadvantages seem great for some environments, configuring multiple shared nothing nodes can offer the following advantages:

- Almost unlimited growth of new nodes in the environment
- Single-node failure does not disrupt other nodes and applications
- Independently configured and managed subsets of the logical database

Shared Memory Systems

Shared memory systems have separate nodes but share a single memory pool. To communicate, they use shared memory accessed through a common bus, which means that shared memory systems are tightly coupled systems. SMP systems usually belong to this category of system type. On shared memory systems, the bandwidth of the shared bus is the feature that limits performance. The lower the bandwidth, the longer the time to synchronize between nodes.

Typical configurations include several nodes accessing the same memory pool and disk areas. Figure 33.2 shows a sample configuration in which a shared bus connects three nodes to shared memory and to each other. The speed of the bus determines the speed of node-to-node, node-to-memory, and node-to-disk access.

FIGURE 33.2.

An example of shared memory configuration.

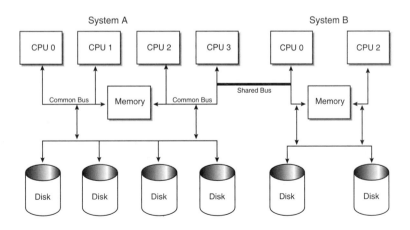

Shared memory configurations provide a cost benefit over loosely coupled systems in that the cost of having shared memory to manage communication across CPUs and nodes is lower than the cost of a high-speed interconnect. In addition, shared memory systems are easier to administer because all the steps to configure shared nothing or shared disk configurations need not be completed.

Two types of memory access are associated with shared memory systems. These access methods refer to the location of the memory pool and associated disks. Because not all nodes in a system necessarily have to use the same shared memory pool, disk access may take place across tightly coupled nodes.

Uniform Memory Access (UMA)

Uniform memory access, or UMA, takes place when a node accesses its own memory pool to retrieve data. (Remember that data must be read from disk into memory before it can be accessed by a process.) *Uniform* is the term used to relate the memory pool to the node.

Nonuniform Memory Access (NUMA)

Nonuniform memory access, or NUMA, occurs when a tightly coupled system must retrieve data from a second tightly coupled system. For example, if system A contains three tightly coupled nodes and system B contains four tightly coupled nodes and system A needs data from system B's disk, system A will perform a nonuniform memory access to retrieve the data, in accordance with parallel server guidelines. Figure 33.3 illustrates two tightly coupled systems and the path the data request must follow in order to perform either a UMA or NUMA request.

FIGURE 33.3.

Two tightly coupled systems connected by a shared bus.

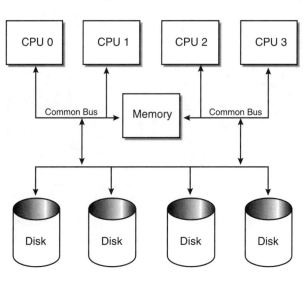

Shared Disk Systems

Shared disk systems are characterized by multiple nodes, each with its own memory pool but sharing common disk storage devices. Each node manages its own memory and must maintain a data cache. Each node communicating across the common bus maintains consistency in the data cache. Because a separate Oracle instance usually runs on each node in this type of configuration, a DLM is necessary to provide locking operations and data consistency.

Communication and consistency across nodes occurs through the common bus, which can be an extremely limiting factor in the capability to speedup or scaleup a system. Unless you can upgrade the bus to perform more functions in the same amount of time, both speedup and scaleup will be limited.

Figure 33.4 shows two nodes configured into a shared disk structure. Each node contains its own memory pool, but the two nodes use the same disks to read and write data.

FIGURE 33.4.

An example of a shared disk configuration.

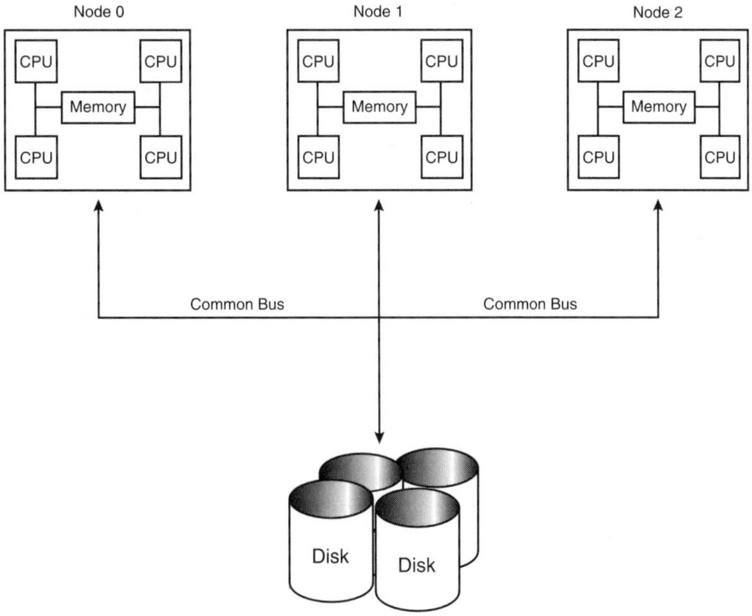

Some advantages of shared disk systems are

■ High data availability, since one node does not exclusively control any peripherals

■ One physical database as opposed to a logical, distributed set of databases

■ Less administrative time required to manage a single system than many systems

Implementing Oracle's Parallel Server

Oracle's Parallel Server runs in conjunction with all hardware configuration options listed previously in this chapter. Additional changes to how the Oracle database kernel works appear in this section, but for the most part, the instance will run almost the same as the standard Oracle database.

To install Oracle Parallel Server, you must first have a hardware platform capable of parallel processing. If it is not able to perform those tasks, you will not be able to install the Parallel Server option. If the hardware is compatible, you install Oracle's Parallel Server through Oracle's installer by selecting the Parallel Server option as either an upgrade or as part of the installation. Then the database administrator must configure the database parameters necessary for Parallel Server to work properly.

The following examples of how Oracle Parallel Server works use a shared disk system with three nodes, each running an Oracle Parallel Server instance. A diagram for this configuration appears in Figure 33.5.

FIGURE 33.5.

Three-node, shared disk system.

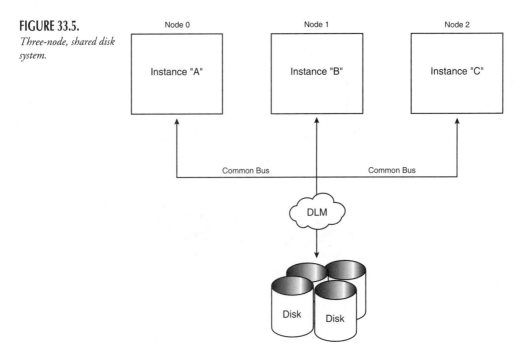

Oracle Parallel Databases

Oracle Parallel Server works within the concept of parallel databases. In a parallel database, the actual database files do not have a one-to-one correspondence with an instance as standard Oracle databases do. A parallel database generally consists of two or more database instances running against a common group of database files. These instances are usually spread across multiple systems, each accessing the same data files.

Each instance not only has all the associated processes database writer (DBWR), log writer (LGWR), and user processes, but also includes a locking (LCK0) process. This process works with the DLM to handle all locking requests and resolutions for database resources on local and remote machines.

Parallel Server Operation Modes

Oracle's Parallel Server can be run in one of two operating modes. Each mode is based on operating requirements and on the task being performed. Sometimes the administrator must switch from one mode to another in order to perform database definition tasks. The two operation modes are

- Exclusive
- Shared

Exclusive Mode

Standard Oracle7 databases and parallel databases both use exclusive mode. *Exclusive* refers to the availability of the database files to another instance. Because the standard Oracle7 database engine can mount only a single instance, and cannot share it, the standard instance can run only in exclusive mode.

Parallel Server can run in all three modes. When run in exclusive mode, all attempts to mount the database files in another instance will fail. This mode is used for creating and recovering the database. At those times, allowing another instance to access the data files is unnecessary—and undesired.

To create the initial database files, you can use instance A for the CREATE DATABASE statement and to add the initial tablespaces. To do so, start instance A in exclusive mode, which is the default. Once the A database is created, it could be shut down and then the STARTUP PARALLEL command could be used to bring the instance and data files up in parallel mode.

Shared Mode

Shared mode is also called *parallel mode*. In this mode, parallel instances are allowed to connect to the database, as well as to perform normal SELECT, INSERT, UPDATE, and DELETE operations. Within shared mode, two additional modes describe the type of shared mode the instance is operating in: single shared mode and multiple shared mode.

Single Shared Mode

When only one instance is configured to run against a database, it is considered to be in single shared mode. In this type of mode, there is no contention for resources by other instances. Likewise there is no need to incur additional overhead caused by having a DLM run in the background. Running in this mode is the same as running in exclusive mode, but single shared mode supports a configuration change to multiple shared mode without reconfiguring the database or having to upgrade to Oracle Parallel Server when the time comes.

If the entire installation is planned for three instances, but at the current time you need only a single instance for accessing the data, you can start instance A in single share mode. Later, you can create additional instances as needed and then start them all in multiple shared mode.

Multiple Shared Mode

Multiple shared mode describes the configuration of running multiple instances against the same database. It is the most common, and generally the most used, type of configuration. In multiple shared configurations, each instance runs with the same System Global Area (SGA) and background processes that standard Oracle databases have, with the addition of an LCK0 process (which handles the DLM locking functions). Each instance has its own redo logs, but all instances share control files, SYSTEM and other tablespaces, and data files.

Handling Locks

In order to process SQL commands, two levels of locking need to occur. The first is at the database level and is identical to that of standard Oracle databases. The second level occurs outside the database when requests for resources take place.

Oracle's Internal Lock Handling

Oracle handles locking on tables and rows within the database internally. Based on the current lock on a data structure, other requests are either placed in a wait status or return an error message stating that a lock request cannot be granted at this time. Table-level locks, for example, cannot be granted when a row-level lock is currently held by a process. The process requesting the table-level lock has the option of either waiting for the row-level lock to be removed or generating an error message.

When the instance must actually write data to a database file, the DLM becomes involved. Although Oracle makes the request, the DLM steps in to handle the intra-instance communication because Oracle instances do not communicate physical data file access information to each other.

For further information on how the DLM handles locks, see the section "Distributed Lock Managers." It explains how the manager works and how Oracle interfaces with the DLM to provide consistent data.

The LCK*x* Process

Parallel Oracle databases have an additional type of background process called the LCK process. This process is responsible for requesting and releasing locks with the DLM. A database can have up to 10 background LCK processes, labeled LCK0–LCK9. Generally only the LCK0 process exists, though systems with a great need for increased performance and high throughput when requesting distributed lock requests may configure more. Added LCK processes will also decrease the amount of time it takes to start and recover the database.

The LCK process handles two types of locks:

- Parallel Cache Management (PCM) locks
- Non-PCM locks

Parallel Cache Management Locks

Parallel cache management (PCM) locks are placed on one or more data blocks and are found in the buffer cache. These locks do not cover row-level locks, but rather the physical resource. Two types of PCM locks schemes exist:

- Hashed locking
- Fine grain locking (default)

Hashed Locking

In hashed locking, a lock is placed on database resources by an instance but is not removed until another instance requests the same lock. Then the lock is relinquished, and the new instance obtains ownership of the lock. In systems with low contention for database resources, hashed locking is a very good method to use.

Fine Grain Locking

Fine grain locking exists when instances allocate resources as needed and deallocate the resource when finished. This mode can sometimes create additional overhead because PCM locks are continually requested and deallocated, but it can also avoid unnecessary contention when resources are shared extensively between instances.

Non-PCM Locks

Locks that do not fit under the category of PCM locks include data dictionary locks, locks on control files, and table and row locks. These locks are all instance specific and do not need to be shared or stored in the parallel cache.

The LCK0 Process

The LCK0 process is nearly identical to all other LCK*x* processes except for the types of locks it will handle. Unlike LCK1–LCK9, the LCK0 process handles non-PCM locks as well as PCM locks. LCK1–LCK9 handle only PCM locks. This limitation is generally not a problem, as non-PCM locks account for less than 10 percent of the total number of locks the LCK processes handle. Sometimes, though, special planning is necessary to ensure that the LCK0 process does not become too busy.

Distributed Lock Managers

In parallel server environments, an Oracle instance must compete with other instances for physical device usage. To handle these types of requests, Oracle designed DLMs. The specifications were handed down from Oracle Corporation to a number of hardware vendors, who have implemented platform-specific DLMs. Oracle works with the DLM, but the DLM is distributed along with the hardware vendor's operating system distribution media. The DLM should be part of either the standard or add-on distribution.

The DLM is responsible for intercepting the physical read/write requests from multiple Oracle instances and deciding whether the request can be fulfilled immediately or should be placed in a queue to be processed when the requested resource becomes available. Since Oracle writes data at the block level, the DLM locks at the data block level and can verify whether a lock exists on the data block in question. If a lock does not prevent the requested lock type, the DLM grants the lock. Otherwise, just like an Oracle instance, the DLM can place the request in a wait queue until the current lock is lifted.

The DLM, in conjunction with the instance background processes, maintains a logical memory structure that tracks the current and requested locks by instance. By searching through its queues in memory, the DLM can determine what types of locks have been granted on database resources, which instance is holding the lock, and correctly fulfill or queue new requests.

> **NOTE**
>
> The DLM does not control any resources at the database level! The Oracle instance itself handles all table and row-level locking. The scope of the DLM is to provide locking at the physical data block layer where multiple instances can share the same resources.

Locking Queues

Inside the DLM are two queues for tracking lock requests:

■ Convert queue
■ Granted queue

The *convert queue* is the location for all lock requests that could not be fulfilled immediately. These requests are placed in this queue and held until either the lock can be granted or the lock is no longer desired. The DLM searches through this queue as locked resources become available, looking for requests waiting for the now-free resource. Once free, the lock is converted to the desired level and placed into the granted queue.

The *granted queue* is the list of all current locks on database resources, based on the resource name and the instance(s) holding locks. Each resource can hold as many locks are there are instances running. (For example, each instance can request a concurrent read.) Before a request is placed in the convert queue, the granted queue is checked by the instance requesting the lock for any lock that would prevent the DLM from granting the requested lock.

Locking Modes

Just like Oracle, the DLM has hierarchical locking modes that can be placed on a database resource, such as a physical data block. Based on the current locks held against a resource, other requests are granted or denied. Table 33.4 contains the types of locks granted by the DLM and their descriptions. The table is based on the hierarchical level of the lock, where X is the highest lock attainable and NL is the lowest.

Table 33.4. DLM lock types.

Name	Description
X	Exclusive mode. X is like the Oracle exclusive locking mode (X) that prevents other processes from reading or writing this resource until the exclusive lock has been lifted. As in Oracle databases, only one process can acquire an exclusive lock on a resource.
PW	Protected write mode. Corresponding to Oracle's sub-shared exclusive lock (SSX), PW prevents other processes from acquiring a write or exclusive lock, but does not prevent protected reads from being acquired on the resource.
PR	Protected read mode. PR is identical to Oracle's shared (S) mode and allows other processes to acquire read locks on the resource, but never write locks. All write requests must be held until the protected read lock is lifted.

continues

Table 33.4. continued

Name	Description
CW	Concurrent write mode. CW is like the Oracle shared exclusive lock and allows other processes to acquire a lock below the protected level (CW, CR, NL). No other process can attain a CW lock on the same resource, such as the data block or row, but can attain a CW lock on a different one.
CR	Concurrent read mode. Corresponding to Oracle's sub-shared lock (SS), CR allows other unprotected reads and writes to be given, but protects the current resource from writes until the CR lock has been released.
NL	Null mode. Identical to the null (N) lock type in Oracle, NL means that a process within an instance plans on locking this resource. NL can also indicate that a process needs ongoing access to this resource. NL will be converted, as needed, to another lock type.

Tracking Locks

To track locks, the DLM uses a structure called the lock value block. This block is stored in each resource block, determined by INIT.ORA parameter settings, and contains locking history. When the first instance in a parallel configuration starts, it will initialize the lock value block to reflect no current locks.

When an instance requests a lock, the DLM will check to see whether the lock can be granted. If it cannot, the DLM places the request in the convert queue to await the resource. If the lock is granted, the DLM adds the locking information to the lock value block and continues with its operation. If an instance requests and is granted an exclusive lock on a resource, the instance takes ownership of the lock value block and can directly write to the newly locked resource.

A lock value block can contain multiple locks. If two instances request concurrent read locks on a resource, both requests will be granted the lock, and both locks, along with instance ids, will be placed in the lock value block.

Summary

This chapter described various ways to configure Oracle Parallel Server and the hardware platforms it can run on. This entire book could be dedicated to explaining how to run, configure, and administer Oracle Parallel Server. The intention here, however, is to provide only a basic outline of the concept of Parallel Server, the possible hardware configurations for a server, how the database is distributed, and how each instance communicates through the DLM. Please refer to Oracle's *Parallel Server Concepts & Administration Guide* for a much more detailed discussion of Oracle Parallel Server.*

35

Trusted Oracle

by Kelly Leigh

Distributed databases offer a wide range of services to environments that benefit from being able to house data in multiple locations. Whether across a LAN or WAN, each node can be administered separately and sometimes more efficiently than a single database as a whole.

In the next sections we discuss the major concepts behind distributed databases and their use. This chapter is not intended to explain advanced administration concepts, but rather to provide an overall picture of what a distributed database is, some of its unique characteristics, and the benefits it can provide. For detailed information, consult the Oracle documentation on *Distributed Server Administration* (volumes I and II).

Distributed Databases

Before trying to understand what distributed processing is and how it is accomplished, it is important to understand the concept of a distributed database. In short, a distributed database is a logical database composed of smaller, independent databases. These smaller databases usually exist on separate computers in the environment. Generally located on the local network, they can also be found on a wide-area network, too.

Each independent database works together to create a single, logical database. Most of the time the actual location of the data, and even the database server, is unknown to the user. Through the application and general naming conventions of the database objects, users and programmers are taught how to get to an object without needing to know its location.

Figure 34.1 shows an example of a distributed database composed of smaller databases and database servers.

Distributed databases work in the context of client/server environments.

The Client/Server Architecture

Client/server architecture is generally the concept of multiple computers accessing a resource offered by yet another computer. The computer that offers the resource is considered the server, while the computer that uses the resource is called the client.

With this type of flexible concept, it is not surprising that a server offering one resource can also become a client when accessing another computer's resource. The most succinct method of naming clients and servers probably falls into one of the following:

- Client: A computer currently accessing a shared resource
- Server: A computer offering the shared resource

One other type of computer described throughout this chapter is called a *database server*. This is a computer responsible for receiving connections to its local database. It, too, can be considered a client, as well as a server, depending on the operation it is performing.

FIGURE 34.1.
A distributed database environment, comprised of smaller databases.

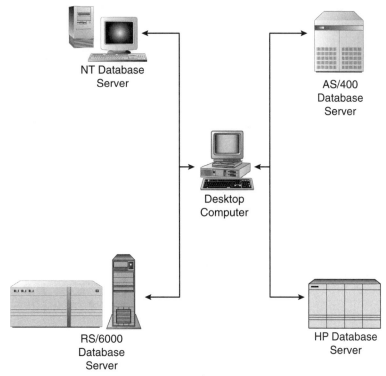

To make this point, let's use the following scenario, which is illustrated in Figure 34.2. There are five computers within this environment, each with a separate purpose. PC1 is a PC used for entering custom orders. DB1 and DB2 both are database servers, offering an order-tracking and inventory database, respectively. PC2 is another PC used for order fulfillment and nightly report generation. Finally, DB3 is the database server where all client names and addresses are located.

When PC1 begins to enter an order, the first thing it must do is a lookup of a customer's name, address, and customer number. PC1 makes a request, as a client, to DB3, now the server, to get the requested information. Once it has been retrieved, the order entry clerk begins to take the order.

Once the first item has been entered, PC1 (once again the client) sends a request to DB2, the server, to check on the available inventory. If there is enough inventory on hand to fulfill the item, the order entry clerk can continue. This goes on until the entire order has been taken.

Once the order is complete and the customer has confirmed all entries, the order entry clerk can press the "update" key. At this time, a request is sent to DB1 to update the customer's records and order history, to DB2 to enter the order information, order number, and tentative shipping date, and to DB3 to decrement the on-hand quantities to track when an order for materials must be placed.

FIGURE 34.2.

*An example client/
server environment.*

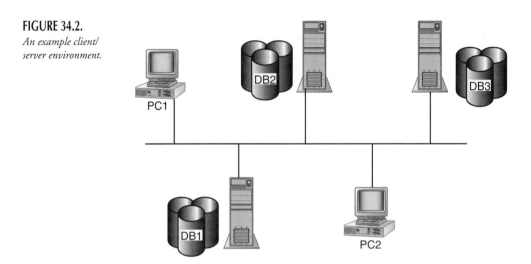

Until now, PC1 has been acting as the client, while all of the database servers have been the servers. Now that the order has been entered and confirmed, the rest of the work happens with the fulfillment clerks. A fulfillment clerk checks the order-tracking screen, searching for orders that must be filled.

As the clerk begins work on the order, a request is made from PC2 to DB2 for all information related to this order. As the clerk packages each item ordered, DB2's order records are updated. Once the order is completely packed and sent to shipping, the order records on DB2 are updated with a status of "filled." Once that happens, DB2 makes a call to DB3 to update the quantity on hand, as well as the actual inventory numbers. PC2 has been a client throughout all of the listed operations, but at the end, when DB2 updates DB3's inventory records, DB2 becomes a client of DB3 for the duration of the update.

Benefits of Distributed Databases

There are many benefits to configuring and using a distributed database environment. Some of them include:

- Transparent data access
- Data replication
- System redundancy/failover
- Heterogeneous computing environments
- Easy data relocation
- Easier database/system administration

Transparent Data Access

Without knowing everything about the data, including location, which instance it resides in, how to log in to that instance, and so on, a distributed database can offer that data transparency. Now the environment seems to be one seamless database instead of multiple, independent database servers.

Data Replication

With distributed databases there are many options for transparently replicating data. With the use of database objects such as views, snapshots, and read-only snapshots, critical data can be distributed among multiple databases. This can alleviate serious performance problems on a single instance by distributing the workload across multiple databases. With the use of read-only snapshots, read operations can be done locally, and updates can be sent to a single database, if desired.

System Redundancy/Failover

Having multiple database servers responsible for replicating data can also provide a form of failover. If one database server becomes unavailable due to system or network problems, users can be routed to a second server where the data also resides. Once the problem has been corrected, changes can be applied to the primary table or view, and users can be redirected to the primary database server. All of this can happen with virtually no interruptions to the normal work flow.

Heterogeneous Computing Environments

With the use of National Language Support, databases within the distributed environment can run in different base languages. Order entry clerks from around the world can work in the same distributed database environment with little or no realization that some of the databases they are selecting from and inserting to are in a language different from their own. This is an excellent feature for companies needing worldwide solutions to their computing needs.

Not only can each database server run with a different base language, but the Oracle version, or even the database type itself, can be different. Both the Oracle version and the other databases in the environment should be verified with Oracle Support to make sure each supports the requirements for a distributed database.

Easy Data Relocation

Because the data location is transparent to the user, data can be relocated to new database servers without needing to notify a group of users. Through the use of views or the applications they are using, they may experience little or no downtime during the relocation, and the application as well as their interactive queries may not need to be changed.

Easier Systems/Database Administration

Because each database server in a distributed environment is independent, or autonomous, it is also administered independently from any other database server. Each server works with others to process queries and distributed transactions, but when administering data, the database, or the system it is running on, does not affect all other database servers.

Database Links

Database links are named paths to other database instances in the current environment, and to other instances physically attached to the network. Database links can be both public and private. Public links are generally set up by the database administrator and are available to all users. Private links can be set up by the administrator or by individual users and are usually intended for the link owner or a group of users with the same database role. By using public and private links, distributed databases initiate SQL queries and updates to remote tables.

Database links are created using the CREATE DATABASE LINK command. Options can be specified for creating a PUBLIC link, the TNS names connect string, and the username/password combination to use when connecting to the remote database.

Example creation statements include the following:

```
CREATE DATABASE LINK inventory.dbs
  CONNECT TO chris IDENTIFIED BY steph863
  USING 'db2`;
CREATE PUBLIC DATABASE LINK customer.dbs
  CONNECT TO scott IDENTIFIED BY tiger
  USING 'db1';
```

By using database links, users see one of the several forms of transparent data access that are available in a distributed environment. Normally the application chooses which links to follow for specific tables, but at other times a user may enter an interactive SQL command specifying a table name/database link combination. To use a database link in a SQL command, issue the command as you would normally, but in the FROM clause, specify the table name, followed by a @, and then the database link. The @database_link tells the instance to select from the table that exists in the specified link. A table with the same name can exist in the user's schema without causing any problems. If the table in the database link is not found, an Oracle ORA-00902: Table not found error is returned.

Example uses of a database link in the command line include the following:

```
SELECT UNIQUE(table_name)
  FROM user_tables@db1.chris.dbs;
UPDATE addresses@db1.dbs
  SET name = 'Melissa Dieckmann',
  STATE = 'KY';
```

It is also important to note that, because database links use the network to connect to remote instances, overuse of a link can degrade query and network performance. If these are limiting factors in the design of the database environment, data replication may be a useful alternative.

Data Replication

When network utilization becomes too high, and a site relies heavily on database links, replication can provide an excellent alternative. It is also an excellent method of providing secondary copies of a master table. By providing a secondary copy, network traffic can be managed more effectively, query and update performance can be drastically improved, and database failure effects can be minimized by providing an alternative copy of a critical table. Replication, then, is the duplication of a table, its supporting objects, and all or a subset of its data in one or more remote databases.

Snapshots

The replicated table (and its objects) is called a *snapshot*. This snapshot is basically a picture of the table in a given point in time. It can be updated in several ways, depending on the needs of the site and the benefits of each type of snapshot.

Snapshots are created by the CREATE SNAPSHOT command and can exist as either a full copy of the table or a subset of the table's rows, like a view. Snapshots exist in two distinct forms:

- Read-only snapshots
- Updateable snapshots

Each form has its advantages and is described in detail below.

NOTE

Because snapshots are created on master tables, it is not possible to apply constraints or modifications to the snapshot itself. The snapshot, once defined, cannot be modified without dropping and re-creating the snapshot.

Also, snapshots cannot contain columns from master tables that have the datatype LONG.

Read-Only Snapshots

A read-only snapshot is a replica of an entire table (called a *master table*), a subset of the table, or a subset of a group of tables, that is placed in a read-only mode. Queries can be submitted against the snapshot, but data can be updated only when the snapshot is updated. Even privileged users receive an error trying to update the snapshot. A read-only snapshot has the following characteristics:

- It is a basic form of replication.
- It enforces a form of "primary site replication."
- It is defined by a distributed query.
- It can reference one or more remote tables.
- It is based on a point in time, so it maintains transactional consistency.
- It provides an excellent form of lookup, or reference, table.

Primary site replication is a method of enforcing the rule that all changes to a table or group of tables happen at a central location, and the snapshot receives those changes on a scheduled basis. Replicating the table in remote databases allows for quick selection of data, but all updates must occur at the master database, which is the database that houses the master table from which the snapshot is refreshed.

Definition of the snapshot is done by specifying the CREATE SNAPSHOT command, using the AS subquery option. This subquery is a distributed query and can follow normal query guidelines. If the query contains functions such as DISTINCT or UNIQUE, or uses aggregate functions, GROUP BY, CONNECT BY, subqueries, joins, or SET operations, the query is considered a complex query. If the query is a simple SELECT statement, the query is considered a simple query.

Transaction consistency, in reference to snapshots, is the name of a method of ensuring consistent tables. If multiple, related snapshots were taken one hour apart, there is a strong likelihood that the data in the second snapshot would be newer, and any references between the tables could be outdated. By taking a snapshot at a point in time, all snapshots that are related can be taken at the same time, and only the data marked up to that time will be added to the snapshot.

Updateable Snapshots

Updateable snapshots can be written to by users with the correct privileges. Unlike read-only snapshots, the guidelines for creating updateable snapshots are fairly strict.

- The subquery must be a simple query (see the preceding section, "Read-Only Snapshots").
- The simple query must span only one master table.

These restrictions allow for simple, efficient updates to the master table, based upon the replication method chosen. An updateable snapshot is created with the same CREATE SNAPSHOT command as a read-only snapshot, but the added clause FOR UPDATE is appended to the command.

Replicated Environments

The configuration of replication in a distributed database configuration consists of one or more replicated environments. Each replicated environment contains the following:

- One replication group
- One master definition site within the group
- One or more master sites within the group
- One or more snapshot sites within the group
- The objects within the replication group

Replication Groups

The replication group is the logical grouping of all sites responsible for replicating a group of objects. Each site has a specific set of responsibilities that relate to the group as a whole. Distributed database environments can have more than one replication group. This is the highest level of the replication structure, excluding that of the distributed database itself.

The Master Definition Site

In order to control changes to the schema objects that are replicated, there can be only one master definition site in the replication group. This site is responsible for all DDL statements that change the format of the replicated table, and its supporting objects (indexes, constraints, and so on). All table modifications must be done from this site and are propagated to the other replication groups and objects, all the way down to the snapshot sites. If the master definition site is down, it is possible to move it to another site in order to perform administrative functions until the original master definition site is returned. A master definition site is also considered a master site.

Master Site

A master site is a site in the replication group that is responsible for pushing all changes to the replicated objects to other master sites. These master sites must receive a full copy of the replicated object. Once received, they are available to the snapshot sites for update and/or retrieval. There can be more than one master site in a replication group, and each one shares most of the same responsibilities.

Snapshot Sites

A snapshot site is an instance that contains one or more snapshots for the replication group. There can be multiple snapshot sites, but each one has a single master site from which it gets snapshot updates. If the snapshot is read-only, it is responsible for retrieving all changes to the master table from the master site, using whatever retrieval mechanism it was configured with. If the snapshot is updateable, it is responsible for working with the master site for writing and retrieving all changes to itself.

Replicated Objects

This is the collection of the replicated tables (and supporting objects) that each snapshot and master site contain.

An Example Replicated Environment

Using the example illustrated throughout this chapter, let's say that the ORDER_HISTORY table from the orders.dbs database, among others, is replicated. This eliminates unnecessary activity in the orders database and cuts down on network traffic during the day. A subset of the replicated environment, consisting of replication group 1, is illustrated in Figure 34.3.

This table's master definition site is the orders.dbs database, the master site is inventory.dbs, and the snapshot site is customer.dbs. This provides three benefits to the order processing environments:

- All administration can be done to the ORDER_HISTORY table in the orders.dbs database. Because it is the master definition site, all changes are propagated to other sites.
- The orders.dbs database has a local copy to run nightly reports on. The snapshot there is refreshed every evening at the close of the business day, and reports run from that snapshot for faster access and no network traffic.

■ The customer.dbs database has a local copy to use as a reference table so customer order inquiries can be handled quickly. All modifications, though, still go to the orders.dbs database, because the snapshot is read-only.

To break up our replication groups into logical partitions, a second replication group is created for the inventory.dbs database. This is a read-only snapshot, as well, of products and product IDs from the database. This is illustrated in Figure 34.4.

FIGURE 34.3.
Example of a replicated environment for the ORDER_HISTORY table.

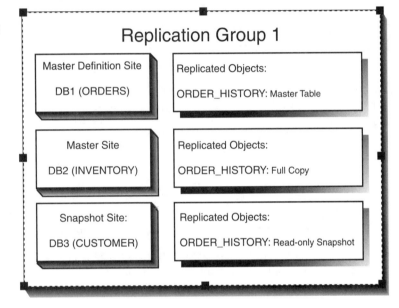

FIGURE 34.4.
Example of a second replicated environment, this time for the INVENTORY database.

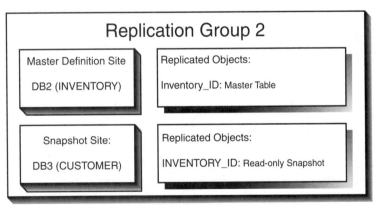

By replicating this inventory table into the customer.dbs database, you accomplish the following:

- Decreased network traffic when looking up valid inventory IDs
- Increased performance because you are running a local transaction
- Created backup copy of the inventory IDs in case the inventory.dbs database fails

Distributed Versus Remote Transactions

To ensure data consistency, Oracle databases implement a form of transaction processing or transaction control. In standard transaction processing, the instance determines whether each transaction is either committed in its entirety or rolled back to its starting point.

For example, when an order entry application enters a new order, it may perform three separate actions.

1. Inserts the order into the order-processing queue.
2. Updates the customer's order history information.
3. Updates the quantity on hand for each product ordered.

If there were a database error that prevented the update of the order-processing queue, it could cause serious problems in the inventory calculations if the quantity on hand were also updated. Most importantly, the data in the database would become inconsistent and unreliable.

To prevent this from happening, transaction processing verifies that all SQL statements in a transaction are successful before committing those changes to the database files. If one INSERT, UPDATE, or DELETE statement fails, the entire transaction is rolled back. (It is possible to prevent this by using a SAVEPOINT in the application, but that is beyond the scope of this discussion.)

A transaction is defined as a group of SQL statements, including SELECT statements, that are terminated by one of the following:

- A COMMIT command
- A ROLLBACK command
- A DDL statement
- A disconnected or ended session

The first two are explicit, or specified ends to the transaction. The last two are implicit, or implied. At the end of an implicit end to a transaction, the instance decides whether or not to commit the transaction or roll it back. At the explicit end of a transaction, the database takes the desired action (COMMIT or ROLLBACK).

In a non-distributed transaction, a single instance is responsible for deciding whether a transaction should be committed or rolled back. In a distributed database, however, each instance must communicate with the other to decide whether the transaction was successful on all nodes or whether it must be rolled back on all nodes.

Local Transactions

A local transaction is completely local to the current database server. In no way are remote nodes affected by the update. This includes being indirectly affected by constraints, triggers, or PL/SQL blocks.

Examples of local transactions include

```
UPDATE product_inventory
  SET item_quantity=500
  WHERE item_id = 17936;
COMMIT;
SELECT SUM(quantity_on_hand)
  FROM product_inventory
  WHERE inventory_id = 17936;
EXIT;
```

Neither of these transactions affects nodes at a remote site.

Remote Transactions

A remote transaction executes entirely against a single, remote node. It affects tables, snapshots, or views against that single node but not the current node. Examples of remote transactions include

```
UPDATE product_inventory@inventory.dbs
  SET item_quantity=500
  WHERE item_id = 17936;
COMMIT;
SELECT SUM(quantity_on_hand)
  FROM product_inventory@inventory.dbs
  WHERE inventory_id = 17936;
EXIT;
```

Notice how a database link has been added to the SELECT and UPDATE statements. In this way, no tables on the local database have been affected, and the SQL statements are now directed to the database listed in the inventory.dbs link.

Distributed Transactions

A distributed transaction is described as a transaction, or group of SQL statements, that involve the update of two or more databases, where at least one of those databases is remote to the issued transaction. Because it affects two or more databases, each instance must communicate with the other in order to decide whether a transaction should be applied or not.

If an update occurs on a remote table as well as a local one, the transaction is considered a distributed transaction, and both instances involved must work together to decide if the entire transaction, should be committed or rolled back. Distributed transactions could look like the following group of SQL statements:

```
UPDATE product_inventory@inventory.dbs
  SET actual_count =
    (SELECT sum(allocated_items)
     FROM processed_orders@inventory.dbs
     WHERE product_id = 1976325)
  WHERE product_id = 1976325;
UPDATE order_products@materials.dbs
  SET order_quantity =
    (SELECT actual_count FROM product_inventory@inventory.dbs
COMMIT;
```

If for some reason the second UPDATE statement fails, the first statement should be rolled back. To do this, a distributed database uses a method called a two-phase commit.

> **NOTE**
>
> If any transaction happens to execute a trigger, constraint, PL/SQL block, or some other function that updates a table in a remote instance, the transaction is then considered a distributed transaction and must follow the rules of a two-phase commit before it can be committed or rolled back.

As the transactions are processed, the global coordinator (the system where the original query originated) creates a session tree. This tree describes the relationship of each system to the other and ultimately defines which system is responsible for issuing the COMMIT or ROLLBACK command.

Session Trees

A session tree is a hierarchical tree defining each node involved in the transaction, to what capacity it is involved, and what role it plays in the transaction. These roles are determined by the following factors:

- Is the transaction remote or local to the node?
- Is the node read-only?
- What is the value of COMMIT_POINT_STRENGTH for that node?

> **NOTE**
>
> COMMIT_POINT_STRENGTH is an INIT.ORA parameter, is set by the database administrator and defines the strength of that node in deciding whether a transaction it is involved in should be committed or rolled back. The higher the value, the higher the strength of

that node. This value might also be considered a level of criticality of data the instance contains. More information on COMMIT_POINT_STRENGTH is listed in the following pages.

Those factors define the role or roles that a node plays in the transaction. The role determines exactly how a node is involved. The five role types are

- Client
- Database server
- Local coordinator
- Global coordinator
- Commit point site

The client and database server roles were defined earlier in the section "The Client/Server Architecture." The other roles are defined in the following sections.

The Local Coordinator

The local coordinator is a node that must reference other nodes in order to complete its part of the transaction. For instance, if a node must reference another node to update a report table, it is considered a local coordinator. Its list of responsibilities include

- Receiving and relaying status information to and from the referenced nodes
- Passing queries and such to those referenced nodes
- Receiving queries from its referenced nodes and passing them on to other nodes involved in those queries
- Returning the query results back to the referenced nodes

The Global Coordinator

The global coordinator is the node where the distributed transaction originated. It is also the node responsible for creating the session tree. Other responsibilities of the global coordinator are

- Sending SQL and remote procedure calls to the directly referenced nodes
- Sending a "prepare" request (see the section on two-phase commits later in this chapter) to all directly referenced nodes, except the commit point site (see the following section)
- Sending a request to the commit point site, if all nodes reply with a "prepared" message, asking for a COMMIT or ROLLBACK on the transaction

The Commit Point Site

The commit point site is the database instance that has the highest COMMIT_POINT_STRENGTH of all the nodes involved in the distributed transaction. The commit point does not receive a "prepare" request from the global coordinator. Instead, it is responsible for giving the final say as to whether the transaction should be committed or rolled back.

Generally, the instance that contains the most critical data in the queries it is involved with has the highest value for COMMIT_POINT_STRENGTH. It is a hierarchical value, with each database server in the distributed environment having a set value. It is set in the INIT.ORA file and does not have to be unique within the distributed environment. Instead, if there are two or more database servers with the same COMMIT_POINT_STRENGTH, the Oracle instances break the tie and nominate one of them to become the commit point site.

The following rules are used to define a commit point site:

■ A node that is read-only in the transaction cannot become the commit point site.

■ The commit point site is not determined until all nodes have reached the point that they are ready to respond to a "prepare" request.

■ If the transaction fails on any referenced node, all nodes are requested to ROLLBACK the transaction, the steps of the two-phase commit are never reached, and a commit point site is never nominated.

Two-Phase Commits

To decide whether all nodes must either COMMIT or ROLLBACK the distributed transaction, Oracle uses a two-phase commit method, called the *prepare/commit mechanism*. This prepare/commit mechanism is completely transparent to all Oracle users and developers. Oracle decides internally whether a transaction can be committed or rolled back and performs the necessary actions.

The node where the transaction originated is called the global coordinator. The global coordinator is responsible for following the steps in the two-phase commit process to decide the proper action for the distributed transaction. The primary phases of the method are

1. Phase I: Prepare
2. Phase II: Commit

Phase I: Prepare

The following steps should be followed in the prepare phase:

■ The global coordinator requests all nodes referenced by the transaction (called *descendants*) to begin the prepare steps (listed next).

■ Each node is asked to prepare checks to see if it or any of its descendants is performing updates to its data.

- If no updates are being performed by the node or its descendants, it responds with a "read-only" status.
- If the node or its descendants are performing updates, all resources necessary to COMMIT or ROLLBACK the transaction are allocated (rollback segments, table locks, and so on).
- The node flushes all necessary information to the redo logs.
- Verification is made that all locks held by the transaction will not be lost if a failure occurs.
- The node responds with a "prepared" status to the global coordinator.
- If the node or one of its descendants cannot allocate all necessary resources, it responds with an "abort" status.

Once all of the nodes have responded to the global coordinator with a status of "prepared," the transaction is considered to be in doubt. It remains in this state until the commit phase has started. Providing there are no media or network failures at this point, this is generally a very short timespan. If any node responds with an "abort" status, all nodes in the transaction are notified to ROLLBACK the transaction.

> **NOTE**
>
> In the prepare phase of a two-phase commit, the node that is considered the commit point site (explained earlier in this chapter) is not included in the prepare steps listed above. It is responsible for giving the final say as to whether to COMMIT or ROLLBACK a transaction and does not need to communicate with the global coordinator until all other affected nodes have reached "prepared" status.

If for any reason a node cannot prepare, the following steps are taken:

- The node releases all locks and database resources allocated for the transaction.
- The node responds to the global coordinator with an "abort" status.
- The global coordinator notifies all affected nodes to release all locks and database resources and ROLLBACK the transaction.

Phase II: Commit

Once all of the nodes have responded with a "prepared" signal, the global coordinator can proceed to Phase II, the commit phase. In this phase, the final decision is made to either COMMIT or ROLLBACK the transaction. The steps are

- The global coordinator checks with the commit point site to make sure it is possible to COMMIT.
- The commit point site commits its data.

■ The commit point site replies to the global coordinator to proceed with the COMMIT.

■ The global coordinator tells all descendants to COMMIT.

A Distributed Transaction Analyzed

In order to illustrate the functions of the session tree, two-phase commits, and the overall distributed transaction, the following scenario will be used. (Refer again to Figure 34.1 for a diagram of how the network, its computers, and its distributed database, are laid out.)

In this order-entry environment, there are three database servers.

■ DB1 is responsible for orders and order tracking.

■ DB2 maintains the current and estimated inventories.

■ DB3 holds all customer information.

When a user from PC1 has taken the entire order and is now submitting the completed order to the servers, it is a distributed transaction because three tasks must be performed.

1. Add the order to the orders.dbs database.

2. Decrement the daily inventory tracking in the inventory.dbs database.

3. Update the client's order history.

The SQL statements issued are as follows:

```
INSERT INTO new_orders@orders.dbs
  (order_num, item_id, item_count, order_date)
  VALUES (18274, 7639, 5, SYSDATE);
INSERT INTO product_inventory@inventory.dbs
  (order_num, item_id, item_count)
  VALUES (18274, 7639, 5);
UPDATE customer_info@customer.dbs
  SET new_order_num = 18274, new_order_date = SYSDATE
  WHERE customer_id = 2239151;
COMMIT;
```

Figure 34.5 shows the session tree in its finished form, as created by customer.dbs, the global coordinator. The steps taken by the global coordinator are listed below.

At the time the order is being taken, the user is connected to the customer.dbs database. The SQL commands for the distributed transaction are entered into the same database, and the following steps are followed to commit the transaction:

Step	Database Server	Actions Taken
1	customer.dbs	Becomes global coordinator because all statements are being issued through its instance. It is also a client to orders.dbs and inventory.dbs because, during the order-taking process, it requests information from these servers, such as next order number and quantity on hand.

Step	Database Server	Actions Taken
		Issues INSERT INTO new_orders@orders.dbs statement. Compares COMMIT_POINT_STRENGTH to that of orders.dbs.
	orders.dbs	Is a server for customer.dbs, by returning next order number before final order updates in this transaction were started.
		Allocates all resources necessary to complete statement, executes statement, but does not commit.
	customer.dbs	Issues INSERT INTO product_inventory@inventory.dbs statement.
	inventory.dbs	Allocates all resources necessary to complete the statement, executes statement, but does not commit.
		Becomes a client because there is a trigger on the product_inventory table to update an audit table back in the customer.dbs database.
		Becomes a local coordinator because it must be the go-between to rollback the audit entries if the transaction fails.
	customer.dbs	Compares COMMIT_POINT_STRENGTH to that of inventory.dbs, notifies orders.dbs that it has the highest COMMIT_POINT_STRENGTH and is now the commit point site.
	customer.dbs	Issues UPDATE customer_info statement, allocates resources but does not commit.
	customer.dbs	Issues the final statement in the transaction, COMMIT.
2	customer.dbs	Because this database server is also the global coordinator, it sends out a "prepare" message as Phase I of the two-phase commit. The message is sent only to inventory.dbs because orders.dbs is the commit point site.
	inventory.dbs	Checks with customer.dbs to verify that the audit information can be written and that the customer.dbs database is "prepared."
		Verifies that it can commit or rollback the transaction and returns a "prepared" to customer.dbs.

continues

Step	Database Server	Actions Taken
	customer.dbs	It knows it is "prepared," so it sends a message to orders.dbs asking whether or not to commit.
	orders.dbs	Agrees that the transaction can be committed, responds to customer.dbs to commit, and issues a COMMIT statement for its portion of the transaction.
	customer.dbs	Issues a COMMIT statement for its part of the transaction and notifies inventory.dbs to commit.
	inventory.dbs	Notifies customer.dbs to commit because it is the local coordinator and then issues a COMMIT for itself.

FIGURE 34.5.

Sample session tree for the customer order transaction.

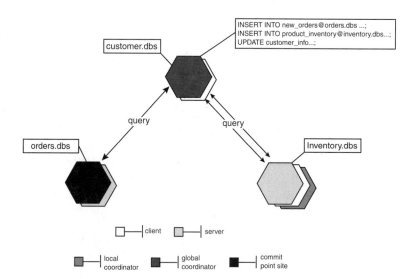

Summary

Distributed database environments can be extremely complex and take a great deal of time and effort to administer effectively. This chapter provided a basic overview of distributed databases and how transactions are processed between them. Further information on managing these types of environments can be found in Oracle's documentation on distributed databases.

35

Trusted Oracle

by Kelly Leigh

Security is an integral part of any Oracle installation. While the standard Oracle7 database provides a very good level of security, it is not all encompassing, nor does it provide the very high levels of security associated with government or military installations and needs. To address this market, Oracle created Trusted Oracle.

Trusted Oracle uses the same security scheme of the standard Oracle database, but adds an additional level of security. Unlike Oracle7, Trusted Oracle is a multilevel secure database management system, or MLS DBMS. It is based on various levels of security that are granted to users and database objects. Based on the compared levels of access, Trusted Oracle grants or denies read and/or write access.

Access Control Methods

Oracle employs two methods to grant or deny database access. The first is called Discretionary Access Control (DAC), and is the first level of access that all Oracle database users must pass. The second, employed only by Trusted Oracle, is called Mandatory Access Control (MAC). This is the control level that allows Trusted Oracle to be a multilevel security system. This type of MAC MLS scheme is also implemented by secure operating systems.

Discretionary Access Control

Discretionary access control (DAC) is common to both Oracle7 and Trusted Oracle. It is handled by the use of the SQL GRANT command at both the database and object level. Once the base-level access to the database is given (permissions to log in, use database resources, and so on), four other privileges can be granted to a user that control object access within the database. These privileges are:

- SELECT
- INSERT
- UPDATE
- DELETE

By granting these options to a user, or to PUBLIC, actions against each database object can be controlled. As a rule, these types of privileges should be granted on a need-only basis. Most sites grant access on the basis of the least amount of access necessary to complete job-related tasks. It is not uncommon, however, to find sites that over-grant privileges to users, thereby creating security problems.

One of the security problems that exists in a discretionary access control situation is illegal propagation of data. Users with CREATE TABLE access in their own schema and SELECT access on secured tables can make a copy of a table by using the CREATE TABLE (table name) AS SELECT * FROM SQL command. Once the command finishes, they can grant access to PUBLIC on the new table and bypass all security that was originally placed on this table's data. What might once have been a highly secure table is now publicly accessible.

While this type of security breach is deliberate and can be limited by the use of views and granting privileges on the view, it cannot be stopped entirely without severely limiting database privileges. By using the Mandatory Access Control features of Trusted Oracle, however, you can make this problem nearly non-existent.

Mandatory Access Control

Trusted Oracle uses both the Discretionary Access Control scheme along with the Mandatory Access Control (MAC) scheme to provide its multilevel security scheme. Users must first be granted access to the database and then SELECT, INSERT, UPDATE, and/or DELETE privileges on a database object before the MAC scheme is tested.

The MAC security scheme is based on the concept of labels. A label is a level of access granted to an object or user on the database system and is defined at the operating system level. A label is broken up into three basic parts:

- Sensitivity
- Integrity (optional)
- Information (optional)

> **NOTE**
>
> Trusted Oracle works with the operating system to provide various levels of security. This requires an MLS-approved operating system that supports the use of labels. Depending on the operating system in use, labels may not support the integrity or information components. Trusted Oracle provides this support, but only in conjunction with the operating system.

MAC Labels: Sensitivity

Sensitivity, or classification, is the basic level of security access. It is defined by the system administrator when the operating system is installed, but also as part of typical maintenance. Each level of classification is defined as a numeric value and an associated character string. Classifications with lower values denote unclassified or less secure data. Higher values denote more sensitive data and should be restricted to fewer users. Table 35.1 shows an example security profile.

Table 35.1. Example security classifications.

Name	Numeric Value	Description
ADMIRAL	80	Top secret, for your eyes only!
GENERAL	60	Highly secure, do not distribute.
CORPORAL	40	Moderately secure, not for general knowledge.
PRIVATE	20	Basic level, not very secure.
NONSECURE	1	Public knowledge, distribute freely.

MAC Labels: Integrity

The integrity portion of a label is optional and is used as a grouping or category. It is defined like the sensitivity level, but must be associated with a unique character string. Since not all information at a specific security level is appropriate for all users in that classification, by adding this additional level of security, access to a database object can be limited further.

Since integrity is considered a grouping or category, it is not hierarchical in nature. Instead of using a greater-than or less-than comparison, integrity values are matched. As long as the user has an integrity that is included in the integrity group assigned to the database object, access is granted. Example integrities are listed in Table 35.2.

Table 35.2. Example integrity categories.

Name	Value	Description
ARMY	1	ARMY-specific information
NAVY	2	NAVY-specific information
AIRFORCE	5	AIR FORCE-specific information
MARINES	7	MARINES-specific information

> **NOTE**
>
> As mentioned above, an integrity is defined in a similar manner to a sensitivity (classification). Unlike sensitivities, the numeric value is used as a unique identification, as opposed to a comparison. An integrity with a value of 5 is no more or less secure than an integrity with a value of 8.

MAC Labels: Information

The information, or marking, portion of a label is also optional. It is not included in the security information in order to grant access, and like integrity, must have a numeric value and a description associated with it. It is simply an indication of the information's use.

Markings can be used to signify how to handle certain information, such as policy information that should be distributed to all members of a group. Assigning an information label of BUDGET might indicate that this information is not for all members of a group. Sample information groupings are listed in Table 35.3.

Table 35.3. Example information groupings.

Name	Value	Description
REPORT	1	General reports and distributions
POLICY	2	Policy information
BUDGET	3	Department budget information

How Labels Control Access

Trusted Oracle works in conjunction with the system's operating system to control access. Once a label is defined at the OS layer and users are granted access, Trusted Oracle takes over by using these labels as valid labels to assign to database objects. Trusted Oracle also handles the security checking by comparing the user's current label with those associated with a requested object.

NOTE

By using the ALTER SESSION SET LABEL command, a user can dynamically change his label to any value within his range (or clearance). Application developers can also dynamically set a label's value through the same command in an application. If this type of functionality is used, it is important to do some sort of error checking to make sure the ALTER SESSION command succeeds. If it does not, other, possibly unrelated, errors may appear.

Trusted Oracle first checks the DAC authorities. If the user does not meet those basic requirements, access is denied, and the MAC portion of security is never checked. If the user passes all DAC requirements, MAC then compares the labels on user and object and assigns a level of domination. The level of domination is determined by comparing the user's label with that of the object.

Levels of Domination

The levels of domination can be broken into the following four groups:

- Strictly dominates
- Dominates
- Does not dominate
- Noncomparable

Access is granted if a user's current label either dominates or strictly dominates the object's label. If the user's current label either does not dominate or is non-comparable, access is denied. To determine the user's level of domination over the objects, use the following rules:

1. The user's label strictly dominates the object's if the sensitivity level is greater than or equal to the object's, and the object's integrity value is a subset of the user's, or is not assigned.

2. The user's label dominates the object's if the sensitivity levels and integrity values of both labels are identical.

3. If the object's sensitivity is greater than the user's, the user's label does not dominate the object's.

4. If neither label dominates the other they are considered noncomparable.

Table 35.4 lists label comparisons and their dominance.

Table 35.4. Label comparisons.

User Label/Object Label	User's Level of Dominance
ADMIRAL/PRIVATE	strictly dominates
ADMIRAL:ARMY/ ADMIRAL	strictly dominates
ADMIRAL:ARMY,NAVY/ GENERAL:ARMY	strictly dominates
PRIVATE:MARINES/ PRIVATE:MARINES	dominates
CORPORAL/CORPORAL	dominates
PRIVATE:MARINES/ ADMIRAL	does not dominate
GENERAL:ARMY,NAVY/ ADMIRAL:AIRFORCE	noncomparable
CORPORAL:MARINES/ GENERAL:ARMY	noncomparable

How Labels Are Assigned

Assigning a label is identical to granting DAC privileges. All labels are associated to access commands using the GRANT command. The key to remember is that the GRANT is labeled with the current MAC label of the user issuing the command.

For example, let's say that the user ORACLE is logged in with the label ADMIRAL. If ORACLE issues a GRANT SELECT, INSERT, UPDATE ON TROOPS TO FRED, FRED must have the ADMIRAL sensitivity in his label to be able to access the TROOPS table. Likewise, if ORACLE issues the GRANT SELECT, UPDATE ON TROOPS TO PUBLIC, while its label was PRIVATE, a huge security breach could be created. Remember that a user's label must dominate the label of an object and have DAC access before any commands can succeed.

Other Access Considerations

Three other privileges in addition to SELECT, INSERT, UPDATE, and DELETE are used in security validation in Trusted Oracle. These privileges are

■ READUP
■ WRITEUP
■ WRITEDOWN

> **NOTE**
>
> These privileges have corresponding privileges that must be granted at the operating system level before they can be used. In other words, granting a user READUP privilege does not necessarily guarantee access. If the tablespace containing the table has a corresponding operating system label that currently dominates the user's label, access is still denied. These privileges do not work outside of the user's operating system clearance levels.

READUP

READUP is a privilege granted to users who need to read data whose label strictly dominates that of the user's current label. For example, let's say there is a reference table called TOP_SECRET_CODES that contains only the name and description of codes used for classified reports. Let's also assume that the data contained in the table was inserted with a label of GENERAL. If a secretary with a current label of CORPORAL is asked to generate these reports for the Admiral on a weekly basis, the secretary would need either a label of GENERAL or higher, or the READUP privilege. This would allow the user to accomplish the given task without granting higher privileges.

WRITEUP

Let's say that the secretary just mentioned must also write to a table that logs every report name, timestamp, and user ID every time a series of reports is run. If the table was created with the label of GENERAL, the secretary also needs GENERAL or higher in his current label to write this information. (Because the table's label strictly dominates the secretary's.) If the secretary were granted WRITEUP privilege, the report would not fail when trying to insert into the timestamp table.

> **NOTE**
>
> Granting WRITEUP privilege to a user does not implicitly grant any other privileges, such as READUP or WRITEDOWN. Each privilege must be granted separately.

WRITEDOWN

The WRITEDOWN privilege grants a user specific rights to write to data that is strictly dominated by the user's current label. At first this sounds redundant, but when used in an application, it can guarantee that a specific function succeeds, provided the user's security clearance at the operating system level is appropriate to allow the transaction.

Trusted Oracle Operating Modes

Trusted Oracle provides two separate operation modes. These modes provide different options for how each instance is set up, their performance benefits, and various security options. Either option runs with MAC security, but depending on which mode an instance is running under, the differences become apparent. These operating modes are instance specific, and some sites may decide to configure several instances, each one running in a different mode, for flexibility.

Trusted Oracle uses the concept of a trusted computing base (TCB) to explain the grouping of security architectures. A TCB is the combination of the operating system, applications, and even the DBMS, all of which create the mechanism by which the total security policy is enforced. In both of Oracle's operating modes, the TCB is layered into two separate groupings: the operating system, which supplies the MAC security to the database files, and the database, which supplies DAC and MAC to the database objects.

DBMS MAC Mode

DBMS MAC mode is a mode in which multiple security labels exist within the same database. Data is ranged between two database variables: DBHIGH and DBLOW. These parameters, respectively, are defined by the lowest label name and highest label name that the database allows connections to and storage of data from. Not only does this define what range of data can be stored in the database, but also the range of users who can access that data.

A DBMS MAC mode where a database is running with a DBLOW of CORPORAL, and a DBHIGH of GENERAL, does not allow users with an active label of PRIVATE or ADMIRAL to have access to the database. In addition, data with those sensitivity labels cannot be stored within the objects of that particular instance.

Instance Configuration

The instance, which encompasses the processes and memory segments, must run at a specific label. This label allows the processes access to all associated database files and devices by dominating the label of those objects. The instance processes should run at the operating system equivalent of DBHIGH, while other processes may run at DBLOW. It is dependent upon what function the process has and whether the process was started by a user or by the instance. Table 35.5 shows each process and the label it should be running under. Processes with a range of priorities are generally started by user processes and receive the label that the user was operating under.

Table 35.5. Instance processes and priorities.

Process Name	Database Equivalent Priority
ARCJ	DBHIGH
CKPT	DBHIGH
Dedicated Server Process	DBLOW to DBHIGH
DBWR	DBHIGH
LCK0	DBHIGH
LGWR	DBHIGH
Listener	DBLOW
PMON	DBHIGH
RECO	DBHIGH
SGA	DBHIGH
SMON	DBHIGH
User Processes	DBLOW – DBHIGH

The instance is created in much the same way a standard Oracle7 instance is created (using the `CREATE DATABASE` command), but does have additional considerations. When creating the database, the effective label should be set to the operating system's equivalent of DBLOW. If the instance runs with a clearance of CORPORAL to GENERAL, the active label should be CORPORAL.

After using the CREATE DATABASE command to create the database, two additional commands are necessary:

```
ALTER DATABASE SET DBMAC ON;

ALTER DATABASE SET DBHIGH 'label name';
```

These commands set the DBMAC mode and then the DBHIGH value. DBLOW does not need to be set because the value is set to the label under which the database was created.

The instance must run at the operating system's equivalent of DBHIGH, so the instance must be brought down—all data files, redo logs, and so on, must be labeled at DBHIGH, and then the instance must be restarted. Further explanation of the data files' security level is provided in the next section.

Database Files

All files associated with the database should be labeled at the operating system's equivalent of DBHIGH, which is set in the instance's INIT.ORA file, or by the ALTER DATABASE command. If the instance is configured with a DBHIGH of GENERAL, the data files for this database should also be labeled GENERAL. The files included in this list are:

- Control files
- Data files
- Redo log files

> **NOTE**
>
> Labeling these files with the equivalent of DBHIGH guarantees that the operating system treats all of the database files with the proper security and also ensures that no data is stored in the database above the value of DBHIGH.

Any data files created at the time the database was created, which include the SYSTEM tablespace's data file, the two redo logs, and the control files, need to be relabeled. If they are not relabeled correctly, the database cannot restart.

Once the instance is running, any subsequent data files added to the database are labeled with DBHIGH. This is because the background processes responsible for all file creations are, or should be, running at that same label.

Tablespaces

Just as in Oracle7, tablespaces are a collection of one or more data files. Each data file must be labeled at DBHIGH, but the tablespace itself is labeled at the user's security label at the time of creation. For example, if logged in with a label of ADMIRAL, any tablespace created during this session also has a creation label of ADMIRAL.

> **CAUTION**
>
> In Trusted Oracle, the data dictionary permanently stores tablespace information. Even if the tablespace is dropped, it cannot be recreated with the same name; it requires a separate security label.

To find the tablespace's creation label, query the DBA_TABLESPACES view with the following command:

```
SELECT rowlabel, tablespace_name
  FROM dba_tablespaces
  WHERE tablespace_name = 'USERS';

ROWLABEL    TABLESPACE_NAME
========    ===============
GENERAL     USERS
```

A tablespace can contain data at any ROWLABEL, but can only store objects labeled between the tablespace's creation label and DBHIGH. Because of this, only objects created at the label GENERAL or above can be stored in the USERS table listed above. Tables and indexes, though, could have data with a ROWLABEL of PRIVATE, because the tablespace's creation label only governs the range of object, not data, that is stored within its file space.

Database Objects

Database objects such as tables and indexes also have creation labels. These labels can be retrieved from the appropriate data dictionary views DBA_TABLES and DBA_INDEXES (or ALL_TABLES, and so on) with a query selecting the table or index name and the ROWLABEL column. For example:

```
SELECT table_name, rowlabel
  FROM dba_tables
  WHERE tablespace_name = 'USERS';

TABLE_NAME    ROWLABEL
==========    ========
ALLY          ADMIRAL
BUDGET_INFO   ADMIRAL:NAVY
```

The tables ALLY, MELISSA, and BUDGET_INFO can store rows with any label. Access to the tables, though, is controlled by the normal DAC and MAC means. Other users who have been given SELECT and INSERT access to BUDGET_INFO, and who meet the label criteria, can either read or write data to the table. If the user meets this access criteria but her label is set to PRIVATE, the table stores data with a label of PRIVATE.

Data Storage

Since a DBMS MAC mode database can store objects and data at multiple labels, it is important to know exactly how to monitor what labels exist in a table's or other object's data. To do this, every database object that stores data has a hidden row called ROWLABEL, and is used in exactly the same manner as it is in DBA_TABLESPACES or DBA_INDEXES.

To find the range of labels in a given table, a query similar to the following can be executed:

```
SELECT UNIQUE(rowlabel)
  FROM BUDGET_INFO;

ROWLABEL
========
PRIVATE
CORPORAL
ADMIRAL
```

The output shows that three separate labels appear in this table. We know from a previous query that the table's creation label was ADMIRAL:NAVY, so it is safe to assume that we have granted several users the WRITEUP privilege to add to this table.

User Administration

User administration is accomplished in the same manner in a Trusted Oracle database as in a standard Oracle7 database. Commands like CREATE USER and GRANT work exactly the same. Additional administration overhead exists, though, when deciding whether a user should be given a database password or identified by the operating system. Oracle recommends that the IDENTIFIED EXTERNALLY option be used on platforms where the database resides wholly on a single system, so that the operating system is responsible for all authentication processes.

Additionally, there is an INIT.ORA parameter, OS_AUTHENT_PREFIX, that allows the user ID in the database to be slightly different from that of the operating system's ID. By assigning a value to the OS_AUTHENT_PREFIX, you append this value to the user's operating system ID to create a unique username.

For example, if the user SATCHWILL were created in the operating system and the OS_AUTHENT_PREFIX were set to ADM, the username in the database would be equated to ADMSATCHWILL and all security verification would be done against this name. For clarity and ease of use, set the OS_AUTHENT_PREFIX to " " when possible. This allows operating system IDs to correspond identically to the database username.

As with all other database objects, usernames are also associated with a creation label. The creation label is given the value of the label at which it was created. If the Oracle administrator creates a user while its active label is ADMIRAL, the newly created user has a creation label of ADMIRAL. This creation label, though, does not explicitly define what range of labels a user can log in under.

A user's range of access to an instance is governed by two things:

- ◼ The value of DBHIGH
- ◼ The creation label of each privilege granted to the user

For example, say the user RED was created with the label CORPORAL. If the GRANT CREATE SESSION TO RED command is issued from a label of GENERAL, the user RED can only gain access to this instance if its effective label is in the range of GENERAL to the value of DBHIGH.

The creation label of a user cannot be changed without dropping and recreating the user. However, because the clearance range is dependent on the ROWLABEL of the GRANT permissions, revoking the privilege and regranting it at a more appropriate level is recommended.

OS MAC Mode

OS MAC mode is a bit easier to understand than DBMS MAC mode is, although its configuration can be a bit awkward at first. Unlike DBMS mode, an OS MAC mode database can only store data and objects at a single label. Because of this, multiple instances may need to be created to handle data with different security labels. In these types of databases, the values of DBHIGH and DBLOW are identical.

To provide a way to share data among multiple databases at different levels of security (database with different labels), an instance can mount the database files that its label dominates, in a read-only mode. In this way data can be read from multiple labels, though the instance is only capable of writing data at its own label.

Instance Configuration

Just as in DBMS mode, the instance is comprised of its processes and memory segments. All of these must run under the same label in which the database is created. There are no configuration differences in the process or data file labels. They should all be the same. Because of this, processes like LGWR or DBWR, which normally run at the equivalent of DBHIGH, run at the same label as the Listener, which normally runs at DBLOW.

Creation of the database is the same as that of an Oracle7 database, by using the CREATE DATABASE command. The command ALTER DATABASE SET DBMAC command is not needed, as the OS MAC mode is the default. Likewise, there is no need to set the values of DBHIGH or DBLOW. They are both set to the label that the database was created under.

The instance must always be started from this label. If the effective label is higher or lower, the database cannot start. Users can only access this database instance if their label dominates, but does not strictly dominate, the instance's label.

While the concepts of primary and secondary databases are available in DBMS MAC mode, only in OS MAC mode do they become critical in the support of multiple instances.

Primary Database

A primary database is the database that an instance mounts for read/write or read-compatible access mode. These database files match the label with which the instance was started. This concept is comparable to a standalone database. All control files, redo logs, and data files that are mounted by a DBMS MAC mode database or a standard Oracle7 database could be considered a primary database.

Secondary Databases

While an OS MAC instance can have only one primary database, it can have many secondary databases. A secondary database is considered a database that belongs to another Oracle instance. A primary database can mount a secondary database under two conditions:

■ The primary database must have mounted its own files in read-compatible mode.

■ The primary database's DBLOW/DBHIGH value must dominate the secondary database's DBHIGH value.

A secondary database can be either an OS MAC mode database or a DBMS MAC mode database, providing it meets the above requirements. The secondary database is mounted in a read-only, or read-secure, mode so that the primary database can read but never write data from it.

For example, if the primary database is labeled at GENERAL, it can mount any secondary database that has a DBHIGH of GENERAL or lower.

Database Management

Database management techniques are similar to that of DBMS MAC mode, where the ROWLEVEL column exists in all data dictionary views and tables, but a few differences do exist:

■ Because an OS MAC database stores only one label of data, clusters can be used.

■ The ROWLABEL columns have the same values.

■ No covert channels exist in OS MAC mode because there is no way to bypass the operating system MAC mode.

■ Users must be authenticated in all instances they access.

Choosing Between Modes

Because of the different modes available and the benefits for each one, it can be difficult to choose exactly which mode to use. Oracle gives the following considerations for choosing between them.

Choosing DBMS MAC Mode

Choose this mode over OS MAC mode when the following requirements exist:

- Multilevel security across labels and applications
- Many different labels exist
- Labels are added and changed when necessary

Choosing OS MAC Mode

Choose OS MAC mode over DBMS MAC mode when these conditions exist:

- Strict MAC enforcement must be adhered to.
- The existence of covert channels is a severe problem.
- Cross-level integrity is not a requirement.
- Only a small number of labels is required.
- Label values are not constantly being added or deleted.
- Data is tiered, where there are greater amounts of data at a low label.

Creating a Security Policy

A security policy is an overall plan of what security methods are going to be employed and how they will be instituted. It should include types of data to be secured, categories of users that will access the data, what their security needs to be, how applications handle the different levels of security, and whether trusted applications can dynamically alter the user's active label to accomplish tasks.

While sounding a bit overwhelming, a security policy is not extremely hard to create. A very thorough policy, however, takes time and trial to refine to the point of being sufficient for all of a business's needs. Each company's security policy is different, based on how secure its data should be. Many government or high security sites spend endless amounts of time on security policy until all loopholes and gaps have been filled.

As an example, a basic security plan might cover:

- The overall policy statement
- Levels of security and their descriptions
- Categories of users and how they fit into the security levels
- Operating system–specific security implementations
- Plans to implement the security policy
- Testing procedures to ensure the policy is accurate

Once the plan has been refined, detailed migration steps can be decided upon. These steps, specifically the ones related to database migration, are used in the migration steps listed later in this chapter.

The security policy decided upon can be as detailed or generic as needed for the installation site. The guidelines in the preceding list are only suggested, and certainly are not completely inclusive. Each site should strive to create a policy that embodies its own goals and policies.

Migrating to Trusted Oracle

Migration to Trusted Oracle is a somewhat involved process. Much of the process is specific to the version of Oracle being migrated from, such as version 6. The other steps involve knowing which mode of operation is going to be used and then exporting and re-importing the data according to specific procedures. The steps for migrating to DBMS mode are different from those of migrating to OS mode, and the following sections outline each migration path.

Migrating to DBMS MAC Mode

In order to migrate to DBMS operation mode, special planning efforts must be made to cover the specific needs of a DBMS MAC Trusted Oracle database—in particular, the list of labels and the database objects associated with them. Since the operating system controls what labels exist and which users have been given rights, the database administrator must work very closely with the system administrator (and security administrator, if one exists) to plan and implement a Trusted Oracle database.

A typical migration follows these steps:

1. Install new hardware/software/DBMS on secured system.
2. Create a full backup of the source database.
3. Copy the backup file(s) to the new system.
4. Create the database objects in advance.
5. Import the backup into the new database.
6. Modify the row labels on each table.
7. Create indexes (if not done in step 4).
8. Shutdown the database and perform a full backup.

Install New Hardware, Software, and DBMS

Installing the new hardware, software, and DBMS is not always done in the first step. Many sites reuse the old hardware as the new secured server. In such a case, the backup of the database should be sent to a temporary holding area until the system has been upgraded, and then restored. The rest of the steps remain the same throughout the migration process.

Create a Full Backup

A full backup is always suggested when migrating or modifying a database to a point where recovery is extremely difficult or not possible. Some administrators consider this a waste of time, trusting luck to keep things going smoothly. However, it is a good idea to create a backup; it can save quite a bit of time and effort in the long run, should problems arise.

The full backup can be done any way desired, but an export format is needed to restore the database objects. Once the export has been completed, it must be transferred to the new system where the Import utility is used to transfer the data from the backup file into the database.

Copy the Backup File(s)

This is a system-specific step based upon what type of platform the new server uses. For some sites, this is actually a tape backup/restore. Others might use the same system and simply upgrade the operating system, leaving some of the data files intact. (At this point, however, a full system backup is usually suggested.)

Create the Database Objects in Advance

This step requires much planning before it can be implemented. Since the MAC level uses the object's creation label as the security label for inserts, it must be the lowest label that can access the object. This is especially true for tables and views. These objects must be created ahead of time so that object definition in the data dictionary has the proper access label. These objects, unlike data, cannot have their creation label modified. Objects must be dropped and re-created to have their creation label changed.

To create these objects in advance, you can use several options. First, you can selectively import objects from the full export of the old database without importing rows or indexes. This entails the following:

1. Alter the current operating system label to match the security label the objects should be created under.
2. Selectively import the database objects belonging under this access label.
3. Repeat steps 1 and 2 until all objects have been created.

Some sites manage a library of SQL scripts that are used to re-create database objects as needed. If such SQL scripts exist, the following steps could be taken to create the database objects:

1. Alter the current operating system label to match the security label the objects should be created under.
2. Start a SQL*Plus session.
3. Execute each SQL script for every object that must be created at this security level.
4. Repeat steps 1 through 3 until all objects for each security label are created.

> **NOTE**
>
> It is a good idea to create the indexes at a later date. If indexes exist, they can have a negative impact on the speed at which the data import runs. Import the data with an `INDEXES = N` option and then create the indexes after all the data has been imported.

Import the Backup

Once the database objects have been created, the data must be imported. Since different labels exist on the database objects, the current label must be set high enough to give access to all objects where data is to be inserted. Oracle suggests setting the current label to the operating system's equivalent of `DBHIGH`, or the highest label at which data exists in the database. Once the data has been imported, all data must have their row label changed to reflect the proper access label. After setting the operating system label to the appropriate value, the import can be accomplished with a command similar to the following:

```
IMP FILE=ORCL.DMP IGNORE=Y FULL=Y INDEXES=N
```

The `IGNORE = Y` clause is used because the database objects have already been created. If `IGNORE = Y` is not used, error messages result.

> **NOTE**
>
> It is probably not a good idea to set the active label to DBHIGH. This value in the database is equated with the value of DBHIGH, but is a valid entry in the ROWLABEL column of tables and indexes. If the value of DBHIGH changes in the future, all data and objects labeled with DBHIGH rather than a valid label may become inaccessible to some users.

Modify the ROWLABEL

Now that the data has been imported, the actual labels of each row must be set. This can be a simple or a difficult process, depending on the access needs of the initial data. To set all rows to the access label of CORPORAL, a SQL command similar to the following can be used:

```
UPDATE classified_data
  SET ROWLABEL='GENERAL';
```

To selectively set the ROWLABEL, use an appropriate SQL command similar to the following:

```
UPDATE classified_data
  SET ROWLABEL='ADMIRAL'
  WHERE subject_matter = 'TOP_SECRET';
```

```
UPDATE classified_data
  SET ROWLABEL = 'GENERAL'
  WHERE subject_matter != 'TOP_SECRET';
```

NOTE

Again, this step is done so that the creation label of the table is set appropriately. There is no way to change the creation label of a database object without dropping it and re-creating it under the appropriate active label.

Create the Indexes

Indexes, just like tables, contain a ROWLABEL column. Since it exists in both places and can be used as part of a table's index to create a unique value, the indexes should be created last. It is possible to create them in one step when importing the backup file, but that slows down the import. It also slows down the previous step of updating the ROWLABEL column of each table and index.

The easiest way to create indexes, if no SQL script exists, is to use the INDEXFILE option of the Import utility to create a SQL script of index creation commands. Steps similar to these can be used:

1. Create the index SQL file with a command similar to IMP FILE=ORCL.DMP INDEXFILE=ORCL.NDX ROWS=N TABLES=N.
2. Create a file for each security label that the indexes should be created with.
3. Set the active label.
4. Start SQL*Plus.
5. Execute the SQL file to create all indexes for this security label.
6. Repeat steps 3 through 5 for each label.

Shutdown the Database

Now that all database objects and data have been imported, it is important to make a full backup of the database at this current revision. This backup represents all the hours necessary to create and update all objects with the proper security levels. The export utility or a cold backup can be used (see Chapter 29, "Developing a Backup and Recovery Plan").

Migrating to OS MAC Mode

Migration to OS mode is a simpler, though more involved, process. Since the architecture of the OS mode database can only hold a single level of data, objects do not have to be created ahead of time. Instead, separate backups of each label of data must be performed. Once that is done, a full import can be done. This is probably the easiest part of the migration.

The greater involvement comes in planning and setting up the database and segregating each instance's files in order to get the best performance from each database. It also comes in separating the tables and objects that belong in each database. Though well worth the effort, this type of migration can be a time consuming and often frustrating process.

A typical migration might follow these steps:

1. Install new hardware/software/DBMS on secured system.
2. Create a backup (export) file for each new database instance.
3. Copy the backup file(s) to the new system.
5. Import each backup into the appropriate database.
6. Shut down the database and perform a full backup.

Install New Hardware, Software, and DBMS

Just as when migrating to DBMS MAC mode, new hardware, software, and DBMS may be required before migrating to OS MAC mode. Many sites may plan to reuse old hardware as the new secured server. If this is the case, the backup of the database should be sent to a temporary holding area until the system has been upgraded and then restored.

Create a Full Backup

Since data is being migrated from a single database to multiple database instances, careful planning must be done in order to import the correct objects (tables, indexes, triggers, packages, and so on) to the correct instance. Unlike a DBMS mode instance, the use of clusters is allowed. This can further increase the difficulty of the backup. Be sure that each object is accounted for and not duplicated unless necessary.

To restore this backup in subsequent steps, an export format using Oracle's export utility is necessary. See Chapter 19, "Export/Import," for more information.

Copy the Backup File(s)

Once again, this step is identical to the copy step when migrating to DBMS mode. Either a tape backup and restore, or FTP can be used to accomplish this step. Some sites do not need to transfer the files.

Import the Backup

Since the instance cannot store data above or below its own label, only three basic steps are needed to import the data to the instance:

1. Change to the appropriate instance.
2. Set the current label to match that of the instance.

3. Import the export file into the instance.
4. Repeat steps 1 through 3 until all data and all instances are populated.

Shutdown the Database

For each instance that has been created and populated, it is a good idea to create a full backup. The export utility or a cold backup can be used, depending on each site's needs.

Trusted Oracle Data Dictionary Reference

Trusted Oracle contains the same data dictionary tables and views that any standard Oracle7 database contains. Except for those tables listed in the next section, only one important difference exists: These views contain a column called ROWLABEL. This is the row-level label associated with each row of data.

The tables/views listed in the following section are specific to Trusted Oracle7.

Further information can be found in Oracle's *Trusted Oracle7 Server Administrator's Guide*.

Views/Tables Specific to Trusted Oracle

ALL_LABELS	A list of all labels the current user holds dominance over
ALL_MOUNTED_DBS	Current list of information on any database currently mounted by this instance
V$SECONDARY	Information pertaining to all secondary databases currently mounted by this instance
V$SYSLABEL	Lists currently mounted database information, including operating mode and DBLOW/DBHIGH values

Modified Views for Trusted Oracle

Table 35.7 lists each data dictionary view that has been modified for the support of Trusted Oracle. The view name and additional columns are listed.

Table 35.7. Modified data dictionary views.

View Name	Added Columns	Column Description
DBA_AUDIT_OBJECT	OBJECT_LABEL	The audited object's label
	SESSION_LABEL	The user's active label
DBA_AUDIT_SESSION	SESSION_LABEL	The audited user's active label
DBA_AUDIT_STATEMENT	SESSION_LABEL	The audited user's active label

continues

Table 35.7. cotinued

View Name	Added Columns	Column Description
DBA_AUDIT_TRAIL	OBJECT_LABEL	The audited object's label
	SESSION_LABEL	The audited user's active label
USER_AUDIT_OBJECT	OBJECT_LABEL	The audited object's label
	SESSION_LABEL	The audited user's active label
USER_AUDIT_SESSION	SESSION_LABEL	The audited user's active label
USER_AUDIT_STATEMENT	SESSION_LABEL	The audited user's active label
USER_AUDIT_TRAIL	OBJECT_LABEL	The audited object's label
	SESSION_LABEL	The audited user's active label

Trusted Oracle `INIT.ORA` Parameter Reference

The parameters listed in Table 35.8 are specific to Trusted Oracle. More detailed information can be found in Oracle's *Trusted Oracle7 Server Administrator's Guide.*

Table 35.8. Trusted Oracle `INIT.ORA` parameters.

Parameter	Value Range	Description
AUTO_MOUNTING	TRUE/FALSE	Automatically mounts a secondary database when any user requests information from an object stored there.
DB_MOUNT_MODE	NORMAL/READ_COMPATIBLE	The default access mode in which the database will be mounted.
LABEL_CACHE_SIZE	50 or greater	The size of the label cache, used to compare label values for MAC.
MLS_LABEL_FORMAT	Any valid label format	Determines the format in which a label will be displayed.
OPEN_MOUNTS	0–255	The maximum number of databases an OS MAC database can mount simultaneously.

Summary

Although Trusted Oracle provides an extremely strict level of security, its implementation must be planned thoroughly with much thought to future growth and the types of data that might be added to the database. Few commercial sites will need this level of security, but it is nice to know that the option is available.

Due to the large differences in how a Trusted Oracle database is administered, be sure to take the time and read through the documentation provided by Oracle. Other third-party books should also help in implementing and administering a Trusted Oracle database.

36

National Language Support

by Kelly Leigh

Oracle's National Language Support (NLS) enables Oracle to become a worldwide player in the database market. Just as its name suggests, NLS is Oracle's support for multiple languages and for language-specific conventions for displaying numbers, dates, and currency. Without this important feature, Oracle would be an English-only database application—unable to provide database solutions for multinational companies.

The many NLS options in Oracle are highly configurable and support both servers and clients running in many of the world's languages. Even more important is that the language barrier becomes nearly seamless to the end users. Without knowing it, users may be entering data into a database whose native language is different from the one in which they are working.

This chapter starts by explaining the background and foundation that allows Oracle to provide NLS in a seamless manner.

EBCDIC and ASCII Character Sets

Thebasic functionality of all character sets is to provide a set of alpha, numeric, and symbolic characters for display on a user's terminal. These items range from the basic letters of the Latin alphabet to the numbers and math symbols across the top of the standard American 101-key keyboard.

A character set is basically a group of display characters, each with an associated unique numeric value. For example, the pipe character (¦) has an associated value of 124 (in decimal notation). Each character in a character set has a unique value within that character set. In order to accommodate the thousands of different characters in all the written languages and the unique groupings of them, many unique character sets have been created.

Various categories of character sets, each with unique properties, enable a single character set to contain all the unique symbols that a given language uses. A single language may have many different character sets so that different types of applications can use the most popular symbols.

The various types of character sets can be grouped into two basic categories: single-byte and multiple-byte. Single-byte character sets generally are used for European languages, such as English, that contain a relatively small number of symbols. Multiple-byte character sets are used for Asian languages, such as Japanese or Chinese, that may require thousands of symbols.

The two categories of single-byte character sets are

- 7-bit
- 8-bit

The two categories of multiple-byte character sets are

- 16-bit
- 32-bit

Each category of single- and multiple-byte character sets can define a maximum number of characters, based on the number of bits used to store each character. Table 36.1 shows the maximum number of characters that can be defined for each character set type.

Table 36.1. Character set storage capacities.

Character Set Type	Maximum Characters
Single-byte 7-bit	128
Single-byte 8-bit	256
Multiple-byte 16-bit	65,536
Multiple-byte 32-bit	131,072

When character sets were first created, two formal standards were developed: ASCII and EBCDIC. These two sets perform the same function: mapping unique symbols to a numeric counterpart. EBCDIC stands for Extended Binary Coded Decimal Interchange Code and is used most on IBM mainframe systems. ASCII is short for American Standard Code for Information Interchange and is mostly used on desktop computers.

ASCII is a 7-bit, single-byte character set. It differs from EBCDIC in the way that the computer stores the values for the symbols in the character set. In short, the computer stores a character in a 1-byte field, which is 8 bits. Without going into too much detail, ASCII uses only 7 of the 8 bits available to store a symbol, which means that an ASCII character set can contain 128 symbols.

EBCDIC uses all 8 bits in the byte to store a symbol's value, which means that an EBCDIC character set can contain up to 256 unique symbols. EBCDIC and ASCII differ in two other ways. First, EBCDIC has a formal mapping for most of the 256 symbols available to it; ASCII does not. Second, even though ASCII and EBCDIC share the same symbols (A–Z, a–z, 0–9, and so on), the numeric values of the symbols are different in each standard, as shown in Tables 36.2 and 36.3. Most character sets have been based on either ASCII or EBCDIC standard mappings.

Table 36.2. ASCII character set.

Dec X_{10}	Hex X_{16}	Binary X_2	ASCII	Dec X_{10}	Hex X_{16}	Binary X_2	ASCII
000	00	0000 0000	null	004	04	0000 0100	♦
001	01	0000 0001	☺	005	05	0000 0101	♣
002	02	0000 0010	☻	006	06	0000 0110	♠
003	03	0000 0011	♥	007	07	0000 0111	•

continues

Table 36.2. continued

Dec X_{10}	Hex X_{16}	Binary X_2	ASCII	Dec X_{10}	Hex X_{16}	Binary X_2	ASCII
008	08	0000 1000	◘	039	27	0010 0111	'
009	09	0000 1001	○	040	28	0010 1000	(
010	0A	0000 1010	◙	041	29	0010 1001	)
011	0B	0000 1011	♂	042	2A	0010 1010	*
012	0C	0000 1100	♀	043	2B	0010 1011	+
013	0D	0000 1101	♪	044	2C	0010 1100	'
014	0E	0000 1110	♫	045	2D	0010 1101	-
015	0F	0000 1111	☼	046	2E	0010 1110	.
016	10	0001 0000	►	047	2F	0010 1111	/
017	11	0001 0001	◄	048	30	0011 0000	0
018	12	0001 0010	↕	049	31	0011 0001	1
019	13	0001 0011	‼	050	32	0011 0010	2
020	14	0001 0100	¶	051	33	0011 0011	3
021	15	0001 0101	§	052	34	0011 0100	4
022	16	0001 0110	▬	053	35	0011 0101	5
023	17	0001 0111	↨	054	36	0011 0110	6
024	18	0001 1000	↑	055	37	0011 0111	7
025	19	0001 1001	↓	056	38	0011 1000	8
026	1A	0001 1010	→	057	39	0011 1001	9
027	1B	0001 1011	←	058	3A	0011 1010	:
028	1C	0001 1100	∟	059	3B	0011 1011	;
029	1D	0001 1101	↔	060	3C	0011 1100	<
030	1E	0001 1110	▲	061	3D	0011 1101	=
031	1F	0001 1111	▼	062	3E	0011 1110	>
032	20	0010 0000	space	063	3F	0011 1111	?
033	21	0010 0001	!	064	40	0100 0000	@
034	22	0010 0010	"	065	41	0100 0001	A
035	23	0010 0011	#	066	42	0100 0010	B
036	24	0010 0100	$	067	43	0100 0011	C
037	25	0010 0101	%	068	44	0100 0100	D
038	26	0010 0110	&	069	45	0100 0101	E

Dec X_{10}	Hex X_{16}	Binary X_2	ASCII	Dec X_{10}	Hex X_{16}	Binary X_2	ASCII
070	46	0100 0110	F	101	65	0110 0101	e
071	47	0100 0111	G	102	66	0110 0110	f
072	48	0100 1000	H	103	67	0110 0111	g
073	49	0100 1001	I	104	68	0110 1000	h
074	4A	0100 1010	J	105	69	0110 1001	i
075	4B	0100 1011	K	106	6A	0110 1010	j
076	4C	0100 1100	L	107	6B	0110 1011	k
077	4D	0100 1101	M	108	6C	0110 1100	l
078	4E	0100 1110	N	109	6D	0110 1101	m
079	4F	0100 1111	O	110	6E	0110 1110	n
080	50	0101 0000	P	111	6F	0110 1111	o
081	51	0101 0001	Q	112	70	0111 0000	p
082	52	0101 0010	R	113	71	0111 0001	q
083	53	0101 0011	S	114	72	0111 0010	r
084	54	0101 0100	T	115	73	0111 0011	s
085	55	0101 0101	U	116	74	0111 0100	t
086	56	0101 0110	V	117	75	0111 0101	u
087	57	0101 0111	W	118	76	0111 0110	v
088	58	0101 1000	X	119	77	0111 0111	w
089	59	0101 1001	Y	120	78	0111 1000	x
090	5A	0101 1010	Z	121	79	0111 1001	y
091	5B	0101 1011	[	122	7A	0111 1010	z
092	5C	0101 1100	\	123	7B	0111 1011	{
093	5D	0101 1101	]	124	7C	0111 1100	¦
094	5E	0101 1110	^	125	7D	0111 1101	}
095	5F	0101 1111	–	126	7E	0111 1110	~
096	60	0110 0000	`	127	7F	0111 1111	Δ
097	61	0110 0001	a	128	80	1000 0000	Ç
098	62	0110 0010	b	129	81	1000 0001	ü
099	63	0110 0011	c	130	82	1000 0010	é
100	64	0110 0100	d	131	83	1000 0011	â

continues

Table 36.2. continued

Dec X_{10}	Hex X_{16}	Binary X_2	ASCII	Dec X_{10}	Hex X_{16}	Binary X_2	ASCII
132	84	1000 0100	ä	163	A3	1010 0011	ú
133	85	1000 0101	à	164	A4	1010 0100	ñ
134	86	1000 0110	å	165	A5	1010 0101	Ñ
135	87	1000 0111	ç	166	A6	1010 0110	ª
136	88	1000 1000	ê	167	A7	1010 0111	º
137	89	1000 1001	ë	168	A8	1010 1000	¿
138	8A	1000 1010	è	169	A9	1010 1001	⌐
139	8B	1000 1011	ï	170	AA	1010 1010	¬
140	8C	1000 1100	î	171	AB	1010 1011	½
141	8D	1000 1101	ì	172	AC	1010 1100	¼
142	8E	1000 1110	Ä	173	AD	1010 1101	¡
143	8F	1000 1111	Å	174	AE	1010 1110	«
144	90	1001 0000	É	175	AF	1010 1111	»
145	91	1001 0001	æ	176	B0	1011 0000	▓
146	92	1001 0010	Æ	177	B1	1011 0001	▓
147	93	1001 0011	ô	178	B2	1011 0010	█
148	94	1001 0100	ö	179	B3	1011 0011	│
149	95	1001 0101	ò	180	B4	1011 0100	┤
150	96	1001 0110	û	181	B5	1011 0101	╡
151	97	1001 0111	ù	182	B6	1011 0110	╢
152	98	1001 1000	ÿ	183	B7	1011 0111	╖
153	99	1001 1001	Ö	184	B8	1011 1000	╕
154	9A	1001 1010	Ü	185	B9	1011 1001	╣
155	9B	1001 1011	¢	186	BA	1011 1010	║
156	9C	1001 1100	£	187	BB	1011 1011	╗
157	9D	1001 1101	¥	188	BC	1011 1100	╝
158	9E	1001 1110	₧	189	BD	1011 1101	╜
159	9F	1001 1111	ƒ	190	BE	1011 1110	╛
160	A0	1010 0000	á	191	BF	1011 1111	┐
161	A1	1010 0001	í	192	C0	1100 0000	└
162	A2	1010 0010	ó	193	C1	1100 0001	┴

Dec X_{10}	Hex X_{16}	Binary X_2	ASCII	Dec X_{10}	Hex X_{16}	Binary X_2	ASCII
194	C2	1100 0010	┬	225	E1	1110 0001	β
195	C3	1100 0011	├	226	E2	1110 0010	Γ
196	C4	1100 0100	─	227	E3	1110 0011	π
197	C5	1100 0101	+	228	E4	1110 0100	Σ
198	C6	1100 0110	╞	229	E5	1110 0101	σ
199	C7	1100 0111	╟	230	E6	1110 0110	μ
200	C8	1100 1000	╚	231	E7	1110 0111	γ
201	C9	1100 1001	╔	232	E8	1110 1000	Φ
202	CA	1100 1010	╩	233	E9	1110 1001	θ
203	CB	1100 1011	╦	234	EA	1110 1010	Ω
204	CC	1100 1100	╠	235	EB	1110 1011	δ
205	CD	1100 1101	=	236	EC	1110 1100	∞
206	CE	1100 1110	╬	237	ED	1110 1101	ø
207	CF	1100 1111	╧	238	EE	1110 1110	∈
208	D0	1101 0000	╨	239	EF	1110 1111	∩
209	D1	1101 0001	╤	240	F0	1110 0000	≡
210	D2	1101 0010	╥	241	F1	1111 0001	±
211	D3	1101 0011	╙	242	F2	1111 0010	≥
212	D4	1101 0100	╘	243	F3	1111 0011	≤
213	D5	1101 0101	╒	244	F4	1111 0100	⌠
214	D6	1101 0110	╓	245	F5	1111 0101	⌡
215	D7	1101 0111	╫	246	F6	1111 0110	÷
216	D8	1101 1000	╪	247	F7	1111 0111	≈
217	D9	1101 1001	╝	248	F8	1111 1000	°
218	DA	1101 1010	╔	249	F9	1111 1001	•
219	DB	1101 1011	█	250	FA	1111 1010	·
220	DC	1101 1100	▄	251	FB	1111 1011	√
221	DD	1101 1101	▌	252	FC	1111 1100	ⁿ
222	DE	1101 1110	▐	253	FD	1111 1101	²
223	DF	1101 1111	▀	254	FE	1111 1110	■
224	E0	1110 0000	α	255	FF	1111 1111	

Table 36.3. EBCDIC character set.

Dec X_{10}	Hex X_{16}	Character	Dec X_{10}	Hex X_{16}	Character	Dec X_{10}	Hex X_{16}	Character
129	81	a	243	F3	3	216	D8	Q
130	82	b	244	F4	4	217	D9	R
131	83	c	245	F5	5	226	E2	S
132	84	d	246	F6	6	227	E3	T
133	85	e	247	F7	7	228	E4	U
134	86	f	248	F8	8	229	E5	V
135	87	g	249	F9	9	230	E6	W
136	88	h	122	7A	:	231	E7	X
137	89	i	123	7B	#	232	E8	Y
145	91	j	124	7C	@	233	E9	Z
146	92	k	125	7D	'	64	40	blank
147	93	l	126	7E	=	76	4C	<
148	94	m	127	7F	"	77	4D	(
149	95	n	193	C1	A	78	4E	+
150	96	o	194	C2	B	79	4F		
151	97	p	195	C3	C	80	50	&
152	98	q	196	C4	D	90	5A	!
153	99	r	197	C5	E	91	5B	$
162	A2	s	198	C6	F	92	5C	*
163	A3	t	199	C7	G	93	5D	)
164	A4	u	200	C8	H	94	5E	;
165	A5	v	201	C9	I	96	60	-
166	A6	w	209	D1	J	97	61	/
167	A7	x	210	D2	K	107	6B	,
168	A8	y	211	D3	L	108	6C	%
169	A9	z	212	D4	M	109	6D	_
240	F0	0	213	D5	N	110	6E	>
241	F1	1	214	D6	O	111	6F	?
242	F2	2	215	D7	P			

Features of National Language Support

Many questions arise when you consider the potential problems in providing support for multiple character sets and languages.

- What kind of problems exist for multinational companies?
- In a client/server environment, does the client's language have to match the server's?
- Are multiple versions of Oracle available for each supported language?
- How does Oracle control the display of currency and date layouts?
- Can data be entered in one language and displayed in another?

Believe it or not, Oracle has addressed all these concerns. The NLS architecture contains two parts:

1. Language-dependent data
2. Language-independent functions

When an Oracle database is installed, a portion of the installation is common to all languages. For the most part, this portion includes the kernel software. Also at the time of installation, a default language must be selected by the installer. Based on this selection, the language-dependent data (for example, documentation and the scripts for database administration) is installed. This architecture allows additional languages to be installed after a database has been created without requiring another install of Oracle. The architecture also allows language-dependent features to be enabled for each session.

Because Oracle has set up language-dependent and language-independent structures, users with different language needs can still run against a common database server. Oracle cannot actually translate from one language to another, but it can handle problems such as

- Regional variations in displaying date formats
- Different currency notations
- Language-specific decimal characters
- Language-specific sort orders
- Multiple calendar types
- Language with context/location sensitive characters

In order to enable these types of options, a few standards must be adopted. First, the database must store data using a common method: all date fields, numeric fields with precision enabled, and so on must have the same storage formats. Second, the storage format must be converted to the desired display format when the formats are different. One way to accomplish this conversion is to use data filters. A second method, which is a bit more complex, is to define a display character set and a storage character set.

The types of display overrides are listed later in this chapter. (The reference section at the end of this chapter explains the override variables in greater detail.)

TIP

Overriding any of these options at the session level changes not only how the various types of data are displayed but also how the database expects them to be inserted from this client/user.

If NLS_NUMERIC_CHARACTERS is changed so that the grouping character is a period (.), inserting the value 101.25 would result in an error because the value, seemingly entered as 101 and 25/100, would actually be interpreted as 101 thousand.

Display and Storage Character Sets

Two separate character set types were created to support the languages (specifically, Arabic and Hebrew) whose alphabets have context-sensitive characters. The use of storage character sets is common to all languages, whereas display character sets are currently used only for these languages.

The *storage character set* defines how data is sent to and received from the Oracle database. All conversions for date, numeric, and other formats are followed as listed above. A *display character set* is used as a translation between the storage character set and the way it appears on the user's terminal.

NLS_LANG is the variable that controls the storage character set. NLS_DISPLAY controls the display character set.

CAUTION

For sites not using Arabic and/or Hebrew, the value of NLS_DISPLAY, which controls the display character set, should not be modified from its installation value.

Oracle does not check the accuracy of these values and will automatically attempt any conversion necessary. If the value of NLS_DISPLAY has been set contrary to the value that is supported at the installation site, unknown problems may occur.

Changing the Date Format

When setting up an Oracle database, you can select values such as a default date format and currency format. These display values are used whenever a user starts a session and requests data to be displayed. You can use the NLS_DATE_FORMAT variable to override the default formats. This variable changes the way the date will be displayed and input into the database.

Changing the Numeric Format

Changing the number format entails changing the grouping character and the decimal character. Normally for the United States, the decimal character is a period (.) and the grouping character is a comma (,). Other countries may follow different conventions. The NLS_NUMERIC_CHARACTERS variable controls these values.

Changing the Language of Oracle Messages

Normally all Oracle error messages and warnings are displayed in the default language of the database. The NLS_LANGUAGE setting changes this value to a session-specific setting, unless it is changed for the entire database in the INIT.ORA parameter file. Changing this value affects the following areas:

■ Messages returned by the database (including messages for SQL*Forms)

■ Day and month names (language-specific)

■ Time and date symbols (the equivalents of the U.S. settings: a.m., p.m., AD, BC)

■ Default sorting sequence

CAUTION

Oracle controls the language of the messages and errors returned by the database. However, the developer must ensure that any text coded into an application is in the appropriate language.

Changing Sort Orders

Sorting is usually accomplished by using a binary sort, which means that characters are sorted according to the character set numeric value (refer again to Tables 36.2 and 36.3). Binary sorts work well for the English alphabet because the letters and numbers were assigned values according to this type of sorting. However, some character sets do not represent their numeric characters in a sequential order. Because of this, the number 4 may have a greater character set numeric value than the number 3 does. The character set numeric value is strictly dependent on the character set being used.

To account for the latter situation, Oracle has implemented a linguistic sort. This type of sort temporarily modifies the character set by changing the numeric equivalents of each character. Reassigning these values for the duration of the sort enables a binary sort to produce the correct values.

You can change the default sort with the NLS_LANGUAGE parameter. If you want to override the default, you need to change the value of NLS_LANG.

> **NOTE**
>
> Linguistic sorts work only on single-byte character sets. Multiple-byte character sets will always be sorted in binary order.

Changing the Default Calendar

Oracle supports the following five calendar types:

- Arabic Hijrah
- Gregorian
- Japanese Imperial
- Persian
- ROC Official

You can change the calendar type by using the `NLS_CALENDAR` variable, which also changes the default date format.

Enabling NLS Features

The way in which an NLS feature is enabled depends on your needs and circumstances. In addition, the process of overriding values adheres to a definite hierarchy. Database administrators and developers must work together to help define where each definition should be made. The definitions of the NLS parameters can exist at these levels and in this order:

1. The `INIT.ORA` parameter file
2. Environment variable settings
3. `ALTER SESSION` commands

The `INIT.ORA` Parameter File

When the database is initially created, the installer either accepts the defaults for the NLS parameters or sets the desired values. After the database has been created, some of these values cannot be changed. You can override them in the environment settings or with `ALTER SESSION` commands, but the database will continue to store them according to the initial settings.

Environment Variable Settings

No matter which platform Oracle is running on, including client/server environments, a user may override the default settings of the database. To do so, the user must enter the operating specific–command to set the value of the NLS parameter before starting the Oracle session.

A UNIX system accomplishes this task with the following command:

```
export NLS_DATE_LANGUAGE = "FRANCE"
setenv NLS_DATE_FORMAT = "MM/DD/YY"
```

On a Windows NT platform, you can change the setting from the Control Panel's System icon.

After the environment variables have been set, when the user connects to the database, Oracle immediately issues an ALTER SESSION SET NLS_DATE_LANGUAGE="FRANCE" command and a NLS_DATE_FORMAT="MM/DD/YY" command before it executes any other command. This procedure enables Oracle to propagate these environment settings into the user's session.

> **CAUTION**
>
> Unless the changes for NLS parameters are modified in the startup files for a user (autoexec.bat for DOS platforms, .login or .profile for UNIX systems, and so on), the current changes may not affect future sessions.
>
> Also, if an application explicitly specifies an ALTER SESSION SET NLS_ command, the values set in the user's environment will be overridden. You need to take this type of override into account when developing applications that use NLS settings that differ from the database defaults.

ALTER SESSION Commands

The ALTER SESSION SET ... command takes precedence over the other two methods of setting NLS parameters. As a rule, this type of command should be used for

- SQL reports
- Applications that require a specific setting to operate properly
- Interactive sessions

You should avoid this option for applications programming. Although it is effective in forcing options to conform to initial standards, future growth or changes in the application program's use may require coding changes to operate correctly. When debugging problems, it is also difficult for other developers to find this type of parameter override unless it is explicitly documented.

NLS Parameter Reference

The following parameters are NLS-specific. Some parameters can be specified only at certain levels. Some of these parameters can be used only as environment variables, whereas others can be specified in the INIT.ORA parameter or as an ALTER SESSION command. See Table 36.4 for the specific uses of each parameter.

Table 36.4. NLS parameter uses.

Parameter	INIT.ORA	Environment	Alter Session
NLS_CALENDAR	Yes	Yes	Yes
NLS_CREDIT	No	Yes	No
NLS_CURRENCY	Yes	Yes	Yes
NLS_DATE_FORMAT	Yes	No	Yes
NLS_DATE_LANGUAGE	Yes	Yes	Yes
NLS_DEBIT	No	Yes	No
NLS_DISPLAY	No	Yes	No
NLS_ISO_CURRENCY	Yes	Yes	Yes
NLS_LANG	No	Yes	No
NLS_LANGUAGE	Yes	No	Yes
NLS_LIST_SEPARATOR	No	Yes	No
NLS_MONETARY_CHARACTERS	No	Yes	No
NLS_NUMERIC_CHARACTERS	Yes	Yes	Yes
NLS_SORT	Yes	Yes	Yes
NLS_SPECIAL_CHARS	Yes	No	No
NLS_TERRITORY	Yes	No	Yes

NLS_CALENDAR

Oracle supports five calendars, and each calendar has a default date format. (Depending on the language the database will be running under, you may need to change the default calendar type.)

You can use the following command to change the calendar type to Persian:

```
ALTER SESSION SET NLS_CALENDAR = "PERSIAN"
```

Default output for the date format would become DD-Month-YYYY. Each calendar has its own default date format, which you can override by using the NLS_DATE_FORMAT setting.

NLS_CREDIT

The value for NLS_CREDIT is used in financial reports to determine whether the value is a credit or debt. The default value is derived from NLS_TERRITORY or from NLS_LANGUAGE if no territory was set. You can override the value for NLS_CREDIT with any string (except for null) of up to 9 bytes.

Valid values are user-definable, for example

```
NLS_CREDIT = "Credit:   "
NLS_CREDIT = " + "
```

NLS_CURRENCY

You can use NLS_CURRENCY to change the local currency symbol, which can be a string of characters or a single character. This setting can be any value you want, regardless of whether it is a true currency symbol. Therefore, the following commands are all valid:

```
ALTER SESSION SET NLS_CURRENCY = "$ ";
ALTER SESSION SET NLS_CURRENCY = "L ";
ALTER SESSION SET NLS_CURRENCY = "My Balance:   ";
```

The local currency symbol is displayed when selecting the number format mask L. The following example uses this type of mask with the third ALTER SESSION command shown previously:

```
SELECT TO_CHAR(balance, 'L999D99') "Balance"
  FROM checking_account
  WHERE account_name = "Kelly's Bank Account";

Balance
=======
My Balance:   100.01
```

NLS_DATE_FORMAT

When setting values to either NLS_LANGUAGE or NLS_TERRITORY, a default value for NLS_DATE_FORMAT is set, based on installation choices. This format is usually in some form of MM-DD-YY where

> MM stands for the two-digit numeric value for the month.
> DD is the two-digit day of the month.
> YY is the last two numbers for the year.
> - is the field separator.

Values for this parameter must be in double quotation marks and can include

```
NLS_DATE_FORMAT = "MM/DD/YYYY"
NLS_DATE_FORMAT = "YY MM DD"
```

NLS_DATE_LANGUAGE

The value of NLS_DATE_LANGUAGE explicitly overrides the value of NLS_LANGUAGE for the spelling of day and month names. The SQL functions TO_CHAR() and TO_DATE() are affected because they return these specific values. The valid values for NLS_DATE_LANGUAGE are identical to the valid values for NLS_LANGUAGE; they are listed in Table 36.5.

The following example illustrates the effects of setting NLS_DATE_LANGUAGE = SPANISH.

The query

```
SELECT TO_CHAR(SYSDATE, 'Day:Dd Month yyyy')
  FROM dual;
```

where today's date is May 24, 1997, returns the following:

```
Sabado:24 Mayo 1997
```

NLS_DEBIT

Similar to NLS_CREDIT, NLS_DEBIT is used in financial reports to show a debit value. If no value is set for NLS_DEBIT, its default value is derived from NLS_TERRITORY, or from NLS_LANGUAGE if no territory is defined. The acceptable values are any strings of up to 9 bytes, except for null.

Example values are

```
NLS_DEBIT = "Debit:  "
NLS_DEBIT = " - "
```

NLS_DISPLAY

This parameter provides context-sensitive character values for the Arabic and Hebrew languages. No default is available for NLS_DISPLAY.

Acceptable values include

```
NLS_DISPLAY = "AR8XBASIC"
NLS_DISPLAY = "AR8HPARABIC8T"
```

> **CAUTION**
>
> If the Oracle database is not using Arabic or Hebrew, setting a value for this parameter can cause unknown results. You should take great care if you set this parameter.

NLS_ISO_CURRENCY

International currency symbols uniquely define a currency value, where local currency symbols do not. Australia and the United States share the same local currency symbol, the $. However, under ISO standards, the international currency symbols are different. (The U.S. international currency symbol is USD, whereas Australia's is AUD.)

If NLS_LANGUAGE is defined, a default value for NLS_ISO_CURRENCY is also defined. You can override its value in two ways:

■ If NLS_TERRITORY is defined, it will provide an alternative ISO currency value.

■ If NLS_ISO_CURRENCY is defined, it overrides the value implied by NLS_TERRITORY.

The acceptable values for this parameter are identical to those of NLS_TERRITORY and are defined in Table 36.5.

NLS_LANG

The NLS_LANG parameter specifies three components: language, territory, and character set. Other NLS parameters can override each parameter, but by specifying all three options in this one parameter, the others do not need to be set individually. Each language has a default territory and character set, which you can omit. The definitions of each component are

Language: The language to use. This setting changes Oracle messages as well as day and month names.

Territory: This setting implies a specific territory within the language area. The territory affects the date format and currency symbols.

Character set: This setting is the default character set, which is specific to the language and territory.

The format for this parameter is

```
NLS_LANG = language_territory.character set
```

The underscore (_) and period (.) characters are used as field separators. If they do not exist or are specified improperly, Oracle may assume the entry is a single language, as opposed to a language, territory, and character set combination.

Valid settings for NLS_LANG include

```
NLS_LANG = AMERICAN
NLS_LANG = FRENCH_CANADA.WE8DEC
```

The values for NLS_LANGUAGE and NLS_TERRITORY override the settings implied or specified by the value of the NLS_LANG parameter.

NLS_LANGUAGE

To set or override the language for server messages; day and month names and abbreviations; symbols for a.m., p.m., AD, and BC; and the default sorting sequence (see NLS_SORT); you can use the NLS_LANGUAGE parameter. The supported languages are listed in Table 36.5.

If the value of NLS_LANGUAGE is set to FRENCH, Oracle's error message for ORA-00942 is

```
ORA-00942:  table ou vue n'existe pas
```

If NLS_LANGUAGE is set to AMERICAN, the error message is

```
ORA-00942:  table or view does not exist
```

NLS_LIST_SEPARATOR

The `NLS_LIST_SEPARATOR` parameter describes the character used to distinguish individual values in a list. A few rules govern the valid values of this parameter:

- The value must be a single-byte character.
- The separator character cannot be the same as a monetary character. (See "NLS_MONETARY_CHARACTERS.")
- The value cannot be the same as a numeric character. (See "NLS_NUMERIC_CHARACTERS.")
- The value cannot be in the set of +, -, <, >.

Valid settings include

```
NLS_LIST_SEPARATOR = '¦'
NLS_LIST_SEPARATOR = '_'
```

NLS_MONETARY_CHARACTERS

These characters indicate monetary units, such as dollars and cents. This parameter is similar to `NLS_NUMERIC_CHARACTERS` in that you must specify two characters in the setting. Default settings are derived from `NLS_TERRITORY`, or from `NLS_LANGUAGE` if the territory has not been defined.

Valid values for this parameter are governed by the following:

- The value must be a single-byte character.
- The separator character cannot be the same as a monetary character.
- The value cannot be the same as a numeric character. (See "NLS_NUMERIC_CHARACTERS.")
- The value cannot be in the set of +, -, <, >.

NLS_NUMERIC_CHARACTERS

The values associated with `NLS_NUMERIC_CHARACTERS` change the default grouping and decimal values. Both are changed at the same time when using this parameter. Defaults for these characters are implied by the value of `NLS_LANGUAGE`, unless `NLS_NUMERIC_CHARACTERS` is set to override the default values.

To change the decimal character to a comma and the grouping character to a period, use the command:

```
ALTER SESSION SET NLS_NUMERIC_CHARACTERS = ",."
```

The decimal character is displayed by using the format mask D, and the grouping character is selected using the format mask G option. These characters must not be the same. Setting both characters to the same value will result in an error and/or unexpected results.

NLS_SORT

By default, most sorts are done in a binary sort pattern. Because character sets for other languages may not define their characters in a numeric order that corresponds with the correct sort order, Oracle provides an override mechanism. This override provides a linguistic sort.

By specifying a value for NLS_SORT, the developer or database administrator can provide a language-correct alternative to the binary sort that may return an invalid sort order. Valid NLS_SORT values are shown in Table 36.5.

NLS_TERRITORY

Not all areas that speak the same language always have the same types of standards. In order to accommodate this variation, Oracle includes a territory with the language settings. Normally this territory is set or implied when a value for NLS_LANGUAGE is defined. To override the territory value, specify a value for the NLS_TERRITORY parameter. Modifying this value changes these settings:

- Default date format
- Start day for the week
- Local currency symbol
- ISO currency symbol
- Decimal character
- Group separator

Oracle's NLS_TERRITORY settings are shown in Table 36.6.

Supported Languages and Territories

The languages that Oracle7.3 currently supports are listed in Table 36.5. The valid territories that this release supports are listed in Table 36.6.

Table 36.5. Languages supported in Oracle7.3.

American	French	Norwegian
Arabic	German	Polish
Brazilian Portuguese	Greek	Portuguese
Bulgarian	Hebrew	Romanian
Canadian French	Hungarian	Russian
Catalan	Icelandic	Simplified Chinese
Croatian	Italian	Slovak
Czech	Japanese	Slovenian
Danish	Korean	Spanish
Dutch	Latin American	Swedish
Egyptian	Spanish	Thai
English	Lithuanian	Traditional Chinese
Finnish	Mexican Spanish	Turkish

Table 36.6. Territories supported in Oracle7.3.

Arabic	Latin
Bulgarian	Lithuanian
Catalan	Norwegian
Croatian	Polish
Czech	Romanian
Danish	Russian
Dutch	Slovak
Finnish	Slovenian
French	Spanish
German	Swedish
German Din	Swiss
Greek	Thai_Dictionary
Hebrew	Thai_Telephone
Hungarian	Turkish
Icelandic	West_European
Italian	

Summary

Understanding the NLS options in Oracle can be a great asset to administrators and programmers alike, especially when working with applications and databases with a large, international user base. While the options are rarely used in small companies, the potential is always there.

IX

Appendixes

A

Annotated SQL Commands

by Kelly Leigh

The SQL commands contained in this section, while not exhaustive, are representative of the most commonly used functions. They are broken down into four categories, with a reference at the end of the appendix for common structures among the command types. The commands are broken into the following categories:

■ Functions

■ System, Session, and Transaction commands

■ DML commands

■ DDL commands

The following pages outline each group, the commands within each group, and the possible parameters for the command. All commands or options that are specific to Oracle7.3 are shown in bold and are indicated with a special *New to Version 7.3* icon.

Some commands share the same command structure, especially those that allocate storage space. The descriptions of commands that use shared structures will reference the section called "Shared Command Structures" at the end of this appendix.

Here are the syntax conventions used to describe the commands in this appendix:

```
COMMAND [parameter] parameter
    OPTION 1
        OPTION 1A
    OPTION 2 [{parameter ¦ KEYWORD}]
    [OPTION 3]
```

Explanation:

COMMAND	The command to be executed.
[parameter]	The *parameter* or KEYWORD in brackets ([ ]) is optional.
parameter	The name or parameter to be substituted.
OPTION 1	One of the available options to the COMMAND.
OPTION 1A	A continuation of OPTION 1.
[OPTION 3]	A nonrequired option.
{number ¦ KEYWORDA KEYWORDB}	User must use either *number* or KEYWORDA KEYWORDB but not both. The choice of options is listed between the braces ({ }).
[{number ¦ KEYWORD}]	These are optional, but use only one.
(See Extent Allocation)	Reference "Extent Allocation" in the "Shared Command Structures" section at the end of this appendix.

> **NOTE**
>
> Options that belong at the same command level are lined up in columns and belong to the column to the left of the option, or to the parent column. In the following example, OPTION 1 and OPTION 2 are grouped together, as are OPTION 1A and OPTION 1B. OPTION 2A, however, belongs to OPTION 2 and is not part of OPTION 1's grouping. (It belongs in the same group as OPTION 2A and OPTION 2B.)
>
> Example:
>
> ```
> COMMAND
>     OPTION 1
>         OPTION 1A
>         OPTION 1B
>     OPTION 2    OPTION 2A
>         OPTION 2B
> ```
>
> In each grouping of subcommands, when the first option (as in OPTION 2A) begins on the same line as the parent option, one or more of the following options are required. In the previous example, OPTION 2A or OPTION 2B is required with OPTION 2.

Functions

The following is a list of functions available to the SQL language. They are divided into the following categories:

- Mathematics
- Character
- Grouping
- Conversion
- Miscellaneous

Mathematics Functions

The mathematics functions listed in Table A.1 are numeric math functions that can be used within a SQL statement and return a numeric-format value. These functions are single-row functions and do not operate in the same way group functions do. (See the section "Group Functions" for further information.)

Table A.1. Numeric math functions.

Function	Description
ABS(*num*)	Returns the absolute value of *num*
CEIL(*num*)	Returns the smallest integer which is >= *num*
COS(*num*)	Gives the cosine of *num* (in radians)
EXP(*num*)	Takes the prefixed *num* to the *num*th power
FLOOR(*num*)	Returns the largest integer that is =< *num*
GREATEST(*expression1* [,*expression2*] ...)	Returns the greatest value of any *expressionX*
LEAST(*expression1* [,*expression2*] ...)	Returns the least value of any *expressionX*
LN(*num*)	Determines the natural log of *num*
LOG(*num1*, *num2*)	Returns the logarithm: base *num1* of *num2*
MOD(*num1* *num2*)	Provides the remainder from dividing *num1* by *num2*
POWER(*num1*, *num2*)	Raises *num1* to the *num2*th power
ROUND(*num1*, [,*num2*])	Rounds *num1* to *num2* decimal places (*num2* is optional and defaults to 0)
SIGN(*num*)	Returns –1 if *num* < 0, 0 if *num* = 0, or 1 if *num* > 0
SIN(*num*)	Gives sine of *num* (in radians)
SINH(*num*)	Provides the hyperbolic sine of *num*
SQRT(*num*)	Shows the square root of *num*
TAN(*num*)	Gives the tangent of *num* (in radians)
TANH(*num*)	Returns the hyperbolic tangent of *num*
TRUNC(*num1* [,*num2*])	Truncates *num1* to *num2* decimal places (*num2* is optional and defaults to 0)

Character Functions

These SQL functions return values for the command issued. Each function, along with a brief description of its use, is described in Tables A.2 and A.3, depending on the type of value returned.

All functions in this section are single-row functions, which means they operate on a single value as opposed to multiple rows. None of the character functions affect the original value passed into them.

Table A.2. Numeric return-value character functions.

Function	Description
ASCII(*string*)	Gives the numeric value of the first character in string
INSTR(*string1*, *string2* [,*num1*[,*num2*]])	Starts with character *num1* in *string1* and returns the position of the *num2* occurrence of *string2*
INSTRB(*string1*, *string2* [,*num1* [,*num2*]])	Starts with byte *num1* in *string1* and returns the position of the *num2* occurrence of *string2*, counting from the start of the string
LENGTH(*string*)	Returns the length of *string* (in characters)
LENGTHB(*string*)	Returns the length of *string* (in bytes)
NLSSORT(*string* [,*nls_sort*])	Sorts *string* according to the *nls_sort* language rule

Table A.3. Character return-value character functions.

Function	Description
CHR(*num*)	Returns the character with the character set value of *num*
CONCAT(*string1*, *string2*)	Concatenates (appends) *string2* to the end of *string1*
INITCAP(*string*)	Capitalizes the first letter of each word in *string*
LOWER(*string*)	Translates all letters in *string* to lowercase
LPAD(string1, *num*[,*string2*])	Left-pads *string1* to *num* characters, cycling through the values of *string2* (which is blank if not specified)
LTRIM(*string1* [,*string2*])	Returns *string1* with first characters of *string* removed, until the first occurrence

continues

Table A.3. continued

Function	Description
	of a character not in *string2*, which defaults to ' ' if not specified
NLS_INITCAP(*string* [,*nls_sort*])	Similar to INITCAP(), but uses *nls_sort*, if specified, to determine sort order of non-ASCII-based character sets
NLS_LOWER(*string* [,*nls_sort*])	Lowers all characters in *string*, using *nls_sort*, if specified, to handle language-specific character handling
NLS_UPPER(*string* [,*nls_sort*])	Returns value of *string* with all characters in uppercase letters. *nls_sort*, if specified, handles any specific language requirements.
REPLACE(*string1*, *string2* [,*string3*])	Replaces each occurrence of *string2* with *string3*, which is in *string1*. This works as a string-deletion if *string3* is not specified.
RPAD(*string1*, *num* [,*string2*])	Right-pads *string1* to *num* characters, cycling through the values of *string2*, which is blank if not specified
RTRIM(*string1* [,*string2*])	Returns *string1* with the last characters of *string1* removed after finding the last character of *string2* within *string1*
SOUNDEX(*string*)	Returns a value that represents the sound of the words in *string*
SUBSTR(*string1*, *num2* [,*num2*])	Returns a set of characters from *string1*, from *num1* to *num2*, or the end of the string if *num2* is not specified
TRANSLATE(*string*, *charset1*, *charset2*)	Translates the value of *string* from the character set of *charset1* into the character set of *charset2*
UPPER(*string*)	Translates all lowercase letters in *string* to uppercase

Group Functions

These functions work on a group of rows collected from a table and generally return a numeric value. The function names and descriptions are listed in Table A.4. All functions listed here ignore non-null values in their calculations.

Table A.4. Group functions.

Function	Description
`AVG([{DISTINCT ¦ ALL}] num)`	Returns the average value of *num*
`COUNT([ALL] *)`	Counts the number of rows returned by a query
`COUNT([{DISTINCT ¦ ALL}] expression)`	Counts the number of rows that fulfill *expression*
`MAX([{DISTINCT ¦ ALL}] expression)`	Returns the maximum value of *expression*
`MIN([{DISTINCT ¦ ALL}] expression)`	Returns the minimum value of *expression*
`STDDEV([{DISTINCT ¦ ALL}] num)`	Displays the standard deviation of *num*
`SUM([{DISTINCT ¦ ALL}] num)`	Sums the values of *num*
`VARIANCE([{DISTINCT ¦ ALL}] num)`	Returns the variance of *num*

Conversion Functions

Conversion functions provide options to convert an input value to an associated output value. Output types are dependent on the function and are listed in Table A.5.

Table A.5. Conversion functions.

Function	Description
`CHARTOROWID(string)`	Converts *string* from a type of CHAR to a related ROWID value
`CONVERT(string, charset1 [,charset2])`	Converts *string* to an equivalent string within the character set *charset1*. If *charset2* is specified, it is used as the source character set.
`HEXTORAW(char)`	Returns a binary RAW datatype from a hexadecimal CHAR number
`RAWTOHEX(raw)`	Converts a value of datatype RAW to an equivalent value in hexadecimal of CHAR datatype
`ROWIDTOCHAR(string)`	Converts *string* from a ROWID datatype to CHAR
`TO_CHAR(string [,format [,nls_num_format]])`	Converts *string* into the format specified by *format*, and optionally

continues

Table A.5. continued

Function	Description
	uses *nls_num_format* as the NLS_NUMBER_FORMAT if specified
TO_DATE(*string* [,*format* [,*nls_lang*]])	Converts *string* to date format, optionally using the date format associated with the *nls_lang*, if given
TO_MULTI_BYTE(*string*)	Converts all single-byte characters in *string* to an equivalent multibyte value
TO_NUMBER(*string* [,*format* [,*nls_lang*]])	Uses *format* as the format for *string* and converts it to an equivalent number. (Uses *nls_lang* to derive values for number and currency symbols.)
TO_SINGLE_BYTE(*string*)	Converts all multibyte characters in *string* to their single-byte equivalents, if they exist

Miscellaneous Functions

These functions provide a different kind of functionality than character or mathematics functions. Because they fall in no particular grouping, they are listed here. Most of the functions from Table A.6 can be used for reporting or debugging.

Table A.6. Miscellaneous functions.

Function	Description
DECODE(*expression*, *search1*, *value1*[, ...] [*default*])	Returns *value1* if expression is equal to *search1*, *search2*, and so on. Otherwise, it returns *default*.
NVL(*expression1*, *expression2*)	Returns *expression2* unless *expression1* != NULL
UID	Displays the unique user ID of the current user
USER	Evaluates to the username of the current user
USERENV('*item*')	Displays the value of the user's environment setting of *item*, based on a set number of items: ENTRYID, LABEL, LANGUAGE, SESSIONID, and TERMINAL

Function	Description
VSIZE(*expression*)	Displays the number of bytes in the internal Oracle representation (parsed) value of *expression*
SYSDATE	Returns the current system date and time

System, Session, and Transaction Commands

These commands are used to alternately modify the system, session, or transaction. These commands are not precisely DML or DDL statements, so they are grouped together here.

ALTER SESSION

ALTER SESSION dynamically changes the characteristics or operating parameters of a user's current session.

```
ALTER SESSION
    ADVISE COMMIT
            ROLLBACK
            NOTHING
    CLOSE DATABASE LINK link-name
    DISABLE COMMIT IN PROCEDURE
    ENABLE COMMIT IN PROCEDURE
    SET GLOBAL_NAMES = {TRUE ¦ FALSE}
        ISOLATION_LEVEL = {SERIALIZABLE ¦ READ COMMITTED}
LABEL = {'label' ¦ DBHIGH ¦ DBLOW ¦ OSLABEL}
        NLS_CURRENCY = 'string'
        NLS_DATE_FORMAT = 'format'
        NLS_DATE_LANGUAGE  = 'language-name'
        NLS_ISO_CURRENCY = territory name
        NLS_LABEL_FORMAT = 'format'
        NLS_LANGUAGE = language-name
        NLS_NUMERIC_CHARACTERS = 'string'
        NLS_SORT = {sort-option ¦ BINARY}
        NLS_TERRITORY = territory-name
        OPTIMIZER_GOAL = {FIRST_ROWS ¦ ALL_ROWS ¦ RULE ¦ CHOOSE}
        SQL_TRACE = {TRUE ¦ FALSE}
```

New To **7.3**

ALTER SYSTEM

ALTER SYSTEM modifies many aspects of the running database, including killing user sessions, forcing cache information to be written to disk, and managing licensing information.

```
ALTER SYSTEM
    ARCHIVE LOG [THREAD number]
        STOP
        START [TO 'location']
        SEQ number
        CHANGE number
        CURRENT
        GROUP number
```

```
        LOGFILE 'filename'
        NEXT
        ALL
CHECKPOINT [{GLOBAL ¦ LOCAL}]
CHECK DATAFILES [{GLOBAL ¦ LOCAL}]
DISABLE DISTRIBUTED RECOVERY
        RESTRICTED SESSION
ENABLE  DISTRIBUTED RECOVERY
        RESTRICTED SESSION
FLUSH SHARED_POOL
HASH_AREA_SIZE
HASH_JOIN_ENABLED
HASH_MULTIBLOCK_IO_COUNT
KILL SESSION 'sid, serial #'
SET RESOURCE_LIMIT = {TRUE ¦ FALSE}
    GLOBAL_NAMES = {TRUE ¦ FALSE}
    LICENSE_MAX_SESSIONS = number
    LICENSE_MAX_USERS = number
    LICENSE_SESSIONS_WARNING = number
    MTS_SERVERS = number
    MTS_DISPATCHERS = 'protocol, number'
    REMOTE_DEPENDENCIES_MODE = 'value'
SWITCH LOGFILE
```

New To
7.3

COMMIT

This command commits changes made by the current session or an in-doubt transaction.

```
COMMIT [WORK] [{COMMENT 'comment' ¦ FORCE 'transaction-ID' [, 'number']}]
```

ROLLBACK

This command rolls back any changes in the current transaction or to a specified SETPOINT.

```
ROLLBACK
        WORK
        TO [SAVEPOINT] savepoint-name
        FORCE 'transaction id'
```

SAVEPOINT

This command sets the name of a point in data modifications to ROLLBACK to, if desired.

```
SAVEPOINT savepoint-name
```

SET ROLE

This command changes the current role for the active session.

```
SET ROLE role-name [IDENTIFIED BY password]
        ALL [EXCEPT role-name [,]]
        NONE
```

SET TRANSACTION

This command changes the characteristics of the current transaction.

```
SET TRANSACTION
        READ ONLY
        READ WRITE
        USE ROLLBACK SEGMENT rollback-segment-name
```

DML Commands

DML, or Data Manipulation Language, commands are those SQL commands that directly modify data within the database. For an explicit listing of what each command is used for, please reference Oracle's *SQL Command Reference*.

INSERT

INSERT is the command used to insert data into tables or views. Column names and values can be specified within the command, or various commands such as AS SELECT ... can be used to bypass the need for specifying data and column names.

```
INSERT INTO [schema.] {table ¦ view} [@database-link] (column [,])
➥VALUES ( expression [,] ¦ subquery )
```

DELETE

DELETE allows a user or program to delete data from a local or remote table or view, using a WHERE clause to limit the amount of data being deleted. See TRUNCATE for a faster, but unrecoverable, method of deleting an entire table's data.

```
DELETE [FROM] [schema.] {table ¦ view} [@database link] [alias]
      WHERE condition
```

SELECT

This command is used to display data from a table or view, with options to narrow down the search through the use of conditions, joins, and groupings.

```
SELECT [{ALL ¦ DISTINCT}] selection-list
    FROM table-list¦ view-list
    WHERE condition
        START WITH condition
        CONNECT BY condition
        GROUP BY expression [,] [HAVING condition]
        UNION select-command
        UNION ALL
        INTERSECT
        MINUS
        FOR UPDATE [OF update list [NOWAIT]]
        ORDER BY expression ¦ position [ ASC ¦ DESC]
```

UPDATE

The UPDATE command is used to modify existing rows in a database's tables. By using this command, the user updates, or changes, the data to the values specified on the command line.

```
UPDATE [schema.] {table ¦ view} [@database-link] [alias]
    SET column = {expression ¦ query}
        (column [,]) = query
    WHERE condition
```

DDL Commands

Data Definition Language (DDL) commands are those commands that modify either the structure of an object or the database in which the objects are stored. These commands include the database creation and administration commands, as well as commands to modify a user's environment.

ALTER CLUSTER

This command alters the characteristics of a cluster within the database.

```
ALTER CLUSTER [schema.]cluster-name
    ALLOCATE EXTENT
        ( [SIZE number [{K ¦ M}]]
          [DATAFILE 'filename']
          [INSTANCE number] )
    SIZE number {K ¦ M}
    (See Extent Allocation)
```

ALTER DATABASE

This command alters various characteristics about the current database (default) or the named database, provided the user has the correct privileges.

```
ALTER DATABASE [database]
    ADD LOGFILE [THREAD number] [GROUP number] 'filename' [,] [SIZE number [{K ¦ M}]
[REUSE]]
    ADD LOGFILE MEMBER 'filename' [SIZE number [{K ¦ M}]] [REUSE]
    ARCHIVELOG
    BACKUP CONTROLFILE TO 'filename' [REUSE]
    BACKUP CONTROLFILE TO 'filename' [REUSE]
    CONVERT
    CREATE DATAFILE 'filename' [,]
        AS 'filename' [,] SIZE number {K ¦ M} [REUSE]
    CREATE STANDBY CONTROLFILE AS 'filename'

    DATAFILE 'filename'
        ONLINE
        OFFLINE [DROP]
    DISABLE THREAD number
    DROP LOGFILE GROUP number [,] ( 'filename' [,] )
    DROP LOGFILE MEMBER 'filename' [,]
    ENABLE [PUBLIC] THREAD number
    MOUNT EXCLUSIVE
```

New To
7.3

```
        PARALLEL
        STANDBY DATABASE [PARALLEL]
NOARCHIVELOG
OPEN
     RESETLOGS
     NORESETLOGS
RECOVER AUTOMATIC [FROM 'location']
     DATABASE
            ACTIVATE STANDBY DATABASE
            RECOVER STANDBY DATABASE
            UNTIL CANCEL
            UNTIL TIME 'date'
            UNTIL CHANGE 'change-number'
            USING BACKUP CONTROLFILE
     TABLESPACE 'tablespace' [,]
     DATAFILE 'filename' [,]
     LOGFILE 'filename'
     CONTINUE [DEFAULT]
     CANCEL
RENAME FILE 'filename' [,] TO 'filename' [,]
RENAME GLOBAL_NAME TO database[.domain]
SET DBMAC {ON ¦ OFF}
     DBHIGH = 'label'
     DBLOW = 'label'
```

ALTER FUNCTION

This command allows a user with the appropriate security to recompile a function.

```
ALTER FUNCTION [schema.]function-name COMPILE
```

ALTER INDEX

This command alters various components of an index, including storage characteristics.

```
ALTER INDEX [schema.]index-name
    DEALLOCATE UNUSED [KEEP integer]
    INITRANS number
    MAXTRANS number
    REBUILD [{PARALLEL integer ¦ NOPARALLEL}]
           [{RECOVERABLE ¦ UNRECOVERABLE}]
    See Storage Allocation
```

ALTER PACKAGE

This command makes it possible to precompile a package before it is called by a user in the database.

```
ALTER PACKAGE [schema.] package-name COMPILE PACKAGE
                                            BODY
```

ALTER PROCEDURE

This command compiles the specified procedure.

```
ALTER PROCEDURE [schema.]procedure-name COMPILE
```

ALTER PROFILE

ALTER PROFILE changes characteristics of a database profile. Based on these characteristics, users can be granted or denied access at threshold points in their sessions.

```
ALTER PROFILE profile-name LIMIT
    COMPOSITE_LIMIT {number ¦ UNLIMITED ¦ DEFAULT¦
    CONNECT_TIME   {number ¦ UNLIMITED ¦ DEFAULT}
    CPU_PER_SESSION  {number ¦ UNLIMITED ¦ DEFAULT}
    CPU_PER_CALL   {number ¦ UNLIMITED ¦ DEFAULT}
    IDLE_TIME  {number ¦ UNLIMITED ¦ DEFAULT}
    LOGICAL_READS_PER_SESSION {number ¦ UNLIMITED ¦ DEFAULT}
    LOGICAL_READS_PER_CALL  {number ¦ UNLIMITED ¦ DEFAULT}
    PRIVATE_SGA  {number [{K ¦ M}] ¦ UNLIMITED ¦ DEFAULT}
    SESSIONS_PER_USER  {number¦ UNLIMITED ¦ DEFAULT}
```

ALTER RESOURCE

This command alters the RESOURCE COST of several components in the database. These resource costs are used to calculate thresholds for resources and profiles.

```
ALTER RESOURCE COST
    CONNECT_TIME number
    CPU_PER_SESSION number
    LOGICAL_READS_PER_SESSION number
    PRIVATE_SGA number
```

ALTER ROLE

This command adds or removes a database password for a role within the currently connected database. The user must have the appropriate privileges to accomplish this task.

```
ALTER ROLE role-name
    IDENTIFIED {BY password ¦ EXTERNALLY}
    NOT IDENTIFIED
```

ALTER ROLLBACK SEGMENT

This command modifies the availability or storage options of a rollback segment.

```
ALTER ROLLBACK SEGMENT
    OFFLINE
    ONLINE
    (See Storage Allocation)
```

ALTER SEQUENCE

This command changes the characteristics of a sequence within the database. These changes take effect immediately.

```
ALTER SEQUENCE [schema.] sequence-name
    INCREMENT BY number
        {MAXVALUE number ¦ NOMAXVALUE}
        {MINVALUE number ¦ NOMINVALUE}
```

```
{CYCLE ¦ NOCYCLE}
{CACHE number ¦ NOCACHE}
{ORDER ¦ NOORDER}
```

ALTER SNAPSHOT

`ALTER SNAPSHOT` can change a snapshot's storage and refresh options.

```
ALTER SNAPSHOT [schema.]snapshot
    REFRESH
        FAST [START WITH 'date'] [NEXT 'date']
        COMPLETE [START WITH 'date'] [NEXT 'date']
        FORCE [START WITH 'date'] [NEXT 'date']
    (See Extent Allocation)
```

ALTER SNAPSHOT LOG

This command modifies the storage characteristics of a snapshot log.

```
ALTER SNAPSHOT LOG ON [schema.]table (See Extent Allocation)
```

ALTER TABLE

This command allows a user to change all aspects of a table's storage, layout, and integrity options.

```
ALTER TABLE [schema.]table-name
➥ADD column datatype [DEFAULT expression][(See Column Constraint)] [,]
        DEALLOCATE UNUSED [KEEP integer]
        DROP
            PRIMARY KEY [CASCADE]
            UNIQUE (column [,])
            CONSTRAINT contraint-name
        MODIFY column datatype [DEFAULT expression]
        ➥(See Column Constraint)] [,]
        (See Extent Allocation)
```

ALTER TABLESPACE

Using this command, a user or administrator with DBA privileges can modify the characteristics of a tablespace within a database. These characteristics include availability and storage options.

```
ALTER TABLESPACE tablespace-name
    ADD DATAFILE 'filename' [SIZE number {K ¦ M}] [REUSE]
BEGIN BACKUP
    COALESCE
    DEFAULT STORAGE (See Storage Allocation)
    END BACKUP
    OFFLINE [{NORMAL ¦ TEMPORARY ¦ IMMEDIATE}]
    ONLINE
    RENAME DATAFILE 'filename' [,] TO 'filename' [,]
    {TEMPORARY ¦ PERMANENT}
```

ALTER TRIGGER

This command modifies the availability status of a trigger.

```
ALTER TRIGGER [schema.]trigger-name
    DISABLE
    ENABLE
```

ALTER USER

ALTER USER can be used to modify a user's password, change a user's security role, and change the amount of disk space a user may have in use at a given time.

```
ALTER USER username
    DEFAULT ROLE role-name [,] [{ALL [EXCEPT role-name [,]] ¦ NONE}]
    DEFAULT TABLESPACE tablespace-name
    IDENTIFIED BY password ¦ EXTERNALLY
    PROFILE profile-name
    QUOTA number [{K ¦ M}]ON tablespace-name ¦ UNLIMITED
    TEMPORARY TABLESPACE tablespace-name
```

ALTER VIEW

This command recompiles a view.

```
ALTER VIEW [schema.]view-name COMPILE
```

ANALYZE

ANALYZE is a performance tool used to evaluate the effectiveness of storage options, index usage, cluster statistics, and to enable the optimizer (if running in cost-based mode) to more effectively optimize queries.

```
ANALYZE
    INDEX [schema.]index
        COMPUTE STATISTICS
        DELETE STATISTICS
        ESTIMATE STATISTICS [{SAMPLE number ROWS ¦ PERCENT}]
        VALIDATE STRUCTURE
    TABLE [schema.]table
        COMPUTE STATISTICS
        DELETE STATISTICS
        ESTIMATE STATISTICS
        [{SAMPLE number ROWS ¦ PERCENT}]
        LIST CHAINED ROWS [INTO [schema.]table-name]
        VALIDATE STRUCTURE [CASCADE]
    CLUSTER [schema.]cluster
        COMPUTE STATISTICS
        DELETE STATISTICS
        ESTIMATE STATISTICS
        [{SAMPLE number ROWS ¦ PERCENT}]
        LIST CHAINED ROWS [INTO [schema.]table-name]
        VALIDATE STRUCTURE [CASCADE]
```

COMMENT

This command adds a comment on a table or a table's column.

```
COMMENT ON
    TABLE [schema.]{table-name ¦ view-name ¦ snapshot-name}
        IS 'comment'
    COLUMN [schema.]{table-name ¦ view-name ¦ snapshot-name} column-name
        IS 'comment'
```

CREATE CLUSTER

This command creates a storage cluster to hold one or more tables. If using Trusted Oracle, refer to the *Administrator's Guide* for restrictions on a cluster's use.

```
CREATE CLUSTER [schema.]cluster-name column-name datatype [,]
    INDEX [HASH IS column-name] [HASHKEYS number]
    SIZE number [{K ¦ M}]
    TABLESPACE tablespace-name
    (See Extent Allocation)
```

CREATE CONTROLFILE

This command creates a new control file for a database.

```
CREATE CONTROLFILE [REUSE]
    [SET] DATABASE database
    LOGFILE [GROUP number] 'filename' [,] [SIZE number [{K ¦ M}]
    ➡RESETLOGS ¦ NORESETLOGS
    DATAFILE 'filename' [,] [SIZE number [{K ¦ M}]
        {ARCHIVELOG ¦ NOARCHIVELOG}
        MAXDATAFILES number
        MAXINSTANCES number
        MAXLOGFILES number
        MAXLOGHISTORY number
        MAXLOGMEMBERS number
```

CREATE DATABASE

This command is used by the administrator to initially create a database.

```
CREATE DATABASE [database]
    {ARCHIVELOG ¦ NOARCHIVELOG}
    CHARACTER SET character-set-name
    CONTROLFILE REUSE
    DATAFILE 'filename' [,] [SIZE number [{K ¦ M}] [,]
    EXCLUSIVE
    LOGFILE [GROUP number] 'filename' [,] [SIZE number [{K ¦ M}] [REUSE] [,]
    MAXDATAFILES number
    MAXINSTANCES number
    MAXLOGFILES number
    MAXLOGHISTORY number
    MAXLOGMEMBERS number
```

CREATE DATABASE LINK

This command creates a link to another Oracle database. These links can be public or private.

```
CREATE [PUBLIC] DATABASE LINK [CONNECT TO username IDENTIFIED BY password]
➥[USING 'connection string']
```

CREATE FUNCTION

This command is used to update or create a user-defined function.

```
CREATE [OR REPLACE] FUNCTION [schema.]function-name (argument [IN]datatype [,] )
➥RETURN datatype {AS ¦ IS}  (PL/ SQL program commands)
```

CREATE INDEX

This command creates an index based on the table and column criteria specified and the storage characteristics that are provided by the index creator or defaulted by the tablespace.

```
CREATE INDEX [schema.]index-name ON
    [schema].table-name (column-name [,] [{ASC ¦ DESC}])
    CLUSTER [schema.]cluster-name
    NOSORT
    TABLESPACE tablespace-name
    (See Extent Allocation)
```

CREATE PACKAGE

This command creates or replaces a custom package and its procedures. Options allow the user to create or replace the entire package or the package body.

```
CREATE [OR REPLACE] PACKAGE [schema.] package-name
    IS (PL/SQL package lines)
    AS (PL/SQL package lines)

CREATE [OR REPLACE] PACKAGE BODY [schema.]package-name
    IS (PL/ SQL package lines)
    AS (PL/SQL package body lines)
```

CREATE PROCEDURE

This command creates and/or replaces a user-defined database procedure.

```
CREATE [OR REPLACE] PROCEDURE [schema.]procedure-name
    ( argument [{IN ¦ OUT ¦ IN OUT}] datatype [,] )
    AS (PL/SQL program body)
    IS (PL/SQL package lines)
```

CREATE PROFILE

This command allows the database administrator to create a new database profile to limit a user's or process's resource utilization. This utilization is based on the definitions of the profile and the RESOURCE COST.

```
CREATE PROFILE profile-name
    LIMIT
    COMPOSITE_LIMIT [{number ¦ UNLIMITED ¦ DEFAULT}]
    CONNECT_TIME [{number ¦ UNLIMITED ¦ DEFAULT}]
    CPU_PER_CALL [{number ¦ UNLIMITED ¦ DEFAULT}]
    CPU_PER_SESSION [{number ¦ UNLIMITED ¦ DEFAULT}]
    IDLE_TIME [{number ¦ UNLIMITED ¦ DEFAULT}]
    LOGICAL_READS_PER_CALL [{number ¦ UNLIMITED ¦ DEFAULT}]
    LOGICAL_READS_PER_SESSION [{number ¦ UNLIMITED ¦ DEFAULT}]
    PRIVATE_SGA [{number [{K ¦ M}] ¦ UNLIMITED ¦ DEFAULT}]
    SESSIONTS_PER_USERS [{number ¦ UNLIMITED ¦ DEFAULT}]
```

CREATE ROLE

This command creates a new database role and allows the user or administrator to define an authentication mode, if desired.

```
CREATE ROLE role-name {IDENTIFIED [BY password ¦ EXTERNALLY] ¦ NOT IDENTIFIED}
```

CREATE ROLLBACK SEGMENT

This command is used by the database administrator to define new rollback segments.

```
CREATE [PUBLIC] ROLLBACK SEGMENT rbs_name
    TABLESPACE tablespace-name
    (See Storage Allocation)
```

CREATE SCHEMA AUTHORIZATION

This command allows the authorized user to issue multiple CREATE and GRANT commands from within the same transaction.

```
CREATE SCHEMA AUTHORIZATION schema
    CREATE TABLE command
    CREATE VIEW command
    GRANT command
```

CREATE SEQUENCE

This command defines a new sequence and its characteristics.

```
CREATE [schema.]sequence-name
    {CACHE number ¦ NOCACHE}
    {CYCLE ¦ NOCYCLE}
    INCREMENT BY number
    {MAXVALUE number ¦ NOMAXVALUE}
    {MINVALUE number ¦ NOMINVALUE}
    {ORDER ¦ NOORDER}
    START WITH number
```

CREATE SNAPSHOT

This command allows the user or administrator to create a snapshot based upon a query. The user must have the authorization to execute the query or else the snapshot is not created.

```
CREATE SNAPSHOT [schema.]snapshot-name
    CLUSTER cluster-name ( column-name [,] )
    REFRESH
        FAST [{START WITH date ¦ NEXT date}]
        COMPLETE [{START WITH date ¦ NEXT date}]
        FORCE [{START WITH date ¦ NEXT date}]
    TABLESPACE tablespace-name
    (See Extent Allocation)
    AS query-command
```

CREATE SNAPSHOT LOG

This command creates a log containing the changes made to the master table of a snapshot.

```
CREATE SNAPSHOT LOG ON [schema.]table-name
    TABLESPACE tablespace-name
    (See Extent Allocation)
```

CREATE SYNONYM

This command defines a local or public synonym for a database object, whether the object is local or accessed through a database link.

```
CREATE [PUBLIC] SYNONYM [schema.]synonym-name
    FOR [schema.]object-name [@database-link]
```

CREATE TABLE

The CREATE TABLE command defines all characteristics of a table, including integrity and check constraints, column names and datatypes, storage options, and so on.

```
CREATE TABLE [schema.]table-name (column-name datatype [DEFAULT expression]
➡[(See Column Constraint)] [,] )
CLUSTER cluster-name ( column-name [,] )
    DISABLE
        UNIQUE (column-name [,]) [CASCADE]
        PRIMARY KEY [CASCADE]
        CONSTRAINT constraint-name [CASCADE]
        ALL TRIGGERS
    ENABLE [{ALL TRIGGERS ¦ (See Integrity Constraint)}]
    TABLESPACE tablespace-name
    (See Extent Allocation)
    AS query-command
```

CREATE TABLESPACE

Database administrators use this option to create new storage areas (tablespaces) in the database for user or administrative data.

```
CREATE TABLESPACE tablespace-name DATAFILE 'filename'
➡[SIZE number {K ¦ M}] [REUSE]
DEFAULT STORAGE (See Storage Allocation)
        {OFFLINE ¦ ONLINE}
        {TEMPORARY ¦ PERMANENT}
```

CREATE TRIGGER

This command creates or replaces a database trigger. Triggers are created by users and administrators depending on what the trigger must do.

```
CREATE [OR REPLACE] TRIGGER [schema.]trigger-name {BEFORE ¦ AFTER}
    DELETE [OR]
    INSERT [OR]
    UPDATE OF column-name [,]
    ON [schema.]table-name
        REFERENCING
            OLD [ AS] old-name [ FOR EACH ROW]
            NEW [ AS] new-name [ FOR EACH ROW]
        WHEN (condition) PL/SQL block
```

CREATE USER

This command defines a new user within a database.

```
CREATE USER username
    DEFAULT TABLESPACE tablespace-name
    IDENTIFIED BY password ¦ EXTERNALLY
    PROFILE profile-name
    QUOTA number [{K ¦ M}] ¦ UNLIMITED ON tablespace-name
    TEMPORARY TABLESPACE tablespace-name
```

CREATE VIEW

This command creates a view, or window, based on a query that may access one or more tables and all or a subset of the columns.

```
CREATE [OR REPLACE] [{FORCE ¦ NOFORCE}] VIEW [schema.]view-name
    [alias [,]]
    AS query-command
    WITH CHECK OPTION
        CONSTRAINT (See Column Constraint)
```

DROP CLUSTER

This command deletes a database cluster and optionally the tables it contains.

```
DROP CLUSTER [schema.]cluster-name INCLUDING TABLES [CASCADE CONSTRAINTS]
```

DROP DATABASE LINK

This command drops the local or public link to another database.

```
DROP [PUBLIC] DATABASE LINK database-link
```

DROP FUNCTION

This command deletes a user-defined function from the database.

```
DROP FUNCTION [schema.]function-name
```

DROP INDEX

This command removes an index and reclaims its storage allocation.

```
DROP INDEX [schema.]index-name
```

DROP PACKAGE

This command is used to drop a package from the database.

```
DROP PACKAGE [BODY] [schema.]package-name
```

DROP PROCEDURE

This command drops a stored procedure from the current database.

```
DROP PROCEDURE [schema.]procedure-name
```

DROP PROFILE

This command drops a user-defined profile.

```
DROP PROFILE profile-name [CASCADE]
```

DROP ROLE

This command drops a custom role.

```
DROP ROLE role-name
```

DROP ROLLBACK SEGMENT

This command allows the administrator to drop a predefined rollback segment, provided it is not in use and is offline.

```
DROP ROLLBACK SEGMENT segment-name
```

DROP SEQUENCE

This command gives the user the ability to drop a previously created sequence.

```
DROP SEQUENCE [schema.]sequence-name
```

DROP SNAPSHOT

This command drops a snapshot.

```
DROP SNAPSHOT [schema.]snapshot-name
```

DROP SNAPSHOT LOG

This command drops a snapshot log for a given master table.

```
DROP SNAPSHOT LOG ON [schema.]table-name
```

DROP SYNONYM

This command drops a user- or administrator-defined synonym.

```
DROP [PUBLIC] SYNONYM [schema.]synonym-name
```

DROP TABLE

This command drops a table and optionally its constraints and reclaims the used data space.

```
DROP TABLE [schema.]table-name [CASCADE CONSTRAINTS]
```

DROP TABLESPACE

This command drops a tablespace and, if desired, all of its contents (indexes, clusters, tables, and so on).

```
DROP TABLESPACE tablespace-name [INCLUDING CONTENTS [CASCADE
CONSTRAINTS]]
```

DROP TRIGGER

This command drops a user-defined trigger from the database.

```
DROP TRIGGER [schema.]trigger-name
```

DROP USER

This command deletes a user from the database, removing all of the user's objects, if desired.

```
DROP USER username [CASCADE]
```

DROP VIEW

This command drops a predefined view to one or more tables without affecting the tables' data.

```
DROP VIEW [schema.]view-name
```

EXPLAIN PLAN

EXPLAIN PLAN is a debugging tool used to view the plan, access paths, and so on, that the database kernel uses to optimize a SQL statement.

```
EXPLAIN PLAN [SET STATEMENT_ID = 'statement-name']
    [INTO [schema.]table-name[@database-link]]
    FOR SQL-statement
```

GRANT

This command gives security access to a user for database access and objects.

```
GRANT system-privilege TO [{username ¦ role-name ¦ PUBLIC}][WITH ADMIN OPTION]
      role-name TO [{username ¦ role-name ¦ PUBLIC}][WITH ADMIN OPTION]
      object-privilege TO [{username ¦ role-name ¦ PUBLIC}][WITH ADMIN OPTION]
      ALL TO [{username ¦ role-name ¦ PUBLIC}][WITH ADMIN OPTION]
```

LOCK TABLE

This command is used to explicitly lock a table for various types of access. Generally, it is advisable to allow Oracle to acquire and release locks.

```
LOCK TABLE [schema.]{table-name ¦ view-name} [@database-link]
➡IN locking-mode MODE [NOWAIT]
```

RENAME

This command renames a database object.

```
RENAME old-name TO new-name
```

REVOKE

This command takes away database privileges to an object or the database.

```
REVOKE system-privilege [,]
    FROM {username ¦ role-name ¦ PUBLIC} [,]
        object-privilege [PRIVILEGES]
        ON [schema.]object-name
        FROM {username ¦ role-name ¦ PUBLIC} [,]
            [CASCADE CONSTRAINTS]
        ALL [PRIVILEGES]
            ON [schema.]object-name
            FROM {username ¦ role-name ¦ PUBLIC} [,]
                [CASCADE CONSTRAINTS]
```

TRUNCATE

This command drops all of the rows in a table and optionally drops the storage allocation. This option is nonrecoverable by a ROLLBACK command.

```
TRUNCATE
    TABLE [schema.]table-name
        [{DROP ¦ REUSE} STORAGE]
    CLUSTER [schema.]cluster-name
        [{DROP ¦ REUSE} STORAGE]
```

Shared Command Structures

The command structures listed here are shared by many commands and are referenced by the expression "(See *Section Name*)" in the preceding command reference sections.

Extent Allocation

Extent allocation refers to the allocation of extents for a database object, as well as the storage options for each extent.

```
INITRANS number

MAXTRANS number

PCTFREE number

PCTUSED number
```

(See *Storage Allocation*)

Storage Allocation

These extensions to the DDL commands alter the storage characteristics of a database object, including the amount of space to allocate, whether to increase the storage allocation, and by how much.

```
STORAGE
   (INITIAL number {K ¦ M}
    FREELISTS number
    FREELIST GROUPS number)
    MAXEXTENTS number
    MINEXTENTS number
    NEXT number {K ¦ M}
    OPTIMAL
        number [{K ¦ M}]
        NULL
    PCTINCREASE number
```

NOTE

The following restrictions apply to the Storage Allocation options:

■ FREELISTS applies only to tables and clusters.

■ FREELIST GROUPS applies only to tables, clusters, and indexes.

■ OPTIMAL is available only on rollback segments.

Column Constraint

Column constraints define integrity and check conditions on a table's or index's column or group of columns.

```
CONSTRAINT constraint-name [NOT] NULL
   UNIQUE
       REFERENCES [schema.]table-name [column-name]
           [ON DELETE CASCADE]
```

```
        CHECK column-name condition
        UNIQUE
        PRIMARY KEY
   DISABLE
   USING INDEX
   TABLESPACE tablespace-name
```

(See *Extent Allocation*)

B

Further Reading

by Kelly Leigh

Experienced Oracle developers and DBAs spend much of their professional careers research-ing, experimenting, testing, and perfecting their own techniques. They can credit their successes to

■ A good measure of ingenuity/creativity

■ Tedious research and experimentation

■ Patience, persistence, and sometimes luck

Everyone who succeeds in this field has a measure of each of these qualities, but we can still broaden our horizons and learn from others who have already been down this road.

You can save much time by examining code and documentation written by experienced indi-viduals. The suggested reading lists that follow are not exhaustive, but they are representative of the types of information that are available.

For additional information, check at your local bookstore and try the various Internet search engines such as http://www.webcrawler.com and http://www.search.com.

Books on Oracle Development

The books listed below are extremely helpful for beginning, intermediate, and advanced Oracle developers, and have been listed here because of their favorable reviews in the press. However, a reviewer's opinion may not be yours, so be sure to browse through any books before you make a purchase. It is possible that the format of the book does not meet your specific likes.

Sams Publishing

Oracle Performance Tuning and Optimization, Wally Talen (ISBN: 0-672-308860-x)

Essential Oracle7, Tom Luers (ISBN: 0-672-30873-8)

Oracle DBA Survival Guide, Joe Greene (ISBN: 0-672-30681-6)

Oracle Unleashed, Sams Publishing (ISBN: 0-672-30872-x)

Teach Yourself Oracle Power Objects in 21 Days, Tom Grant (ISBN: 0-672-30868-1)

Developing Client/Server Applications with Oracle Developer/2000, Paul Hipsley (ISBN: 0-672-30852-5)

Developing Personal Oracle7 for Windows 95 Applications, David Lockman (ISBN: 0-672-31025-2)

Oracle Press

Oracle: The Complete Reference, George Koch and Kevin Loney (ISBN: 0-07-882097-9)

Oracle Workgroup Server Handbook, Thomas B Cox (ISBN: 0-07-881186-4)

Tuning Oracle, M.J. Corey, M. Abbey, and D. J. Dechichio Jr. (ISBN: 0-07-881181-3)

Power Objects Handbook, Bruce Kolste and David Peterson (ISBN: 0-07-882089-9)

Oracle Developer's Guide, David McClanahan (ISBN: 0-07-882087-1)

Oracle Backup and Recovery Handbook, Rama Velpuri (ISBN: 0-07-882106-1)

Oracle Developer/2000 Handbook, Robert J. Muller (ISBN: 0-07-882180-0)

O'Reilly and Associates

Oracle Performance Tuning, Peter Corrigan and Mark Gurry (ISBN: 1-56590-048-1)

Oracle PL/SQL Programming, Steven Feuerstein (ISBN: 0-672-30886-x)

Addison-Wesley

Introduction To Oracle Designer 2000, Carrie Anderson and David Wendelken

Relational Database Management with Oracle, Second Edition, Rolland (ISBN: 0-201-56520-x)

Rapid Development with Oracle CASE, Billings (ISBN: 0-201-63344-2)

WWW Usenet Groups

The World Wide Web contains millions of lines of code and documentation on almost every topic imaginable. Participating in Usenet discussion groups (news groups) can help you fix problems and find solutions to various business needs. Although each news group has a specific discussion topic, members occasionally discuss miscellaneous topics. The following Usenet groups are taken from the hundreds of news groups listed on the Web.

You can access news groups with specialized news group readers, as well as with the latest version of Netscape Navigator. Members of CompuServe or America Online also have relatively easy access to most news groups. You do not need to become a member of a news group, but you must find a news group server that provides access to the desired news group.

Usenet News Groups Related to Oracle and Oracle Development

`comp.databases.oracle`	The SQL database products of the Oracle Corporation
`comp.databases.oracle.misc`	Oracle-related topics
`comp.databases.oracle.server`	Oracle database administration/server
`comp.databases.oracle.tools`	Oracle software tools/applications
`comp.databases.rdb`	Oracle RDB
`relcom.comp.dbms.oracle`	Oracle DBMS discussions
`comp.soft-sys.powerbuilder`	Discussions on PowerBuilder

Usenet News Groups Related to Database Issues

`comp.databases`	Database and data management issues and theory
`comp.databases.object`	Object-oriented paradigms in database systems
`comp.databases.olap`	Analytical processing, multidimensional DBMS, EIS, DSS
`comp.databases.theory`	Advances in database technology

Oracle-Related Mailing Lists

Mailing lists differ from news groups in three important ways:

■ Mailing lists send mail directly to your e-mail account.

■ Mailing lists are usually moderated, so the topic is more likely to be adhered to.

■ To become a member of a mailing list, you must add your name to its distribution list.

You can join a mailing list by sending a message to a special account on the server that supports that list and requesting that your e-mail address be added to the list. Follow these steps to subscribe to the mailing lists mentioned here.

1. Send an e-mail message to the account listed under the list's description.

2. In the body of the e-mail, include the following

   `SUBSCRIBE (list name) (your full name)`

   For example: `SUBSCRIBE Oracle-sig-HP Kelly D. Leigh`

If disk space or mail volume is a big concern for you, then news groups are an excellent alternative to mailing lists.

Oracle RDBMS Mailing Lists

List Name	Description	Subscription Address
DecRdb-l	General Oracle RDB information discussions	listserv@ccvm.sunysb.edu
Oracle-sig-SUN	Oracle on SUN platforms	listserv@netcom.com
Oracle-sig-IbmRs6000	Oracle on IBM RS/6000 platforms	listserv@netcom.com
Oracle-sig-DEC	Oracle on DEC platforms	listserv@netcom.com
Oracle-sig-HP	Oracle on HP platforms	listserv@netcom.com

Other Oracle-Related Mailing Lists

List Name	Description	Subscription Address
OraWeb-L	World Wide Web and Oracle discussions	majordomo@labyringh.net.au
OCSig-l	Oracle Designer/2000 (CASE) discussions	listserv@fatcity.com
OCSig-Warehouse-l	Data warehousing discussions	listserv@fatcity.com

Web Pages and Links

Hundreds of sites on the World Wide Web pertain to Oracle and its use. A tiny sampling follows. Note that these links were in operation at the time this book was published, but these pages may have been modified or discontinued by the time you read this appendix. We made every effort to choose sites that appeared to be stable and long-standing.

Sites Maintained by Oracle Corporation

http://www.oracle.com—Oracle's home page

http://www-govt.us.oracle.com—Oracle Government home page

http://omo.us.oracle.com—Jimmy's Garage, Oracle Media Objects home page

http://support.oracle.com—Oracle's Support Page

http://www.oramag.com—Oracle Magazine Interactive

http://www.oracle.com/products/trial/—Oracle Trial Software

http://commerce.us.oracle.com/oraStore/—Oracle Store

http://www.oracle.ru/—Oracle Business Alliance

Oracle-Related Sites

http://www.steview.com—Oracle developer's page

http://tiburon.us.oracle.com/odp—Another Oracle developer's page

http://www.all-4-one.com/hot_links.html—An excellent collection of Oracle links

http://www.informant.com—Home page to reach *Oracle Informant,* a magazine dedicated to Oracle and its development

http://tiburon.us.oracle.com/odp/public/library/cr/html/cr_whhite.html—Oracle white papers

http://www.oracle.com/corporate/press/html/—Oracle press releases

http://www.us.oracle.com/support/bulletins/—Oracle technical bulletins

http://www.pinpub.com/level3/l3nod.htm—Oracle developer

http://www.elmwood.com/oracle/d2ksig—Designer 2000 special interest group

http://www.dbmsmag.com—*DBMS* magazine

Oracle Users Groups

http://www.ioug.org—International Oracle Users Group - America

http://www.ougf.fi/eoug/—EOUG - Europe Oracle Users Groups

http://www.aa.gov.au/ANZORA.html—ANZORA - Australia and New Zealand Oracle Users Group

http://www.ougf.fi/eoug/egypt—EGOUG - Egypt Oracle Users Group `http://www.uk.oracle.com/europe/southafr/SAOUG/home.html`—SAOUG - South African Oracle Users Group

`http://www.ccas.ru/~prz/hp2.html`—EAOUG - Euro-Asian Oracle Users Group

`http://www.oracle.co.jp/Customer/JOUG/`—JOUG - Japan Oracle Users Group

`http://www.metasys.com/coug/coug.htm`—COUG - Charlotte Oracle Users Group

`http://www.roman.com/coug/`—COUG - Chicago Oracle Users Group

`http://www.oug.com/OUG/DEVOUG`—DEVOUG - Delaware Valley Oracle Users Group

`http://www.doug.org`—DOUG - Dallas Oracle Users Group

`http://www.tensor.net/fworacle`—FWOUG - Fort Worth Oracle Users Group

`http://www.tacticsus.com/~gouser/`—GOUG - Georgia Oracle Users Group

`http://www.southwind.com/gcoug`—GCOUG - Gulf Coast Oracle Users Group

`http://www.cois.com/houg`—HOUG - Houston Oracle Users Group

`http://www.rti.in.net/inoug/inoug.htm`—INOUG - Indiana Oracle Users Group

`http://ns-cic2.lanl.gov/abm/OracleWelcome.html`—LANLOUG - Los Alamos National Laboratory Oracle Users Group

`http://www.moug.igt.ort`—MOUG - Midwest Oracle Users Group

`http://www.clark.net/pub/soh/maoug.htm`—MAOP - Mid Atlantic Oracle Users Group

`http://www.state.me.us/bis/dba/msoug/msoug.htm`—MSOUG - Maine's Oracle Users Group

`http://sunsite.unc.edu/ncoug`—NCOUG - North Carolina Oracle Users Group

`http://wwwmfgsys.com/njoug/njoug.html`—NJOUG - New Jersey Oracle Users Group

`http://www.nocoug.org`—NoCOUG - Northern California Oracle Users Group

`http://cornerstone.aasp.net/noug`—NOUG - Northeast Oracle Users Group

`http://www.ioug.org/nwoug`—NWOUG - NorthWest Oracle Users Group

`http://www.nyoug.org/nyoug`—NYOUG - New York Oracle Users Group

`http://www.ppoug.org`—PPOUG - Pikes Peak Oracle Users Group

`http://www.ioug.org/nwoug/psoug.html`—PSOUG - Puget Sound Oracle Users Group

`http://www.interealm.com/p/rmoug/index.html`—RMOUG - Rocky Mountain Oracle Users Group

`http://www.edo.com/sacoug`—SACOUG - Sacramento Oracle Users Group

`http://www.scoug.org`—SCOUG - South Central Oracle Users Group `http://sunsite.unc.edu/ncoug/seoug/seoug.htm`—SEOUG - Southeast Oracle Users Group

`http://www.pubsvc.dsr.com/sdoug`—SDOUG - San Diego Oracle Users Group

`http://www.ugn.com/sfoug1.htm`—SFOUG - South Florida Oracle Users Group

`http://www.carnac.com/sloug.html`—SLOUG - St. Louis Oracle Users Group

`http://mail.irm.state.fl.us/orclusr1.html`—TAOUG - Tallahassee Area Oracle Users Group

`http://www.barr.com/tcoug/index.html`—TCOUG - Twin Cities Oracle Users Group

`http://www.crtnet.com/voug/index.htm`—VOUG - Virginia Oracle Users Group

Source Code and Helpful Programs via FTP

Many developers use FTP to share their programs with other users, free of charge. You can reach these sites in a number of ways, including Netscape, Internet Explorer, and command-line FTP programs. Usually, all you need is an Internet connection.

FTP Sites

`ftp://ftp.oracle.com/pub`—Oracle Corporation

`ftp://ftp.uni-oldenburg.de/pub/Oracle`—University of Oldenberg's Computer Science Center

`ftp://ftp.bf.rmit.edu.au`—Royal Melbourne Institute of Technology

C

Glossary

by Gigi Wadley

alias   A temporary name for a table or column within a SQL statement, which is used to refer to the associated table elsewhere in the same statement.

ANALYZE   A SQL command that collects statistics about a table, cluster, or index for the optimizer and stores it in the data dictionary.

ANSI   The American National Standards Institute (ANSI) sets standards for the Structure Query Language (SQL).

archive   The process of saving data for future use; specifically, archives save data found in redo logs in the event the logs are needed to restore a database.

argument   Expressions within the parentheses of a function, supplying values to the function.

array processing   Array processing allows batch processing instead of row-by-row processing.

BIND PHASE   The part of SQL processing where variables are made known to the database.

BIND variable   A variable in a SQL statement that must be replaced with a valid value for the statement to execute properly.

b-tree   A high-performance indexing structure used by Oracle.

block   Basic unit of storage (physical and logical) for all Oracle data.

buffer   A scratchpad, usually stored in memory, where commands are stored.

chained blocks   A second or subsequent Oracle block designated to store table data when the original block is out of space.

chained row   A row that is stored in more than one database block.

checkpoint   A point at which, on a session basis, changed blocks are written to the database.

child   In a tree-structured data, a child is a node that is the immediate descendant of another node.

clause   A major section of a SQL statement, which is begun by a keyword such as SELECT, INSERT, UPDATE, DELETE, FROM, WHERE, ORDER BY, GROUP BY, or HAVING.

client   A general term for a user that requires the services of another application or computer.

cluster   A means of storing together data from multiple tables when the data in those tables contains common information and is likely to be accessed together.

column constraint   An integrity constraint placed on a column of a table.

composite key   A foreign or primary key composed of multiple columns.

concatenation   The joining of CHAR values, represented by the operator ¦¦.

concurrency   A term that means multiple users accessing the same data.

consistency   A term requiring that all related data be updated together in proper order.

constraint   A rule or restriction concerning a piece of data that is enforced at the data level rather than the application level.

context area   The working area in memory where Oracle stores the current SQL statement. This area also holds the state of the cursor.

control file   An administrative file that is required to start and run the database.

correlated query   A subquery that is executed repeatedly, once for each row selected by the main query.

cursor   A work area in memory where Oracle stores the current SQL statement. It is also referred to as the *context area*.

Data Control Language (DCL)   Statements that control access to the data and statements database. These statements are GRANT, CONNECT, GRANT SELECT, GRANT UPDATE on, and REVOKE DBA.

Data Definition Language (DDL)   Statements that allow the creation and deletion of database objects. CREATE and DROP are the two most frequently used DDL statements.

data locks   After executing a SQL statement, the data that satisfies the statement is locked in one of several modes. With implicit locks, the operator never has to lock rows; with explicit locks, the operator has to request the lock.

Data Manipulation Language (DML)   Statements that allow the manipulation of data within the database. SELECT, INSERT, DELETE and UPDATE are the primary DML statements.

deadlock   Deadlocks occur when two processes are trying to access the same row and are waiting on each other. Oracle resolves deadlocks by rolling back the work of one process.

deferred rollback   A rollback segment that is unable to be applied to a tablespace because the tablespace is offline.

distributed database   A collection of databases that share information but can be operated and managed separately.

dual   A table with one row and column which stores system date (sysdate) and the current user (user).

entity   A person, place, or thing that is represented by a row within a table.

entity-relationship diagram (ERD)   A diagramming tool used to show the relationship between two or more sets of data (entities).

exclusive lock   An exclusive lock allows a user to query data but not change it, which is different from a share lock because it does not permit another user to place any lock on the same data.

executable SQL statement   A statement that the database can execute to take action on the database. The three different types of executable statements in Oracle are DML, DDL, and DCL statements.

file   An area of storage where database data is kept. In Oracle, at least one physical file is required but several files might exist in multiple tablespaces. A file is a part of a tablespace.

foreign key   A primary key in a related table. This key can be made of more than one column.

import   An Oracle utility that retrieves data from an export file into an Oracle database. So "to import" is to move data from an export file into a table.

index   An index is used to impose uniqueness upon data to speed up database searches.

instance   An instance involves being able to run Oracle to access a database. Instances usually have unique names and IDs.

integrity constraints   Rules and restrictions placed on data to ensure accuracy.

key   A column or combination of columns that identifies a row.

leaf   A leaf belongs to a tree-structured table; it is a row that has no child row.

Log Writer Process (LGWR)   Responsible for writing entries to the redo log on disk.

media recovery   In the event of hardware failure, the type of recovery that occurs is media recovery. This type of recovery does not allow reading or writing of data.

nesting   The placing of a statement, clause, or query within another statement.

node   A node can be represented by a row in a tree-structured table.

object   An item in the database such as a table, index, procedure, trigger, or synonym.

online backup   The archiving of Oracle data while the database is still running.

operator   An operator is used in an expression to perform an operation, such as addition or comparison, and is typically a reserved word or character.

optimizer   An optimizer decides the best way to use tables and indexes. It is a part of the Oracle kernel.

parent   A node that has descendants in a tree-structured data.

parse   Parsing a cursor involves mapping the SQL statement for optimal use.

physical block   A storage location on a disk.

precompiler   A precompiler reads SQL statements and translates them into statements a normal compiler can interrupt.

primary key   A primary key uniquely identifies a row of data in a table. A primary key may be one or multiple columns.

process monitor (PMON)   There are five background processes used by a multiprocess database system. The background process that is responsible for recovery when a process accessing the database fails is the process monitor.

read consistency   Read consistency assures that all data encountered by a transaction will be the same throughout the transaction.

record locking   Record locking stops two or more users from updating the same row at the same time.

recursive calls   A nested request of the RDMBS. Oracle utilizes recursive calls during auditing.

referential integrity   A property that indicates that the values from one column will depend on values from another column. Constraints enforce referential integrity.

remote database   A remote database resides on a remote computer that is accessible through a database link.

resource   A database object that may be locked. Rows and tables can be locked by a user, but data dictionary tables, cache, and files can be locked by RDBS.

session   A series of events that occur between the time a user connects to SQL and disconnects.

share lock   A share lock permits other users to query data but not change it.

single process   A mode of operation that allows the user to access only one database at a time.

statement   A statement is comprised of SQL instructions to Oracle that may have clauses and conditions.

Structured Query Language   The American National Standards Institute's (ANSI) industry-standard language to manipulate information stored in relational databases. Oracle utilizes ANSI SQL.

synonym   A synonym is an alias name given to an Oracle table, view, or sequence, which can be referred to by any SQL command.

syntax   The grammatical rules for writing computer language such as SQL.

System Global Area (SGA)   While a Oracle database is running, the System Global Area (SGA) is the center of activity. The size of the SGA depends on the system's needs.

system monitor process (SMON)   A multiprocess database system uses five background processes, one of which is the system monitor process. Its primary responsibility is recovery and cleanup of temporary segments.

transaction   A sequence of SQL statements is considered to be a transaction. To make transactions permanent in a database, the COMMIT command is used; to restore the data, the command ROLLBACK is used.

transaction lock   A transaction lock indicates that a transaction is holding rows to be processed.

tree-structured query   A tree-structured query results in a hierarchical representation of the data. The clause CONNECT BY provides this type of result. This type of query is typically used in organizational charts.

tuple   A synonym for *row*.

two-phase commit   Distributed transactions are managed by Oracle in a feature called two-phase commit. This feature guarantees that a transaction is valid at all sites even if an error has occurred, and the data will not change until a final action command, such as COMMIT or ROLLBACK, is issued.

unique index   An index that could be a single column or comprised of several columns that uniquely identifies a row of data in a table. Indexing a table decreases searching time for queries.

unique key   A unique key can be a single column or several columns that uniquely identify each row of data in a table.

unit of work   A unit of work is equivalent to a *transaction*. A transaction can be comprised of several SQL statements.

username   A word that identifies you to the host computer's operating system or Oracle. A password also is required to gain access to systems.

view   An object that is a logical representation of a single or multiple tables. It has no storage but can be used just like a single table.

I

Index